READINGS ON COMMUNICATING WITH STRANGERS

READINGS ON COMMUNICATING WITH STRANGERS

EDITED BY

William B. Gudykunst
California State University, Fullerton

Young Yun Kim
University of Oklahoma

McGraw-Hill, Inc.
New York   St. Louis   San Francisco   Auckland   Bogotá
Caracas   Lisbon   London   Madrid   Mexico   Milan   Montreal
New Delhi   Paris   San Juan   Singapore   Sydney   Tokyo   Toronto

READINGS ON COMMUNICATING WITH STRANGERS

1 2 3 4 5 6 7 8 9 0 DOC DOC 9 0 9 8 7 6 5 4 3 2 1

ISBN 0-07-025140-1

This book was set in Goudy Old Style by Better Graphics, Inc.
The editors were Hilary Jackson and John M. Morriss;
the production supervisor was Denise L. Puryear.
The cover was designed by Rafael Hernandez.
Project supervision was done by The Total Book.
R. R. Donnelley & Sons Company was printer and binder.

Library of Congress Cataloging-in-Publication Data

Readings on communicating with strangers / edited by William B.
  Gudykunst, Young Yun Kim.—[1st ed.]
    p.   cm.
  ISBN 0-07-025140-1
    1. Intercultural communication.   2. Intergroup relations.
  I. Gudykunst, William B.   II. Kim, Young Yun.
  HM258.R34   1992
  158'.27—dc20   91-20075

Permissions Acknowledgments

by International Communication Association. Reprinted by permission of Sage Publications, Inc.

pages 273–284: Abridged from William B. Gudykunst and Stella Ting-Toomey, "Nonverbal Dimensions and Context-Regulation," *Culture and Interpersonal Communication*, pp. 117–133, copyright © 1988 by Sage Publications, Inc. Reprinted by permission of Sage Publications, Inc.

pages 284–297: Abridged from David Matsumoto, Harald G. Wallbott, and Klaus R. Scherer, "Emotions in Intercultural Communication," in M. Asante and W.B. Gudykunst (Eds.), *Handbook of International and Intercultural Communication*, pp. 225–246, copyright © 1989 by Sage Publications, Inc. Reprinted by permission of Sage Publications, Inc.

pages 302–308: Abridged from William B. Gudykunst, "Applying our Knowledge and Skills," *Bridging Differences: Effective Intergroup Communication*, pp. 135–142, copyright © 1991 by Sage Publications, Inc. Reprinted by permission of Sage Publications, Inc.

pages 308–317: From "Cognitive and Dyadic Processes in Intergroup Contact" (pp. 280–289) by Terrence L. Rose, in *Cognitive Processes in Stereotyping and Intergroup Behavior*, edited by D.L. Hamilton, 1981, Hillsdale, New Jersey: Lawrence Erlbaum Associates, Inc. Copyright 1981 by Lawrence Erlbaum Associates, Inc. Reprinted by permission.

pages 318–336: From Letty Cottin Pogrebin, "The Same and Different," *Among Friends*, New York: McGraw-Hill, 1987. Reprinted by permission of The Wendy Weil Agency, Inc. Copyright © 1987 by Letty Cottin Pogrebin. As abridged in John Stewart, *Bridges not Walls*, New York: McGraw-Hill, 1989.

pages 336–345: Abridged from Adrian Furnham, "The Adjustment of Sojourners," in Y.Y. Kim and W.B. Gudykunst (Eds.), *Cross-Cultural Adaptation*, pp. 43–61, copyright © 1988 by Sage Publications, Inc. Reprinted by permission of Sage Publications, Inc.

pages 345–357: Abridged from Young Yun Kim, "Facilitating Immigrant Adaptation: The Role of Communication," in T.L. Albrecht and M.B. Edelman (Eds.), *Communicating Social Support*, pp. 192–211, copyright © 1987 by Sage Publications, Inc. Reprinted by permission of Sage Publications, Inc.

pages 371–381: Abridged from Young Yun Kim, "Intercultural Communication Competence: A Systems-Theoretic View," in S. Ting-Toomey and F. Korzenny (Eds.), *Cross-Cultural Interpersonal Communication*, pp. 259–275, copyright © 1991 by the Speech Communication Association. Reprinted by permission of Sage Publications, Inc.

pages 382–392: Abridged from William B. Gudykunst, "Being Perceived as a Competent Communicator," *Bridging Differences: Effective Intergroup Communication*,

Contents

CHAPTER 8

VERBAL BEHAVIOR   222

CHAPTER 9

NONVERBAL BEHAVIOR   272

PART 4

Interaction with Strangers

CHAPTER 10

INTERPERSONAL RELATIONSHIPS
WITH STRANGERS   301

CHAPTER 11

STRANGERS ADAPTATION   334

CHAPTER 12

COMMUNICATING EFFECTIVELY
WITH STRANGERS   369

CHAPTER 13

BECOMING INTERCULTURAL   399

CHAPTER 14

BUILDING COMMUNITY   421

Preface

Since the publication of the first edition of *Communicating with Strangers*, many instructors using the book have told us that they wished there were a reader to accompany the text. They all indicated that the text is not sufficient when they are teaching intercultural communication at the upper division and/or graduate levels. Our main purpose in preparing this volume was to address these requests.

While this reader is designed specifically to supplement the second edition of *Communicating with Strangers*, we believe it is compatible with other introductory texts. We have written an introduction for each chapter that provides the conceptual foundation for the articles included. One criterion we used in selecting the articles was that the article elaborate on an important concept presented in *Communicating with Strangers*. Since the reader may be using other texts, we have "borrowed" some of the introductory material for each of the chapters from the text. While this results in some redundancy for students using our text and this reader, we believe the redundancy helps reinforce important points and places the readings in context.

In selecting the readings, we looked for articles that examined cross-cultural differences in communication *and* articles that looked at communication between people from different groups. We used a "culture (and ethnic group) general" approach in selecting the readings. That is, we selected readings which illustrated the concepts across cultures and/or ethnic groups. We do not include readings on any specific cultures or ethnic groups, which would have made the reader prohibitively long and could have been perceived as ethnocentric. We believe that the general readings included provide the foundation necessary to understand communication with strangers from specific cultures and/or ethnic groups.

We selected only articles dealing with intercultural and/or interethnic communication. The concepts being discussed, however, apply equally to our communication with strangers who differ based on other group memberships (e.g., gender groups, homosexual-heterosexual, ablebodied-disabled, social classes). Our decision not to include readings on these areas was based on several factors. To adequately cover differences based on other group memberships, we would have had to include several additional readings in many chapters (e.g., there would have to be readings on each of the group memberships in the chapter on sociocultural influences and additional readings in the chapters on verbal and nonverbal behavior, as well as the chapter on intercultural relationships). This, again, would have made the book too long. More important, our discussion with instructors who teach the introductory intercultural communication course suggests that the vast majority of instructors focus on culture and ethnicity. We, therefore, decided to cover these two areas comprehensively.

In selecting aritcles, we tried to balance the contribution of the article (e.g., clarifying the concepts in the text), its comprehensiveness (e.g., the range of material covered in the article), and its readability. Since the study of intercultural communication is interdisciplinary, we have included articles by authors from many different disciplines. There are articles by communication scholars studying intercultural communication, as well as articles by sociologists, social psychologists, anthropologists, psychiatrists, and cross-cultural psychologists. Several readings are by Canadian and European authors, and they reflect contemporary approaches to the study of intergroup behavior outside the United States.

Most of the readings were class tested in a large general education section of intercultural communication at California State University, Fullerton. Based on student comments, several articles were omitted and others were substituted. We believe that the readings included cover the major concepts and are accessible to upper division undergraduates. Some of the articles may challenge readers, but none of the readings is overly difficult.

In preparing the articles for inclusion, we have abridged most readings. We were careful to ensure that none of the omitted material was necessary to understand the point of the article. Since we believe that the language used is related closely to how the message is interpreted, we edited articles, where necessary, so that they are gender neutral. While this makes the reading a little awkward in some points, we believe that this is important to presenting a nonsexist attitude.

Before concluding, we want to thank Stella Ting-Toomey, Richard Wiseman, and Sandra Sudweeks for their comments and suggestions on the readings included. We also want to thank our editor at McGraw-Hill, Hilary Jackson, for her support in the development of this volume. We hope you find the readings enjoyable and useful in improving your communication with strangers.

William B. Gudykunst
Young Yun Kim

Introduction

Our purpose in preparing this reader is to provide a set of readings that covers the important concepts in the study of intercultural communication. This reader is designed primarily to supplement an intercultural communication text. In order to provide a framework for the readings which follow, we would like to outline our approach to the study of intercultural communication.

To begin, we see the processes underlying intracultural communication (between people from the same culture) and intercultural communication (between people from different cultures) to be the same. Similarly, the processes underlying intraethnic communication (between people from the same ethnic group) and interethnic communication (between people from different ethnic groups) are the same. Our interactions with others always are based on the way we categorize them until we "get to know them." We can classify others into many different categories. Initial categories we use include, but are not limited to, "from the same culture" or "from a different culture"; "from the same ethnic group" or "from a different ethnic group." We usually use more specific categories. A person from a different culture might be categorized as a member of his or her culture (Chinese, Mexican, French, etc.). We also categorize people from our own culture or ethnic group whom we do not know. To illustrate, if we are from the north and the other person is from the south, we may categorize him or her as a "southerner."

Whether they are from a different culture (or ethnic group) or from our own culture (or ethnic group), people we do not know share one thing in common—they are not members of our ingroups. Ingroups, as we use the term here, are groups which are important to us. We use "communicating with strangers" to refer to the common communication process underlying intracultural, intercultural, intraethnic, and interethnic communication when we do not know the other person. Strangers, as we use the term, are people we do not know who are not members of our ingroups.

Our purpose in the remainder of this introduction is to outline how we organize the study of communicating with strangers. In the following section, we present a model (see Figure 1) designed to organize the elements influencing our communication with strangers.

AN ORGANIZING MODEL

To begin, it is necessary to define briefly the elements in the model. Messages involve the transmission of information from one person to another. Since it is impossible to transmit electrical impulses directly from one's brain to that of another person, it is necessary for us to put messages into codes that can be transmitted. Messages can be encoded into many forms, but for the purpose of our analysis two are most relevant: language (verbal codes) and nonverbal behaviors (we exclude codes such as mathematics, music, etc.). The use of language is mostly a conscious activity, while the use of nonverbal behavior is mostly an unconscious activity. That is, we generally are not aware of the messages we are encoding nonverbally through our gestures, facial expressions, or tones of voice, to name only a few.

To a certain extent, message decoding is the opposite of message encoding. When we decode a message, our interpretation depends on what the other person says verbally, what nonverbal behavior the other person exhibits, our own encoded messages, our "conceptual filters" (discussed below), and the context in which the message is received.

We see the encoding and decoding of communication messages to be an interactive process influenced by cultural, sociocultural, and environmental factors. This is illustrated in Figure 1 by the way the center circle, which contains the interaction between encoding and decoding of messages, is surrounded by three other circles representing cultural, sociocultural, and psychocultural influences. The circles are drawn with dashed lines to indicate that the elements affect, and are affected by, the other elements. The two persons represented in the model are surrounded by a dashed box representing the environmental influences. This box is drawn with a dashed rather than a solid line because the immediate environment in which the communication takes place is not an isolated or "closed system." Most communication between people takes place in a social environment that includes other people who also are engaging in communication, and these environmental factors also influence the communication that takes place.

The message/feedback between the two communicators is represented by the lines from one person's encoding to the other person's decoding and from the second person's encoding to the first person's decoding. Two message/feedback lines are shown to indicate that anytime we communicate we are simultaneously engaged in encoding and decoding of messages. In other words, communication is not static; we do not encode a message and do nothing until we receive feedback. Rather, we are processing incoming stimuli (decoding) at the same time as we are sending (encoding) messages.

The cultural, sociocultural, psychocultural, and environmental influences on communication serve as conceptual filters for our encoding and decoding of messages. By conceptual filters we mean mechanisms that affect the number of alternatives from which we choose when we encode and decode messages. Our conceptual filters influence the stimuli to which we pay attention and how we choose to interpret those stimuli when we decode incoming messages. To communiate effectively with strangers, we must understand how our conceptual filters influence our communication and how the strangers' conceptual filters influence their communication.

The cultural factors that influence our communication with strangers include the unconscious assumptions we are taught as part of our socialization as children.

FIGURE 1. An organizing model for studying communication with strangers

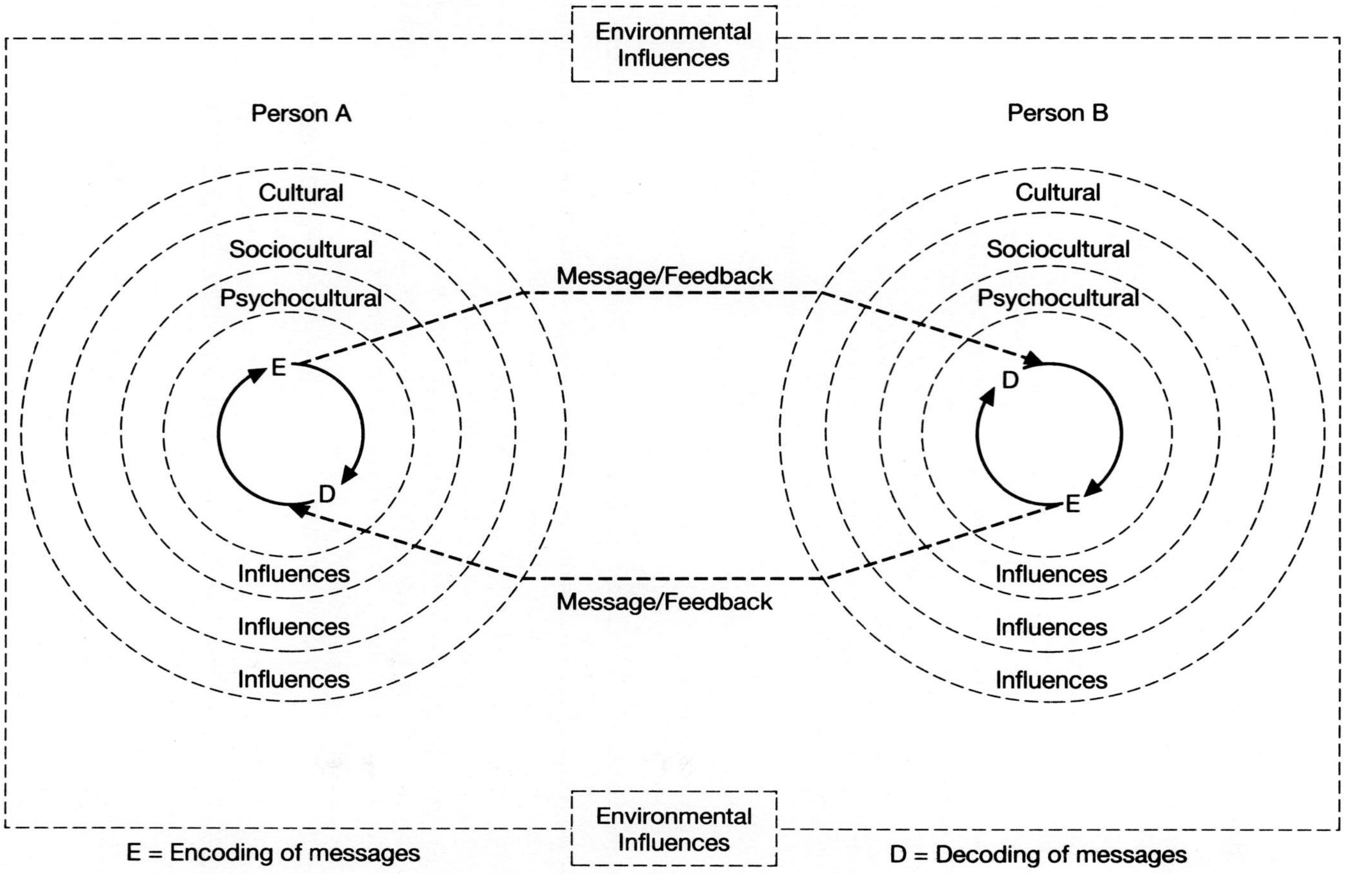

E = Encoding of messages   D = Decoding of messages

These assumptions include how the self is defined, people's relationships to one .
another, and their relationships to the environment and supernatural phenomena.
The cultural influences on our behavior also include the values we hold and the norms
and rules guiding our communication.

The sociocultural factors that influence our communication with strangers
include our membership in social groups, our role expectations, and our definitions of
interpersonal relationships. The various groups of which we are members, for example, enforce sets of expected behaviors (norms and rules) and have shared values and,
therefore, affect how we communicate with strangers (and how they communicate
with us).

The variables included under the psychocultural influences include the categorization and stereotyping processes, as well as our intergroup attitudes, particularly
ethnocentrism and prejudice. Our stereotypes and intergroup attitudes create expectations for how we think strangers will behave.

The environment in which we communicate influences our encoding and
decoding of messages. The geographical location, climate, and architectural setting,
as well as our perceptions of the environment, influence how we interpret incoming
stimuli and the predictions we make about strangers' behavior. Since strangers may
have different perceptions and orientations toward the environment, they may interpret behavior differently in the same setting.

PLAN FOR THE BOOK

We begin in Part I by looking at concepts we believe are critical to communicating
effectively with strangers—uncertainty and anxiety reduction. Uncertainty involves
the inability to predict and/or explain strangers' behavior. Anxiety refers to the
"nervous" feelings we have when we communicate with strangers. It is impossible to
communicate effectively if uncertainty and anxiety are high. Communicating effectively with strangers requires that we be able to manage our uncertainty and anxiety so
that we can accurately predict and explain strangers' behavior.

The readings in Chapter 2 are designed to provide a foundation for studying the
processes influencing our communication with strangers. The reading on the concept
of the stranger provides an excellent overview of what it means to be a stranger and
illustrates how mindfulness contributes to effective communication. We believe that
individuals must be mindful if we are going to manage their anxiety and accurately
predict and/or explain strangers' behavior. The final article in this chapter illustrates
the differences between categorization and particularization of strangers. We believe
that particularizing strangers is one way to become mindful of our behavior when we
communicate with them.

We use the model presented above to organize Parts II and III of the book. In
Part II, we look at the major influences on communication—cultural, sociocultural,
psychocultural, and environmental. The readings included are designed to present

detailed information on the major factors influencing our communication in each of these areas.

More specifically, the readings in Chapter 3 explain the major dimensions in which cultures vary (e.g., individualism-collectivism). In Chapter 4, we present readings on the sociocultural influences on our behavior with an emphasis on how our social identities (the part of our identity based on our group memberships) influences our communication. Chapter 5 contains readings on the psychocultural influences on our communication. We have included readings on stereotyping, prejudice-tolerance, and improving intergroup relations in this chapter. Chapter 6 in Part II focuses on the environmental influences on our communication.

The readings in Part III focus specifically on the encoding (verbal and nonverbal) and decoding processes. The readings in Chapter 7 focus on how we make sense of strangers' behavior (the attribution process) and how we perceive people from different cultures. Chapter 8 contains articles on cultural variations in verbal behavior and how we use language when we communicate with strangers. In Chapter 9, we present readings on cultural variations in nonverbal behaviors and emotions.

We conclude in Part IV by presenting readings on the different types of interaction we have with strangers. The readings in Chapter 10 are designed to provide insights into how we develop interpersonal relationships with strangers. In Chapter 11, we present readings on how strangers adapt to new cultural environments. Chapter 12 contains articles on improving the effectiveness of our communication with strangers. Chapter 13 includes two readings on becoming intercultural. Finally, Chapter 14 contains three articles on building community with strangers.

READINGS ON
COMMUNICATING
WITH STRANGERS

PART 1

CONCEPTUAL FOUNDATIONS

CHAPTER 1

Central Concepts

Our expectations regarding how people from other cultures and ethnic groups will behave are based on how we categorize them (e.g., he is Japanese; she is Mexican-American). Our use of social categories, however, is not limited to our communication with people from different cultures and ethnic groups. We categorize others when we communicate with people from our own culture or ethnic group, but the categories are different (e.g., that person is a woman; he is a waiter; she or he is a "friend of a friend").

Until we "know" others (e.g., know what they think, what their attitudes are, how they behave), our interactions with them must be based on our expectations regarding how people in the category in which we place them will behave. Our initial interactions with people from our own groups and with people from other groups, therefore, are relatively similar. There are, of course, some differences. We experience more anxiety, for example, when people come from different ethnic groups than when they are from our ethnic group. To be able to talk about the similarities in the underlying communication process, we (Gudykunst & Kim, 1984, 1992) use *communicating with strangers* to refer to our communication with people who are not members of our own groups and who are "different" (on the basis of culture, ethnicity, gender, age, or other group memberships).

There are many reasons why we communicate with strangers. We communicate to inform someone about something, to entertain another person, to change another person's attitudes or behavior, and to support our self-conceptions, to name only a few of the possibilities. It is impossible to examine all the functions in a book like this. We, therefore, focus on two specific functions that are related closely to improving the effectiveness of our communication with strangers: reducing uncertainty and reducing anxiety.

Interacting with strangers is a novel situation for most people. Because these types of interactions do not occur frequently, they create ambiguity. Our attempts to deal with the ambiguity of new situations involves a pattern of information-seeking (uncertainty reduction) and tension (anxiety) reduction (Ball-Rokeach, 1973).

When we reduce uncertainty about others and ourselves, understanding is possible. Understanding involves obtaining information, knowing, comprehending,

and interpreting (Berger et al., 1976). Three levels of understanding can be differentiated: description, prediction, and explanation. Description involves delineating what
is observed in terms of its physical attributes (i.e., drawing a picture in words).
Prediction involves projecting what will happen in a particular situation, and explanation involves stating why something occurred.

We make predictions and create explanations all the time when we communicate. We rarely describe others' behavior, however. When we communicate with
others we typically decode messages by attaching meaning to or interpreting them. We
do not stop to describe what we saw or heard before we interpret it. Rather, we
interpret messages as we decode them. The problem is that we base our interpretations
on our life experiences, culture, or ethnic group memberships. Because our life
experiences differ from the other person's, this often leads to misinterpretations and
ultimately to misunderstandings.

Anxiety refers to feelings of being uneasy, tense, worried, or apprehensive about
what might happen in a particular communication encounter. It is an affective (i.e.,
emotional) response, not a cognitive or behavioral response like uncertainty. Whereas
uncertainty results from our inability to predict strangers' behavior, anxiety is a
function of our anticipation of negative consequences (Stephan & Stephan, 1985).

Our ingroups are groups with which we identify that are important to us. If we
define our religious group as important and identify with being members of our
religion, for example, it is one of our ingroups. Other religious groups then become
outgroups for us. We may identify with many ingroups. When we interact with
another person, we categorize that person as being a member of an ingroup or an
outgroup. We experience more uncertainty and anxiety when we communicate with
members of outgroups than when we communicate with members of ingroups.

There are numerous other factors that affect the amount of uncertainty and
anxiety we experience in a particular situation. The degree to which we are familiar
with the situation and know how to behave, the expectations we have for our own and
others' behavior, and the degree to which we perceive ourselves to be similar to the
other person, for example, influence our levels of uncertainty and anxiety. Our ability
to reduce our uncertainty and anxiety, in turn, influences the degree to which we can
communicate effectively.

We do not mean to imply that we want to reduce our uncertainty and anxiety
totally when we communicate with strangers. Low levels of uncertainty and anxiety
are not functional (see Byrne & Kelley, 1981). If anxiety is too low, we do not care
enough to perform well. If uncertainty is too low, we get bored. Moderate levels of
uncertainty and anxiety are desirable for effectiveness and adaptation.

The two readings in this chapter are designed to examine the reduction of
uncertainty and anxiety in more detail. In the first reading, Charles Berger outlines
why reducing uncertainty is important. He also overviews research on uncertainty
reduction in intercultural contexts. The second reading focuses on intergroup anxiety.
Stephan and Stephan outline the antecedents and consequences of our anxiety in
communicating with people from different groups.

REFERENCES

Ball-Rokeach, S. (1973). From pervasive ambiguity to definition of the situation. *Sociometry*, 36, 378–389.

Berger, C. R., Gardner, R., Parks, M., Shulman, L., & Miller, G. (1976). Interpersonal epistemology and interpersonal communication. In G. Miller (Ed.), *Explorations in interpersonal communication.* Beverly Hills, CA: Sage.

Byrne, D., & Kelley, K. (1981). *An introduction to personality* (3rd ed.). Englewood Cliffs, NJ: Prentice-Hall.

Gudykunst, W. B., & Kim, Y. Y. (1984). *Communicating with strangers: An approach to intercultural communication.* New York: McGraw-Hill.

Gudykunst, W. B., & Kim, Y. Y. (1992). *Communicating with strangers: An approach to intercultural communication* (2nd ed.). New York: McGraw-Hill.

Stephan, W.G., & Stephan, C. W. (1985). Intergroup anxiety. *Journal of Social Issues, 41*, 157–166.

Communicating under Uncertainty

Charles R. Berger

. . . Although economists, political scientists, sociologists, and psychologists have recognized the centrality of uncertainty in human affairs, communication researchers in general and interpersonal communication researchers in particular have only recently begun to acknowledge the importance of uncertainty in human communication. Early communication researchers (e.g., Berlo, 1960) did discuss Shannon and Weaver's (1949) mathematical theory of information, which deals with uncertainty in communication systems, however, such discussions did little to motivate either theory building or empirical research aimed at exploring the role played by uncertainty in human communication. Several psychologists (Heider, 1958; Kelly, 1955; Thibaut & Kelley, 1959) discussed the role played by uncertainty in interpersonal relationships, but these discussions had little impact upon communication researchers interested in the study of interpersonal processes. Thus, the main impact of Thibaut and Kelley's (1959) analysis of interpersonal relationships was their explication of the roles played by exchanges of rewards and costs in relationship development (e.g., Roloff, 1981). Their discussion of uncertainty was virtually ignored by communication researchers.

This state of affairs changed in 1975 when Calabrese and I (Berger & Calabrese, 1975) advanced an axiomatic theory designed to explain certain communication phenomena that we observed during initial interactions. We felt then, as we feel

Source: Abridged from chapter with same title in M. E. Roloff & G. R. Miller (Eds.), *Interpersonal Processes.* Newbury Park, CA: Sage, 1987.

today, that a number of events occurring in such initial encounters can be explained in terms of uncertainty and uncertainty reduction. Although the theory was originally developed to explain certain initial interaction phenomena, it has recently been expanded to explain aspects of established romantic relationships (Parks & Adelman, 1983) and intercultural encounters (Gudykunst, Yang, & Nishida, 1985). These studies, as well as several others, have demonstrated three important points: First, uncertainty levels are important in relationships beyond the initial stages of their formation. Second, uncertainty is also important in communication contexts other than interpersonal ones. Third, and not surprisingly, the theory, as proposed by Berger and Calabrese (1975), contains some propositions of dubious validity.

A decade has elapsed since publication of the original theory, and it seems appropriate to see what directions it has taken and to sketch how it might be developed in the future. Thus the two primary goals of the present chapter are to assess the evolution of the theory since its inception and to plot some potential courses of future development. When the theory was first discussed (Berger & Calabrese, 1975), there was no official name given to it. Some dubbed it "initial interaction theory" while others called it "uncertainty theory." More recent discussions have used the term "uncertainty reduction theory" (URT). This more inclusive label seems to capture best the evolutionary direction of the theory

THEORETICAL EVOLUTION

The Nature of Uncertainty

Just as it is the bane of political and economic decision-makers, uncertainty is also a potential hobgoblin of interpersonal relationships. The task of interacting with a stranger, who in theory can behave and believe in a very large number of alternative ways and whose actions and beliefs remain to be explained, presents interactants with complex predictive and explanatory problems. These problems pertain both to understanding the other person in an interaction and understanding oneself. To interact in a relatively smooth, coordinated, and understandable manner, one must be able both to predict how one's interaction partner is likely to behave, and, based on these predictions, to select from one's own repertoire those responses that will optimize outcomes in the encounter. Uncertainty is not reduced for its own sake. Political and economic planners as well as communicators seek to reduce their uncertainties about their environments so that they can respond to these environments in ways that will assure goal achievement (e.g., Miller & Steinberg, 1975).

The idea that uncertainty is a function of the number of alternatives present in a situation and their relative likelihood of occurrence is, of course, taken directly from information theory (Shannon & Weaver, 1949). However, Berger and Calabrese (1975) extended this notion of uncertainty to include explanation. Thus uncertainty is a function of both the ability to predict and the ability to explan actions of other *and* of self. This explanatory component was added because of the importance accorded causal explanation by various attribution theorists (Heider, 1958; Jones & Davis, 1965; Kelley, 1967, 1971). This broader conceptualization of uncertainty holds that persons obtain information that allows them to increase their predictive certainty before they become concerned with the problem of why certain behaviors have or have not occurred. Berger, Gardner, Parks, Schulman, and Miller (1976) pointed out that obtaining the knowledge necessary for reducing explanatory uncertainty might be both more difficult and time consuming than acquiring information necessary for the reduction of predictive uncertainty. A similar discussion of levels of knowing was presented by Miller and Steinberg (1975) at about the same time.

This basic conceptualization of the uncertainty construct remains intact. Furthermore, Berger (1975) was able to demonstrate how information exchanged early in interactions can foster predictions about unknown attributes of the other (*proactive attributions*) and explanations of subsequent conduct during ongoing interactions (*retroactive attributions*). This distinction between proactive and retroactive attributional activity was incorporated into Clatterbuck's (1979) CLUES scale, which has been employed in a number of studies examining the relationships between uncertainty and other variables. Recently, Gudykunst and Nishida (1986) have modified the CLUES scale to increase its cross-cultural generalizability. . . .

Communication and Uncertainty

Given the many combinations of verbal and nonverbal behaviors and the ranges of subtle modulations of these behaviors available to most normal interactants, it is amazing persons are able to carry out as many meaningful interactions with others as they apparently do. Of course, psychotherapists, organizational and media consultants, and others whose job it is to improve communication skills are quick to point out that persons playing a variety of roles fail to discharge their duties as they should because of "communication breakdowns" or "failures to communicate." Though such breakdowns and failures are certainly real and should be expected given the complex nature of communicative transactions, more often than not persons are able to achieve their interaction goals successfully. If the reader doubts the veracity of this assertion, consider all of the mundane interactions that most of us have during the course of an average day. Encounters with shopkeepers, ticket agents, waiters, coworkers, and a host of others usually go off without a hitch.

Communication and uncertainty are inextricably intertwined. Communicative actions are those things interactants frequently wish to predict and less frequently seek to explain, and it is through observations of communicative conduct that predictions and explanations are derived. This reciprocal relationship is central to URT. Axioms of the original theory posited reciprocal causal relationships between amount of communication and uncertainty and between nonverbal affiliative expressiveness and uncertainty; specifically, uncertainty is reduced as these variables increase, and decreases in uncertainty are responsible for increases in both verbal and nonverbal communication.

Although these relationships still seem somewhat plausible, Berger and Bradac

(1982) recognized that there are circumstances under which communicative action might actually increase uncertainty. Persons are perfectly capable of acting in ways calculated to cloud their intentions in the eyes of others. Goffman (1969) presents an insightful analysis of how persons employ *covering moves* to mask their true intent and how observers employ *uncovering moves* to ascertain actual intentions. However, persons can deploy *counter-uncovering moves* to foil the uncovering moves made by observers. This process of increasing uncertainty through communicative action may not be intentional. Given certain combinations of alternative choices and specific contexts, some communicative choices might actually increase uncertainty because of the number of alternative interpretations available to observers. As Jones and Davis (1965) have argued, since positive actions can be motivated by either sincere or ulterior motives, they are not as reliable for making inferences about underlying dispositions as are negative behaviors that we assume are not motivated by ulterior motives.

In addition to the above possibilities, Planalp and Honeycutt (1985) have studied events that increase uncertainty in ongoing relationships. In their survey, respondents had little difficulty thinking of events that increased their uncertainty about persons whom they thought they knew well. These events—namely, competing relationships, unexplained loss of close contact, sexual behavior, deception, change in personality and values, and betraying confidence—exerted strong impacts upon cognitive, affective, and communication variables. In addition, a majority of the relationships studied became more distant or were terminated as a result of the events. Unfortunately, the way in which participants were asked to report on uncertainty-increasing events in their relationships may have biased them toward thinking about negative rather than positive events, although a few respondents did report positive events. This is an important point since persons can be pleasantly surprised by certain events in such relationships. Nevertheless, this study is significant because it supports the notion that communication does not always act to reduce uncertainty in relationships.

It is probably safe to assume that reduced communication between persons can impair their ability to predict and explain each other well. This prediction challenges the well-known aphorism, absence makes the heart grow fonder. Under the present view, absence and reduced interaction between persons are likely to lead to increased relational difficulties, especially when the individuals involved in the relationship are experiencing considerable change in their individual lives. . . .

The relationship between uncertainty and communication is not simple. Lack of opportunity to communicate most certainly has the effect of raising uncertainty levels; however, the opportunity to interact may or may not produce reductions in uncertainty. Although it is safe to assume that communication is necessary for the reduction of uncertainty—unless, of course, one believes uncertainty can be reduced through ESP—the relationships between uncertainty and communication posited here differ from those advanced by Berger and Calabrese (1975). Moreover, the present discussion suggests that sheer volume of communication is probably not a good predictor of uncertainty reduction. Indeed, the quality rather than the quantity of information exchanged between interactants should have a greater impact upon the reduction of mutual uncertainties.

Social Context and Uncertainty Reduction

Berger and Calabrese (1975) suggested that the social context of interactions might provide uncertainty-reducing information. For example, persons first meeting at a political rally might begin their conversation by talking about the candidate rather than exchanging the usual biographic and demographic information; however, exchanges of such information might occur later in the same interaction. In this situation uncertainty is reduced by both parties making inferences about the reasons for the other's presence at the rally. Most likely, persons would assume that others present at such a rally support the candidate, thus making the candidate a safe topic for a conversational opening.

Rubin (1977) varied the interaction context to see how it would affect the number and types of questions asked by interactants. In the ambiguous condition, persons were asked to form a general impression of others by asking them questions. In the specific condition, persons were asked to form impressions of their partners in terms of how they thought the partners would perform on a library job. Persons in the latter condition also were told to form their impressions by asking questions. This study revealed two findings relevant to the present issue: First, more questions were asked in the ambiguous context; second, more demographic questions were asked in the ambiguous context. In addition to these findings, Rubin (1979) reported that interactions in the ambiguous context lasted significantly longer than those in the specific context, and postinteraction ratings revealed that persons in the ambiguous context felt they had greater insight into their partners' personalities.

These findings support the notion that uncertainty can be reduced by the context of the interaction. Interactants in the ambiguous context faced the problem of reducing their uncertainties about their partners along many more dimensions than those in the specific context. To accomplish this task, they had to spend more time interacting with their partners and they had to ask them more questions. In addition, the questions they asked were primarily biographic and demographic. Answers to these broad background questions can be used to make inferences about attitudes and opinions not yet revealed in the conversation (Berger, 1975). Interestingly, the increased interaction time in the ambiguous context led interactants to feel they had a better grasp of their partners' personalities than did interactants in the specific context. This finding is not too surprising given the conversational task in the specific condition—that is, to form an impression of a person as a potential library assistant.

Although Rubin's findings clearly show the uncertainty-reducing properties of interaction contexts, the social context may increase interactants' uncertainty levels under certain conditions. One can imagine circumstances in which persons might structure interaction situations to maximize the uncertainty levels of the persons involved. Individuals may be intentionally misled so they do not discover a hidden agenda, or so many potential agendas are rendered possible that persons have a difficult time understanding exactly which one is operating at a given time. Thus the social context, like communicative action, can sometimes be used to raise uncertainty levels.

Uncertainty Reduction Strategies

Thus far we have examined the roles played by both communication and the interaction context in the uncertainty reduction process. There are, however, additional routes to uncertainty reduction. First, persons bring considerable knowledge with them to any interaction situation: information about persons in the form of person prototypes (Cantor & Mischel, 1977), role schemas, and typical event sequences or scripts (Abelson, 1981; Schank & Abelson, 1977). This knowledge enables the individuals to begin to understand others involved in the social situation and provides the procedural knowledge necessary to conduct the interaction. Such knowledge is vital for the conduct of most interactions (Abelson, 1981; Schank, 1982; Schank & Abelson, 1977; Winograd, 1980). Also in this long-term memory are schemas for the acquisition of new knowledge (i.e., procedural routines for acquiring new information). Obviously, such new information *must* be acquired if a relationship is to develop. This kind of procedural knowledge is extremely powerful because it enables us to acquire new knowledge. It is to these knowledge acquistion routines that I now turn.

In the original version of URT, Berger and Calabrese (1975) were not concerned with strategies for reducing uncertainty. Subsequently, attention was directed toward these knowledge acquisition strategies (Berger, 1979; Berger & Bradac, 1982; Berger et al., 1976). These presentations advanced a typology of information-gaining strategies consisting of three broad strategy classes: passive, active, and interactive. *Passive* strategies are those in which the uncertainty reducer gathers information about a target through unobtrusive observation. *Active* strategies involve the observation of targets' responses to manipulations of the interaction environment but no direct interaction between observers and targets. Also included in this category is the acquisition of information about a target from third-party sources. Finally, *interactive* strategies involve direct, face-to-face contact between the information seeker and the target. . . .

Research conducted to investigate knowledge acquisition strategies has revealed several important findings. Studies aimed at illuminating the passive strategies (Berger & Douglas, 1981; Berger & Perkins, 1978, 1979) suggest that when persons wish to acquire information about a target person using unobtrusive observation, they prefer to observe the target in social rather than solitary situations. In addition, social situations in which the target is highly involved in interaction with others are judged to be more informationally rich than social situations in which the target is relatively uninvolved with the others present. Finally, persons anticipating interaction with the target person consider informal social contexts to be potentially more informative than formal contexts. These findings suggest that informal, active social contexts are perceived to place fewer situational constraints on target persons and thus to be more informative about the target persons; in short, one can find out more about individuals conversing with others at a party than by observing them at a funeral or sitting in a room alone. . . .

Interactive strategies for knowledge acquisition have received the bulk of our recent research attention. In a series of studies (Berger & Kellermann, 1983, 1985; Kellermann & Berger, 1984) we have sought to discover the information-seeking devices used during face-to-face interactions. Berger and Kellermann (1983) found three principal strategies: question asking, disclosure, and relaxation of the target. Interestingly, persons attempting to acquire large amounts of information do not necessarily ask any more questions than persons seeking to have a "normal conversation." Instead, persons in the high information-seeking mode ask their targets more questions concerned with explanations for their behavior and their future goals and plans. Moreover, persons interested in knowledge acquisition take advantage of floor possession to ask questions of their targets. . . .

Berger and Kellermann (1985) have discovered a series of *offensive* and *defensive* tactics that persons use to foil information-seeking attempts of others during the parry and thrust of conversations. Offensive tactics include focusing the conversation on the information seeker and asking the information seeker as many questions as possible. Such tactics prevent the seeker from querying the target. Defensive tactics include giving minimal and ambiguous responses to questions and giving off unaffiliative nonverbal behaviors. We are currently in the process of examining how information seekers respond to the communicative parries employed by their conversational partners. We suspect that patterns of strategy and countermeasure deployment emerge over time. One critical focus of this research is upon the *iterative mechanisms* underlying these exchanges through time.

For persons to conduct relatively coordinated interactions with others, they need person, role, and procedural knowledge. If the relationship is to progress beyond an initial interaction, interactants must acquire more specific information about each others' personalities, attitudes and preferences, and values. Persons can employ perceptual, cognitive, and communicative routines to acquire the needed information for understanding both their relational partners and themselves. Since the acquisition of such information is vital for continuance of the relationship, researchers need to gain an understanding of the strategies persons use to acquire it. Studies of these strategies will both add to our fund of knowledge about uncertainty reduction and enable us to aid those who have difficulty gaining understanding of others and themselves. . . .

Uncertainty in Intercultural Encounters

Some intercultural communication researchers have found uncertainty to be a fruitful starting point for their research. Gudykunst and Kim (1984) note the likelihood of elevated uncertainty when persons interact interculturally. This fact has been frequently invoked to explain the dismal history of U.S.-U.S.S.R. relations since World

War II. This line of reasoning implies that relationships between the two superpowers would be considerably more amiable if persons on both sides gained greater understanding of the history and culture of the other nation. Such an understanding would presumably facilitate communication between the two nations and lower the probability of aggression.

Intuition suggests that uncertainty should be more pervasive in intercultural interactions; however, uncertainty and the strategies for its reduction probably vary across cultures. Some research has addressed this particular issue. Gudykunst (1983) employed Hall's (1976) notions of high- and low-context communications to examine cultural differences in the way uncertainty is handled in relationships. In distinguishing between high- and low-context communications, Hall (1976) asserts,

> A high-context (HC) communication or message is one in which most of the information is either in the physical context or internalized in the person, while very little is in the coded, explicit part of the message. A low-context (LC) communication is just the opposite, i.e., the mass of information is vested in the explicit code. (p. 79)

In Hall's system, such Asian cultures as those of China, Korea, and Japan are high-context cultures while those of the United States, Germany, Switzerland, and Scandinavia tend to be low-context.

Gudykunst (1983) compared the responses of members of HC and LC cultures to a hypothetical situation which asked them to indicate what they would do upon meeting a stranger from their own culture at a party. Results revealed that members of HC cultures (1) are more cautious in initial interactions with strangers, (2) make more assumptions about strangers, and (3) ask more questions of strangers than do their LC culture counterparts. These findings led Gudykunst (1983) to conclude that while there are differences in uncertainty reduction strategies between HC and LC cultures, members of both types of cultures reduce their uncertainties by seeking background information from their interactive partners.

Gudykunst and Nishida (1984) reported that Japanese and American students asked to imagine themselves interacting with a stranger from a different culture indicated they would be more likely to ask questions of their partner and disclose more information about themselves than did persons asked to imagine themselves interacting with a stranger from their own culture. These findings support the idea that intercultural interactions are more uncertainty prone than intracultural interactions. Gudykunst and Nishida (1984) found no support for the proposition that cultural similarity by itself is related to interpersonal attraction. Instead, they found that the combination of cultural and attitudinal dissimilarity tends to lower estimates of interpersonal attraction, suggesting that in the intercultural context, similarities and attraction are not related in simple ways.

In a study already cited, Gudykunst et al. (1985) found consistent relationships between uncertainty and attraction across three kinds of relationships within three cultures. Attraction was positively associated with reduced uncertainty. We have noted, however, that under some conditions, reduced uncertainty might not lead to increased attraction; in fact, Gudykunst et al.'s (1985) version of URT suggests that attraction determines uncertainty reduction (i.e., we find out more about persons whom we like and less about persons whom we dislike). While this relationship is quite plausible, there is most likely some kind of complex, reciprocal relationship between these two variables. Nevertheless, the evidence adduced in this study, as well as that reported by Clatterbuck (1979), is impressive in its consistency across relationship types and cultures.

In addition to the relationship between uncertainty and attraction, Gudykunst et al. (1985) found no support for the propositions that (1) amount of communication reduces uncertainty, and (2) perceived similarities between persons reduce uncertainty. We have already considered why amount of communication may not be a good predictor of uncertainty reduction. Why perceived similarity fails to predict uncertainty reduction is not clear, although Clatterbuck (1979) noted that the similarity variable did not perform well as a predictor of CLUES scores. Perhaps similarity has a direct impact upon attraction which, in turn, affects uncertainty reduction with similarity exerting no direct effect on uncertainty. Further research is needed to resolve this particular problem. Finally, Gudykunst et al. (1985) report that the use of interactive strategies of uncertainty reduction is associated with increased attributional confidence. This finding coincides with Gudykunst and Nishida's (1984) finding that persons experiencing uncertainty in a culturally dissimilar interaction employ interactive strategies to a greater extent than do persons interacting with others from similar cultures.

Anyone who has traveled in another culture knows the havoc that uncertainty creates in daily living. Action sequences that are routine in one's own culture become obsolete. Driving, riding buses, making telephone calls, and ordering food may require learning new routines. Such learning requires considerable energy; thus, the fatigue that frequently plagues foreign travelers, usually attributed to "jet lag," may also result from the increased cognitive effort required to cope with new uncertainties. Moreover, even interethnic interactions within one's own country may be rendered effortful by uncertainty. As Simard (1981) pointed out in her study of Canadian Francophones and Anglophones, both groups "perceive it as more difficult to know how to initiate a conversation, to know what to talk about during the interaction, to be interested in the other person, and to guess in which language they should talk" (p. 179) when they interact with each other. The potential stress engendered by uncertainty in such encounters is worthy of research attention in its own right.

Uncertainty and Social Support

As just suggested, uncertainty can breed both stress and anxiety. It is also the case that uncertainty reduction can alleviate these aversive states. When persons are unsure of what is likely to occur, they are unable to respond adaptively so as to control their outcomes in the situation. Consider the individual who has been biopsied for a suspicious lump. The critical question is whether the growth is malignant; however, given no knowledge of the biopsy results, the individual can do little but worry about them. Once the individual knows the test findings, he or she can take action. Obviously, if the lump is benign, no action is necessary; however, even if it is malignant the individual can act to deal with the situation. Persons apparently find waiting for such results *more* stress provoking than receiving bad news. URT would predict that knowing is preferable to not knowing since persons can try to control outcomes when they are certain of their options. It is also obvious, however, that in the biopsy example, learning that one has cancer would probably increase stress and anxiety. What is being argued here, however, is that stress and anxiety will be greater when the results are unknown because of inability to respond adaptively to the situation.

Albrecht and Adelman (1984) have suggested that the positive role played by social networks in reducing stress and anxiety can be explained by uncertainty reduction. They propose that when persons communicate with others who share their plight, stress is alleviated because uncertainty is reduced by such interactions. Support networks provide the distressed individual with information that makes the environment more stable and predictable. When persons share their problems, they can assist each other in developing cognitive and action strategies; for example, persons may literally *learn* how to be parents of terminally ill children or how to deal with a terminal illness of their own. The acquisition and internalization of such information enable persons to respond to their environments more adaptively, and hence to gain more control over their outcomes. . . .

REFERENCES

Abelson, R. (1981). Psychological status of the script concept. *American Psychologist, 36,* 715–729.

Albrecht, T. L., & Adelman, M. B. (1984). Social support and life stress: New directions for communication research. *Human Communication Research, 11,* 3–32.

Berger, C. R. (1975). Proactive and retroactive attribution processes in interpersonal communication. *Human Communication Research, 2,* 33–50.

Berger, C. R. (1979). Beyond initial interaction: Uncertainty, understanding, and the development of interpersonal relationships. In H. Giles & R. St. Clair (Eds.), *Language and social psychology* (pp. 122–144). Oxford: Blackwell.

Berger, C. R., & Bradac, J. J. (1982). *Language and social knowledge: Uncertainty in interpersonal relations.* London: E. E. Arnold.

Berger, C. R., & Calabrese, R. J. (1975). Some explorations in initial interaction and beyond: Toward a developmental theory of interpersonal communication. *Human Communication Research, 1,* 99–112.

Berger, C. R., & Douglas, W. (1981). Studies in interpersonal epistemology III: Anticipated interaction, self-monitoring and observational context selection. *Communication Monographs, 48,* 183–196.

Berger, C. R., & Kellermann, K. A. (1983). To ask or not to ask: Is that a question? In R. N. Bostrom (Ed.), *Communication yearbook 7* (pp. 342–368). Newbury Park, CA: Sage.

Berger, C. R., & Kellermann, K. A. (1985). *Personal opacity and social information gathering: Seek, but ye may not find.* Paper presented at the annual convention of the International Communication Association, Honolulu, HI.

Berger, C. R., & Perkins, J. (1978). Studies in interpersonal epistemology I: Situational attributes in observational context selection. In B. Ruben (Ed.), *Communication yearbook 2* (pp. 171-184). New Brunswick, NJ: Transaction Books.

Berger, C. R., & Perkins, J. (1979). *Studies in interpersonal epistemology II: Self-monitoring, involvement, facial affect, similarity and observational context selection.* Paper presented at the annual convention of the Speech Communication Association, San Antonio, TX.

Berger, C. R., Gardner, R. R., Parks, M. L., Schulman, L. W., & Miller, G. R. (1976). Interpersonal epistemology and interpersonal communication. In G. R. Miller (Ed.), *Explorations in interpersonal communication* (pp. 149-171). Newbury Park, CA: Sage.

Berlo, D. K. (1960). *The process of communication.* New York: Holt, Rinehart & Winston.

Berlyne, D. (1960). *Conflict, arousal, and curiosity.* New York: McGraw-Hill.

Cantor, N., & Mischel, W. (1977). Traits as prototypes: Effects on recognition memory. *Journal of Personality and Social Psychology, 35,* 38-48.

Clatterbuck, G. W. (1979). Attributional confidence and uncertainty in initial interaction. *Human Communication Research, 5,* 147-157.

Goffman, E. (1969). *Strategic interaction.* Philadelphia: University of Pennsylvania Press.

Gudykunst, W. B. (1983). Uncertainty reduction and predictability of behavior in low- and high-context cultures: An exploratory study. *Communication Quarterly, 31,* 49-65.

Gudykunst, W. B., & Kim, Y. Y. (1984). *Communicating with strangers.* Reading, MA: Addison-Wesley.

Gudykunst, W. B., & Nishida, T. (1984). Individual and cultural influences on uncertainty reduction. *Communication Monographs, 51,* 23-36.

Gudykunst, W. B., & Nishida, T. (1986) Attributional confidence in low- high-context cultures. *Human Communication Research, 12,* 525-549.

Gudykunst, W. B., Yang, S. M., & Nishida, T. (1985). A cross-cultural test of uncertainty reduction theory: Comparisons of acquaintances, friends, and dating relationships in Japan, Korea, and the United States. *Human Communication Research, 11,* 407-455.

Hall, E. T. (1976). *Beyond culture.* Garden City, NY: Doubleday.

Heider, F. (1958). *The psychology of interpersonal relations.* New York: John Wiley.

Hogarth, R. (1980). *Judgement and choice: The psychology of decision.* New York: John Wiley.

Jones, E. E., & Davis, K. E. (1965). From acts to dispositions: The attribution process in person perception. In L. Berkowitz (Ed.), *Advances in experimental social psychology* (Vol. 2, pp. 219-216). New York: Academic Press.

Kellermann, K. A., & Berger, C. R. (1984). Affect and the acquisition of social information: Sit back, relax, and tell me about yourself. In R. N. Bostrom (Ed.), *Communication yearbook 8* (pp. 412-445). Newbury Park, CA: Sage.

Kelley, H. H. (1967). Attribution theory in social psychology. In D. Levine (Ed.), *Nebraska Symposium on Motivation* (Vol. 15, pp. 192-237). Lincoln: University of Nebraska Press.

Kelley, H. H. (1971). *Attribution in social interaction.* Morristown, NJ: General Learning Press.

Kelly, G. A. (1955). *The psychology of personal constructs.* New York: Norton.

Lalljee, M., & Cook, M. (173). Uncertainty in first encounters. *Journal of Personality and Social Psychology, 26,* 137-141.

Mehrabian, A., & Wiener, M. (1966). Non-immediacy between communicator and object of communication in a verbal message. *Journal of Consulting Psychology, 30,* 420-425.

Miller, G. R., & Steinberg, M. (1975). *Between people: A new analysis of interpersonal commu-nication.* Chicago: Science Research Associates.

Nisbett, R. E., & Ross, L. (1980). *Human inference: Strategies and shortcomings of social judgment.* Englewood Cliffs, NJ: Prentice-Hall.

Parks, M. R., & Adelman, M. B. (1983). Communication networks and the development of romantic relationships: An expansion of uncertainty reduction theory. *Human Commu-nication Research, 10,* 55-79.

Planalp, S., & Honeycutt, J. M. (1985). Events that increase uncertainty in personal rela-tionships. *Human Communication Research 11,* 593-604.

Roloff, M. E. (1981). Interpersonal communications: The social exchange approach. Newbury Park, CA: Sage.

Rubin, R. B. (1977). The role of context in information seeking and impression formation. *Communication Monographs, 44,* 81-90.

Rubin, R. B. (1979). The effect of context on information seeking across the span of initial interactions. *Communication Quarterly, 27,* 13-20.

Schank, R. C. (1982). *Dynamic memory.* Cambridge: Cambridge University Press.

Schank, R. C., & Abelson, R. (1977). *Scripts, goals, plans and understanding.* Hillsdale, NJ: Lawrence Erlbaum.

Scheidel, T. M. (1977). Evidence varies with phases of inquiry. *Western Journal of Speech Communication, 41,* 20-31.

Shannon, C., & Weaver, W. (1949). *The mathematical theory of communication.* Urbana: University of Illinois Press.

Sherblom, J., & Van Rheenen, D. E. (1984). Spoken language indices of uncertainty. *Human Communication Research, 11,* 221-230.

Simard, L. (1981). Cross-cultural interaction. *Journal of Social Psychology, 113,* 171-192.

Thibaut, J. W., & Kelley, H. H. (1959). *The social psychology of groups.* New York: John Wiley.

Winograd, T. (1980). What does it mean to understand language? *Cognitive Science, 4* 209-241.

Intergroup Anxiety

Walter G. Stephan and Cookie White Stephan

. . . A woman who works for a large corporation is asked by her boss to entertain a group of her counterparts from a large Japanese conglomerate. She has no experience with Japanese people and is afraid she will make embarrassing mistakes or offend her guests.

A black freshmen at an engineering school in the East finds that all the members of his physics lab group are white. He worries that they will be prejudiced and reject him.

An Anglo construction worker moves to the Southwest in search of work. He is hired by a construction company and finds that his entire crew is comprised of

Source: Abridged from *Journal of Social Issues,* 1985, *41(3),* 157-175.

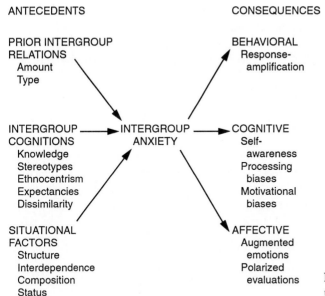

FIGURE 1 A model of intergroup anxiety.

Hispanics. He is afraid they might try to get rid of him by interfering with his work or beating him up if they don't like him.

A white suburban housewife decides that she should invite her new neighbor over for coffee. Her neighbor is the first black to move into the neighborhood. She is concerned that her friends will be angry with her for doing this, but she decides to do it anyway.

These are examples of situations in which the members of one group experience *intergroup anxiety*, anxiety stemming from contact with outgroup members. Individuals often experience intergroup anxiety before interacting with people from a different culture. It is also common within cultures, for example, in contacts between members of different racial and ethnic groups, and between members of nonstigmatized and stigmatized groups (e.g., the handicapped). While these may be the most common settings for intergroup anxiety, it can potentially occur in interactions between the members of any two socially defined groups. . . .

In this article we propose a model encompassing the antecedents and consequences of intergroup anxiety (see Figure 1). Intergroup anxiety is important because it accounts for many of the unique characteristics of intergroup interaction. In the model we hypothesize that intergroup anxiety is created by three sets of factors: prior intergroup relations (e.g., the amount and conditions of prior contact), prior intergroup cognitions (e.g., knowledge of the outgroup, stereotypes, prejudice, expectations, and perceptions of dissimilarity), and situational factors (e.g., amount of structure, type of interdependence, group composition, and relative status).

We also hypothesize that the anxiety created by these factors affects the behavior (e.g., amplification of normative responses), cognitions (e.g., cognitive and motivational biases, heightened self-awareness), and affective reactions (e.g., augmented emotional reactions and evaluations) of members of both ingroup and outgroups. . . .

INTERGROUP ANXIETY

Like other types of anxiety, intergroup anxiety stems from the anticipation of negative consequences. People appear to fear four types of negative consequences: negative psychological or behavioral consequences for the self, and negative evaluations by members of the outgroup and the ingroup.

Feared Negative Consequences

Negative Psychological Consequences for the Self In intergroup interactions, people experience a variety of self concerns. They often fear embarrassment due to their own or others' behavior (as in the above example of the woman asked to entertain Japanese businesspeople). People may also be worried about feeling incompetent, confused, or not in control. People frequently anticipate discomfort, frustration, and irritation due to the awkwardness of intergroup interactions. In addition, loss of self-esteem is feared in some situations; in others, people are concerned that their sense of group identity will be threatened. Further, people sometimes worry that they will feel guilty if they behave in ways that offend or harm others. In unusual cases people actually fear acceptance by a disliked outgroup.

Negative Behavioral Consequences for the Self Members of ingroups may fear that outgroup members will take advantage of, exploit, or dominate them. This is especially true for members of low-status groups who fear discrimination from high-status groups. Ingroup members may also fear physical harm or verbal conflict (as in the example of the Anglo construction worker who fears his co-workers). In some contexts, people worry about performing poorly in the presence of outgroup members.

Negative Evaluations by Outgroup Members Ingroup members frequently fear rejection in intergroup interactions. Members of low-status groups often expect the outgroup to act as if the ingroup is inferior by displaying scorn or disdain (as in the example of the black engineering student). Ingroup members may also fear disapproval, ridicule, or being negatively stereotyped.

Negative Evaluations by Ingroup Members People commonly fear that members of their own group will disapprove of their interactions with outgroup members. They may be concerned that ingroup members will reject them or apply other sanctions (as in the example of the housewife and her new neighbor). In some instances, ingroup members fear being identified with the outgroup. While many of these sources of intergroup anxiety can affect interaction with ingroup members, ingroup members do not experience as much anxiety when interacting with members of their own group.

Intergroup anxiety can be distinguished from other related concepts such as culture shock, xenophobia, shyness, and social anxiety. Originally, culture shock referred to the anxiety that travelers experience upon losing the social cues that guide interaction in their own culture (O'Berg, 1960). Intergroup anxiety extends the concept of culture shock to include interactions with members of different groups *within* a culture, as well as between cultures. Also, intergroup anxiety is occasioned by a wide range of feared consequences, not simply the loss of cues to social interaction. Xenophobia is clinically defined as an irrational fear of foreigners or strangers. By contrast, intergroup anxiety often has a basis in reality. People sometimes do make embarrassing mistakes, are taken advantage of, and are rejected by ingroup or out-group members in intergroup interactions. Intergroup anxiety differs from shyness and social anxiety in two ways: (1) it is specific to members of certain outgroups and may not apply to ingroup members, and (2) it has a range of consequences broader than a simple reluctance to engage in interaction.

ANTECEDENTS OF INTERGROUP ANXIETY

The antecedents of intergroup anxiety can be divided into three broad categories: prior relations between the groups, prior cognitions concerning the outgroup, and the structure of the interaction.

Prior Intergroup Relations

The most important aspect of prior intergroup relations is the contact that has occurred between the groups. Both the amount of prior contact and the conditions under which the contact has occurred affect intergroup anxiety.

Amount of Contact Where contact between groups has been minimal, future interactions will produce high levels of intergroup anxiety. When two groups have had extensive contact where roles are well-defined, norms evolve for the conduct of intergroup relations. Where clear norms for interaction are clear, intergroup anxiety will generally be low—at least within the contexts governed by these norms. In the 1950s, for instance, blacks and whites who worked together in coal mines developed work relations that involved relatively little strain, but this lack of strain did not extend to interactions above ground (Minard, 1952).

Conditions of Contact If prior relations between the groups have been characterized by conflict, then even in situations where the norms are clear anxiety may be high.

The members of two or more groups whose economic or political interests conflict tend to experience more anxiety when interacting than do members of groups whose interests coincide.

Prior status differences between groups also promote interaction anxiety. High-status groups tend to regard low-status groups as inferior and may disdain interaction with their members. They may also fear the resentment of low-status groups, feel guilty about their own advantaged position, or justify their advantaged status by disparaging the outgroup. Such concerns may account for the findings in laboratory studies that whites display elevated galvanic skin responses (GSR) in the presence of blacks (e.g., Rankin & Campbell, 1955; Vidulich & Krevanick, 1966).

Members of low-status groups are likely to experience anxiety because they anticipate inferior treatments or exploitation. They may resent members of high-status groups and be concerned that their resentment will manifest itself. Conversely, if the members of the low-status group accept some aspects of their lower status, they may fear interaction with outgroup members because they regard themselves as inferior. As Braddock (1985) suggests, concerns about interacting and competing with whites may be one reason why blacks who have attended segregated schools are less likely to attend integrated colleges than are blacks who have attended desegregated schools.

Mediating Variables for Contact Individuals' acceptance of the ingroup's perceptions mediate the effects of the historical relationship between groups. In general, ingroup members share the views of their own group, especially if they have little prior personal contact with the outgroup. However, there are exceptions. For instance, an individual who is aware that the ingroup regards itself as inferior, but who does not share this view, will experience less anxiety about intergroup interaction than one who accepts the ingroup's view. Also, some ingroup members may have extensive contact with an outgroup, even though contact is atypical. Such prior contact should reduce anxiety about interacting with the outgroup. Similarly, some individuals experience little conflict in their interactions with outgroup members, even though relations between the groups are generally characterized by conflict. This prior positive contact will also reduce intergroup anxiety.

Prior Intergroup Cognitions

A second category of determinants of intergroup anxiety consists of prior intergroup cognitions. We here focus on "outgroup schemata"—cognitive structures that organize ingroup members' knowledge about the outgroup. Outgroup schemata contain knowledge about the culture of the other group, stereotypes and prejudices concerning outgroups, ethnocentric beliefs, expectations for intergroup interaction, and perceptions of ingroup–outgroup differences.

The knowledge that members of two groups have about one another is determined, in part, by the amount and the conditions of prior contact. In the absence of prior contact the ingroup is largely ignorant of the outgroup, and its schemata are relatively simple. Increasing contact leads to more complex and better articulated views of the outgroup (Triandis & Vassilou, 1972).

Knowledge of Subjective Culture When two groups have had little prior contact, anxiety about interacting with the other group may be high because each group is ignorant of the other's values, norms, roles, and nonverbal behaviors. Such knowledge of the other group's subjective culture (Triandis, 1972) often consists of information about norms and values that even members of the ingroup may have difficulty articulating.

When members of two groups lack information about each other's subjective culture, members of both groups may justifiably feel incompetent about interacting with one another. They may fear making mistakes, being misunderstood, or being rejected. They may also experience uncertainty, confusion, and stress during interaction, making such interactions frustrating and unsatisfactory. When the two groups do not share the same language, their interaction is complicated even further. One study of the relationship between ignorance and anxiety, found that whites responded with anxiety when they became aware of their ignorance about the subjective culture of blacks (Randolph, Landis & Tzeng, 1977).

Stereotypes and Prejudice Many outgroup stereotypes and beliefs reflect a negative variety of perceptual and motivational biases, including biased labeling of group similarities and differences (LeVine & Campbell, 1972), social comparisons that favor the ingroup (Brewer, 1979a), and projection. Negative stereotypes about outgroups create anxiety, because they lead ingroup members to expect negative behaviors. People are unlikely to anticipate positive interaction with members of disliked outgroups. Several studies have found that prejudice toward blacks is correlated with GSR arousal in reaction to blacks, thus providing evidence that prejudice can create anxiety (Porier & Lott, 1967; Vidulich & Krevanick, 1966).

Ethnocentrism Ethnocentrism, the belief that the ingroup is superior to the outgroup, is a particularly important aspect of ethnic relations (LeVine & Campbell, 1972). So basic is ethnocentrism to intergroup relations that perceived superiority has been found even in minimal interactions between members of arbitrarily created groups (Brewer, 1979b; Tajfel, 1978). The effects of perceived superiority are similar to those of perceived higher status: people who regard themselves as superior experience anxiety concerning interaction with others who are regarded as inferior.

Expectations Scripts, norms, and other expectations reduce anxiety if positive behaviors are expected; they increase anxiety if negative behaviors are expected. For instance, the executive with Japanese guests mentioned at the beginning of this article might assume that similar positive scripts for attending concerts exist in both cultures. Therefore, she probably would not be anxious if she took her guests to a concert. On the other hand, taking her guests to a night club could occasion considerable anxiety, since the social script for night-clubbing is more ambiguous and negative behavior such as inebriation could occur.

Perceptions of Ingroup-Outgroup Differences In the absence of prior interaction, ingroup members are apt to assume that outgroup members are different from them. In addition, assimilation and contrast effects are likely to exaggerate real group differences, leading people to believe within-group homogeneity and between-group differences are greater than they actually are. Assumed and actual dissimilarity will lead ingroup members to believe they do not know how to interact with outgroup members. It may also lead them to anticipate disliking outgroup members and being disliked by them (Gonzales, Davis, Loney, LuKena, & Junghans, 1983). The greater the assumed or actual difference, the more anxiety ingroup members are likely to feel.

Structure of the Situation

The last category of antecedents to be discussed consists of situational factors: (1) amount of structure—from highly structured to highly unstructured situations; (2) type of interdependence—cooperative, competitive, or no interdependence; (3) group composition—the ratio of ingroup to outgroup members; and (4) relative status—the effects of differential status within the interaction.

Amount of Structure In general, unstructured interactions (e.g., getting acquainted) will evoke more intergroup anxiety than structured situations (e.g., completing a task in which there are predetermined roles for each person). In structured situations, roles and norms provide people with guides for their behavior. Because structure lowers ambiguity, it decreases anxiety.

Type of Interdependence Considerable research suggests that intergroup interaction is more positive when the reward structure of the situation is cooperative rather than competitive or individual (Slavin, 1985). The positive interaction inherent in cooperation stems from shared goals; when ingroup members gain, so do outgroup members. The negative interaction typical of competition is derived from its zero-sum goal structure: what ingroup members gain, the outgroup members must lose. Generally, cooperative interdependence lowers anxiety, compared to competition or no interdependence at all. However, during the initial phases of interaction, cooperation may lead to considerable anxiety due to the close contact and coordination required. For instance, the members of an interracial football team may not be at ease with one another at the beginning of the season, but as the season progresses they should become more at ease. By contrast, even at the end of the season the team members are unlikely to be equally at ease with other-race members of competing teams.

Group Composition Anxiety will be higher in situations in which the rate of outgroup to ingroup members is high than where the ratio is low. When the ratio is high, the norms and values of the outgroup are likely to dominate. In such situations, the group identity of ingroup members becomes salient (McGuire & McGuire, 1982) and ingroup members may fear discrimination. When the ratio of outgroup to ingroup members is low, the ingroup members will typically have more control over the interaction and will experience less anxiety as a consequence.

Relative Status We have previously discussed the effects of prior status differences between groups. In this section we address the effects of status differences within the interaction situation. Deviations from equal status among the participants tend to increase anxiety. Status disequilibria favoring the ingroup will cause ingroup members less anxiety than those favoring the outgroup. When individuals' status within the interaction differs from their perceived status outside the interaction, anxiety will also be increased, especially if the individuals' status within the group is lower than their status outside the group. . . .

CONSEQUENCES OF INTERGROUP ANXIETY

Next we turn to the consequences of intergroup anxiety. Intergroup anxiety is important because it potentially has negative effects on intergroup relations. While the consequences depend to some extent on the specific feared outcomes, we argue that general patterns of responses occur regardless of the origin of the anxiety. . . .

Behavioral Consequences

Normative response patterns will be amplified in interactions where intergroup anxiety is high. This hypothesis is derived from drive theory (Hull, 1951). As drive increases, so does the intensity of habitual responses to a situation. Since anxiety contributes to drive, it tends to energize dominant responses. We first discuss avoidance, the most common behavioral response, and then examine the role of social norms.

Avoidance The dominant response to many forms of anxiety is avoidance, because it so often reduces anxiety. Thus intergroup anxiety leads to the avoidance of intergroup interaction when it is possible (e.g., Pancer, McMullen, Kabatoff, Johnson, & Pond, 1979). If avoidance is not possible, interaction is frequently terminated as quickly as possible.

For example, avoidance is exhibited by members of nonstigmatized groups toward the stigmatized. The nonstigmatized often act as though interaction with the stigmatized will result in their contamination by the stigma (Goffman, 1963). Some societies have explicit norms regarding avoidance, as was the case for high-caste Hindus contact with untouchables. In relations between other groups—such as relations between nonhandicapped and handicapped people or between mental patients and "normals"—avoidance norms appear to be implicit.

Intergroup Interaction Norms In interaction between the members of two groups with a history of mutual relations, normative behavioral responses will be amplified by intergroup anxiety. As anxiety increases, norms will be followed in more rigid and exaggerated ways. For example, if the norm prescribes or condones politeness, then individuals will be more polite as they become more anxious. If past relations have been negative and norms of outgroup rejection have evolved, then high anxiety should amplify rejection. In general, norms for intergroup interaction prescribe behavior that is formal and superficial, because such behavior appears to reduce anxiety and minimizes negative outcomes.

Status differences between groups are often associated with normative response patterns. High-status groups may have norms that prescribe discrimination against members of low-status groups. Since anxiety amplifies normative behavior, high anxiety can lead members of high-status groups to become more arrogant or condescending. The most extreme discrimination, arrogance, and condescension occur when an ingroup's superior status is threatened by an outgroup. This could explain the rudeness of tourists from industrialized countries who travel to developing countries and find to their surprise that the residents do not regard themselves as inferior.

Among the dominant responses of members of low-status groups who experience anxiety in intergroup interactions are submission and ingratiation. Such behaviors help avoid negative treatment by members of a high-status group.

The Absence of Intergroup Interaction Norms In the absence of intergroup interaction norms, ingroup norms for the treatment of unfamiliar ingroup members will be elicited. If these norms call for suspicion as they often do, suspicion will be intensified, even to the point of paranoia when ingroup members experience high anxiety. In contrast, if norms call for quiet reserve, then under high anxiety reserved behavior will become intensified.

Such amplified normative responses may contribute to group stereotypes. In interactions where anxiety is high, the members of each group observe members of the other group behaving in consistent and distinctive ways. Neither group, however, is likely to be aware that much of the behavior they observe is caused by the anxiety generated by their own presence. They are therefore likely to base trait inferences about the other group on these behaviors. The stereotype held by Americans that the English are cold and snobbish, and the stereotype held by the English that Americans are forward and intrusive, may have their origins in exaggerated behaviors produced by intergroup anxiety. Such stereotypes have a kernel of truth that even the ingroup recognizes.

Another common response to the absence of intergroup interaction norms is social incompetence, which may be manifested in extreme withdrawal, hesitance, or confusion. For example, it has been suggested that the confused behavior of white liberals toward blacks is due to social incompetence brought about by anxiety (Poskocil, 1977). White liberals may feel guilty about the past treatment of blacks by whites, and may be concerned that their own behavior will confirm blacks' negative stereotypes of whites. In consequence, they do not know how to behave: whether to be ingratiating, to behave as if the other person were not black, to be overly agreeable no matter what the situation, or to confess their discomfort. Caught among such conflicting options, they cannot do anything with ease. One common response to such feelings of incompetence is imitation. When ingroup members fear rejection from the outgroup, they often pattern their behavior after the behavior of outgroup members. . . .

Finally, when specific negative consequences are feared, these fears can lead to preemptive behavior. A fear of hostility, for instance, may lead to the preemptive use of aggression (Snyder & Swann, 1978). Thus, when ingroup members anticipate rejection they themselves may become rejecting and turn the expectation into a self-fulfilling prophecy. Anxiety should amplify such responses.

Cognitive Consequences

Three types of cognitive consequences of intergroup anxiety are information-processing biases, motivational biases, and self-awareness.

Information Processing Biases Intergroup anxiety will increase schematic processing and simplify information processing. If scripts for outgroup interaction or expectations based on stereotypes exist, these schematic structures will be used to process the behavior of outgroup members. Expected behaviors will be attended to, while small deviations are unlikely to be noticed or remembered (cf. Marcus & Sentis, 1982). In addition, people may actively seek out information confirming their expectations about outgroup members (Carver & de la Garza, 1984; Wilder & Allen, 1978). Thus, when anxiety is high, intergroup interaction will typically lead the ingroup to perceive that its expectations have been confirmed. However, extremely unusual or negative outgroup behavior may command attention. Since attributions typically follow the focus of attention, strong trait inferences would be expected in such situations (cf. Rothbart & John, 1985).

The arousal that anxiety creates will generally narrow the focus of attention (Easterbrook, 1959). Since attention is allocated to a narrow range of topics, the individual will allocate less attention to other information. Under these conditions, much social information will be minimally processed, and biases can enter the inference process. Thus intergroup anxiety should be associated with an increased reliance on cognitive strategies that involve simplified and biased processing of information about others. . . . . .

Motivational Biases Heightened anxiety will increase concerns for self-esteem, particularly when people feel that their self-esteem is threatened by the interaction. Threats to self-esteem lead ingroup members to make both ego-defensive and ego-enhancing attributions for their own behavior. For example, they tend to justify negative behaviors they may direct toward the outgroup (Katz & Glass, 1979; Katz, Glass, & Cohen, 1973).

The perception of threats to one's group identity will increase the tendency toward ingroup bias in the evaluation of group differences. Traits on which the ingroup is perceived to be superior receive more attention than traits on which the outgroup is perceived superior. Thus, intergroup anxiety feeds ethnocentrism by leading people to emphasize the "superior" characteristics of their own group.

Self-awareness Intergroup anxiety will intensify either private or public self-awareness (Buss, 1980; Scheier & Carver, 1983). The type of self-awareness elicited depends on the origin of the anxiety. If ingroup members fear negative psychological consequences for the self, they will experience intense private self-awareness—i.e., direct their attention toward internal states and standards. Private self-awareness leads one to evaluate the self and others in terms of one's personal standards. It may account for the extreme rejection of the customs of an outgroup that is characteristic of culture shock. Other effects of self-awareness, such as resistance to persuasion and to conformity may also be heightened. Thus, intensified private self-awareness may account for the tendency of some people to behave in self-righteous ways in intergroup situations (e.g., the ugly American).

When ingroup members fear negative evaluations by outgroup or ingroup members, their attention is focused outward and they will experience public self-awareness (awareness of the self as an object of others' attention). Public self-awareness leads people to evaluate their behavior in terms of norms and standards relevant to the situation (Buss, 1980). Three sets of norms can influence intergroup interactions. First, if norms for intergroup interaction exist, ingroup members will evaluate their behaviors against these norms. Second, if the ingroup members know the norms and standards of the outgroup, and if relations between the groups are not antagonistic, they may use these norms to evaluate their own behavior. Finally, if ingroup norms exist for relations with outgroup members, these norms may be used to evaluate behavior.

The set of norms used depends on factors such as the salience and clarity of the norms, the cost and rewards of complying with the norms, and the presence of other ingroup members. For instance, a lone black student in a class of white students would probably conform to his or her perceptions of the white norms, but the black student's behavior might change to conform to ingroup norms if several of his or her friends were in the class. If ingroup members find that they are not behaving appropriately when judged against the norms they are using, they may change their behavior to conform to the norms, justify their failure to conform, switch to a different set of norms, or denigrate the norms or themselves. Determining which avenue would be taken is a project for future empirical study.

Affective Consequences

We will discuss two affective consequences of intergroup anxiety: amplified emotional and evaluative reactions.

Emotional Reactions The arousal generated by intergroup anxiety will transfer readily to other emotions elicited in the situation. This transfer leads to augmented emotional responses during the interaction and amplified evaluative responses afterwards. Positive interactions will produce strong positive emotions, while negative interactions will have the opposite effect. Among the positive emotions are relief, joy, or even love; negative emotions frequently include fear, hate, resentment, guilt, disgust, or righteous indignation.

Participants in intergroup interactions are likely to overreact to slight provocations or misunderstandings. Because frustration is a common feature of such interactions, expressions of anger can surface more easily in intergroup than in ingroup interactions—particularly if the groups have a history of conflict or if ethnocentrism, negative stereotypes, or strong prejudices exist. Due to the misunderstandings, frustration, and conflicts that often occur, amplified negative emotions are more likely than positive ones.

Evaluative Reactions Intergroup anxiety will amplify evaluative responses toward outgroup members. Amplified negative evaluations occur in interactions in which ingroup members experience negative emotions or outcomes (Blanchard, Adelman, & Cook, 1975). In addition, negative evaluations are likely where outgroup members have violated the norms, scripts, or expectations held by the ingroup (Costrich, Feinstein, Kidder, Maracek, & Pascale, 1975), particularly if the norm violations are costly for the ingroup (Gergen & Jones, 1963). Whereas an outgroup's violation of norms leads to negative evaluations, its conformity does not lead to particularly positive evaluations.

Positive outcomes or the experience of positive emotions in intergroup interactions will lead to amplified positive evaluations (Gibbons, Stephan, Stephenson & Petty, 1981; Linville & Jones, 1980). Thus, when ingroup members are extremely anxious about interacting with outgroup members but the interaction goes well, the relief and other positive emotions that ingroup members experience will be translated into highly favorable evaluations. Such a process could help account for the frequency with which servicemen fall in love in foreign countries. . . .

REFERENCES

Blanchard, F. A., Adelman, & Cook, S. W. (1975). Effect of group success and failure upon interpersonal attraction in cooperating interracial groups. *Journal of Personality and Social Psychology, 31,* 1020–1030.

Braddock, J. H. (1985). School desegregation and black assimilation. *Journal of Social Issues, 41(3)* 9–22.

Brewer, M. B. (1979a). The role of ethnocentrism in intergroup conflict. In W. Austin & S. Worchel (Eds.), *The social psychology of intergroup relations* (pp. 71–84). Monterey, CA: Brooks/Cole.

Brewer, M. B. (1979b). In-group bias in the minimal group situation: A cognitive motivational analysis. *Psychological Bulletin, 86,* 307–324.

Brewer, M. B., & Miller, N. (1984). Beyond the contact hypothesis: Theoretical perspectives on desegregation. In N. Miller & M. B. Brewer (Eds.), *Groups in contact: The psychology of desegregation* (pp. 281–302). New York: Academic Press.

Buss, A. (1980). *Self-consciousness and social anxiety.* San Francisco, CA: Freeman.

Carver, C. S., & de la Garza, N. (1984). Schema-guided information search in stereotyping of the elderly. *Journal of Applied Social Psychology, 14,* 69–81.

Costrich, N. J., Feinstein, J., Kidder, L., Maracek, J., & Pascale, L. (1975). When stereotypes hurt: Three studies of penalties for sex–role reversals. *Journal of Experimental Social Psychology, 11,* 520–530.

Easterbrook, J. A. (1959). The effect of emotion on cue utilization and the organization of behavior. *Psychological Review, 66,* 83–201.

Gergen, K. J., & Jones, E. E. (1963). Mental illness, predictability, and affective consequences as stimulus factors in person perception. *Journal of Abnormal and Social Psychology, 6,* 95–104.

Gibbons, F. X., Stephan, W. G., Stephenson, B., & Petty, C. R. (1981). Contact relevance and reactions to stigmatized others: Response amplification vs. sympathy. *Journal of Experimental Social Psychology, 16,* 591–605.

Goffman, E. (1963). *Stigma.* Englewood Cliffs, NJ: Prentice-Hall.

Gonzales, M. H., Davis, J. M., Loney, G. L., LuKena, C. K., & Junghans, C. M. (1983). Interactional approach to interpersonal attraction. *Journal of Personality and Social Psychology, 44,* 1192–1197.

Hull, C. L. (1951). *Essentials of behavior.* New Haven, CT: Yale University Press.

Katz, I., & Glass, D. G. (1979). An ambivalence-amplification theory of behavior toward the stigmatized. In W. Austin & S. Worchel (Eds.), *The social psychology of intergroup relations* (pp. 55–70). Monterey, CA: Brooks/Cole.

Katz, I., Glass, D. G., & Cohen, S. (1973). Ambivalence, guilt, and the scapegoating of minority group victims. *Journal of Experimental Social Psychology, 9,* 423–436.

LeVine, R. A., & Campbell, D. T. (1972). *Ethnocentrism: Theories of conflict, ethnic attitudes and group behavior.* New York: John Wiley and Sons.

Linville, P. W., & Jones, E. E. (1980). Polarized appraisals of outgroup members. *Journal of Personality and Social Psychology, 38,* 689–703.

Marcus, H., & Sentis, K. (1982). The self in social interaction. In J. Suls (Ed.), *Psychological perspectives on the self* (Vol. I, pp. 41–70). Hillsdale, NJ: Erlbaum.

McArthur, L. Z., & Soloman, L. K. (1978). Perceptions of an aggressive encounter as a function of the victim's salience and the perceiver's arousal. *Journal of Personality and Social Psychology, 36,* 1278–1290.

McCauley, C., & Stitt, C. L. (1978). An individual and quantitative measure of stereotypes. *Journal of Personality and Social Psychology, 36,* 929–940.

McGuire, W. J., & McGuire, C. V. (1982). Significant other in the self-space: Sex differences and developmental trends in the social self. In J. Suls (ed.), *Psychological perspectives on the self* (Vol. I, pp. 71–96). Hillsdale, NJ: Erlbaum.

Minard, R. D. (1952). Race relationships in the Pocahontas coal field. *Journal of Social Issues, 8,* 29–44.

O'Berg, K. (1960). Cultural shock: Adjustment to new cultural environments. *Practical Anthropology, 7,* 177–182.

Pancer, S. M., McMullen, L. M., Kabatoff, R. A., Johnson, K. G., & Pond, C. A. (1979). Conflict and avoidance in the helping situation. *Journal of Personality and Social Psychology, 37,* 1406–1411.

Pettigrew, T. F. (1979). The ultimate attribution error: Extending Allport's cognitive analysis of prejudice. *Personality and Social Psychology Bulletin, 5,* 461–476.

Porier, G. W. & Lott, A. J. (1967). Galvanic skin response and prejudice. *Journal of Personality and Social Psychology, 5*, 253-259.

Poskocil, A. (1977). Encounters between black and white liberals: The collision of stereotypes. *Social Forces, 55*, 715-727.

Randolph, G., Landis, D., & Tzeng, O. C. S. (1977). The effects of time and practice upon cultural assimilator training. *International Journal of Intercultural Relations, 1*, 105-119.

Rankin, R. E., & Campbell, D. T. (1955). Galvanic skin response to Negro and White experimenters. *Journal of Abnormal and Social Psychology. 51*, 30-33.

Rothbart, M., & John, O. (1985). Social categorization and behavioral episodes: A cognitive analysis of the effects of intergroup contact. *Journal of Social Issues, 41(3)*, 81-103.

Scheier, M. F., & Carver, C. S. (1983). Two sides to the self: One for you and one for me. In J. Suls & A. G. Greenwald (Eds.), *Psychological perspectives on the self* (Vol. II, pp. 123-159). Hillsdale, NJ: Erlbaum.

Slavin, R. E. (1985). Cooperative learning: Applying contact theory in desegregated schools. *Journal of Social Issues, 41(3)*, 45-62.

Snyder, M., & Swann, W. B., Jr. (1978). Behavioral confirmation in social interaction: From social perception to social reality. *Journal of Experimental Social Psychology, 14*, 148-162.

Stephan, W. G. (1985). Intergroup relations. In G. Lindzey & E. Aronson (Eds.), *Handbook of social psychology* (Vol. III, pp. 599-659). New York: Random House.

Stephan, W. G., & Rosenfield, D. (1979). Black self-rejection: Another look. *Journal of Educational Psychology, 71*, 708-716.

Stephan, W. G., & Stephan, C. W. (1984). The role of ignorance in intergroup relations. In N. Miller & M. B. Brewer (Eds.), *Groups in contact: The psychology of desegregation* (pp. 229-257). New York: Academic Press.

Tajfel, H. (1978). *Differentiation between social groups.* London: Academic Press.

Triandis, H. C. (1972). *The analysis of subjective culture.* New York: John Wiley and Sons.

Triandis, H. C., & Vassilou, V. (1972). Frequency of contact and stereotyping in two cultures. *Journal of Personality and Social Psychology, 7*, 316-328.

Vidulich, R. N., & Krevanick, F. W. (1966). Racial attitudes and emotional response to visual representation of the Negro. *Journal of Social Psychology, 68*, 82-93.

Wilder, D. A., & Allen, V. L. (1978). Group membership and preference for information about others. *Personality and Social Psychology Bulletin, 4*, 106-110.

CHAPTER 2

Issues in the Study of Intercultural Communication

When we communicate, we make "predictions" about the outcomes of our communication (Miller & Steinberg, 1975). Outcomes include, but are not limited to, whether the other person will respond as we expect him or her to respond and whether we will get along with the other person. Our predictions about others' behavior allow us to know what to expect when we communicate with them. We are highly aware of some of our predictions, but we are not highly aware of most of the predictions we make.

Miller and Steinberg (1975) contend that we use three different types of "data" in making predictions about others: *cultural, sociological,* and *psychological.* People in any culture generally behave consistently because of the norms, rules, and values of their culture. This regularity allows cultural information to be used in making predictions. Miller and Sunnafrank (1982) point out that "knowledge about another person's culture—its language, beliefs, and prevailing ideology—often permits predictions of the person's probable response to messages . . . . Upon first encountering . . . [another person], cultural information provides the only grounds for communicative predictions" (p. 226). If we are introduced to a person from the United States, we can make certain assumptions about the person's understanding of introduction rituals. We implicitly predict, for example, that if we stick out our right hand to shake hands, she or he will do the same.

Our predictions are based on the category in which we place the other person (e.g., member of my culture, not a member of my culture). One of the major cognitive tools we use to define ourselves in terms of the world in which we live is social categorization. Social categorization refers to the way we order our social environment (i.e., the people with whom we come in contact) by grouping people in a way that makes sense to us (Tajfel, 1978). We may, for example, divide people into women and men, white and nonwhite, black and nonblack, "Americans" and foreigners, to name only a few of the sets of categories we use. In categorizing others and ourselves, we become aware of being members of social groups.

When we communicate with strangers, we cannot base our predictions of their behavior on *our* cultural rules and norms. This inevitably will lead to misunderstanding. If we want to communicate effectively, we must use our knowedge of the strangers' culture to make our predictions. If we have little or no knowledge of *their* culture, we have no basis for making accurate predictions. "This fact explains the uneasiness and perceived lack of control most people experience when thrust into an alien culture; they not only lack information about the individuals with whom they must communicate, they are bereft of information concerning shared cultural norms and values" (Miller & Sunnafrank, 1982, p. 227).

Sociological predictions also are based on memberships in or aspirations to particular social groups or social roles. Miller and Sunnafrank (1982) argue that sociological data are the principal kind used to predict behavior of people from our own culture (when we communicate intraculturally). Group memberships based on ethnicity, gender, religion, disabilities, gender orientation, and so on, are used to predict others' behavior. We use our stereotypes of these groups to make unconscious predictions of how members of the different groups will behave. Roles such as professor, physician, clerk, supervisor, for example, also provide a basis for the sociological predictions we make because we expect people in these positions to behave in certain ways.

When we base our predictions on cultural or sociological information, we are assuming that the people within the category (e.g., the culture or ethnic group) are similar. Although individuals within a category share similarities (e.g., there are similarities shared by people born and raised in the United States, such as the value freedom), individuals within each of the categories also differ. When we are able to discriminate how individuals are similar to and different from other members of the same category, we are using psychological data to make predictions. This process also is referred to as "particularization." The use of psychological data involves taking the specific person with whom we are communicating and her or his attitudes, values, and feelings, as well as how she or he will respond to our messages, into consideration when we make our predictions.

Miller and Steinberg (1975) point out that we use cultural and sociological data in the vast majority of the interactions we have. There is nothing "wrong" with this. It is natural, and it is necessary to allow us to deal with the complexity of our social environment. Imagine going into a restaurant and having to "get to know" your waiter or waitress so that you could make psychological predictions about his or her behavior before you could place your order. This would complicate our lives and is not necessary. We can communicate effectively with a waitress or waiter without using psychological data. Sociological data are all that are necessary to get our order correct. We know from experience with the waiter/waitress role how he or she will behave. The same is true for most other role relationships that do not involve extended interaction (e.g., with clerks, mechanics, and so on).

When we communicate frequently with someone in a specific role relationship, using psychological data becomes important. Physicians who treat all patients alike (i.e., use only sociological data) will not be very effective. Successfully treating patients requires knowledge of them both as patients and as individuals. Physicians must know enough about individual patients to be able to predict how they will respond to particular treatments and medications similarly to and differently from other patients. Communicating effectively with strangers also requires differentiating individuals from the groups of which they are members. Relying completely on cultural and/or sociological data when communicating with strangers over an extended period of time inevitably leads to misunderstandings. Effective communication requires that some psychological data be used.

Effective communication with strangers also requires that we are mindful of our communication. Langer (1989) isolates three qualities of mindfulness: "(1) creation of new categories; (2) openness to new information; and (3) awareness of more than one perspective" (p. 62). She points out that we cannot become mindful by stopping our categorization of others; "categorizing is a fundamental and natural human activity. It is the way we come to know the world. Any attempt to eliminate bias by attempting to eliminate the perception of differences is doomed to failure" (p. 154).

Langer (1989) argues that what we need to do is learn to make more, not fewer, distinctions. To illustrate, Langer uses an example of people who are in the category "cripple." If we see all people in this category as the same, we start treating the category in which we place a person as his or her identity. If we draw additional distinctions within this category (i.e., create new categories), on the other hand, it stops us from treating the person as a category. If we see a person with a "lame leg," we do not necessarily treat her or him as a "cripple."

Openness to new information and awareness of more than one perspective are related to focusing on the process, rather than the outcome. Langer argues that

> an outcome orientation in social situations can induce mindlessness. If we think we know how to handle a situation, we don't feel a need to pay attention. If we respond to the situation as very familiar (as a result, for example, of overlearning), we notice only minimal cues necessary to carry out the proper scenarios. If, on the other hand, the situation is strange, we might be so preoccupied with the thought of failure ("what if I make a fool of myself?") that we miss nuances of our own and others' behavior. In this sense, we are mindless with respect to the immediate situation, although we may be thinking quite actively about outcome related issues. (p. 34)

Langer believes that focusing on the process (e.g., how we do something) forces us to be mindful of our behavior and pay attention to the situations in which we find ourselves. It is only when we are mindful of the process of our communication that we can determine how our interpretations of messages differ from others' interpretations of those messages. When we are mindful we can see how others might not interpret our messages the way we meant them to be interpreted.

The first reading in this chapter deals with the concept of the stranger. Levine summarizes how the concept of the stranger has been used in the past and how we react to strangers. He points out, for example, that because strangers are not part of the ingroup, our response involves high levels of uncertainty and anxiety.

The final two readings in this chapter deal with the issue of mindfulness and the dialectic between categorization and particularization. In the second reading, Langer describes what she means by mindfulness and outlines how we can apply in it in our communication with others. In the third reading, Billig discusses how the processes of categorization and particularization are interlinked.

REFERENCES

Langer, E. (1989). *Mindfulness*. Reading, MA: Addison-Wesley.
Miller, G., & Steinberg, M. (1975). *Between people*. Chicago: Science Research Associates.
Miller, G., & Sunnafrank, M. (1982). All is for one but one is not for all. In F. Dance (Ed.), *Human communication theory*. New York: Harper & Row.
Tajfel, H. (1978). Social categorization, social identify, and social comparisons. In H. Tajfel (Ed.), *Differentiation between social groups*. London: Academic Press.

The Sociology of the Stranger
Donald N. Levine

In sociology, as in other disciplines (if not more so), certain concepts bear a special freight for being linked so closely with major figures in the history of the field. . . . In the case of the sociological concept of the stranger, the relevant association is of course to Georg Simmel. . . .

Simmel is perhaps most widely known among anglophone social scientists for his six-page excursus on the stranger. What is less well known is that this "classic essay" originally appeared as a note, a mere digression, in a long chapter entitled "Space and the Spatial Ordering of Society."[1] . . .

It is likely that the excursus, as a stimulus both to studies of the role of the stranger and to work on the related concept of social distance, has been cited in more social scientific research than any of Simmel's writings . . . .

[I]f we are now to . . . transform the sociology of the stranger from a random collection of very uneven forays into a substantial body of codified knowledge, we can learn a good deal from the many writings which have taken Simmel's formulations as a key point of reference, even though they were headed in so many different directions.

Let me begin by referring to the work of Robert E. Park, a man who did so much to make Simmel's work known in American sociology in the 1920s and who produced the first English translation of *Der Fremde*.[2] In his seminal essay of 1928 "Human Migration and the Marginal Man," Park cited Simmel's definition of the stranger and

Source: Adapted from "Simmel at a Distance: On the History and Systemnatics of the Sociology of the Stranger," Chapter 1 in W. Shack and E. Skinner (Eds.), *Strangers in African Societies* (Berkeley: University of California Press, 1979).

proceeded to delineate a concept of the marginal man [or woman] as its equivalent—an equivalence illustrated by his remark that "the emancipated Jew was, and is, historically and typically the marginal man [or woman]. . . . He [or she] is, par excellence, the 'stranger,' whom Simmel, himself a Jew, has described with such profound insight and understanding."[3]

Commenting on this adaptation of Simmel's concept, Alvin Boskoff has recently observed: "Park borrowed the concept of the stranger and applied it to the phenomena of migration and culture contact in complex society. Briefly, Park suggested that various kinds of deviant behavior (crime, delinquency, illegitimacy) reflected the experience of persons who, by migrating, had given up old values but had not adequately acquired the norms and skills of their new setting."[4]

It should be clear, however, that in the borrowing Park altered the shape of the concept: his "marginal man" [or woman] represents a configuration notably different from Simmel's "stranger." Thinking of the experience of ethnic minorities in zones of culture contact in American cities, Park conceived the marginal man [or woman] as a racial or cultural hybrid—"one who lives in two worlds, in both of which he [or she] is more or less of a stranger"—one who aspires to but is excluded from full membership in a new group. Simmel's stranger, by contrast, does not aspire to be assimilated; he [or she] is a potential wanderer, one who has not quite got over the freedom of coming and going. Where Park's excluded marginal man [or woman] was depicted as suffering from spiritual instability, intensified self-consciousness, restlessness, and malaise, Simmel's stranger, occupying a determinate position in relation to the group, was depicted as a successful trader, a judge, and a trusted confidant.

In his extended study *The Marginal Man*, Park's student Everett Stonequist indicated his awareness that Park's "marginal man" [or woman] was not identical with Simmel's "stranger." He observed, first, that marginality need not be produced by migration, but could also come about through internal changes like education and marriage. More explicitly, he stated:

> The stranger, [Simmel] writes, first appears as a trader, one who is not fixed in space, yet settles for a time in the community—a "potential wanderer." He [or she] unites in his [or her] person the qualities of "nearness and remoteness, concern and indifference." . . . This conception of the stranger pictures him [or her] as one who is not intimately and personally concerned with the social life about him [or her]. His [or her] relative detachment frees him [or her] from the self-consciousness, the concern for status, and the divided loyalties of the marginal man [or woman].[5]

Stonequist went on to note that the distinctive properties of the stranger identified by Simmel get lost once an individual moves into the position of being a marginal person.

In spite of Stonequist's clarity about this distinction, there has persisted in the literature a tendency to confuse the marginal man [or woman] concept with Simmel's "stranger."[6] Thus more than a decade later Everett Hughes uncritically repeated Park's view that Simmel's passages on the stranger referred to the same phenomenon as the marginal man [or woman].[7] And Boskoff, with comparable carelessness, glossed Simmel's stranger as "vulnerable to internal uncertainties."[8] Seeking to "re-examine the ubiquitous concept of 'marginal man [or woman]," Peter Rose did so by asking "how the 'stranger' in the midst of alien territory adapts to community life." After interviewing former urban Jews in several small towns in upstate New York, Rose concluded that their position could more aptly be described as one of duality rather than marginality, for they felt "we have the best of both." Rose considered his findings to provide evidence against the applicability of the concept of marginality, and to refute the view of "Stonequist [sic], Park, and others [who] have characterized the Jew as a disturbed marginal man [or woman], an eternal stranger [here Rose footnotes Simmel!] unable to reconcile the traditions of his [or her] people with the counter-forces of the majority world."[9] In making this point, Rose, like Hughes and Boskoff, was misreading Simmel through the distorting lens formed by Park. What he actually found was that the Jews in question were not adequately characterized by Park's concept of marginality, but that they might indeed be characterized in terms of Simmel's concept of the stranger.

If Stonequist's distinction between marginality and strangerhood was made only to be lost, it was inadvertently recovered by Paul C. P. Siu. In his investigation of Chinese laundrymen [or women] in Chicago, originally carried out as a study of "marginality," Siu was dismayed to find that "none of the Chinese laundrymen [or women] I studied could be considered a marginal man [or woman]." In this case, however, Siu did not use those findings to invalidate Simmel's conception of the stranger. Rather, he returned to Simmel to raise the question whether the marginal man [or woman] might not more aptly be viewed as one of a possible larger number of variant types of stranger. Siu then proposed a new type, the sojourner—who, in contrast to the bicultural complex of the marginal man [or woman], clings to the culture of his [or her] own ethnic group—and added a few notes on still another type of stranger, the settler.[10] The way was thus opened for a more differentiated view of phenomena previously lumped together under the diffuse categories of strangerhood or marginality.

Another related step, albeit in a different direction, had been taken around the time of Stonequist's study. Margaret Mary Wood's *The Stranger: A Study in Social Relationships* drew freely on Simmel, but adopted a definition of the stranger that was clearly differentiated from Simmel's:

> We shall describe the stranger as one who has come into face-to-face contact with the group for the first time. This concept is broader than that of Simmel, who defines the stranger as "the man [or woman] who comes today and stays tomorrow, the potential wanderer, who although he [or she] has gone no further, has not quite got over the freedom of coming and going." For us the stranger may be, as with Simmel, a potential wanderer, but he [or she] may also be a wanderer who comes today and goes tomorrow, or he [or she] may come today and remain with us permanently.[11]

In other words, Wood's topic was not the sojourner but the newly arrived outsider, and her concern was with those internal adjustments by which different types of groups adapt to his [or her] arrival in their midst. Her work might well have laid the groundwork for an extensive sociology of the stranger, in which Simmel's formulations would properly have been understood as referring to a special type; but as S. Dale McLemore stresses in a spirited review of some of the voluminous literature related to Simmel's essay, subsequent sociologists of the stranger tended to cite Simmel as the primary point of reference for the topic and, even when citing Wood, tended to miss the distinction between Wood's newly arrived outsider and Simmel's stranger.[12] Thus Julian Greifer, in the course of reconstructing the evolution of ancient Jewish attitudes toward the stranger, defines the stranger as one who "has come into face to face contact with the group for the first time," and in the next sentence refers to this stranger "as described by Georg Simmel."[13] Oscar Grusky similarly confuses the new arrival with Simmel's stranger by using the latter concept in describing the position of a newcomer in a line of administrative succession.[14]

In this context it is instructive to examine an experimental study which claims to draw inspiration from Simmel, "The Stranger in Laboratory Culture" by Dennison Nash and Alvin W. Wolfe. In a series of experiments in which a Rorschach card stimulus was presented to small groups of subjects over a number of "epochs," Nash and Wolfe sought to create a role which "would seem to approximate in the laboratory Simmel's description of the stranger." The hypothesis they tested, however, sprang from the ideas of Park, Stonequist, and others concerning the peculiar creativity of the marginal man [or woman]. What they found was that the "strangers" proved to be less innovative than other participants in the experiment.[15]

In spite of the experimental rigor with which this study was carried out, its value is limited by the double conceptual confusion on which it rests. It seeks to verify Simmel's formulations about the stranger by using hypotheses devised, not by Simmel, but by others concerned with a different social type, the marginal man [or woman]; and to do so by constructing an experimental role modeled, not on Simmel's "stranger," but on the still different type of the newly arrived person. Nash and Wolfe were led by their unexpected findings to draw a distinction between persons socialized in a marginal situation and persons introduced into such a situation briefly as adults. The distinction seems useful, and broadly parallels the distinctions noted above between the marginal man [or woman] and the newly arrived—neither of which, it should be clear, replicates Simmel's own concept of the stranger.

In a study which remains more faithful to Simmel's formulations, Robert Zajonc has in effect recovered the distinction between the "stranger" and the newly arrived. Linking Simmel's ideas about the stranger's relative independence from local customs with frustration-aggression theory, Zajonc hypothesized that insofar as strangers are expected to conform to host culture norms and find this expectation disturbing due to conflicts with values brought from their home culture, they will tend to express aggression against those norms; and that such criticism is facilitated by their unique position as stranger in the host society, and further reduces the need to conform by devaluing the norms in question. "This relationship," Zajonc notes, "hinges upon the unique role of the stranger, and it *consequently cannot be expected to hold for the newly arrived.*"[16] His second hypothesis, then, is that "attitudinal aggression as a result of frustration in conformity will be greater for strangers with long residence [Simmel's 'stranger'] than for those with short residence [the 'newly arrived']"—a hypothesis that is supported by his findings.

If the materials just reviewed reflect a tale of distinctions lost and distinctions regained, other studies which remain fairly faithful to Simmel's own conception of the stranger suggest a story of distinctions still struggling to be born. One such distinction concerns whether generalizations about strangers are to refer to a category of persons or to members of a collectivity. The former usage appears, for example, in several papers which examine the effects of social detachment on moral and cognitive orientations. Lewis A Coser, noting that "what Georg Simmel said about the stranger applies with peculiar force to the eunuch: 'He is not radically committed to the unique ingredients and peculiar tendencies of the group,'" has argued that the detachment of the eunuch-stranger from all group involvements makes him [or her] an ideal instrument for carrying out a ruler's subjective desires; and then extended the point to cover uncastrated but politically impotent aliens, such as the court Jews of Baroque Germany and Christian renegades who served Ottoman sultans.[17] A kindred theme is examined in papers by Arlene Kaplan Daniels and Dennison Nash which consider the ways in which the stranger's lack of social affiliations affect the degree of objectivity which social scientists can have in field research.[18]

In other writings whose authors are no less concerned to associate their work with Simmel's essay, strangers are referred to chiefly as members of ethnic communities. In *Immigrants and Associations,* for example, Lloyd A. Fallers has assembled a collection of papers on Chinese, Lebanese, and Ibo immigrant communities. Generalizing from these papers, Fallers observes that stranger communities exhibit a typical pattern: "a socially segregated and hostilely-regarded community of kinship units, knit together and defended by associational ties."[19] Similarly, Edna Bonacich has set forth "A Theory of Middleman [or woman] Minorities" to account for the development and persistence of communities of this sort.[20] Elliott P. Skinner assesses Simmel's portrayal of strangers as mobile and "opportunistic" by examining the situation of alien ethnic communities in three West African societies.[21] The idea that free-floating individual strangers and those organized in ethnic communities might have quite different properties is a possibility which cannot be explored so long as the same concept is used to refer indiscriminately to both sets of phenomena.

Other distinctions of considerable analytic importance are submerged beneath the ambiguous concept of "distance" which Simmel used with such memorable effect in his excursus. The stranger relationship, Simmel tells us, involves a distinctive blend of closeness and remoteness: the stranger's position *within* a given spatial circle is fundamentally affected by the fact that he [or she] brings qualities into it that are derived from the *outside.*

Generations of readers have been haunted by the imagery of distance contained in this and related passages. Some have been lured by the promise implicit in the metaphor of social distance—that social relations could somehow be represented in mathematical terms analogous to those used to represent physical space—into constructing instruments for the measurement of social distance. Although certain sociologists have become aware of the highly ambiguous character of the metaphor of social distance—one could cite, for example, the four distinct social distance scales of Westie, the four quite different social distance scales of Kadushin, and the two still different social distance scales of Laumann—none has sought to specify and relate the particular dimensions of social distance represented in the position of the stranger.[22]

A step in that direction, however, was taken by McFarland and Brown in their paper on "Social Distance as a Metric." They write that Simmel's stranger was

> described as having elements of both nearness and distance. The nearness comes from features held in common with the observer, and the distance comes from the observer's awareness that the features held in common are common to all men [and women] or at least to large groups of men [and women]. Simmel's use of the concept does not lend itself either to quantification or to a clear analogy with physical distance since in his usage two people can simultaneously be "near" and "distant." His concept of social distance actually seems to be a mixture of two different concepts: features held in common, and the degree of specificity or generality of these common features.[23]

This interpretation does serious injustice to Simmel's excursus in two respects. For one thing, it attends to only one of the meanings of distance actually used in Simmel's essay. As Simmel himself observed in a different context, there are "very manifold meanings encompassed by the symbol of 'distance.'"[24] In the stranger essay, Simmel employs his formula concerning the mixture of nearness and remoteness in at least *three* quite different senses. He says, first, that "the appearance of this mobility within a bounded group occasions that synthesis of nearness and remoteness which constitutes the formal positions of the stranger."[25] In this passage, Simmel is referring to distance in the sense of *interactional proximity:* the stranger is near in that he [or she] interacts with numerous members of the group, he [or she] is remote in that he [or she] does so incidentally and not by virtue of well-established expectations based on ties of kinship, community, or occupation.

In another passage, discussing the quality of objectivity inherent in the position of the stranger, Simmel goes on to equate the distinction between remoteness and nearness with "indifference and involvement." In this context, distance is used to refer to the degree of *emotional attachment* between actors. It is only toward the end of the essay that he comes to the usage which McFarland and Brown single out, distance in the sense of the degree of *generality of features held in common.*

In rejecting Simmel's usage as metrically unviable, since it conceived of people as being simultaneously near and far in the same relationship, McFarland and Brown do further injustice to the scientific fruitfulness of the Simmelian formulation. On the contrary, I would argue that Simmel's paradoxical formulation not only makes great social psychological sense but is indeed the key to opening up a proper sociology of the stranger.

If people can be close to or remote from one another in many ways (and the task of mapping all those ways remains on the agenda of social psychology), it is the simultaneous pressure of characteristics of closeness and remoteness along any of those dimensions—the very dissonance embodied in that dualism—that makes the position of strangers socially problematic in all times and places. When those who would be close, in any sense of the term, are actually close, and those who should be distant are distant, everyone is "in his [or her] place." When those who should be distant are close, however, the inevitable result is a degree of tension and anxiety which necessitates some special kind of response.

Two psychological mechanisms would appear to underlie this universal need, separation anxiety and group narcissism. The common observation that "the child's dread is brought into existence by the approach of a 'stranger'" can be grounded in a primal experience: the infant's dread of losing its mother aroused by the appearance of a strange person in her place.[26] In that paradigmatic situation, one who should be distant appears to be taking the place of one who should be close, and the result is immediate apprehension.

Compounding this primal anxiety is the response represented by Freud's formulation concerning the narcissism of small differences: "In the undisguised antipathies and aversions which people feel towards strangers with whom they have to do we may recognize the expression of self-love—of narcissism. This self-love works for the self-assertion of the individual, and behaves as though the occurrence of any divergence from his [or her] own particular lines of development involved a criticism of them and a demand for their alteration."[27]

To translate all this into the terms of a more general group psychology: group members derive security from relating in familiar ways to fellow group members and from maintaining their distance from nonmembers through established insulating mechanisms. In situations where an outsider comes into the social space normally occupied by group members only, one can presume an initial response of anxiety and at least latent antagonism. A systematic sociology of the stranger might therefore organize itself around the types of response to this frequent social dilemma.

Logically prior to the question of the host's response, however, is the question of how the stranger himself [or herself] seeks to relate to the host group. One thing to be learned from our brief review of the literature is that the stranger concept has been used to refer to a number of distinct social phenomena, phenomena which may have quite different properties. Some of these differences reflect the variety of modes of acceptance which strangers try to elicit from host groups.

Wood's discussion affords a point of departure for formulating these distinctions. In her words, "for us the stranger may be, as with Simmel, a potential wanderer, but he [or she] may also be a wanderer who comes today and goes tomorrow, or he [or she] may come today and remain with us permanently."[28] If, however, a properly sociological interest in the stranger concept is to understand it as referring to a distinctive type of relationship—as Wood herself, like Simmel, maintains—then *perhaps the critical variable here is not the length of time spent in the host community, but the type of relationship which the stranger aspires to establish with the host group.* In other words, the stranger may wish merely to *visit* the host community, remaining an outsider throughout his [or her] visit; or he [or she] may desire *residence* in the host community without becoming assimilated into it—to be in the group but not of it; or he [or she] may aspire to gain *membership* as a fully integrated participant in the host community.

Whatever his [or her] aspirations, the appearance of an outsider is likely to arouse feelings of anxiety and at least latent antagonism. More accurately, perhaps, it could be said to arouse pronounced ambivalence: positive feelings related to the proximity, anxiety and hostile feelings related to the fact that one who should be distant is close by. The host's response will therefore be described as compulsive, reflecting the reality of a persisting ambivalence underlying all stranger relationships and the related fact that these relationships are invested with a particularly high degree of affect. It will be compulsively friendly if positive feelings predominate, compulsively antagonistic if negative ones are dominant.

Taking this dichotomy into account enables us to incorporate Stonequist's distinction between marginal men [and women] and strangers readily and, indeed, to classify each of the three types of stranger orientations just distinguished according to whether it is reciprocated in a primarily positive or negative form. The following typology of stranger relationships may then be generated by cross-classifying the two variables in question.[29] Each of these types, finally, should be further distinguished according to whether it is being taken to refer to strangers as *individuals* or as *collectivities*.

A Typology of Stranger Relationships

Host's Response to Stranger	Stranger's Interest in Host Community		
	Visit	**Residence**	**Membership**
Compulsive Friendliness	Guest	Sojourner	Newcomer
Compulsive Antagonism	Intruder	Inner Enemy	Marginal Man [or Woman]

This typology provides the basis for developing an analytic paradigm, one organized here with respect to three basic questions which appear to define the main areas of interest in this field:

1. What are the characteristic properties of each of these types of stranger relationship?
2. What factors are associated with the process by which persons enter into one or another of these types of relations?
3. What factors account for the changes which move persons from one of these types of relation into another?

The accompanying outline, "Paradigm for the Sociology of the Stranger," is designed to provide a means for organizing existing empirical materials and for

Paradigm for the Sociology of the Stranger

I. Characteristics of Each Type of Stranger
(Guest, Intruder, Sojourn, Inner Enemy, Newcomer, Marginal Man)
A. Individual strangers
   1. Personal characteristics (detachment, insecurity, etc.)
   2. Typical relations with host (used as confidants, king's men, etc.)
B. Stranger collectivities
   1. Internal characteristics (high levels of participation in voluntary associations, etc.)
   2. Typical relations with hosts (residentially segregated, used as scapegoats, etc.)

II. Factors Affecting Assumption of Each Type of Stranger Status
A. Factors affecting aspirations of stranger
   1. Reasons for leaving home (alienation, boredom, calling, disaster, economic hardship, political oppression, etc.)
   2. Conditions of entrance into host group (amount of prestige, movable resources, special skills, etc.)
B. Factors affecting response of host
   1. Extent of stranger-host similarity (ethnicity, language, race, region, religion, value orientations, etc.)
   2. Existence of special cultural categories and rituals for dealing with strangers
   3. Criteria for group or societal membership (classificatory kinship, religion, citizenship, professional certification, etc.)
   4. Conditions of local community (age, size, homogeneity, degree of isolation, etc.)

III. Factors Affecting Shifts in Stranger Status
A. Factors affecting orientations of strangers
   1. Changing conditions at home
   2. Changes in stranger's control of resources in host community
B. Factors affecting response of host
   1. Changes in criteria of group membership (from tribal affiliation to national citizenship, etc.)
   2. Changes in local community conditions (increasing unemployment, political unrest, etc.)

articulating a set of specific questions for future research. I shall conclude with a few comments on various parts of the paradigm.

I. A more comprehensive typology of stranger status would include variant and specialized forms within each generic type. This would facilitate the incorporation of material that might not appear at first glance to belong to the subject. Consideration of the stranger as visitor, for example, should include whatever may exist on the sociology of tourism. The Sojourner category would encompass most of what has been discussed as "middle-man [or woman] minorities." The analysis of the Newcomer would include materials on problems of succession in large organizations as well as studies on the assimilation of immigrants. The Marginal Man [or woman] would include such problematic positions as that of the Homecomer, as described by Alfred Schutz, and the kindred phenomenon of the *estranged* native, discussed in recent papers by Edward A. Tiryakian and Elliott P. Skinner.[30]

I.A. The precise nature of Simmel's contribution in *Der Fremde* can now be specified. It dealt almost exclusively with the question of the characteristics of the status of the *individual Sojourner*. For the most part these concerned his [or her] relations with the host group: his [or her] freedom from its conventional constraints, the fluidity of his [or her] relations with host group members, and the ease with which he [or she] establishes a relationship of confidant with them. Wood did, in fact, make the point that the characteristics enumerated by Simmel should *not* be presumed to exist in all stranger relationships, but only in those in which the stranger does not seek to become a regular group member. Nor would they obtain when the host group expresses a compulsively antagonistic attitude toward the stranger, though Simmel's account does call attention to the host's underlying ambivalence toward Sojourners.

I.B. Much of the literature on strangers in concerned with the characteristics of Sojourner communities. Thus, Fallers speaks of the tendency of Sojourners to form a great number of interlinked voluntary associations. Wood describes the tendency of old-timers within Sojourner communities to be anxious about those newly arrived from their homeland, because the latter may not appreciate the precarious circumstances under which the Sojourners live and by some untoward act may trigger an antagonistic reaction from the host group. Howard Becker writes that such communities tend to form counter-ideologies which depict themselves as superior or chosen in defense against the low regard in which they are held by the host communities.[31]

II.A.1. I know of no studies concerning the range of motivations involved in becoming a stranger, though Robert Michels long ago enumerated some points which bear on the question.[32] It seems likely, however, that the type of status acquired by strangers will be significantly affected by whether the stranger views the host community as an asylum from political or religious persecution or natural disaster, as a market for special skills and services, as a reference group attractive because of special moral or other cultural features, as a group of infidels to be converted, or as a source of stimulating adventures.

II.B.2. Some cultures may know very well how to deal with Guests, but lack any institutionalized procedures for accommodating Sojourners. Some may be able to integrate legitimate immigrants as Newcomers, but can only define short-term visitors as Intruders. There is a huge and fascinating range of variability here, all the way from the custom of those Northern Australian tribesmen who reportedly speared any stranger from an unknown tribe unless he [or she] came accredited as a sacred messenger, to that of the ancient Jews, who were told to leave the gleanings of their harvests for the poor and the strangers, and were admonished, "if a stranger sojourn with thee in your land, ye shall not vex him [or her]; but the stranger that dwelleth with you shall be unto you as one born among you, and thou shalt love him [or her] as thyself; for ye were strangers in the land of Egypt."[33] This is an ethic toward Guests, if not Sojourners, which was likewise highly developed in Arabian culture and represented among the Amhara of northern Ethiopia by the concept *ye-egziabher ingida*, a "guest of God."

II.B.3. The potential interest of this topic may be illustrated by considering the quite disparate ways in which different ethnic groups within Ethiopia relate to strangers. In this respect, as in so many others, the traditional patterns of the Amhara and Galla (Oromo) stand in sharp contrast. Although the Amhara, guided by their concept of the "guest of God," are customarily inclined to receive legitimate visitors with extremely considerate hospitality, they find it difficult to integrate Newcomers, and often even Sojourners, into their local communities—a process which Galla communities in many parts of the country are reported to do almost effortlessly. I would attribute this difference in good part to the different criteria for local group membership in the two traditions. In a traditional Amhara community full-fledged status is related to the possession of *rist*—rights to the use of land inherited through an ambilineal descent system—and no outsider, lacking genealogical affiliations through which he [or she] might establish some legitimate claim to *rist*, can expect to acquire that status. Galla traditions, by contrast, derive from a style of life that historically (and among the Borana today) may be described as serially sedentary. Local camps were formed and reformed periodically on a voluntary basis; neighbors were chosen with respect to qualities of cooperativeness and personal friendship.[34]

II.B.4. Wood has dealt with the topic of the preceding section in the part of her book on "The Stranger and the Social Order." The part of her book with perhaps the most enduring value, however, is the section entitled "The Stranger and the Community Pattern." There she provides a wealth of propositions on the differential effects on the reception of strangers produced by such factors as whether the host communities consist of natives or foreigners; whether they are frontier settlements or retarded districts; whether they are homogeneous in culture or highly diverse; whether they are rural, small towns, or large cities.

III. The topical salience of the sociology of the stranger is of course related to the dramatic shifts in the position of strangers experienced in so many of the new states of Africa and Asia following independence. In many instances, Guests have been redefined as Intruders; Newcomers of long standing have been turned into Marginal Men [or Women]; and most dramatically, Sojourners have been transformed into Inner Enemies, and subjected to harassment, expulsion, and even assassination. There is a great need for studies which can illuminate the dynamics of these fateful changes, studies which will consolidate and extend the pioneering analyses of this topic by Skinner and Bonacich in the papers cited above.

In conclusion, I wish to note that the sociology of strangerhood articulated by this paradigm is limited by its adherence to one essential feature of Simmel's conception: the depiction of strangerhood as a figureground phenomenon, in which the stranger status is always defined *in relation to a host*. Other kinds of phenomena, however, have been linked with this concept, namely, those in which *both* parties to a relationship are labeled strangers. In this usage, strangerhood is defined simply as a function of the degree of unfamiliarity existing between the parties. In Lyn Lofland's elaboration of this notion, individuals are strangers to one another simply when they lack personal, biographical information about one another. Following this definition, Lofland and others have produced some interesting insights by analyzing the modern urban milieu as a "world of stranger."[35] Applying a similar model at the collective level, relations between ethnic groups have been conceived in terms of attitudes and transactions between stranger communities, and analyzed with respect to the degrees of stereotyping, prejudice, and receptivity that obtains in their relationships.[36]

Important though such topics are, there is a danger that in characterizing the content of strangerhood so broadly, what has always been most fascinating about this subject may become obscured. The continuing relevance of Simmel's essay is its focus on what happens when people bring *into a group* qualities not inherent in it. "The stranger," writes Edward Tiryakian, "brings us into contact with the limits of ourselves . . . he [or she] makes us aware of ourselves by indicating the boundaries of selfhood."[37] The experience of and responses to this mixture of closeness and remoteness, of threat and excitement, is a distinctive social formation which continues to demand attention wherever there are firmly bounded groups and others who step across their boundaries.

NOTES

1 *Soziologie* (Leipzig: Duncker and Humblot, 1980), Chapter Nine.
2 The next few pages are drawn from "Simmel's Influence on American Sociology: I," by D. N. Levine, E. B. Carter, and E. M. Gorman, published in the *American Journal of Sociology*, vol. 81, no. 4 (1976), pp. 813–845.
3 *American Journal of Sociology*, vol. 33, no. 8 (1928), p. 892.
4 *Theory in American Sociology* (New York: Thomas Y. Crowell, 1969), pp. 282–283.
5 E. Stonequist, *The Marginal Man* (New York:: Scribner's, 1937), pp. 177ff.
6 One exception to this tendency is Ernest Mowrer's *Disorganization: Personal and Social* (Philadelphia: Lippincott, 1942), whose chapter "The Nonconformist and the Rebel" faithfully reproduces Stonequist's distinction between strangers and marginal men.
7 E. Hughes, "Social Change and Status Protest: an Essay on the Marginal Man," *Phylon*, vol. 10, no. 1 (1949), pp. 58–65.
8 A. Boskoff, *Theory in American Sociology*, p. 282.

9 "Strangers in Their Midst: Small-town Jews and Their Neighbors," in *The Study of Society*, edited by P. I. Rose (New York: Random House, 1967), pp. 463-479.

10 "The Sojourner," *American Journal of Sociology*, vol. 58, no. 1 (1952), pp. 34-44.

11 Wood, *The Stranger: a Study in Social Relationships* (New York: Columbia University Press, 1934), pp. 43-44.

12 S. Dale McLemore, "Simmel's 'Stranger': A Critique of the Concept," *Pacific Sociological Review*, vol. 13, no. 2 (1970), pp. 86-94.

13 J. Greifer, "Attitudes to the Stranger: A Study of the Attitudes of Primitive Society and Early Hebrew Culture," *American Sociological Review*, vol. 10, no. 6 (1945), p. 739.

14 O. Grusky, "Administrative Succession in Formal Organizations," *Social Forces*, vol. 39, no. 2 (1960), pp. 105-115.

15 D. Nash and A. W. Wolfe, "The Stranger in Laboratory Culture," *American Sociological Review*, vol. 22, no. (1957), pp. 400-405.

16 "Aggressive Attitudes of the 'Stranger' as a Function of Conformity Pressures," *Human Relations*, vol. 5, no. 2 (1952), pp. 205-216.

17 L. A. Coser, "The Political Functions of Eunuchism," *American Sociological Review*, vol. 29, no. 6 (1964), pp. 880-885.

18 A. K. Daniels, "The Low-caste Stranger in Social Reserach," in *Ethics, Politics, and Social Research*, edited by G. Sjoberg (Cambridge, Mass.: Schenkman, 1967), pp. 267-296; D. Nash, "The Ethnologist as Stranger," *Southwestern Journal of Anthropology*, vol. 19, no. 1 (1963), pp. 149-167.

19 *Immigrants and Associations* (The Hague: Mouton, 1967), pp. 12ff.

20 "A Theory of Middleman Minorities," *American Sociological Review*, vol. 38, no. 5 (1973), pp. 583-594.

21 "Strangers in West African Societies," *Africa*, vol. 33, no. 4 (1963), pp. 307-320.

22 C. Kadushin, "Social Distance Between Client and Professional," *American Journal of Sociology*, vol. 67, no. (1962), pp. 517-531; F. Westie, "A Technique for the Measurement of Race Attitudes," *American Sociological Review*, vol. 18, no. 1 (1953), pp. 73-78; and E. O. Laumann, *Prestige and Association in an Urban Community* (Indianapolis: Bobbs-Merrill, 1966).

23 McFarland and Brown, "Social Distance as a Metric: A Systematic Introduction to Smallest Space Analysis," in *Bonds of Pluralism*, edited by E. O. Laumann (New York: Wiley, 1973), p. 215.

24 *Soziologie*, p. 321. See also *Conflict and the Web of Group Affiliations*, translated by K. H. Wolff and R. Bendix (Glencoe, Ill.: Free Press, 1955), p. 105.

25 *Georg Simmel On Individuality and Social Forms*, edited and with an Introduction by D. N. Levine (Chicago: University of Chicago Press, 1971), p. 145.

26 Freud, *Group Psychology and the Analysis of the Ego*, translated by J. Strachey (New York: Liveright, 1949), p. 86.

27 *Ibid.*, pp. 55ff.

28 Wood, *The Stranger*, p. 43.

29 The resulting characterization of the Marginal Man is congruent with that of R. K. Merton, who, cross-classifying two somewhat different variables, depicts the Marginal Man as one who aspires to a group but is defined as ineligible for membership by the group. See his *Social Theory and Social Structure*, 2nd ed. (Glencoe, Ill.: Free Press, 1957), p. 290.

30 A. Schutz, "The Homecomer," *American Journal of Sociology*, vol. 50, no. 5 (1945), pp. 369-376. E. A. Tiryakian, "Perspectives on the Stranger," in *The Rediscovery of Ethnicity*,

edited by S. TeSelle (New York: Harper and Row, 1973). E. P. Skinner, "Theoretical Perspectives on the Stranger," paper presented to Conference on Strangers in Africa, Smithsonian Conference Center, Belmont, Maryland, October 1974.

31 *Man in Reciprocity* (New York: Praeger, 1956).

32 "Materialism zu einer Sociologie des Fremden," *Jahrbuch für Sociologie,* I (1925).

33 Leviticus 19: 9-10, 33-34.

34 For a more extensive treatment of the structural contrasts between Amhara and Oromo societies, see D. N. Levine, *Greater Ethiopia: The Evolution of a Multiethnic Society* (Chicago: University of Chicago Press, 1974), Chapters Eight through Ten.

35 L. Lofland, *A World of Strangers* (New York: Basic Books, 1973). See also V. Packard, *A Nation of Strangers* (New York: McKay, 1972).

36 See R. M. Williams, Jr., *Strangers Next Door: Ethnic Relations in American Communities* (Englewood Cliffs, N.J.: Prentice-Hall, 1964).

37 Tiryakian, "Theoretical Perspectives on the Stranger," p. 57.

The Nature of Mindfulness

Ellen J. Langer

Our life is what our thoughts make it.
Marcus Aurelius, *Mediations*

When Napoleon invaded Russia, he appeared to the world as a brilliant conquering hero, yet again proving his military genius by daring to march against a giant. But behind the proud banners and eagles, he carried a dangerous mindset, a determination to have Russia, to have Russia no matter what the cost in human life. As Tolstoy describes him in *War and Peace,* Napoleon had no use for alternatives; his determination was absolute.

Opposite Napoleon stood the old Russian bear of a general, Kutuzov, a mellowed veteran who liked his vodka and had a habit of falling asleep at state occasions. An uneven match, or so it would appear.

As Napoleon's army advanced, Kutuzov let his army fall back, and then fall back some more. Napoleon kept coming, deeper into Russia, farther from his supply lines. Finally, as Kutuzov knew would happen, a powerful ally intervened: the Russian winter. The French army found itself fighting the cold, the wind, the snow, and the ice.

When Napoleon at least achieved his single, obsessive goal—Moscow—there was no one there for him to conquer. Everyone had left. The Russians had set their holy city on fire to greet the invader. Once more Kutuzov played the seeming loser.

Source: From Chapter 5 in E. J. Langer, *Mindfulness* (Reading, MA: Addison-Wesley, 1989).

He knew that an apple should not be picked while it is green. It will fall of itself when ripe, but if plucked unripe the apple is spoilt, the tree is harmed, and your teeth are set on edge. . . . He knew that the beast was wounded as only the whole strength of Russia could have wounded it, but whether it was mortally wounded or not was still an undecided question.[1]

At that moment, when Napoleon had no choice but to retreat—from the burned city, from the winter—the mindful old general attacked. He appealed to Mother Russia, an appeal that Stalin was to use with similar success years later. He appealed to the people to save their land, and that appeal revived all of Russia. The French had everything against them, including the Cossacks, who rode down off the winter steppes. Mother Russia prevailed, just as she would when Hitler was to repeat Napoleon's mistake.

In the character of Kutuzov we can find portrayed the key qualities of a mindful state of being: (1) creation of new categories; (2) openness to new information; and (3) awareness of more than one perspective.

In each case, Napoleon's blind obsession provides a vivid mirror image, a portrait of mindlessness. First of all, Kutuzov was flexible: Evacuating a city would usually fall under the category of defeat, but for him it became the act of setting a trap. Second, his strategy was responsive to the news of Napoleon's advance, while Napoleon did not seem to be taking in information about Kutuzov's moves. Finally, while Napoleon saw his rapid advance and march on Moscow only from the point of view of conquering enemy terrain, Kutuzov could also see that an "invasion" in the context of winter and distance from supplies could be turned into a bitter route.

CREATING NEW CATEGORIES

Just as mindlessness is the rigid reliance on old categories, mindfulness means the continual creation of new ones. Categorizing and recategorizing, labeling and relabeling as one masters the world are processes natural to children. They are an adaptive and inevitable part of surviving in the world.[2] Freud recognized the importance of creation and mastery in childhood:

Should we not look for the first traces of imaginative activity as early as in childhood? The child's best-loved and most intense occupation is with his [or her] play or games. Might we not say that every child at play behaves like a creative writer, in that he [or she] creates a world of his [or her] own, or rather, re-arranges the things of his [or her] world in a new way which pleases him [or her]?[3]

The child's serious re-creation can become the adult's playful recreation.

As adults, however, we become reluctant to create new categories. As we saw earlier, our outcome orientation tends to deaden a playful apaproach. If I asked you to make a list of what you did yesterday, what would you say? Think about it for a moment, then think of what you would say if I offered you money for each item in your answer. Did you list your day in large chunks at first—breakfast, work, lunch, phone calls? Most people will say, for example, that they "ate breakfast" rather than "bit, chewed, and swallowed a piece of toast" and so on, even when offered a reward for a longer list of activities.

Without psychotherapy or a crisis as motivation, the past is rarely recategorized. We might from time to time call upon different episodes from the past to justify a present situation or grievance, but it rarely occurs to us to change the way the events or impressions were intially stored.

For example, take a couple, Alice and Fred, whom you see quite often. Sometimes you hear them fight a bit. You don't pay attention; don't all couples quarrel? Now you learn that they are getting a divorce. You call to mind all the evidence that explains this outcome. "I knew it, remember how they used to fight? Their fights were vicious." On the other hand, perhaps you hear that they have just celebrated their silver anniversary. "Isn"t that nice," you say, "they have such a solid marriage; they hardly ever quarrel and when they do, they always make up so sweetly to each other." While we pick and choose in our store of memories, the original categorizing of what we saw remains the same. In this case, we remember certain behavior as a quarrel. It might come to mind as vicious or playful, but we identify it as a quarrel nonetheless. We don't recategorize the original behavior and say that rather than quarreling, perhaps they were engaging in foreplay or playing a game or practicing a role for a play. Initially, the behavior labeled "quarrel" may have been open to several interpretations. Once it is stored in memory as a quarrel it is not likely to be recategorized, even though it may be called up or left behind to help make some case.

When we make new categories in a mindful way, we pay attention to the situation and the context. If I need someone to help me fix a high ceiling, a tall person might be best. On the other hand, maybe someone who is 5 feet, 2 inches, would be more appropriate—if he [or she] is a mountain climber, doesn't mind ladders, and so forth. Breaking down categories of skills to more precise distinctions is a useful approach for a personnel manager. In a very noisy environment a clever programmer who is deaf might be a better job candidate than a person of equal ability but of normal hearing. If sitting for long periods of time is necessary, someone confined to a wheelchair may not mind the sedentary work as much as the next applicant. A simple list of general skills free of context would mask these and many more differentiated distinctions.

Most strong opinions rest on global categories. If we describe someone we dislike intensely, a single statement usually does it. But if, instead, we are forced to describe the person in great detail, eventually there will be some quality we appreciate. This is true of objects or situations as well, and is one way of changing an intolerable situation: We can try to have the good without the bad. Take, for example, someone who hates New England winters. If he [or she] lets his [or her] thoughts become more differentiated, he [or she] may discover that what he [or she] really dislikes is feeling restricted by heavy winter clothing. A well-insulated jacket or a better heater in his [or her] car might change his [or her] outlook. Or, consider a couple arguing over whether to get an air conditioner. She can't stand the heat but he objects violently because he gets "air conditioner colds" all the time in the office. Perhaps the air in the office is too dry, or the attic of their house needs an exhaust fan, and so on. A mindful attitude may not avoid all need for compromise, but then again, it might. In any case, it can significantly reduce the margin of conflict. In a domestic setting and, as we will see later, in the workplace or in the realm of prejudice, mindful new distinctions and differentiated categories can smooth the way we get along.

WELCOMING NEW INFORMATION

A mindful state also implies openness to new information. Like category making, the receiving of new information is a basic function of living creatures. In fact, lack of new information can be harmful. Research on sensory deprivation shows that, if confined to an unstimulating environment for a long time, such as a submarine or a specially designed, stimulus-free chamber, we suffer a variety of psychological problems. Also, if exposed to patterns of stimulation that are perceived as repeated and unvarying, the sensory system often shuts down, since it is not "receiving" anything new.

A model of mindful receptivity is the inertial navigation system in modern aircraft. This device is constantly receiving new information, constantly letting the pilot know where the plane is at any particular moment. We have a similar mechanism operating within us as we walk or balance ourselves in other ways. Our minds, however, have a tendency to block out small, inconsistent signals.

For example, if a familiar quotation is *altered* so that it is made nonsensical (but retains sufficient structural familiarity), someone reading it out loud is likely to read the *original* quote. Even though what she [or he] was reading was not on the page in front of her [or him], she [or he] is likely to express great confidence that the the quote was indeed read accurately.[4] (Reread the last sentence, and note the double *the.*) In contrast, mindfully engaged individuals will actively attend to changed signals. Behavior generated from mindful listening or watching, from an expanding, increasingly differentiated information base, is, of course, likely to be more effective.

Consider a relationship between two business partners, Mr. X and Mrs. Y. Perhaps they sense that although the business is growing, misunderstandings are multiplying as well. Mr. X notices that Mrs. Y is categorizing him as rigid. Attuned to subtleties, he feels a lack of approval. Realizing that he and Mrs. Y are very different, but that she may see his style as inappropriate rather than different, he explains his behavior from his own point of view, saying how hard he tries to be consistent and predictable. Mrs. Y accepts Mr. X's depiction of his behavior, now realizing the value of a business partner she can depend upon, instead of seeing these same qualities as rigid. Mrs. Y was able to make this switch because she, too, was open to cues, to another point of view. In the strongest relationships, this sets up a continuous feedback loop that keeps the partnership, marriage, or team in balance, like an aircraft.

MORE THAN ONE VIEW

Openness, not only to new information, but to different points of view is also an important feature of mindfulness. For years, social psychologists have written about the differences between the perspective of an actor [or actress] and that of an observer.[5] For instance, we are likely to blame circumstances for our own negative behavior: "The subway always makes me late." If the very same behavior is engaged in by someone else, however, we tend to blame that individual: "He [or she] is chronically behind schedule."

Once we become mindfully aware of views other than our own, we start to realize that there are as many different views as there are different observers. Such awareness is potentially liberating. For instance, imagine that someone has just told you that you are rude. You thought you were being frank. If there is only one perspective, you can't both be right. But with an awareness of many perspectives, you could accept that you are both right and concentrate on whether your remarks had the effect that you actually wanted to produce. If we cling to our own point of view, we may be blind to our impact on others; if we are too vulnerable to other people's definitions of our behavior, we may feel undermined, for observers are typically less flattering of us that we are of ourselves. It is easy to see that any single gesture, remark, or act between people can have *at least* two interpretations: spontaneous versus impulsive; consistent versus rigid; softhearted versus weak; intense versus overemotional; and so on.

This list should not give the impression that for every act there are two set, polarized interpretations. As we said, there are potentially as many interpretations as there are observers. Every idea, person, or object is potentially simultaneously many things depending on the perspective from which it is viewed. A steer is steak to a ranger, a sacred object to a Hindu, and a collection of genes and proteins to a molecular biologist. Nor does being mindful mean that we can plan certain defined ways of interacting with others that will produce certain outcomes; rather, it means that we remain aware that the various possible perspectives will never be exhausted. We can see this on a grand scale or in the most ordinary circumstances. The nuclear accident at Chernobyl was portrayed in many different colors, from a "heroic sacrifice to the benefit of mankind" to "gross and destructive negligence."[6]

Closer to home, we can see how one set of circumstances gives rise to more than one view: "I go regularly to visit my mother—every week, for years now, every week—like clockwork," says a grown-up son. His elderly mother sees things differently: "He's so unpredictable, I never even know what day of the week he's coming. For years now, sometimes it's Monday, sometimes it's not until Friday. I never know."[7]

Or take the couple in Woody Allen's film *Annie Hall*, who were asked by their respective therapists how often they made love. "Hardly ever," says the man, "no more than three times a week." "Constantly," says the woman, "at least three times a week."

As observers, we judge behavior according to whether, as actors [or actresses], we could or would do the same thing. If I take a basketball shot from the outer key (and make it), I am looked at as though I took a risk. What that means is that my *perceived* competence exceeded someone else's estimates of her [or his] own competence. It does not mean that I took more of a risk than someone else would have, had she [or he] felt as confident as I. I took the shot because I believed I could make it. However, since the observer would not have risked the shot and does not know my perceived level of competence, she [or he] presumes that I'm a *risk taker.* Enjoying the compliment, I do not argue. But being aware of all these elements is in the nature of mindfulness.

In trying to develop a limber state of mind, it helps to remember that people may have perfectly good reasons for behavior we consider negative. Even if their reasons are hard for us, as observers, to discern, people are rarely *intentionally* stingy, grim, choosy, inflexible, secretive, lax, indiscreet, rash, or fussy, for example. No one tries to cultivate unpleasant qualities. Take the same list and imagine yourself in a situation where the word might be applied to you. If you bought someone a present on sale, for instance, would you than see yourself as stingy or thrifty? If you took your children out of school early one Friday in spring, would you see yourself as irresponsible or fun-loving? Virtually all behavior can be cast in a negative or a more tolerable or justifiable light.[8]

The consequences of trying out different perspectives are important. First, we gain more choice in how to respond. A single-minded label produces an automatic reaction, which reduces our options. Also, to understand that other people may not be so different allows us empathy and enlarges our range of responses. We are less likely to feel locked into a polarized struggle.

Second, when we apply this open-minded attitude to our own behavior, change becomes more possible. When I used to do clinical work, it often seemed odd to me that many people in therapy not only had strong motivation to change (hence their visits to me), but the desired behavior was already in their repertoires. What was stopping them? In looking back, now I realize that, often, they were probably trying to change behavior (for example, "being impulsive") that they actively enjoyed, but from another point of view ("being spontaneous"). With this realization, changing one's behavior might be seen not as changing something negative but as making a choice between two positive alternatives (for example, "being reflective" versus "being spontaneous").

One of my students, Loralyn Thompson, and I tested the hypothesis that the reason some people have a hard time changing their behavior, no matter how hard they seem to try, is that they really value that behavior under a different name.[9] Using a list of negative traits, such as rigid, grim, gullible, and the like, we asked people to tell us whether they had tried to change this particular quality about themselves and succeeded or failed, or whether the description was irrelevant to them. Later we had people tell us how much they valued each of a number of traits such as consistency, seriousness, trust, and so on, which were the mirror opposites of the negative traits.

Our hypothesis was confirmed. People valued specific qualities that, when negatively framed, were the very things they wanted most to change about themselves but had failed to change. Being aware of these dual views should increase our sense of control and our success in changing behavior (if we still feel that the behavior is undesirable).

. . .

CONTROL OVER CONTEXT: THE BIRDMAN OF ALCATRAZ

The increased control made possible by mindfulness can also help us change contexts. Irving Janis, John Wolfer, and I investigated the influence on pain of a single-minded view of the hospital setting.[10] Patients are often certain that pain is inevitable in a hospital. Caught in such a mindset, they assume that, without the help of medication, pain cannot be controlled. In our experiment, we tried to learn whether people could control their experience of pain by putting it in a different, more optimistic context.

Patients who were about to undergo major surgery were taught to imagine themselves in one of two situations: playing football or preparing for a dinner party. In the midst of a rough skirmish on the football field, bruises are hardly noticed. Similarly, cutting oneself while rushing to prepare dinner for ten people who will be arriving any minute might also be something one would hardly notice. In contrast, a paper cut suffered while reading a dull magazine article quickly becomes the focus of attention. Through examples of this sort, participants in the study were taught that, rather than being inevitable, much of the pain we experience appears to be context-dependent.

Hospital staff, unaware of our hypothesis, monitored the use of medication and length of stay for the participating patients in this experimental group and in control groups. Those patients who were taught to reinterpret the hospital experience in nonthreatening ways took fewer pain relievers and sedatives and tended to leave the hospital sooner than the untrained patients. The same hospital experience seen through psychologically different eyes is not the same experience, and the difference could be measured in lower doses of medication and quicker recoveries. This reappraisal technique effectively loosened the hospital mindset and, by showing that pain was not a certainty, gave the participants more control over their convalescence.

Even the most apparently fixed and certain situations can become subject to control if viewed mindfully. The Birdman of Alcatraz was sentenced to life in prison with no hope of reprieve. All the world was cut off from him; one empty, grim day followed the next, as he stared at the flocks of birds flying outside his window. One morning a crippled sparrow happened into his cell, and he nursed it back to health. The bird was no longer just a bird; for him it was a particular sparrow. Other prisoners, guards, visitors started giving him birds and he learned more and more about them. Soon he had a veritable aviary in his cell. He became a distinguished authority on bird diseases, noticing more and more about these creatures and developing more and more expertise. Everything he did was self-taught and original.

Instead of living a dull, stale existence in a cell for forty-odd years, the Birdman of Alcatraz found that boredom can be just another construct of the mind, no more certain than freedom. There is always something new to notice. And he turned what might have been an absolute hell into, at the least, a fascinating, mindful purgatory.

PROCESS BEFORE OUTCOME

. . . a preoccupation with outcome can make us mindless. Turning this observation around, as we have with all our definitions of mindlessness, we can see mindfulness as a process orientation. Consider a scientist who feels stupid for not having read a journal article that is being discussed heatedly among his colleagues. A mindless hindsight makes him [or her] feel this way. He [or she] sees himself [or herself] as having had the choice of either reading or not reading the important article, and having stupidly made the wrong choice. Had he [or she] been less fixated on the outcome of the choice, he [or she] might have realized that the choice had not been between reading the article and doing nothing, but rather between reading the article or working in the lab, taking a much-needed rest, or reading to his [or her] daughter. This is another example of the *faulty comparisons* described in the previous chapter. Awareness of the process of making real choices along the way makes it less likely that we will feel guilty in retrospect. After all, mindful choices are perceived to offer some benefit, or why would we intentionally make them? On occasion, after learning the consequences of a choice, we may wish we had chosen differently, but we still tend not to be quite as hard on ourselves when we know why we did what we did.

A true process orientation also means being aware that every outcome is preceded by a process. Graduate students forget this all the time. They begin their dissertations with inordinate anxiety because they have seen other people's completed and polished work and mistakenly compare it to their own first tentative steps. With their noses deep in file cards and half-baked hypotheses, they look in awe at Dr. So-and-so's published books as if it had been born without effort or false starts, directly from brain to printed page. By investigating how someone got somewhere, we are more likely to see the achievement as hard-won and our own chances as more plausible.

Our judgments about the intelligence of others can be distorted by an emphasis on outcome. In an informal inquiry, my students and I asked people to evaluate the intelligence of scientists who had achieved an "impressive" intellectual outcome (such as discovering a new planet or inventing a new drug). When the achievement was described as a series of steps (and virtually all achievements can be broken down in this way), they judged the scientist as less smart than when the discovery or invention was simply named. People can imagine themselves taking steps, while great heights seem entirely forbidding.

A process orientation not only sharpens our judgment, it makes us feel better about ourselves. A purely outcome orientation can take the joy out of life. Take playing golf. First you learn to keep your head low and not to bend your arm. You keep trying and you lower your score. But imagine that you read about clubs that would decrease your score by a third. Wouldn't you buy them? The fourth hole in four rather than six strokes—that's playing. Now to get better golf balls. Ah, down to three strokes. Finally a new ball is invented, so refined that it finds its way to the hole on one stroke. What a game, a hole in one on each stroke. What game?

In a game, we can understand that process—if not being everything—is really all that matters. But it may be the same for the rest of our lives. In business, would it be nice always to be assured of success? What if every business plan worked out, without stumbling blocks or irritation? At first it might seem appealing, like the Midas touch. What would such a life be like? A corporate nursing home? According to the Japanese, big business has a lot to learn from kindergarten children. In some Japanese firms, the thinkers and innovators are specifically encouraged to be *process-oriented*—the results can come later.[11] Bell Labs, with its focus on research, was said to be free from a drive toward products, at least until the breakup of AT&T.

MINDFULNESS EAST AND WEST

The definitions of mindfulness in this chapter, especially the process orientation just discussed, will remind many readers of various concepts of mindfulness found in Eastern religion. Students in my classes who are knowledgeable about such fields are continually drawing parallels. While there are many similarities, the differences in the historical and cultural background from which they are derived, and the more elaborate methods, including meditation, through which a mindful state is said to be achieved in the Eastern traditions should make us cautious about drawing comparisons that are too tidy.

My work on mindfulness has been conducted almost entirely within the Western scientific perspective. Initially, my focus was on mindlessness and its prevalence in daily life. As can be seen in the order of chapters so far in this book, the notion of mindfulness develops gradually by looking at aspects of mindlessness and then at the other side of the coin. Only after a series of experiments demonstrating the costs of rigid mindsets and single-minded perspectives do I begin to explore the enormous potential benefits of a mindful attitude in aging, health, creativity, and the workplace.

Behind Eastern teachings of mindfulness lies an elaborate system of cosmology developed and refined over time. The moral aspect of mindfulness (the idea that the mindful state achieved through meditation will lead to spontaneous right action[12]) is an essential part of these philosophies. It reaches into matters too complex for the scope of this book. Since many qualities of the Eastern concepts of mindfulness and of the one being described in this book are strikingly similar, however, we might hope that some of the moral consequences striven for by the Eastern disciplines might also result from mindfulness as understood in this Western form and context.

As an example of the semantic and philosophical tangles that arise if we try to compare Eastern and Western views of the mindful state, consider the activity of creating new categories. While this is a form of mindfulness in our definition, it appears to be in direct opposition to what one does during meditation.[13] In meditation, the mind becomes quieter and active thought is discouraged. In some forms of meditation, thoughts and images that come to mind are considered unimportant and are relinquished as soon as one discerns their presence. At the same time, in many Eastern views, the proper meditation techniques are said to result in a state that has been called *de-automatization*.[14] In this state, old categories break down and the individual is no longer trapped by stereotypes. Such freedom from rigid distinctions is very similar to the mindfulness being described in this book. This one example should show why, not being fully trained in Eastern thought, I leave it to others to tease out the similarities and differences between the two concepts of mindfulness. If a reader is familiar with a particular Eastern discipline, she or he may enjoy making comparisons, in both technique and result.

NOTES

1 L. Tolstoy, *War and Peace*, 1869 trans. Louise and Aylmer Maude (Oxford: Oxford University Prerss, 1983).

2 J. Bruner, J. Goodnow, and G. Austin, *A Study of Thinking* (New York: Wiley, 1956); R. Brown, *Words and Things* (New York: Free Press, 1958).

3 S. Freud (1907). "Creative Writers and Daydreaming," in *The Standard Edition of the Complete Psychological Works of Sigmund Freud*, ed. J. Strachey, vol. 9 (London: Hogarth Press, 1959), 143–144.

4 E. Langer and C. Weinman, "Mindlessness, Confidence and Accuracy" (1976), as described in B. Chanowitz and E. Langer, "Knowing More (or Less) Than You Can Show: Understanding Control Through the Mindlessness/Mindfulness Distinction," in *Human Helplessness*, ed. M. E. P. Seligman and J. Garber (New York: Academic Press, 1980).

5 E. Jones and R. Nisbett, "The Actor and the Observer: Divergent Perceptions of the Causes of Behavior," in *Attributions: Perceiving the Causes of Behavior*, ed. E. Jones et al. (Morristown, NJ: General Learning Press, 1972).

6 I. Lindahl, "Chernobyl: The Geopolitical Dimensions," *American Scandinavian Review* 75, no. 3 (1987): 29–40.

7 These points of view are different in another way that is important in the study of psychology. The more specific the level of analysis, the greater the likelihood of unpredictability. The study of personality does not generally pay attention to the individual's prototypical level of analysis. As in the example cited, differences on this dimension, whether stemming from trait or even state, may give rise to interpersonal difficulty.

8 If one makes a *conscious decision* to consider alternative frames for complex negative information in this way, one cannot sensibly be accused of "rationalizing."

9 E. Langer and L. Thompson, "Mindlessness and Self-Esteem: The Observer's Perspective," Harvard University (1987).

10 E. Langer, I. Janis, and J. Wolfer, "Reduction of Psychological Stress in Surgical Patients," *Journal of Experimental Social Psychology* 11 (1975): 155–165.

11 R. Pascale and N. Athos, *The Art of Japanese Management* (New York: Simon & Schuster, 1981).

12 S. Druker, "Unified Field Based Ethics: Vedic Psychology's Description of the Highest Stage of Moral Reasoning," *Modern Science and Vedic Science,* in press.

13 See E. Langer, *Minding Matter* (chapter 2, note 6) for a discussion of the latent vs. expressed modes of mindfulness. Only the expressed mode is being considered in this book.
14 A. Deikman, "De-automatization and the Mystic Experience," *Psychiatry* 29 (1966): 329–343.

Categorization and Particularization
Michael Billig

. . . Cognitive social psychologists have devoted much effort to searching for the basic units of thought. . . .

The particular process which cognitive social psychologists have concentrated upon is that of categorization. By basing theories of thinking upon the importance of categorization, psychologists have tended to construct one-sided theories of thinking. These theories seem to describe prejudiced and bureaucratic styles of thought, and opposing aspects of thought are correspondingly neglected. It is one-sided to suggest that as humans all we can do in our thoughts is to categorize information. It is at this point that the spirit of Protagoras will be invoked, in order to put the other side. The concept of categorization needs to be reversed in order to show that the conflicting process—that of particularization—is just as psychologically important. Instead of building a psychological portrait principally upon the single, and unopposed, process of categorization, the tensions between categorization and particularization will be seen as central. Thinking will be viewed in terms of the conflicts between these two processes. . . .

CATEGORIZATION AND COGNITIVE SOCIAL PSYCHOLOGY

Social psychologists who employ a cognitive perspective have set themselves the task of understanding how people make sense of their worlds. . . . A basic assumption relates to the importance of cognition in human activity. This very assumption serves to distinguish the cognitive theorist from other theoretical persuasions. For instance, cognitive theorists will distance themselves from behaviorists, who tend to view the person as the unthinking respondent to outside stimuli. They will look askance at the more lurid stories produced by those motivational theorists who see the person as being powered by emotional forces.

The cognitive approach does not merely rest upon the assumption that thinking is important for understanding human action, but it also makes assumptions about the

Source: Abridged from M. Billig, *Arguing and Thinking: A Rhetorical Approach to Social Psychology* (pp. 118–134) (Cambridge, England: Cambridge University Press, 1987).

nature of thought. One of the leading textbooks in the area has discussed the assumptions at the root of the cognitive approach in the following way: "The individual is an active processor of information", and "the effect of a stimulus depends on how it is categorized and interpreted by the perceiver" (Eiser, 1980, p. 8). Eiser's characterization of the cognitive approach is revealing. He uses four typical phrases: 'the individual', 'processor of information', 'categorized' and 'perceiver'. These terms are of importance to cognitive social psychologists, who tend to see thinking, or cognition, in terms of isolated individuals, processing perceptual information by means of categories. It will be suggested that this view tends to produce a psychology which is one-sided and essentially non-rhetorical. Above all, it produces a psychology of thinking which removes some of the essential ingredients of thought from cognition. [1]

Much of the discussion will concentrate upon the notion that as thinkers we impart meaning by categorizing the information which our senses provide. Accordingly, cognitive theorists in social psychology have tended to assume that categorization is a basic unit of thinking. At its simplest level, categorization involves the placing of a particular object, or entity, within a general category. To say that 'this cup is red', or that 'stealing is wrong' or that 'Socrates was Greek' is to make a categorization. In each case, an entity—whether object, action or person—has been placed into a wider, or general, category. This cup has been categorized as belonging to the wider category of red objects, stealing to the category of wrongful actions and Socrates to the category of Greeks. In the last example, the use of the past tense indicates a more subtle categorization, as Socrates is inserted into the subcategory of deceased Greeks. All three statements involve locating a particular entity in a more general category. This is something which we do all the time, when we use language to make statements about entities. If we talk about anything, rather than make grunts or gestures, we can be sure that we will be using categories, and, thereby, making categorizations.

Psychologists have pointed to the link between categorizing objects and making judgements of similarity. To say that 'this cup is red' implies that this cup resembles, in some way, other cups also categorized as red, and differs from green, blue and yellow ones. Eleanor Rosch, who in recent years has probably done more than any other psychologist to awaken interest in categorization, has defined a category in terms of judgements of similarity: "A category exists whenever two or more distinguishable objects or events are treated equivalently" (Mervis and Rosch, 1981, p. 89). . . .

Rosch, in studying categorization, has little doubt that she is studying a fundamental aspect of cognition. According to Rosh et al. "one of the most basic functions of all organisms is the cutting up of the environment into classifications by which nonidentical stimuli can be treated as equivalent" (1976, p. 382) and, in consequence, it is asserted that "categorization may be considered one of the most basic functions of living creatures" (Mervis and Rosch, 1981, p. 89). Other cognitive social psychologists also affirm the importance of categorization for thinking, and, indeed, for survival in general. Wilder describes categorization as "a pervasive cognitive process" (1981, p. 213), and Cantor et al. call categorization "a fundamental quality of cognition". Its psychological importance arises "because categoriziation schemes allow us to structure and give coherence to our general knowledge about people and the social world, providing expectations about typical patterns of behaviour and the range of likely variation between types of people and their characteristic actions and attributes" (Cantor *et al.*, 1982, p. 34). It can be noted that Cantor *et al.* refer to 'schemes'. Some cognitive social psychologists talk of 'schemas' or 'schemata', rather than categorizations, and schemata resemble categories but are generally held to be more complex and abstract. Like categories, schemata provide means for incorporating the particular instance into a more general framework. Fiske and Taylor state that "a schema contains abstract knowledge about types of people and events as a class, not a representative of every instance ever encountered" (1984, p. 179), and Anderson (1985) suggests that schemata are organizations of categories. (For an excellent discussion schemata and categories, and their relations to the social sciences, see Casson, 1983). Because schemata, in social psychological theory, are considered as forms of categories, many of the same psychological assumptions apply to the application of schemata as to categorization. In particular, there is the same implication that, if psychologists can uncover the principles of categorization or the application of schemata, they will have laid bare the basic units of thought. . . .

PREJUDICED AND BUREAUCRATIC THINKING

From the assumptions of the cognitive approach, a rather narrow and unflattering image of the thinker can be drawn. This image is a very different one from the imaginative user of witcraft described in the last chapter. Unlike the crafty and witty arguer, dodging and weaving in the momentum of debate, the categorizing thinker appears as a rather dull person, destined to plod through the procedures of thought. The person as a categorizer of information can be compared either to a prejudiced individual, whose errors arise from a narrow thoughtlessness, or to a bureaucrat, who seeks little more than well-ordered routines. Both these metaphors—the thinker as a bigot, and the thinker as a bureaucrat—will be explored in this section, in order to illustrate the one-sidedness of categorization theory. The connections between categorization and prejudice are made by social psychologists themselves, but the unflattering image of the thinker as a bureaucrat is one that is being ascribed here to the cognitive approach.[2] . . .

(1) Categorization and Prejudice

Social psychologists adhering to a cognitive approach sometimes tend to see all thought as being inherently prejudiced, or, at least, they suggest that prejudice arises from the normal processes of categorization, which are assumed to lie at the basis of all thought. The very notion of categorization, as used by cognitive social psychologists, seems to invite this link with prejudiced thought. It is implied that reality is being distorted and simplified, when stimuli are categorized. The real world, existing objectively outside our perceptions, is assumed to be composed of infinitely different stimuli. Yet these infinite differences become simplified by categorization, and, therefore, the act of categorizing implies that objectively different stimuli are being perceived as if they were similar. This translation of objective differences into psychological similarities is necessary for perception, and it enables the overwhelming amount of information in the world to be reduced to manageable proportions. Fiske and Taylor refer to the model of the "cognitive miser": because "people are limited in their capacity to process information" they must take cognitive "shortcuts", and "consequently, errors and biases stem from inherent features of the cognitive system" (1984, p. 12).

Experimental evidence has been produced to show how categorization can simplify and distort the stimulus world. When stimuli are labelled, subjects will tend to underestimate the differences between stimuli falling under the same label and to overestimate the differences of stimuli from different categories (e.g., Tajfel and Wilkes, 1963 and 1964). In other words, the imposition of a category label leads subjects to overlook, and even to misperceive, the objective differences between stimuli which are grouped together. There is a serious implication from this sort of experimental evidence and from Rosch's definition of a category. This is the implication that all categories are distorting simplifications. Since language is a repository of categories, this implies that language functions to impoverish the richness of the outside world. Language does not create a complex, and infinitely rich, world of meaning, but shuts out complexity to protect the stability of the perceiver and to help in the task of processing information.

This image of thinking seems to be very similar to the image of prejudice, as traditionally discussed by social psychologists. The prejudiced person does not perceive social groups as they are, but is guided by prior conceptions and biases. These operate rather like the shortcuts of the "cognitive miser". The full richness of the social world is shut out by the imposition of stereotypes, or group schemata, and variety is reduced to simple categorical distortions. The prejudiced person exaggerates the extent to which members of the same group are similar to one another, and at the same time chooses to view people belonging to different groups as being very different. For instance the early work on stereotypes held by Americans suggested that Italians were seen to be excitable and violent (Katz and Braly, 1933). This stereotype glossed over the infinite differences between individual Italians, and imposed a composite picture on the whole group. In addition, the stereotype of the Italians was distinguished from that of the Germans ('ruthlessly efficient') or that of the Turks ('cruel') or whatever. The result was that the similarities between Italians, Germans, Turks, etc. were neglected.

If all thinking is assumed to be based upon distorting categorizations, then the implication is that stereotyping is merely an instance of normal cognitive processes. In fact, a number of cognitive social psychologists have accepted this implication.

According to Taylor, "stereotyping is the outgrowth of normal cognitive processes" (1981, p. 83) and Wilder claims that "ingroup/outgroup bias may be a consequence of normal categorization processes" (1981, p. 232). . . .

(2) Bureaucratic Model of Thought

Generally speaking, the categorization approach leads to a rather limited view of thought. The typical thinker is seen as an individual who is faced with a complex and untamed stimulus world, which must be caught by the net of an appropriate categorization or scheme. For example, if confronted by a stimulus, we ask ourselves "Is there an active schema for this event?". If the answer is 'yes', then all is safe, but if the answer is 'no', then we must search a bit harder in order to "find appropriate scheme" (Hastie, 1981, p. 45). Once the scheme has been found, the event can be categorized, and we will achieve the security of possessing instructions to tell us how to react. The untamed stimulus world will have been safely domesticated, as the complexities of the original stimulus fall away, leaving it to be remembered as just another instance of the schema.

A parallel can be drawn between the image of the thinker to emerge from this approach and a parodied image of the bureaucrat. Both need rules for dealing with the world. As Taylor and Crocker state, in a passage already cited, schemata "tell the social perceiver" what to look for. Low-level bureaucrats also have instructions telling them how to conduct themselves. In both cases the instructions forestall the panic which can occur, when it is discovered that there is no appropriate "active schema" to deal with the situation in hand. The parallel can be pursued by imagining that our bureaucrat deals with members of the public who wish to attract the attention of the bureaucracy. Both the perceiver and the bureaucrat are faced with the problem of processing the messiness of the outside world into orderly categories, and both tackle the problem in a similar way. The bureaucrat cannot treat each individual case as if it were unique, but each case must be placed into bureaucratically suitable pigeon-holes. Members of the public must fill out appropriate forms, which extract the information of interest to the bureaucracy. In this way the messy features of the general public's lives can become suitably regularized. Irrelevant information, for which there is no appropriate question on the official form, will be weeded out, and need never come to the attention of the bureaucratic system. Similarly, categories or schemata, like the official forms, serve to weed out the irrelevant stimuli and to organize the relevant features into ways which can be easily processed by the higher authorities of the system. Just as the bureaucrat will pass on the suitably completed forms to the higher cortical reaches of the bureaucratic system, so the processed information of the schema system will pass along the corridors of the nervous system: as Taylor and Crocker assert, "schemas determine what information will be encoded or retrieved from memory" (1981, p. 98). In this way, the individual case will lose its sense of uniqueness, to become just another instance of the official form, or schematic category, to be processed. This is inevitable, because both the bureaucrat and the ideal perceiver of the cognitive approach do not have the time to deal with each member of the public as a unique case. In both instances there is an image of inflexibility. All the bureaucrat or thinker can do is to impose pre-set categories which turn disorder into order. Our bureaucrat must follow the rules of the system, and the schemata equip the perceiver with rules to be followed, in order to escape the dangerous messiness of the outside world.

The bureaucratic image is particularly apt, because cognitive theorists tend to talk about the advantages of categorization in the way that a bureaucrat might defend office procedures. Thus, categorization and schemata theorists talk about the organization, order, management, and efficiency which are brought by schematic procedures to the stimulus world. For example, we are told that categorization "lends organization to our social world" (Hamilton, 1979, p. 56) and that it serves "to stabilize, make predictable and make manageable the individual's view of the world" (Snyder, 1981a, p. 183). Another cognitive theorist praises "the efficiency" of a cognitive system which provides such "stability" (Rothbart, 1981), p. 178). Those who describe thinking in terms of computer processes cannot help but strengthen the bureaucratic metaphor. Information is deposited into, and retrieved from, 'files' (e.g., Abelson, 1979; Schank, 1981). Quite literally these are the same sort of files which the modern bureaucrat uses in the name of mechanized efficiency. . . .

CATEGORIZATION AND PARTICULARIZATION

The problem with the categorization approach to cognition is that, from one-sided assumptions, a one-sided image of the person has been developed. . . . If a psychological theory concentrates upon a single principle, it often pays to reverse that principle. The notion of categorization as a fundamental unit of thought represents such a single principle. In consequence, the very principle of categorization itself will be reversed, and an opposing principle, that of particularization, will be proposed. Following from this, the assumptions of categorization theory can also be reversed. The intention is not to show that the original assumptions are erroneous or based upon badly constructed experiments. Instead, the broad aim is to show that Protagoras's maxim can be profitably applied to psychological theory itself, and the reverse case can be put to the categorization theory. The reversals of psychological assumptions, surprising as it may be, can turn out to be just as reasonable as the originals. What is more, these reversals can be attained within the broad domain of a cognitive approach and without wandering to the theoretically alien territory of behaviourism or motivational theory.

The obvious way to start reversing the assumptions of the categorization approach is to begin with the notion of categorization itself. The reversal does not take the form of denying that people categorize objects, for such a denial would clearly be absurd. In addition, it would be out of keeping with Protagoras's maxim, which states that the reversal does not replace the original but complements it. Therefore the aim of the reversal is to point to a process which seems to be the reverse of categorization and which might be just as fundamental to human cognition. The reverse of categorization will be described as 'particularization'. Categorization refers to the process by which a particular stimulus is placed in a general category: as a result of this process, the particular stimulus is robbed of its particularity, to become merely an instance of the general category. On the other hand, one might hypothesize that there is a reverse process: a stimulus need not be treated as being equivalent to other stimuli, but might be considered in its particularity. For instance such a stimulus might be extracted from a category into which it had previously been placed, or it might have been kept separate in the first place from that category and from all other stimuli. In either case, it can be said that the stimulus has been particularized.

The bureaucratic metaphor can be used to illustrate the differences between the two processes. We have already encountered the parody of the bureaucrat operating office procedures according to the strict demands of categorization. However, the bureaucrat, who routinely hands out standard forms to members of the public in order to process their cases in routine ways, might decide to do things differently when faced by a relative or a generous business contact. Instead of making them, or their documents, wait their turn, the bureaucrat may exploit the rules. A special case may be created and reasons may be found why the relative or business contact is different from the other members of the public. To create the special case, the bureaucrat must pay attention to the special features of the instance and must treat these special features as special. In consequence, the 'special case' is not robbed of its particularity. To achieve this, the bureaucrat will have needed to use wit and ingenuity to oppose routine categorization by particularization, and the same skills will be required should the special case be challenged by others.

The argument that categorization was the fundamental process of thought rested upon a number of assumptions, whose reasonableness was taken for granted. For example, cognitive social psychologists normally accept as intuitively obvious the notion that the stimulus environment demands simplification. However, the same sort of assumptions, which are used to justify the importance of categorization, can be turned around in order to justify the importance of the reverse process of particularization. For instance, Rosch, in arguing for the fundamental importance of categorization, states that "it is to the organism's advantage not to differentiate one stimulus from others when that differentiation is irrelevant to the purposes at hand" (1978, p. 29). The reversal of this assumption is equally plausible: it can be asserted that it is to the organism's advantage to be able to differentiate a special stimulus from the others when that differentiation is relevant to the purposes at hand.

Similarly it is not difficult to reverse Allport's statement about [hu]mankind having a natural propensity for prejudice because of the 'normal and natural' tendency to form categorizations and generalizations. Equally impressive would be a pronouncement to the effect that [hu]mankind has a natural propensity for tolerance because of a natural tendency to form particularizations and to make special cases. In neither case would anyone deny that humans have the abilities assumed by the respective statements, whether it is to form generalizations or to make special cases. Moreover, it would seem to be a political, or moral, decision to regard mankind as having more of a natural propensity for prejudice than for tolerance or vice versa. The evidence from cognitive psychology need not be taken as being conclusive in either direction.

A further two examples should be sufficient to show the ease with which the assumptions of the categorization approach can be reversed. In a typical statement, which seems to dismiss particularization as it stresses categorization, Rothbart asserts that "the amount of cognitive effort that would be required to treat every new stimulus as unique would lead us to be overwhelmed by events and would render us virtually immobile in a world that required action" (1981, p. 175). Just as plausibly it could be suggested that we would run the risk of being overwhelmed by a world which required action if no unique stimulus could be treated as being unique, but instead every unique stimulus had to be considered as similar to others. Lastly there is that statement by Mervis and Rosch, which directly links categorization with the need to cope with the infinite differences existing in the world: "Without any categorization an organism could not interact profitably with the infinitely distinguishable objects and events it experiences" (1981, p. 94). Again the statement seems eminently reasonable, and again an equally reasonable reversal can be made. For instance, it could be asserted that without particularization an organism could not interact profitably with the infinitely similar objects and events which it experiences. Nor is the concept of the infinite similarity of objects any more unreasonable than the assumption of their infinite differences. As Protagoras remarked to Socrates, "everything resembles everything else up to a point" (*Protagoras*, 331). If there are infinite ways of distinguishing between objects, then there must be infinite ways of finding them similar. At the very least, any two objects must resemble each other in infinite ways: there will be an infinite number of characteristics which neither possesses, and therefore the two objects are similarly non-possessors of these infinite characteristics.

However, there is no need to go into intricate arguments about infinite similarities and infinite differences. The basic point is a much simpler one. All the arguments which accord a special place to the process of categorization in cognition can be countered by similar arguments for the importance of the opposing process of particularization. Thus, if we need to put particulars into categories, in order to survive as perceiving and thinking beings, so then we need also to be able to pick out particulars. These reversals are not intended to suggest that we need to construct a cognitive approach on the basis of particularization, in order to rival the theories built upon categorization. The result of any such endeavour would be equally one-sided. What the ease of reversal does imply is that we should not necessarily accord a privileged status to the one process of categorization. Instead, we should examine cognition in terms of two opposing processes: categorization and particularization.[3]

It can be argued that the two processes are deeply interrelated, so much so that the ability to categorize presupposes the ability to particularize. Here, the notions of infinite similarities and infinite differences may be illustrative. If there are infinite ways of organizing the stimulus world in terms of similarities and differences, then we need to select appropriate patterns of similarities and differences, and reject a whole host of others. The notion of 'selection' is a crucial one in cognitive psychology. Any perceptual system which is attempting to categorize incoming information must engage in some form of selection. This point has been well made by Erdelyi in his review of theories about perceptual categorization. He writes that selection is "pervasive" in perception, and at all levels of the perceptual system information is selected (1974, p. 12). If we have a choice of ways of categorizing the stimulus arrays with which we are faced, then selection is involved in arriving at one appropriate categorization. This sort of selection is akin to what we have been calling particularization. Out of all possible categories, one is treated as uniquely appropriate, and it must be fished out of the general pool of categories. Thus, in order to categorize something by putting it into an appropriate category, we must have particularized that category. In this way, categorization depends upon the opposing process of particularization. . . .

Categorization and particularization, inasmuch as they refer to human thought processes, are not to be considered as two distinct capabilities, as separate, for example, as the olfactory and visual senses. The two processes are interrelated, at least as far as linguistic categories and particularities are concerned. In order to use categories, we must be able to particularize and vice versa. The paradox is that these two processes seem to pull in opposite cognitive directions: the one pulls towards the aggregation of things and the other towards the uniqueness of things. The result is that the human mind is equipped with the two contrary skills of being able to put things into categories and to treat them as special. Thus, our thought processes are not held in the thrall of a single process, which inevitably leads to a distorting narrow-mindedness. Nor do our basic cognitive processes merely function to provide psychological stability and order. They also provide the seeds of argumentation and deliberation, as our logoi of categorization are always liable to be opposed by our anti-logoi of particularization. However, in order to see how this might operate, we need to move from the perceptual metaphor, used in much cognitive psychology, to consider directly logoi and their negations. . . .

NOTES

1 The individualist and perceptual themes in cognitive psychology have been forcefully criticized by Moscovici. . . . Moscovici stresses the social nature of thought by discussing ideas, beliefs and attitudes in terms of 'social representations' (Moscovici, 1984 . . .). According to Moscovici, the argumentative common-places which are discussed by rhetorical theorists (see Chapter 8) would be forms of social representations. The notion of common sense, as used in Chapter 8, is very close to Moscovici's concept of social representation. The principal difference is that 'common-places' and 'common sense', because they are linked to rhetorical theory, point towards the contrary and argumentative aspects of cognition much more directly than does 'social representation'. However, it might be profitable to explore the rhetorical dimensions of this theoretically important concept of social representations.

2 Many of the themes discussed in this section are elaborated in greater detail in Billig (1985). Although this section might give the impression that all of cognitive social psychology is dominated by the images of the prejudiced person and of the bureaucrat, this would be misleading. In particular, attribution theory is not discussed. At the root of attribution theory, which examines how people ascribe causes to events, is the image of the person as a scientist . . . . Although attribution theory might appear to postulate that the ordinary

person is a scientist in their thinking, much of the emphasis of the research suggests that ordinary people think unscientifically, because they show many of the biases which are outlined by categorization theorists . . . . Antaki (1985) specifically argues that attribution theory, as normally conceived, is ill-equipped to deal with the rhetorical aspects of cognition.

3 A further example of the one-sided bias in cognitive theory is provided by the current interest in metaphor. In an extremely perceptive article, which emphasizes the metaphorical nature of much psychological science, Lakoff and Johnson argue that human thinking "is fundamentally metaphorical in character" (1981, p. 193). A similar point is made by I. A. Richards in *Philosophy of Rhetoric*. A metaphor points to the similarity between two things or concepts, and thus it could be called the tropic expression of the principle of categorization. Metaphor can be contrasted with metonymy, which highlights the particular features of a category of things. Thus metonymy is the tropic expression of particularization. Although it might just as reasonably be asserted that human thinking is fundamentally metonymic, cognitive psychologists have paid nowhere near as much attention to metonymy as they have to metaphor.

REFERENCES

Abelson, R. P. (1979). Differences between belief and knowledge systems. *Cognitive Science*, 3, 355–366.

Adorno, T. W., Frenkel-Brunswick, E., Levinson, D. J. and Sanford, R. N. (1950). *The Authoritarian Personality*. New York: Harper and Row.

Altemeyer, R. A. (1981). *Right-Wing Authoritarianism*. Manitoba: University of Manitoba Press.

Allport, G. W. (1958). *The Nature of Prejudice*. Garden City: Anchor Books.

Antaki, C. (1985). Ordinary explanations in conversation. *European Journal of Social Psychology*, 15, 213–230.

Anderson, J. R. (1985). *Cognitive Psychology and its Implications*. New York: W. H. Freeman.

Bartlett, F. (1932). *Remembering*. Cambridge: Cambridge University Press.

Billig, M. (1985). Prejudice, Categorization and Particularization. *European Journal of Social Psychology*, 15, 79–103.

Cantor, N., Mischel, W. and Schwartz, J. (1982). Social knowledge: structure, content, use and abuse. In *Cognitive Social Psychology*, ed. A. H. Hastorf and A. M. Isen. New York: Elsevier.

Casson, R. W. (1983). Schemata in cognitive anthropology. *Annual Review of Anthropology*, 12, 429–462.

Eiser, J. R. (1980). *Cognitive Social Psychology*. London: McGraw-Hill.

Erdelyi, M. H. (1974). A new look at the New Look: perceptual defence and vigilance. *Psychological Review*, 87, 215–251.

Fiske, S. T. and Taylor, S. E. (1984). *Social Cognition*. New York: Random House.

Greenwald, A. G. (1980). The totalitarian ego: fabrication and revision of personal history. *American Psychologist*, 35, 603–618.

Hamilton, D. L. (1976). Cognitive biases in the perception of social groups. In *Cognitive and Social Behavior*, ed. J. S. Carroll and J. W. Payne. Hillsdale: Lawrence Erlbaum.

Hamilton, D. L. (1979). A cognitive-attributional analysis of stereotyping. In *Advances in Experimental Social Psychology*, ed. L. Berkowitz. New York: Academic Press.

Katz, D., & Braly, K. W. (1933). Racial stereotypes and 100 college students. *Journal of Abnormal and Social Psychology*, 28, 280–290.

Lakoff, G. and Johnson, M. (1981). The metaphorical structure of the human conceptual system. In *Perspective on Cognitive Science*, ed. D. A. Norman. Hillsdale: Lawrence Erlbaum.

Mervis, C. B. and Rosch, E. (1981). Categorization of natural objects. *Annual Review of Psychology*, 32, 89–115.

Moscovici, S. (1984). The phenomenon of social representations. In *Social Representations*, ed. R. M. Farr and S. Moscovici. Cambridge: Cambridge University Press.

Rokeach, M. (1960). *The Open and Closed Mind*. New York: Basic Books.

Rosch, E. (1978). Principles of categorization. In *Cognition and categorization*, ed. E. Rosch and B. Lloyd. New Jersey: Lawrence Erlbaum.

Rosch, E., Mervis, C. B., Gray, W. D., Johnson, D. M. and Boyes-Braem, P. (1976). Basic objects in natural categories. *Cognitive Psychology*, 8, 382–439.

Rothbart, M. (1981). Memory processes and social beliefs. In *Cognitive Processes in Stereotyping and Intergroup Behavior*, ed. D. L. Hamilton. Hillsdale: Lawrence Erlbaum.

Schank, R. C. (1981). Language and memory. In *Perspectives on cognitive theory*, ed. D. A. Norman. New Jersey: Lawrence Erlbaum.

Showers, C. and Cantor, N. (1985). Social cognition: A look at motivated strategies. *Annual Review of Psychology*, 36, 275–305.

Snyder, M. (1981a). On the self-perpetuating nature of social stereotypes. In *Cognitive Processes in Stereotyping and Intergroup Behavior*, ed. D. L. Hamilton. Hillsdale: Lawrence Erlbaum.

Tajfel, H. (1981). *Human Groups and Social Categories*. Cambridge: Cambridge University Press.

Tajfel, H. and Wilkes, A. L. (1963). Classification and quantitative judgment. *British Journal of Psychology*, 54, 101–114.

Tajfel, H. and Wilkes, A. L. (1964). Salience of attributes and commitments to extreme judgments in the perception of people. *British Journal of Social and Clinical Psychology*, 2, 40–49.

Taylor, S. E. (1981). A categorization approach to stereotyping. In *Cognitive Processes in Stereotyping and Intergroup Behavior*, ed. D. L. Hamilton. Hillsdale: Lawrence Erlbaum.

Taylor, S. E. and Crocker, J. (1981). Schematic bases of social information processing. In *Social Cognition*, ed. E. T. Higgins et al. Hillsdale: Lawrence Erlbaum.

PART 2

INFLUENCES ON THE PROCESS OF COMMUNICATING WITH STRANGERS

CHAPTER 3

Cultural Influences on Communication

There is no agreement among social scientists on how to define culture. Culture can be seen as including everything that is human-made (e.g., Herskovits, 1955) or as a system of shared meanings (e.g., Geertz, 1973), to name only two possible views. Culture also has been equated with communication. Hall (1959), for example, believes that "culture is communication and communication is culture" (p. 169).

Although there are many definitions of culture, it is necessary to select one to guide our analysis. Keesing's (1974) definition is long, but not overly technical:

> Culture, conceived as a system of competence shared in its broad design and deeper principles, and varying between individuals in its specificities, is then not all of what an individual knows and thinks and feels about his [or her] world. It is his [or her] theory of what his [or her] fellows know, believe, and mean, his [or her] theory of the code being followed, the game being played, in the society into which he [or she] was born. . . . It is this theory to which a native actor [or actress] refers in interpreting the unfamiliar or the ambiguous, in interacting with strangers (or supernaturals), and in other settings peripheral to the familiarity of mundane everyday life space; and with which he [or she] creates the stage on which the games of life are played.
> . . . But note that the actor's [or actress'] "theory" of his [or her] culture, like his [or her] theory of his [or her] language may be in large measure unconscious. Actors [or actresses] follow rules of which they are not consciously aware, and assume a world to be "out there" that they have in fact created with culturally shaped and shaded patterns of mind. We can recognize that not every individual shares precisely the same theory of the cultural code, that not every individual knows all the sectors of the culture . . . even though no one native actor [or actress] knows all the culture, and each has a variant version of the code. Culture in this view is ordered not simply as a collection of symbols fitted together by the analyst but as a system of knowledge, shaped and constrained by the way the human brain acquires, organizes, and processes information and creates "internal models of reality." (p. 89)

Culture, therefore, refers to a "system of knowledge" that is shared by a large group of people. Our culture tells us how to interpret others' behavior and provides guidelines for our behavior.

The "borders" between cultures usually, but not always, coincide with political boundaries between countries. To illustrate, we can speak of the culture of the United States, the Japanese culture, and the Mexican culture. When we refer to subdivisions of a "national" culture, we use the term *subculture*. Subculture implies that the group shares some of the larger national culture, but has some values or customs that differ from the larger culture. To illustrate, we can speak of ethnic subcultures or an "artistic" subculture. Although the focus of this book is on communicating with people from different national cultures and ethnic subcultures, everything said applies to other subcultures as well.

In order to understand similarities and differences in communication across cultures, it is necessary to have a way of talking about how cultures differ. It does not make any sense to say that "Jiro communicates indirectly because he is a Japanese" or that "Adrian communicates directly because he is from the United States." This does not tell us why there are differences in the way people communicate in the United States and in Japan. There has to be some aspect of the cultures in Japan and the United States that are different, and this difference, in turn, explains why Japanese communicate indirectly and people from the United States communicate directly. In other words, there are variables on which cultures can be different or similar that can be used to explain communication across cultures. We will refer to these variables as "dimensions of cultural variability."

There are several different views of how cultures differ. It is impossible to include readings on all the dimensions of cultural variability. We, therefore, focus on those which we have found most useful in understanding similarities and differences in communication across cultures. In the first reading in this chapter Triandis outlines the differences between individualistic and collectivistic cultures. Individualistic cultures like the United States emphasize the importance of the individual over the group. Collectivistic cultures, in contrast, emphasize the importance of the group over the individual. People in collectivistic cultures draw a sharper distinction than people in individualistic cultures between being a member of an ingroup and being a member of an outgroup.

In the second reading, Hall discusses low- and high-context communication. In low-context communication, the emphasis in interpreting a message is placed on the content of the message. In high-context communication, the emphasis in interpreting the message is placed on the context in which the message is transmitted. Low-context communication tends to be very direct, whereas high-context communication tends to be indirect. This dimension of cultural variability explains the differences between direct communication in the United States and indirect communication in Japan in the example just presented.

In the final reading in this chapter, Hofstede presents the four dimensions of cultural variability he isolated in his large cross-cultural study. The four dimensions are individualism-collectivism (previously discussed), uncertainty avoidance, power distance, and masculinity-femininity. In high uncertainty avoidance cultures people try to avoid uncertainty whenever possible. In low uncertainty avoidance cultures people accept a certain amount of uncertainty as part of life. In high power distance cultures people see inequalities between people as natural, whereas in power distance cultures people see equality as the natural state. Finally, in highly masculine cultures there are highly differentiated sex roles, and in feminine cultures there is little differentiation in what males and females are expected to do.

These dimensions of cultural variability can help us understand and predict strangers' behavior. If we are from an individualistic culture and know that a stranger is from a collectivistic culture, for example, we can predict that she or he will draw a sharper distinction between being a member of an ingroup or an outgroup than we will. Knowing this, in turn, will allow us to predict how the stranger might respond to us if he or she defines us as a member of an outgroup.

REFERENCES

Geertz, C. (1973). *The interpretation of cultures.* New York: Basic Books.
Hall, E. T. (1959). *The silent language.* New York: Doubleday.
Herskovits, M. (1955). *Cultural anthropology.* New York: Knopf.
Keesing, R. (1974). Theories of culture. *Annual Review of Anthropology, 3,* 73-97.

Collectivism v. Individualism:
A Reconceptualisation of a Basic Concept in Cross-Cultural Social Psychology
Harry Triandis

Perhaps the most important dimension of cultural difference in social behaviour, across the diverse cultures of the world, is the relative emphasis on individualism v. collectivism. In individualist cultures, most people's social behaviour is largely determined by personal goals, attitudes, and values of collectivities (families, co-workers, fellow countrymen [or women]). In collectivist cultures, most people's social behaviour is largely determined by goals, attitudes, and values that are shared with some collectivity (group of persons). . . .

THE THEORETICAL FRAMEWORK

Definitions

Gould and Kolb (1964) defined *individualism* as 'belief that the individual is an end in himself [or herself], and as such ought to realise his [or her] "self" and cultivate his [or her] own judgement, notwithstanding the weight of pervasive social pressures in the

Source: Abridged from chapter with same title in G. K. Verma & C. Bagley (Eds.), *Cross-Cultural Studies of Personality, Attitudes and Cognition* (pp. 60-95). London: Macmillan, 1988.

direction of conformity'. This definition seems to be too narrow to encompass the phenomena described above. We thus define *Collectivism* as great emphasis on: (a) the views, needs, and goals of the ingroup rather than of oneself, (b) social norms and duty defined by the ingroup rather than behaviour to get pleasure, (c) beliefs shared with ingroup rather than on beliefs that distinguish oneself from the ingroup, and (d) great readiness to cooperate with ingroup members. In the case of extreme collectivism individuals do not have *personal* goals, attitudes, or values. Social roles are the building blocks of society and the performance of duties associated with roles is the path to salvation, which is a personal goal (Shweder and Bourne, 1982). This definition subsumes ideas such as high interdependence, interpersonal sensitivity, conformity, readiness to be influuenced by others, mutual sympathy, *personalismo* (wanting to deal only with others who are personally known to one), self-sacrifice for ingroup members, and external control. The emphasis is on the ingroup—i.e., a group of people who influence an individual's behaviour, so that the individual chooses the goals of this group, or subjugates his [or her] personal goals to theirs. The ingroup may be very narrow (e.g., just the nuclear family), slightly broader (extended family and friends), or rather broad (members of the army, countrymen [or women], members of a political party). This conceptualisation suggests that there are different kinds of collectivism, and size of the ingroup is one of the relevant parameters.

Extreme collectivism occurs when the individual's and the ingroup's needs, goals, attitudes, and values are indistinguishable. The person then enjoys doing what the ingroup demands. In such a case, the individual and the culture are both collectivist. When there is non-overlap between individual goals and the goals of the ingroup one might have an individualist culture (where most people act with reference to their own goals) or a collectivist culture (where most people subjugate their personal goals to the goals of the ingroup) and one can also imagine situations where an individualist lives in a collectivist or an individualist culture.

It is important to note here that in collectivist cultures the incompatibility of personal and ingroup goals or values is not reflected in conflict between the individual and a specific member of the ingroup; rather the individual feels that the ingroup is like a person and pushes toward a direction away from his or her personal goals. Others are seen as representatives of the ingroup rather than as individuals.

In the definition of collectivism presented above we use the ingroup as a central concept. 'Ingroups' are here conceived as groups of people about whose welfare one is concerned, with whom one is willing to cooperate without demanding equitable returns, and separation from whom leads to discomfort or even pain. Exactly who is included in one's ingroup is quite variable. Some cultures have very narrow ingroups—e.g., the nuclear family. Other cultures have very wide ingroups—e.g., Asians. Among the persons who are likely to be included in some definitions of ingroups are parents, siblings, spouses, children, other relatives, friends, co-workers, neighbours, members of particular political, scientific, or religious group, fellow nationals, and so on. In some cultures special groups may be included in the ingroup— e.g., the kibbutz for some Israelis.

In collectivist societies ingroups are defined through tradition. In individualist societies people create their own ingroups (Hsu, 1971). They tend to explore other groups and to colonise them. One finds missionaries, colonies, and people spending a lot of time in specialised groups (e.g., chess-clubs) in societies that are individualistic. In individualistic societies ingroups are thus defined by individuals rather than by tradition.

Now consider the areas of concern, influence, and norm-imposition of the ingroup. In extremely collectivist societies the ingroup dominates all aspects of a person's life. By contrast in individualist societies only certain aspects of a person's life are influenced by ingroups. The nuclear family may thus influence how one spends one's 'pocket money', but not how one invests; the work group may determine when one gets to work, but not what one does while at work; the government may determine how much one pays in taxes but not what deductions one will claim, and so on. These examples indicate that the *breadth* of influence is an important variable. In collectivist societies the influence is broad. While few sources (e.g., the family) are influential, they do have an influence on a wide range of behaviours. In individualist societies there are many sources of influence, and each of them has a narrow sphere of influence. Furthermore, since there are many groups an individual can afford to ignore some of them. If he [or she] is rejected for non-conformity by some, he or she will be accepted by others. S/he can always acquire new ingroups. Conformity is thus not a great virtue in individualist societies.

This conceptualisation, then, results in the following variables that are relevant for the analysis of individualism-collectivism: (a) the number of ingroups; (b) the extent of the sphere of influence of each ingroup; (c) the depth of this influence. In general, the more ingroups there are the narrower is the extent of influence and the lesser the depth of influence of each.

Collectivist societies are characterised by one or two ingroups, and one can think of different kinds of collectivism by identifying different rank-orders of importance of these ingroups. The *patriot* puts nation ahead of family; the *familist* puts family ahead of work-group or country; the *organisation man* [or woman] puts the company ahead of family; the *party member* puts the political party ahead of the family or work-group. In some cultures, particular ingroups are all-important: in Japan the work-group; in traditional China the extended family; in the USSR the communist party, and so on.

These considerations, then, lead to the definition of different kinds of collectivism and individualism.

First we define *basic collectivism* as occurring when one ingroup totally determines a very large number of behaviours of the person. The larger the *number* of behaviours determined by the group the more collectivism. The converse—when no ingroup determines any of the person's behaviour—is extreme *basic individualism*.

Second, we consider the *number* of ingroups that influence a person's behaviour. If *no* ingroup determines any of the person's behaviours this is basic individualism. If *one* ingroup determines it, either totally or in part we have the general case of *basic collectivism*. In basic collectivism there is no norm or role conflict. If two or three ingroups influence the person's behaviour there is an opportunity for the person to consult with them, balance the views of each, and decide. Such a situation is essentially individualistic. *Consultative individualism* thus occurs when two or more ingroups influence behaviour. The larger the number of ingroups that influence behavior the more individualistic is the person. If in a culture it is appropriate to consult a large number of ingroups, this is a very individualistic culture.

Third, if ingroups do influence some behaviours, we can consider a matrix one side of which includes behaviours and the other side various kinds of ingroups. If there is substantial influence by one or more ingroups on one or more behaviours we have a case of *contextual collectivism* (Hui, 1984). The stronger such influences, the greater the degree of collectivism. Contextual collectivism is specific. A patriot whose family life is regulated by the needs of the state would thus exhibit 'family—state collectivism'. A worker who decides what kind of car to drive, on the basis of the views of his co-workers, would be a 'transportation—work group collectivist'. According to this conceptualisation there are an infinitely large number of such collectivisms, but in describing a culture it will probably be sufficient to sample some of the major ingroups and behaviours.

In analysing the sphere of influence of a group one can consider behaviours that are susceptible to ingroup influence. Among the most important are who to marry, what religious beliefs to hold, what language to speak, who can be one's friends, what kind of education one should acquire, what kind of work should one do, where to live, in what shops to trade, and to what political party one is to belong. However, ingroup influence may extend beyond these areas, to aesthetic judgements, to what food to eat, and so on. In highly-collectivist cultures—e.g., the Amish or the Dukabors—the ingroup regulates almost all areas of social behaviour. By contrast, highly-individualistic cultures allow individuals much freedom, and ingroups can control a very limited range of social behaviour.

The main dimensions relevant to an analysis of social organisation in general, and to collectivism in particular, are thus the following:

1. How many ingroups influence an individual's social behaviour? The more these ingroups, the greater is the individualism of the culture.
2. How easy is it for the individual to become a member of these ingroups? The easier it is, the more individualistic the culture.
3. What is the size of these ingroups? In individualistic cultures small ingroups are found in affiliative settings; in achievement settings the ingroups are of any size. In collectivist cultures the ingroups are of any size in affiliative settings (e.g., Mardi Gras), but the achievement settings usually have small ingroups. However, modifications have been observed—e.g., the Japanese large firm is often seen as an ingroup by its members.
4. How many behaviours are completely determined by ingroup norms? When many are controlled by ingroup norms, that is characteristic of collectivism.
5. Is behaviour mostly predictable from norms and roles? In collectivist cultures norms rather than the attitude toward the act or the perceived consequences of the behaviour control and predict the behaviour.
6. Are the majority of the perceived consequences of social behaviour other-oriented (characteristic of collectivism) or self-oriented (characteristic of individualism)?

This conceptualisation of collectivism allows for a wide range of measurements. Specifically, if one takes a sample of different kinds of behaviours one can determine for each behaviour the extent to which it is under the influence of social factors—such as norms, roles, or interpersonal agreements—or under the influence of hedonistic tendencies—such as the affect toward the behaviour itself (Triandis, 1976; 1980). The greater the influence of the former the more collectivist the individual; the greater the influence of the latter the more individualist the individual. Societies where the majority consists of collectivists can be called collectivist.

Triandis (1980) conceptualised behavioural intentions (self-instructions on how to act) as a function of social factors (norms, roles, interpersonal agreements), the affect toward the behaviour, and the perceived consequences of the behaviour. Clearly, the first of these factors is collectivist, and the other two individualist, though the last factor can have societal relevance (when the perceived consequences have relevance for others).

In a study of the perceptions of wrongdoing, the collectivist Japanese gave greater emphasis to the actor's role position and the act's social context, while the individualist Americans emphasised only the actor's [or actress's] deed *per se* (Hamilton and Saunders, 1983).

In population studies done in Mexico and the US Davidson *et al.* (1976), found the lower-class Mexican women more influenced by the social factor, while the upper-class Mexican women were like American women—mostly influenced by the perceived consequences factor.

Antecedents of Individualism and Collectivism

Collectivism is conceptually linked to ethnocentrism. It is thus possible to list many of the propositions of LeVine and Campbell (1972), substituting the concept of collectivism for the concept of ethnocentrism. Space does not allow a complete listing, but the following dozen propositions are illustrative.

1. The greater the real threat to the ingroup the greater the collectivism (the phenomenon that patriotism emerges mostly in wartime).
2. The greater the real threat to the ingroup, the greater the awareness of the ingroup, and the tightening of the ingroup boundaries.
3. When natural resources are in short supply the society will be more collectivist, but under extreme deprivation individualism emerges.
4. The more similar ingroups are perceived to be to outgroups, the more individualist will be the society, and vice-versa.
5. When membership in outgroups is closed, individuals will be more collectivist.
6. Groups offering their members greater rewards for membership will be found in collectivist cultures, and vice-versa. (The greater levels of sacrifice of parents in collectivist cultures, and the high levels of child abuse in individualist cultures, are consistent with this proposition).
7. The more frustrating the environment, the more collectivist the society, but when frustration is extreme individualism emerges.

8. The more ingroup norms place restraint on impulse the more collectivist the culture, and vice versa.
9. The more severe the socialisation process the more collectivist the society, and vice-versa.
10. The greater the population density, the greater the residential proximity and crowdedness, the greater the collectivism.
11. The more collectivist the society the more authoritarian the family, the more severe the sanctions of those who defy authority, the more approval of repressive leaders, the greater the emphasis on obedience, and the greater the use of physical punishment, and vice-versa (LeVine and Campbell, p. 150).
12. The more mutual liking there is within the ingroup the greater the collectivism, and vice-versa.

In addition to propositions inspired from theories of ethnocentrism, one can derive propositions from other fields:

1. The smaller the size of the family the more individualistic the child.
2. The greater the family solidarity, the more collectivist the child.
3. The more autonomy in child-rearing, the more individualistic the child.
4. The more exposure to different kinds of groups, ideologies and viewpoints, the more individualist the child.
5. The more mobility (either social or across national boundaries, as among migrants) the greater the individualism (findings by Forgas, Morris and Furnham, 1982, support this).
6. The more success is defined in individual rather than group terms, the more individualistic the society, and vice-versa.
7. The more hedonistic the society the more individualistic it will be, and vice-versa.
8. The more primary group identification, the more collectivist the society (data by Madsen and Lancy, 1981, support this).

Consequents of Individualism and Collectivism

Individualism is strongly linked to high GNP (Hofstede, 1980; Adelman and Morris, 1967). Yet, as the moderately collectivist Japanese have demonstrated, this link is not inevitable. If one can expand the 'Am I competent?' question to also ask 'Am I a good member of the ingroup?' one can have a society that is more balanced. This is, according to DeVos (1973), the way the Japanese define themselves—as both competent and good ingroup members. By contrast, Americans tend to overemphasise competence and to underemphasise ingroup membership, with undesirable consequences. Naroll (1983) reviews a broad literature linking what he calls 'moralnets' to a variety of social phenomena. Weak moralnets occur when the patterns of interdependence, sharing, and interpersonal concern are weak. People in weak moralnets are more likely to have heart disease, and they are more likely to die. Weak moralnets are linked to mental illness, alcohol abuse, suicide, divorce, homicide, teenage pregnancies, child abuse, crimes, and so on.

Naroll quotes studies which show that when a high school senior reported strong interpersonal links with five or more households of similar background, there was a lower probability of divorce or desertion in that family, and a lower probability of delinquency.

Strong social support systems, such as Alcoholics Anonymous, have repeatedly been found to be associated with the overcoming of interpersonal difficulties or undesirable habits. Janis (1983) shows the importance of social support for stopping smoking, and for losing weight. Gottlieb (1983) shows the health-protective effects of social support. Those who receive social health support are more likely to persist at a task under unfavourable conditions (Sarason, Levine, Basham and Sarason, 1983).

While extreme forms of individualism have undesirable consequences, extreme forms of collectivism are equally debilitating. Banfield (1958), discussing his observations in rural Southern Italy, argues that cultures where all associations are limited to family and tribe cannot develop a modern economy. Industrialisation requires corporate organisations. Such organisation cannot be limited to a narrow ingroup.

Banfield describes what he calls the 'amoral familism' of that part of Italy as characterised by the action principle: 'maximise the material, short-range advantage of the nuclear family; assume that all others will do likewise' (p. 85). Amoral familism is due to the high death rate, the patterns of land tenure, and the lack of an extended family, characteristic of this culture. There are no voluntary organisations, so very little gets done that can benefit the community. The authorities consist of individuals whose only concern is how to enrich themselves. Writing to the authorities is considered offensive (the authority essentially says: 'how dare you interfere with my work'). The upper class is highly individualistic, concerned with maximising their own benefits. Thus, no one furthers the interests of the community, unless by chance they happen to overlap with own interests. Some officials are concerned with the community only because they perceive that as 'their job'. There are no checks or controls on officials and the government in Rome.

In such societies there is no self-sacrifice for the organisation, no trust in others. Laws are disregarded unless punishment is probable. Bribes for officials are common. Officials who claim to be concerned with the welfare of the community are considered frauds. Votes are cast to maximise family gain. Nothing that will benefit the community but not the self/ingroup directly is voted for. Punishment is perceived as good, because 'it keeps people from sinning'. Those punished do not feel guilty, only unlucky. No one feels obligated to do anything for a collective larger than the nuclear family.

Such a picture suggests collectivism in a very narrow band of situations (areas) and extreme individualism (maximise own benefit) in every other area. The contradiction that the society is both highly collectivist (because of the great importance of the ingroup) and individualistic, because many people behave individualistically, can be handled by the conceptualisation of multiple kinds of individualism and collectivism presented above.

The need to make distinctions among different kinds of individualism is apparent from the following anecdote: the musical director appointed to the Philadelphia

Orchestra, one of the top ten orchestras in the world, in 1982 was Italian Ricardo Muti. In an interview with the French magazine *L'Express* (September 1982 issue) he was asked why Italy has produced such a large number of great conductors, including himself, and no major orchestras. He said that 'Italians are too individualistic to play well in an orchestra'. Presumably, in an orchestra one has to adjust well to others, which meant adjustment in the area of work-relationships. Italians may be low in the extent they are influenced by work relationships. By contrast, Americans, who get the world's top individualism scores in Hofstede's (1980) work, have five of the ten top orchestras in the world. How come? GNP may be relevant, but perhaps more useful is to note that Americans are consultative individualists and Italians are family collectivists and outside the family basic individualists.

Quite similar to the Italian situation described by Banfield, is the situation in rural Greece. Triandis and Vassiliou (1972) collected multi-method data from interviews, observations, questionnaires and tests, and did experiments to obtain some impression of the cultural differences between Greece and the US. They identified the Greek ingroup (family and friends) as relatively narrow, a source of protection, social insurance, and the setting within which one can relax. Relations with outgroup members (everybody else) are suspicious, competitive, and uncooperative. Ingroup authorities are accepted; outgroup authorities are rejected, defied, undermined, resented. The strongest tie is the parent—child link; in the US the stronger tie is the spouse—spouse link. In Greece children remain interdependent with parents as long as the parents live. In the US children are encouraged to become independent, to do 'their own thing', once they have reached a certain age.

In Greece there is much intimacy in ingroup roles, and much more conflict in roles such as landlord—tenant and boss—subordinate than is perceived in the US. In Greece the self is entangled with the ingroup. Achievement is not individual achievement but the achievement of the ingroup. If a member of the ingroup achieves fame, that is wonderful because it elevates the ingroup and puts down the outgroup. Within the ingroup, influence such as criticism is acceptable. But criticism from the outgroup is rejected, and a facade of arrogance, dogmatism, and an all-knowing personality is presented. Social control is considered good (Triandis and Vassiliou, pp. 324–5). In responding to a variety of attitude items the Greeks had lower variance than the corresponding US samples, and they indicated they did not mind being judged by the organisations to which they belonged. The concepts *Freedom* and *Progress* were conceived in collection terms (national) in Greece and individual terms in the US. The major values in the US were found to be achievement and efficiency; the major values in Greece were good social relations and social control.

These observations suggest the hypothesis that similar patterns of collectivism and individualism would be found in most of the Mediterranean rural societies.

In a study of role perceptions in Java and the US Setiadi (1984) found that the most important factor in Java was obedience, while the most important factor in the US was enjoyment (have fun together). This is quite consistent with the collectivist hierarchial structure of Java.

While both extremes of individualism and collectivism are apparently undesirable; it is not at all clear how different levels of this dimension are linked to social phenomena. This appears to be a research area of high priority.

Rianoshek (1980, p. 105) argues that increased independence and interdependence go hand in hand. All human relationships involve both. There are some relationships that might be called symbiotic-dependent, as in the tradition male-female roles in Western society, where each depends on the other, and the relationship is symbiotic. As both partners move toward independence, by playing both the instrumental and expressive roles of marriage, they develop more interdependence. Both can be both nurturant and dominant at different points in time. Such a conceptualisation, far from seeing the neoindividualist as influenced by the self, sees the person operating in a highly coordinated social network.

This conception would suggest the hypothesis that levels of influence from self as well as others may be best conceptualised as orthogonal dimensions. It may be that there are cultures where only minimal influence can be traced to conscious individual processes or group arguments; there may be other cultures where people respond very consciously to their own needs, attitudes and concerns of others; still other cultures may show a strong individualist and a weak collectivist or a weak individualist and a strong collectivist influence. Such a view accommodates both individualistic and collectivistic tendencies. The problem of how to accommodate such tendencies seems to be of world-wide importance, as seen by the fact that it is the focus of attention of Soviet as well as Western observers (Lawler, 1980; Zotova, 1974). The survival advantages of certain kinds of collectivism (e.g., the Arapesh as summarised by Lee, 1976) consider it the lowest form of humanity for a hunter to eat his own kill; what is ideal is that each will eat what someone else has killed. (Obviously this maximises the chances that everyone will eat). Yet to the extent that collectivism inhibits economic development (Adelman and Morris, 1967) one must regulate it. At this point, we are not in a position to determine the desirable limits of collectivism. The more promising strategy is to examine how certain societies that are relatively successful (e.g., the Japanese) manage this variable. It is also instructive to review how collectivism operates in different US subcultures.

Within the US Hispanics and Hawaiians are apparently more collectivist than the mainstream. Reviews of the attributes of such groups (e.g., Triandis, 1983; Gallimore, Weiss and Finney, 1974) can help us understand how they function. Increased understanding has implications for helping such groups in their economic development, since many changes which lead to development will increase individualism and those problems associated with it.

In addition, it is useful to examine the effects of collectivism on social behaviour. Studies conducted by Leung (1983) suggest that collectivists are more likely to employ *equality* rather than *equity* principles in distributing resources. A similar conclusion is suggested by data from India and the US.

Leung also found that collectivists (Chinese University of Hong Kong students) behave very differently when they divide resources between themselves and a friend than when they divide resources between themselves and unknown fellow students; by contrast, individualists (American students) do not behave very differently toward these two kinds of persons. A similar point can be derived from the work of Nomura and Bar[n]lund (1983) who found that Japanese subjects reported that they criticise their parents quite actively, but criticised aquaintances rather passively, while American subjects used active methods of criticism toward both types of targets.

Collectivists attempt to maximise harmony in ingroup situations so they prefer to use the equality principle; they are also more attracted, according to Leung's data, to people who allocate rewards equally between themselves and friends. Individualists, in Leung's studies, are more attracted toward individuals who use the equity principle in allocating rewards between themselves and friends.

Other kinds of differences in social behaviour have also been noted. For example, Hiniker (1969) found that in studies of forced compliance Chinese subjects show much compliance but little attitude change. It is as if behaviour and attitudes have been decoupled. Behaviour is under the control of contemporary social forces such as norms, the other person's behaviour, and interpersonal agreements. Attitudes reflect values, and the history of the person's exchanges with others, over a long period of time.

There is a large literature (see Knight, 1981; Wetherell, 1982 for example) showing that in games, where rewards are divided; children from collectivist cultures prefer to maximise joint profit, while children from individualist cultures prefer to maximise the difference between ingroup and outgroup profit. The former thus tend to be cooperative, the latter competitive. Hewstone and Jaspers (1982) reviewed evidence that attributions are influenced by the social group of which the other belongs to, and this phenomenon is particularly strong in collectivist societies. . . .

CONCLUSION

In this paper we outlined some of the attributes that distinguish members of individualist and collectivist cultures. We reviewed a broad literature that is related to these constructs, and also literature that reports measurements of the constructs. The construct is central to many analyses of social systems and promises to be an important one for the social sciences.

REFERENCES

Adelman, I. and Morris, C. T. (1967) *Society, Politics and Economic Development: A Humanistic Approach*, Baltimore: Johns Hopkins Press.

Banfield, E. C. (1958) *The Moral Basis of a Backward Society*, Glencoe, Ill.: Free Press.

Davidson, A. R., Jaccard, J. J., Triandis, H. C., Morales, M. L. and Diaz-Guerrero, R. (1976) 'Cross-cultural model testing: Toward a solution of the etic-emic dilemma,' *International Journal of Psychology*, 11, 1–13.

DeVos, G. A. (1973) *Socialization for Achievement: Essays on the Cultural Psychology of the Japanese*, Berkeley, Cal.: University of California Press.

Forgas, J. P., Morris, S. L. and Furnham, A. (1982) 'Lay explanations of wealth: Attributions for economic success', *Journal of Applied Social Psychology*, 12, 381–97.

Gallimore, R., Weiss, L. and Finney, R. (1974) 'Cultural differences in delay of gratification: A problem of behavioral classification', *Journal of Personality and Social Psychology*, 30, 72–80.

Gottlieb, B. H. (1983) 'Social support as a focus for integrative research in psychology', *American Psychologist*, 38, 378–87.

Gould, J. and Kolb, W. L. (1964) *A Dictionary of the Social Sciences*, Glencoe, Ill.: Free Press.

Hamilton, V. L. and Saunders, J. (1983) 'Universals in judging wrongdoing: Japanese and Americans compared', *American Sociological Review*, 48, 199–211.

Hewstone, M. and Jaspers, J. M. F. (1982) 'Intergroup relations and attribution processes', in Tajfel, H. (ed.), *Social Identity and Intergroup Relations*, Cambridge: Cambridge University Press.

Hiniker, P. J. (1969) 'Chinese reactions to forced compliance: Dissonance reduction or national character?', *Journal of Social Psychology*, 77, 157–76.

Hofstede, G. (1980) *Culture's Consequences: International Differences in Work-related Values*, Beverley Hills, Cal.: Sage.

Hsu, F. L. K. (1971) 'Psychological homeostasis and jen: Conceptual tools for advancing psychological anthropology', *American Anthropologist*, 73, 23–44.

Hui, C. C. H. (1984) 'Individualism-collectivism and distributive behavior', doctoral dissertation, Department of Psychology, Champaign, Ill: University of Illinois.

Janis, I. L. (1983) 'The role of social support in adherence to stressful decisions', *American Psychologist*, 38, 143–60.

Knight, G. P. (1981) 'Behavioral and sociometric methods of indentifying cooperators, competitors and individualists: Support for the validity of the social orientation construct', *Development Psychology*, 17, 430–3.

Lawler, J. (1980) 'Collectivity and individuality in Soviet educational theory', *Contemporary Educational Psychology*, 5, 163–74.

Lee, D. (1976) *Valuing the Self: What Can We Learn from Other Cultures?*, Englewood Cliffs, N. J.: Prentice-Hall.

Leung, K. (1983) 'The impact of cultural collectivism on reward allocation', unpublished M.A. thesis, Department of Psychology, Champaign, Ill.: University of Illinois.

LeVine, R. A. and Campbell, D. T. (1972) *Ethnocentrism: Theories of Conflict, Ethnic Attitudes and Group Behavior*, New York: Wiley.

Madsen, M. C. and Lancy, D. F. (1981) 'Cooperative and competitive behavior', *Journal of Cross-cultural Psychology*, 12, 389–408.

Naroll, R. (1983) *The Moral Order*, Beverley [Hills], Cal.: Sage.

Nomura, N. and Bar[n]lund, D. (1983) 'Patterns of interpersonal criticism in Japan and the United States', *International Journal of Intercultural Relations*, 7, 1–18.

Rianoshek, R. (1980). 'A comment on Sampson's "Psychology and the American Ideal" ', *Journal of Personality and Social Psychology*, 38, 105–7.

Sarason, I. G., Levine, H. M., Basham, R. B. and Sarason, B. R. (1983) 'Assessing social support: the social support questionnaire', *Journal of Personality and Social Psychology*, 44, 127–39.

Setiadi, B. N. (1984) 'Schooling, age, and culture as moderators of role perceptions', doctoral dissertation, Champaign–Urbana: University of Illinois.

Shweder, R. A. and Bourne, E. J. (1982) 'Does the concept of person vary cross-culturally?', in

Marsella, A. J. and White, G. M. (eds), *Cultural Conceptions of Mental Health and Therapy*, Boston: D. Reidel, pp. 97–137.

Triandis, H.C. (1976) *Variations in Black and White Perceptions of the Social Environment*, Urbana, Ill: University of Illinois Press.

Triandis, H. C. (1980) 'Values, attitudes and interpersonal behavior', in Howe, H. and Page, M. (eds), *Nebraska Symposium on Motivation, 1979*. Lincoln, Neb: University of Nebraska Press.

Triandis, H. C. (1983) "Allocentrism vs. ideocentrism: A major cultural difference between Hispanics and Mainstream in the US', Technical Report 16, Department of Psychology, Champaign, Ill.: University of Illinois.

Triandis, H. C., Leung, K., Villareal, M. J. and Clack, F. L. (1985) 'Allocentric versus idiocentric tendencies: Convergent and discriminant validation', *Journal of Research in Personality*, 19, 395–415.

Triandis, H. C. and Vassiliou, V. (1972) 'A comparative analysis of subjective culture', in Triandis, H.C. (ed.), *The analysis of subjective culture*, New York: Wiley, pp. 299–338.

Wetherell, M. (1982) 'Cross-cultural studies of minimal groups: Implications for the social identity theory of intergroup relations', in Tajfel, H. (ed.), *Social Identity and Intergroup Relations*, Cambridge: Cambridge University Press.

Zotova, O. I. (1974) 'Development of the theory of groups in Soviet psychology', *Studia Psychologica*, 16, 278–82.

Context and Meaning

Edward T. Hall

One of the functions of culture is to provide a highly selective screen between [people] and the outside world. In its many forms, culture therefore designates what we pay attention to and what we ignore.[1] This screening function provides structure for the world and protects the nervous system from "information overload."[2] Information overload is a technical term applied to information-processing systems. It describes a situation in which the system breaks down when it cannot properly handle the huge volume of information to which it is subjected. Any mother who is trying to cope with the demands of small children, run a house, enjoy her husband, and carry on even a modest social life knows that there are times when everything happens at once and the world seems to be closing in on her. She is experiencing the same information overload that afflicts business managers, administrators, physicians, attorneys, and air controllers. Institutions such as stock exchanges, libraries, and telephone systems also go through times when the demands on the system (inputs) exceed capacity. People can handle the crunch through delegating and establishing priorities; while institutional solutions are less obvious, the high-context rule seems to apply. That is, the only way to increase information-handling capacity without increasing the mass and

Source: Abridged from Chapter 6 in E. T. Hall, *Beyond Culture* (pp. 74–90). New York: Doubleday, 1976.

complexity of the system is to program the memory of the system so that less information is required to activate the system, i.e., make it more like the couple that has been married for thirty-five years. The solution to the problem of coping with increased complexity and greater demands on the system seems to lie in the pre-programming of the individual or organization. This is done by means of the "context-ing" process. . . .

Like a number of my colleagues, I have observed that meaning and context are inextricably bound up with each other. While a linguistic code can be analyzed on some levels independent of context (which is what the machine translation project tried to accomplish), *in real life the code, the context, and the meaning can only be seen as different aspects of a single event.* What is unfeasible is to measure one side of the equation and not the others.[3]

Earlier, I said that high-context messages are placed at one end and low-context messages at the other end of a continuum. A high-context (HC) communication or message is one in which most of the information is either in the physical context or internalized in the person, while very little is in the coded, explicit, transmitted part of the message. A low-context (LC) communication is just the opposite; i.e., the mass of the information is vested in the explicit code. Twins who have grown up together can and do communicate more economically (HC) than two lawyers in a courtroom during a trial (LC), a mathematician programming a computer, two politicians drafting legislation, two administrators writing a regulation, or a child trying to explain to his mother why he [or she] got into a fight.

Although no culture exists exclusively at one end of the scale, some are high while others are low. American culture, while not on the bottom, is toward the lower end of the scale. We are still considerably above the German-Swiss, the Germans, and the Scandinavians in the amount of contexting needed in everyday life. While complex, multi-institutional cultures (those that are technologically advanced) might be thought of as inevitably LC, this is not always true. China, the possessor of a great and complex culture, is on the high-context end of the scale.

One notices this particularly in the written language of China, which is thirty-five hundred years old and has changed very little in the past three thousand years. This common written language is a unifying force tying together half a billion Chinese, Koreans, Japanese, and even some of the Vietnamese who speak Chinese. The need for context is experienced when looking up words in a Chinese dictionary. To use a Chinese dictionary, the reader must know the significance of 214 radicals (there are no counterparts for radicals in the Indo-European languages). For example, to find the word for star one must know that it appears under the sun radical. To be literate in Chinese, one has to be conversant with Chinese history. In addition, the spoken pronunciation system must be known, because there are four tones and a change of tone means a change of meaning; whereas in English, French, German, Spanish, Italian, etc., the reader need not know how to pronounce the language in order to read it. Another interesting sidelight on the Chinese orthography is that it is also an art form.[4] To my knowledge, no low-context communication system has ever been an art form. Good art is always high-context; bad art, low-context. This is one reason why good art persists and art that releases its message all at once does not.

The level of context determines everything about the nature of the communication and is the foundation on which all subsequent behavior rests (including symbolic behavior). Recent studies in sociolinguistics have demonstrated how context-dependent the language code really is. There is an excellent example of this in the work of the linguist Bernstein,[5] who has identified what he terms "restricted" (HC) and "elaborated" (LC) codes in which vocabulary, syntax, and sounds are all altered: In the restricted code of intimacy in the home, words and sentences collapse and are shortened. This even applies to the phonemic structure of the language. The individual sounds begin to merge, as does the vocabulary, whereas in the highly articulated, highly specific, elaborated code of the classroom, law, or diplomacy, more accurate distinctions are made on all levels. Furthermore, the code that one uses signals and is consistent with the situation. A shifting of code signals a shift in everything else that is to follow. "Talking down" to someone is low-contexting him [or her]—telling him [or her] more than he [or she] needs to know. This can be done quite subtly simply by shifting from the restricted end of the code toward the elaborated forms of discourse.

From the practical viewpoint of communications strategy, one must decide how much time to invest in contexting another person. A certain amount of this is always necessary, so that the information that makes up the explicit portions of the message is neither inadequate nor excessive. One reason most bureaucrats are so difficult to deal with is that they write for each other and are insensitive to the contexting needs of the public. The written regulations are usually highly technical on the one hand, while providing little information on the other. That is, they are a mixture of different codes or else there is incongruity between the code and the people to whom it is addressed. Modern management methods, for which management consultants are largely responsible, are less successful than they should be, because in an attempt to make everything explicit (low-contexting again) they frequently fail in their recommendations to take into account what people already know. This is a common fault of the consultant, because few consultants take the time (and few clients will pay for the time) to become completely contexted in the many complexities of the business.

There is a relationship between the world-wide activism of the sixties and where a given culture is situated on the context scale, because some are more vulnerable than others. HC actions are by definition rooted in the past, slow to change, and highly stable. Commenting on the need for the stabilizing effect of the past, anthropologist Loren Eiseley[6] takes an anti-activist position and points out how vulnerable our own culture is:

> Their world (the world of the activist), therefore, becomes increasingly the violent, unpredictable world of the first men [and women] simply because, in lacking faith in the past, one is inevitably forsaking all that enables [hu]man[s] to be a planning animal. For man's [and woman's] story,[7] in brief, is essentially that of a creature who has abandoned *instinct* and replaced it with cultural tradition and the hard-won increments of contemplative thought. The lessons of the past have been found to be a reasonably secure construction for proceeding against an unknown future.[8]

Actually, activism is possible at any point in the HC–LC continuum, but it seems to have less direction or focus and becomes less predictable and more threatening to institutions in LC systems. Most HC systems, however, can absorb activism without being shaken to their foundations.

In LC systems, demonstrations are viewed as the last, most desperate act in a series of escalating events. Riots and demonstrations in the United States, particularly those involving blacks,[9] are a message, a plea, a scream of anguish and anger for the larger society to *do something*. In China (an HC culture), the Red Guard riots apparently had an entirely different significance. They were promulgated from the top of the social order, not the bottom. They were also a communication from top to bottom: first, to produce a show of strength by Mao Tse-tung; second, to give pause to the opposition and shake things up at the middle levels—a way of mobilizing society, not destroying it. Chinese friends with whom I have spoken about these riots took them much less seriously than I did. I was, of course, looking at them from the point of view of one reared in a low-context culture, where such riots can have disastrous effects on the society at large.

Wherever one looks, the influence of the subtle hand of contexting can be detected. We have just spoken of the effects of riots on high- and low-context political systems, but what about day-to-day matters of perception? On the physiological level of color perception, one sees the power of the brain's need to perceive and adjust everything in terms of context. As any interior designer knows, a powerful painting, print, or wall hanging can change the perceived color of the furnishings around it. The color psychologist Faber Birren[10] demonstrated experimentally that the perceived shade of a color depends upon the color context in which it occurs. He did this by systematically varying the color of the background surrounding different color samples.

Some of the most impressive demonstrations of the brain's ability to supply missing information—the function of contexting—are the experiments of Edwin Land, inventor of the Land camera. Working in color photography using a single red filter, he developed a process that is simple, but the explanation for it is not. Until Land's experiments, it was believed that color prints could be made only by superimposing transparent images of three separate photographs made with the primary colors—red, blue, and yellow. Land made his color photographs with two images: a black-and-white image to give light and shadow, and a single, *red* filter for color. When these two images were projected, superimposed on a screen, even though red was the only color, they were perceived in full color with all the shades and gradations of a three-color photograph![11] Even more remarkable is the fact that the objects used were deliberately chosen to provide no cues as to their color. To be sure that his viewers didn't unconsciously project color, Land photographed spools of plastic and wool and geometric objects whose color would be unknown to the viewer. How the eye and the visual centers of the brain function to achieve this remarkable feat of internal contexting is still only partially understood. But the actual stimulus does only part of the job.

Contexting probably involves at least two entirely different but interrelated processes—one inside the organism and the other outside. The first takes place in the brain and is a function of either past experience (programmed, internalized contexting) or the structure of the nervous system (innate contexting), or both. External contexting comprises the situation and/or setting in which an event occurs (situational and/or environmental contexting).[12] . . .

In summary, regardless of where one looks, one discovers that a universal feature of information systems is that meaning (what the receiver is expected to do) is made up of: the communication, the background and preprogrammed responses of the recipient, and the situation. (We call these last two the internal and external context).

Therefore, what the receiver actually perceives is important in understanding the nature of context. Remember that what an organism perceives is influenced in four ways—by status, activity, setting, and experience. But in [hu]man[s] one must add another crucial dimension: *culture*.

Any transaction can be characterized as high-, low-, or middle-context. HC transactions feature preprogrammed information that is in the receiver and in the setting, with only minimal information in the transmitted message. LC transactions are the reverse. Most of the information must be in the transmitted message in order to make up for what is missing in the context (both internal and external).

In general, HC communication, in contrast to LC, is economical, fast, efficient, and satisfying; however, time must be devoted to programming. If this programming does not take place, the communication is incomplete.

HC communications are frequently used as art forms. They act as a unifying, cohesive force, are long-lived, and are slow to change. LC communications do not unify; however, they can be changed easily and rapidly. This is why evolution by extension is so incredibly fast; extensions in their initial stages of development are low-context. To qualify this statement somewhat, some extension systems are higher on the context scale than others. A system of defense rocketry can be out of date before it is in place and is therefore very low-context. Church architecture, however, was for hundreds of years firmly rooted in the past and was the material focus for preserving religious beliefs and ideas. Even today, most churches are still quite traditional in design. One wonders if it is possible to develop strategies for balancing two apparently contradictory needs: the need to adapt and change (by moving in the low-context direction) and the need for stability (high-context). History is replete with examples of nations and institutions that failed to adapt by holding on to high-context modes too long. The instability of low-context systems, however, on the present-day scale is quite new to mankind. And furthermore, there is no reservoir of experience to show us how to deal with change at this rate.

Extensions that now make up most of [our] world are for the most part low-context. The question is, How long can [we] stand the tension between [ourselves] and [our] extensions? This is what *Future Shock* [13] and *Understanding Media* [14] are all about. Take a single example, the automobile, which completely altered the American scene in all its dimensions—exploded communities, shredded the fabric of

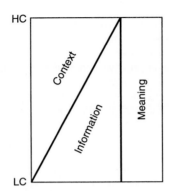

relationships, switched the rural-urban balance, changed our sex mores and church-going habits, altered our cities, crime, education, warfare, health, funerals. (One undertaker recently experimented with drive-in viewing of the corpse!)

In summary:

The screens that one imposes between oneself and reality constitute one of the ways in which reality is structured.

Awareness of that structure is necessary if one is to control behavior with any semblance of rationality. Such awareness is associated with the low-context end of the scale.

Yet there is a price that must be paid for awareness—instability, obsolescence, and change at a rate that may become impossible to handle and result in information overload.

Therefore, as things become more complex, as they inevitably must with fast-evolving, low-context systems, it eventually becomes necessary to turn life and institutions around and move toward the greater stability of the high-context part of the scale as a way of dealing with information overload.

NOTES

1 *The Hidden Dimension* discusses this quality of culture in more detail.
2 Meier (1963).
3 The linguist Noam Chomsky (1968) and his followers have tried to deal with the contexting feature of language by eliminating context and going to so-called "deep structure." The results are interesting but end up evading the main issues of communication and to an even greater extent stress ideas at the expense of what is actually going on.
4 For further information on Chinese, see Wang (1973).
5 Bernstein (1964).
6 Eiseley (1969).

7 I do not agree with Eiseley's generalizing about all of [hu]mankind, because activism, like everything else, has to be taken in context. As we will see, LC cultures appear to be more vulnerable to violent perturbations than HC cultures.

8 Saul Bellow's (1974) article on the role of literature in a setting of changing times is also relevant to this discussion. Bellow makes the point that for some time now there has been a conscious effort on the part of avant-garde Western intellectuals to obliterate the past. "Karl Marx felt in history the tradition of all dead generations weighing like a nightmare on the brain of the living. Nietzsche speaks movingly of 'it was,' and Joyce's Stephen Dedalus also defines history as a 'nightmare from which we are trying to awaken.'" Bellow points out, however, that there is a paradox that must be met, for to do away with history is to destroy one's own part in the historical process. It is reasonably certain, however, that what these men [and women] were trying to do was to redefine context in order to reduce its influence on men's [and women's] actions. Simply to do away with the past would lead to an incredibly unstable society, as we shall see.

9 Black culture is much higher on the context scale than white culture, and one would assume from our model that riots do not have the same meaning for blacks as they do to the white society in which the blacks are imbedded.

10 Birren (1961).

11 For further details on this fascinating set of experiments, see Land (1959).

12 These distinctions are completely arbitrary and are for the convenience of the writer and the reader. They do not necessarily occur in nature. The inside-outside dichotomy has been struck down many times, not only by the perceptual transactionalists ,(Kilpatrick, 1961) following in Dewey's footsteps but in my own writings as well. Within the brain, experience (culture) acts on the structure of the brain to produce mind. It makes little difference *how* the brain is modified; what is important is that modification does take place and is apparently continuous.

13 Toffler (1970).

14 McLuhan (1964).

REFERENCES

Bellow, Saul. "Machines and Story Books," *Harper's Magazine*, Vol. 249, pp. 48–54, August 1974.

Berstein, Basil. "Elaborated and Restricted Codes: Their Social Origins and Some Consequences." In J. Gumperz and Dell Hymes (eds.). The Ethnography of Communication, *American Anthropologist*, Vol. 66, No. 6, Part II, pp. 55–69, 1964.

Birren, Faber. *Color, Form and Space*. New York: Reinhold Publishing Corp., 1961.

Chomsky, Noam. *Language and Mind*. New York: Harcourt, Brace & World, Inc., 1968.

Eisley, L. "Activism and the rejection of History," *Science*, Vol. 165, p. 129, July 11, 1969.

Kilpatrick, F. P. *Explorations in Transactional Psychology* (contains articles by Adelbert Ames, Hadley Cantril, William Ittelson, and F. P. Kilpatrick). New York: New York university Press, 1961.

Land, Edwin H. "Experiments in Color Vision," *Scientific American*, Vol. 200, No. 5, May 1959.

Mc Luhan, Marshall. *Understanding Media*. New York: McGraw-Hill Book Co., Inc., 1964.

Meier, Richard. "Information Input Overload: Features of Growth in Communications-Oriented Institutions," *Libri* (Copenhagen), Vol. 13, No. 1, pp. 1-44, 1963.

Toffler, Alvin. *Future Shock*. New York: Bantam Books, Inc., 1970.

Wang, William. "The Chinese Language," *Scientific American*, Vol. 228, No. 2, February 1973.

Cultural Dimensions in Management and Planning

Geert Hofstede

. . . Management deals with a reality that is [hu]man-made. People build organizations according to their values, and societies are composed of institutions and organizations that reflect the dominant values within their culture. Organization theorists are slowly realising that their theories are much less universal than they once assumed: theories also reflect the culture of the society in which they were developed.

In this respect, the notion of a "Western" culture which justified universal "Western" modern management methods is also crumbling. It has become more and more clear that managing in different Western countries like Germany, France, Sweden or U.K. is not the same activity and that many usual generalizations are, in fact, not justified. By the same token, speaking of an "Asian" or "Middle-Eastern" type of management is not justified. There is a need among international managers and management theorists for a much deeper understanding of the range of culture-determined value systems that, in fact, exists among countries, and should be taken into account when transferring management ideas from one country to another. . . .

CULTURE AND MANAGEMENT

"Culture" has been defined in many ways. My own preferred definition is that culture is the collective programming of the mind which distinguishes the members of one group or society from those of another. Culture consists of the patterns of thinking that parents transfer to their children, teachers to their students, friends to their friends, leaders to their followers, and followers to their leaders. Culture is reflected in the meanings people attach to various aspects of life; their way of looking at the world and their role in it; in their values, that is, in what they consider as "good" and as "evil"; in their collective beliefs, what they consider as "true" and as "false"; in their artistic expressions, what they consider as "beautiful" and as "ugly". Culture, although basically resident in people's minds, becomes crystallized in the institutions and tangible products of a society, which reinforce the mental programmes in their turn. Management within a society is very much constrained by its cultural context, because

Source: Abridged from *Asia Pacific Journal of Management*, January 1984, pp. 81-98.

it is impossible to coordinate the actions of people without a deep understanding of their values, beliefs, and expressions.

Management is a symbolic activity: that is, managers influence other persons through wielding symbols that have meaning for these persons and motivate them towards the desired actions. An example of such a symbol is a memorandum written by the manager to announce a change in procedure. Its effect depends on a complex set of pre-programmed interpretations by the receivers: whether they can read, whether they understand the language used, whether they respect the legitimacy of this decision by this manager, whether they consider the style of the memo appropriate to their status, whether they are accustomed to react on written messages, whether they consider themselves as competent to take the requested steps, etc.

Taking into account the cultural side of management presupposes an understanding of the way people's minds can be programmed differently by their different life experiences. Patterns and models of behaviour between subordinates and superiors, among colleagues, and towards clients in the work situation have been set outside the work situation: between children and parents in the family (starting right at birth), among siblings and friends, between students and teachers, among citizens and authorities. The assumption of a collective programming of people's minds does not mean that everybody in a society is programmed in exactly the same way (there are wide differences among individuals and among subgroups of individuals) but the collective programming which I call culture should be seen as a collective component shared in the minds of otherwise different individuals and absent in the minds of individuals belonging to a different society. . . .

THE SCOPE OF CULTURAL DIFFERENCES AROUND THE WORLD

The cultural systems of nations and of their subdivisions are very complex and cannot be described in simple terms. It takes years to understand a single cultural system if one is not born to it. Even the cultural system in which we are born cannot [be] said to be understood by us in a way which we can explain to others because we participate in it unconsciously. The author of this study has been involved for more than fifteen years in a large research project across many nations aimed at detecting some elements of structure in their cultural systems, in particular those that most strongly affect behaviour in work situations.

The manifestations of culture I studied were answers on paper-and-pencil questions about values collected by psychologists within a large multinational business enterprise among the employees of its subsidiaries in 67 countries. I compared the distribution of answers from one country to another, at first for the 40 largest subsidiaries, afterwards for over 50 subsidiaries (see Hofstede, 1980 and 1983). As I always compared employees in similar occupations and, besides, the individuals were all employed by subsidiaries of the same multinational corporation, the national differences in this material could not be due to either occupation or employer but had to be due to nationality, to the mental programmes that people brought with them when starting to work for this employer.

The research project used the answers on 32 value statements. Subsequent statistical analysis showed that the differences among countries reflected the existence of four underlying value dimensions along which the countries could be positioned. The four dimensions represent elements of common structure in the cultural systems of the countries. They are based on four very fundamental issues in human societies to which every society has to find its particular answers. The position of a country on each of the four dimensions could be indicated by a score, the range of scores represented the range of different answers to the four issues actually found.

Individualism versus Collectivism

Individualism stands for a preference for a loosely knit social framework in society wherein individuals are supposed to take care of themselves and their immediate families only. Its opposite, Collectivism, stands for a preference for a tightly knit social framework in which individuals can expect their relatives, clan, or other in-group to look after them in exchange for unquestioning loyalty (it will be clear that the word "collectivism" is not used here to describe any particular political system). The fundamental issue addressed by this dimension is the degree of interdependence a society maintains among individuals. It relates to people's self-concept: "I" or "we".

Large versus Small Power Distance

Power Distance is the extent to which the members of a society accept that power in institutions and organizations is distributed unequally. This affects the behaviour of the less powerful as well as the more powerful members of society. People in Large Power Distance societies accept a hierarchical order in which everybody has a place which needs no further justification. People in Small Power Distance societies strive for power equalization and demand justification for power inequalities. The fundamental issue addressed by this dimension is how a society handles inequalities among people when they occur. This has obvious consequence for the way people build their institutions and organizations.

Strong versus Weak Uncertainty Avoidance

Uncertainty Avoidance is the degree to which the members of a society feel uncomfortable with uncertainty and ambiguity. This feeling leads them to beliefs promising certainty and to maintaining institutions protecting conformity. Strong Uncertainty Avoidance societies maintain rigid codes of belief and behaviour and are intolerant towards deviant persons and ideas. Weak Uncertainty Avoidance societies maintain a more relaxed atmosphere in which practice counts more than principles and deviance is more easily tolerated. The fundamental issue addressed by this dimension is how a society reacts on the fact that time only runs one way and that the future is unknown:

whether it tries to control the future or to let it happen. Like Power Distance, Uncertainty Avoidance has consequences for the way people build their institutions and organizations.

Masculinity versus Femininity

Masculinity stands for a preference in society for achievement, heroism, assertiveness, and material success. Its opposite, Femininity, stands for a preference for relationships, modesty, caring for the weak, and the quality of life. This fundamental issue addressed by this dimension is the way in which a society allocates social (as opposed to biological) roles to the sexes.

Some societies strive for maximum social differentiation between the sexes. The norm is then that men are given the more outgoing, assertive roles and women the caring, nurturing roles. As in all societies most institutions are populated by men. Such maximum-social-differentiation societies will permeate their institutions with an assertive mentality. Such societies become "performance societies" evident even from the values of their women. I have called these societies "masculine". (In the English language, "male" and "female" are used for the biological distinctions between the sexes: "masculine" and "feminine" for the social distinction. A man can be feminine, but he cannot be female.)

Other societies strive for minimal social differentiation between the sexes. This means that some women can take assertive roles if they want to but especially that some men can take relationship-oriented, modest, caring roles if they want to. Even in these societies, most institutions are populated by men (maybe slightly less than in masculine societies). The minimum-social-differentiation societies in comparison with their opposite, the maximum-social-differentiation societies, will permeate their institutions with a caring, quality-of-life orientated mentality. Such societies become "welfare societies" in which caring for all members, even the weakest, is an important goal for men as well as women.

I have called such societies "feminine". "Masculine" and "feminine" are relative qualifications: they express the relative frequency of values which in principle are present in both types of societies. The fact that even modern societies can be differentiated on the basis of the way they allocate their social sex role is not surprising in the light of anthropological research on non-literate, traditional societies in which the social sex role allocation is always one of the essential variables. Like the Individualism-Collectivism dimension, the Masculinity-Femininity dimension relates to people's self-concept: who am I and what is my task in life?

Although the four dimensions were originally derived from data on the values scored by multinational corporation employees, subsequent research has shown that the same or closely similar dimensions could be found in other research data, collected by different researchers with different methods from different sources: from groups of students, from random samples of entire national populations, from statistics compiled by international bodies like the World Health Organization. Thus, there is solid evidence that the four dimensions are, indeed, universal. Together they account only for a small part of the differences in cultural systems around the world, but this small part is important if it comes to understand the functioning of work organizations and the people within them. This is the domain of management.

Fifty countries and three multi-country regions could be given index scores on each of the four dimensions on the basis of their local employees' values data collected by the multinational corporation. These scores are collected in Exhibit 1. They are always relative scores in which the lowest country is situated around zero and the highest around 100.

IMPLICATIONS OF CULTURAL DIFFERENCES FOR MANAGEMENT: INDIVIDUALISM VERSUS COLLECTIVISM

In Exhibit 1, virtually all less economically developed countries score closer to the Collectivist end of the scale while the more economically developed countries score closer to the Individualist end of the scale. There will therefore be an Individualism-Collectivism gap in virtually any transfer of management skills from a more to a less economically developed country. This gap becomes evident in a number of respects.

a. The validity of economic theories based on self-interest,
b. The validity of psychological theories based on self-actualization,
c. The nature of the employer-employee relationship: whether this is considered as calculative or as morally based,
d. Priority in business to the task or to the relationship,
e. The role of family in the work situation, [and]
f. The importance of face and of harmony.

The Validity of Economic Theories Based on Self-Interest

The historical roots of modern capitalist economics were laid in late 18th century Great Britain by David Hume (1711-1776) and especially by Adam Smith (1723-1790). Both their followers and their critics have rarely disputed the assumption, made explicitly by Smith, that each individual is motivated by self-interest. In Exhibit 1, we see that Great Britain (GBR) scores very high on Individualism (rank 48 out of 50). Although Britain in the 18th century was certainly less individualist than it is at present, there is much historical evidence that relative to other countries it represented a very individualist culture even then.

In countries nearer to the Collectivism end of the Individualism-Collectivism scale, the assumption that each individual is motivated by self-interest is culturally untenable. In a collectivist culture, the individual is motivated by group interests. The group can be the extended family, the clan, the tribe, or some other type of in-group with which people have learned to identify. Economic behavior in such a society will be incomprehensible, and irrational to those who assume self-interest to be the

EXHIBIT 1 Value of the Four Indices for Fifty Countries . . . and Three Regions.

Country	Individualism	Power distance	Uncertainty avoidance	Masculinity
Argentina	46	49	86	56
Australia	90	36	51	61
Austria	55	11	70	79
Belgium	75	65	94	54
Brazil	38	69	76	49
Canada	80	39	48	52
Chile	23	63	86	28
Colombia	13	67	80	64
Costa Rica	15	35	86	21
Denmark	74	18	23	16
Equador	8	78	67	63
Finland	63	33	59	26
France	71	68	86	43
Germany (F R)	67	35	65	66
Great Britain	89	35	35	66
Greece	35	60	112	57
Guatemala	6	95	101	37
Hong Kong	25	68	29	57
Indonesia	14	78	48	46
India	48	77	40	56
Iran	41	58	59	43
Ireland	70	28	35	68
Israel	54	13	81	47
Italy	76	50	75	70
Jamaica	39	45	13	68
Japan	46	54	92	95
Korea (S)	18	60	85	39
Malaysia	26	104	36	50

ultimate motive. Individuals who have a job will not spend their earnings themselves but share them with needy relatives. On the other hand, there is no shame in being dependent on others and living off their incomes. In a religion like Buddhism, mortification of material needs is seen as a higher goal than satisfaction of material needs and monks who go around begging for food have high status. Culture also affects the attractiveness of economic systems: free-market capitalism in culturally collectivist countries often appeals less than systems of state capitalism and state socialism. These are political choices but underneath are cultural choices.

The Validity of Psychological Theories Based on Self-Actualization

Modern managerial psychology has largely been developed in another very individualist country, the United States of America (rank 50 out of 50 in Exhibit 1). Especially popular has become the theory of Abraham H. Maslow (1900–1970) that

EXHIBIT 1 (*Cont.*)

Country	Individualism	Power distance	Uncertainty avoidance	Masculinity
Mexico	30	81	82	69
Netherlands	80	38	53	14
Norway	69	31	50	8
New Zealand	79	22	49	58
Pakistan	14	55	70	50
Panama	11	95	86	44
Peru	16	64	87	42
Philippines	32	94	44	64
Portugal	27	63	104	31
South Africa	65	49	49	63
Salvador	19	66	94	40
Singapore	20	74	8	48
Spain	51	57	86	42
Sweden	71	31	29	5
Switzerland	68	34	58	70
Taiwan	17	58	69	45
Thailand	20	64	64	34
Turkey	37	66	85	45
Uruguay	36	61	100	38
U S A	91	40	46	62
Venezuela	12	81	76	73
Yugoslavia	27	76	88	21
Regions				
East Africa[1]	27	64	52	41
West Africa[2]	20	77	54	46
Arab Ctrs[3]	38	80	68	53

[1] Ethiopia, Kenya, Tanzania, Zambia
[2] Ghana, Nigeria, Sierra Leone
[3] Egypt, Iraq, Kuwait, Lebanon, Libya, Saudia Arabia, UAE

human needs follow a hierarchy, with physiological needs at the lowest level, followed by safety needs, belongingness needs, esteem needs (both self-esteem and esteem from others), and, at the highest level, "self-actualization" (Maslow, 1970). Self actualization means that the individual realizes his or her full potential in whatever field he or she chooses. The way the hierarchy works is that people are supposed to be motivated by the lower needs until these are reasonably satisfied, then the next higher need steps in. Self-actualization needs represent the top of the motivation pyramid and can never be fully satisfied.

Maslow, and his followers even more, have presented the need hierarchy as a human universal. Self-actualization as the supreme need, however, is the typical choice of an individualist culture. In a more collectivist culture, people will rather have a supreme need for actualizing their in-group which may in fact require giving all for self-effacement, filial piety, the maintenance of harmony with others, and similar behaviour very different from what is usually associated with self-actualization. Maslow would probably classify these with belongingness. Maslow's ranking of self-actualization and esteem over belongingness represents in itself a cultural choice based on Maslow's U.S. middle class culture which is strongly individualist.

In more collectivist cultures, "belongingness" may have to come above ego-needs like self-actualization and esteem. Moreover, the relative importance of safety needs is probably culturally dependent: it relates to a culture's level of Uncertainty Avoidance (to be discussed later on). In strongly uncertainty avoiding culture, safety needs may also have to be ranked on a higher level than ego-needs. In transferring management skills from one culture to another, fundamental psychological assumptions about human motivation have to be revised.

The Nature of the Employer-Employee Relationship

In individualist cultures, the relationship between the employee and employer is a business relationship based on the assumption of mutual advantage: it can be called a calculative relationship. Either party can terminate it if it can exchange it for a more advantageous deal elsewhere. Employees are "labour", in economic theory a "factor of production" and part of a "labour market". All these concepts are typical products of individualist cultural thinking.

In more collectivist cultures, the relationship between the employee and employer has a moral component. It is felt to be similar to the relationship of a child with its extended family where there are mutual traditional obligations: on the side of the employer, protection of the employee, almost regardless of the latter's performance; on the side of the employee, loyalty toward the employer. Changing employers is often socially disapproved of. We recognise many of these features in employment practices in Japan, which scores as the most collectivist among the wealthy countries. The movement of labour in these cultures only very imperfectly follows market mechanisms because of this moral component.

The distinction between calculative and moral relationships (Etzioni, 1975) can obviously also be applied within cultures. In individualist countries, certain employment relationships still have moral components; some employers do feel responsible for their employees, some employees do demonstrate considerable loyalty towards their employers. In collectivist cultures, there is also exploitation of labour by employers who do not respect traditional obligations because they consider workers as outgroup members as well as calculative disloyalty among some employees. Culture accounts for part of the difference in employer-employee relationships but there are other contributing factors.

Priority in Business to the Task or to the Relationship

In individualist cultures, it is felt to be "right" that in business all people should be treated alike: friendships and enmities should not affect business deals. Business considerations should have precedence over personal friendships and preferences. Business behaviour, to use a sociological term, should be universalist. Of course, this norm is often violated but such violations are considered objectionable.

In collectivist cultures, even in business, people think in terms of "we" (our family, tribe, organization) and "they" (the others). Relations, friends, tribesmen [or women] get better deals than strangers and this is the way it should be. It is normal and right. The sociological term for such behaviour is particularist. Considerations of personal trust and relationships should have precedence over business considerations. Whereas in individualist cultures, it is felt that the task should have priority over the relationships; in collectivist cultures, it is felt that the relationships should have priority over the task.

When a person—say, a manager—from an individualist culture wants to work in a collectivist culture, he or she will have to learn that before a task can be completed, he or she has to "invest" in personal relationships of trust. This will take time (from a few minutes to a few years, depending on the culture and on the type of relationship), which in the individualist culture would be considered as time wasted, but which in the collectivist culture represents an essential investment. Also, it means that in the collectivist cultures an integration is necessary between business life and private life. The latter playing a role in developing the relationship which is essential in business life. If the proper time is spent and the relationship is successfully established, the business partner is adopted in one's circle of friends and relatives. This is a lasting tie on the basis of which business can be done from then onwards much more quickly and effectively and mistakes will be more easily tolerated.

Investing in personal relationships in most collectivist cultures also involves the giving of presents and the rendering of services, practices which in an individualist culture would be considered as bribes. In a collectivist, particular society, bribing is generally more socially acceptable than in an individualist society. This is a cultural difference and no reason for people from more individualist societies to feel morally superior. Most collectivist societies have informal norms as to what bribes are to be given in what situations: these often represent an essential part of the economic system and of the compensation of civil servants who otherwise could not survive. "Corruption" starts where people abuse their position to extort bribes which surpass the informal norm.

The Role of the Family in the Work Situation

In an individualist society, nepotism is generally considered objectionable. Sometimes rules even forbid the employment of close relatives in the same department or organization. In a collectivist society, the domain of work and the domain of family interests cannot so easily be separated. Employers know that behind every employee there is an extended family and that it would be unacceptable for one member to be rich while others are needy. Salaries are shared with relatives if necessary. If a vacancy occurs at work, employees will volunteer unemployed relatives to fill it.

Employing many members of a family is generally considered desirable rather than undesirable. It fits the pattern of employee loyalty which is, at the same time, family loyalty. The tendency to employ relatives exists also on the employer side. Many enterprises in collectivist cultures are family-owned and family-run with members of the owning family often occupying all key positions. This need not be dysfunctional: the relatives' loyalty can compensate for a possible lack of technical competence. Even in individualist countries, effective family-owned and family-run enterprises survive.

The Importance of Face and Harmony

In individualist countries, openness and directness in work relations is often considered a virtue. Conflict resolution is preferred over conflict suppression. There are forms of management training which try to teach people to be open and direct (sensitivity training is an example). In collectivist cultures with their tightly knit and predetermined social framework, there is generally an extensive set of expectations of how people should behave towards each other. Violating these expectations would threaten the so-important social framework. Therefore, the maintenance of the proper forms and of harmony is usually considered preferable over openness where openness could lead to disharmony.

In order to preserve harmony, the truth may have to be strained a bit. Disagreement may be more effectively expressed in indirect ways than in direct confrontation. "Face" is the English translation of a Chinese term which indicates both the front part of the head and the dignity based on a correct relationship between a person and the collectivities to which one belongs. Most collectivist cultures are very face-conscious and loss of face can be felt to be more painful than physical maltreatment. Maintaining harmony consists in avoiding anybody's loss of face. Loss of face can often be avoided by having contentious issues handled by a third party, a go-between. In most collectivist cultures, therefore, it is not a virtue to be open and direct. People from individualist cultures who want to operate in collectivist environments should learn the art of indirect communication.

DIFFERENCES ALONG THE DIMENSION OF POWER DISTANCE

To a somewhat lesser extent than in the case of the Individualism-Collectivism dimension, the Power Distance dimension tends to separate the more economically developed countries from the less developed ones: smaller Power Distances for the more developed countries, larger for the less developed countries. Usually but not always, in the transfer of management skills from a more to a less economically developed country, there will also be Power Distance gap. This gap becomes evident in:

a. The need for subordinate consultation versus the acceptability of paternalistic management,
b. The meaning of status differences,
c. Respect for old age,

d. Ways of redress in case of grievances, . . . [and]
e. The feasibility of appraisal systems in general.

The Need for Subordinate Consultation versus the Acceptability of Paternalistic Management

In all cultures, models of behaviour are carried over from one domain of life to the other. Thus, if we compare cultures, we find within each a certain consistency between superior-subordinate relationships at work, teacher-student relationships at school, and parent-child relationships in the family. In cultures lower on the Power Distance scale, the average parent is likely to encourage independence in his or her children from an early age onwards. Teachers encourage independence in students who are free to contradict them and superiors are expected to encourage independence in subordinates. There is often a norm that a good superior is one who consults his or her subordinates. This "consultation-ism" may be carried so far that there are extensive consultation rituals (meetings) even in cases where the *de facto* contribution of subordinates to decision is likely to be very small.

In cultures higher on the Power Distance scale, parent-child relationships are different. There is a norm of filial piety: loyalty, respect, and devotion to parents is considered a supreme virtue. This leads to an expectation of obedience by children, at least formally, and obedience which is supposed to last for life, even after the children have grown up. This formal dependence of children, even adult children, on parents carries forward into the relationship between teachers and students. Students are expected to show respect to teachers, and to treat them as sources of wisdom, never openly disputing their teachings. One-way, ex-cathedra teaching is customary in such a cultural setting.

If we then move to the work organizations, it is normal that superior-subordinate relationships are modelled after the same pattern of subordinate dependence. This pattern is expected and considered comfortable by superior and subordinate alike. A good superior is expected to behave like a good father (or mother) towards subordinates: *paternalism* is the norm.

Paternalism in Small Power Distance cultures has an unfavorable connotation. Power differences between superiors and subordinates are associated with power abuse. There is not, however, necessarily more power abuse in large Power Distance cultures than in Small Power Distance ones. A paternalistic superior who respects the norms of his or her society for the behaviour of a good father or mother does not abuse power; a consultative superior who manipulates consultation rituals does.

The dependence relationship of subordinates on superiors is also likely to carry over to the relationship of citizens to authorities. Political democracy is less likely to be found in large Power Distance societies. This does not mean that democratic ideals do not appeal to people in large Power Distance societies. The word "democracy" has acquired a strong symbolic value for people the world over but its use has been inflated: It is used as a label to cover the most diverse systems of government. In large Power Distance societies, rulers *de facto* are less likely to consult with citizens.

The Meaning of Status Differences

In cultures low on the Power Distance scale, status differences are considered undesirable. Powerful people are not supposed to look powerful: wealthy people are not supposed to demonstrate their wealth in conspicuous consumption. Also, power and wealth need not coincide. Powerful people need not be wealthy and wealthy people need not be powerful.

In cultures high on the Power Distance Scale, both superiors and subordinates expect power differences to be translated into visible differences in status. Status differences contribute to the superior's authority and to the subordinate's respect for it; actually, they even contribute to the subordinate's status in the outside world. Power and wealth do tend to coincide and, the status derived from one, reinforces the status derived from the other.

An additional difference is that in Small Power Distance societies, what status there is tends to be achieved status, based on the personal merit of the achiever, on what one has done. In large Power Distance societies, status is often ascribed status based on rank, ancestry, wealth: on who one is supposed to be, regardless of how one got there. This carries over into the attitudes of students with regard to examinations. In Small Power Distance societies, an exam tends to be seen as a proof of mastering a subject (achievement). In large Power Distance societies, it is seen more as an entry certificate to a higher status group (ascription). In some cases this can lead to practices of actually buying diplomas.

Respect for Old Age

In large Power Distance societies, the importance of paternal and maternal authority, which subsists throughout life, implies a respect for the older person, both within work organizations and in social life outside. People may try to look older than they are. In small Power Distance societies, age tends to be negatively evaluated, old people often are not taken seriously and it is normal to try to look younger than one is. People from large Power Distance societies are often shocked at the lack of respect for old people in small Power Distance societies.

Ways of Redress in Case of Grievances

In cultures low on the Power Distance scale, it is generally felt desirable to maintain a system of checks and balances against power abuse. In work organizations there are usually established channels for handling grievances by subordinates, in such a way that the complaining subordinate will not suffer, not even if the complaint is considered unjustified.

In cultures high on the Power Distance scale, such grievance channels are generally missing and very difficult to establish. The power of the superior is more absolute and the act of complaining to a third party may expose the subordinate to reprisals from the superior, so it is generally not done. There are, however, often indirect ways of making grievances known. When there is no way of redress for the individual, there may still be collective redress. If many subordinates hold the same grievance and the superior is supposed to have infringed upon the collectivist norm of good superior behaviour, they can at least in some cultures collectively resist the superior. This is a very serious matter and leads to considerable loss of face on the latter's part. . . .

The Feasibility of Appraisal Systems in General

A cornerstone of leadership in small Power Distance cultures is the process of appraising subordinate performance. Skills in subordinate appraisal are one of the first things a newly nominated first-line superior has to learn. Appraisal systems developed in low Power Distance countries generally call for a superior-subordinate interview at least once a year with the corresponding openness, directness, and two-way communication.

Under the discussion of Individualism versus Collectivism, limitations have been shown for openness and directness in collectivist societies with a strong concern for face-saving and harmony. Most of these societies are large Power Distance as well which means that two-way communication between superior and subordinate is unlikely to occur. In this situation, the entire approriateness of this type of appraisal system becomes doubtful.

This is an area *par excellence* for the development of local approaches fitting local cultural traditions. The way subordinates are appraised and corrected should be consistent with the way benevolent parents correct their children. In order to avoid loss of face on the side of the subordinate, negative appraisals may have to be given indirectly, for example through the withdrawal of a favour or through a third person as a go-between.

DIFFERENCES ALONG THE DIMENSION OF UNCERTAINTY AVOIDANCE

On this dimension, both less and more economically developed countries are widely dispersed so that cultural differences between countries involved in the transfer of management skills can be large or small, positive or negative with regard to Uncertainty Avoidance. They may have consequences for:

a. The emotional need for formal and informal rules to guide behaviour,
b. Formalization, standardization, and ritualization of organizations,
c. Implicit models of organizations,
d. Types of planning used,

e. The meaning of time,
f. Appeal of precision and punctuality,
g. The showing or hiding of emotions, and
h. Tolerance for deviant ideas and behaviour.

The Emotional Need for Formal and Informal Rules to Guide Behaviour

The extent to which people feel that behaviour should follow fixed rules differs from one culture to another. In cultures high on the Uncertainty Avoidance scale, behaviour tends to be rigidly prescribed either by written rules or by unwritten social codes. The presence of these rules satisfies people's emotional need for order and predictability in society. Even if people break the rules by their own behaviour, they will feel that it is right that the rules exist. "Law and order" are important symbols in such a society: they satisfy deep emotional needs in people. People feel uncomfortable in situations where there are no rules. If the outcome of the negotiation is not predictable, they are not very good negotiators.

In cultures low on the Uncertainty Avoidance scale, there will also be written and unwritten rules but they are considered more a matter of convenience and less sacrosanct. People are able to live comfortably in situations where there are no rules and where they are free to indulge in their own behaviour. If existing rules are not kept in these societies, people are more prepared to change the rules. People here are more pragmatic, even opportunistic, and comfortable in negotiations where the outcome is not a *priori* clear. . . .

Formalization, Standardization, and Ritualization of Organizations

In organizations, the emotional need for rules (even if they are not actually kept) means a preference for formalization of structure, standardization of procedures, and "ritualization" of behaviour (see below). Other factors being equal, we can expect more formalization, standardization and ritualization in strong Uncertainty Avoidance countries than in weak Uncertainty Avoidance countries. In the process of transferring management skills, differences in the cultural need for formalization, standardization and ritualization may lead to deep misunderstandings and to the ineffectiveness of practices developed in one culture whenever transferred to another. If the sending culture is relatively informal and the receiving one relatively formal, there will be a need for formalization of structures in the receiving country which would be considered superfluous and irritating in the sending country. If the sending country is relatively formal and the receiving country relatively informal, structures and procedures may have to be loosened up before they can be expected to work in the receiving country.

Ritualization of behaviour refers to the extent to which it is important to speak the proper words, dress in the proper way, perform the proper acts in given situations. In organizations, it is visible in when and how meetings are conducted, memos are written, plans and budgets are specified, forms and reports are issued, experts are nominated. Meetings, memos, reports, experts often serve ritual ends as much as (or even more than) decision-making ends. The rituals are important because they maintain people's emotional equilibrium (their feeling that things are as they should be), if they are in line with the surrounding culture. Japanese organizational rituals do not fit in a British organization or vice-versa.

Implicit Models of Organizations

We saw that Uncertainty Avoidance relates to formalization: the degree of structure in the social environment with which people feel comfortable. Power Distance relates to the degree of inequality with which people feel comfortable and in organizations this translates into more or less centralization of decisions. Other things being equal, organizations in large Power Distance countries will be more centralized than organizations in small Power Distance societies . . . Professor O. J. Stevens . . . has studied the "implicit models of organizations" in the minds of French, German and British business school students. He discovered that the French . . . conceive of an organization as a "pyramid of people", with the highest boss at the top and everyone else in his or her proper place below, interacting according to the rules. In . . . Germany . . . we can expect organizations to be formalized but less centralized. Professor Stevens discovered that the Germans conceive of an organization as a "well-oiled machine", whose operation is predetermined by the rules, without the need of hierarchical interventions in daily operations. In . . . Great Britain . . . we can expect organizations to be neither very centralized nor very formalized. Stevens found the British to conceive of an organization as a "village market" in which actors negotiate and where outcomes are neither predetermined by hierarchy nor by procedures . . . [D]iscussions with Asian scholars lead us to believe that the Asian's implicit model of an organization is a "family", in which authority is clearly centralized in the "parents", but outcomes are not predetermined by procedures.

The four types of implicit models of organizations (pyramid, machine, market, family) mean that there is not one best way of organizing. It depends on the surrounding culture. Organizations are symbolic structures which will be effective if the symbols used are properly interpreted by the people inside and around the organization. If individuals are transferred to a different cultural environment, the symbols may have to be changed in order to maintain effectiveness.

Types of Planning Used

All kinds of planning presupposes a certain level of economic development. Traditional societies at a low level of economic development tend to be fatalistic. Life experience in these societies provides many good reasons for this. People in this situation have had little chance to affect their future and to better themselves. Their religious convictions tend to be that man is not supposed to affect his or her future in a major way for the future is in the hands of God or gods.

There are differences however in the types of religious convictions found in more and in less Uncertainty Avoiding traditional societies. In the more Uncertainty Avoiding ones, God or the gods are seen as difficult to please and threatening. In the less Uncertainty Avoiding traditional societies, God or the gods are seen as more easy to communicate with. There is also a stronger belief in the factor of luck which is visible in the greater popularity of games of chance in such cultures. Neither situation is conducive to the use of planning methods as preached and sometimes practised in more economically developed countries. For example, systems of preventive maintenance meet with resistance in most traditional societies. Something tends to be repaired only after it has broken down.

Among the more economically developed countries, we still find cultural differences in planning practices. In the more Uncertainty Avoiding cultures, short- and medium-term scheduling and planning get more top management attention than in less Uncertainty Avoiding cultures. On the other hand, it has been shown that the idea of strategic planning—rethinking the fundamental goals and activities of an organization—is more popular in *less* Uncertainty Avoiding cultures like Great Britain than in *more* Uncertainty Avoiding cultures like France . . . because strategic planning presupposes a tolerance for great ambiguity and for taking distance from the certainties of the past. This popularity of strategic planning in less uncertainty avoiding countries does not mean, however, that organizations in such countries deal with environmental changes more effectively. At least, there is no hard evidence for it.

The Meaning of Time

In traditional societies with a low rate of change, time is generally not a scarce resource. Life in such societies is relatively unhurried and time is conceived as circular (returning in itself) rather than linear. However, more Uncertainty Avoiding traditional societies like Mexico are more hurried than less Uncertainty Avoiding societies where meditation is more popular (like India).

With economic development, the conception arises of time as a scarce resource. Again there is a difference between more and less Uncertainty Avoiding developed countries. In the former, life tends to be more hurried than in the latter and it is more difficult for people to relax and do nothing. A feeling prevails that time is money and that it should be mastered and exploited. Japan and France are examples. In the less Uncertainty-Avoiding, developed countries, time is a framework for orientation rather than something to be mastered. Life is less hurried. Examples are Great Britain and Sweden.

Appeal of Precision and Punctuality

In more traditional societies, the expected degree of punctuality depends on the social relationship: one is more punctual towards a superior than towards a subordinate. In general, time is not seen as a scarce resource and there are fewer clocks. There is less of a stress on punctuality. In the more Uncertainty Avoiding traditional societies, precision and punctuality have a ritual meaning in the performance of certain religious ceremonies.

Of course, modern technology demands precision and punctuality. Economical and technical development has everywhere been accompanied by a process of learning of technical precision. Nevertheless, among the more Uncertainty Avoiding developed countries, precision and punctuality come more naturally than among the less Uncertainty Avoiding ones. The success of a country like Japan in the precision industries is supported by the strong Uncertainty Avoidance in its culture.

The Showing or Hiding of Emotions

Regardless of a country's level of economic development, in more Uncertainty Avoiding cultures the expression of emotions is more easily tolerated than in less Uncertainty Avoiding ones. This is because the urge to avoid uncertainty in human life that is itself essentially uncertain provokes a nervous tension for which society should provide outlets. More Uncertainty Avoiding cultures like those of Mediterranean Europe and Latin America come across as noiser and more emotional than less Uncertainty Avoiding cultures like those of Asia or Northern Europe. The outlets of emotions in more Uncertainty Avoiding societies may be limited to certain situations, like the Japanese drinking parties after business hours, or during games and ceremonies.

Becoming emotional, pounding the table, raising one's voice can be perfectly acceptable for a manager in a more Uncertainty Avoiding culture but it is likely to lead to a complete loss of respect from others in a less Uncertainty Avoiding culture. This is one of the pitfalls in the interaction of people from different cultures.

Tolerance for Deviant Ideas and Behaviours

More Uncertainty Avoiding societies do not like deviants. What or who is different is considered dangerous. Such societies have a low level of social tolerance. In organizations this can be a problem because the deviant is often the source of innovations. The confirmed "organization man [or woman]" is not an innovator. Differences of opinion on business, scientific, or political issues in Uncertainty Avoiding countries are associated with personal antipathies. If you disagree with a person, you cannot be friends.

On the other hand, in less Uncertainty Avoiding societies people feel less upset by deviant behaviour or ideas and are more tolerant although this tolerance may take the form of simply ignoring the deviant. Such societies are likely to produce more innovative ideas but not necessarily to take more action upon them.

In the transfer of management skills, those that represent innovations will be more easily welcomed in the less Uncertainty Avoiding cultures, but possibly taken more seriously in the more Uncertainty Avoiding countries.

DIFFERENCES ALONG THE DIMENSION
OF MASCULINITY VERSUS FEMININITY

On Masculinity-Femininity, like on Uncertainty Avoidance, both less and more economically developed countries are widely spread and cultural differences in the transfer of management skills can go either way. This dimension relates to:

a. Competitiveness versus solidarity, equity versus equality, sympathy for the strong or for the weak,
b. Achievement motivation versus relationship motivation,
c. Concepts of the quality of work life,
d. Career expectations,
e. Acceptability of macho manager behaviour, and
f. Sex roles in the work place.

Competitiveness versus Solidarity, Equity versus Equality, Sympathy for the Strong or for the Weak

In describing the Masculinity versus Femininity dimension, Masculinity is associated with a performance society and Femininity with a welfare society. There are profound value differences here which divide more developed countries amongst themselves and less developed countries amongst themselves. U.S.A. and Germany are examples of performance societies with a masculine ethos: Sweden and the Netherland of welfare societies with a feminine ethos. In a masculine society, competitiveness between people is seen as a good thing: the strong should win. In a feminine society, solidarity between people is seen as a good thing: the strong should help the weak and social justice is an important value. A masculine society believes in equity: rewards according to performance. A feminine society believes in equality: reward according to need. The public hero in a masculine society is the superman [or woman], the successful achiever. In a feminine society, the public sympathy goes to the underdog, the sufferer. Obviously, the contrast between the two sets of values is seldom as black and white as just described: both value sets are present in any society but the percentage of people preferring one over the other differs from one society to another.

Management methods are not value-free. Management as developed within one culture will have absorbed values from that culture which need not be supported by people from other cultures to which management is transferred. Moreover, there is no evidence whatsoever that one value system is economically more effective than the other. In the long run, countries with more masculine value systems have not been more successful than countries with more feminine value systems. What counts is only that a country is managed according to the value systems of its people. The trouble is that management experts going abroad often hold positions which they do not recognize as such which are immaterial to the success of management, and dysfunctional in the other society to which they move. It is important to gain insight into the dominant value systems of the receiving country and of the sending country, of the match or mismatch between these, and of the corrections that have to be made in transferring value-laden management methods.

Achievement Motivation versus Relationship Motivation

Cultural differences in motivation patterns were already discussed in the beginning of this chapter under Individualism-Collectivism. It was shown that "self-actualization" as a presumed need (Maslow) is a product of an individualist society. Another need stressed by another U.S. psychologist, David McClelland (1961), is the need for achievement. McClelland has postulated this need to be a condition for economic development. He has identified its strength for a large number of countries by a content analysis of the stories that were given as reading material to young children in the schools of these countries.

A comparison of McClelland's achievement motivation scores with the four culture dimensions shows that McClelland's achievement motivation stands for a combination of weak Uncertainty Avoidance and strong Masculinity. This combination is found among other Anglo countries and their former colonies.

Like in the case of Maslow described earlier, McClelland's universal theory of human motivation is in fact a value choice in which the value system dominant in the U.S. middle class (McClelland's own) is held up as a model to the rest of the world. In fact, McClelland's prediction (made in 1960) that countries with strong achievement motivation would show the greatest economic growth has not come true. There have been fast and slow growing countries with all combinations of Uncertainty Avoidance and Masculinity. Japan did not score high in achievement motivation in McClelland's data.

We can interpret the combination of dimensions in such a way that weak Uncertainty Avoidance stands for a willingness to take risks and to innovate. Its opposite stands for a concern with security and stability. Masculinity stands for a stress on performance and its opposite. Femininity, for a stress on relationships. Dominant motivation patterns differ among countries. No combination is intrinsically better or more conducive to economic development than the other although, in a given historical context, a particular combination will affect the ways in which a country can solve its problems.

Concepts of the Quality of Work Life

We saw that the culture of feminine societies is more quality-of-life oriented. The quality of life is considered more important in the more-developed, feminine societies. It can also be asserted that masculine and feminine societies hold different ideas about what represents work of high quality. This is evident from contrasting the ways for "humanization of work" used in North America and in Northern Europe.

In North America, the dominant objective is to make individual jobs more interesting by providing workers with an increased challenge. This grew out of the earlier "job enlargement" and "job enrichment". In countries like Sweden and

Norway, the dominant objective is to make group work more rewarding by allowing groups to function as self-contained social units (semi-autonomous groups) and to foster cooperation among group members. Humanization of work means "masculinization" in North America but "femininization" in Sweden.

In the less developed countries, concern for the quality of work life is often considered a luxury. If it comes to developing management models for a poor country, however, it is important to choose a model that potentially leads to a high quality work life in terms of the country's prevalent value system.

Career Expectations

The symbolic meaning of a career is greater in masculine than in feminine countries. Careers fit in a competitive, performance oriented system. In the less competitive feminine societies some people will also make careers, but the general level of ambitions will be lower, and "having made a career" is less important for people's self-concept.

In transferring management ideas, it should be realized that the meaning and the appeal of careers differs from one culture to another. Obviously, the types of careers sought are also culture specific. The attractiveness of different jobs varies somewhat from one culture to another.

Acceptability of Macho Manager Behaviour

In some cultures, the ideal picture of a manager is a masculine, aggressive hero with superhuman qualities, taking fast important decisions, admired by his followers and his women, crushing his adversaries. Trying to live up to such an ideal will lead to demonstrations of manliness in managers which fit the Spanish term *machismo*. In a masculine culture, such behaviour may be acceptable to many and functional, even if the manager in reality is not as much of a superman as the ideal he tries to live up to. The same behaviour in a feminine culture would disqualify the manager as a ridiculous braggart who cannot be taken serious. In reverse, a managerial style developed in a feminine culture may be too modest to be efficacious in a masculine environment.

Sex Roles in the Work Place

In some countries, like Japan, sex roles in the work place are extremely rigid. What jobs can be taken by men and what jobs by women is strictly predetermined. There are very few female managers or politicians or professors in Japan. On the Masculinity scale, Japan [ranks] 50 out of 50 [Exhibit 1].

In other masculine countries women are admitted to traditionally male work roles. Such women tend to adopt masculine values and behaviour. Only in more feminine countries are men admitted to traditionally female work roles such as nursing and nursing management. Which roles are considered appropriate for men and which for women is culturally determined. In the transfer of management, ideas about sex roles from one country may have to be profoundly revised in order to be functional for another country.

CONCLUSION

This paper has discussed a number of management and planning aspects that are culturally constrained. Effectiveness within a given culture, and judged according to the values of that culture, asks for management skills adapted to the local culture. There is a need for the application of anthropological concepts to the field of management in order to help in the development of locally effective ways of management and planning.

REFERENCES

Hofstede, G. (1980). *Culture's consequences: International differences in work related values.* Beverly Hills, CA: Sage.

Hofstede, G. (1983). Dimensions of national cultures in fifty cultures and three regions. In J. B. Deregowski, S. Dziurawiec, and R. C. Annis (Eds.), *Expications in cross-cultural psychology.* Lisse, The Netherlands: Swets and Zeitlinger.

Maslow, A. H. (1970). *Motivation and personality.* New York: Harper & Row.

McClelland, D. C. (1961). *The achieving society.* Princeton, NJ: Van Nostrand Reinhold.

CHAPTER 4

Sociocultural Influences on Communication

Miller and Steinberg (1975) argue that we should limit the use of the term *interpersonal communication* to those encounters in which most of the predictions we make about others are based on psychological data. They contend that when most of our predictions about another person are based on cultural or sociological data (using social categorizations) we are engaging in *noninterpersonal communication*. Another way of thinking about this is to say that we are engaging in *intergroup communication* (*intercultural communication* is a form of intergroup communication). The distinction between these two "types" of communication is important and deserves further discussion. To explain the differences it is necessary to talk about the self-concept or how we define ourselves.

Our self-concept consists of two components: our personal identity and our social identity (Tajfel, 1978). Our personal identity includes those aspects of our self-definition that make us unique individuals. You may, for example, see yourself as a caring person who wants to improve relations between people from different groups. Our personal identities are derived from our unique individual experiences, our values, our attitudes, and our feelings. Our social identities, in contrast, are derived from our shared memberships in social groups.

Our communication behavior can be based on our personal and our social identities. In a particular situation, we may choose (either consciously or unconsciously) to define ourselves through our communication as unique persons or as members of groups. When our communication behavior is based mostly on our personal identities, interpersonal communication can be said to take place. When we define ourselves mostly in terms of our social identities (including our cultural and ethnic identities), intergroup communication can be said to occur.

Tajfel and Turner (1979) believe that behavior can vary from being "purely intergroup" to "purely interpersonal." They contend that pure intergroup communication can take place. An air force bomber crew that does not draw any distinctions among the people on whom they are dropping bombs (i.e., they see them all as the "enemy") is one example of pure intergroup communication. If the members of the bomber crew start drawing distinctions among the people on whom they are dropping bombs (e.g., recognizing that some of them are children), they would no longer be engaged in pure intergroup communication.

Pure interpersonal communication, in contrast, cannot occur, according to Tajfel and Turner. They argue, and we concur, that group memberships influence even the most intimate forms of communication. Consider the communication between two lovers. Although it might seem that group memberships and social identities would not influence this form of communication, they do. Whether we define ourselves as heterosexual, homosexual, or bisexual (part of our social identities), for example, influences the gender of the partners we select and the way we communicate with them.

Thinking of interpersonal and intergroup communication as varying along a continuum or being a dichotomy oversimplifies the nature of the communication process. In actuality, our personal *and* social identities influence all our communication behavior, even though one may predominate in a particular situation. When our social identities have a greater influence than our personal identities on our behavior, however, there is an increased chance of misunderstandings because we are likely to interpret others' behavior based on our group memberships and not take into consideration their individual attitudes, values, and feelings.

In order to overcome the potential for misunderstandings that can occur when our social identities predominate, we must recognize that we share a common identity with strangers (i.e., we are all humans). At the same time, we must acknowledge our differences and try to understand them and how they influence our communication. This involves the process of negotiating our identities through our communication with strangers.

The first reading in this chapter focuses on differences in communication when our communication is based on our social and personal identities. In this reading, Tajfel and Turner outline their social identity theory of intergroup behavior. This theory can be used to understand communication between people of different cultures and different ethnic groups, as well as communication between males and females, able-bodied and disabled, and so forth.

In the second reading, Ting-Toomey discusses the role of identity in forming relationships with strangers. She discusses how the way we negotiate identities varies across cultures. Ting-Toomey also looks at how our identities influence the way we express our feelings and how we use them to protect ourselves when we communicate.

REFERENCES

Miller, G., & Steinberg, M. (1975). *Between people*. Chicago: Science Research Associates.

Tajfel, H. (1978). Social categorization, social identity, and social comparisons. In H. Tajfel (Ed.), *Differentiation between social groups*. London: Academic Press.

Tajfel, H., & Turner, J. (1979). An integrative theory of intergroup conflict. In W. Austin & S. Worchel (Eds.), *The social psychology of intergroup relations*. Monterey, CA: Brooks/ Cole.

The Social Identity Theory of Intergroup Behavior
Henri Tajfel and John C. Turner

. . .

THE SOCIAL CONTEXT OF INTERGROUP BEHAVIOR

Our point of departure for the discussion to follow will be an a priori distinction between two extremes of social behavior, corresponding to what we shall call interpersonal versus intergroup behavior. At one extreme (which most probably is found in its pure form only rarely in real life) is the interaction between two or more individuals that is fully determined by their interpersonal relationships and individual characteristics, and not at all affected by various social groups or categories to which they respectively belong. The other extreme consists of interactions between two or more individuals (or groups of individuals) that are fully determined by their respective memberships in various social groups or categories, and not at all affected by the interindividual personal relationships between the people involved. Here again, it is probable that pure forms of this extreme are found only infrequently in real social situations. Examples that might normally tend to be near the interpersonal extreme would be the relations between wife and husband or between old friends. Examples that would normally approach the intergroup extreme are the behavior of soldiers from opposing armies during a battle, or the behavior at a negotiating table of members representing two parties in an intense intergroup conflict. . . .

[T]he main empirical questions concern the conditions that determine the adoption of forms of social behavior nearing one or the other extreme. The first—and obvious—answer concerns intergroup conflict. It can be assumed, in accordance with our common experience, that the more intense is an intergroup conflict, the more likely it is that the individuals who are members of the opposite groups will behave toward each other as a function of their respective group memberships, rather than in terms of their individual characteristics or interindividual relationships. This was precisely why Sherif (1967, for example) was able to abolish so easily the interindividual friendships formed in the preliminary stages of some of his field studies when, subsequently, the individuals who had become friends were assigned to opposing groups.

An institutionalized or explicit conflict of objective interests between groups, however, does not provide a fully adequate basis, either theoretically or empirically, to account for many situations in which the social behavior of individuals belonging to distinct groups can be observed to approach the "group" extreme of our continuum. The conflict in Sherif's studies was "institutionalized" in that it was officially arranged

Source: Abridged from chapter with same title in S. Worchel & W. G. Austin (Eds.), Psychology of intergroup relations (pp. 7–17). Chicago: Nelson-Hall, 1986.

by the holiday camp authorities; it was "explicit" in that it dominated the life of the groups; and it was "objective" in the sense that, given the terms of the competition, one of the groups had to be the winner and the other group the loser. And yet, there is evidence from Sherif's own studies and from other research that the institutionalization, explicitness, and objectivity of an intergroup conflict are not necessary conditions for behavior in terms of the "group" extreme, although they will often prove to be sufficient conditions. One clear example is provided by our earlier experiments (Tajfel, 1970; Tajfel et al., 1971), which we shall discuss briefly below, in which it was found that intergroup discrimination existed in conditions of minimal in-group affiliation, anonymity of group membership, absence of conflicts of interest, and absence of previous hostility between the groups.

Other social and behavioral continua are associated with the interpersonalintergroup continuum. One of them may serve to summarize a quasi-ideological dimension of attitudes, values, and beliefs that may be plausibly hypothesized to play a causal role in relation to it. This dimension will also be characterized by its two extremes, which we shall refer to as "social mobility" and "social change." These terms are not used here in their sociological sense. They refer instead to individuals' belief systems about the nature and the structure of the relations between social groups in their society. They belief system of "social mobility" is based on the general assumption that the society in which the individuals live is a flexible and permeable one, so that if they are not satisfied, for whatever reason, with the conditions imposed upon their lives by membership in social groups or social categories to which they belong, it is possible for them (be it through talent, hard work, good luck, or whatever other means) to move individually into another group that suits them better. A good example of this system of beliefs, built into the explicit cultural and ideological traditions of a society, is provided in the following passage from Hirschman (1970):

> The traditional American idea of success confirms the hold which exit has had on the national imagination. Success—or, what amounts to the same thing, upward social mobility—has long been conceived in terms of evolutionary individualism. The successful individual who starts out at a low rung of the social ladder, necessarily leaves his [or her] own group as he [or she] rises; he [or she] "passes" into, or is "accepted" by, the next higher group. He [or she] takes his [or her] immediate family along, but hardly anyone else. (pp. 108-9)

At the other extreme, the belief system of "social change" implies that the nature and structure of the relations between social groups in the society is characterized by marked stratification, making it impossible or very difficult for individuals, as individuals, to divest themselves of an unsatisfactory, underprivileged, or stigmatized group membership. The economic or social realities of a society may be such (as, for example, in the case of the millions of unemployed during the Depression of the 1930s) that the impossibility of "getting out" on one's own, as an individual, becomes an everyday reality that determines many forms of intergroup social behavior. But even this example is still relatively extreme. Many social intergroup situations that contain, for whatever reasons, strong elements of stratification perceived as such may tend to move social behavior away from the pole of interpersonal pattern toward the pole of intergroup patterns. This is as true of groups that are "superior" in a social system as of those that are "inferior" in it. The major characteristic of social behavior related to this belief is that, in the relevant intergroup situations, individuals will not interact *as* individuals, on the basis of their individual characteristics or interpersonal relationships, but as members of their groups standing in certain defined relationships to members of other groups. . . .

The continuum of systems of beliefs discussed so far represents one conjecture as to one important set of subjective conditions that may shift social behavior toward members of out-groups between the poles of "interpersonal" and "intergroup" behavior within particular situations and societies. To conclude this part of our preliminary discussion, we must characterize briefly two further and overlapping continua, which can be considered as encompassing the major consequences of social behavior that approaches one or the other end of the interpersonal-intergroup continuum. They both have to do with the variability or uniformity within a group of behavior and attitudes concerning the relevant out-groups. The first may be described as follows: The nearer are members of a group to the "social change" extreme of the belief-systems continuum and the intergroup extreme of the behavioral continuum, the more uniformity they will show in their behavior toward members of the relevant out-group; an approach toward the opposite extremes of both these continua will be correspondingly associated with greater in-group variability of behavior toward members of the out-group. The second statement is closely related to the first: the nearer are members of a group to the "social change" and the "intergroup" extremes, the more they will tend to treat members of the out-group as undifferentiated items in a unified social category, rather than in terms of their individual characteristics. . . .

SOCIAL CATEGORIZATION AND INTERGROUP DISCRIMINATION

The initial stimulus for the theorizing presented here was provided by certain experimental investigations of intergroup behavior. The laboratory analogue of real-world ethnocentrism is in-group bias—that is, the tendency to favor the in-group over the out-group in evaluations and behavior. Not only are incompatible group interests not always sufficient to generate conflict (as concluded in the last section), but there is a good deal of experimental evidence that these conditions are not always necessary for the development of competition and discrimination between groups (Brewer, 1979; Turner, 1981), although this does not mean, of course, that in-group bias is not influenced by the goal relations between the groups.

All this evidence implies that in-group bias is a remarkably omnipresent feature of intergroup relations. The phenomenon in its extreme form has been investigated by Tajfel and his associates. There have now been in addition to the original studies (Tajfel, 1970; Tajfel et al., 1971) a large number of other experiments employing a similar procedure . . . all showing that the mere perception of belonging to two distinct groups—that is, social categorization per se—is sufficient to trigger intergroup discrimination favoring the in-group. In other words, the mere awareness of the presence of an out-group is sufficient to provoke intergroup competitive or discriminatory responses on the part of the in-group.

In the basic paradigm the subjects (both children and adults have acted as subjects in the various studies) are randomly classified as members of two nonoverlapping groups—ostensibly on the basis of some trivial performance criterion. They then make "decisions," awarding amounts of money to pairs of other subjects (excluding self) in specially designed booklets. The recipients are anonymous, except for their individual code numbers and their group membership (for example, member number 51 of the X group and member number 33 of the Y group). The subjects, who know their own group membership, award the amounts individually and anonymously. The response format of the booklets does not force the subjects to act in terms of group membership.

In this situation, there is neither a conflict of interests nor previously existing hostility between the "groups." No social interaction takes place between the subjects, nor is there any rational link between economic self-interest and the strategy of in-group favoritism. Thus, these groups are purely cognitive, and can be referred to as "minimal."

The basic and highly reliable finding is that the trivial, ad hoc intergroup categorization leads to in-group favoritism and discrimination against the out-group. Fairness is also an influential strategy. There is also a good deal of evidence that, within the pattern of responding in terms of in-group favoritism, maximum difference (MD) is more important to the subjects than maximum in-group profit (MIP). Thus, they seem to be competing with the out-group, rather than following a strategy of simple economic gain for members of the in-group. Other data from several experiments also show that the subjects' decisions were significantly nearer to the maximum joint payoff (MJP) point when these decisions applied to the division of money between two anonymous members of the in-group than when they applied to two members of the out-group; that is, relatively less was given to the out-group, even when giving more would not have affected the amounts for the in-group. Billig and Tajfel (1973) have found the same results even when the assignment to groups was made explicitly random. This eliminated the similarity on the performance criterion within the in-group as an alternative explanation of the results. An explicitly random classification into groups proved in this study to be a more potent determinant of discrimination than perceived interpersonal similarities and dissimilarities not associated with categorization into groups. . . .

SOCIAL IDENTITY AND SOCIAL COMPARISON

Many orthodox definitions of "social groups" are unduly restrictive when applied to the context of intergroup relations. For example, when members of two national or ethnic categories interact on the basis of their reciprocal beliefs about their respective categories and of the general relations between them, this is clearly intergroup behavior in the everyday sense of the term. The "groups" to which the interactants belong need not depend upon the frequency of intermember interaction, systems of role relationships, or interdependent goals. From the social-psychological perspective, the essential criteria for group membership, as they apply to large-scale social categories, are that the individuals concerned define themselves and are defined by others as members of a group.

We can conceptualize a group, in this sense, as a collection of individuals who perceive themselves to be members of the same social category, share some emotional involvement in this common definition of themselves, and achieve some degree of social consensus about the evaluation of their group and of their membership in it. Following from this, our definition of intergroup behavior is basically identical to that of Sherif (1967, p. 62): any behavior displayed by one or more actors [or actresses] toward one or more others that is based on the actors' [or actresses'] identification of themselves and the others as belonging to different social categories.

Social categorizations are conceived here as cognitive tools that segment, classify, and order the social environment, and thus enable the individual to undertake many forms of social action. But they do not merely systematize the social world; they also provide a system of orientation for *self-reference*: they create and define the individual's place in society. Social groups, understood in this sense, provide their members with an identification of themselves in social terms. These identifications are to a very large extent relational and comparative: they define the individual as similar to or different from, as "better" or "worse" than, members of other groups. It is in a strictly limited sense, arising from these considerations, that we use the term *social identity*. It consists, for the purposes of the present discussion, of those aspects of an individual's self-image that derive from the social categories to which he [or she] perceives [her- or] himself as belonging. With this limited concept of social identity in mind, our argument is based on the following general assumptions:

1. Individuals strive to maintain or enhance their self-esteem: they strive for a positive self-concept.
2. Social groups or categories and the membership of them are associated with positive or negative value connotations. Hence, social identity may be positive or negative according to the evaluations (which tend to be socially consensual, either within or across groups) of those groups that contribute to an individual's social identity.
3. The evaluation of one's own group is determined with reference to specific other groups through social comparisons in terms of value-laden attributes and characteristics. Positively discrepant comparisons between in-group and out-group produce high prestige; negatively discrepant comparisons between in-group and out-group result in low prestige.

From these assumptions, some related theoretical principles can be derived:

1. Individuals strive to achieve or to maintain positive social identity.
2. Positive social identity is based to a large extent on favorable comparisons that can

be made between the in-group and some relevant out-groups: the in-group must be perceived as positively differentiated or distinct from the relevant out-groups.

3. When social identity is unsatisfactory, individuals will strive either to leave their existing group and join some more positively distinct group and/or to make their existing group more positively distinct.

The basic hypothesis, then, is that pressures to evaluate one's own group positively through in-group/out-group comparisons lead social groups to attempt to differentiate themselves from each other (Tajfel, 1978a; Turner, 1975b). There are at least three classes of variables that should influence intergroup differentiation in concrete social situations. First, individuals must have internalized their group membership as an aspect of their self-concept: they must be subjectively identified with the relevant in-group. It is not enough that the others define them as a group, although consensual definitions by others can become, in the long run, one of the most powerful causal factors determining a group's self-definition. Second, the social situation must be such as to allow for intergroup comparisons that enable the selection and evaluation of the relevant relational attributes. Not all between-group differences have evaluative significance (Tajfel, 1959), and those that do vary from group to group. Skin color, for instance, is apparently a more salient attribute in the United States than in Hong Kong (Morland, 1969); whereas language seems to be an especially salient dimension of separate identity in French Canada, Wales, and Belgium (Giles and Johnson, 1981; Giles and Powesland, 1975). Third, in-groups do not compare themselves with every cognitively available out-group: the out-group must be perceived as a relevant comparison group. Similarity, proximity, and situational salience are among the variables that determine out-group comparability, and pressures toward in-group distinctiveness should increase as a function of this comparability. It is important to state at this point that, in many social situations, comparability reaches a much wider range than a simply conceived "similarity" between the groups.

The aim of differentiation is to maintain or achieve superiority over an out-group on some dimensions. Any such act, therefore, is essentially competitive. Fully reciprocal competition between groups requires a situation of mutual comparison and differentiation on a shared value dimension. In these conditions, inter-group competition, which may be unrelated to the objective goal relations between the groups, can be predicted to occur. . . .

REFERENCES

Bass, B. M., & Dunteman, G. (1963). Biases in the evaluation of one's group, its allies and opponents. *Journal of Conflict Resolution, 7,* 16–20.

Berkowitz, L. (1962). *Aggression: A social psychological analysis.* New York: McGraw-Hill.

Berry, J. W., Kalin, R., & Taylor, D. M. (1977). *Multiculturalism and ethnic attitudes in Canada.* Ottawa: Min. Supply & Services.

Billig, M., & Tajfel, H. (1973). Social categorization and similarity in intergroup behavior. *European Journal of Social Psychology, 3,* 27–52.

Bourhis, R. Y., Giles, H., & Tajfel, H. (1973). Language as a determinant of Welsh identity. *European Journal of Social Psychology, 3,* 447–460.

Brewer, M. B. (1979). In-group bias in the minimal intergroup situation: A cognitive-motivational analysis. *Psychological Bulletin, 86,* 307–324.

Brigham, J. C. (1971). Ethnic stereotypes. *Psychological Bulletin, 76,* 15–38.

Dizard, J. E. (1970). Black identity, social class and black power. *Psychiatry, 33,* 195–207.

Festinger, L. (1954). A theory of social comparison. *Human Relations, 7,* 117–140.

Friedman, N. (1969). Africa and the Afro-American: The changing Negro identity. *Psychiatry, 32*(2), 127–136.

Giles, H., & Johnson, P. (1981). The role of language in ethnic group relations. In J. C. Turner and H. Giles (Eds.), *Intergroup behavior.* Oxford: Basil Blackwell.

Giles, H., & Powesland, P. F. (Eds.) (1975). *Speech style and social evaluation.* London: Academic Press.

Gregor, A. J., & McPherson, D. A. (1966). Racial preference and ego identity among white and Bantu children in the Republic of South Africa. *Genetic Psychology Monographs, 73,* 217–254.

Harris, S., & Braun, J. R. (1971). Self-esteem and racial preference in black children. *Proceedings of the 79th Annual Convention of the American Psychological Association.*

Hirschman, A. O. (1970). *Exit, voice and loyalty: Responses to decline in firms, organizations and states.* Cambridge, MA: Harvard University Press.

Hraba, J., & Grant, G. (1970). Black is beautiful: A re-examination of racial preference and identification. *Journal of Personality and Social Psychology, 16,* 398–402.

Kidder, L. H., & Steward, V. M. (1975). *The psychology of intergroup relations.* New York: McGraw-Hill.

Morland, J. K. (1969). Race awareness among American and Hong Kong Chinese children. *American Journal of Sociology, 75,* 360–374.

Sherif, M. (1967). *Group conflict and co-operation.* London: Routledge and Kegan Paul.

Tajfel, H. (1959). Quantitative judgements in social perception. *British Journal of Psychology, 10,* 16–29.

Tajfel, H. (1970). Experiments in intergroup discrimination. *Scientific American, 223*(5), 96–102.

Tajfel, H. (1978a). The achievement of group differentiation. In H. Tajfel (Ed.), *Differentiation between social groups: Studies in the social psychology of intergroup relations.* London: Academic Press.

Tajfel, H. (1982b). The social psychology of intergroup relations. *Annual Review of Psychology, 33,* 1–39.

Tajfel, H., Billig, M. G., Bundy, R. P., & Flament, C. (1971). Social categorization and intergroup behavior. *European Journal of Social Psychology, 1,* 149–178.

Thibaut, J. (1950). An experimental study of the cohesiveness of under-privileged groups. *Human Relations, 3,* 251–278.

Tomlinson, T. M. (Ed.). (1970). Contributing factors in black politics. *Psychiatry, 32*(2), 137–281.

Turner, J. C. (1975a). Social categorization of social comparisons in intergroup relations. Unpublished doctoral dissertation, University of Bristol.

Turner, J. C. (1975b). Social comparison and social identity: Some prospects for intergroup behavior. *European Journal of Social Psychology, 5,* 5–34.

Turner, J. C. (1982). Towards a cognitive redefinition of the social group. In H. Tajfel (Ed.), *Social identity and intergroup relations.* Cambridge: Cambridge University Press.

Vaughn, G. (1978). Social change and intergroup preferences in New Zealand. *European Journal of Social Psychology, 8*, 297–314.

Wilson, W., & Miller, N. (1961). Shifts in evaluations of participants following intergroup competition. *Journal of Abnormal and Social Psychology, 63*, 428–431.

Identity and Interpersonal Bonding
Stella Ting-Toomey

. . .

IDENTITY PERSPECTIVES

. . .

Cultural Variability Perspective

The cultural variability perspective is concerned primarily with how definable dimensions of a culture affect identity conceptions and relationship development. Dimensions of cultural variability influence the underlying social structures and norms of a situation, and the social norms, in turn, influence how one should or should not behave in a certain manner (Gudykunst & Ting-Toomey, 1988). The identity salience dimension, Shich is defined as the "degree to which an individual's relationships to particular others depended upon his or her being a given kind of person . . . playing a particular role, and having a particular identity" (Stryker, 1987, p. 97), depends heavily on the cultural context in which the encounter takes place. How one constructs and presents a "self" in a relationship is, to a large degree, situationally-dependent and culturally-dependent.

On a more specific level, when one examines the cultural variability dimensions that have been isolated by theorists in different disciplines, the one cross-cultural dimension that appears to have strong etic endorsement is individualism-collectivism (Gudykunst, 1987; Hofstede, 1980; Hofstede & Bond, 1984; Hui, 1988; Hui & Triandis, 1986; Ting-Toomey, 1988a; Triandis, Bontempo, & Betancourt et al., 1986; Triandis, Bontempo, Villareal, Asai, & Lucca, 1988). Individualism-collectivism refers to the culturally grounded "cluster of attitudes, beliefs, and behaviors toward a wide variety of people" (Hui & Triandis, 1986, p. 240). In an etic analysis of the dimension in nine cultures (Chile, Costa Rica, France, Greece, Hong Kong, India, Indonesia, the Netherlands, and three ethnic samples in the United States), Triandis et al. (1986) uncovered four stable etic factors: Individualism has two factors

Source: Abridged from chapter with same title in M. K. Asante & W. B. Gudykunst (Eds.), *Handbook of International and Intercultural Communication* (pp. 351–373). Newbury Park, CA: Sage, 1989.

(*separation from ingroups* and *self-reliance with hedonism*) and collectivism has two factors (*family integrity* and *interdependability with sociability*).

Overall, members of the individualistic cultures (such as Australia and the United States) tend to place a high emphasis on the "I" identity over the "we" identity, the "I" assertion over the group assertion, and tend to maintain a considerable social distance between the "I" identity and ingroup social influences. Conversely, members of the collectivistic cultures (such as China and Japan) tend to place a high premium on the "we" identity over the "I" identity, the group assertion over the individualistic assertion, and tend to be more susceptible to ingroup influences than members in the individualistic cultures. Triandis (1986) argued that there are two types of collectivism: "simple" collectivism and "contextual" collectivism. "Simple" collectivism allows members to choose how to behave when multiple ingroups are relevant, while "contextual" collectivism designates an ingroup influence that is specific. In addition, while the boundary conditions between ingroups and outgroups are fairly diffused and loosely structured in individualistic cultures, the boundary conditions between ingroups and outgroups, and also between memberships in various ingroups (e.g., kin, coworkers, neighbors), are more sharply defined and tightly structured in collectivistic cultures (Triandis et al., 1986).

In a recent study, for example, Triandis et al. (1988) found that individualism in the United States is reflected in (a) *self-reliance with competition,* (b) *low concerns for ingroups,* and (c) *distance from ingroups.* In addition, a higher-order factor analysis suggests that *subordination of ingroup goals to personal goals* may be the most important aspect of individualism in the United States. In comparison, samples from two collectivist cultures (Japan and Puerto Rico) indicate that "which ingroup is present, in what context . . . , and what behavior (e.g., paying attention to the views of others, feelings similar to others, competing with others)" are critical to role enactment and performance (Triandis et al., 1988, p. 336). Furthermore, the psychological dimension of idiocentrism-allocentrism (e.g., the personality dimension equivalent to individualism and collectivism, respectively) also asserts influence on individuals' behavior within cultures. Overall, allocentric individuals reported more social support and perceived a better quality of such support than idiocentric individuals, while idiocentric individuals reported being more lonely. Related research by Gudykunst and Nishida (1986) and Gudykunst, Yoon, and Nishida (1987) obtained results similar to Triandis et al.'s study (1986). For example, Gudykunst, Yoon, and Nishida (1987) found that members of collectivistic cultures (Japan and Korea) perceive greater social penetration (personalization and synchronization) in their ingroup relationships than do members of individualistic cultures (United States). Their data further revealed that perceived outgroup relationships in collectivistic cultures are influenced by either "simple" collectivism or "contextual" collectivism. Overall, the Korean culture exhibits "simple" collectivistic patterns, while the Japanese exhibits "contextual" collectivistic patterns.

In cross-cultural interpersonal conflict literature, Chua and Gudykunst (1987), Leung (1988), and Ting-Toomey (1985) observed that members of individualistic cultures tend to use a direct conflict communication style and a solution-orientation style, and members of collectivistic cultures tend to use an indirect conflict communication style and a conflict-avoidance style. In addition, collectivists tend to use the equality norm (the equal distribution norm) with ingroup members and use the equity norm (the deservingness norm) with outgroup members more than individualists (Leung & Bond, 1984; Leung & Iwawaki, 1988). Collectivists also display stronger preference for conflict mediation and bargaining procedure than individualists (Leung, 1987). Preferences for a direct conflict style, for the use of the equity norm, and for the direct settlement of disputes reflect the salience of the "I" identity in individualistic cultures; while preferences for an indirect conflict style, for the use of the equality norm, and for the use of mediation procedures reflect the salience of the "we" identity in the collectivistic cultures.

Ting-Toomey (1985, 1988a) developed a theory of face-negotiation and cross-cultural conflict styles. Conflict is viewed as an identity-bound concept in which the "faces" or the "situated identities" of the conflict interactants are called into question. Based on the two dimensions of self-concern focus versus other-concern focus and positive-face need (inclusion need) versus negative-face need (autonomy need), twelve theoretical propositions were developed to account for the relationship between cultural variability and conflict style. The first four propositions, for example, were as follows:

(1) Members of individualistic cultures would tend to express a greater degree of self-face maintenance in a conflict situation than would members of collectivistic cultures.

(2) Members of collectivistic cultures would tend to express a greater degree of mutual-face or other-face maintenance than would members of individualistic cultures.

(3) Members of individualistic cultures would tend to use more autonomy-preserving strategies (negative-face need) in managing conflict than would members of collectivistic cultures.

(4) Members of collectivistic cultures would tend to use more inclusion-seeking strategies (positive-face need) in managing conflict than would members of individualistic cultures.

. . .

Ethnolinguistic Identity Perspective

The ethnolinguistic identity perspective (Beebe & Giles, 1984) is concerned mainly with group membership influences on identity salience vis-à-vis the critical role of language. Giles and Johnson (1981), for example, argue that language plays a critical role in shaping the ethnic/cultural identity salience dimension for individuals. Giles, Bourhis, and Taylor (1977) contend that perceived ethnolinguistic vitality influences the degree to which individuals will act as an ethnic/cultural group member in an intergroup encounter situation. Perceived high ethnolinguistic vitality means individuals perceive their own ingroup language as assuming a high-status position and as receiving wide-based institutional support from the language community. Perceived low ethnolinguistic vitality means individuals perceive their own ingroup language as assuming a low-status position and as receiving narrow-based institutional support from the government, education, industry, and the mass media (for a detailed review on ethnolinguistic identity, see Chapter 5, Franklyn-Stokes & Giles, in this volume; Gudykunst, in press; Chapter 9, Gudykunst & Gumbs, in this volume).

In addition to the issue of ethnic/cultural identity salience dimension, Tajfel's (1978) and Turner's (1987) social identity theory argues for the critical role of social identity salience in the formation of an individual's self-concept. Tajfel (1978, p. 63) states: "Social identity is that *part* of an individual's self-concept which derives from his [or her] knowledge of his [or her] membership in a social group (or groups) together with the value and emotional significance attached to that membership." Incorporating the main ideas in ethnolinguistic identity theory and social identity theory, Gudykunst (in press) identifies five factors that influence ethnolinguistic identity development: (a) the strength of ingroup identification, (b) the salience and overlaps of multiple group memberships, (c) the valence of intergroup comparisons, (d) the permeability of ingroup/outgroup boundaries, and (e) the perceived vitality of ingroup language. According to Gudykunst (1988), the more secure and positive members of a group feel about their identity, the more positive the intergroup comparisons, the more tolerant and receptive they are toward members of other groups. He further theorizes that an increase in the strength of strangers' ethnolinguistic identities will produce an increase in their attributional confidence regarding the behaviors of other groups' members. He contends that secure ethnolinguistic identity, positive expectations, perceived group similarity, shared intergroup networks, interpersonal salience, second-language competence, and personality factors affect the reduction of uncertainty and anxiety in intergroup encounter processes. Reducing uncertainty and anxiety, in turn, influences intergroup-interpersonal adaptation and effectiveness. Identity security, in short, brings about confidence in oneself to initiate the exploration of the world of a stranger, and the exploration, in turn, brings about greater knowledge and understanding of the stranger's background and normative culture.

Members who are secure in their ethnolinguistic identities will have an overall sense of positive self-concept. They will be likely to take risks in strangers' interaction. They will also be likely to explore and cultivate deeper levels of intergroup relationship with outgroup members, and will be more receptive to move the relationship to different bonding stages such as close friendship, romantic relationship, or marital relationship than members with insecure ethnolinguistic identities. There exists, of course, an optimal level of the ethnolinguistic identification process. Members who are at the extreme far ends of the continuum of identification will have either extreme marginal identities or extreme ethnocentric identities. Secure ethnolinguistic identification in this chapter means a healthy, optimal level of cultural role identities and social role identities that constitute the integral part of an individual's positive sense of "self." . . .

INTERGROUP-INTERPERSONAL BONDING PROCESS

A Convergent Approach

Bochner (1984, p. 583), in discussing the functions of human communication in interpersonal bonding, proposes five specific functions of relational communication: "(1) to foster favorable impressions; (2) to organize the relationship; (3) to construct and validate a conjoint world view; (4) to express feelings and thoughts; and (5) to protect vulnerabilities." As intercultural communication researchers, however, we cannot discuss the interpersonal bonding process adequately unless the dynamics of intergroup factors are taken into consideration. The factors of language, ethnolinguistic identity salience, preconceived expectations of outgroup members, and the boundary conditions between ingroup and outgroup members are critical to the development of the evolving, long-term relationships of the intergroup-interpersonal dyad.

In order to examine the bonding ties between members of two ethnic or cultural communities, we have to make some basic assumptions. For example, the intergroup members have a common means (i.e., a common language) to communicate with one another. They are in close proximity with one another, they have the opportunities to communicate, and they have a sense of reciprocal awareness of the other's presence (Ting-Toomey, 1981, 1986a). The first intergroup bonding question asks: What are the conditions that promote the initiation of intergroup-interpersonal encounters?

The theories and research based on ethnolinguistic identity theory can provide initial observations to answer this question. Under the conditions that intergroup comparisons are positive, ethnolinguistic identities are strong, and group boundaries are permeable, members of culture X are more likely to venture out to initiate contact with members of culture Y, and vice versa. As Axiom 1 in Gudykunst's (1988) intergroup uncertainty reduction theory indicates: Strangers' positive ethnolinguistic identities are more likely to increase attributional confidence regarding outgroup members' behavior and decrease initial anxiety they experience with outgroup members' contact. The axiom, however, *only* holds when members of the outgroup are perceived as "typical" and when ethnic status is activated.

Nevertheless, while ethnolinguistic identities serve as a critical factor during the initial intergroup contact phase, it does not assume equal values and equal statuses during actual interactions in all cultures. In some cultures, personal identity salience outweighs the importance of role identity salience. In other cultures, cultural role and social role identities are of paramount importance to one's sense of "self" and personhood construction. Explaining these differences is where the cultural variability perspective can facilitate our understanding of the intergroup-interpersonal bonding process.

Applying the individualism-collectivism theoretical dimension, we can state the basic assumption that members of individualistic cultures will place a greater emphasis on the salience of personal identities over role identities, while members of collectivistic cultures will place a greater emphasis on the salience of role identities over personal identities during the intergroup encounter process. For example, members of individualistic cultures will emphasize personal identity factors such as personal ideals or achievements during initial attraction stages, while members of collectivistic cultures will emphasize role identity factors such as educational or occupational background during initial intergroup encounters. This basic assumption, in turn, influences how intergroup members attune to different aspects of the encounter—to foster favorable impressions, to validate a conjoint worldview, to organize the relationship, to express feelings and thoughts, and to protect relational vulnerabilities (Bochner, 1984).

Fostering Impressions

Impression management is critical to the cultivation of intergroup-interpersonal ties. Both the cultural norms of the encounter situation and the identity negotiation process between the two individuals will have a profound influence on the further development of the relationship. If the intergroup encounter takes place in a heterogeneous, individualistic culture, norms and rules will assert relatively less pressures on the dyad than if the intergroup encounter takes place in a homogeneous, collectivistic culture like Japan. Beyond the contextual setting of the encounter, the identity negotiation process between the two individuals will be critical to the further evolution of the relationship. While interpersonal attraction variables such as physical attraction, personality attraction, perceived attitudinal similarity, and close proximity may be necessary conditions for the intergroup-interpersonal bonding process to occur, identity negotiation and reciprocal support are the vital conditions that propel the intergroup relationship forward, moving toward an individualized relationship that is "close, deep, personal and intimate" (Bochner, 1984, p. 544; Cushman & Cahn, 1985; Ting-Toomey, 1986a).

In attempting to foster a favorable impression, especially during actual initial encounters, the intergroup dyad has to grapple with two sets of problems: self-presentation versus other-validation. This section focuses on the self-presentation dimension, while the next section contains a discussion of the other-validation dimension.

In terms of self-presentation acts, there are four possible intergroup impression presentation options: (a) member categorizes or identifies self as a typical cultural member, and behaves typically; (b) member categorizes or identifies self as an atypical cultural member, and behaves atypically; (c) member categorizes or identifies self as a typical cultural member, but acts atypically; and (d) member categorizes or identifies self as an atypical cultural member, but acts typically. All four options probably are influenced more by the dyadic partner's perceptions and interpretations than by the member's projected sense of self in the encounter. The partner's knowledge of the culture, the degree of favorableness toward the outgroup, the levels of expectations of the role enactment from outgroup member, and the degree of tolerance of ambiguity will create either a positive or a negative climate for the initial intergroup contact. Past intergroup literature (Hewstone & Brown, 1986) has indicated that positive feelings toward outgroup members as a whole are more likely to be generated from intergroup interaction involving an outgroup member who is perceived as typical of his or her group rather than from interaction involving an outgroup member who is perceived as atypical. We may want to qualify this finding, however, by adding on the variables of degree of favorable outgroup attitude and the valence of typical/atypical outgroup member's behavior. A favorable outgroup attitude, in conjunction with desirable typical/atypical outgroup member's behavior, will promote further inter-group-interpersonal relationship development, while an unfavorable outgroup attitude, with undesirable typical/atypical outgroup member's behavior, will impede further relationship progress. . . .

The construction of personhood in individualistic cultures is based on intrinsic qualities and characteristics, while the construction of personhood in collectivistic cultures is tied closely to the sociocultural webs of the system. As Shweder and Bourne (1984, pp. 191–192) summarize, in the individualistic cultures, "each person is conceived of as . . . a monadic replica of general humanity. A kind of sacred person-alized self is developed and the individual qua individual is seen as inviolate, a supreme value in and of itself. The 'self' becomes an object of interest *per se*," whereas in collectivistic cultures, the "context-dependent, occasion-bound concept of the person" is expressed through "(a) no attempt to distinguish the individual from the status s(he) occupies; (b) the view that obligations and rights are diffentially appor-tioned by role, group, etc.; (c) a disinclination to ascribe intrinsic moral worth to persons merely because they are persons." . . .

Validating the Other

Accurate coorientation and reciprocal, mutual support of identities occur in conjunc-tion with fostering favorable impressions. Mutual validation and confirmation is vital to further relational growth and progress (Ting-Toomey, 1986a). Three issues (iden-tity validation, the content of validation, and the means of validation) are of central concern in the intergroup-interpersonal validation process.

As mentioned in the previous section, identity presentation can come in different forms. Likewise, identity validation can take on different shapes. To validate someone's identities, we have to obtain the following identity information about the other group members: (a) the extent to which he or she identifies with cultural role categories, social role categories, or personal identity categories; (b) the salience (important-unimportant) and the valence (positive-negative) in which he or she identifies with different role types; and (c) the consistency and frequency distributions in which he or she enacts each role category. Beyond obtaining the basic relational knowledge, the members have to possess a certain degree of attributional confidence in themselves to infer whether the obtained information is accurate or inaccurate.

Ethnolinguistic identity theory suggests some initial predictions. Members who are secure about their ethnolinguistic identities are more confident in their predictions of the outgroup members' behavior, while members who are insecure about their ethnolinguistic identities are probably less confident in their predictions of outgroup members' behavior. Members who are secure in their own identities possess a sense of awareness, knowledge, and acceptance of their own self and behavior. Members who are self-aware are also likely to be alert and aware of their outer environment. Self-awareness leads to other-awareness, self-knowledge leads to other-knowledge, and self-acceptance leads to other-acceptance and tolerance. Members who have strong ethnolinguistic identities will be more ready to engage in an active information-seeking process concerning strangers' behavior than members who have weak ethnolinguistic identities. Members who are secure in their identities are not afraid of losing their "selves" in the searching process, while members who are insecure in their identities will have a high apprehension level in losing their "selves" in interactions with dissimilar strangers.

Cross-cultural studies of uncertainty reduction (Gudykunst & Nishida, 1984, 1986) indicate that the individualism-collectivism dimension influences uncertainty reduction content and uncertainty reduction modes of intergroup-interpersonal communication. Members of individualistic cultures tend to reduce uncertainty in the personal identity salience area, while members of collectivistic cultures tend to reduce uncertainty in the role identity salience area. Personal identity salience means a set of self-definitional personal identities that are derived from unique, idiosyncratic individual characteristics (e.g., active-passive, fast-slow). Role identity salience is conceptualized as a set of self-definitional role identities that are derived from cultural and/or social membership categories (Ting-Toomey, 1986a).

Applying the results of cross-cultural studies of uncertainty reduction to the intergroup-interpersonal validation process, the findings suggest that members of individualistic cultures are more likely to validate an outgroup member's personal identity salience, while members of collectivistic cultures are likely to validate an outgroup member's role identity salience. Furthermore, previous work (Hall, 1983; Okabe, 1983; Ting-Toomey, 1985, 1988a) reveals that members of individualistic cultures tend to use a direct, verbal mode of communication to reduce relational uncertainty, while members of collectivistic cultures tend to use an indirect, nonverbal mode of communication to reduce uncertainty. Individualistic cultures are low-context cultures and collectivistic cultures are high-context cultures (Hall, 1983). Low-context cultures emphasize direct verbal assertion, explicit meanings, and personal identity interactions, and high-context cultures value indirect verbal assertion, implicit meanings, and role identity interaction. In terms of intergroup modes of validation, members of low-context, individualistic cultures are likely to engage in a direct, explicit verbal mode of identity validation, while members of high-context, collectivistic cultures are likely to engage in an indirect, implicit nonverbal mode of identity validation.

Finally, social networks play a critical role in the intergroup-interpersonal identity validation process. According to Triandis et al. (1988, p. 325), in collectivist cultures, "the ingroup's influence on behavior is broad, profound, and diffuse; in the individualist [cultures] it is narrow, superficial, and specific." In individualistic cultures, identity validation is a private, dyadic affair, while in the collectivistic cultures, identity validation is embedded within the approval of family and social networks. Identity validation is an intensive affair in individualistic cultures, while identity validation is a diffused activity in collectivistic cultures. . . .

Organizing the Relationship

Organizing the relationship refers to how the intergroup couple establishes rules for the relationship, and the rules "constitute the *definition of the relationship* and form the organizational basis for controlling *what* actions will take place in the relationship, as well as *how* thoughts and feelings may be expressed" (Bochner, 1984, p. 591; Duck, 1985). Different levels of rules concerning how a relationship should be conducted are reflective of basic cultural ideologies and themes surrounding the structure, content, and meanings of a relationship. According to Bochner (1984), there are four types of bonding rules: (a) common consent rules, (b) idiosyncratic rules, (c) explicit or implicit rules, and (d) metarules. *Common consent rules* are rules that are learned during primary socialization process via family interaction (i.e., are determined culturally). *Idiosyncratic rules* are rules that reflect the private beliefs concerning what is fair and just in the relationship by the involved parties. *Explicit* or *implicit rules* are prior agreement rules that are either publicly acknowledged or publicly denied to a third party outside the relationship. Finally, *metarules* are rules about who may set the rules, and also about rules against seeing or knowing about certain rules in the relationship (Bochner, 1984, pp. 591–592).

Common consent rules are rules with high normative cultural forces. They constitute the cultural "scripts" of what it means to be a "good" friend, what it means to be a "dating" couple, or what it means to be a "harmonious" family. Argyle (1986), in a series of studies testing 33 common rules in four cultures (Britain, Hong Kong, Italy, and Japan), found that respect for privacy is a basic rule regulating all rela-' tionships across cultures. In addition, there are more rules about obedience, avoiding loss of face, maintaining harmonious relations in groups, and restraining emotional expression in the collectivistic cultures than in the individualistic cultures.

The issue of privacy-regulation is related directly to identity respect and the identity validation process. With respect to the influence of cultural variability on privacy negotiation, we can predict that members of individualistic cultures probably display a higher privacy need in interpersonal relationships than members of collectivistic cultures. Members of individualistic cultures treasure autonomy and freedom in a relationship, while members of collectivistic cultures value mutual interdependence and restraint. While the dialectic of freedom and restraint is present simultaneously in all intimate relationships, cultural variability will influence members' preference for one end of the dialectic over another. In addition, members of individualistic cultures will be likely to articulate their need for privacy or privacy respect, while members of collectivistic cultures will be subdued about it. Privacy respect is a reflection of respect extended to the personhood of "I"; whereas privacy regulation, in the context of the collectivistic cultures, may mean dyadic privacy away from kinship network and social network influences, but may not necessarily mean the separate, autonomous privacy between the "you" and the "I."

Idiosyncratic rules are private beliefs concerning what constitutes "fairness" in a relationship. According to Leung and Iwawaki (1988), collectivists typically follow the "equality norm" in reward allocation, while individualists typically follow the "equity norm" in reward distribution. The equality norm requires an equal allocation of a reward among the participants of their input to the obtaining of the reward, while the equity norm requires that reward distribution should be proportional to participants' input (Leung & Iwawaki, 1988, p. 36). In the initial intergroup-interpersonal attraction phase, members of individualistic cultures will probably practice the equity norm of self-deservingness, while members of collectivistic cultures will probably practice the equality norm for the sake of preserving relational harmony and solidarity. In addition, there are differences in the reciprocity norm in intergroup relationship development across cultures. The reciprocity norm in individualistic cultures means *individualized* responsibilities and exchange obligations, whereas in collectivistic cultures, it means *role* responsibilities and exchange obligations (Ting-Toomey, 1986a). To be attracted to a member of a collectivistic culture means to take on additional responsibilities and obligations toward the member's social networks. In terms of the *explicit-implicit rules*, while violation of relational rules in the public may be acknowledged explicitly in individualistic, low-context cultures, violation of relational rules will be noticed but may not be acknowledged explicitly in collectivistic, high-context cultures. To acknowledge relational rules' breakdowns in public will bring on enormous "loss of face" to members of the collectivistic cultures. . . .

Expressing Thoughts and Feelings

According to Bochner (1984, p. 600), *expressive communication* refers to "messages that signify emotive and subjective experiences such as feelings, private sentiments, and personal qualities." Beyond normative rules of the culture, second-language competence is critical to expressive communication in intergroup encounters. The normative rules of individualistic, low-context cultures stress verbal expressive communication, while the normative rules of collectivistic, high-context cultures emphasize nonverbal affiliative expressiveness (Gudykunst & Nishida, 1984; Okabe, 1983; Ting-Toomey, 1985). Second-language competence is critical for collectivists who are attracted to individualists, especially when the intergroup encounter takes place in individualistic, low-context cultures. On the other hand, nonverbal affiliative expressiveness is of paramount important for individualists who are attracted to collectivists, and, particularly when the intergroup encounter takes place in collectivistic, high-context cultures. As Gudykunst, Nishida, and Chua's (1987) study indicates, perceived second-language competence for the Japanese in the United States is correlated positively with the social penetration process of greater perceived personalization, greater perceived synchronization, and less perceived difficulty with U.S. members. The cultural context of expressive communication asserts strong influence over the critical role of second-language competence. While relational commitment will be expressed through verbal forms of communication in individualistic, low-context cultures, relational commitment will be expressed through subtle forms of nonverbal communication in collectivistic, high-context cultures.

The perceived ethnolinguistic identity dimension is also linked positively with second-language competence. The more secure and positive individuals feel about their identities, the greater the perceived competence in the outgroup language, and also the more receptive they are of members of other groups (Hall & Gudykunst, 1986). Members with secure ethnolinguistic identities tend to take more risks with cultivating second-language competence and intergroup relationship competence. Successes in both areas probably act as a feedback loop to reinforce the security of the group members' identities.

Expressive communication or relational openness, however, does not follow a unidirectional trajectory in the development of intergroup-interpersonal relationships. As Bochner (1984, p. 610) comments, "the dialectical qualities of interpersonal communication make it obvious that things are not always what they seem; yet interactants sometimes are pressured to act as if things are. . . . Talk may inhibit what it exhibits—expressiveness mandating protectiveness, revealing necessitating concealing, openness petitioning discretion, weakness used to dominate, freedom as a constraint." . . .

Protecting Vulnerabilities

The sense of the "self" is the most vulnerable and the most sacred in any type of intimate relationships. In the individualistic cultures, the "I" identity is most vulnerable to attack and to relational hurts. In the collectivistic cultures, the "face" identity is most sensitive to hurts and violations. To hurt someone's "I" identity in individualistic cultures means direct violation of the other person's sense of personal privacy, the betrayal of private information to a third person, or the bringing up of deeply personal taboo topics that hurt the other person's ego. To hurt someone's "face" identity in the collectivistic cultures means verbally assaulting the other person's face in front of a third party, separating the other person's connection with family and kinship network ties, or bringing up taboo topics that deal with ingroups' ineffectiveness or inadequacy.

Respecting and protecting relational vulnerabilities requires high role-taking ability. High rhetorically sensitive persons (Hart, Carlson, & Eadie, 1980; Ting-Toomey, 1988), high self-monitoring persons (Snyder, 1987), or allocentric personality types (Triandis et al., 1988) probably possess a higher role-taking ability than low rhetorically sensitive persons, low self-monitoring persons, or idiocentric personality types. Members who are secure in their ethnolinguistic identities are also good role-takers because their sense of identity security will push them to take relational risks more easily than members with insecure ethnolinguistic identities. Members with ambivalent or insecure ethnolinguistic identities will have a harder time taking on the perspective of the other person because they have to spend time and energy struggling with their own identity problems and definitions. In addition, members of collectivistic cultures are probably better role-takers than members of individualistic cultures because members in collectivistic cultures have been socialized in cultural systems that emphasize a high other-orientation rather than a high I-orientation. Anticipating the other person's need, empathizing with the other's response, and learning the discretion and sensitivity of when to speak and when to remain silent are some of the fundamental training that collectivists receive early on in their family socialization process (Clancy, 1986).

Finally, we also can predict that people with secure ethnolinguistic identities have few relational taboo topics, while people with insecure ethnolinguistic identities will have many relational taboo topics. If individuals do not feel secure about their ethnolinguistic identities, then conversations surrounding both the role identity salience dimension and the personal identity salience dimension will oftentimes becomes strained and awkward. Taboo topics and vulnerable feelings along these two dimensions will also accumulate. . . .

REFERENCES

Altman, I., Vinsel, A., & Brown, B. (1981). Dialectical conceptions in social psychology: An application to social penetration and privacy regulation. In L. Berkowitz (Ed.), *Advances in experimental social psychology*. New York: Academic Press.

Argyle, M. (1986). Rules for social relationships in four cultures. *Australian Journal of Psychology, 38*, 309-318.

Beebe, L. M., & Giles, H. (1984). Speech accommodation theories: A discussion in terms of second-language acquisition. *International Journal of the Sociology of Language, 46*, 5-32.

Bochner, A. (1984). The functions of human communication in interpersonal bonding. In C. Arnold & J. Bower (Eds.), *Handbook of rhetorical and communication theory*. Boston: Allyn & Bacon.

Bochner, A. (1985). Perspectives on inquiry: Representation, conversation, and reflection. In M. Knapp & G. Miller (Eds.), *Handbook of interpersonal communication*. Beverly Hills, CA: Sage.

Burke, P. (1980). Measurement requirements from an interactionist perspective. *Social Psychology Quarterly, 43*, 18-29.

Chua, E., & Gudykunst, W. (1987). Conflict resolution style in low- and high-context cultures. *Communication Research Reports, 4*, 32-37.

Clancy, P. (1986). The acquisition of communicative style in Japanese. In B. Schieffelin & E. Ochs (Eds.), *Language socialization across cultures*. Cambridge: Cambridge University Press.

Collier, M., & Thomas, M. (1988). Cultural identity: An interpretive perspective. In Y. Kim & W. Gudykunst (Eds.), *Theories in intercultural communication*. Newbury Park, CA: Sage.

Cushman, D., & Cahn, D. (1985). *Communication in interpersonal relationships*. Albany: State University of New York Press.

Duck, S. (1985). Social and personal relationships. In M. Knapp & G. Miller (Eds.), *Handbook of interpersonal communication*. Beverly Hills, CA: Sage.

Giles, H., Bourhis, R., & Taylor, D. (1977). Towards a theory of language in ethnic group relations. In H. Giles (Ed.), *Language, ethnicity and intergroup relations*. London: Academic Press.

Giles, H., & Johnson, P. (1981). The role of language in ethnic group relations. In J. Turner & H. Giles (Eds.), *Intergroup behavior*. Chicago: University of Chicago Press.

Gudykunst, W. (1987). Cross-cultural comparisons. In C. Berger & S. Chaffee (Eds.), *Handbook of communication science*. Newbury Park, CA: Sage.

Gudykunst, W. B. (1988). Uncertainty and anxiety. In Y. Y. Kim & W. B. Gudykunst (Eds.), *Theories in intercultural communication*. Newbury Park, CA: Sage.

Gudykunst, W. B. (in press). Cultural variability in ethnolinguistic identity. In S. Ting-Toomey & F. Korzenny (Eds.), *Language, communication, and culture: Current directions*. Newbury Park, CA: Sage.

Gudykunst, W. B., & Nishida, T. (1984). Individual and cultural influences on uncertainty reduction. *Communication Monographs, 51*, 23-36.

Gudykunst, W. B., & Nishida, T. (1986). Attributional confidence in low- and high-context cultures. *Human Communication Research, 12*, 525-549.

Gudykunst, W. B., Nishida, T., & Chua, E. (1987). Perceptions of social penetration in Japanese-North American dyads. *International Journal of Intercultural Relations, 51*, 256-278.

Gudykunst, W. B., & Ting-Toomey, S., with Chua, E. (1988). *Culture and interpersonal communication*. Newbury Park, CA: Sage.

Gudykunst, W. B., Yoon, Y. C., & Nishida, T. (1987). The influence of individualism-collectivism on perceptions of communication in ingroup and outgroup relationships. *Communication Monographs, 54*, 295-306.

Hall, B. J., & Gudykunst, W. B. (1986). The intergroup theory of second language ability. *Journal of Language and Social Psychology, 5*, 291-302.

Hall, E. (1983). *The dance of life*. New York: Doubleday.

Hart, R., Carlson, R., & Eadie, W. (1980). Attitudes toward communication and the assessment of rhetorical sensitivity. *Communication Monographs, 47*, 1-20.

Hewstone, M., & Brown, R. (1986). Contact is not enough: An intergroup perspective on the "contact hypothesis." In M. Hewstone & R. Brown (Eds.), *Contact and conflict in intergroup encounters*. London: Basil Blackwell.

Hofstede, G. (1980). *Culture's consequences: International differenes in work-related values*. Beverly Hills, CA: Sage.

Hofstede, G., & Bond, M. (1984). Hofstede's culture dimensions: An independent validation using Rokeach's value survey. *Journal of Cross-Cultural Psychology, 15*, 417-433.

Hui, C. (1988). Measurement of individualism-collectivism. *Journal of Research in Personality, 22*, 17-36.

Hui, C., & Triandis, H. (1986). Individualism-collectivism: A study of cross-cultural researchers. *Journal of Cross-Cultural Psychology, 17*, 225-248.

Leung, K. (1987). Some determinants of reactions to procedural models for conflict resolution: A cross-national study. *Journal of Personality and Social Psychology, 53*, 898-908.

Leung, K. (1988). Some determinants of conflict avoidance. *Journal of Cross-Cultural Psychology, 19*, 125-136.

Leung, K., & Bond, M. (1984). The impact of cultural collectivism on reward allocation. *Journal of Personality and Social Psychology, 47*, 793-804.

Leung, K., & Iwawaki, S. (1988). Cultural collectivism and distributive behavior. *Journal of Cross-Cultural Psychology, 19*, 35-49.

Marsella, A., DeVos, G., & Hsu, F. (Eds.). (1985). *Culture and self: Asian and Western perspectives.* New York: Tavistock.

Okabe, R. (1983). Cultural assumptions of East and West: Japan and the United States. In W. Gudykunst (Ed.), *Intercultural communication theory: Current perspectives.* Beverly Hills, CA: Sage.

Parks, M. (1985). Interpersonal communication and the quest for personal competence. In M. Knapp & G. Miller (Eds.), *Handbook of interpersonal communication.* Beverly Hills, CA: Sage.

Shweder, R., & Bourne, E. (1984). Does the concept of the person vary cross-culturally? In R. Shweder & R. LeVine (Eds.), *Culture theory: Essays on mind, self, and emotion.* Cambridge: Cambridge University Press.

Snyder, M. (1987). *Public appearances, private realities.* New York: Friedman.

Stryker, S. (1987). Identity theory: Development and extentions. In K. Yardley & T. Honess (Eds.), *Self and identity: Psychosocial perspective.* Chichester, England: John Wiley.

Tajfel, H. (1978). Social categorization, social identity, and social comparison. In H. Tajfel (Ed.), *Differentiation between social groups.* London: Academic Press.

Ting-Toomey, S. (1981). Ethnic identity and close friendship in Chinese-American college students. *International Journal of Intercultural Relations, 5,* 383–406.

Ting-Toomey, S. (1984). Qualitative methods: An overview. In W. Gudykunst & Y. Kim (Eds.), *Methods for intercultural communication research.* Beverly Hills, CA: Sage.

Ting-Toomey, S. (1985). Toward a theory of conflict and culture. In W. Gudykunst, L. Stewart, & S. Ting-Toomey (Eds.), *Communication, culture, and organizational processes.* Beverly Hills, CA: Sage.

Ting-Toomey, S. (1986a). Interpersonal ties in intergroup communication. In W. Gudykunst (Ed.), *Intergroup communication.* London: Edward Arnold.

Ting-Toomey, S. (1986b). Japanese communication patterns: Insider versus the outsider perspective. *World Communication, 15,* 113–126.

Ting-Toomey, S. (1988a). Intercultural conflicts: A face-negotiation theory. In Y. Kim & W. Gudykunst (Eds.), *Theories in intercultural communication.* Newbury Park, CA: Sage.

Ting-Toomey, S. (1988b). Culture and interpersonal relationship development: Some conceptual issues. In J. Andersen (Ed.), *Communication yearbook* (Vol. 12). Newbury Park, CA: Sage.

Ting-Toomey, S. (1988c). Rhetorical sensitivity style in three cultures: France, Japan, and the United States. *Central States Speech Communication Journal, 38,* 28–36.

Triandis, H. C. (1986). Collectivism vs. individualism: A reconceptualization of a basic concept in cross-cultural psychology. In C. Bagley & G. Verma (Eds.), *Personality, cognition, and values: Cross-cultural perspectives of childhood and adolescence.* London: Macmillan.

Triandis, H., Bontempo, R., Betancourt, L., Bond, M., Leung, K., Brenes, A., Georgas, J., Hui, H., Marin, G., Setiadi, B., Sinha, J., Verma, J., Spangenberg, J., Touzard, H., & Montmollin, G. (1986). The measurement of the etic aspects of individualism and collectivism across cultures. *Australian Journal of Psychology, 38,* 257–267.

Triandis, H., Bontempo, R., Villareal, M., Asai, M., & Lucca, N. (1988). Individualism and collectivism: Cross-cultural perspectives on self-ingroup relationships. *Journal of Personality and Social Psychology, 54,* 323–338.

Turner, J. C. (1987). *Rediscovering the social group.* London: Basil Blackwell.

CHAPTER 5

Psychocultural Influences on Communication

The psychocultural influences on our communication include our stereotypes of other cultures and ethnic groups and our intergroup attitudes, especially prejudice. Our stereotypes and intergroup attitudes create expectations for how strangers will behave. Our expectations involve our anticipations and predictions about how others will communicate with us. Understanding the expectations we have for strangers' behavior is critical to communicating effectively with strangers.

Our stereotypes result from our social categorizations. They are the "pictures" we have for the various social categories we use. Hewstone and Brown (1986) isolate three essential aspects of stereotypes:

1. Often individuals are categorized, usually on the basis of easily identifiable characteristics such as sex or ethnicity.
2. A set of attributes is ascribed to all (or most) members of that category. Individuals belonging to the stereotyped group are assumed to be similar to each other, and different from other groups, on this set of attributes.
3. The set of attributes is ascribed to any individual member of that category. (p. 29)

Stereotyping is a natural result of the communication process. We cannot not stereotype. Anytime we categorize others our stereotype of that category is activated.

One intergroup attitude, prejudice, is particularly important in creating expectations. Prejudice involves making a prejudgment based on membership in a category. Whereas prejudice can be positive or negative, there is a tendency for most of us to think of it as negative. Consistent with this view, Allport (1954) defined negative

133

ethnic prejudice as "an antipathy based on a faulty and unflexible generalization. It may be felt or expressed. It may be directed toward a group as a whole, or toward an individual because he [or she] is a member of that group" (p. 10).

We tend to think of prejudice in terms of a dichotomy; either I am prejudiced or I am not. It is more useful, however, to think of the strength of our prejudice as varying along a continuum from low to high. This suggests that we all are prejudiced to some degree. We also are all racist, sexist, agist, etc., to some degree. As with ethnocentrism, this is natural and unavoidable. It is the result of our being socialized as members of our ingroups. Even people with low levels of prejudice prefer to interact with people who are similar to themselves because such interactions are more comfortable and less stressful than interactions with strangers.

We also can think of prejudice as varying along a second continuum ranging from very positive to very negative. We tend to be positively prejudiced toward our ingroup and negatively prejudiced toward outgroups. It is possible, however, to be positively prejudiced toward outgroups and negatively prejudiced toward an ingroup. The positive or negative direction of our prejudice must be taken into consideration in trying to understand our reactions to violations of our expectations.

In today's society, it generally is not acceptable to make overt prejudiced comments in public. It may be acceptable within some ingroups, but in public talk people try to present themselves as "nonprejudiced." If we are going to make a negative comment about people who are different, we preface our comment with a claim of not being prejudiced.

The readings in this chapter are designed to help you understand how our expectations for strangers' behavior are created. In the first reading, Hamilton, Sherman, and Ruvolo discuss stereotypes and how they influence our behavior. More specific, they look at how stereotypes create expectations of strangers and how they will behave.

The second reading by Billig and his associates focuses on how our prejudice and tolerance are manifested in our communication. They illustrate the things we do in conversations to avoid looking prejudiced.

The final reading focuses on how we can change our expectations of strangers' behavior. Brewer and Miller discuss the conditions when our contact with strangers will lead to changes in our expectations.

REFERENCES

Allport G. (1954). *The nature of prejudice*. New York: Macmillan.

Hewstone, M., & Brown, R. (1986). Contact is not enough. In M. Hewstone & R. Brown (Eds.), *Contact and conflict in intergroup encounters*. Oxford: Blackwell.

Stereotype-Based Expectancies:
Effects on Information Processing and Social Behavior

David L. Hamilton, Steven J. Sherman, and Catherine M. Ruvolo

. . .

Juan Garcia, 23, was arrested Saturday night and charged with attempted murder following an incident outside the Big Dipper, a local pub. Garcia allegedly stabbed Frank Jordan, a 33-year-old construction worker, with a knife following a heated argument, inflicting a severe stomach wound. Although there were no eyewitnesses to the stabbing, patrons in the pub reported that Garcia and Jordan had begun arguing with each other at the pub, that the argument became more intense and a few punches were thrown, and that they were then seen leaving the bar together, yelling obscenities at each other. Later, following questioning at the scene by Lt. Thomas O'Reilly, Garcia and a police officer were seen shoving each other, after which Garcia was handcuffed and taken off in a squad car.

Observers of the incident described above—both casual bystanders at the pub and police officers whose task is to determine what happened—are faced with a complex situation. They all either see or subsequently learn about a sequence of behaviors whose meaning and causes are of considerable importance. Yet each of them has available only fragmentary information to use in determining what happened and why. Somehow this information must be used to construct (or reconstruct) an understanding of the events that transpired. Further complicating this task is the fact that one of the central participants, Juan Garcia, as an Hispanic, is a member of a group about whom many of the perceivers would hold stereotypic beliefs. Those beliefs may influence the way in which that "understanding" is (re)constructed and what new information is solicited.

This article is concerned with how perceivers use and seek information to develop an understanding of such incidents, and it focuses on the influence of stereotype-based expectancies on this process. We define a stereotype as a cognitive structure containing the perceiver's knowledge and beliefs about a social group and its members. As such, a stereotype is an important source of expectancies about what the group as a whole is like as well as about attributes that individual group members are likely to possess. The discussion examines the impact of these expectancies on processing information about and behavior toward members of stereotyped groups.

To address these issues, we adopt an information processing framework for understanding social perception. In this view, a number of cognitive processes influence observers' use of available information, and each of these processes may facilitate or impede achieving an accurate understanding of the persons and events to which that information pertains. For present purposes we can differentiate among three

Source: From *the Journal of Social Issues*, 1990, 46(2), 35–60.

categories of cognitive effects: (a) information acquisition and elaboration, (b) information seeking and hypothesis testing, and (c) behaviorial direction. The next three sections discuss these consequences of stereotype-based expectancies in detail. Each section summarizes relevant research findings to illustrate the variety of ways that such expectancies could affect perceptions of and decisions about Juan Garcia and the incident described at the outset. There is also discussion of how these consequences might be prevented or undermined. The final section then considers some more general implications of stereotypic expectancies, their functioning, and their consequences.

In adopting an information processing framework, we are assuming that the same general mechanisms underlie expectancy effects in most, if not all, contexts. Therefore the following analysis is not limited to any particular stereotype or stereotyped group, nor to any particular social problem or context. Adopting this approach does *not* assume that manifestations of expectancy effects will be the same in all contexts, but it *does* assume that differences between contexts are likely to be quantitative, rather than qualitative, in nature.

COGNITIVE CONFIRMATION
OF STEREOTYPIC EXPECTANCIES

As perceivers we actively contribute to the way we come to understand the persons and events that are the fabric of our social lives. The information available constitutes a springboard for a number of processes that embellish and add meaning to what we have seen or learned about those persons and events.

The perceiver's attention to the available information is necessarily selective. Properties both of the perceiver (e.g., momentary goals, generalized beliefs, current mood states) and of the information (e.g., importance for immediate goals, salience, self-relevance) can affect what the perceiver attends to. The information initially acquired then becomes the basis for several processes by which perceivers expand and elaborate their understanding of the meaning of persons and events. Thus, perceivers interpret the meaning of a target person's behaviors; they make inferences about people's abilities, motives, and personality attributes; they make causal attributions about why certain events occurred; and they react affectively to the persons and events they observe. All of these processes are subject to the influence of stereotype-based expectancies. These processes are of crucial importance in social perception because it is the information *as elaborated* in these ways that becomes represented in memory and hence available to guide the perceiver's subsequent judgments and behaviors.

As a consequence of the influence of stereotypes on these processes, the perceiver's mental representation of the available information can differ in significant ways from the actual information on which that representation is based. In many cases these discrepancies are of little import, for stereotypes, based on our accumulated social knowledge, are generally useful in helping us comprehend the often ambiguous and incomplete information we acquire in the course of social interaction. In other cases, however, the effects of stereotypes on these processes can result in more serious misconceptions and biases that may have undesirable consequences and ramifications. It is important, therefore, that we understand the mechanisms that underlie these potentially biasing effects, as well as the role that stereotype-based expectancies can play in their manifestation. Becasue of their importance in a number of social domains, the present article is focused on understanding the processes that mediate these adverse consequences of stereotypes.

Effects of Expectancies on Information Processing

Social behavior is often ambiguous. Much of what we learn about others is open to alternative interpretations. The person's motives, goals, and other internal states often are not clear; whether a particular behavior was freely chosen or enacted out of obligation frequently cannot be determined; and the situational constraints on the actor's [or actress's] behavior often are not apparent. Therefore the perceiver must impose some meaning on this information. Research has shown that stereotypic expectancies can affect perceivers' interpretations of such ambiguous occurrences. For example, both Duncan (1976) and Sagar and Schofield (1980) have shown that behaviors whose meanings are unclear (e.g., one person giving a mild shove to another during a heated discussion; one child poking another with a pencil) are more likely to be interpreted as aggressive when performed by a Black than by a White person. Similarly, Darley and Gross (1983) showed that socioeconomic class stereotypes influenced perceivers' interpretation of a girl's academic performance. Thus behaviors, as they are initially encoded, can take on different meaning as a result of the stereotypes the perceiver holds about the relevant social groups to which the actors belong.

This initial encoding, however, is only the beginning of the process by which the perceiver develops an understanding of the information being processed. That information then constitutes the basis for inferences, attributions, and evaluative reactions that give further meaning to the facts that have been acquired. And again, stereotypic expectancies can guide these processes. Once an individual's group membership is recognized, the relevant stereotype provides the basis for inferring additional "knowledge" of what else is likely to be true of the individual (Schneider & Blankmeyer, 1983), what was true of the person in the past (Snyder & Uranowitz, 1978), and what is likely to be true of the individual in the future (Bodenhausen & Wyer, 1985). These inferences, which many have strong evaluative overtones, would then become a part of the perceiver's cognitive representation of that person.

One particularly important social inference process is attribution, the perceiver's inference regarding the causal origin of an observed behavior. Attribution theories propose that the perceiver makes a fundamental distinction between whether the cause of a behavior resides within the actor [or actress] (personality attributes, attitudes, motivational goals) or reflects the influence of external constraints to which the actor responded. In many contexts the cause of an observed behavior is ambiguous, and here again stereotype-based expectancies have been shown to influence this inference (Bodenhausen, 1988; Deaux, 1976; Hewstone & Jaspers, 1982; Ugwuegbu, 1979).

Stereotypic expectancies can also affect the patterns that are perceived in the information available (Hamilton & Rose, 1980). In one study subjects read sentences describing members of occupational groups, each person being described by two personality traits, some of which were stereotypic of the groups. Each trait described members of each group equally often, so there were no empirical associations between traits and groups. Nevertheless, when subsequently asked to estimate how often each trait had described members of each group, subjects overestimated the frequency with which stereotypic traits had described members of the associated group. In another study, where the traits actually did describe some groups more often than others, subjects were more likely to detect the relationship if the trait-group association was stereotypic than if it was not. Expectancies, then, can influence not only the processing of individual pieces of information but also the associations that are perceived in the information that is acquired.

All of the expectancy-driven processes discussed above have one common element that is important for understanding the effect of stereotypes on information processing. Specifically, all of these processes are biased in the direction of maintaining the preexisting belief system, that is, the very sterotype that initiated these biasing mechanisms. These processes, then, can produce the *cognitive confirmation* of one's stereotypic beliefs. Although the actual information available may not confirm the stereotype, the observer's perceptual experience is consistent with those beliefs. Thus, returning to the scenario involving Juan Garcia, a patron at the bar who believes that Hispanics are aggressive might be more likely (a) to interpret Juan's pushing Frank aside as an aggressive act, (b) to evaluate Juan's behavior negatively, and (c) to assign primary causal responsibility for the incident to Juan, rather than Frank, even though the patron did not see how the incident began. These information processing mechanisms, then, can serve to perpetuate stereotypic beliefs even in the absence of confirmatory evidence.

Mediating Mechanisms

Although these findings clearly reflect biases based on preexisting stereotypes, it is important to understand the particular mechanisms underlying these effects. One possibility is that expectancies influence the perceiver's *interpretation* of the available information as it is encoded. Alternatively, expectancies may exert their influence primarily on the *retrieval* of information from memory, at the time judgments are made. Finally, it is possible that information consistent with expectancies is more extensively *processed* in some way(s), with the consequence that it is more likely to be retained (or more of it will be retained), and hence it will be available to affect subsequent judgments. Of course, all three effects may occur, but it is important to consider the research evidence relevant to each one.

The first mechanism focuses on the initial encoding of information. A concept (e.g., a stereotype), once activated, will be used to interpret new information that is acquired. We have already referred to studies indicating that stereotypic expectancies can bias the initial interpretation of ambiguous behavioral information (Darley &

Gross, 1983; Duncan, 1976; Sagar & Schofield, 1980). In addition, research on priming has shown that stereotypic concepts, once activated, can influence the interpretation of new information about a target person (Devine, 1989).

The second possible mechanism is that expectancies have a biasing effect on the retrieval of information from memory. There is actually a "family" of possible retrieval effects, three of which are briefly mentioned here. First, a stereotype that is activated at the time of retrieval may selectively guide the search for the retrieval of information from memory. This mechanism would produce biased recall of stereotype-consistent information. Thus, a witness to the bar incident may remember that Juan pushed Frank, but not recall that Frank pushed Juan first. Although expectancy manipulations introduced at the time of retrieval have been shown to produce results of this kind, typically these effects are either nonexistent or quite small, particularly in comparison to the magnitude of the same manipulation's effect when presented prior to the stimulus information (Bodenhausen, 1988; Zadny & Gerard, 1974). Second, memory may be subject to "reconstructive" processes such that information, as retrieved from memory at a later time, may be distorted and biased in the direction of the stereotype that is activated at the time. Although evidence for the reconstructive consequences of stereotype activation is limited, findings from related studies suggest that such effects need to be investigated (see Alba & Hasher, 1983; Ross & Conway, 1985). Third, with the passage of time, the perceiver may be unable to differentiate accurately information that was actually presented from stereotype-consistent inferences based on that information. This inability to distinguish between what is *known* to be true and what is *believed* to be true has been demonstrated in a stereotype-relevant context by Slusher and Anderson (1987). Thus, when later asked by police or by a lawyer in a trial proceeding, a witness might be genuinely convinced that he saw a knife in Juan's hand, when in fact he is now unable to recognize that this was an inference he made in mentally reconstructing the incident.

Evidence supporting the third mechanism—that expectancies influence the nature and extent of processing of expectancy-relevant information—is more plentiful, although not without its own ambiguities. This research has typically assessed subjects' recall for expectancy-relevant information as an indicator of its differential processing. A number of studies have shown that subjects recall expectancy-consistent information better than information irrelevant to the expectancy (Rothbart, Evans, & Fulero, 1979; Stangor & Ruble, 1989). If that information is better retained, and if it is retrieved and used at the time judgments are made, then those judgments would be biased in an expectancy-consistent direction.

Why would information consistent with a stereotype be more likely to be remembered? First, because it conforms to what the perceiver already believes to be true, expectancy-consistent information may be more "believable," and hence be given greater credibility as information worth retaining. Second, because it easily fits into an existing cognitive structure, it may trigger more inferences about the target person. If so, then the expectancy-consistent information would become associated in memory with other, inferred qualities that may subsequently provide additional retrieval cues.

There is, however, a body of evidence indicating that information that is inconsistent with a prior expectancy is recalled better than either expectancy-consistent or irrelevant information (Srull & Wyer, 1989). The explanation of this effect is that, because inconsistent information does not fit with the expectancy, the perceiver thinks about the inconsistent item in relation to what else is known about the person, thereby forming an elaborate network of associations involving the inconsistent item(s). Although the accumulated evidence provides considerable support for this view, recent findings also suggest limits to its applicability. For example, both the perceiver's processing goals (Srull, 1981) and the complexity of the stimulus information (Hamilton, Driscoll, & Worth, 1989) influence the occurrence of the effect. Moreover, the passage of time may actually reverse this effect, as subjects seek to bolster their initial expectancy (Wyer & Martin, 1986). Finally, and particularly relevant here, this inconsistency effect appears to be weaker (or nonexistent) when the expectancy pertains to a group rather than to an individual (Srull, Lichtenstein, & Rothbart, 1985; Stangor & Ruble, 1989).

Even if inconsistent information is recalled better, this does not mean that it will have a greater impact on judgments. Inconsistent information may be given extended processing (Hemsley & Marmurek, 1982) as the perceiver tries to explain the inconsistency (Hamilton, 1988; Hastie, 1984) but it may then be discounted or attributed to situational factors (Crocker, Hannah, & Weber, 1983). If so, then it would not be viewed as having important implications for one's perception of the actor, and hence would not strongly influence the perceiver's judgments. In addition, the differential recallability of certain kinds of information will affect judgments only when those judgments are based on information retrieved from memory at the time judgments are made. Many social judgments are made "on-line" as the information is acquired (Hastie & Park, 1986), and in these cases factors other than recallability (e.g., primacy effects) can have greater impact on judgments.

Do Stereotypes Influence Judgments of Individuals?

Stereotypes by definition pertain to groups. They are conceptions that summarize the attributes assumed to be most characteristic of a group as a whole. An important question, therefore, concerns the extent to which these group-level beliefs are applied to individual group members. Unfortunately, the answer to this question is not straightforward.

When the perceiver encounters an individual group member, two kinds of information are available for use in making judgments of that person—the perceiver's stereotype of the group to which the target person belongs, and specific "individuating" information about this particular target person. The question posed above concerns the relative importance of these two kinds of information for the perceiver's judgments. If stereotypes strongly affect perceptions of individual group members, then their effect on judgments would be general, pervasive, and relatively immune to change in the face of contradictory information concerning individual group members. In contrast, if judgments of individuals are driven by individuating information, then the consequences of stereotypes would be less severe and would be limited to perceptions of the group as an entirety (or to individuals about whom little individuating information was available). The research evidence at this point does not provide a thorough answer to the question, but it is clear that neither of these extreme positions is viable.

The issue was first investigated empirically by Mann (1967) and Brigham (1971), who found substantial discrepancies between the attributes subjects endorsed as describing a group and those they endorsed as describing individual members of the group. Locksley and her colleagues (Locksley, Hepburn, & Ortiz, 1982; Locksley, Borgida, Brekke, & Hepburn, 1980) argued that judgments of individuals are based primarily on individuating information, whereas stereotypes have relatively little impact on judgments of individuals and are influential only at the level of group perceptions. In one study subjects read descriptions of male and female target persons who engaged in assertive or nonassertive behavior, and then rated the person's overall assertiveness. Results showed that subjects' judgments were primarily determined by the nature of the target person's behavior, regardless of stereotypic expectancies based on gender. Thus, although females in general are perceived as less assertive than males, a woman who behaved assertively was rated as being as assertive as a man who performed the same behavior. Locksley et al. (1980) concluded that even "a *single* instance of moderately diagnostic behavioral information is sufficient to swamp the effects of social category information" (p. 830).

Subsequent research, however, has shown that the issue is more complex that Locksley et al.'s analysis would imply. Several factors appear to be relevant. First, the relative importance of the group and individual information will be a function of the diagnosticity of each for the judgment made. Locksley et al.'s experiments created conditions in which the group category (females) was only moderately diagnostic for the trait in question (assertiveness), but the behavioral information had high diagnosticity. Krueger and Rothbart (1988) showed that both group stereotypes and individual behavior information influenced judgments, and found that individuating information eliminated social category effects only when the former clearly conveyed stable, trait-like behavioral information.

Second, the complexity of the judgment task can affect one's use of stereotypes in making judgments (Bodenhausen & Lichtenstein, 1987; Bodenhausen & Wyer, 1985). Stereotypes had greater impact on judgments that required considering and weighing complex and diverse information (e.g., a verdict in a legal trial) than they did on trait inferences based on the same information. Reliance on stereotypes in making judgments thus serves as a heuristic strategy, facilitating the judgment process under complex and difficult conditions.

Third, the relation between the individuating information and the group stereotype also affects their relative influence. Fiske, Neuberg, Beattie, and Milberg (1987) have shown that stereotypes have more impact on judgments of a target person when the specific information describing that person is ambiguous, consistent with the stereotype, or uninformative. On the other hand, when the individuating information is inconsistent with stereotypic expectancies, judgments of the target person are more likely to be based on properties of that information.

In sum, the question is not *whether* stereotypes influence judgments of individuals, but rather *when* such effects are manifested. Recent theoretical models (Brewer, 1988; Fiske & Neuberg, 1990) offer potentially useful frameworks for investigating the complexities of this issue.

Undermining the Effects of Expectancies on Processing and Judgment

We have seen, then, that stereotypes operate as a source of expectancies about what a group as a whole is like (e.g., Hispanics) as well as about what attributes individual group members are likely to possess (e.g., Juan Garcia). Their influence can be pervasive, affecting the perceiver's attention to, encoding of, inferences about, and judgments based on that information. And the resulting interpretations, inferences, and judgments typically are made so as to be consistent with the preexisting beliefs that guided them. Are these expectancy effects invariant? Are we destined always to rely on the social categories we construct, so that information will always be slanted by the processing and judgmental biases discussed above? Will we always "see" what we already "believe"?

One of the benefits of an information processing analysis of stereotype effects is that it permits identification of the cognitive mechanisms that mediate their influence. In particular, if the mediating processes do not occur, then the stereotypic expectancy should not produce an effect. This knowledge may than permit us to (a) anticipate the conditions under which various effects are more and less likely to be manifested and (b) devise strategies for undermining these effects by affecting the necessary underlying mechanisms.

As noted earlier, in most contexts, the perceiver has available two kinds of information about a target person—information about the individual's attributes or behaviors, and information about that person's membership in some stereotyped group. Stereotypic expectancies are influential to the extent that information processing and judgments are based on the group membership information rather than on the individuating information. The implication, then, is that these effects can be reduced if greater importance is attached to the information pertaining specifically to the target person. For example, the biasing role of stereotypes in guiding attention to the interpretation of new information about target persons might be diminished if the perceiver's attention can be directed away from the target person's membership in a stereotyped group and focused instead on other information about the person. Similarly, if attributions were based on the evidence pertinent to the specific behavioral event in question, rather than on stereotype-based inference, the influence of these expectancies would be less evident. And if evaluative judgments were based on individuating information rather than on category memberships, then stereotypes would have less impact on social perceptions. In this view, then, efforts aimed at undermining the influence of stereotypic expectancies should focus on strategies for decreasing the salience of and reliance on the target person's group membership, and increasing the salience and perceived importance of specific information about the target person's attributes and behaviors.

EXPECTANCIES AS HYPOTHESES: EFFECTS ON INFORMATION SEEKING

The perceiver not only reacts to extant stimuli but also *elicits* information from others in order to test his or her beliefs and to evaluate their validity. The nature of that active information seeking is also subject to bias.

Stereotype-based expectancies operate as initial and tentative hypotheses that are then to be assessed—to be confirmed or disconfirmed in light of subsequent information. However, these hypotheses influence the information sought in order to test them. The questions that are asked, the inferences that one draws from answers to these questions, and the point at which one stops seeking further information are all influenced by the initial hypothesis. For example, in questioning Juan Garcia and the witnesses, Lt. O'Reilly may ask certain questions, or he may frame questions in one way rather than another. Similarly, lawyers during a trial may ask certain questions of Juan Garcia and the witnesses, depending on their initial hypotheses about what transpired, and depending on their goals. These hypotheses and goals are in part determined by the stereotypes that are held about Juan Garcia.

There is now a well-developed literature concerned with how stereotype-based expectancies may guide the information-gathering strategies that people employ as they test their initial hypotheses. This research provides evidence for certain biases in which, as hypotheses are tested, a preference is shown for seeking certain kinds of information while ignoring other kinds.

Diagnostic Questioning Strategy

Trope and his colleagues (Bassok & Trope, 1984; Trope & Bassok, 1982, 1983) suggest that people test their hypotheses by asking the most diagnostic questions about events—that is, questions for which the answer will be most likely to distinguish between the truth or falsity of the hypothesis. In other words, this view holds that the initial hypothesis or expectancy does *not* bias information seeking. Thus, whether one's initial hypothesis is that Juan Garcia is innocent or guilty, the same questions will be asked of Juan and of witnesses, and these questions will be the ones that are most diagnostic of Juan's guilt or innocence.

Hypothesis-Confirmation Strategies

Despite this focus on diagnostic information, information seekers have an additional tendency to seek hypothesis-confirming information—a bias that can lead to erroneous conclusions about the truth value of the hypothesis. Such a bias is important when hypotheses are based on stereotypes because it can serve as a basis for the maintenance of stereotypic beliefs. In fact, when hypotheses have a motivational basis (as may often be true for stereotypic beliefs), hypothesis-confirmation strategies are more likely (Kunda, 1989).

The most widely cited evidence for the use of hypothesis-confirmation strategies comes from a study by Snyder and Swann (1978b). Their subjects were asked to test a hypothesis about the personality characteristics of a target person (e.g., is he [or she] an introvert?). Subjects were allowed to choose from a list of questions in order to assess the truth value of the hypothesis. There was a strong tendency for subjects to search for evidence that would confirm the hypothesis in question. For example, when testing an extravert hypothesis, subjects chose questions such as "What would you do if you wanted to liven things up at a party?" When testing an introvert hypothesis, subjects chose such questions as "What do you dislike about loud parties?" Thus, subjects asked questions that assumed the truth value of the hypothesis being tested.

Because of hypothesis-confirmatory strategies (see Klayman & Ha, 1987; Skov & Sherman, 1986), people often ask questions where the overall likelihood of a "yes" answer under the hypothesis is high and where the conclusion to be drawn from this "yes" answer is that the hypothesis is supported. Consider, for example, trying to determine whether Juan Garcia is, in general, an aggressive man (character information relevant to the trial). The questioner holds an initial hypothesis that Juan is aggressive and is thus likely to ask a question for which a large majority of aggressive people would answer "yes" (say 90%) and for which a moderate number of nonaggressive people (say 50%) would also answer "yes." Such a question might be "Have you ever felt so angry that you wanted to punch someone?" Assume, for the sake of simplicity, that there are an equal number of aggressive and nonaggressive people in the world. Given this assumption, the overall likelihood of getting a "yes" answer from a randomly chosen person in the population is very high (70%). Moreover, a "yes" answer will serve as support for aggressiveness, and thus such support will occur far more frequently than will support for a conclusion of nonaggressiveness. The bias in choice of questions (due to the preexisting hypothesis) affects the likelihood of obtaining supportive evidence.

It thus appears that hypothesis-confirmation strategies are used in choosing questions in order to verify hypotheses. In questioning Juan Garcia and the witnesses, the police *want* accurate information in order to arrive at a correct and unbiased conclusion. They should, then, adopt a diagnosing strategy—one where the best possible information is obtained. However, the research evidence indicates that an initially held hypothesis—in this case, initial expectancies based on stereotypes—may well bias the questions that are asked (and thus the conclusions that are drawn). An "innocent until proven guilty" initial expectancy will lead to a very different line of questioning than will a "probably guilty" expectancy.

If accurate information would be most useful, why would hypothesis-confirmation strategies be employed? Several reasons, both motivational and non-motivational in nature, can be offered. As an example of the latter, questions about the hypothesis may simply be easier to process than questions about the alternative, and questions where a "yes" answer confirms the hypothesis are easier to process than questions where a "no" answer confirms the hypothesis (Clark & Chase, 1972). Another possibility is that holding an expectancy makes information that would be true under that expectancy more accessible. This differential accessibility of hypothesis-consistent information could underlie hypothesis-confirmatory strategies.

An additional reason for hypothesis-confirmation strategies is motivational in nature. Hypotheses may operate like wishes (Kunda, 1989). We adopt many hypotheses and hold many expectancies (e.g., a healthy life, a successful career) because we want them to be true. We also want to believe that they *are* true. In testing our hypotheses, therefore, one kind of error (false rejection of the desired hypothesis) is more costly than the other kind of error (false acceptance of the alternative). By asking questions that are very likely to get a "yes" answer under the hypothesis and where a "yes" answer would confirm this hypothesis (or questions that are very likely to get a "no" answer under the hypothesis and where a "no" answer would confirm the hypothesis), subjects ensure that they will falsely accept the hypothesis more often than they will falsely rejct it. The wish to believe in the hypothesis is thus fulfilled. Because many hypotheses and expectations develop out of wishes, the confirmatory strategies they foster may generalize to *all* initial hypotheses (even those in which there is little personal investment). That is, we may adopt hypothesis-confirming strategies as a general principle for hypothesis testing.

Misleading Questions

There is another way in which stereotype-based expectancies may introduce biases into the question asking process. These expectancies may lead to assumptions that find their way into questions that indicate the truth value of the assumptions. For example, a policeman might assume that Juan Garcia is violent. He might ask Juan "What did you do after the feeling of violence overtook you?" Such misleading questions can affect the inferences of listeners (e.g., jurors) and can even affect the memories of actual witnesses. In one study (Loftus, 1975) witnesses saw slides of an automobile accident during which a car went past a "Yield" sign. Some subjects were asked "How fast was the car going when it ran the 'Stop' sign?" Later, these subjects actually (mis)remembered that they saw the car go through a "Stop" sign. More subtle misleading questions can cause inaccurate memory for important events during a crime. According to Loftus and Greene (1980), the misleading information actually replaces the original information in memory so that witnesses are quite confident that they are reporting the events accurately.

Similarly, the wording of questions can lead witnesses to reconstruct their memories for events, and the wording of questions is often guided by the particular initial hypothesis that is held. Loftus and Palmer (1974) asked some subjects "About how fast were the cars going when they smashed into each other?" Other subjects were asked "About how fast were the cars going when they bumped into each other?" The former subjects judged the speed of the cars to be significantly greater, and they later (mis)remembered having seen broken glass during the accident. Thus, a question to Juan Garcia about where he was standing when he smashed the victim in the face (as opposed to slapped the victim in the face) would leave jurors, and even witnesses themselves, with quite different representations and memories of the events. And, of course, these different representations could have effects on later judgments.

Conclusions Drawn from the Answers to Questions

We have seen how initial hypotheses and expectations can lead to biases in information seeking. Does such a bias in question *asking* necessarily lead to errors of *inference* once the answers to the questions are ascertained? Not always. For example, preferring to ask questions where a "yes" answer confirms a hypothesis over questions where a "no" answer confirms the hypothesis in no way ensures perceived confirmation of the hypothesis. A "no" answer to the former type of question should disconfirm the hypothesis just as well as a "yes" answer will confirm it.

Some strategies will, however, necessarily lead to errors of inference. Asking only questions where it is known a priori that confirmation is likely, and avoiding questions where rejection of the hypothesis is likely, will obviously lead to a false belief in the hypothesis. Likewise, asking questions where anyone's answer would confirm the hypothesis will also lead to perceived confirmation. Snyder and Swann's (1978b) question about "What would you do to liven up a party?" is such a question. Both introverts and extraverts will answer this question in a way that will make them appear extraverted, and thus the extravert hypothesis will be perceived as confirmed.

Sometimes a bias in question asking that need not lead to faulty perceptions of hypothesis confirmation does have this effect because of people's judgmental inadequacies. For example, people prefer to ask questions where the likelihood of a "yes" answer under the hypothesis is higher than the likelihood of a "yes" answer under the alternative, and where the overall likelihood of a "yes" answer is high (Skov & Sherman, 1986). Thus, given a hypothesis of honesty, people prefer to ask questions where 90% of honest people would say "yes" and only 50% of dishonest people would say "yes" (whereas equally diagnostic questions where 50% of honest people and 90% of dishonest people would say "yes" are avoided). In this case, the likelihood of a "yes" answer is high (70% overall), and inferences of honesty (from "yes" answers) will be more frequent than inferences of dishonesty (from "no" answers). However, although the likelihood of an answer indicative of honesty is high, these inferences of honesty should be held with little confidence. Because of their frequency, "yes" answers are rather undiagnostic of honesty. On the other hand, although the likelihood of a "no" answer (an indication of dishonesty) is low, the inference of dishonesty in this case should be made with high certainty—"no" is a highly diagnostic answer to the question. However, research has shown that people are quite insensitive to differences in the diagnostic value of the answers to questions (Slowiaczek, Klayman, Sherman,

& Skov, 1989). In the above example they are just as confident of honesty given a "yes" answer as they are of dishonesty given a "no" answer. Thus, the bias in question asking, combined with an insensitivity to the diagnostic value of the answers to the questions, almost ensures that this strategy of information seeking will lead to a perception that the initial hypothesis is supported.

Stopping Information Seeking: When Do We Have Enough Evidence?

Information seeking is instigated in order to test initial hypotheses and either to confirm or disconfirm them. However, at some point this information seeking must stop so that decisions can be made—decisions about whether or not to hire someone, whether someone is an introvert or an extravert, or whether someone is innocent or guilty of a crime. As with the initiation and the direction of question asking, the cessation of information seeking is also influenced by initial expectancies. People seem willing to stop seeking information sooner when indications are in favor of hypothesis confirmation than when there is equivalently diagnostic information that is opposed to the initial hypothesis. It is as though the initial expectancy has a decided advantage that must be overcome by additional evidence before abandoning it (Van Wallendael, 1988). In the case of Juan Garcia, for example, the police may have stopped asking questions of Juan and of the witnesses relatively quickly and concluded that he should be arrested—as soon as the evidence tilted in favor of his guilt, their working hypothesis. For a different suspect presumed by the police to be innocent, initial information suggesting guilt might not lead to such quick cessation of questioning. Instead, additional information might be sought until the balance of evidence tilted toward innocence (the initial working hypothesis), at which point questioning would be stopped.

Undermining Information Seeking Effects

We have seen how stereotype-based expectancies operate as initial working hypotheses and bias the question-asking process, the conclusions that are drawn from the questions asked, and the point at which information seeking stops. Given our current understanding of these biases, it becomes important to ask what can be done in order to reduce or eliminate them. How can we prevent stereotype-based expectancies from biasing the information-gathering process?

In the past several years, scientists working in the judgment and decision-making area have become increasingly aware of the limitations of human decision making and of the biases and errors that pervade the decision-making process. These realizations have been coupled with suggestions about how to eliminate or reduce these errors and biases (Nisbett, Krantz, Jepson, & Fong, 1982; Paulos, 1988). The best solution seems to be better education. Our current educational system at the high school and college levels is woefully lacking in courses that discuss judgment and decision making. Nisbett et al. (1982) suggest programs in which simple probabilistic models and statistical heuristics will be incorporated into everyday reasoning. With regard to information-gathering strategies, an understanding of several simple rules would go a long way toward reducing errors and biases. "Consider the alternatives and not just the hypotheses" and "Use both stereotype (base-rate) and individuating information" are two examples. Finally, the very understanding of how expectations guide the information-seeking process and how expectancies can become reality (both perceived and actual) would constitute important steps in improving human judgment and decision making.

BEHAVIORAL CONFIRMATION
OF STEREOTYPIC EXPECTANCIES

Besides their effects on information processing and information seeking, expectancies also affect social interaction—both the behavior of the person holding the expectancy and the behavior of the target of the expectancy. This section focuses on the behavioral ramifications of social expectancies. . . .

As Thomas and Thomas (1928, p. 572) stated, "If men [or women] define situations as real, they are real in their consequences." That is, a person's belief can cause reality to conform to that belief. The belief becomes a "self-fulfilling prophecy"—an expectancy for which behavioral confirmation by the target is induced through the actions of the perceiver. By definition, in order for an expectancy to be self-fulfilling, it must induce expectancy-confirming behavior from the target person.

Snyder, Tanke, and Berscheid (1977) demonstrated how a stereotype-induced expectancy can elicit expectancy-confirming behavior. Male subjects were shown a photograph of an attractive or unattractive female with whom they presumably would interact. This manipulation activated subjects' beliefs about their partners' sociability (Berscheid & Walster, 1974). Each male subject then conversed with a randomly assigned female partner on a telephone, and the interaction was tape-recorded. Subjects who thought they were interacting with attractive women were themselves more outgoing and friendly as they talked with their partners. This in turn elicited more friendly responses from their female interactants. Thus, expectancies based on the attractiveness stereotype affected the perceiver's behavior, which then influenced the target's behavior.

Earlier we discussed how an expectancy can bias the way social information is interpreted. It is important to note, however, that in Snyder et al.'s (1977) study the targets' sociability was rated differently *not* because of perceptual biases but because of actual behavioral differences. The tape recordings of the interactions were rated by naive, unbiased judges who detected differences in the targets' sociability: target persons whom their male partners believed to be attractive were in fact more friendly and sociable. This, then, is a true self-fulfilling prophecy: the target person's behavior provided actual behavioral confirmation of the expectancy.

Perceivers can influence a person with whom they interact by constraining the person's behaviors. However, perceivers typically do not recognize this influence or take it into consideration when interpreting the target's behavior. Although a target person's behavior may be affected by perceiver-induced constraints, it is often interpreted by the perceiver as a manifestation of the target's personality (Gilbert & Jones, 1986; Jones, 1979).

The Self-Fulfilling Prophecy Process

Although various authors have identified different stages in this social interaction sequence (Darley & Fazio, 1986; Jones, 1986; Jussim, 1986), all agree that three major steps are necessary for an expectancy to be self-fulfilling. First, an expectancy must be activated. As discussed earlier, one important source of expectancies is stereotypes about social groups. Thus, any time a target person is perceived to be a member of a stereotyped group, the perceiver's stereotype-based expectancies about that group can be of potential influence.

Second, the activation of this stereotype must affect how the perceiver will act toward the target (Rubovits & Maehr, 1973; Snyder et al., 1977; Word, Zanna, & Cooper, 1974). In the scenario involving Juan Garcia, the police officer first on the scene sees a Hispanic man. If the officer holds a stereotypic belief that Hispanics are prone to violence, he [or she] might then approach Juan accordingly, for example, with his [or her] billy club raised. Thus the stereotype of Hispanics being aggressive could affect the officer's behavior.

Word et al. (1974) demonstrated the effect of racial stereotypes on perceivers' behavior. White subjects interacted with both Black and White confederates in a simulated job interview. When interviewing Blacks, subjects emitted a pattern of nonverbal cues conveying negative evaluation that they did not emit to the White confederates: they conducted shorter interviews, maintained less eye contact, and had higher rates of speech errors with the Black interviewees. Because the confederate interviewees were trained to behave in a uniform manner, the differences in perceivers' behavior toward the Black and White confederates were due only to the perceivers' stereotype-based expectancies. Similar effects have been reported by others (e.g., Jones & Panitch, 1971; Neuberg, 1989).

Given that an expectancy affects the perceiver's behavior toward the target person, the third step in the self-fulfilling process is the effect of the perceiver's behavior on the target's behavior. Returning to the initial example, suppose that Juan, on seeing a police officer approaching with billy club poised, clenches his fists in preparation for an anticipated aggressive act on the part of the officer. By expecting aggressiveness, the officer has "caused" an aggressive reaction and, as a consequence, Juan's behavior becomes consistent with the officer's prior beliefs.

What empirical evidence do we have for this effect on the target's behavior? In a second study conducted by Word et al. (1974), confederates were trained to use the two different interview styles that subjects had manifested in the first study. The first style was the manner in which subjects interviewed Black confederates, conveying nonverbally a negative evaluation (short interview length, little eye contact, and more speech disfluencies). The second style was the way in which subjects interviewed White confederates (expressing a positive evaluation by increased interview length, more eye contact, and fewer speech errors). Word et al. (1974) found that subjects who were interviewed by a confederate using the negative interview style actually performed less well in the interview (as rated by independent judges). Thus the positive or negative interview style produced actual differences in interviewee performance. This effect on the target person's behavior has been shown in a number of other experiments (e.g., Neuberg, 1989; Snyder et al., 1977; Snyder & Swann, 1978a).

The three steps just described, although a simplification, capture the essential aspects of the self-fulfilling prophecy process. The effects of expectancies on behavior can be very subtle. For example, as shown in Snyder et al.'s (1977) study, face-to-face interaction is not required for behavioral confirmation to occur. Moreover, expectancy-confirming behavior can be elicited nonverbally through the perceivers' body position, eye contact, and speech characteristics (Neuberg, 1989; Word et al., 1974).

It is important to recognize that the terms "perceiver" and "target" are arbitrarily assigned; each interactant is both a perceiver of the other and a target of the other's expectancies. Taken to the extreme, we can imagine an interaction in which each person "becomes" what the other expects of him or her. Because each person in an interaction is a perceiver, each has the ability to "create" the behavior that he or she expects from the other. However, each person is also the target of the other's expectancies, and his or her behavior will be affected by the expectancies held by the other. Thus, two people can interact in such a way as to bring to reality the mental image that each one has of the other.

Beyond the Initial Interaction

Not only can an expectancy affect the behavior of both the perceiver and the target in a social interaction, but the consequences of the self-fulfilling prophecy can extend beyond that interaction setting itself. For example, in Snyder and Swann's (1978a) study, perceivers' beliefs that their partners were hostile induced greater hostility from the target persons—a self-fulfilling prophecy. In addition, these targets, when led to believe that their hostility was a function of their personality and not the situation, acted in a hostile manner when interacting with new, unbiased perceivers. The effect of the first perceiver's expectancy remained strong enough to affect the target's subsequent interactions.

In addition to a target person's behavior being molded by a perceiver's expectancy, his or her self-concept may also be affected. In an experiment by Fazio, Effrein, and Falender (1981), subjects were interviewed in a biased manner that made them appear either introverted or extraverted. Following the interview, subjects' self-descriptions corresponded to the way they were induced to perform in the interview. Subjects who were led to appear introverted rated themselves more introverted, whereas subjects induced to appear extraverted rated themselves more extraverted. Thus a perceiver's expectancy can affect not only the behavior of a target person but also the target's own self-perception.

The consequences of the self-fulfilling prophecy for the perceiver can extend beyond the initial setting as well. Following the behavioral confirmation of an expectancy, a perceiver is likely to subscribe to his or her beliefs even more strongly. The perceiver not only believes that the expectancy about the target person is correct, but also may regard this "confirmation" as "evidence" that the stereotype about the target person's social group is accurate as well. In this light, the self-fulfilling prophecy may contribute to the persistence of social stereotypes and the difficulty of dispelling them. This possibility is suggested by a study (Swann & Snyder, 1980) in which perceivers were instructed to teach a card trick to another person, who was labeled as either high or low in ability. Although the low-ability targets actually outperformed the high-ability targets (due to teachers' increased effort), the perceivers rated the high-ability targets as more successful. Thus the perceiver's expectancy about the target person, rather than the actual performance, determined the perceiver's rating. This finding, of course, does not mean that perceivers are oblivious to the behavior of persons with whom they interact (Jussim, 1989). It does, however, demonstrate the potentially powerful ramifications of perceiver expectancies.

Undermining the Self-Fulfilling Prophecy

Although the effects of expectancies can permeate many aspects of social information processing and interaction, they are not inevitable. Recent research has identified factors that can undermine this process. . . .

Research has investigated both target variables and perceiver variables that can influence whether an expectancy will lead to behavioral confirmation. For example, targets with a high degree of certainty in their self-concept were not influenced by a perceiver's expectancies about them (Swann & Ely, 1984), and targets who were made aware of a perceiver's negative expectancy were successful in modifying the perceiver's perceptions of them on that attribute (Hilton & Darley, 1985). Similarly, if the perceiver anticipates working with the target person (Darley, Fleming, Hilton, & Swann, 1988) or is motivated to form an accurate impression of the target (Neuberg, 1989), an initial expectancy has less directive effect on the perceiver's behavior, decreasing the likelihood of confirmatory behavior from the target. In other circumstances the perceiver may be motivated to avoid expectancy confirmation. For example, one who perceives a target person as hostile or temperamental might behave in a calm and friendly manner so as to avoid the target's manifesting the perceived qualities. Thus, the perceiver's goals in the interaction context can interact with expectancies in determining whether a self-fulfilling outcome will occur.

STEREOTYPE-BASED EXPECTANCIES: SOME CONCLUDING THOUGHTS

Like other cognitive structures we develop as a product of our experiences, stereotypes are cognitive categories that contain our accumulated knowledge, beliefs, and expectancies about particular social groups (Hamilton & Trolier, 1986). And like other cognitive structures, one of the most important functions of these categories is that they permit us to expand on our current knowledge in a variety of ways. As described above, stereotype-based expectancies can influence the way we process the information we receive, seek additional information, and guide our behavioral interactions with others. These processes have important functional value as we adapt to our social world. In addition, however, they present the potential for bias and hence the opportunity for error. And there's the rub.

The stereotypes we develop about social groups are belief systems that evolve through a variety of processes. They are the product of what we learned in our early years, they reflect the values of our peer groups and our culture, and they incorporate the knowledge we have acquired and the beliefs we have formed through our own experiences. In this sense they are cognitive constructions. To the extent that what we have learned and experienced and inferred about a particular group is representative of the group and its members, the resulting stereotype will reflect the predominant characteristics of the group. In this sense the stereotype may be, to some degree at least, an accurate characterization of the group. Any such accuracy, of course, would be limited to statements about the group as a whole, as group-level characterizations cannot be equally accurate of all individuals who comprise the group. Moreover, to the extent that cognitive and/or motivational biases enter into the development of stereotypic beliefs, that stereotype will be, at least partially, an inaccurate representation of the information on which it is based. And if that stereotype then influences judgments of the group as a whole, or of individual group members, then those judgments will be vulnerable to inaccuracy.

Expectancy effects will not inevitably result in inaccuracies in judgment and representation; stereotypic "knowledge" may reflect the actual predominant characteristics of a group. However, to the extent that the stereotype provides an inappropriate characterization of the group, and to the extent that it is indiscriminantly applied to individual group members, then these expectancy effects can result in inaccurate judgments and potentially discriminatory behaviors. Moreover, stereotypic beliefs may achieve some degree of accuracy because they bring about expectancy-consistent behavior. For instance, if parents and teachers subscribe to the belief that women are poor in mathematics, their behavior may in fact create that reality and then maintain it. Thus the belief reflects the truth, but it is not a necessary truth, and therein lies the insidious nature of stereotypes. In this sense, achieving "accuracy" may not be an ultimate virtue. Finally, as a consequence of the processes discussed in this article, group members will be perceived as sharing important attributes in common, and the stereotype holder will therefore tend to behave in the same manner toward various group members. To the extent that stereotyped-based expectancies bring about such uniformity in both perception and behavior, they can also impose constraints on opportunities for change.

One particularly important characteristic of the processes and biases discussed above is their confirmatory nature. In virtually all cases these processes serve to maintain the status quo. That is, they preserve the beliefs or expectancies that generated the effects. To the extent that stereotypes are simplified, overgeneralized, and/or inaccurate characterizations of these groups, then this aspect of expectancy effects takes on serious ramifications. This confirmatory property of expectancy-based effects would contribute to the persistence of stereotypes, the conviction with which they are held, and their resistance to change.

Given these adverse consequences of stereotypic expectancies, a variety of important questions arise concerning their role in specific social contexts as well as what can be done to prevent or to diminish these effects. Thus, for example, one might wonder if stereotypic expectancies would have more or less influence in a trial proceeding than they would in a job interview, or a teacher-student interaction, or a therapist-client relationship. If stereotypes have differential impact in these situations, why? Within any given context, what factors determine whether expectancies will have large or small effects on various outcome measures? And what steps can be taken to undermine or reduce the adverse effects of stereotypes on social judgments and interactions? Earlier sections of this article considered efforts for undermining specific mechanisms involved in expectancy effects. Here we consider more general questions concerning strategies for limiting these effects.

The questions raised above are important, and social science research will ultimately need to provide answers to them. One approach to answering them would be to investigate, within a given context, those factors that govern the manifestation of expectancy effects. Such research can be effective in devising strategies that, if implemented, might moderate the effects of stereotypes on the outcomes of central importance in that domain. In contrast, the research discussed in this article reflects an alternative approach, one that seeks to understand the processes by which expectancy effects come about and exert their influence. Identifying these underlying mechanism would then aid in understanding the social conditions that are likely to spawn or to inhibit the consequences of stereotypic expectancies, as well as in formulating strategies for undermining those effects.

Although this approach has not focused on developing specific policies or interventions to this end, the research evidence does suggest certain guidelines that would be important in developing such programs. These guidelines would include the following:

1. Stereotypic expectancies are more likely to be influential when stimulus cues to group membership are salient. Attention to such cues can increase categorization of others into stereotyped groups and can result in differential perceptions of "token" minorities within a group. To the extent that the salience of group

membership cues is reduced, and the salience of other types of stimulus information is enhanced, the effect of stereotypes on social perceptions will be reduced.

2. Sterotypic expectancies are more likely to be influential in the absence of individuating information about the target person. To the extent that target-specific information can be provided and made salient, the effect of stereotypes on information processing and judgment will be reduced.

3. Stereotypic expectancies are more likely to be influential when the individuating information about a target person is ambiguous and open to interpretation. To the extent that such information can be made specific, clear, and unambiguous, the effect of stereotypes on information processing and judgment will be reduced.

4. Stereotypic expectancies are more likely to be influential when information about a target person is sought rather than given. Stereotypes can bias the perceiver's attention to and recruitment of expectancy-confirming information about group members. To the extent that an unbiased pattern of information about the target person is provided and attention to that information is assured, the effect of stereotypes on selective information seeking will be reduced.

5. Stereotypic expectancies are more likely to be influential when the behavior of the stereotype holder is unconstrained. Stereotypes can be expressed in a variety of ways—in overt statements reflecting opinions and evaluations, in the kinds of questions asked of a target person, and in the nonverbal behavior displayed in the target person's presence. These expressions are less likely to occur when behavior is constrained either by social norms (e.g., when there are sanctions against expressions of stereotypic beliefs) or by structural aspects of the situation (e.g., when interviewers are trained to follow a prescribed procedure). To the extent that the behavior of the stereotype holder is constrained in nonbiasing ways, the effects of stereotypes on interpersonal behavior will be reduced.

One general principle can be seen as underlying these guidelines. Specifically, to the extent that the social context can be arranged such that diagnostic individuating information can be both provided and utilized, the effects of stereotypes on social perception and behavior will be diminished. Thus, although the information processing approach focuses on investigating the processes and mechanisms underlying the manifestation of stereotypes, the results of that research can be used to deduce some potentially useful principles for preventing or circumscribing those manifestations.

REFERENCES

Alba, J. W., & Hasher, L. (1983). Is memory schematic? *Psychological Bulletin*, 93, 203–231.

Bassok, M., & Trope, Y. (1984). People's strategies for testing hypotheses about another's personality: Confirmatory or diagnostic? *Social Cognition*, 2, 199–216.

Berscheid, E., & Walster, E. (1974). Physical attractiveness. In L. Berkowitz (Ed.), *Advances in experimental social psychology* (Vol. 7, pp. 157–215). New York: Academic Press.

Bodenhausen, G. V. (1988). Stereotypic biases in social decision making and memory: Testing process models of stereotype use. *Journal of Personality and Social Psychology*, 55, 726–737.

Bodenhausen, G. V., & Lichtenstein, M. (1987). Social stereotypes and information process-ing strategies: The impact of task complexity. *Journal of Personality and Social Psychology*, 52, 871-880.

Bodenhausen, G. V., & Wyer, R. S., Jr. (1985). Effects of stereotypes on decision making and information-processing strategies. *Journal of Personality and Social Psychology*, 48, 267-282.

Brewer, M. B. (1988). A dual process model of impression information. In T. K. Srull & R. S. Wyer, Jr. (Eds.), *Advances in Social Cognition* (Vol. 1, pp. 1-36). Hillsdale, NJ: Erlbaum.

Brigham, J. C. (1971). Ethnic stereotypes. *Psychological Bulletin*, 76, 15-33.

Clark, H. H., & Chase, W. G. (1972). On the process of comparing sentences against pictures. *Cognitive Psychology*, 3, 472-517.

Crocker, J., Hannah, D. B., & Weber, R. (1983). Person memory and causal attributions. *Journal of Personality and Social Psychology*, 44, 55-66.

Darley, J. M., & Fazio, R. H. (1980). Expectancy confirmation processes arising in the social interaction sequence. *American Psychologist*, 35, 867-881.

Darley, J. M., Fleming, J. H., Hilton, J. L., & Swann, W. B., Jr. (1988). Dispelling negative expectancies: The impact of interaction goals and target characteristics on the expec-tancy confirmation process. *Journal of Experimental Social Psychology*, 24, 19-36.

Darley, J. M., & Gross, P. H. (1983). A hypothesis-confirming bias in labeling effects. *Journal of Personality and Social Psychology*, 44, 20-33.

Deaux, K. (1976). Sex: A perspective on the attribution process. In J. H. Harvey, W. J. Ickes, & R. F. Kidd (Eds.), *New directions in attribution research* (Vol. 1, pp. 335-352). Hillsdale, NJ: Erlbaum.

Devine, P. G. (1989). Stereotypes and prejudice: Their automatic and controlled components. *Journal of Personality and Social Psychology*, 56, 5-18.

Duncan, B. L. (1976). Differential social perception and attribution of intergroup violence: Testing the lower limits of stereotyping of Blacks. *Journal of Personality and Social Psychology*, 34, 590-598.

Fazio, R. H., Effrein, E. A., & Falender, V. J. (1981). Self-perceptions following social interaction. *Journal of Personality and Social Psychology*, 41, 232-242.

Fiske, S. T., & Neuberg, S. (1990). A continuum model of impression formation: From category-based to individuating processes as a function of information, motivation, and attention. In M. P. Zanna (Eds.), *Advances in experimental social psychology* (Vol. 23, pp. 1-74). New York: Academic Press.

Fiske, S. T., Neuberg, S. L., Beattie, A. E., & Milberg, S. J. (1987). Category-based and attribute-based reactions to others: Some informational conditions of stereotyping and individuating processes. *Journal of Experimental Social Psychology*, 23, 399-427.

Gilbert, D. T., & Jones, E. E. (1986). Perceiver-induced constraint: Interpretations of self-generated reality. *Journal of Personality and Social Psychology*, 50, 269-280.

Hamilton, D. L. (1988). Causal attribution viewed from an information processing perspective. In D. Bar-Tal & A. W. Kruglanski (Eds.), *The social psychology of knowledge* (pp. 359-385). Cambridge, England: Cambridge University Press.

Hamilton, D. L., Driscoll, D. M., & Worth, L. T. (1989). Cognitive organization of impres-sions: Effects of incongruency in complex representations. *Journal of Personality and Social Psychology*, 57, 925-938.

Hamilton, D. L., & Rose, T. L. (1980). Illusory correlation and the maintenance of stereotypic beliefs. *Journal of Personality and Social Psychology*, 39, 832-845.

Hamilton, D. L., & Trolier, T. K. (1986). Stereotypes and stereotyping: An overview of the cognitive approach. In J. Dovidio & S. L. Gaertner (Eds.), *Prejudice, discrimination, and racism* (pp. 127–163). New York: Academic Press.

Hastie, R. (1984). Causes and effects of causal attribution. *Journal of Personality and Social Psychology, 46,* 44–56.

Hastie, R., & Park B. (1986). The relationship between memory and judgment depends on whether the judgment task is memory-based or on-line. *Psychological Review, 93,* 258–268.

Hemsley, G. D., & Marmurek, H. H. C. (1982). Person memory: The processing of consistent and inconsistent person information. *Personality and Social Psychology Bulletin, 8,* 433–438.

Hewstone, M., & Jaspars, J. M. F. (1982). Intergroup relations and attribution processes. In H. Tajfel (Ed.), *Social identity and intergroup relations* (pp. 99–133). Cambridge, England: Cambridge University Press.

Hilton, J. L., & Darley, J. M. (1985). Constructing other persons: A limit on the effect. *Journal of Experimental Social Psychology, 21,* 1–18.

Jones, E. E. (1979). The rocky road from acts to dispositions. *American Psychologist, 34,* 107–117.

Jones, E. E. (1986). Interpreting interpersonal behavior: The effects of expectancies. *Science, 234,* 41–46.

Jones, S. C., & Panitch, D. (1971). The self-fulfilling prophecy and interpersonal attraction. *Journal of Experimental Social Psychology, 7,* 356–366.

Jussim, L. (1986). Self-fulfilling prophecies: A theoretical and integrative review. *Psychological Review, 93,* 429–445.

Jussim, L. (1989). Teacher expectations: Self-fulfilling prophecies, perceptual biases, and accuracy. *Journal of Personality and Social Psychology, 57,* 469–480.

Klayman, J., & Ha, Y. W. (1987). Confirmation, disconfirmation, and information in hypothesis-testing. *Psychological Review, 94,* 211–228.

Krueger, J., & Rothbart, M. (1988). The use of categorical and individuating information in making inferences about personality. *Journal of Personality and Social Psychology, 55,* 187–195.

Kunda, Z. (1989). *The case for motivated reasoning.* Unpublished manuscript, Princeton University.

Locksley, A., Borgida, E., Brekke, N., & Hepburn, C. (1980). Sex stereotypes and social judgment. *Journal of Personality and Social Psychology, 39,* 821–831.

Locksley, A., Hepburn, C., & Ortiz, V. (1982). Social stereotypes and judgments of individuals: An instance of the base-rate fallacy. *Journal of Experimental Social Psychology, 18,* 23–42.

Loftus, E. F. (1975). Leading questions and the eyewitness report. *Cognitive Psychology, 7,* 560–572.

Loftus, E. F., & Greene, E. (1980). Warning: Even memory for faces may be contagious. *Law and Human Behavior, 4,* 323–334.

Loftus, E. F., & Palmer, J. C. (1974). Reconstruction of automobile destruction: An example of the interaction between language and memory. *Journal of Verbal Learning and Verbal Behavior, 13,* 585–589.

Mann, J. W. (1967). Inconsistent thinking about group and individual. *Journal of Social Psychology, 71,* 235–245.

Neuberg, S. L. (1989). The goal of forming accurate impressions during social interactions:

Attenuating the impact of negative expectancies. *Journal of Personality and Social Psychology, 56,* 374–386.

Nisbett, R. E., Krantz, D. H., Jepson, C., & Fong, G. T. (1982). Improving inductive inference. In D. Kahneman, P. Slovic, & A. Tversky (Eds.), *Judgment under uncertainty: Heuristics and biases* (pp. 445–459). New York: Cambridge University Press.

Paulos, J. A. (1988). *Innumeracy.* New York: Hill & Wang.

Ross, M., & Conway, M. (1985). Remembering one's own past: The construction of personal histories. In R. M. Sorrentino & E. T. Higgins (Eds.), *Motivation and cognition: Foundations of social behavior* (pp. 122–144). New York: Guilford.

Rothbart, M., Evans, M., & Fulero, S. (1979). Recall for confirming events: Memory processes and the maintenance of social stereotypes. *Journal of Experimental Social Psychology, 15,* 343–355.

Rubovits, P. C., & Maehr, M. L. (1973). Pygmalion Black and White. *Journal of Personality and Social Psychology, 25,* 210–218.

Sagar, H. A., & Schofield, J. W. (1980). Racial and behavioral cues in Black and White children's perceptions of ambiguously aggressive acts. *Journal of Personality and Social Psychology, 39,* 590–598.

Schneider, D. J., & Blankmeyer, B. L. (1983). Prototype salience and implicit personality theories. *Journal of Personality and Social Psychology, 44,* 712–722.

Skov, R. B., & Sherman, S. J. (1986). Information-gathering processes: Diagnosticity, hypothesis-confirmatory strategies, and perceived hypothesis confirmation. *Journal of Experimental Social Psychology, 22,* 93–121.

Slowiaczek, L. M., Klayman, J., Sherman, S. J., & Skov, R. B. (1989). *Information selection and use in hypothesis testing: What is a good question, and what is a good answer?* Unpublished manuscript.

Slusher, M. P., & Anderson, C. A. (1987). When reality monitoring fails: The role of imagination in stereotype maintenance. *Journal of Personality and Social Psychology, 52,* 653–662.

Snyder, M., & Swann, W. B., Jr. (1978a). Behavioral confirmation in social interaction: From social perception to social reality. *Journal of Experimental Social Psychology, 14,* 148–162.

Snyder, M., & Swann, W. B., Jr. (1978b). Hypothesis-testing processes in social interaction. *Journal of Personality and Social Psychology, 36,* 1202–1212.

Snyder, M., Tanke, E. D., & Berscheid, E. (1977). Social perception and interpersonal behavior: On the self-fulfilling nature of social stereotypes. *Journal of Personality and Social Psychology, 35,* 656–666.

Snyder, M., & Uranowitz, S. W. (1978). Reconstructing the past: Some cognitive consequences of person perception. *Journal of Personality and Social Psychology, 36,* 941–950.

Srull, T. K. (1981). Person memory: Some tests of associative storage and retrival models. *Journal of Experimental Psychology: Human Learning and Memory, 7,* 440–463.

Srull, T. K., Lichtenstein, M., & Rothbart, M. (1985). Associative storage and retrieval processes in person memory. *Journal of Experimental Psychology: Learning, Memory, and Cognition, 11,* 316–345.

Srull, T. K., & Wyer, R. S. (1989). Person memory and judgment. *Psychological Review, 96,* 58–83.

Stangor, C., & Ruble, D. N. (1989). Strength of expectancies and memory for social information: What we remember depends on how much we know. *Journal of Experimental Social Psychology, 25,* 18–35.

Swann, W. B., Jr., & Ely, R. J. (1984). A battle of wills: Self-verification versus behavioral confirmation. *Journal of Personality and Social Psychology, 46,* 1287–1302.

Swann, W. B., Jr., & Snyder, M. (1980). On translating beliefs into action: Theories of ability and their application in an instructional setting. *Journal of Personality and Social Psychology, 38,* 879–888.

Thomas, W. I., & Thomas D. S. (1928). *The child in America: Behavior problems and programs.* New York: Knopf.

Trope, Y., & Bassok, M. (1982). Confirmatory and diagnosing strategies in social information gathering. *Journal of Personality and Social Psychology, 43,* 22–24.

Trope, Y., & Bassok, M. (1983). Information gathering strategies in hypothesis-testing. *Journal of Experimental Social Psychology, 19,* 560–576.

Ugwuegbu, D. C. E. (1979). Racial and evidential factors in juror attribution of legal responsibility. *Journal of Experimental Social Psychology, 15,* 133–146.

Van Wallendael, L. R. (1988). *Diagnosticity and information use in decision making.* Paper presented at Psychonomic Society meeting, Chicago.

Word, C. O., Zanna, M. P., & Cooper, J. (1974). The nonverbal mediation of self-fulfilling prophecies in interracial interaction. *Journal of Experimental Social Psychology, 10,* 109–120.

Wyer, R. S., Jr., & Martin, L. L. (1986). Person memory: The role of traits, group stereotypes, and specific behaviors in the cognitive representation of persons. *Journal of Personality and Social Psychology, 50,* 661–675.

Zadny, J., & Gerard, H. B. (1974). Attributed intentions and informational selectivity. *Journal of Experimental Social Psychology, 10,* 34–52.

Prejudice and Tolerance

Michael Billig, Susan Condor, Derek Edwards, Mike Gane, David Middleton, & Alan Radley

> You'd think at our ages we wouldn't be colour prejudiced because we've been to school with them. But we're not really. Things have happened. Just silly things happen, and it turns us against them.

This is a fifteen-year-old girl speaking, living in the West Midlands of England. Wendy and her friend had been expressing their support for the unambiguously racist political party, the National Front. They had been justifying this support with tales about the violence of West Indians, the shortages of jobs caused by immigration, and the differentness of Asians. In outlining these tales, Wendy and her friend had been displaying the signs which psychologists normally associate with prejudice. They were advocating discrimination against non-whites, for both believed that non-whites should be expelled from Britain. Both made free use of stereotypes, as they described West Indians and Asians in simple terms. No doubt a standard attitude questionnaire

Source: Abridged from Chapter 7 in M. Billig, S. Condor, D. Edwards, M. Gane, D. Middleton, and A. Radley, *Ideological Dilemmas* (pp. 100–123). London: Sage, 1988.

might have been given, and these supporters of the National Front would have provided the answers which psychologists would have little trouble in defining as prejudiced.

It is not difficult to view prejudice in a comparatively undilemmatic way, which assumes that the unprejudiced are liberal, healthy and egalitarian, whereas the prejudiced are the repositories of the very opposite values. The classic psychological approach to prejudice, *The Authoritarian Personality* by Adorno et al. (1950), tends to view prejudice in such a relatively straightforward manner. The prejudiced person was seen as psychologically unhealthy, and a bundle of complexes, as compared with the tolerant individual. Whereas the unprejudiced person could cope with the ambiguities and the equalities of modern life, the prejudiced individual hankers after rigidly authoritarian structures. If the unprejudiced person stands for freedom, the prejudiced person, like Wendy, is drawn toward the politics of totalitarianism. However, as previous chapters have suggested, such an image may be too simple, for equality and authority, illness and health, and freedom and necessity are not so easily separated. Modern celebrations of equality have not eradicated authority. Even a celebration of health does not dispel the spectre of illness. Similarly, as this chapter will argue, prejudice is not undilemmatically straightforward; there is a dialectic of prejudice. If there is a dialectic of equality which includes authority, and one of health which includes illness, the dialectic of prejudice is even more dramatic in its revelation of the dark side of the ideological tradition of the Enlightenment.

The dilemmatic aspects of prejudice will be explored by looking at one aspect of the topic which has tended to be ignored by psychologists: the meaning of 'prejudice' itself. Most psychologists study prejudice by examining the images which people have of other groups or by looking at people's reactions to other group members. In so doing they avoid studying the meaning of prejudice itself. It needs to be recognized that prejudice is not merely a technical concept to be found in the writings of psychologists, but a concept used in everyday discourse, as the comments of Wendy illustrate. It is not a simple concept, and her usage indicates ambivalence. She was accepting the moral evaluation attached to the notion of 'prejudice': that it is wrong to be prejudiced, just as it is assumed to be wrong to be undemocratic or tyrannical or to encourage illness. If she did not accept this moral theme, there would be little point in her denial that she was 'really' prejudiced. Yet at the same time she was expressing— and, what is most important, she realized that she was expressing—views which might be considered to be prejudiced.

. . . Today, 'prejudice' refers particularly to irrational feelings or attitudes which are held against social groups. When social scientists write books about prejudice, they primarily have in mind these sorts of intergroup prejudices. Thus Gordon Allport's classic work *The Nature of Prejudice* was an analysis of racial and national prejudices. Not only were the psychological and social roots of such prejudices examined, but there was an overall moral evaluation: such prejudices were to be eradicated in the name of tolerant rationality. Social psychologists frequently define prejudice in a way that suggests that the essence of the concept is to be found in racial and national attitudes. For example Harding et al., in their contribution to the

Handbook of Social Psychology, state that 'by *prejudice* we mean an ethnic attitude in which the reaction tendencies are predominantly negative' (1969: 1022). The same sort of definition is to be found in popularly used textbooks of social psychology. For instance, Perlman and Cozby (1983: 417) define prejudice 'as a negative attitude towards members of socially defined groups'. Forsyth (1987: 614) has the following entry for 'prejudice' in the glossary of his textbook: 'An attitude toward an ethnic, racial or other social group.' In all these works, there is an assumption of obvious morality: prejudice is not merely to be analysed psychologically, it is also to be condemned. . . .

The language of the young girl, quoted at the beginning of the chapter, was full of the division between 'us' and 'them'. This is a division which, as she herself recognized, should disappear if the enlightened opposition to 'prejudice' were the sole guiding principle. Her language emphasized the ideological dilemma she faced when talking of classmates of a darker coloured skin. 'They' were like 'us', but unalike: 'our' neighbours, yet felt to be different; 'our' workmates, yet competitors for scarce jobs. Perhaps 'they' would have become just like 'us', but 'things' happen. Yet again, 'things' do not always happen. Immediately after the interview, conducted at school, this young supporter of a racist party, and of compelling all of 'them' to leave 'our country', was to be seen walking arm in arm with a young Asian girl, chatting and laughing in easy friendship.

AMBIVALENCE AND RACIAL DISCOURSE

There is considerable evidence that nowadays people in the West generally do not speak about race in an unambiguous way. The evidence comes from studies which have conducted attitudinal surveys and from those which have analysed the patterns of actual speech. For example, American investigators of white attitudes towards blacks have talked of 'modern' or 'symbolic' racism (McConahay, 1986; . . .). The results from these surveys suggest that the 'modern', or 'symbolic', racist is unlikely to hold attitudes which outrightly demean black people as being racially inferior. Name-calling and racial insults are avoided by the modern racists, who nevertheless express strong opposition to moves to advance the position of blacks within American society. This opposition is typically justified in terms of traditional values, and, in particular, in terms of values of equality and fairness. The modern racist believes that black people are 'getting more than they deserve' and are receiving unfairly generous, and thereby unequal, privileges. In this way, the crude sentiments of 'rednecked' racism are avoided, in an attitudinal pattern which claims for itself a degree of reasonableness (see also the studies on racial ambivalence by Katz, Wackenhut and Hass, 1986).

Investigators such as McConahay and Sears claim that this outwardly 'reasonable' expression of racism is basically a modern, post-1960s development. Nevertheless, there is evidence to suggest that the difference between old-fashioned rednecked racism and 'modern racism' may be exaggerated. This is a point made by Weigel and Howes (1985), who have compared the items on older and modern surveys of racial attitudes, and have found that there is not such a great qualitative difference between the two. Billig (1982, 1985) has re-examined some of the responses of the classicly bigoted persons in Adorno et al.'s *The Authoritarian Personality* (1950). These authoritarians, who supposedly showed a predilection for unambiguously hostile views against minorities, nevertheless hedged and qualified their views with a veneer of reasonableness. As Adorno noted in *The Authoritarian Personality*, even bigoted authoritarians were aware of the social norm against being prejudiced, or at least against appearing to be prejudiced. Perhaps the most striking evidence that the the older rednecks were never completely uninhibited in their prejudices comes from Myrdal's *An American Dilemma* (1944). Researching at a time when racial discrimination was practised both *de jure* and *de facto* throughout the south of the United States, Mydral found that even whites who defended the discriminatory laws of their states displayed an indirectness in talking about blacks. Words were picked with care, and there was, above all, a desire to appear unprejudiced: 'When talking about the Negro problem, everybody—not only the intellectual liberals—is thus anxious to locate race prejudice outside himself [or herself] (p. 37).

Similar patterns have been noted by modern researchers who have examined ordinary discourse of race in a number of different settings. Wetherell and Potter (1986) and McFadyen and Wetherell (1986) have looked at the way in which middle-class New Zealanders talk about Maoris. Their respondents did not cling to a single, monolithically unfavourable stereotype (or 'prototype') of 'the Maori', in the way that the old-fashionedly prejudiced person supposedly did. Instead, ostensibly liberal respondents managed to introduce innuendoes and to cast aspersions in the most polite and outwardly 'reasonable' ways. Similar patterns have been said to characterize the way in which white Britons talk about non-whites living in Britain: the crudities of National Front propaganda are avoided, but 'they', despite the good qualities of some of 'them', are held to be different from 'us' and would, on the whole, be better off back in 'their' own countries. . . .

Van Dijk (1984) has given an extremely detailed and fascinating analysis of comments made in interviews by working-class Dutch people about immigrants to Holland. Van Dijk points to the complex ways in which the interviewees expressed their views. On the whole, they had unfavourable things to say about immigrants, but rarely did the respondents present wholly unfavourable views. Delicate elisions, qualifications and shifts of topic were normal. Often questions which were aimed at eliciting negative attitudes did not produce direct answers. Van Dijk (1984: 65) offers the example of an interviewee who was asked whether he had ever had an unpleasant experience with blacks. He replied:

> I have nothing against foreigners.
> But their attitude, their aggression is scaring.
> We are no longer free here. You have to be careful.

Just as Myrdal noted in the prewar deep south of the United States, there is a reluctance to plunge into a denunciation of the other. There is a denial of prejudice ('I have nothing against foreigners'). As in the comments of the young British girl at the beginning of the chapter, there is implication that things have occurred beyond the control of the 'unprejudiced' speaker: 'their' attitudes and 'their' aggression are the cause of the views, rather than any biases within the speaker. Moreover, these 'causes' have destroyed one of the values of the Enlightenment: 'we' are no longer free, 'they' are the enemies of freedom.

One of the aspects of racial discourse which van Dijk notes is the way that contrary themes are introduced, often with a connecting 'but'. The interviewee has nothing against foreigners, but. . . . There is, according to van Dijk, a give-and-take in the exchanges between interviewer and interviewee, paralleling a give-and-take between positive and negative comments about immigrants: 'The interviewee agrees with or accepts some positive point of the interviewer (and thereby shows cooperation and tolerance) but at the same time wants to express his/her own negative experience or evaluations' (1984: 148–9). Van Dijk refers to this as 'an "on the one hand" and "on the other hand" strategy of opinion formulation' (p. 152). In van Dijk's analysis, there is a tendency to view this strategy in terms of the interpersonal moves of a conversation, in which a prejudiced, working-class interviewee wishes to impress a tolerant, middle-class interviewer. Van Dijk suggests that there is a contradiction between expressing racist views openly and conforming to the norms of polite conversation. Speakers will wish to present themselves in a favourable light, and will, in consequence, avoid the unalloyed expression of their racist views. In consequence, the goals of self-expression and self-presentation 'may sometimes conflict: a direct or "honest" expression of the beliefs or the opinions from the speaker's situation model may lead to a negative social evaluation of the speaker by the hearer' (p. 117).

Although it may be the case that some interviewees might hedge their 'true' views in this situation, the ambivalence of their remarks cannot be solely attributed to the conflict between attitude and impression management. One must ask why respondents assumed that the utterance of racist comments would make such a bad impression. Evidence suggests that the respondents were not paying lip-service to norms of politeness, which were foreign to themselves but which they knew the interviewer held. Instead, these were norms which they themselves shared. Just like the girl quoted earlier, there was a recognition of the moral inappropriateness of being 'prejudiced'. In a public opinion survey in Britain, Airey (1984) reports that the majority of the population believed that there was substantial prejudice against Asians and West Indians. Yet most respondents believed that other people were more prejudiced than themselves. Prejudice might be perceived as being consensual, but it was not recognized as being social acceptable. In other words, racial prejudice was not something to admit of the self, even if people believed that it was widespread; prejudice was, as Myrdal noted, to be located outside the self. . . .

According to Billig (1982 and 1986b) it is necessary to understand this sort of discourse in its rhetorical context. The two-handedness of the 'on the one hand, on the other hand' formulation is a form of prolepsis, which is aimed to deflect potential criticism in advance. Having stated an opposition to racism or to prejudice, the way is then opened for an expression of racist and prejudiced views. One might say that this rhetorical device is a signal indicating the existence of dilemmatic thought, or of an ideological pattern which is itself two-sided, rather than possessing the narrow one-sidedness by which Marx and Engels characterized traditional nationalism. Two contrary themes are expressed simultaneously, but not necessarily with equal force, in this ideology. To use the terminology of discourse analysis, it could be said that two contrary 'linguistic repertoires' are being used within the same two-handed statement. . . . The availability of such contrary repertoires indicates a divide within prevailing ideology. . . .

PREJUDICE AND REASONABLENESS

The notion of 'prejudice' has been a central concept in social psychology, as Samelson (1978, 1986) has made clear in his historical accounts of the development of modern research in the topic. Although social psychologists have offered many different definitions of the term 'prejudice', most have sought to preserve, at least in a refined form, the ordinary meanings of the term. In consequence, the social psychological definitions are broadly consonant with the use by the young girl who denied that she was really colour prejudiced. As has been mentioned, a number of definitions actually specify that prejudice refers to attitudes towards ethnic groups. Most definitions also include the idea that prejudices are irrational, or wrongly formed, attitudes. For example, Allport in *The Nature of Prejudice* defined 'prejudice' as 'thinking ill of others without sufficient warrant', and he stressed that prejudices, unlike unprejudiced beliefs, are especially resistant to change in the face of relevant evidence. Aronson in *The Social Animal* defines 'prejudice' as 'a hostile or negative attitude toward a distinguishable group based on generalizations derived from faulty or incomplete information' (1976: 174).

The term 'prejudice', therefore, refers not only to the contents of the belief but also to the way in which it is formed. Some authors, including Allport, have stressed that emotional factors may play an important part in producing the unsound judgements of prejudice. He refers to the 'feeling-tone', or emotional antipathy, which often accompanies prejudice. On the other hand much modern social psychology, under the influence of the general cognitive movement in psychology, has tended to concentrate upon the unsoundness of the judgemental processes, rather than upon the 'feeling-tones' (Hamilton, 1979, 1981;) . . . Despite the lack of attention to the 'feeling-tones', modern cognitive theory continues to associate 'prejudice' with a deficiency in judgment which leads to erroneous conclusions, especially about social groups. In this way, the very notion of 'prejudice' raises psychological problems about the holding of erroneous and irrational beliefs. For example, Bethlehem, in his textbook on the topic of prejudice, takes a cognitive perspective. He suggests that 'the fundamental problem of prejudice, from the point of view of the cognitive psychologist, is to explain how it comes about that people make judgements and apparently believe things, or act as though they believe them, in the absence of adequate evidence' (1985: 2). . . .

Moscovici (1976) has suggested that psychological ideas, originating as technical theories, often become diffused into popular consciousness. Certainly it is true that 'prejudice' is not the conceptual property of the specialist intellectual, whether Enlightenment philosopher or modern psychologist. The term is well understood, and frequently used in everyday talk. Moreover, in everyday talk the term retains its psychological implication. The comments by the young girl at the beginning of this chapter suggest a naive psychology. She declares that she is not 'prejudiced'. In this way she denies that there is any psychological or irrational cause of her beliefs. Instead it is external events—the things that happen—which give rise to the beliefs. She suggests that the beliefs are not really prejudiced, for, lacking an internal psychological cause, they reflect the external world, not the internal psychology of the believer. Similarly, Myrdal's comment on the racist southerners shows the care with which they sought to locate the source of their beliefs outside their selves, and thereby to present themselves and their beliefs as rational. Van Dijk's respondents similarly denied their own 'prejudices', and thereby they were denying that there was anything wrong, psychologically or morally, with their selves. . . .

The tag 'I'm not prejudiced but . . .' indicates this dissociation from the irrationalities of 'prejudice'. Hewitt and Stokes (1975) have described this linguistic move as 'credentialling': the speaker wishes to avoid being branded negatively and, in the case of prejudice, as being someone who harbours unreasonable antipathies. In this way, speakers can present themselves and their views as being reasonable, determined by the facts that happen in the world rather than by irrational feelings. Beyond the issue of self-presentation, there is an argumentative or rhetorical dimension. If views are to be presented as being rational and unprejudiced, then they must be seen to be justified, or at least to be justifiable. Thus the complaints which follow the 'but' in 'I'm not prejudiced but . . .' must appear as arguments, for which reasons are expected to be given.

Van Dijk noted that many of his respondents, who voiced complaints about immigrants, did so in two ways. They told stories about events which may or may not have happened to themselves, or they formulated their views in terms of abstract generalizations. Both these forms convey the image of reasonableness: the story implies that the expressed belief is based upon external happenings, and the abstract generalization further distances the psychological feelings of the speaker from the expressed conclusion. Both forms were apparent in the discussion groups of Cochrane and Billig (1984). Wendy, the young girl quoted previously, used both forms freely to justify why she felt that non-whites should be expelled from Britain. Wendy's stories include personal events, involving violent fights between gangs of whites and blacks. Her boyfriend had been picked on by black gangs, and 'They chased my boyfriend's brother with a metal bar.' There had been trouble at the local disco: 'I don't suppose you believe this, but there was one with a shotgun last night—a coloured with a shotgun.' And someone had been seriously hurt: 'There was one boy, he was unconscious, just lying on the floor and people just trampling all over him.' Then there were generalizations about immigration and unemployment: 'You can't go into a factory, it's just all Indians.' her friend, Tracy, agreed vigorously: 'It's getting us to resent 'em more and more.' The syntax tells its own psychological story: 'we' are not resenting 'them' of our own accord, but something, and more often than not 'them' themselves, are getting 'us' to do the resenting.

This general style of discourse allows, even demands, that sympathy should be shown to the targets of the stories and generalizations. 'Best friends' might be produced to show that the speaker has no personal prejudices. Nor is there necessarily any hypocrisy in this. Wendy, herself, was clearly friendly with non-white girls in her class. In articulating her National Front view that all non-whites should be expelled, she commented

> I'm not being colour prejudiced, you know. I've got friends, who I would like to stay in this country. But if it was either get 'em all out, or keep the odd ones here and keep 'em all in, I'd rather get 'em all out.

The style is to express reluctance: hard choices, conflicting with non-prejudiced feelings, are being forced upon 'us' from outside. Wendy even spoke about having had a 'half-caste' boyfriend. She had been called names by other white girls. It hadn't been right, all that name-calling. But it happens. She was asked whether she would think of having a non-white boyfriend in the future. Her answer was two-sided. First, there were her feelings: 'I suppose I might, you know, if I met somebody who I really liked.' But then, external to her, were the things that might happen: 'But, then it's gonna cause that much trouble that I think I'd say no. Because, you know, my parents are going to resent me.' The feelings of her parents were converted into one of the facts of the world. In this way her discourse could still claim to be based upon the rhetoric of fact, and not upon that of prejudice, but nevertheless it could still incorporate prejudices uncritically. . . .

THE SYMBOL OF IRRATIONAL PREJUDICE

In the modern discourse of 'race', contradictory themes are apparent. Wendy, like many of the adolescents observed by Cochrane and Billig (1984), and in common with the respondents of van Dijk (1984), simultaneously expressed views which seemed to be ever contradicting themselves. Complaints against 'immigrants' or 'foreigners' would be made, only to be followed by concessions. Blame would be mingled with sympathy, as tolerant themes follow upon those of prejudice. Seldom in the discussion groups of Cochrane and Billig would there be direct confrontation between those who only voiced tolerant sentiments and those who clung to unalloyed prejudice. More common were discussions in which all shared the contrary themes, and all chipped in with remarks which added the 'but . . .' qualifications to previous assertions. Nor did it matter whether it was the same or a different speaker who had made the previous statement which seemed in need of qualification. The members of the discussion group would argue with their own assertions just as much as they did with those of others, whose contrary assertions they largely shared in any case.

This form of agreement by disagreement occurred when all shared the contrary themes of 'reasonable prejudice'. Nevertheless, this form of discourse must be prepared to argue with those who express 'unreasonable prejudice'. If one of the themes of reasonable prejudice is a rejection of 'prejudice', then it needs a symbol of unreasonable 'prejudice' from which to distance itself and with which to argue, in order to prove its own unprejudiced reasonableness. Those who deny their own prejudice need, implicitly or explicitly, to envisage a boundary between their own unprejudiced selves and the prejudiced bigot. In other words, the reasonable discourse of prejudice needs its unreasonably prejudiced Other.

Wendy's comments, and those of her friend Tracy, made it clear that there were certain sorts of activities of which they did not approve. Wendy mentioned name-calling of the sort which she had suffered when she had dated a non-white. Tracy said that her sister went out with a half-caste boy: 'She gets called all sorts of names, which aren't very nice. I wouldn't repeat them, I don't think it is fair.' In the same way, she said that 'If a Jamaican boy comes up and puts his arm around you, then you get called names—you're "wog-bait", that's what they call you. It isn't fair, is it?' Nor was it 'fair' for gangs of white boys to search out and beat up young Jamaicans. All this could be conceded. In fact, it needed to be conceded, if there were to be such a thing as 'prejudice' located outside of the self.

These young girls were not inventing the forms and themes of their discourse. Despite the talk of personal experiences of discos and boyfriends, the basic forms are discernible in the discourse of respectable politicians. Like Wendy and her friend, modern politicians need to deny prejudice, and thereby they need the symbol of prejudiced behaviour from which to distance themselves. The notion of a boundary becomes evident in their discourse, when it is perceived that one of their number has transgressed the codes of reasonable discourse. For example, in 1986 a Conservative MP [member of Parliament] was widely reported as having referred to West Indians as 'bone idle and lazy'. Fellow party members instantly recognized this as a piece of unreasonably prejudiced name-calling. In attacking the transgression, they could defend their own contrary reasonableness with a qualifying 'but . . .':

> Mr Teddy Taylor, joint secretary of the Conservative backbench home affairs committee, said: 'I have always been regarded as being on the right wing of the Conservative Party and one who wants strict immigration control. But I think this kind of bone-headed racial abuse is uncalled for because many of the problems facing West Indians are a direct result of the way we brought them into this country.
> (*Guardian*, 2 September 1986)

One should note how this condemnation of name-calling includes a lay psychological diagnosis of the name-caller. The person who utters abuse is 'bone-headed', and thereby fails to show the intellect of rational judgement. Yet the condemnation of prejudice, and the sympathy for the problems of West Indians, do not rest unqualified. They accompany the call for 'strict' immigration control. In this way a politely respectable elision between 'race' and 'immigration' is effected, so that 'immigration', not 'race', can be talked about. The resulting discussion of 'strict control' is then about such reasonable matters as the facts of 'overpopulation', 'numbers' and the movements of population. In such discourse there need be no explicit mention of 'race' or anything else, which overtly smacks of the language of prejudice. Instead there is ostensibly little more than the language of fact and number. . . .

The reasonably prejudiced may be caught in the dilemma of possessing contrary ways of talking about 'them', drawing upon opposing themes of tolerance and prejudice, sympathy and blame, nationalism and internationalism. In this sense their discourse, and indeed their thinking, possesses a dilemmatic quality. The unreasonable know no such dilemma. Many of the National Front supporters in Cochrane and Billig's discussion groups were delighting in their own prejudices, freed from any restraining reasonableness. There were few expressions of regret in their claims that 'they' (or worse) should be expelled in order to relieve the level of unemployment; instead, they would employ the violent language of 'kicking out', 'booting out', 'getting rid of' to describe an event to which they looked forward. The unambiguously prejudiced had few inhibitions about name-calling. In fact they frequently played their undilemmatic parts in order to taunt the sensibilities of the reasonably prejudiced, as well as to express their own strong feelings. One skinhead insisted upon repeating the catch-phrase "BM [British Movement] boys are big and brave, each deserves a nigger slave.' Others would twist every conversation around to joky remarks about 'Pakis' and the smell of curry, so sabotaging the themes of reasonableness. Psychological condemnation seemed to be invited by violently expressed obsessions: 'Wogs smell like six-month-old shit; Pakis smell like curry which has been mixed with shit and piss; their breath stinks like the local fucking sewers; all our teachers are bastards.'

It would be tempting to presume that this is the 'real' voice of racism: the protective coating of liberalism has been removed, with the unconscious aspects of racism, freed from the superego of tolerance, becoming conscious. However, there is one aspect of this unashamed racism which should be noted. It is no more 'real' than the liberal themes of the reasonably prejudiced are 'unreal' strategies of self-presentation. In fact the unabashed prejudice lacks reality, for it is unbelievable, even to the believer. As Sartre noted in his essay 'Portrait of the anti-semite', extreme bigots do not fully believe their own bigotry, and constantly seem to be operating at a level of ferocious joking. The same joky quality has been noted in extreme fascist propaganda (Lowenthal and Gutterman, 1949; Billig, 1978: 169). . . .

'STILL WE OUGHT NOT TO BURN THEM'

. . . For the reasonably prejudiced . . . the dilemmas were clear: prejudice was to be avoided, but there were 'problems' to be faced; 'they' (the immigrants, the non-whites, the Asians, the blacks, the foreigners) were the problem, but of course 'they' had 'their' problems too. The language of prejudice and that of the avoidance of prejudice continually conflict. Conjunctions such as 'but' or 'still' show how these opposing themes can coexist grammatically and dilemmatically within the same sentence. . . .

The very tones of ambivalence are caught in Voltaire's writings. His stereotyping and sociological dismissal of Jews might be far cruder than anything Wendy said. Yet the symbol of enlightened philosophy shared similar ambivalences of 'prejudice' with the young working-class supporter of a fascist party. Above all there was the same two-handedness which expressed, but denied, prejudice. As Voltaire wrote about the Jews, whom we 'tolerate' but from whom 'we' receive nothing but prejudice:

> In short, we find in them only an ignorant and barbarous people, who have long united the most sordid avarice with the most detestable superstition and the most invincible hatred for every people by whom they are tolerated and enriched. Still we ought not to burn them. (p. 94)

REFERENCES

Adorno, T. W., E. Frenkel-Brunswik, D. J. Levinson, and R. N. Sanford (1950) *The Authoritarian Personality*. New York: Harper & Row.

Allport, G. W. (1954) *The Nature of Prejudice*. Garden City: Anchor Books.

Altemeyer, R. (1981) *Right-Wing Authoritarianism*. Manitoba: University of Manitoba Press.

Aronson, E. (1976) *The Social Animal*. New York: Freeman.

Barker, M. (1981) *The New Racism*. London: Junction Books.

Berkeley, G. (1972) 'Prejudices and opinions', in *Chamber's Readings in English Literature*. Edinburgh William & Robert Chambers.

Bethlehelm, G. (1985) *A Social Psychology of Prejudice*. Aldershot: Gower.

Billig, M. (1978) *Fascists: A Social Psychological View of the National Front*. London: Academic Press.

Billig, M. (1982) *Ideology and Social Psychology*. Oxford: Basil Blackwell.

Billig, M. (1985) 'Prejudice, categorization and particularization: From a perceptual to a rhetorical approach', *European Journal of Social Psychology*, 15: 79–103.

Billig, M. (1986b) 'Very ordinary life and the young conservatives', in H. Beloff (ed), *Getting into Life*. London: Meuthen.

Cochrane, R., and Billig, M. (1984) 'I'm not National Front, but . . .', *New Society*, 68: 255–8.

Diderot, D. (1966) *Encyclopedie ou dictionnaire raisonne* (1757). Stuttgart: Friedrich Frommann.

Edelman, M. (1977) *Political Language*. New York: Academic Books.

Forbes, H. D. (1986) *Nationalism, Ethnocentrism and Personality*. Chicago: University of Chicago Press.

Forsyth, D. R. (1987) *Social Psychology*. Belmont: Brooks/Cole.

Gadamer, H. G. (1979) *Truth and Method*. London: Sheed & Ward.

Hamilton, D. (1979) 'A cognitive-attributional analysis of stereotyping', in L. Berkowitz (ed), *Advances in Experimental Social Psychology* vol. 12. New York: Academic Press.

Hamilton, D. (1981) 'Stereotyping and intergroup behavior: some thoughts on the cognitive approach', in D. Hamilton (ed), *Cognitive Processes in Stereotyping and Intergroup Behavior*. Hillsdale, NJ: Lawrence Erlbaum.

Harding, J., B. Kunter, H. Proshansky and I. Chein (1969) 'Prejudice and ethnic relations', in G. Lindzey (ed), *Handbook of Social Psychology*. New York: Addison-Wesley.

Hazlitt, W. (1934) 'Prejudice' (1930). In *The Complete Works* vol. XX. London: Dent.

Hewitt, J. P. and R. Stokes (1975) 'Disclaimers', *American Sociological Review*, 40:1~11.

Katz, I., J. Wackenhut and R. G. Haas (1986) 'Racial ambivalence, value duality and behavior', in J. F. Dovidio and S. L. Gaertner (eds), *Prejudice, Discrimination, and Racism*. Orlando: Academic Press.

Lowenthal, L. and N. Gutterman (1949) *Prophets of Deceit*. New York: Harper & Row.

Marx, K. and F. Engels (1968) *The Communist Manifesto*, in *Selected Works*. London: Lawrence & Wishart. (Original, 1848.)

McFadyen, R. and Wetherell, M. (1986) 'Categories in discourse'. Paper presented at Social Psychology Section, British Psychology Conference, Sussex.

Moscovici, S. (1976) *La Psychanalyse, son image et son public*. Paris: Presses Universitaires de France.

Myrdal, G. (1944) *An American Dilemma*. New York: Harper.

Perlman, D. and P. C. Cozby (1983) *Social Psychology*. New York: Holt, Rinehart & Winston.

Reeves, F. (1983) *British Racial Discourse*. Cambridge: Cambridge University Press.

Samelson, F. (1978) 'From "race psychology" to "studies in prejudice": some observations on the thematic reversal in social psychology', *Journal of the History of the Behavioral Sciences*, 14: 265~78.

Samelson, F. (1986) 'Authoritarianism from Berlin to Berkeley: On social psychology and history', *Journal of Social Issues*, 42: 191~208.

Selznick, G. and S. Steinberg (1969) *The Tenacity of Prejudice*. New York: Harper.

Sennett, R. and J. Cobb (1977) *The Hidden Injuries of Class*. Cambridge: Cambridge University Press.

Van Dijk, T. A. (1984) *Prejudice in Discourse: An Analysis of Ethnic Prejudice in Cognition and Conversation*. Amsterdam: Benjamins.

Van Dijk, T. A. (1986) 'When majorities talk about minorities', in M. McLaughlin (ed), *Communication Yearbook 9*. Beverly Hills: Sage.

Van Dijk, T. A. (1987) 'Discourse and power'. Unpublished paper, Department of General Literary Studies, University of Amsterdam.

Voltaire (n.d.) *A Philosophical Dictionary* vol. 2. London: E. Truelove.

Weigel, R.H. and P.W. Howes (1985) 'Conceptions of racial prejudice: symbolic racism reconsidered', *Journal of Social Issues*, 41: 117~38.

Wetherell, M. and J. Potter (1986) 'Discourse analysis and the social psychology of racism', *Newsletter of the Social Psychology Section of the British Psychological Society*, 15: 24~9.

Contact and Cooperation
When Do They Work?

Marilynn B. Brewer and Norman Miller

Although the social-science-based justification for the *Brown* decision of 1954 was framed primarily in terms of its effect on the achievement and self-esteem of minority children, it is generally agreed that a major societal goal of desegregation is improved

Source: Abridged from Chapter 16 in P. A. Katz and D. A. Taylor (Eds.), *Eliminating Racism* (pp. 315~326). New York: Plenum Press, 1988.

intergroup relations (Stephan, 1978). Presumably, what we mean by this is not simply that we can create conditions in which members of different ethnic groups coexist temporarily without conflict. What most of us have in mind when we think of improving intergroup relations is that any positive effects of contact will extend beyond the contact situation to reduce intergroup conflict and prejudice in general.

Despite the practical importance of generalization effects, relatively little research on desegregation has focused on this aspect of the contact hypothesis. Interventions (such as the cooperative learning technique . . .) have been directed toward improving intergroup acceptance within the desegregated setting. Whether the positive effects observed within the treated classrooms will persist in time or will generalize to other settings and/or children remains an open question. Ironically, it may be the case that some of the factors that most effectively promote positive intergroup behavior within a given situation actually *reduce* the probability of generalization to other times and places. A closer look at the nature of generalization effects and the processes underlying them will clarify why this may be true.

TYPES OF GENERALIZATION

What does it mean for the effects of a particular experience with intergroup contact to generalize to the group as a whole? We distinguish among three different types of generalization effects:

1. *Change in attitudes toward the social category.* This is the most direct form of generalization, where positive experiences with individual members of a broad social category lead to alterations in the affect and stereotypes associated with the group as a whole.
2. *Increased complexity of intergroup perceptions.* This form of generalization involves a change in the perceived heterogeneity of category structure. Instead of perceiving the out-group category as a relatively homogeneous social group, the individual comes to recognize variability among category members. Attitudes toward the category as a whole may not be altered, but affect and stereotypes are differentiated among various "subtypes" of the general category.
3. *Decategorization.* In this form of generalization, the meaningfulness of the social category itself is undermined. Based on the frequency or intensity of exposure to individual members of a social group, the utility of category membership as a basis for identifying or classifying new individuals is reduced.

These three forms of generalization correspond to the distinction drawn by Brewer and Miller (1984) among three different levels of intergroup interaction: (a) category-based; (b) differentiated; and (c) personalized. Each of these implies different cognitive processes occurring at the time of intergroup contact. Considering each in turn, we will illustrate how different conditions of contact may promote or inhibit different types of generalization.

Category-Based Generalization

In his programmatic research on the contact hypothesis, Cook (1984, 1985) was particularly interested in testing whether positive contact experiences would generalize to intergroup attitudes. Consistent with the specifications of the contact hypothesis, he found that intensive, equal-status interaction in cooperative groups could succeed in promoting cross-ethnic liking and respect within such groups, even among persons who were highly prejudiced at the outset. In most cases, however, these effects did not extend to measures of racial prejudice in general. Such findings led Cook (1984) to speculate that

> attitude change will result from cooperative interracial contact only when such contact is accompanied by a *supplementary* influence that promotes the process of generalization from favorable contact with individuals to positive attitudes toward the group from which the individual comes. (p. 163; italics added)

In the absence of such special influence, there is apparently a strong tendency for individuals to isolate the contact experience from other cognitions, and to regard the individuals they come to know and like as special exceptions rather than representatives of their social group.

In Cook's experiments, the "supplementary influence" that helped promote generalized attitude change was one in which group norms supporting racial equality and nondiscrimination were *explicitly* articulated in association with pleasant experiences with members of the out-group. At least two problems can be noted in this solution to the problem of generalization. First, it requires that the contact situation be engineered in such a way as to ensure that the interpersonal experience will be uniformly pleasant, so that any generalized attitude change will be in the desired direction. Such conditions are not easily achieved, at least not in ways that permit interactions that are not highly constrained or superficial.

Second, this mode of enhancing generalization depends on category-based information-processing. The out-group member in the interaction must be perceived as representative of his or her social category if attitudes developed toward that individual are to be generalized to the group as a whole. In a laboratory experiment on contact effects, for instance, Wilder (1984) found that pleasant interaction with a *typical* student of another college resulted in more positive attitudes toward the out-group college in general, but interaction with an *atypical* (i.e., counterstereotypical) member produced no generalization. This was true even though the atypical student was liked better than the typical student.

Thus, categorical generalization of contact experiences occurs only when the superordinate category membership of the out-group individual is salient in the contact situation. As a consequence, the distinctiveness of the social category itself may be reinforced during the course of the interaction. In the long run, such maintenance of in-group–out-group category distinctions may determine any immediate positive effects on intergroup attitudes.

Differentiation and Complexity

In general, it is unlikely that firmly established category stereotypes will be substantially altered on the basis of a few interactions with category members that disconfirm stereotypical expectancies. Instead, individuals appear to handle such discrepant experiences through a process of *subtyping:* the creation of a new, counterstereotypical subcategory that is differentiated from the category as a whole (Weber & Crocker, 1983). As Rothbart and John (1985) put it:

> Contact and familiarity permit a more differentiated encoding of the stimulus person, and this very process of individuation serves to insulate the attributes associated with the category from those of the individual. This process leads to the unhappy prediction that inferences from the individual to the group should decline with increasing familiarity with that individual, particularly when the individual is perceived as generally atypical of the group. (p. 94)

Such subtyping processes may not alter stereotypes about characteristics of the group as a whole, but they may enhance perceived diversity or variability among category members. This provides another way in which individual contact experiences may generalize to perceptions of the group as a whole. Following contact with out-group members who do not conform to category stereotypes, the individual may not necessarily develop a more favorable perception of the group as a whole but may view that group as more complex or differentiated than previously.

Quattrone (1986) pointed out that the perception of variability within a group can take at least two forms. *Dimensional variability* refers to the extent to which individual differences are perceived to exist with respect to a particular trait characteristic. Even though a specific trait may be considered "typical" of a social group, group members may vary in the extent to which they possess that trait. Perceptions of such variability can range from the idea that "all" group members are essentially the same on this dimension to a recognition that individuals within the group are distributed across all points on the dimension. Group stereotypes may also be characterized by *taxonomic variability*. This term refers to the extent to which the category is differentiated into distinctive subtypes, each subtype being represented by a unique configuration of characteristic traits.

Both dimensional variability and taxonomic variability are measures of the complexity of the cognitive representation of a social category, and both are likely to be increased by contact with diverse category members. It is important to note, however, that exposure to diversity alone is not sufficient to ensure greater differentiation of category representations. It is also necessary that the perceiver *pay attention* to information that distinguishes one category member from another. Thus, the generalization of contact experiences to an increase in category complexity requires conditions in which individual differences are made salient and participants are motivated to encode and remember such individuating information.

There is some reason to believe that changes in the complexity of intergroup perception may lead to changes in the evaluation of the group as a whole. A series of studies by Linville (1982; Linville & Jones, 1980) demonstrated that category complexity is associated with reduced polarization of affect toward category members. Individuals with more complex (differentiated) representations of a social category were less extreme in their positive or negative evaluations of a category member than were individuals with less complex representations. Further, Wilder (1978) found that the presence of a dissenter (i.e., an individuated member) in an otherwise homogeneous out-group increased reward allocations to all out-group members, compared to a condition in which no dissenter was present. It should be noted, however, that the generalization of category complexity effects depends on the perceiver's being *aware of* category diversity at the time a judgment about an out-group person is made. If no cuing of category subtypes is present, the individual may fall back on generalized attitudes toward the superordinate category when making evaluations of individuals in new situations.

Personalization and Decategorization

Both of the processes of generalization discussed thus far rely on some type of categorization effect for their effectiveness. The contact experience generalizes to new situations if it modifies the individual's cognitive representation of the out-group category—either the representation of what is typical of the category or the representation of category variability. Another way to look at the effects of intergroup contact is to consider the extent to which interpersonal interaction reduces awareness of category distinctions or group membership—what Brewer and Miller (1984) referred to as "decategorization."

Decategorization occurs to the extent that interrelations in the contact situation are personalized rather than category-based. Personalized interactions are ones in which category identity is replaced as the basis for classifying other individuals in favor of information that is self-relevant and not necessarily correlated with category membership. Such interactions are characterized by information processing that is "piecemeal" rather than category-based (Fiske & Pavelchak, 1985). In piecemeal processing, impressions are abstracted from incoming information about the individual rather than being derived from preexisting category stereotypes.

Differentiation is a necessary but not sufficient condition for personalization and decategorization. Obviously, before information can be personalized, individual differences must first be recognized. However, categories may be differentiated into subtypes or distinct individual members without eliminating superordinate category identity. (For instance, one may learn to discriminate accurately among different presidents of the United States but still classify all of them as occupants of a specialized role in terms of their relationship to oneself.)

With personalization, category identity becomes subordinate to individual identity rather than vice versa. To illustrate this distinction, consider the statement "Janet is a nurse." This description can be psychologically represented in one of two ways. It could mean that Janet is subordinate to (i.e., a specific instance of) the general category of nurses. Or it could mean that being a nurse is subordinate to (i.e., a particular characteristic of) the concept of Janet. The former interpretation is an

example of category-based individuation, and the latter is an example of personalization. In this sense, personalized contact is the polar opposite of category-based
interaction, and the conditions that promote decategorization are antithetical to the
categorical generalization of contact effects.

Reduction of Category-Based Interaction

Interpersonal contact will be category-based to the extent that the category membership of the participants is made salient in the contact situation. Physical
distinctiveness is one basis for category salience but not its sole determinant. (A
person wearing a green shirt in a room full of people with pink shirts is physically
distinct, but it is unlikely that such an individual would be placed in a category of
"green shirt wearers.") Categorization is more likely to occur when categories are
characterized by what Brewer and Campbell (1976) called "convergent boundaries,"
in which group identities based on many different distinctions—for example, religious, economic, and political—all coincide. When social category membership is so
multiply determined, the probability is high that at least one cue to category identity
will be relevant in almost any social situation.

   Tajfel (1978) gave particular emphasis to the structure of intergroup relations at
the societal level as a critical determinant of category salience. Of most relevance is
the presence of intense conflict of interest between groups (as in the relation between
two rival football teams) or the existence of a fairly rigid system of social stratification
within the society that establishes differences in status between the social categories.
According to Tajfel, an individual's feelings of positive social identity are deeply
affected by the prevailing differences in status between social groups. For those who
belong to categories with superior status, the importance of maintaining category
distinctiveness will depend on how secure the established status relationship is. When
high status is secure, one's own category identity will not be particularly salient in
most social situations. However, if status differentials are perceived to be insecure or
threatened, the need to preserve category distinctiveness may be high for members of
both high- and low-status groups.

   Group structure within the contact situation is also an important factor in
category salience, particularly the relative proportion of members of the different
social categories that are represented. In general, in fairly large social groupings, a
relatively equal representation of two social categories makes category distinctions less
salient, whereas the presence of a clear minority enhances awareness of category
identity. . . . The so-called solo effect (Taylor, Fiske, Etcoff, & Ruderman, 1978)
illustrates the extent to which the category identity of a single member of a distinctive
social group is made salient when embedded in an otherwise homogeneous social
environment. The effects of minority-majority representation also interact with differences in group status to determine the extent to which category differentiation is
important to the members of the respective groups. Majority groups with an insecure
or negative self-image and minority groups with a positive self-image have been found
to display the greatest degree of discrimination against out-groups, whereas majority

groups with a secure positive self-image and minority groups with a negative self-image show relatively little discrimination (Espinoza & Garza, 1985; Moscovici & Paicheler, 1978).

The effects of category size and group composition are more complex in situations in which more than two distinguishable social categories are present. Based on perceptual factors alone, we hypothesize that the salience of particular category distinctions will vary as a function of the ratio of category size to total group size. If a fairly large group is divided into several categories of relatively equal size, those categories will provide a useful way of "chunking" the social environment, and category differentiation will be highly salient (each category, in effect, being treated as a distinctive minority). When several different social categories are equally represented in a much smaller social group, however, category salience should be substantially lowered. When the representation of any one social category is small relative to that of other categories, the distinctiveness of that category may be highly salient, whereas distinctions among the other categories will be less apparent.

The conditions that characterize desegregation in a variety of social settings typically have a number of features conducive to category-based social interaction. First of all, the groups involved are usually social categories that are differentiated by convergent boundaries, including distinctions in cultural, economic, linguistic, and physical features. In addition, these objective group differences tend to be confounded with status in the larger social system, often under conditions in which the existing status structure is under threat. Moreover, desegregation frequently occurs within a political context that affects groups differentially and brings individuals into the situation as representatives of their respective social categories. Finally, the immediate social structure tends to be one of disproportional (majority-minority) representation of the different groups and thereby makes category identity perceptually salient as well as emotionally significant.

If personalized rather than category-based interactions are the goal of desegregation, then the contact situation must be designed to eliminate or overcome the features that promote category salience. In effect, the situation must reduce information processing that is category-based and must promote, instead, attention to personal or individual information that is not correlated with category membership. In our view, many of the cooperative interventions designed for implementation in classroom settings are not adequate to achieve this goal. A cooperative task structure by itself is not sufficient to guarantee personalized interaction within heterogeneous groups or to ensure that such interactions will generalize to new situations. In general, we hypothesize (Brewer & Miller, 1984) that the effects of categorization on social interaction will be reduced most successfully when (a) the nature of the interaction in the contact situation promotes an interpersonal rather than a task-oriented approach to fellow participants, and (b) the basis for the assignment of roles, status, social functions, and subgroup composition in the situation is perceived to be category-independent rather than category-related.

The paradox in all of this is that successful decategorization, by its very nature, reduces the possibility of category-based generalization, in either form. To the extent that relationships with individual members of an out-group are highly personalized, they are also insulated from category-based prejudices and stereotypes. Cook's experiments (1984) provide an illustrative case of conditions that promote personalized interactions that did not extend to attitudes toward the group as a whole. Nevertheless, in our view, such interactions have the most promise for reducing intergroup conflict in the long run. Frequent individualization of out-group members results in a loss of meaning and utility of the broader category distinction. Note, however, that such effects cannot be expected to follow from single contact experiences. Generalized decategorization depends both on personalization within contact situations and replication across situations. . . .

REFERENCES

Brewer, M. B., & Campbell, D. T. (1976). *Ethnocentrism and intergroup attitudes: East African evidence*. New York: Halsted Press (Sage Publications).

Brewer, M. B., & Miller, N. (1984). Beyond the contact hypothesis: Theoretical perspectives on desegregation. In N. Miller & M. Brewer (Eds.), *Groups in contact: The psychology of desegregation*. New York: Academic Press.

Cohen, E. G. (1982). Expectation states and interracial interaction in school settings. *Annual Review of Sociology, 8*, 209–235.

Cohen, E. G. (1984). The desegregated school: Problems in status power and interethnic climate. In N. Miller & M. Brewer (Eds.), *Groups in contact: The psychology of desegregation*. New York: Academic Press.

Cook, S. W. (1984). The desegregated school: Problems in status power and interethnic climate. In N. Miller & M. Brewer (Eds.), *Groups in contact: The psychology of desegregation*. New York: Academic Press.

Cook, S. W. (1985). Experimenting on social issues: The case of school desegregation. *American Psychologist, 40*, 452–460.

DeVries, D. L., Slavin, R. E., Fennessey, G. M., Edwards, K. J., & Lombardo, N. M. (1980). *Teams-games-tournament: The team learning approach*. Englewood Cliffs, NJ: Educational Technology Publications.

Espinoza, J. A., & Garza, R. T. (1985) Social group salience and interethnic cooperation. *Journal of Experimental Social Psychology, 21*, 380–392.

Fiske, S. T., & Pavelchak, M. A. (1985). Category-based versus piecemeal-based affective responses: Developments in schema-triggered affect. In R. Sorrentino & E. T. Higgins (Eds.), *The handbook of motivation and cognition: Foundations of social behavior*. New York: Guilford Press.

Johnson, D. W., Johnson, R., & Maruyama, G. (1984). Goal interdependence and interpersonal attraction in heterogeneous classrooms: A metalysis. In N. Miller & M. Brewer (Eds.), *Groups in contact: The psychology of desegregation*. New York: Academic Press.

Linville, P. W. (1982). The complexity-extremity effect and age-based stereotyping. *Journal of Personality and Social Psychology, 42*, 193–211.

Linville, P. W., & Jones, E. E. (1980). Polarized appraisals of out-group members. *Journal of Personality and Social Psychology, 38*, 689–703.

Miller, N., Brewer, M. B., & Edwards, K. (1985). Cooperative interaction in desegregated settings: A laboratory analogue. *Journal of Social Issues, 41(3)*, 63–79.

Moscovici, S., & Paicheler, G. (1978). Social comparison and social recognition: Two complementary processes of identification. In H. Tajfel (Ed.), *Differentiation between social groups*. London: Academic Press.

Quattrone, G. A. (1986). On the perception of a group's variability. In S. Worchel & W. Austin (Eds.), *Psychology of intergroup relations*. Chicago: Nelson-Hall.

Rabin, I. (1985). *The effect of external status characteristics on intergroup acceptance*. Unpublished dissertation, University of Southern California.

Rogers, M. (1982). *The effect of interteam reward structure on intragroup and intergroup perceptions and evaluative attitudes*. Unpublished dissertation, University of Southern California.

Rothbart, M., & John, O. (1985). Social categorization and behavioral episodes: A cognitive analysis of the effects of intergroup contact. *Journal of Social Issues, 41(3)*, 81–104.

Slavin, R. E. (1985) Cooperative learning: Applying contact theory in desegregated schools. *Journal of Social Issues, 41(3)*, 45–62.

Stephan, W. (1978). School desegregation: An evaluation of predictions made in Brown vs. Board of Education. *Psychological Bulletin, 85*, 217–238.

Tajfel, H. (1978). Social categorization, social identity and social comparison. In H. Tajfel (Ed.), *Differentiation between social groups*. London: Academic Press.

Taylor, S. E., Fiske, S. T., Etcoff, N. L., & Ruderman, A. J. (1978). Categorical and contextual bases of person memory and stereotyping. *Journal of Personality and Social Psychology, 36*, 778–793.

Warring, D., Johnson, D. W., Maruyama, G., & Johnson, R. (1985). Impact of different types of cooperative learning on cross-ethnic and cross-sex relationships. *Journal of Educational Psychology, 77*, 53–59.

Weber, R., & Crocker, J. (1983). Cognitive processes in the revision of stereotypic beliefs. *Journal of Personality and Social Psychology, 45*, 961–977.

Wilder, D. A. (1978). Reduction of intergroup discrimination through individuation of the outgroup. *Journal of Personality and Social Psychology, 36*, 1361–1374.

Wilder, D. A. (1984). Intergroup contact: The typical member and the exception to the rule. *Journal of Experimental Social Psychology, 20*, 177–194.

CHAPTER 6

Environmental Influences on Communication

The environment in which interaction occurs obviously influences the communication taking place. The environmental influence on our behavior is so strong that Lewin (1936) includes it as one of the two factors in his definition of behavior: $B = f(P,E)$, where B = behavior, P = person, and E = environment. In other words, Lewin believes the behavior in which we engage is a function of us and the person with whom we are communicating, as well as of the environment within which the interaction takes place.

Lewin divides the environment into the physical environment and the psychological environment, or what people think about the physical environment. Both aspects of the environment influence communication. To illustrate the influence of the psychological environment, we need only look at the research on the impact of different types of rooms on behavior. According to Saarinen (1948), when we enter a room, we rarely feel indifferent about it. Research by Mintz (1956) suggests prolonged exposure to an "ugly" room brings about such reactions "as monotony, fatigue, headache, sleep, discontent, irritability, hostility, and avoidance of the room" (p. 466). Exposure to a "beautiful" room, on the other hand, brings about "feelings of comfort, pleasure, enjoyment, importance, energy, and a desire to continue [the] activity" (p. 466). Mintz's study illustrates one important aspect of the environment's influence on our behavior; namely, that we are not always aware of its influence.

The physical setting in which communication occurs defines what is proper. Obviously, such settings as an office behind closed doors, an elevator, a living room, a bedroom, and a formal dining room suggest different forms of communication within any particular culture. People within a culture are taught during the socialization process what it is appropriate to talk about in each of these different settings. As Deutsch (1954) observes, "it is evident that behavior settings are 'coercive' primarily because there exists shared frames of reference of collective action as to what is appropriate behavior in a given behavior setting or with a given behavior-object" (p. 194). (The preceding should not be taken to suggest the same communication cannot occur in different settings, because it can and does.) The setting in which the communication occurs also performs the additional function of defining boundaries about how to interpret messages. The same message transmitted in different settings can have two entirely different meanings. A physician asking a member of the opposite sex to remove his or her clothes, for example, means one thing in a physician's office, but an entirely different thing in a bedroom; only the context tells the receiver how to interpret the message. A "social act is always interpreted in relation to some normative context" (Deutsch, 1961, p. 398).

With respect to communication with strangers, the physical setting takes on increased importance for at least two reasons. First, what is appropriate behavior in a particular setting can differ across cultures. In some cultures (e.g., the United States) being in the living room of a home calls for informal conversation, whereas in other cultures (e.g., Colombia) being in the living room calls for formal behavior. Second, when we communicate with strangers, the strangers are often in a physical setting unfamiliar to them. The strangers, therefore, may not know what behavior is expected in that setting.

In the first reading in this chapter, Pandey reviews research on the environment, culture, and behavior. Pandey looks at the natural environment, the "built" environment (e.g., architecture), and the social environment.

In the second reading, Hall discusses our attitudes toward time and how they influence our behavior. Hall draws a distinction between cultures with monochronic (e.g., do one thing at a time) and polychronic (e.g., do many things at the same time) orientations. He also discusses what happens when a person with one orientation interacts with a person who has a different orientation.

REFERENCES

Deutsch, M. (1954). Field theory in social psychology. In G. Lindzey (Ed.), *The handbook of social psychology* (Vol. 1). Reading, MA: Addison-Wesley.

Deutsch, M. (1961). The interpretation of praise and criticism as a function of their social context. *Journal of Abnormal and Social Psychology, 62*, 391–400.

Lewin, K. (1936). *Principles of topological psychology.* New York: McGraw-Hill.

Mintz, N. (1956). Effects of aesthetic surroundings II. *Journal of Personality, 41*, 459–466.

Saarinen, E. (1948). *The search for form.* New York: Reinhold.

The Environment, Culture, and Behavior

Janak Pandey

. . . . The physical environment influences people and their cultures and, in turn, is influenced by them. Altman and Chemers (1980a, p. 1) suggest that people, cultures, and physical environments form a social "system." These parts of the system work together in an integrated way. We may take houses as an example. Houses created by people in different parts of the world differ a great deal in design, materials used, neighborhoods, and ecological context. For example, homes in the Middle East have high ceilings to minimize the effects of oppressive heat, but, in Alaska, Eskimo igloos are designed to conserve heat to provide protection from freezing temperatures and wind. Although modern architectural science has had a tremendous impact on house building, some cultural considerations may be found to influence the design of houses. In India, houses are frequently oriented toward sacred directions, ignoring the topographical suitability of the land. The quality and design of the houses depend on the economic prosperity of a society and its individuals. The physical environment and culture affect each other reciprocally. The understanding of relationships among the members (people, culture, environments) of this trio has applied value for architects and designers, planners, policymakers, and all those who influence environments.

CONCEPTUALIZING ENVIRONMENT, CULTURE, AND BEHAVIOR

Herskovits (1948), an anthropologist, defined *culture* simply as "the [hu]man-made part of the human environment." This definition, according to Triandis (1980, p. 2), includes "both physical objects (roads, buildings, and tools that constitute *physical culture*), and subjective responses to what is [hu]man-made (myths, roles, values, and attitudes), which constitute *subjective culture*." Subjective responses, however, may also be toward the natural environment (mountains, rivers, deserts, and so on). This definition of culture and its physical and subjective dimensions reveals a very close relationship with the environment. White (1949) emphasizes symbolic behavior, especially language, that helps in the transmission of wisdom concerning skills for coping with the environment. Culture appears in people's perceptions, beliefs, values, norms, customs, and behaviors as well as in objects and the physical environment. Home designs, layouts of villages, communities, and cities, public buildings and places reflect the values and beliefs of a culture. The concept of culture indicates ways of behaving and relating to the environment. It is important to understand how different aspects of culture affect and are affected by the physical environment.

　　　The effect of environment on behavior was well recognized by Kurt Lewin (1951, p. 25), who stated "that behavior (B) is a function of the person (P) and the environment (E), B = (P, E)." In his formula, he considered person and environment

Source: Abridged from Chapter 12 in R. W. Brislin (Ed.), *Applied Cross-Cultural Psychology* (pp. 254–277). Newburg Park, CA: Sage, 1990.

as interdependent variables. Lewin's assertion regarding the relationship between person and environment is widely accepted. Sinha has argued that, despite acceptance of the role of environment in behavior, the discipline of psychology has given relatively more importance to individual variables than to the environment. Various psychological processes such as perceptions, cognitions, attitudes, beliefs, and abilities, both physical and mental, are affected by environmental influences. Recognizing the importance of environmental variables, Sinha (1981, p. 27) comments: "The nature of environment provides the necessary inputs, stimulation, and experiential base for the development of perceptual skills of various kinds." In addition, overt behaviors that help to achieve privacy and to control territories, migrations, use of land, and so forth act in relation to the environment.

Human geographers argue that, because all food, clothing, shelter, and other material things that surround people are derived from things produced by the earth, it becomes important to examine people's natural surroundings, called "the human habitat." The characteristics of various habitats result from the interplay of earth's surface features, water, vegetation, and soil. People's experience in making a living from earth resources has differed in various geographical areas of the world, leading to changes in habitats and cutlure. Therefore, some human geographers, cultural anthropologists, cross-cultural psychologists, and others have advocated comparative study. We may identify three major domains of environments:

(1) natural environments (geographical features, landscapes, wilderness, disasters, pollution, energy sources, flora and fauna, and so on);
(2) built environment (buildings, architectures, roads, cities, communities, farms, technology, and so on); and
(3) social environment (territory, crowding, space, and so on). . . .

NATURAL ENVIRONMENT

The ability of human beings to adapt, individually and socially, to naturally or artificially occurring conditions of their environment is striking. Some geographers and historians have tried to account for the rise and fall of civilizations on the basis of the strategies used to adapt to environmental conditions. For example, Toynbee (1962) suggested that the environment (topography, climate, vegetation, water, and so on) presents a challenge to its inhabitants. Responses of the inhabitants to their environment may be adaptive, maladaptive, or creative. Rural people in India and some other regions of the world burn dried animal dung for heating and cooking in the absence of an adequate supply of firewood. This response could be first considered adaptive and creative, but in the long run such a practice destroys the environment because the dung is no longer available for use as a fertilizer. There is a very delicate relationship between people and their natural environment.

Whiting (1964), in his study of the role of the environment in the development of culture and individual personality, found that in tropical climates diets are mostly based on fruits and roots, leading to low consumption of protein. To compensate for protein deficiency, children depend on mother's milk, and, therefore, weaning in such regions takes place quite late. Children, because of long periods of breast-feeding, develop very strong bonds to their mothers. Whiting has tried to show causal influences of climate on culture and personality development. Some others, like Barry, Bacon, and Child (1957), have argued that the relationships of culture and personality to the environment are mostly bidirectional and interdependent. They argue that nonnomadic agricultural cultures seem to emphasize dependence, responsibility, and obedience in child-rearing practices. Hunter/gatherer cultures, on the other hand, emphasize independence and innovation. People who are stationed at one place in an organized community, rural or urban, require structured organization, and, therefore, they require obedience and compliance. On the other hand, hunter/gatherers inculcate independence and resourcefulness in their children, so that children can face unpredictable environmental demands. It seems that an environment provides fertile soil for the development of a culture and an individual that can best survive in that particular environment.

In the process of adaptation to the environment, equilibrium is achieved through the dual processes of adaptation (changes in people and culture) and adjustment (changes in the environment). It is important to mention that, in many cases, this equilibrium is threatened when we fail to take a long-term perspective on the aftereffects of changes in the environment in which we live. For example, uncontrolled use of various kinds of pesticides may provide the short-term advantage of increased production of a crop, but it may produce long-term negative effects such as loss of lives of birds and the introduction of new diseases in man, animals, and plants. It may lead to long-term deleterious effects on the ecological balance between humans and environment. The killing of frogs in the paddy fields of Kerala, India, for export to earn money and to meet Western demands for a food delicacy creates an imbalance in the ecology of the paddy fields, leading to an increase in the population of insects (no longer eaten by frogs) that destroy the crops. . . .

BUILT ENVIRONMENT

The *built environment* refers to what people create in the form of homes, hospitals, schools, communities, cities, roads, parks, and other modifications of the natural environment. It seems that humans are by nature builders. We are continuously in the process of planning, designing, and constructing private and public buildings and other facilities. The built environment, once created, constantly influences our interpersonal relationships. Our experiences of the built environment help us to reshape and construct our future environment.

The built environment is greatly influenced by natural environmental factors such as climate, landscape, available resources, and culture. For example, Rapoport (1969) has related home and community design to cultural factors. For example, in the Dogon and Bambara communities (Niger, Africa), people build villages in pairs to represent heaven and earth. They believe that the world is created spirally, and, therefore, agricultural fields are arranged in spirals. Rapoport (1969) has mentioned that, in some Baltic countries, villages are designed in a manner to relate to heavenly bodies like the path of the sun. The streets in the village run north-south, and doors and facades of the houses face east-west to receive preferred sun positions during the day. Some cultures emphasize privacy, and, therefore, homes are often surrounded by walls (Iran, India, Japan). In several African communities too, people build walls around their houses or clusters of houses to maintain privacy and territoriality.

The growth and demand for space is a major force in the development and preservation of the environment. Unfortunately, because of unabated population growth, particularly in India and other developing countries, usable land has shrunk significantly in size and proportion (Pandey & Nagar, 1987). With the exception of only a small percentage of affluent people, a larger percentage of the population in developing countries are facing greater problems of housing due to overcongestion in cities and, in some countries, even in villages. The growth of slums in the developing countries is primarily the result of excessive population growth and poverty. Although the built environment is influenced by cultural characteristics, variables like available space, density of population, economic resources, building materials, and so forth determine the design and construction of houses, public facilities (parks, schools, hospitals, roads), villages, and cities.

In his chapter on residential environments, Tognoli (1987) identified some salient sociocultural functions of the home. First, the home is the central place of human existence and provides a sense of rootedness and attachment. Second, the home includes aspects of heritage and connections with one's origin. Third, the home provides privacy, security, and ownership. Fourth, an individual develops self-identification of belonging and a feeling of control. Individuals decorate their homes according to their personalities and cultures. Fifth, home provides a context for social and family relations. Sixth, home is conceptualized as a sociocultural unit (Rapoport, 1969). According to Rapoport, any conceptualization of home is highly culture-bound. House-settlement complexes must be examined in relation to activities that occur there, and these activities have some commonality and differences across cultures. Altman and Chemers (1980a, 1980b) consider home as the outcome of the "interplay" of environmental and cultural factors. Tognoli (1987) suggests that physical factors such as climate and house construction materials and techniques are less important than primary sociocultural factors such as style of life, social structure and hierarchy, ways of fulfilling basic needs, family structure, position of women and men, privacy, territoriality, social relations, and so forth.

The term *housing* is a pluralistic concept and it has been used in the context of neighborhoods. The residents of a neighborhood value compatibility for their social adjustment. For example, in India's traditional villages, one may find houses built together among people of similar caste and/or among people who have similar professions. The hierarchy of castes is also easily observable in the segregation of houses of different castes. The design and size of homes differ in the same culture due to professional differences and structure of the families. For example, a farmer's house in a village will be different from the house of a carpenter or a barber. Housing is linked with race and class issues in the United States and in many other developed countries.

Although, in the United States, segregation and discrimination have been found in housing, some scholars have noted that residents of a desegregated community managed to maintain a stable neighborhood when residents were of an equal social status (Heuman, 1979).

SOCIAL ENVIRONMENTS

Our reactions and adjustments in various environments are most severely and most often affected by the other people who surround us. Our use of personal space, decisions about territories, sense of privacy, and reactions to crowding are determined by the people with whom we interact in various physical environments. Privacy, personal space, territoriality, and crowding are environmental issues, but they are highly social and cultural in nature.

With the pioneering work of Hall (1966) and Sommer (1969) on personal space and the equally compelling and popular work of Ardrey (1966) on territoriality, the initial understanding of how animals as well as human beings use and react to physical space in the actual or implied presence of others began to show signs of theoretical development. From then onward, scholars have made significant headway in theorizing and empirically demonstrating how people in a densely populated environment tend to regulate their spatial needs and thus reduce the discrepancy between desired and attained levels of privacy so as to overcome mismatches between their needs and environmental demands. For instance, it is often noticed that, in a crowded rural Indian home, some inhabitants tend to sleep outdoors in summer, partly to attain desired privacy. They also tend to adjust their timing with other residents (sleeping, eating, staying at home) as a way to reduce the adverse effects of crowding-related annoyance. The objective here is not to review all the interrelated studies on personal space, territorial behavior, privacy regulation, and crowding but just to highlight some studies to support a coherent theme regarding the impact of physical environment on social behaviors in varied cultural contexts.

Proxemics

The term *proxemics* was first used in a cross-cultural context by an anthropologist, Edward Hall (1966). The use of this term largely centered on the characterization of interpersonal distance in various cultural groups. However, the concept has become broadened: It incorporates the role of various spatial factors and is used as a determinant as well as a consequent of social behavior.

With some exceptions (Altman, 1975), most scholars have attempted to use the concepts of crowding, personal space, privacy, and territoriality interchangeably and have tried to unite them in a single broad theoretical framework of proxemics. Crowding-related effects are often explained by scholars in terms of personal space violation (Worchel & Teddlie, 1976), and privacy regulations, in terms of territorial behavior. Irwin Altman (1975) emphasized the importance of privacy and viewed it as a dialectic process in his theory of the environment-behavior interface. Utilizing a transactional perspective, Altman and his colleagues have identified several important characteristic features of this concept (Altman & Chemers, 1980a, 1980b). They conceived privacy as a dynamic interplay between the opposing forces of openness and closedness. Irrespective of the cultural setting, people have a general tendency to open or close the level of social interaction and thus regulate their social contact with others. We can see this in our own lives. Sometimes we want solitude, and thus we make ourselves unavailable even to our friends by closing curtains and doors. At other times, we make ourselves open to visual surveillance and social interaction. In addition, openness and closedness vary over time and across situations and are viewed as boundary-control processes.

To achieve privacy and to regulate the quality of social interaction, a series of behavioral mechanisms are used: verbal, paraverbal, and nonverbal behaviors. Another distinctive feature of privacy is selective control. This suggests that we all seek optimum privacy, and any deflection from an optimal degree of openness of the self to others is perceived by the individual as mentally harmful and socially undesirable. It seems plausible to expect that culturally universal processes to manage desired privacy are operative across different cultures (Lonner, 1980). However, specific behavioral mechanisms used to regulate privacy might differ across diverse cultures because of different norms, sanctioned behavioral patterns, and cultural styles. In the Muslim culture, young women cover their faces with veils while going out, and, in North Indian traditional societies, curtains are used to keep women circulating in the house from being noticed by visitors.

Crowding

The unabated increase in the population of the world and issues related to population growth are receiving a great deal of attention by behavioral scientists, demographers, policymakers, and concerned lay people. An initial study carried out by Calhoun (1962) on overpopulation among rodents (to be described below) did not attract a lot of immediate research attention. However, since the 1970s, a great deal of work has been done on crowding and spatial behavior, and some elaborate reviews (Baum & Paulus 1987; Paulus & Nagar, in press; Sundstromm, 1978) are available.

The term *crowding* has been operationalized in a variety of ways depending upon the nature of the study to be carried out. In the laboratory setting, crowding is generally equated with density. Various forms of density can be manipulated, such as (a) spatial density and (b) social density that reduces interpersonal distance, to bring about crowding-related effects. This objective indicator of crowding resulting from density manipulation has been used across different cultures (Griffitt & Veitch, 1971; Jain, 1987; Paulus, Annis, Seta, Schkade, & Matthews, 1976). Stokols (1972) made an important distinction between density and crowding. He considers density in terms of a physical parameter of population concentration. Density in physical terms can be measured in terms of number of people in a limited space, in terms of number of people per square acre, or by census data. Stokols (1972) pointed out that density can be an important antecedent condition of crowding; it is not at all a sufficient condition. Crowding, a subjective feeling, is often experienced when density causes stress and discomfort. Another way of distinguishing density from crowding is to imagine two people in a small room with 10 others. One person may feel "crowded," the second quite comfortable, even though the objective density is the same. . . .

The role of cultural coping mechanisms in response to density and crowding has been noted by many scholars (Altman & Chemers, 1980a, 1980b; Michelson, 1970; Rapoport, 1980). For instance, Rogler (1967) investigated squatter families in Colombia and Peru. These communities evolved their own methods of privacy regulation to overcome the ill effects of density. For instance, strong reactions to intrusion, the seclusion of children, and the rejection of newcomers were the methods for coping employed by these communities. The same theme emerges in analyses of crowding in Mexican slums, where people did not visit one another's home. People's need to be with others was satisfied through day-to-day proximity. The same people's efforts to obtain privacy were assisted through the avoidance of home visits. . . .

REFERENCES

Altman, I. (1975). *The environment and social behavior*. Monterey, CA: Brooks/Cole.

Altman, I., & Chemers, M. M. (1980a). *Culture and environment*. Monterey, CA: Brooks/ Cole.

Altman, I., & Chemers, M. M. (1980b). Cultural aspects of environment-behavior relationships. In H. C. Triandis & R. W. Brislin (Eds.), *Handbook of cross-cultural psychology* (Vol. 5, pp. 355–393). Boston: Allyn & Bacon.

Ardrey, T. (1966). *The territorial imperative*. New York: Athaneum.

Barry, H., Bacon, M., & Child, I. (1957). A cross-cultural survey of some sex differences in socialization. *Journal of Abnormal Psychology, 55*, 327–332.

Baum, A., & Paulus, P. B. (1987). Crowding. In D. Stokols & I. Altman (Eds.), *Handbook of environmental psychology* (Vol. 1, pp. 533–570). New York: John Wiley.

Calhoun, J. B. (1962). Population density and social pathology. *Scientific American, 206*, 139–148.

Griffitt, W., & Veitch, R. (1971). Hot and crowded: Influences of population density and temperature on interpersonal affective behavior. *Journal of Personality and Social Psychology, 17*, 92–98.

Hall, E. T. (1966). *The hidden dimension*. New York: Doubleday.

Herskovits, M. J. (1948). *Man and his works*. New York: Knopf.

Heuman, L. F. (1979). Racial integration in residential neighborhoods: Towards more precise measures and analysis. *Evaluation Quarterly, 3*(1), 59–79.

Jain, U. (1987). *The psychological consequences of crowding*. New Delhi: Sage.

Lewin, K. (1951). *Field theory in social science*. New York: Harper & Row.

Michelson, W. (1970). *Man and his urban environment: A sociological approach*. Reading, MA: Addison-Wesley.

Panday, J., & Nagar, D. (1987). Experiences of indwelling and outdwelling crowding and social psychological consequences. *Social Science International, 3*, 1–9.

Paulus, P. B., Annis, A., Seta, J., Schkade, J., & Matthews, R. W. (1976). Density does affect task performance. *Journal of Personality and Social Psychology, 34*, 248–253.

Paulus, P. B., & Nagar, D. (1987). Environmental influences on social interaction and group development. In C. Hendrick (Ed.), *Review of personality and social psychology* (Vol. 9, pp. 68–90). Beverly Hills, CA: Sage.

Paulus, P. B., & Nagar, D. (in press). Environmental influences on groups. In P. B. Paulus (Ed.), *Psychology of group influence*. Hillside, NJ: Lawrence Erlbaum.

Rapoport, A. (1969). *House form and culture*. Englewood Cliffs, NJ: Prentice-Hall.

Rapoport, A. (1980). Cross-cultural aspects of environmental design. In I. Altman, A. Rapoport, & J. F. Wohlwill (Eds.), *Environment and culture*. New York: Plenum.

Rogler, L. H. (1967). Slum neighborhood in Latin America. *Journal of Inter-American Studies, 9*, 507–528.

Sinha, D. (1981). Towards an ecological framework of deprivation. In D. Sinha, R. C. Tripathi, & G. Misra (Eds.), *Deprivation: Its social roots and psychological consequences*. New Delhi: Concept.

Sommer, R. (1969). *Personal space*. Englewood Cliffs, NJ: Prentice-Hall.

Stokols, D. (1972). On the distinction between density and crowding: Some implications for future research. *Psychological Review, 79*, 275–278.

Sundstromm, E. (1978). Crowding as a sequential process: Review of research on the effects of population density on humans. In A. Baum & Y. M. Epstein (Eds.), *Human response to crowding*. Hillsdale, NJ: Lawrence Erlbaum.

Tognoli, J. (1987). Residential environments. In D. Stokols & I. Altman (Eds.), *Handbook of environmental psychology* (Vol. 2, pp. 655–690). New York: John Wiley.

Toynbee, A. (1962). *The study of history*. New York: Oxford University Press.

Triandis, H. C. (1980). Introduction. In H. C. Triandis & W. W. Lambert (Eds.), *Handbook of cross-cultural psychology* (Vol. 1, pp. 1–14). Boston: Allyn & Bacon.

White, L. (1949). *The science of culture*. New York: Grove.

Whiting, J. W. M. (1964). Effects of climate on certain cultural processes. In W. H. Goodenough (Ed.), *Explorations in cultural anthropology*. New York: McGraw-Hill.

Worchel, S., & Teddlie, C. (1976). The experience of crowding: A two factor theory. *Journal of Personality and Social Psychology, 34*, 30–40.

Monochronic and Polychronic Time

Edward T. Hall

Lorenzo Hubbell, trader to the Navajo and the Hopi, was three quarters Spanish and one quarter New Englander, but culturally he was Spanish to the core. Seeing him for the first time on government business transactions relating to my work in the 1930s, I felt embarassed and a little shy because he didn't have a regular office where people could talk in private. Instead, there was a large corner room—part of his house adjoining the trading post—in which business took place. Business covered everything from visits with officials and friends, conferences with Indians who had come to

Source: Abridged from Chapter 3 in E. T. Hall, *The Dance of Life* (pp. 41–47). New York: Doubleday, 1983.

see him, who also most often needed to borrow money or make sheep deals, as well as
a hundred or more routine transactions with store clerks and Indians who had not
come to see Lorenzo specifically but only to trade. There were long-distance telephone
calls to his warehouse in Winslow, Arizona, with cattle buyers, and his brother,
Roman, at Ganado, Arizona—all this and more (some of it quite personal), carried on
in public, in front of our small world for all to see and hear. If you wanted to learn
about the life of an Indian trader or the ins and outs of running a small trading empire
(Lorenzo had a dozen posts scattered throughout northern Arizona), all you had to do
was to sit in Lorenzo's office for a month or so and take note of what was going on.
Eventually all the different parts of the pattern would unfold before your eyes, as
eventually they did before mine, as I lived and worked on that reservation over a five-
year period.

It was prepared for the fact that the Indians do things differently from AE
[American-European] cultures because I had spent part of my childhood on the Upper
Rio Grande River with the Pueblo Indians as friends. Such differences were taken for
granted. But this public, everything-at-once, mélange way of conducting business
made an impression on me. There was no escaping it, here was another world, but in
this instance, although both Spanish and Anglos had their roots firmly planted in
European soil, each handled time in radically different ways.

It didn't take long for me to accustom myself to Lorenzo's business ambiance.
There was so much going on that I could hardly tear myself away. My own work
schedule won out, of course, but I did find that the Hubbell store had a pull like a
strong magnet, and I never missed an opportunity to visit with Lorenzo. After driving
through Oraibi, I would pull up next to his store, park my pickup, and go through the
side door to the office. These visits were absolutely necessary because without news of
what was going on life could become precarious. Lorenzo's desert "salon" was better
than a newspaper, which, incidentally, we lacked.

Having been initiated to Lorenzo's way of doing business, I later began to notice
similar mutual involvement in events among the New Mexico Spanish. I also observed the same patterns in Latin America, as well as in the Arab world. Watching my
countrymen's reactions to this "many things at a time" system I noted how deeply it
affected the channeling and flow of information, the shape and form of the networks
connecting people, and a host of other important social and cultural features of the
society. I realized that there was more to this culture pattern than one might at first
suppose.

Years of exposure to other cultures demonstrated that complex societies organize
time in at least two different ways: events scheduled as separate items—one thing at a
time—as in North Europe, or following the Mediterranean model of involvement in
several things at once. The two systems are logically and empirically quite distinct.
Like oil and water, they don't mix. Each has its strengths as well as its weaknesses. I
have termed doing many things at once: Polychronic, P-time. The North European
system—doing one thing at a time—is Monochronic, M-time.[1] P-time stresses involvement of people and completion of transactions rather than adherence to preset
schedules. Appointments are not taken as seriously and, as a consequence, are

frequently broken. P-time is treated as less tangible than M-time. For polychronic people, time is seldom experienced as "wasted," and is apt to be considered a point rather than a ribbon or a road, but that point is often sacred. An Arab will say, "I will see you before one hour," or "I will see you after two days." What he [or she] means in the first instance is that it will not be longer than an hour before he [or she] sees you, and at least two days in the second instance. These commitments are taken quite seriously as long as one remains in the P-time pattern. . . .

Though M-time cultures tend to make a fetish out of management, there are points at which M-time doesn't make as much sense as it might. Life in general is at times unpredictable; and who can tell exactly how long a particular client, patient, or set of transactions will take. These are imponderables in the chemistry of human transactions. What can be accomplished one day in ten minutes, may take twenty minutes on the next. Some days people will be rushed and can't finish; on others, there is time to spare, so they "waste" the remaining time.

In Latin America and the Middle East, North Americans can frequently be psychologically stressed. Immersed in a polychronic environment in the markets, stores, and souks of Mediterranean and Arab countries, one is surrounded by other customers all vying for the attention of a single clerk who is trying to wait on everyone at once. There is no recognized order as to who is to be served next, no queue or numbers to indicate who has been waiting the longest. To the North European or American, it appears that confusion and clamor abound. In a different context, the same patterns can be seen operating in the governmental bureaucracies of Mediterranean countries: a typical office layout for important officials frequently includes a large reception area (an ornate version of Lorenzo Hubbell's office), outside the private suite, where small groups of people can wait and be visited by the minister or his [or her] aides. These functionaries do most of their business outside in this semipublic setting, moving from group to group conferring with each in turn. The semiprivate transactions take less time, give others the feeling that they are in the presence of the minister as well as other important people with whom they may also want to confer. Once one is used to this pattern, it is clear that there are advantages which frequently outweigh the disadvantages of a series of private meetings in the inner office.

Particularly distressing to Americans is the way in which appointments are handled by polychronic people. Being on time simply doesn't mean the same thing as it does in the United States. Matters in a polychronic culture seem in a constant state of flux. Nothing is solid or firm, particularly plans for the future; even important plans may be changed right up to the minute of execution.

In contrast, people in the Western world find little in life exempt from the iron hand of M-time.[2] Time is so thoroughly woven into the fabric of existence that we are hardly aware of the degree to which it determines and coordinates everything we do, including the molding of relations with others in many subtle ways. In fact, social and business life, even one's sex life, is commonly schedule-dominated. By scheduling, we compartmentalize; this makes it possible to concentrate on one thing at a time, but it also reduces the context. Since scheduling by its very nature selects what will and will not be perceived and attended, and permits only a limited number of events within a given period, what gets scheduled constitutes a system for setting priorities for both people and functions. Important things are taken up first and allotted the most time; unimportant things are left to last or omitted if time runs out.

M-time is also tangible; we speak of it as being saved, spent, wasted, lost, made up, crawling, killed, and running out. These metaphors must be taken seriously. M-time scheduling is used as a classification system that orders life. The rules apply to everything except birth and death. It should be mentioned, that without schedules or something similar to the M-time system, it is doubtful that our industrial civilization could have developed as it has. There are other consequences. Monochronic time seals off one or two people from the group and intensifies relationships with one other person or, at most, two or three people. M-time in this sense is like a room with a closed door ensuring privacy. The only problem is that you must vacate the "room" at the end of the allotted fifteen minutes or an hour, a day, or a week, depending on the schedule, and make way for the next person in line. Failure to make way by intruding on the time of the next person is not only a sign of extreme egocentricism and narcissism, but just plain bad manners.

Monochronic time is arbitrary and imposed, that is, learned. Because it is so thoroughly learned and so thoroughly integrated into our culture, it is treated as though it were the only natural and logical way of organizing life. Yet, it is *not* inherent in [hu]man's biological rhythms or his [or her] creative drives, nor is it existential in nature.

Schedules can and frequently do cut things short just when they are beginning to go well. For example, research funds run out just as the results are beginning to be achieved. How often has the reader had the experience of realizing that he [or she] is pleasurably immersed in some creative activity, totally unaware of time, solely conscious of the job at hand, only to be brought back to "reality" with the rude shock of realizing that other, frequently inconsequential previous commitments are bearing down on him [or her]?

Some Americans associate schedules with reality, but M-time can alienate us from ourselves and from others by reducing context. It subtly influences how we think and perceive the world in segmented compartments. This is convenient in linear operations but disastrous in its effect on nonlinear creative tasks. Latino peoples are an example of the opposite. In Latin America, the intelligentsia and the academicians frequently participate in several fields at once—fields which the average North American academician, business, or professional person thinks of as antithetical. Business, philosophy, medicine, and poetry, for example, are common, well-respected combinations.

Polychronic people, such as the Arabs and Turks, who are almost never alone, even in the home, make very different uses of "screening" than Europeans do. They interact with several people at once and are continually involved with each other. Tight scheduling is therefore difficult, if not impossible.

Theoretically, when considering social organization, P-time systems should demand a much greater centralization of control and be characterized by a rather shallow or simple structure. This is because the leader deals continually with many people, most of whom stay informed as to what is happening. The Arab fellah [or woman] can always see his [or her] sheik. There are no intermediaries between man [or woman] and sheik or between man [or woman] and God. The flow of information as well as people's need to stay informed complement each other. Polychronic people are so deeply immersed in each other's business that they feel a compulsion to keep in touch. Any stray scrap of a story is gathered in and stored away. Their knowledge of each other is truly extraordinary. Their involvement in people is the very core of their existence. This has bureaucratic implications. For example, delegation of authority and a buildup in bureaucratic levels are not required to handle high volumes of business. The principal shortcoming of P-type bureaucracies is that as functions increase, there is a proliferation of small bureaucracies that really are not set up to handle the problems of outsiders. In fact, outsiders traveling or residing in Latin American or Mediterranean countries find the bureaucracies unusually cumbersome and unresponsive. In polychronic countries, one has to be an insider or have a "friend" who can make things happen. All bureaucracies are oriented inward, but P-type bureaucracies are especially so. . . .

NOTES

1 *Beyond Culture* by Edward T. Hall, 1976 (pp. 17–20, 150–51, Anchor Press/Doubleday), also discusses these two time systems.
2 The exceptions are the large and important minorities who trace their origins to Spain (Spanish Americans, Cubans, Puerto Ricans, Hispanos from Mexico, as well as other parts of Latin America). The P-pattern tends to be associated with binding family ties, with large groups of relatives. One wonders if it is not an artifact of informal culture in such a situation as that of almost a hundred relatives arriving without notice or on very short notice and making demands. The Jews, the Arabs, and the Spanish share close family ties and extensive networks of friends as a cultural characteristic, and, though there are exceptions, all tend to be polychronic.

PART 3

THE ENCODING AND DECODING PROCESSES

CHAPTER 7

Decoding of Messages

Humans are active organisms. In making sense of our environment, we create meaning. A large class of social objects, such as our concepts of love, friendship, beauty, and freedom, "exist" only as created and collectively understood meanings. The perceptions of our environment as offering opportunities, as threatening, or as irrelevant are somewhat arbitrary because their meaning is a function of our interpretations of the environment; they are not an "objective" reality. In many cases such meanings cannot be derived simply from knowledge of such objective qualities. Through the process of decoding, we appraise the things and people around us and try to assess what meanings they may have. Because other people and objects are perceived and interpreted in terms of their meanings for us, it follows that our definitions and classifications reflect only in part the "real" nature of things.

When we decode a message, our interpretation depends on what the other person says verbally, what nonverbal behavior the other person exhibits, the messages we send to others, our conceptual filters, and the context in which the message is received. In other words, how we interpret the messages encoded by strangers is a function of what they have encoded, what we had previously encoded, the context in which we are communicating, and our conceptual filters.

Heider (1958) originally raised the question of how we make sense of our own and others' behavior and how our interpretations shape our responses to behavior. He believed that we act as "naive" or "intuitive" scientists when we are trying to make sense of the world. Briefly, Heider suggests that we are motivated by practical concerns such as our need to simplify and comprehend our environment, and to predict others' behavior and reduce our anxiety about the encounter. In order to meet these needs, we try to get beneath external appearances to isolate properties of others that will help us explain their behavior. Heider believes that others' motives are the dispositions we use most frequently in giving meaning to our experiences. He also points out that it is not our experiences per se, but our interpretations of our experiences that constitute our "reality."

Heider's explanation of how we make sense of others' behavior (i.e., make attributions) does not take into account that we are members of social groups. It, therefore, is necessary to look at how our group memberships influence the way we make sense of others' behavior. When group membership is taken into consideration,

195

we are concerned with how members of one social group explain the behavior of their own members and members of other social groups.

Hewstone and Jaspars (1984) isolate three propositions regarding the social nature of attributions:

(1) Attribution is social in origin (e.g., it may be created by, or strengthened through, social interaction, or it may be influenced by social information).

(2) Attribution is social in its reference or object (e.g., an attribution may be demanded for the individual characterized as a member of a social group, rather than in purely individual terms; or for a social outcome, rather than any behavior as such).

(3) Attribution is social in that it is common to the members of a society or group (e.g., the members of different groups may hold different attributions for the same event). (pp. 379–380; italics omitted)

Hewstone and Jaspars argue that we enhance our social identities when we make social attributions and that our social attributions usually are based on the social stereotypes we share with other members of our ingroups.

To illustrate the way in which we process incoming stimuli consider a situation where strangers are visiting Japan and are invited into a Japanese home. In a Japanese home, people are expected to remove their shoes before entering the house. The strangers may see the Japanese family's shoes by the door but not attribute any meaning to the stimuli and, therefore, walk into the house with shoes still on their feet. When the Japanese hosts become upset, the strangers will have no idea what they did wrong. The strangers' cultural backgrounds have limited the stimuli to which they attribute meaning, thereby influencing the interpretations they make about the situation. The Japanese host will, in all likelihood, attribute the strangers lack of knowledge to their cultural background.

The readings in this chapter focus on two issues that are central to decoding incoming messages from strangers. In the first reading, Jaspars and Hewstone outline the attribution process that occurs when we communicate with strangers. They illustrate the differences in the attributions we make when communicating with members of our ingroups and our outgroups.

In the second reading, Oddou and Mendenhall review research on person perception across cultures. They isolate major cognitive variables such as cognitive complexity and category width and illustrate how these variables influence the way we perceive strangers.

REFERENCES

Heider, F. (1958). *The psychology of interpersonal relations*. New York: Wiley.

Hewstone, M., & Brown, R. (1986). Contact is not enough. In M. Hewstone & R. Brown (Eds.), *Contact and conflict in intergroup encounters*. Oxford: Blackwell.

Hewstone, M., & Jaspars, J. (1984). Social dimensions of attributions. In H. Tajfel (Ed.), *The social dimension* (Vol. 2). Cambridge: Cambridge University Press.

Cross-Cultural Interaction, Social Attribution and Inter-Group Relations

Jos Jaspars and Miles Hewstone

. . . .

ATTRIBUTION THEORY IN SOCIAL PSYCHOLOGY

It is not our intention, nor would it be possible, to give here a complete exposition of attribution theory as it has developed in social psychology over the last 10-15 years. We merely want to highlight those issues in attribution theory which are of direct relevance to the study of cross-cultural interaction and intergroup relations. . . .

According to Kelley, attribution theory "is a theory about how people make causal explanations, about how they answer questions beginning with 'why'" (Kelley, 1973, p. 107). He goes on to point out that the theory developed in social psychology as a means of dealing with questions which are concerned with the causes of observed behaviour, as seen by the man [or woman] in the street. Such causes can, broadly speaking, either be sought in a characteristic of the person or in the environment. The theory deals both with the question of self-perception and with the perception of the behaviour of others. The crucial question for attribution theory, as far as the perception of others is concerned, is to specify how an observer arrives at a causal understanding of observed behaviour. Which information does the observer use? Kelley (1973) outlines two different cases depending upon the amount of information available to the attributor. In the first case the attributor has information from multiple observations, thus permitting him or her to observe and respond to the *covariation* of an observed effect and its possible cause. In the second case the attributor has information from only a single observation which makes it necessary for him or her to take account of the *configuration* of factors that are plausible causes for the observed effect.

Following suggestions made earlier by Heider (1958, p. 297) and Duncker (1945, p. 64) Kelley argues that it is convenient to conceptualize the process of causal attribution of observed behaviour (in the case of covariation) as a common-sense replica of analysis of variance. In this model the factors are *persons, entities* and *time/ modalities*. Each factor contributes a particular kind of information: from persons we derive *consensus* information, from entities we derive *distinctiveness* information, from times/modalities we derive *consistency* information. The covariation principle suggests that the effect is seen as caused by the factor with which it covaries and experiments conducted by McArthur (1972) and others (see Kelley and Michela, 1980) confirm that consistency, consensus and distinctiveness do indeed affect the attribution of causality in the way predicted by Kelley, although not all factors are of equal importance.

Source: Abridged from Chapter 6 in S. Bochner (Ed.), *Cultures in Contact* (pp. 127-156). Elmsford, NY: Pergamon, 1982.

The discussion of Kelley's three informational criteria (consensus, consistency and distinctiveness) leads to a more general question, concerning "psychological epistemology", i.e. the veridicality of our beliefs and judgements of the world. A person can, according to Kelley, know that his or her perceptions, judgements and evaluations of the world are true to the extent that he/she can confidently make an entity attribution. Of particular importance for the study of stereotypes is Kelley's liberal interpretation of the process of causal attribution when he writes that:

> the ascription of an attribute to an entity amounts to a particular causal explanation of effects associated with that entity—reactions or responses to it, judgments and evaluations of it, etc. So all judgments of the type 'Property x characterizes Entity y' are viewed as causal attributions (Kelley, 1973, p. 107).

This is certainly a somewhat questionable and elastic use of the notion of causal explanation since it is by no means evident that any attribute ascribed to an entity is always seen by the man [or woman] in the street as actually producing the effects associated with that entity. For instance, an attribute may be seen as nothing more than a shorthand expression for the observed actions of a person. It may well be that the ascription of an attribute to an entity may have the function of a causal attribution, but it seems reasonable to make a distinction between such implicit attributions and attributions which are explicitly based on inferences from observed behaviour. We should also be aware that we are talking about the explanation of behaviour and not about the explanation of the direct or indirect effects of individual or collective behaviour; however, these effects may influence the process of inferring the causes of the behaviour which produces the effects. In fact the theory of Heider (1958), expressed in his naive analysis of action, and the Correspondent Inference theory of Jones and Davis (1965) take the relations between action and outcome into account.

Thus far we have referred to Kelley's model for multiple observations, and his taxonomy of relevant information, but on what principles does the observer operate when only single observations are available? Kelley has suggested two principles or causal schemata which observers may use to arrive at causal attributions in this latter case. The first principle is known as the discounting principle and states that the role of a given cause in producing a given effect is discounted if other plausible causes are present. The second principle is called the augmentation principle and refers to the familiar idea that when there are known to be constraints, costs, sacrifices or risks involved in taking an action the action is attributed more to the actor [or actress] than it would be otherwise. The discounting principle and the augmentation principle are examples of what Kelley calls a multiple sufficient cause schema and a compensatory cause schema. A more complete discussion of these and other schemata need not detain the present argument (see Kelley, 1972). It is, however, important to point out here that Kelley holds that the layman [or woman] has a repertoire of such schemata available for trying to interpret social reality. He goes on to emphasize the importance of considering the interplay of these schemata and new information which rests on covariation of "cause" and "effect". It appears that existing causal preconceptions are much more powerful determinants of causal attributions than are observed covariations. Furthermore, simple, main effects schemata are preferred over more complex ones.

Emerging from this brief outline of attribution theory there are three main points which appear relevant to the study of cross-cultural interactions:

(1) The suggestion that when multiple observations are available an observer will attribute the cause of the observed behaviour to either something in the person or to the situation on the basis of the covariation of the behaviour across actors [or actresses], entities and times (occasions).
(2) An observer will experience his or her judgement as true to the extent that consensus, distinctiveness and consistency information provide for an entity attribution.
(3) In addition to basing attributions upon observed covariation of the factors mentioned, an observer will be influenced in his or her judgement by causal schemata such as the discounting principle, the augmentation principle, and so on.

Although there is a great deal of similarity between Kelley's theory of causal attribution, Heider's naive-analysis-of-action model and Jones's correspondent inference theory, there are a number of relevant differences which are important for the study of attribution processes in cross-cultural interaction. Heider's theory is, in essence, equal to Kelley's theory because one can argue that Kelley merely elaborates Heider's suggestions that causal analysis is "in a way analogous to experimental methods" (Heider, 1958, p. 297). However, Heider originally discussed phenomenal causality as an example of unit formation. Actor [or actress] and act, act and outcome, cause and effect were seen as examples of dynamic *Gestalt* formation or kinematic integration (Michotte, 1946). In this view it seems less important for causal attribution that covariation across persons, entities and times occurs. Rather, Heider argues, *Gestalt* factors like proximity, contiguity and *Prägnanz* (good form) will determine whether a causal attribution is made to the person or to the situation. On the basis of these *Gestalt* principles Heider also shows that in general a person attribution is much more likely than a situation attribution. But person attribution does not only occur because it more often makes a good *Gestalt*. Heider quotes with approval Fauconnet's rhetorical question: "Is a first and personal cause anything else but a cause conceived in such a way, that it can be held responsible, that it can furnish something fixed and constant to which sanction can be applied" (Heider, 1944, p. 361). The fact that a person is seen as a first or "local" cause beyond which we do not retrace the chain of causal inferences implies that (the effects of) the behaviour can much more easily and justifiably be annulled by "destroying" the absolute origin of the effects. This motivational basis of causal attribution processes has even wider implications in the case of inter-group behaviour. If the choice in causal attribution is between a person and a situation attribution, "person" and "situation" are constituted, in the case of intergroup relations, by members of in- and out-groups. Attributing the cause of certain events to an out-group or (one of) its members and blaming them as scapegoats then "exonerates the members of the ingroup from any blame for their conditions and prevents a lowering of the selfesteem of the ingroup members" (Heider, 1944, p. 369).

In his *Psychology of Interpersonal Relations* (Heider, 1958), Heider adds to this

Gestalt analysis of personal causality the criterion of equifinality. Personal causality is then equated with intentionality for which the fact that different acts may lead to the same outcome (equifinality) is a clear indication. Thus in addition to the criteria which Kelley has formulated for causal attribution we now have Heider's *Gestalt* principles and the notion of equifinality as another set of possible independent variables which may influence causal attribution. Research by Michotte (1946) and more recent research (Kelley and Michela, 1980) have shown that these factors do indeed have an influence on causal attributions.

Finally, before we can turn to the question of ethnic stereotyping and intergroup relations, we have to consider several criteria put forward by Jones and Davis (1965) and Jones (1979) for inferring dispositions from acts. In their theory of correspondent inferences Jones and Davis have suggested that the fewer distinctive reasons an actor [or actress] has for an action, and the less these reasons are widely shared in the culture, the more informative is that action about the identifying dispositions of the actor [or actress]. More specifically, Jones and Davis argue that the disposition or the intention governing an action is indicated by those of its consequences not common to the alternative actions and the fewer such noncommon effects, the less ambiguous is the attribution of the intention or the disposition (*the non-common effects* principle). The second factor which affects causal attribution, according to Jones and Davis, is the observer's beliefs about what other actors [or actresses] would do in the same situation (*social desirability*). If few persons would have acted as the actor [or actress] does, the action is seen as revealing a person's intentions and dispositions. Thus in Western culture it may mean little that a man holds open a door for a woman; if the same man slammed the door in the woman's face, we might learn more about his true intentions and dispositions. Thirdly, Jones and Davis suggest that the observer makes a personal attribution if the action affects the actor [or actress] personally (*hedonic relevance*). Thus if our Western man holds the door for a woman whom we know he is "interested" in, we might make a person attribution. Research based on correspondent inference theory has by and large confirmed that these factors do indeed affect causal attribution to persons.

Having considered some of the relevant basic principles of attribution theory we are now ready to consider the implications of an attributional approach to cross-cultural interaction, ethnic stereotyping and the study of inter-group relations in general.

ATTRIBUTION THEORY, CROSS-CULTURAL INTERACTION AND INTER-GROUP RELATIONS

Basic Distinctions

Before embarking on this ambitious synthesis a few basic distinctions are necessary. First of all it is important to distinguish between situations in which in-group members or individuals belonging to one culture are indeed in interaction with members of the out-group or other culture and situations where no direct contact exists. In the first case it seems natural to proceed from Kelley's *covariation* model of attribution; in the second case Kelley's *configurational* approach makes more sense. This is not to say that one should not pay attention to the causal schemata which people bring into cross-cultural interaction. Such schemata may in effect be extremely important, but from a theoretical point of view it makes sense to develop the pure case where people interact with members of other groups about whom they do not have any clear preconceptions and consider in the second instance how attributions based on observed covariation are affected by pre-existing causal notions.

In the second place we should take into account the nature of cause and effect in particular attributions. Attribution theory as formulated by Kelley, Heider and Jones has been applied mainly to the explanation of observed behaviour in terms of more or less permanent latent dispositions of persons and situations. It is concerned with the inference of an unobservable cause from observable behaviour. In certain cases we are, however, not interested in the explanation of the behaviour as such, but in the explanation of the effect or outcomes of behaviour or even in the (social) conditions which are characteristic of a group of individuals. It makes quite a difference whether we want to understand why someone makes certain political statements, why an accident happens or why someone is unemployed.

The attribution process becomes more complex when we are dealing with the explanation of social conditions which are used to characterize an individual. A state of affairs which we describe as unemployment is clearly not to be taken as behaviour (although it does refer to or imply a particular behaviour), nor is it to be seen necessarily as the outcome of the behaviour of the person who may be characterized by it. When a person or a group of people is unemployed, someone or something either directly or indirectly is seen as the cause, but such a cause is often only an intermediate cause which may be traced back to another first or ultimate cause (Fincham and Jaspars, 1980). In the case of unemployment we can give the state, a Conservative policy or the poor management of an employer as the cause of unemployment, but policies or management decisions can be seen as caused by practices and attitudes of workers. A social condition can thus be explained by indirectly attributing the cause of this condition to personal dispositions (attitudes of workers) or more directly to external social factors such as a government policy or a management decision. . . .

One final consideration should be mentioned before we discuss the application of attribution theory to inter-group relations and cross-cultural interaction. In many inter-group relations studies subjects are asked to judge themselves and members of particular out-groups on a number of personality attributes. From an attributional perspective such a procedure short-circuits, so to speak, the attribution process by not presenting subjects with the particular acts committed by individual members of the out-group or in-group. If such stereotype ratings are to be interpreted as the result of attributional processes, which is how Kelley interprets them (Kelley, 1973), we will have to consider such judgements as implicit attributions which are inherent in stereotypes. Such implicit attributions may, however, turn out to be quite different from explicit attributions based on observed behaviour or events. Sometimes studies confuse such attributions with simple descriptions of actual behaviour which may reflect misconceptions.

Covariation and Attribution in Cross-Cultural Interaction, or on How to Shake Hands with a Foreigner

In his hilarious handbook for beginners and advanced pupils on *How to be an Alien*, George Mikes (1966) describes the complexities of what is seemingly the simplest form of cross-cultural interaction: when to shake hands with an Englishman [or woman]. Starting from this simple example it is easy to see how attributions based on observed covariation may deviate from the general predictions of Kelley (1973). The easiest way to illustrate this point is to consider Kelley's "covariation cube" with the added distinction that at least one of the persons in the cube belongs to a group or culture different from that of the other persons in the cube. . . . If we consider the attributor as belonging to the same group as the actor(s) [or actress(es)] s(he) observes, Kelley's analysis of variance predicts that an entity attribution will be made when all persons observed show the behaviour (consensus) all the time (consistency) with respect to the same entity (distinctiveness). A handshake is therefore interpreted as a consistent social custom which is elicited by the behaviour of another person or the social occasion (circumstance). However, if we now consider the situation where the people who meet belong to different cultural groups, which differ with respect to this particular custom, we see that the behaviour also covaries with the social categories describing the differences between the groups. Since the same social occasion does not elicit the response in one group, but does so consistently and uniformly with members of the other social group a person attribution or an attribution to something in persons belonging to the same group is much more likely. In other words when an Englishman [or woman] does not extend his [or her] hand to greet a Polish visitor to Britain who is used to this custom, the latter may attribute the former's response as a sign of some personal quality of English people, such as unfriendliness.

Stereotyping an out-group member in this way can thus be explained as person attribution which is confounded with social category attribution. This is a prediction which follows directly from Kelley's analysis of variance model in which the person is nested within a social category distinction.

We should notice, however, that cross-cultural covariation also leads to person attribution. "We shake hands because we're friendly, they don't because they are unfriendly." If the context is not cross-cultural it seems perfectly natural to expect a situational explanation of the kind which explains such greeting behaviour as pre-scribed by social custom. This conclusion suggests immediately an interesting inter-pretation, which can be derived from Jones's correspondent inference theory. Jones and Davis (1965) and Jones (1979) have suggested that the attribution of a personal disposition is more likely to occur when behaviour is out of role, i.e., does not conform to custom or normative expectations. In the case of greeting behaviour it is easy to see that not performing the required or expected behaviour will be explained in terms of the other person's attitudes or intentions. If such behaviour occurs in someone belonging to a different social or cultural category the person attribution is associated with belonging to that different category.

Heider's *Gestalt* approach to the naive analysis of action strengthens even more the case for person attribution in cross-cultural interaction since it suggests that the person and his or her acts form a stronger *Gestalt* than the act and situational factors which also determine it. This will certainly be the case when the process of social categorization is enhanced by highly salient characteristics of group membership in cross-cultural interaction. In Heider's terminology such a situation will increase the "*Prägnanz*" of personal characteristics when searching for an explanation of manifested behaviour.

Summarizing thus far our extension of attribution theory to cross-cultural interaction we argue that:

(1) Behaviour of members of other groups perceived as out-of-role and unexpected from the perspective of one's own group is more likely to lead to person attribution.
(2) Since social categorization in terms of cultural differences is probably very salient in such situations, the person attribution will be associated with the perceived difference in culture.
(3) The same behaviour which gives rise to person attribution cross-culturally may lead to a situational attribution within a particular group or culture because social categorization does not covary with the behaviour, but is constant.

Until now we have only considered cross-cultural interaction which brings to the fore differences in behaviour between members belonging to different cultural groups. What if such differences do not exist or the only difference which exists concerns the fact that individuals belong to different groups?

The prediction which follows from our cloven covariation cube . . . is obvious and in line with the explanations which have been offered for the actor [or actress]—observer differences in attribution at the individual level. Cross-cultural interaction could lead to in-group—out-group differentiation in attribution based on cognitive factors as suggested by Jones and Nisbett (1972). It seems reasonable to argue that an observer in cross-cultural interaction has more information about the behaviour of the members of his or her culture or group than about persons belonging to another culture or group. Paraphrasing Kelley and Michela (1980) one might say that the observer may know nothing more about the actor [or actress], who belongs to a different group or culture, than his or her behaviour in a limited range of situations, but the observer knows of the behaviour of in-group members in many situations and is aware of its cross-situational variability. At the individual level this hypothesis has been tested directly for the actor [or actress]—observer difference (Lay *et al.*, 1974; Lenauer, Sameth and Shaver, 1976; Nisbett *et al.*, 1973; for a review see Monson, in press). The social extension of the actor [or actress]—observer difference in attribution to in-group out-group differences suggests immediately that perceived cross-situational variability of behaviour could directly be tested at the group level. The further suggestions made by Nisbett *et al.* (1973, stdy 3) that there is a gradient of dispositional attribution which relates inversely to the total amount of information available about other persons, can also be directly extended to the group level when we are considering differences in dispositional attribution with respect to more than one out-group.

It has also been suggested that the actor [or actress]-observer difference may be explained cognitively by a difference in visual perspective, in that the actor [or actress] attends to his or her task while the observer attends to the actor's [or actress'] behaviour. Attempts to manipulate the perspective of the observer, e.g. by showing the actor [or actress] a videotape replay of his or her behaviour, have shown that this leads indeed to less situational attribution (e.g., Eisen, 1979; Storms, 1973). An analogous change in perspective is possible in cross-cultural interaction when we compare newcomers' judgements of their own group with the judgements of people who have already spent some time in the other culture. One would expect those who have already spent some time in the new culture to have developed a different perspective, to look upon the newcomers as out-group members and to make more dispositional attributions than the newcomers themselves will do.[3]

Apart from the cognitive explanation we have suggested for in-group—out-group differences in attribution we should also consider, just as in the case of actor- [or actress]-observer differences, whether motivational factors might be involved in this social attribution process. A plausible common-sense hypothesis which has been tested in several actor- [or actress]-observer studies is that an actor [or actress] is egocentrically concerned with receiving credit for actions which have positive consequences and avoiding blame for actions which lead to negative outcomes. If such an egocentric motivation were to play a role, we could expect internal actor [or actress] attribution and external observer attribution in the case of positive behaviour and the reverse in the case of negative behaviour. Results of various studies (see Kelley and Michela, 1980; Monson, in press) are, however, contradictory in the sense that the effect has only been found in some studies and not in others.

One reason why the results of these studies are not so clear-cut is perhaps that there are processes at work which operate, in part, at cross-purposes. There is in the first place Nisbett's (Jones and Nisbett, 1972) cognitive theory which predicts an actor- [or actress]-observer main effect. The egocentric theory predicts an interaction effect of the actor- [or actress]-observer difference and outcome valence. But there is also the correspondent inference theory developed by Jones and Davis which predicts that there is a greater likelihood of dispositional attribution when the effects are highly desirable for the actor [or actress]. In fact, Jones and Davis generate rather confusing predictions in this respect, since they also argue that out-of-role (e.g. socially undesirable) behaviour leads to dispositional attribution. For simplicity, our predictions deal just with their first prediction.

Systematically we therefore have the complex expectations, shown in Table 7, for actor- [or actress]-observer differences in attribution. If we assume that the three processes just described are of equal strength in their effect on attribution we have to predict an interaction effect of the actor- [or actress]-observer difference and outcome valence in the sense that one's own negative behaviour will be different from all other conditions in that it will lead to more situational attribution. One could in general not expect a difference between self and other attribution for positive behaviour or an effect of outcome valence for attributions made by an observer. However, if under particular circumstances the effects of the three processes are of unequal strength any of these theories could be confirmed. It is therefore not easy to say which conditions would favour one or the other of the theories mentioned. It has been suggested by

TABLE 7 Actor- [or Actress]-Observer Differences in
Attribution Based on Nisbett's Cognitive Theory (C),
Snyder's Egocentrism Model (E) and Jones and Davis's
Hedonic Relevance Hypothesis (H)

| | | Outcome | |
		Positive	Negative
Actor	C	Situational	Situational
[or Actress]	D	Dispositional	Situational
	H	Dispositional	Situational
Observer	C	Dispositional	Dispositional
	D	Dispositional	Situational
	H	Situational	Dispositional

Snyder, Stephan and Rosenfield (1976) that a competitive situation would favour an egocentric attribution, because the tendency to attribute own gain to a personal disposition will be strengthened by the tendency to make a dispositional attribution for the other's loss. In general one might expect the egocentric hypothesis to become more important when the observer is affected in one way or another by the behaviour of the actor [or actress]. The desirability hypothesis might apply especially when the difference between actor [or actress] and observer vanishes because they share a common viewpoint. If outcomes refer to acts which are *socially* desirable one might argue that both actor [or actress] and observer will agree in this respect and infer that in general people want to do good things and only do bad things intentionally.

The last considerations bring us back to the original question which we set out to answer in this section: will the same behaviour be attributed differently if it is shown by an in-group or an out-group member? The answer to this question can now be qualified. We do expect dispositional attribution of behaviour by out-group members and situational attribution of behaviour by in-group members, especially when there are only intrinsic outcomes. However, when behaviour is clearly perceived as positive or negative we expect that positive behaviour of in-group members and negative behaviour of out-group members will be dispositionally attributed, whereas negative behaviour of in-group members and positive behaviour of out-group members will be situationally attributed. In addition to this we expect that, irrespective of in-group--out-group membership, socially desirable behaviour will be more strongly attributed to person dispositions. We would expect the same attributional processes to take place when positive or negative social conditions are attributed with in-group--out-group categorization.

Social Attribution and Culturally Determined Causal Schemata

In the previous sections we have looked at the possible transformations of attribution theory when actual interaction takes place between persons belonging to different social and cultural groups, or categories. In many cases we seem to be willing to make inferences about other people's behaviour on the basis of indirect information. The classical studies on stereotypes refer very often to national or cultural groups who have never, or only rarely, been in contact with each other (e.g. Katz and Braly, 1933). Clear stereotypes certainly appear to exist in such circumstances, but the genesis of these stereotypes must be considered as different from stereotypes which might emerge through cross-cultural interaction. It seems even more likely that the latter kind of stereotypes, and the attributional process they imply, are more basic in the sense that no-one ever enters into cross-cultural interaction without any preconceptions about the other culture. For this reason Le Vine and Campbell (1972) consider stereotypes between autonomous, independent groups as distinct from stereotypes held by ethnic groups which are integrated within a single political and economic order. LeVine and Campbell argue that in the first situation, when little or no actual opportunity for mutual observation exists, the groups are more ambiguous stimuli for each other and allow more autistic perception, "These fantasies may represent the wishes or fears of the in-group and may serve the group's need for solidarity, dominance or self-esteem or its members' individual motives" (LeVine and Campbell, 1972, p. 165).

It is precisely at this point that Kelley's ideas about causal schemata and Tajfel's theory of inter-group relations appear to complement each other. If there is, as Tajfel (1978) argues, a need for positive social identity which a person can achieve through social comparison based on social categorization, there are at least two ways in which a positive social identity can contribute to, for example, a high self-esteem via configurational attribution processes, as suggested by Kelley. The first case is represented by situations in which we are concerned with the common-sense explanation of social events which can be cast in an attributional schema analogous to the internal-external distinction made by Kelley in his configuration model. At the level of explanations for individual behaviour or interpersonal events the internal-external distinction is equated with the differentation in personal and (social) situational causes. When considering the internal-external distinction at the group level the out-group becomes the situational and the in-group the "personal" cause. Once we accept this interpretation of attribution theory at the inter-group level Kelley's discounting principle can easily explain the scapegoat phenomenon to which Heider has already referred in attributional terms. It follows from the discounting principle that attributing the cause of certain events to an out-group excludes in-group attribution, and hence may exonerate the in-group from any blame for their social conditions and thus prevent a lowering of the self-esteem of in-group members. An extension of the discounting principle to positive social events would follow in the same way. A victory by one's own group over another is probably more often interpreted as the result of own strength than as weakness in the adversary.

However, other causal schemata are probably called upon in other circumstances. External events probably require a multiple necessary cause schema, but it would be interesting to see whether such a schema is less likely to be invoked at the group level than at the individual or inter-personal level. Thus far we have made a distinction between in-group and out-group which is analogous to the person-situation distinction in attribution theory. However, the parallel can also be drawn in another way. One might equally well ask whether behaviour of in-group members or events directly or indirectly "caused" by in-group members are interpreted in a different way from similar actions or events related to out-group members. The predictions one could offer here are similar to the ones which were discussed for the covariation model. Assuming that one is more familiar with situational factors which can potentially explain behaviour and social events of in-group members a discounting principle is more likely to operate for out-group behaviour, whereas a multiple necessary cause schema can be called upon to explain in-group behaviour.

In the previous example we only discussed the common-sense explanations of one and the same social event or social act which could either be attributed to the in-group or out-group, or to personal or situational causes. In many situations we are confronted with a perceived or reported difference between in-group and out-group which calls for an explanation. We have already discussed this problem for the situation in which one is actually able to observe covariation of "cause" and "effect". However, if the (reported) observation is confined to one instance, a configurational explanation has to be sought. In this case we have to realize that, just as in the situation of selective cross-cultural interaction, the information which is available to the individual may have been selectively acquired or transmitted. In this case selectivity takes on a different form. We would like to put forward the hypothesis that where information is transmitted via news media a bias in the form of extreme instances takes place (for evidence of this bias see Husband, 1977). If news media are biased towards reporting extreme events, the consequence of this is that the likelihood of reporting positive (or negative) instances associated with one or the other group is very high. Given such reported instances, people will, according to Tversky and Kahnemann (1974), ignore the base rate of such instances, forget that such extreme instances are very rare and infer that there are large differences between in-group and out-group which call for an explanation. The inferred association of such differences with particular out-groups can be understood also as a non-common effect according to Jones and Davis's correspondent inference theory which leads to person rather than situational attribution. . . .

SUMMARY AND CONCLUSIONS

. . . The major contribution of this chapter, as we see it, is the emphasis we have put upon the fact that ethnic stereotypes or, in general, evaluative judgements of in- and out-group members should be seen as the outcome of an attribution process and not simply as distorted perceptions. Such a view makes clear why such personal evaluations occur in the first place. We have argued that in an inter-group situation behaviour which would normally lead to situational (entity) attribution, will lead to person attribution because of the added covariation with the observable social categorization. Such an effect, we have argued, will increase in strength because the interaction which takes place between individuals belonging to different ethnic groups is very often highly selective in nature.

It also follows from an attributional point of view that different attributions will be made for in- and out-group members when observers are confronted with exactly the same behaviour by an in-group or an out-group member. We have pointed out, however, that a simple actor- [or actress]-observer model of these differences is not tenable, and we have argued that one should take the nature of the behaviour into account in making predictions and especially the outcome of such behaviours for both actor [or actress] and "receiver".

We have also argued that even when cross-cultural interaction is limited to single interaction or to indirect information, attribution theory is applicable. In particular, it appears to be reasonable to assume that causal schemata such as discounting may play an important role because they can enhance the observer's social identity along positively valued dimensions. . . .

NOTES

1 This [reading] was made possible by a Social Science Research Council grant to the second author.
2 We would like to point out that this [reading] is itself the product of cross-cultural interaction between the authors, since one of them is English and the other Dutch. True to our theory of social attribution, each of us is therefore happy to accept personally any credit for the good points of this [reading], and to blame any errors on the other.
3 One of us who has now spent a few years in England as a Dutchman is regularly confronted with compatriot tourists visiting Oxford, whose behaviour he is sometimes inclined to regard as "typically Dutch", attributing it to such national characteristics as "uncouth, loud, etc.". Of course, he is willing to admit that his own behaviour may be seen in the same way by Englishmen.

REFERENCES

Duncker, K. (1945) On problem-solving. *Psychological Monographs*, 58, (5; whole no. 270).
Eisen, S. V. (1979) Actor-observer differences in information inference and causal attribution. *Journal of Personality and Social Psychology*, 37, 261–72.
Fincham, F. D. and Jaspars, J. M. F. (1980) Attribution of responsibility: from man-the-scientist to man-as-lawyer, *Advances in Experimental Social Psychology*, vol. 13 (Edited by Berkowitz, L.). Academic Press, New York.
Heider, F. (1944) Social perception and phenomenal causality. *Psychological Review*, 51, 358–74.
Heider, F. (1958) *The Psychology of Interpersonal Relations*. Wiley, New York.
Husband, C. (1977) News media, language and race relations: a case study in identity maintenance. *Language, Ethnicity, and Intergroup Relations* (Edited by Giles, H.). Academic Press, London.
Jones, E. E. (1979) The rocky road from acts to dispositions. *American Psychologist*, 34, 107–17.
Jones, E. E. and Davis, K. E. (1965) From acts to dispositions: the attribution process in person

perception. *Advances in Experimental Social Psychology*, vol. 2 (Edited by Berkowitz, L.). Academic Press, New York.

Jones, E. E. and Nisbett, R. E. (1972) *The Actor and the Observer: Divergent Perceptions of the Causes of Behaviour*. General Learning Press, New Jersey.

Katz, D. and Braly, K. (1933) Racial stereotypes of 100 college students. *Journal of Abnormal and Social Psychology*, 28, 280–90.

Kelley, H./H. (1967) Attribution theory in social psychology. *Nebraska Symposium on Motivation*, 15, 192–238.

Kelley, H. H. (1972) *Causal Schemata and the Attribution Process*. General Learning Press, New Jersey.

Kelley, H. H. (1973) The processes of causal attribution. *American Psycholigist*, 28, 107–28.

Kelley, H. H. and Michela, J. L. (1980) Attribution theory and research, *Annual Review of Psychology*, vol. 31 (Edited by Rosenzweig, M. R. and Porter, L. M.).

Lay, C. H., Ziegler, M., Hershfield, D. L. and Miller, D. T. (1974) The perception of situational consistency in behaviour: Assessing the actor–observer bias. *Canadian Journal of Behavioral Science*, 6, 376–84.

Lenauer, M., Sameth, L. and Shaver, P. (1976) Looking back at oneself in time: another approach to the actor-observer phenomenon. *Perceptual and Motor Skills*, 43, 1283–7.

Levine, R. A. and Campbell, D. T. (1972) *Ethnocentrism: Theories of Conflict, Ethnic Attitudes and Group Behaviour*. Wiley, New York.

Mann, J. F. and Taylor, D. M. (1974) Attribution of causality: role of ethnicity and social class. *Journal of Social Psychology*, 94, 3–13.

McArthur, L. A. (1972) The how and what of why: some determinants and consequences of causal attributions. *Journal of Personality and Social Psychology*, 22, 171–193.

Michotte, A. E. (1946) *La perception de la causalité*. J. Vrin, Paris. (Translation: *The Perception of Causality*. Basic Books, New York, 1963.)

Mikes, G. (1966) *How To Be An Alien*. Penguin, Harmondsworth.

Monson, T. C. Implications of the traits vs. situations controversy for differences in the attributions of actors and observers, *Attribution Theory and Research: Conceptual, Developmental and Social Dimensions* (Edited by Jaspars, J., Fincham, F. and Hewstone, M.). Academic Press, London. In press.

Nisbett, R. E., Caputo, C., Legant, P. and Maracek, J. (1973) Behaviour as seen by the actor and as seen by the observer. *Journal of Personality and Social Psychology*, 27, 154–64.

Snyder, M. L., Stephan, W. G. and Rosenfield, D. (1976) Egotism and attribution. *Journal of Personality and Social Psychology*, 33, 435–41.

Storms, M. D. (1973) Videotape and the attribution process: reversing actors' and observers' points of view. *Journal of Personality and Social Psychology*, 27, 165–75.

Tversky, A. and Kahneman, D. (1974) Judgment under uncertainty: heuristics and biases. *Science*, 185, 1124–31.

Person Perception in Cross-Cultural Settings

Gary Oddou and Mark Mendenhall

. . . The purpose of this paper . . . is to review two kinds of empirical literature; (a) that which has specifically investigated the relationship of cognitive characteristics and processes to cross-cultural interaction, and (b) that which represents a sampling of literature investigating cognition and perception not specifically studying cross-cultural issues, but which supplements our understanding of this very under-researched field and which suggests significant implications for understanding cross-cultural interaction. . . .

COGNITIVE SIMILARITY: CATEGORIZATION OF STIMULI

Part of the perceptual process is concerned with the cognitive "perspective" of an individual. *How* an individual categorizes perceptual information and *what* one's categories are certainly influence one's perceptions. Perceptual categorization is perhaps one of the most fruitful components of understanding cognitive similarity between cultures and relating it to cross-cultural attribution and adjustment (Detweiler, 1975, 1978, 1980). In defining category, Bruner (1957) described it as "a set of specifications regarding what events will be grouped as equivalent—rules respecting the nature of the criterial cues required, the manner of their combining, their inferential weight, and the acceptance limits of their variability" (p. 1330).

Bruner (1957) identified five important reasons for this categorization process:

1. To reduce the complexity of the environment.
2. To identify the objects (e.g. behaviors, etc.) in the environment.
3. To reduce the necessity for constant learning and reclassifying.
4. To construct a ready knowledge of appropriate and inappropriate action depending on the situation (i.e. the classification of accident, for example, calls for a particular type of action depending on the type and severity of the accident).
5. To relate classes of events to understand relationships among variables.

Bruner (1957) also mentioned that the categories by which a person "sorts out and responds to the world about him [or her] reflects deeply the culture into which he [or she] is born" (p. 10). The implication of cultural-based categorizing is that people from different cultures learn to attach meaning and learn to expect certain responses according to learned experience or socialization.

In order to understand the effects of categories used in perceptual processing, Triandis (1959, 1960a, b) found that the more similar the categories are that people use, the more effective the interpersonal communication and attractiveness. Triandis' studies were *intra*cultural, however.

Source: Abridged from *International Journal of Intercultural Relations,* 1984, 8, 77–96.

Korten (1974) investigated perceptual categorization with subjects from different cultures. Korten compared university students in Ethiopia and the United States and the similarity of their systems of perceptual organization. Korten found that the two groups categorized their perceptions using different classification categories. For example, to describe people they knew, Ethiopian students' statements characterized such categories as *opinions and beliefs* and *interpersonal relations*. Their American counterparts tended to describe their acquaintances in terms of *abilities and knowledge, cognitive-emotional style,* and *interpersonal style.*

If Triandis' and Korten's studies are accurate, combining their findings could lead one to posit that people from different cultures do sometimes process and categorize information differently, thereby encouraging ineffective communication and low interpersonal attractiveness. Certainly, research on stereotyping and intergroup attractiveness supports such a notion (Billig & Tajfel, 1973; . . .). Further, using different categories to process information may lead to stress and frustration, which can adversely affect problem solving (Glass & Singer, 1972; Glass, Singer, & Friedman, 1969) and acculturation (Tucker & Benson, 1979).

No doubt the way one categorizes information determines what information is kept or discarded (Bruner, 1957; Rosch, 1975, 1977). Even in one's own culture, categorization can result in an important loss of information. A graphic illustration of loss due to categorization is with colors. Out of a reported 7,500,000 colors in the world, there are about 4,000 English words to represent all these colors (Triandis, 1965). Of the 4,000 words, only 8 (the primary colors) are commonly used to represent all the colors—a ratio of one word to 937,500 colors!

Another example of information loss due to categorization, and one which is intercultural, concerns labels for snow. It is commonly known that the Eskimo has 26 different words to describe different kinds of snow. Obviously, survival in their environment demands a more specific knowledge of snow and its forms than in the typical American's environment, where snow generally is seen on a continuum of wet to dry. A conversation about snow between an Eskimo and an American might well lead to erroneous conclusions and misattributions.

Regarding the possible effect cultural-based categories may have on one's ability to effectively interact with people from other cultures, Szalay (1981) has stated, "The more we consider our views and experiences to be absolute and universal, the less prepared we are to deal with people who have different backgrounds, experiences, culture, and therefore different views of the universe" (p. 138).

Further, Triandis (1964) has stated that "Once a category is stabilized, subjects are likely to experience positive or negative reinforcements in connection with this category. As a result, people will learn to experience positive and negative affect states in the presence of the category" (pp. 6–7), thereby learning to keep, modify or discard categories or possibly even their system of categorizing. Receiving positive or negative feedback about how one "sees" the world and categorizes it, as one would in a foreign culture, would also influence one's attitude about the experience and people in the foreign culture. . . .

Category Width

Another important way in which individuals vary in categorizing stimuli is the width of the categories. As Detweiler (1975) explains:

> Category width (CW) is a measure of individual consistency in the breadth or range of perceptual categories, and is based on Pettigrew's (1958) conceptions. The major idea is that on many types of judgments (such as brightness of sky, the weight of objects, etc.), individuals consistently use narrow, moderate, or wide categories for classification. For example, can a vehicle with five wheels still be called a car? Can a one inch opening in a wall with glass in it be called a window? A narrow categorizer would probably not be willing to so classify these objects. . . . A broad categorizer should be willing to classify these somewhat discrepant objects as car and window . . .

It is of interest to the researcher to investigate the impact of category width on attribution and adjustment. Detweiler (1975) researched the relationship between category width and interpretation of behavior in a simulated cross-cultural context. American subjects were given short stories with positive or negative outcomes. The culture of the individual in the photo (the "actor" [or "actress"] in the story) given to the subjects was systematically varied to be an American or a foreigner (e.g., Haitian, etc.). Narrow and broad categorizers were then asked to respond to questions measuring the actor's [or actress'] intention, the locus of responsibility for the outcome in the story, the reasons for the actor's [or actress'] behavior, and the actor's [or actress'] dispositional trait similarity or dissimilarity to the respondent's. The results showed that narrow categorizers tended to make stronger, more confident attributions of intention and responsibility, and to attribute more undesirable personal traits to the foreigner when the outcome in the story was negative.

In a similar study, Detweiler (1978) investigated the influence of category width on attributions or persons of different cultures. Trukese and American subjects appraised persons of liked and disliked nationalities who were confrontive and aggressive in a story the subjects read. For both Americans and Trukese, the most negative inferences were made by narrow categorizers about persons from disliked nations. The broad categorizers had the least difference in attributions between persons of liked and disliked nations. . . .

Cognitive Differentiation

A concept very closely related to category width is cognitive differentiation; that is, the degree to which an individual differentiates between stimuli (i.e., the *number* of categories used to construct one's social reality rather than the *width* of the categories).

Werner (1948) was one of the first individuals to emphasize the importance of psychological and cognitive differentiation. He conceived of human development as a phenomenon that becomes increasingly differentiated and better integrated with age; advanced systems are more differentiated and integrated than primitive systems.

Some of the first empirical research with cognitive differentiation in cross-cultural research was done by Witkin, Dyk, Faterson, Goodenough, and Karp (1962).

Using varoius perceptual tests, they determined that the types of perceivers range from (a) those who perceive holistically without differentiation of figure and ground (field-dependence) to (b) those who discriminate, analyze, and differentiate (field-independence).

It has been suggested that the overall orientation toward field-dependence (FD) or field-independence (FI) originates from a physiological or cultural basis (Dawson, 1967; Witkin, 1967). It is the influence of the cultural basis that is of most interest here. Societies that emphasize conformity seem to have higher mean FD scores, while those that emphasize independence have higher FI scores (Dawson, 1967). Generally, agricultural societies require much more cooperation and emphasize obedience; fishing and hunting societies, however, emphasize independence, initiative, and self-discipline (Berry, 1976; Berry & Annis, 1974; Witkin & Berry, 1975).

In support of these conclusions, Berry (1966) found that the Temne, a highly obedience-oriented society, had high FD scores and the Eskimo, a hunting society had high FI scores. Similar findings have been found by others (Witkin & Berry, 1975). Apparently, the socialization experience within each culture seems to account for the difference in field orientation. Other differences between groups of people were found by Holtzman, Diaz-Guerrero, and Swartz (1975) who have shown Texan children to be more field-independent than Mexican children.

It appears from this research that cultures differ in the degree of differentiation. It also seems that an important distinguishing variable between FI and FD societies is whether the society emphasizes conformity or independence.

However, the relationship between the actual state of differentiation of a society (i.e., the number and kinds of stimuli existing in a society) and a corresponding primary mode of perception (FI or FD) of the people in the society has only been indirectly investigated (Berry, 1976). One might hypothesize, for example, that the average American would perceive more differentially than the Arabic nomad because the perceptual field of most Americans is much more complex (i.e., having a greater range of stimuli). How such socialized perception might affect cross-cultural interaction has been alluded to earlier (Detweiler, 1975, 1978, 1980; Glass, Singer, & Friedman, 1969; Tucker & Benson, 1979).

One area of differentiation in which cultures have been found to differ significantly is in roles and institutions (Foa & Foa, 1974). Bochner (1976), for example, compared religious role salience and differentiation in four cultures (Pakistani Moslems, Javenese Moslems, Thai Buddhists, and Philippine Catholics). Subjects were asked to complete 10 sentences beginning with, "I am _____." A measure of salience was determined by rank order of any religious reference (e.g., I am a *believer of God*) in the list of 10 sentences. The further up in the list, the more salient the role of religion. Degree of differentiation was measured by the *number* of references to religion. Bochner found that cultures differed in degree of religious role salience and differentiation. He suggested, therefore, that in these four cultures, cultural confrontation might be a result of differentiation of religion and salience differences rather than any actual doctrinal discrepancies. . . .

SALIENCE OF STIMULUS

In addition to understanding how cognitive differentiation affects perception and acculturation, it is of interest to know how the salience of certain stimuli affect one's perception. McArthur (1971) and Taylor and Fiske (1978) have found that perceivers do attend differentially to salient or distinctive stimuli and that such attention can have pronounced influences on social perception.

Variables such as physiognomy, color, customs, architecture, and so on can all represent salient stimuli to the person who does not share aspects of those same variables in his/her own culture. Such salience of features can provide the stimulus for categorizing others into in-groups and out-groups, for example, and for developing stereotypes. As Campbell (1967) stated:

> The greater the real difference between groups on any particular custom, detail of physical appearance, or item of material culture, the more likely it is that the feature will appear in the stereotyped imagery each group has of the other. (p. 281)

Although Campbell (1967) used the words "real differences," it can be safely assumed that perceived differences *are* "real" differences.

Cognitive psychologists have known for some time that perceivers attend to novel or distinctive stimuli more than to familiar stimuli (Langer, Taylor, Fiske, & Chanowitz, 1976).

How the Langer et al. study relates to cross-cultural perception is fairly obvious. A foreigner in a new culture sees many things as distinct from his/her own culture. The differences in cultures may become salient features simply because they are novel and because the foreigner focuses more attention on them. The saliency effect may become extremely important in forming the foreigner's impressions and conclusions about the people and their behavior in the new culture. Other things of the culture, less salient but equally important and common in the culture, may be omitted from the foreigner's consideration in creating a picture of the culture and making attributions about the people.

A related issue is one's perspective of saliency. When a foreigner moves into a new culture, the foreigner is often as salient to the hosts as the host people are to the foreigner. For example, a black tribe of Africans may view a visiting Caucasian just as novelly as the Caucasian views the African tribe. Further, it is possible that in many situations, the host people themselves may modify their normal behavior to deal with the foreigner in an attempt to be helpful or to determine the foreigner's needs. Likewise, the foreigner often modifies her/his normal behavior (i.e., that which is normal in her/his own culture) in order to deal with those situations that have no normal definition in the foreigner's own culture. For example, because there is no real equivalent to the Egyptian marketplace in the United States, the American in Egypt might well create new, abnormal behaviors for an American in order to deal with the heretofore unconfronted marketplace situation. To the degree this argument is accurate, misperceptions on both sides are reflective of unusual or abnormal behavior for both sides. In a sense, there is a behavioral interaction effect, upon which stereotypes are based, misattributions made, and varying affective states experienced.

In one study indirectly investigating saliency effect, Kim (1978) studied Korean immigrants' cognitive complexity by looking at the apparent saliency of perceptions of similarities and differences in friendship patterns between Koreans and Americans. The Koreans were living in Chicago and were sampled through mailed questionnaires. Kim obtained a composite score of perceptual complexity by summing the respondent's number of areas of dimensions of similarities and differences in friendshipping patterns between Korea and the United States. The assumption was that the ability to compare interpersonal relationship patterns is a reflection of the individual's overall cognitive complexity in perceiving the host culture.

The results show that newer immigrants were able to point out differences between cultures more often than similarities. However, Kim found a linear, though somewhat S-shaped curve for length of stay and increasing cognitive complexity. During the first 3 years, the immigrants' perception progressed steadily toward increasing complexity (i.e., increasing perceived similarities and differences in friendshipping patterns); then plateaued during the next 5 years; then increased again after about 9 years of living in the United States.

From the 7th to the 9th years, the number of friendship differences described by the immigrants was approximately equal to the number of similarities enumerated— the first time in the 9 years that the number of differences did not outnumber the similarities. One could conclude, then, that differences between cultures were immediately more salient but less so with increased exposure to Chicagoans.

Kim's research is useful in terms of delineating factors related to acculturation. For example, Kim found that length of stay, cognitive complexity, level of satisfaction, and positive attitude toward the United States were all linearly related. The results seem to point toward the efficacy of teaching similarities between cultures in cross-cultural adaptation training (Oddou & Mendenhall, 1982), thereby quickening the perceptual process described in Kim's research. Such training may serve to help one organize one's perceptual framework before actually experiencing the stimuli in the new culture, thus increasing the likelihood of seeing similarities. . . .

Categorization into in-groups and out-groups depends on finding some salient criterion or criteria by which separation of two groups can be made. Skin color, sex, physiognomy, intelligence, and many other variables can provide stimulus for such a cognitive division. With regard to separation of cultures by stereotypes, cultural characteristics and customs are typically the criteria that divide members of two cultures. However, it should be noted that evidence exists that indicates *inter*cultural differences may not be the only basis for the division between two cultures and for resulting stereotypes. Rather, *intra*cultural differences, such as occupational status or socio-economic level, may also underly cultural division (Feldman & MacDonald, 1980; Lambert, 1982).

Regardless of the origin of the division, once the division has taken place, the literature indicates that an individual tends to favor his/her own group in nearly every respect and disfavors the other group, attributing more positive attributes to one's own group and more negative ones to the other (Allen & Wilder, 1975; . . .). Furthermore, such research has firmly established that the favoring of one's group can be attributed to the existence of a *perceived* out-group, regardless of any *actual* differences among people that would merit division.

To give further support to other findings, Allen and Wilder (1979) and Billig and Tajfel (1973) determined to see whether perceived belief dissimilarity caused the same favor-disfavor dichotomy with *temporary* groups *arbitrarily* categorized. Their results were positive. Allen and Wilder (1979) also investigated the kind of belief statements that were more likely to cause a division between two groups or cultures. Their results show that perceived belief dissimilarity was stronger on task-relevant belief items, which supports the notion that perception of similarities and differences is at the behavioral level rather than the conceptual level.

In a somewhat similar study, Wilder and Allen (1978) investigated the effects of perceptual categorization of people into in-group or out-group divisions. They found that such categorization has implications for group motivation. Members of a group preferred learning about their similarities to other in-group members and dissimilarities to out-group members.

Although this study did not include ethnic or cross-cultural groups, the implications are fairly certain. Being a member of a group apparently only serves to strengthen one's ties with other in-group members by emphasizing similarities, while further alienating one from out-group members by emphasizing dissimilarities. However compelling the findings, one must still be cautious when interpreting Wilder and Allen's (1978) conclusions. In their research, Wilder and Allen used ad hoc groups rather than preexisting groups formed from some previous dividing criterion arising from the natural development and contact of each group (as in the case of blacks and whites in the United States). Such experimentation as Wilder and Allen's (1978) should be extended to existing groups for increased generalizability.

ILLUSORY CORRELATIONS IN PERSON PERCEPTION

As mentioned earlier in this paper, categorization of stimuli is highly functional. It organizes information about relationships between variables, facilitates retention, and acts as predictor of in-group and out-group members' behavior.

However, the classification process can also be deceptive. It can cause one to "see" relationships that are not really there.

In intergroup research on stereotypes, for example, the researcher is very interested in how individuals develop correlational relationships. Just how does one come to stereotype one group as lazy, another as shrewd, and so on?

Forming accurate correlational relationships requires an accumulation of instances of co-occurrences between variables, storage of this information over time, and accurate judgment as to the actual degree and kind of association. Given this complex process, it is not surprising that judgments about relationships between behaviors or other features of a different culture are often inaccurate. In previous material reviewed about salience of stimuli, we learned that certain kinds of stimuli are overweighted; others are underweighted in the process of perceiving, encoding, and storing. Such selective attentional processes can easily distort the actual kind and frequency of the two apparent covarying behaviors or events (Quattrone & Jones, 1980).

Researchers (Tversky & Kahneman, 1973) have empirically shown that subjective estimates of degree of association are based on retrieval of *relevant* instances from memory, a process they found to be subject to distortion. Unlike Tversky and Kahneman, however, Treisman and Schmidt (1982) found memory retrieval not to be the cause of illusory association. Instead, they discovered that attentional overloading causes an individual to make illusory associations.

However, in both cases (Treisman & Schmidt, 1982; Tversky & Kahneman, 1973), the research dealt with perception of objects in a laboratory and not people in a real world setting. Therefore, one must hold tentative these findings to person-perception phenomena, though the parallel is an appealing one.

Assuming such a parallel exists, it would suggest that because the individual entering a new culture for the first time is subject to numerous new stimuli, the more likely the individual will suffer from attentional overload, thereby increasing the tendency to make illusory correlations. Conversely, the individual who has had substantial exposure to the different culture—and who is sensitive to the acculturation process—has had time to accumulate instances of covariation, store them, and more accurately judge their relationship.

Thus, the inexperienced or unprepared individuals who become frustrated and leave the culture soon after initiation may be leaving with and because of many inaccurate conclusions about the people of that culture. The fact that other evidence (Kim, 1978) seems to show an individual initially sees more differences than similarities might imply that inaccurate conclusions drawn from stimulus overload (Triesman & Schmidt, 1982) are ones focusing on differences—and perhaps negative aspects—in the new culture.

In other research (Hamilton & Gifford, 1976) it was found that cognitive mechanisms involving information processing about co-occurring events with differential frequencies can distort the actual association of those variables. In two different experiments, Hamilton and Gifford (1976) tested the relationship between majority-minority group, group trait desirability, and perceived trait frequency. They varied the majority and minority group and also the number of desirable and undesirable traits. In both cases, they found that whichever group was designated as the minority group was also associated with the fewer number of traits regardless of the trait desirability; similarly, the arbitrarily assigned majority group was associated with the larger number of traits regardless of the trait desirability.

Conclusions about the perceived association of a group with a trait are probably often inaccurate, especially for the tourist, who is only briefly exposed to the people and culture. The literature clearly supports the notion that low frequency of contact with a group results in more [inaccurate] stereotyping than frequent contact (Everett, Stening, & Longton, 1981; Stening, 1979; Triandis & Vassiliou, 1967).

The conclusion that stereotypes are or can be formed as a result of cognitive processes and perceptual misinterpretations is not to deny the importance of socially learned stereotypes (Allport, 1954). It may well be that invalid associations are first developed largely through perceptual processes and thereafter socially transferred from one generation to the next.

Perceptual illusions can also be based on nonsocial stimulus factors. Brislin and Keating (1976) investigated the differential effects of a three-dimensional Ponzo illusion on different cultures. The Ponzo illusion is an effect that supposedly occurs because of the differences in peoples' natural or typical environment. Reportedly, people from carpentered environments, that is, environments that characterize converging lines, are more susceptible to such an illusion.

Brislin and Keating had a house built in a natural setting in Hawaii. They then placed two boards sticking upward in the sand at two different points next to the house, varying the position of one of the boards to be closer or farther from the other one. Subjects recruited were from the continental United States (staying in Hawaii at the time), from a large urbanized area in the Philippines, and from the Pacific Islands. Each group of individuals were asked to judge the length of the two boards in relation to each other. Results indicated Pacific Islanders were significantly more accurate than the other two groups, apparently being less susceptible to the illusion of a carpentered effect. . . .

CONCLUSION

Because of the apparent diversity of research undertaken and the findings reviewed, the following tentative conclusions and hypotheses (denoted by asterisks) generated by the findings are given in an attempt to provide some coherent view of the field:

1. Wide categorizers and FI perceivers apparently acculturate more easily.
2. Wide categorizers attribute less intention and responsibility to the "actor" [or "actress"] and have less confidence in their conclusions when judging a foreigner who is associated with negative outcomes.
3. Foreigners in a new culture tend to notice novel features (i.e., dissimilarities) more than others and tend to weight those features more heavily in judging their frequency. Therefore, foreigners sometimes misjudge the frequency of the feature. The apparent focusing on dissimilarities seems to encourage negative conclusions about the culture.
4. Individuals favor their own group and disfavor the out-group. Such a division seems to influence subsequent learning (i.e., similarities about the in-group; dissimilarities about the out-group), which serves to reinforce the strength of the division.
5. Under certain conditions, things other than ethnicity might be more important criteria for group division (e.g., occupational status, religious saliency).
6. Categorization is both functional and dysfunctional. It helps predict behavior and retain information; however, some of the information may be illusory due to

overestimation of differential frequency of the associated variables, overweighting of salient stimuli, attentional overload, and different environmental conditions.

*7. Frequency of contact between cultures correlates with the amount of stereotyping (i.e., low contact leads to high stereotyping; high contact to low stereotyping).

*8. Cultures differ in their degree of differentiation by the amount and different kinds of stimuli in the environment—social and physical. There is probably a correlation between a culture's degree of stimuli differentiation and the typical member's primary mode of perception (FD or FI). There is also probably a correlation between the degree of cultural differentiation and the type of perceiver that acculturates most easily. Those with high FI scores may acculturate more easily in a highly differentiated society, whereas both FI and FD perceivers probably acculturate with similar ease or difficulty in a culture low in differentiation (other things being equal).

*9. There is probably a dual level of analysis of people's behavior: (a) the behavior itself, and (b) the reason for the behavior (e.g., attitudes, intentions). According to research, the behaviorial level seems more important in defining differences and similarities between two groups. Furthermore, stereotypes seem to be mostly at the behavioral level.

*10. The reasons for entering a new culture and the length of time expected to be in the culture probably influence long-term learning and satisfaction in the new culture.

*11. FI perceivers are possibly less subject to illusory association than FD perceivers with regard to differential frequency of association of variables and attentional overload. FD perceivers are possibly less subject to illusory association with respect to overweighting of apparently salient stimuli.

*12. In a one-to-one or one-to-many exchange in which each party is foreign to the other, there is probably a behavioral and perceptual interaction effect where both parties are exhibiting and perceiving "abnormal" behaviors in reaction to the "abnormal" situation (i.e., one in which two different cultures meet). . . .

REFERENCES

Allen, V., & Wilder, D. Categorization, belief similarity, and intergroup discrimination. *Journal of Personality and Social Psychology*, 1975, **32**, 971–977.

Allen, V., & Wilder, D. Group categorization and attribution of belief similarity. *Small Group Behavior*, 1979, **10**, 73–80.

Allport, G. *The nature of prejudice*. Cambridge, MA: Addison-Wesley, 1954.

Berry, J. W. *Human ecology and cognitive style*. New York: Wiley, 1976.

Berry, J. W., & Annis, R. C. Acculturative stress: The role of ecology, culture and differentiation. *Journal of Cross-Cultural Psychology*, 1974, **5**, 382–406.

Billig, M., & Tajfel, H. Social categorization and similarity in intergroup behavior. *European Journal of Social Psychology*, 1973, **3**, 27–52.

Bochner, S. Religious role differentiation as an aspect of subjective culture. *Journal of Cross-Cultural Psychology*, 1976, **3**, 3–19.

Brislin, R., & Keating, C. Cultural differences in the perception of a three-dimensional Ponzo illusion. *Journal of Cross-Cultural Psychology*, 1976, **1**, 397–411.

Bruner, J. On perceptual readiness. *Psychological Review*, 1957, **64**, 123–152.

Cambell, D. Stereotypes and the perception of group differences. *American Psychologist*, 1967, **22**, 817–829.

Dawson, J. Cultural and physiological influences upon spatial-perceptual processes in West Africa. *International Journal of Psychology*, 1967, **2**, 115–128.

Detweiler, R. On inferring the intentions of a person from another culture. *Journal of Personality*, 1975, **43**, 591–611.

Detweiler, R. Culture, category width, and attributions: A model building approach to the reasons for cultural effects. *Journal of Cross-Cultural Psychology*, 1978, **9**, 259–284.

Detweiler, R. Intercultural interaction and the categorization process: A conceptual analysis and behavioral outcome. *International Journal of Intercultural Relations*, 1980, **4**, 275–293.

Everett, J., Stening, B., & Longton, P. Stereotypes of the Japanese manager in Singapore. *International Journal of Intercultural Relations*, 1981, **5**, 277–289.

Foa, U., & Foa, G. *Societal structures of the mind.* Springfield, IL: Thomas, 1974.

Glass, D., & Singer, J. *Urban stress: Experiments on noise and social stressors.* New York: Academic Press, 1972.

Glass, D., Singer, J., & Friedman, L. Psychotic cost of adaptation to an environmental stressor. *Journal of Personality and Social Psychology*, 1969, **12**, 200–210.

Hamilton, D., & Gifford, R. Illusory correlation in interpersonal perception: A cognitive basis of stereotypic judgments. *Journal of Experimental Social Psychology*, 1976, **12**, 392–407.

Holtzman, H., Diaz-Guerrero, R., & Swartz, S. *Personality development in two cultures.* Austin: University of Texas Press, 1975.

Kim, Y. A communication approach to the acculturation process: A study of Korean immigrants in Chicago. *International Journal of Intercultural Relations*, 1978, **2**, 197–223.

Korten, F. The influence of culture and sex on the perception of persons. *International Journal of Psychology*, 1974, **9**, 31–44.

Langer, E., Taylor, S., Fiske, S., & Chanowitz, B. Stigma, staring and discomfort: A novel-stimulus hypothesis. *Journal of Experimental Social Psychology*, 1976, **12**, 451–463.

McArthur, L. What grabs you? The role of attention in impression formation and causal attribution. A paper presented at the Ontario Symposium on Personality and Social Psychology, Ontario, Canada, 1971.

Oddou, G., & Mendenhall, M. The A-R-C cross-cultural training approach for pre-expatriate managers. Unpublished manuscript, 1982.

Quattrone, G., & Jones, E. The perception of variability with ingroups and outgroups: Implications for the law of small numbers. *Journal of Personality and Social Psychology*, 1980, **38**, 141–152.

Rosch, E. Universals and cultural specifics in human categorization. In R. Brislin, S. Bochner, & W. Lonner (Eds.), *Cross-cultural perspectives on learning.* New York: Halsted Press, 1975.

Rosch, E. Human categorization. In N. Warren (Ed.), *Advances in cross-cultural psychology.* (Vol. 1). London: Academic Press, 1977.

Stening, B. Problems in cross-cultural contact: A literature review. *International Journal of Intercultural Relations*, 1979, **3**, 269–314.

Szalay, L. Intercultural communication—A process model. *International Journal of Intercultural Relations*, 1981, **5**, 133–146.

Taylor, S., & Fiske, S. Salience, attention, and attribution: Top of the head phenomenon. In L. Berkowitz (Ed.), *Advances in experimental social psychology*. Vol. 10. New York: Academic Press, 1978.

Treisman, A., & Schmidt, H. Illusory conjunctions in the perception of objects. *Cognitive Psychology*, 1982, **14**, ·107–141.

Triandis, H. Cognitive similarity and interpersonal communication in industry. *Journal of Applied Psychology*, 1959, **43**, 321–326.

Triandis, H. Cognitive similarity and communication in a dyad. *Human Relations*, 1960, **13**, 175–183. (a)

Triandis, H. Some determinants of interpersonal communication. *Human Relations*, 1960, **13**, 279–287. (b)

Triandis, H. Cultural influences upon cognitive processes. In L. Berkowitz (Ed.), *Advances in experimental social psychology*. Vol. 1. New York: Academic Press, 1964.

Triandis, H., & Vassilou, V. Frequency of contact and stereotyping. *Journal of Personality and Social Psychology*, 1967, **7**, 316–318.

Tucker, M., & Benson, P. The prediction of intercultural adjustment: A longitudinal validation. Paper presented at the Annual Meeting of the Society for Intercultural Education, Training and Research, 1979.

Tversky, A., & Kahneman, D. Availability: A heuristic for judging frequency and probability. *Cognitive Psychology*, 1973, **5**, 207–232.

Werner, H. *Comparative psychology of mental development*. New York: International University Press, 1948.

Wilder, D., & Allen, V. Group membership and preference for information about others. *Personality and Social Psychology Bulletin*, 1978, **4**, 106–110.

Witkin, H., & Berry, J. Psychological differentiation in cross-cultural perspective. *Journal of Cross-Cultural Psychology*, 1975, **6**, 4–87.

Witkin, H., Dyk, R., Faterson, H., Goodenough, D., & Karp, S. *Psychological differentiation*. New York: Wiley, 1962.

Witkin, H. Cognitive style approach to cross-cultural research. *International Journal of Psychology*, 1967, **2**, 233–250.

CHAPTER 8

Verbal Behavior

Because it is impossible to transmit electrical impulses directly from one's brain to that of another person, it is necessary for us to put messages into codes that can be transmitted. Messages can be encoded into many forms, but for the purpose of our analysis two are most relevant: language (verbal codes) and nonverbal behaviors. (We exclude codes such as mathematics, music, etc.; nonverbal behavior is discussed in the next chapter.)

Language is one of the major vehicles through which we encode messages. Obviously, languages can differ from culture to culture. Culture and language are closely intertwined, with each influencing the other. Our language is a product of our culture, and our culture is a product of our language. The language we speak influences what we see and think, and what we see and think, in part, influences our culture.

When a baby enters the world, he or she begins to perceive that people in the environment behave in rather stable ways toward objects and toward each other. The baby also begins to see that adults employ special linguistic patterns. Through the gradual development of knowledge and the use of language, the child eventually learns to behave in the manner set forth by his or her elders and hence comes to understand and participate in that culture. The particular code the child learns, in turn, exerts a powerful influence on his or her interaction with the environment. By specifying or highlighting what in the environment is relevant or irrelevant, the code influences the nature of the child's experience.

In communicating with strangers from another linguistic or cultural group, the degree of shared meaning is likely to be minimal. This is particularly the case when the differences between two linguistic systems are considerable. An English-speaking person, for example, will have fewer commonalities with a Chinese-speaking stranger than with a German-speaking stranger, because the Chinese language is less related than the German language to English.

The relationship between language and culture was emphasized first by Boas (1911). He did this in a simple and obvious way by analyzing the lexicons of two languages, revealing the distinctions made by people of different cultures. A common example is the different degree of refinement in the vocabulary to describe snow. To most North Americans, snow is just one part of the weather, and their vocabulary is basically limited to two terms: snow and slush. In the Eskimo language, there are more than 20 terms, each of which describes snow in a different state or condition. This multiplicity of terms clearly reveals a dependence on an accurate vocabulary to describe what is not just a part of the weather but a major environmental feature for Eskimos. Since Boas's time, anthropologists have developed extensive knowledge and insights into this important relationship between language and culture.

The readings in this chapter are designed to help you better understand the way language influences our communication with strangers. In the first reading, Gudykunst and Ting-Toomey examine differences in verbal communication styles across cultures. They look at direct and indirect styles, as well as elaborate versus succinct and personal versus contextual styles of communication.

In the second reading, Philipsen examines the communal function of language in four specific cultures. He discusses male speech in a major city in the United States, speech as it is used on television talk programs, speech in Appalachia, and speech in Israel.

In the third reading, Edwards looks at how our attitudes toward language influence our communication with strangers. More specifically, he looks at how our attitudes toward dialects and accents and the vitality of minority languages affect our interactions with strangers.

In the final reading, Giles, Mulac, Bradac, and Johnson review research on the speech accommodation process. They isolate the factors that determine whether we converge or diverge toward the strangers with whom we communicate.

REFERENCES

Boas, F. (1911). Introduction. In *Handbook of American Indian languages* (Vol. 40). Washington, DC: Smithsonian Institute.

Verbal Communication Styles
William B. Gudykunst and Stella Ting-Toomey

. . . This [reading] focuses on verbal communication styles. . . .

Style is a meta-message that contextualizes how individuals should accept and interpret a verbal message. Verbal style carries the tonal coloring of a message. It is expressed through shades of tonal qualities, modes of nonverbal channels, and consistent thematic developments in the discourse process. Of the four stylistic modes of verbal interaction, the research evidence on the direct-indirect style dimension is the most extensive and persuasive.

Source: Abridged from Chapter 5 in W. B. Gudykunst and S. Ting-Toomey, *Culture and Interpersonal Communication* (pp. 99–115). Newbury Park, CA: Sage, 1988.

DIRECT VERSUS INDIRECT STYLE

The direct-indirect style refers to the extent speakers reveal their intentions through explicit verbal communication. The direct verbal style refers to verbal messages that embody and invoke speakers' true intentions in terms of their wants, needs, and desires in the discourse process. The indirect verbal style, in contrast, refers to verbal messages that camouflage and conceal speakers' true intentions in terms of their wants, needs, and goals in the discourse situation. Okabe (1983) differentiates rhetorical style differences between Japan and the United States as follows:

> Reflecting the cultural value of precision, [North] Americans' tendency to use explicit words is the most noteworthy characteristic of their communicative style. They prefer to employ such categorical words as "absolutely," "certainty," and "positively." . . . The English syntax dictates that the absolute "I" be placed at the beginning of a sentence in most cases, and that the subject-predicate relation be constructed in an ordinary sentence. . . . By contrast, the cultural assumptions of interdependence and harmony require that Japanese speakers limit themselves to implicit and even ambiguous use of words. In order to avoid leaving an assertive impression, they like to depend more frequently on qualifiers such as "maybe," "perhaps," "probably," and "somewhat." Since Japanese syntax does not require the use of subject in a sentence, the qualifier-predicate is a predominant form of sentence construction. (p. 36)

Johnson and Johnson (1975) make a similar observation, pointing out that "a child raised in a Japanese family learns that he [or she] should not call attention to himself [or herself] by being loud, conceited, or self-centered. Children who take verbal initiative are generally not rewarded, for the [Japanese American] subculture usually extols the quiet child as the good child" (p. 457). The language socialization process of Japanese children is aimed at fostering the norm of *enryo*, a ritualized verbal self-deprecation process for the purpose of maintaining group harmony. Johnson and Johnson also note that "the verbal styles of modal [North] Americans can be described as reflecting notions of individual worth, the positive value of assertiveness, and the tendency to conceptualize relationships as egalitarian" (p. 458). The language socialization process of North American children is cultivated toward the achievement of honesty. The norm of honesty reinforces the importance of using words and messages that reflect one's true intentions and values.

Clancy's (1986) observations of how verbal communication styles are learned by Japanese children supports the "intuitive, indirect communication" model concerning Japanese mother-child interaction. By using indirection in making and refusing requests, 2-year-olds are taught not to hurt the feelings of another person early in their lives, and they learn the subtleties of face-giving and face-threatening behaviors through modeling their mothers' behaviors. In addition, Japanese mothers typically use rhetorical questions to state their disapprovals and indicate disapproval mainly by their tone of voice and context. The norms of empathy and conformity are viewed as the primary reasons why Japanese children acquire the style of indirect verbal communication when interacting with other children and their mothers (Clancy, 1986).

Similar observations have been advanced by Hsu (1981) concerning the differences in communication styles between Chinese and North Americans. He notes that

> the [North] American emphasis on self-expression not only enables the [North] American child to feel unrestrained by the group, but also makes him [or her] confident that he [or she] can go beyond it. The Chinese lack of emphasis on self-expression not only leads the Chinese child to develop a greater consciousness of the status quo but also serves to tone down any desire on his [or her] part to transcend the larger scheme of things. (p. 94)

. . . The value orientation of individualism propels North Americans to speak their minds freely through direct verbal expressions. Individualistic values foster the norms of honesty and openness. Honesty and openness are achieved through the use of precise, straightforward language behaviors. The value orientation of collectivism, in contrast, constrains members of cultures such as China, Japan, and Korea from speaking boldly through explicit verbal communication style. Collectivistic cultures like China, Japan, and Korea emphasize the importance of group harmony and group conformity. Group harmony and conformity are accomplished through the use of imprecise, ambiguous verbal communication behaviors.

Katriel (1986) examined direct and indirect style usage in Israeli Sabra culture. She argues that members of Israeli Sabra culture use the direct style of *dugri* speech (or "straight talk") to achieve the cultural functions of sincerity, assertiveness, naturalness, solidarity, and anti-style. According to Katriel (1986), *dugri* speech in Hebrew "involves a conscious suspension of face-concerns so as to allow the free expression of the speaker's thoughts, opinions, or preferences that might pose a threat to the addressee" (p. 11). To Hebrew speakers, the use of *dugri* speech implies the concern for sincerity in the sense of being true to oneself. To Arab speakers, the use of *dugri* speech implies the concern for honesty by stating the information truthfully without concealments and embellishments. As Katriel (1986) summarizes:

> What stands in the way of truth-speaking in the Hebrew *dugri* mode is sensitivity to face concerns, interpreted as lack of courage and integrity. What stands in the way of truth speaking in the Arabic *dugri* mode is the high value placed on smoothness in interpersonal encounters as well as the ever-present temptation to embellish the facts for rhetorical purposes in the service of self-interest. (p. 12)

Israeli Sabra culture is a low-context, direct verbal style culture, while the Arab-speaking culture is a high-context, indirect verbal style culture.

In comparing Israeli verbal style with North American verbal style, Katriel (1986) borrows Gibson's (1966) term of "tough talk" style to characterize North American verbal interaction process. According to Gibson (1966), three speech styles can be found in contemporary North American prose: the "tough talk" style, the "sweet talk" style, and the "stuffy talk" style. He suggests that

> the Tough Talker . . . is a man [or woman] dramatized as centrally concerned with himself [or herself]—his [or her] style is I-talk. The Sweet Talker goes out of his [or

her] way to be nice to us—his [or her] style is you-talk. The Stuffy Talker expresses
no concern either for himself [or herself] or for his [or her] reader—his [or her] style
is it-talk. (p. x)

Building upon the "tough talker" concept, Katriel (1986) proposes that there are
both similarities and differences between the North American "tough talker" and the
Israeli Sabra culture's "straight talker." On the interactional level, both "tough talker"
and "straight talker" are concerned more with preserving their own face than their
addressee's face. They both share similar attitudes in terms of using the direct style to
fulfill the "antistyle" function. They both are concerned with the faithful projections
of their feelings concerning the issues being discussed. On the cultural-meaning level,
however, Katriel observes that the form of "tough talk" is "to be read as a reaction
against established cultural patterns after the First World War, whereas *dugri*
speech . . . is part of the reaction to cultural patterns associated with Diaspora life
and European tradition" (p. 101). While both "tough talk" and "straight talk" reflect
the interactional patterns of individualistic, low-context cultures, the cultural under-
pinnings and the historical-cultural logics that give rise to such stylistic variations may
vary from one culture to the next.

In contrast to "tough talk" and "straight talk," Arab-speaking communities can
be characterized as engaging in "sweet talk." According to Katriel (1986), the cultural
ethos of *musayra* (meaning roughly to go along, to humor, to accommodate oneself)
characterizes Arab communication patterns. One of her informants reported that the
concept of *musayra* "is in the blood of every Arab person" (p. 111). As Katriel
summarizes:

> It seems that the indirectness of style associated with the ethos of *musayra* is shared
> by men and women alike, although differences are found in the contexts, manner,
> and norms of style enactment of the two genders. The high value placed on *musayra* ,
> on metaphorically "going with" the other, on humoring, on accommodating oneself
> to the position or situation of the other, reflects a concern for harmonious social
> relations and for the social regulation of interpersonal conduct. (p. 111)

The verbal communication patterns of the Arab-speaking communities, therefore, are
reflective of some of the fundamental norms and values in collectivistic, high-context
cultures.

Cohen (1987) supports Katriel's (1986) observation. He identifies the dimension of direct-indirect style as the one of the four key dimensions that poses serious
communication problems in diplomatic relations between Egypt and the United
States. After analyzing several autobiographical accounts that produce dissonance
between Egyptian and North American diplomats, Cohen concluded that the values
of collectivism and conformity in Egyptian culture influence the use of indirect,
smoothing style in Egyptian diplomatic relations, while the values of individualism
and self-assertion in U.S. cultures influence the use of the direct, cut-and-dry style in
U.S. diplomatic relations. According to Cohen, the former is a shame-oriented,
mutual-face concern culture, while the latter is a guilt-oriented, individual-face
concern culture. . . .

ELABORATE VERSUS SUCCINCT STYLE

Different cultural assumptions underlie the dimension of verbal elaborate style and verbal succinct style. This dimension encompasses three verbal stylistic variations: elaborate style, exacting style, and succinct style. The dimension deals with the quantity of talk that is valued in different cultures. The elaborate style refers to the use of rich, expressive language in everyday conversation. The exacting style echoes the concept of Grice's (1975) "quantity maxim," which in effect states that one's contribution in language interaction ought to be neither more nor less information than is required. Finally, the succinct style includes the use of understatements, pauses, and silences in everyday conversation.

The linguistic patterns of people in Arab cultures reflect the use of an elaborate style of verbal communication. As Shouby (1970) comments on the Arab language, "fantastic metaphors and similes are used in abundance, and long arrays of adjectives to modify the same word are quite frequent" (p. 700). Wolfson's (1981) analysis of compliments supports this observation. According to Wolfson, Iranian and Arabic speakers' compliments typically are filled with metaphors, proverbs, and cultural idioms, while North American English speakers' compliments typically are very exacting and ritualized. To illustrate, an Arabic speaker in Wolfson's study complimented her friend's child by saying, "She is like the moon and she has beautiful eyes" (Wolfson, 1981, p. 120).

In analyzing the language style differences between Arab speakers and North American English speakers, Prothro (1970) concluded that "statements which seem to Arabs to be mere statements of fact will seem to [North] Americans to be extreme or even violent assertions. Statements which Arabs view as showing firmness and strength on a negative or positive issue may sound to North Americans as exaggerated" (p. 711). Almaney and Alwan (1982) analyzed the forms of assertion (*tawkid*) and exaggeration (*mubalaqha*) in Arabic language, concluding that

> the built-in mechanism of assertion in language affects the Arabs' communication behavior in at least two ways. First, an Arab feels compelled to overassert in almost all types of communication because others expect him [or her] to. If an Arab says exactly what he [or she] means without the expected assertion, other Arabs may still think that he [or she] means the opposite. For example, a simple "No" by a guest to the host's request to eat more or drink more will not suffice. To convey the meaning that he [or she] is actually full, the guest must keep repeating "No" several times, coupling it with an oath such as "By God" or "I swear to God." Second, an Arab often fails to realize that others, particularly foreigners, may mean exactly what they say even though their language is simple. To the Arabs, a simple "No" may mean the indirectly expressed consent and encouragement of a coquettish woman. On the other hand a simple consent may mean the rejection of a hypocritical politician. (p. 84)

Cohen (1987) agrees with Almaney and Alwan's (1982) summary of the Arabic language. He argues that the Arabs' proclivity for verbal exaggerations and elaborations have done more to complicate Egyptian-North American international relations than almost anything else. The fact that Arabic is considered a "sacred and holy language" and that "Islam forbids the depiction of living beings in visual form" probably constitute the reasons why an elaborated style of language is the primary vehicle for both creative and political expressions (Adelman & Lustig, 1981; Almaney & Alwan, 1982).

Similar to the exaggerated style of Arabic language is the "crooked" style of Ilongot traditional oratory articulated eloquently by Rosaldo (1973, 1980). According to Rosaldo, the Ilongot oratory also employs abundant use of metaphors, flowery expressions, and elaborate rhythms in its language system. The purpose of using such an elaborate style of speech is to negotiate relational equality and social harmony, whereas the use of "plain talk" is reserved for power assertion and relational dominance.

At the opposite end of the continuum from the elaborate style is the succinct style. Johnson and Johnson (1975) compared Japanese-American and Caucasian language interaction in Hawaii. They contend that Japanese-Americans often use indirection, circumlocution, and silence in their everyday language interaction. This is consistent with Hall's (1983) position that *ma*, or silence, is dominant in Japanese communication. According to Hall, *ma* in Japanese speech means that "it is the silences between words that also carry meaning and are significant" (p. 208). The concept of *ma*, however, is much more than pausing between words; it is rather a semicolon that reflects the inner pausing of the speaker's reflective state. Through *ma*, interpersonal synchrony is made possible.

Ting-Tommey (1980) studied language patterns in Chinese-American families. She found that members of tradition-oriented Chinese families use talk as a status resource while they use silence as an affiliative-power strategy. Members of modern-oriented Chinese families, in contrast, use talk as a distributional resource and use silence as a conversational-regulations strategy.

Wiemann, Chen, and Giles (1986) recently have begun a series of cross-cultural studies on the beliefs about talk and silence in different cultures. Based on their Beliefs About Talk Survey, they found that Caucasian-Americans perceive talk as more important and enjoyable than Chinese-Americans and native-born Chinese. Caucasian-Americans also perceive using talk as a means of social control, while native Chinese tend to perceive silence as a control strategy. Finally, native Chinese are more tolerant of silence in conversation than Caucasians or Chinese-Americans.

Similar to Asian cultures, Basso (1970) found that the concept of silence occupies a central role in the Apache culture in the United States. Silence is appropriate in the contexts of uncertain and unpredictable social relations. Silence is preferred over talk when the status of the focal participant is marked by ambiguity and the fixed role expectations lose their applicability. Basso also argues that members of the Navajo and Papago Indian tribes exhibit similar silent behavior under the same conditions as Apaches.

The use of an elaborate style characterizes many Middle Eastern communication patterns. The use of an exacting style is characteristic of people in many Northern European cultures and the U.S. culture, and the use of a succinct verbal communication style is characteristic of people in many Asian cultures and some American Indian cultures in North America. Middle Eastern cultures such as Egypt, Iran, Lebanon, and Saudi Arabia are moderate on Hofstede's (1980) uncertainty avoidance dimension and are high-context cultures. Denmark, Sweden, Germany, and the United States are low to moderate on Hofstede's (1980) uncertainty avoidance dimension and are low-context cultures. Finally, Korea, Japan, Taiwan, and Thailand are relatively high on Hofstede's (1980) uncertainty avoidance dimension and are high-context cultures. . . .

PERSONAL VERSUS CONTEXTUAL STYLE

Verbal personal style is individual-centered language, while verbal contextual style is role-centered language. Verbal personal style refers to the use of certain linguistic devices to enhance the sense of "I" identity, and verbal contextual style refers to the use of certain linguistic signals to emphasize the sense of "role" identity. In the verbal personal style, meanings are expressed for the purpose of emphasizing "personhood," while in the verbal contextual style, meanings are expressed for the purpose of emphasizing prescribed role relationships.

Gumperz, Aulakh, and Kaltman (1982) analyzed conversational styles in an East Indian English-speaking community and a British English-speaking community, observing that Indian English is very contextual-based, while British English is very individualistic-based. In British English, the use of personal pronouns and the use of temporal and spatial locatives (e.g., then, there) are vital in sentence constructions, whereas in Indian English, these linguistic devices are not emphasized. They concluded:

> In some cases explicit textual referents need not be present at all; where they are present and particularly where there are multiple possible referents, speakers use pragmatic rules very different from those of Western English. The general nature of the contrast is that Indian English users rely to a greater extent on shared assumptions about speakers' knowledge of the situation being talked about, rather than on structural features of the explicit textual context. (pp. 46–47)

Mishra (1982) concurs with the contextual nature of Indian English. She observes that speakers of Indian English like to provide many minor contextual points of a story before advancing the thesis of the story, while speakers of British English tend to first provide the topical thesis of the story, then proceed to provide relevant information.

Young (1982) analyzed Chinese discourse styles, making a similar observation. Rather than relying on a preview statement to orient the listener to the overall direction of the discourse, Chinese discourse relies heavily on contextual cues and tends to use single word items such as "because," "as," and "so" to replace whole clause connectives commonly used in English, such as "in view of the fact that," "to begin with," or "in conclusion" (Young, 1982, p. 79).

In commenting on the Japanese language, Okabe (1983) contends that English is a person-oriented language, while Japanese is a status-oriented language. The key distinction is that a person-oriented language stresses informality and symmetrical power relationships, while a status-oriented or contextual-oriented language emphasizes formality and asymmetrical power relationships:

> [North] Americans tend to treat other people with informality and directness. They shun the formal codes of conduct, titles, honorifics, and ritualistic manners in the interaction with others. They instead prefer a first-name basis and direct address. They also strive to equalize the language style between the sexes. In sharp contrast, the Japanese are likely to assume that formality is essential in their human relations. They are apt to feel uncomfortable in some informal situations. The value of formality in the language style and in the protocol allows for a smooth and predictable interaction for the Japanese. (Okabe, 1983, p. 27)

In other words, the Japanese language tends to put conversational members in the proper role positions and in the proper status hierarchical levels. The English language tends to emphasize the "personhood" of the conversationalists and aims for informality and symmetrical power distributions.

Similarly, Yum (1987b) notes that the Korean language accommodates the Confucian ethical rules of hierarchical human relationships; it has special vocabularies for different sexes, for different degrees of social status, for different degrees of intimacy, and for different formal occasions. The correct usage of the proper language style, for the proper types of relationships, and in the proper contexts are the sure signs of a learned person in the Korean culture (Yum, 1987b). She also argues that the Korean language is a context-based language because the cultural ethos of Korean communication style is based on the key concept of *uye-ri*. Three clusters of meanings define *uye-ri*. The first cluster includes justice, righteousness, a just cause, duty, morality, probity, and integrity. The second cluster refers to obligation, a debt of gratitude, loyalty, and faithfulness. The third cluster concerns the importance of proper relationships between people, such as the employer and employee relationship or friendship.

The philosophical orientation of *uye-ri* governs the contextual parameters of Korean language usage. The following three categories, for example, demand different degrees of formality in Korean verbal interaction: (1) those people who are from the same exclusive group and with whom one has developed close personal relationships over an extended period, (2) those whose background is such that they can draw upon *uye-ri* but who are not personally well-known, and (3) those who are unknown strangers (Yum, 1987b). The first category includes those who went to the same high school and were in the same class and have become close friends. The second category includes those who went to the same high school and with whom one has become acquainted but who are not necessarily close friends. Finally, the last group is the stranger group, the members of which one can ignore and bypass without necessarily engaging in active verbal communication. Formal language style is used when status differential is involved and relational distance is far. Informal language style is practiced when status differential is minimal and the relational distance is close. Park (1979) arrives at a similar conclusion, suggesting that the Korean language is a "situation-oriented" language in which propriety and harmony are preserved through status-oriented verbal communication style.

Status-oriented verbal style also has been uncovered as a major theme in Albert's (1972) study of the cultural patterning of speech behavior in Burundi. Based on fieldwork research, she finds that members in Burundi use different degrees of formal speech style in accordance to caste, age and sex, kinship, friendship, contiguous residence, or political-economic ties. She observes that

> distinctions are made according to the social roles of those present: the degree of formality, publicity or privacy, and the objectives of the speech situation. Together, social role and situational prescriptions determine the order of precedence of speakers, relevant conventions of politeness, appropriate formulas and styles of speech, including extralinguistic signs, and topics of discussion. Socialization and sanctions are also determined by the social role-situational complexes within which discourse occurs. (p. 86)

The style of speaking reflects the overall values and patterns of a culture. In the Burundi case, the contextual style of speaking is preferred over the personal style of speaking. Contextual style of speaking refers to the use of language to reflect hierarchical social order and asymmetrical role positions. The personal style of speaking refers to the use of language to reflect egalitarian social order and symmetrical relational positions. . . .

INSTRUMENTAL VERSUS AFFECTIVE STYLE

The instrumental verbal style is sender-oriented language usage and the affective verbal style is receiver-oriented language usage. The instrumental style is goal-oriented in verbal exchange. The instrumental style relies heavily on the digital level to accomplish goal objective and the affective style relies heavily on the analogic level to negotiate relational definition and approval.

Ramsey (1984) commented on the Japanese interaction style, proposing that

> the Japanese value catching on quickly to another's meaning before the other must completely express the thought verbally, or logically. *Haragei* (*hara*—belly, and *gei*—sensitivity or subtleness) is referred to as the Japanese way of communication. *Haragei* means heart-to-heart communication or guessing the inner thoughts of the other. *Ishin denshin* (intuitive sense) is an additional referent for this preference. (pp. 142–143)

The affective-intuitive style of the Japanese verbal communication pattern places the burden of understanding on both the speaker and the listener. While the Japanese speaker actively monitors the reactions of the listener, the listener is expected to display intuitive sensitivity toward meanings beyond words. Verbal expressions are presented only as hints to reality, but they never are expected to be perceived as accurate facts that capture the totality of reality.

Okabe (1983) uses the term *erabi* (selective) worldview to represent the instrumental nature of verbal communication style in the U.S. culture, while he uses the term *awase* (adjustive) worldview to represent the affective-intuitive nature of verbal communication style in the Japanese culture. *Erabi* worldview holds that "human beings can manipulate their environment for their own purpose as the speaker consciously constructs his or her message for the purpose of persuading and producing attitude change"; the *awase* worldview assumes that human beings will "adapt and aggregate themselves to the environment rather than change and exploit it, as the speaker attempts to adjust himself or herself to the feelings of his or her listeners" (Okabe, 1983, pp. 36–37). The *erabi* worldview segregates the roles of speaker and listener into distinct categories, while the *awase* worldview integrates the roles of speaker and listener into a highly interdependent relationship. Both speaker and listener are expected to use their "intuitive sense" to interpret the multifarious nuances that are being transmitted in the ongoing dialogue.

This "intuitive sense" also finds its way into the Korean language. According to Park (1979), the Koreans place a high emphasis on the concept of *nunchi* in everyday verbal communication. *Nunchi* refers to the intuitive sense by which Koreans can detect whether others are really pleased or are really satisfied concerning the ongoing dialogue. According to Kim (1975), *nunchi* is an "interpretation of others' facial expressions or what they say plus—mysterious 'alpha' hidden in the inner hearts" (p. 7). Similar to Japanese verbal communication patterns, the affective-intuitive style characterizes the Korean verbal communication pattern. As Park observes:

> In an instrumental communication pattern, like that of the [North] Americans, people assert themselves or make themselves understood by talking . . . whereas in a situation communication style like that of Koreans or Japanese, people try to defend themselves either by vague expressions or by not talking. [North] Americans try to persuade their listeners in the step-by-step process [regardless of] whether their listeners accept them totally. But a Korean or a Japanese tends to refuse to talk any further in the course of a conversation with someone once he [or she] decides that he [or she] cannot accept the other's attitude, his [or her] way of thinking and feeling in totality. (pp. 92–93)

Morris's (1981) ethnographic work on Puerto Rican discourse processes uncovered five key points concerning Puerto Rican language style that closely resembles both Korean and Japanese language style:

(1) In Puerto Rican society, one's place and one's sense of oneself depend on an even, disciplined, and unthreatening style of behavior. . . .

(2) In language one must take great care not to put oneself or others at risk, and one must reduce the risk of confrontation to the lowest degree possible. This implies a systematic blurring of meaning—that is, imprecision and indirectness. . . .

(3) This implies a constant problem of interpretation, testing, probing, second-guessing, and investigation, but conducted indirectly. . . .

(4) The personal value of the individual—and so the validity of his [or her] words—will be determined by what he [or she] actually *does*, not by what he [or she] says. . . .

(5) Information does not come in discrete "bits," but as complex indicators of fluid human relationships, the "bits" being inextricable from the constant, implicit negotiation of meaning. Information is sought in the flow of talk, the exchanging of clues, and the sharing and the referring. (pp. 135–136)

The predominant style of Puerto Rican discourse, therefore, is affective-intuitive in orientation. It is listener-oriented, and oftentime what is not said is as important as what is being said. Affective intuition is used to infer and interpret the hidden implications of the verbal message.

Moving beyond the subdued affective style, Adelman and Lustig (1981) notice that native Arab speakers in Saudi Arabia tend to use a dramatic affective style of verbal communication in their everyday discourse. They note that "Arabic intonation patterns carry unwanted affective meanings when used in speaking English. . . . The intonation for exclamatory sentences in Arabic is much stronger and emotional than in English. Further, the higher pitch range of Arabic speakers conveys a more emotional tone than does English spoken by a native speaker" (p. 353). Beyond paralinguistic style differences, Cohen (1987) comments on proxemic behavior differences concerning Arab speakers and North American English speakers:

The Arab need for personal contact with his [or her] interlocutor is associated with an outlook that defines relationships in affective and familiar, not instrumental, terms. Once again we are back to the individual and the group. The [North] Americans' distaste for tactile intimacy with strangers is clearly linked with the cultural primacy of personal autonomy and "privacy." Close contact with someone who is, literately, not one's intimate, constitutes an invasion of one's living space. When Arab representatives meet, whether as friends or rivals, they do so as brothers. They embrace, hold hands, acquire a strong physical sense of the other's presence. Anything else leaves them "cold," uncomfortable and unable to relate to the issue at hand. Personal chemistry may not ensure a successful negotiation in the Arab world, but its absence makes life more difficult. (p. 41)

Arabs, therefore, use an affective style of verbal communication that emphasizes heavily on expressive nonverbal behavior. Whereas, for the North Americans, the digital level of verbal communication is the prime concern for effective face-to-face communication. . . .

REFERENCES

Adelman, M., & Lustig, M. (1981). Intercultural communication problems as perceived by Saudi Arabian and American managers. *International Journal of Intercultural Relations, 5,* 349–364.

Albert, E. (1972). Culture patterning in Burundi. In J. Gumperz & D. Hymes (Eds.), *Directions in sociolinguistics.* New York: Holt, Rinehart, and Winston.

Almaney, A., & Alwan, A. (1982). *Communicating with the Arabs*. Prospect Heights, IL: Waveland.

Basso, K. (1970). To give up on words: Silence in western Apache culture. *Southern Journal of Anthropology, 26*, 213–230.

Clancy, P. (1986). The acquisition of communicative style in Japanese. In B. Schieffelin & E. Ochs (Eds.), *Language socialization across cultures*. Cambridge: Cambridge University Press.

Cohen, R. (1987). Problems of intercultural communication in Egyptian-American diplomatic relations. *International Journal of Intercultural Relations, 11*, 29–47.

Gibson, W. (1966). *Tough, sweet, and stuffy: An essay on modern American prose styles*. Bloomington: Indiana University Press.

Grice, H. (1975). Logic and conversation. In P. Cole & J. Morgan (Eds.), *Syntax and semantics: Vol. 3 Speech acts*. New York: Academic Press.

Gumperz, J., Aulakh, G., & Kaltman, H. (1982). Thematic structure and progression in discourse. In J. Gumperz (Ed.), *Language and social identity*. Cambridge: Cambridge University Press.

Hall, E. T. (1976). *Beyond culture*. New York: Doubleday.

Hall, E. T. (1983). *The dance of life*. New York: Doubleday.

Hofstede, G. (1980). *Culture's consequences*. Beverly Hills, CA: Sage.

Hsu, F. (1981). *Americans and Chinese* (3rd ed.). Honolulu: University of Hawaii Press.

Johnson, C., & Johnson, F. (1975). Interaction rules and ethnicity. *Social Forces, 54*, 452–466.

Katriel, T. (1986). *Talking straight: Dugri speech in Israeli Sabra culture*. Cambridge: Cambridge University Press.

Keenan, E. (1974). Norm-makers, norm-breakers: Uses of speech by men and women in a Malagasy community. In R. Bauman & J. Sherzer (Eds.), *Explorations in the ethnography of speaking*. Cambridge: Cambridge University Press.

Kim, K. (1975). Cross-cultural differences between Americans and Koreans in nonverbal behavior. In H. Sohn (Ed.), *The Korean language: Its structure and social projection*. Honolulu: University of Hawaii Press.

Mishra, A. (1982). Discovering connections. In J. Gumperz (Ed.), *Language and social identity*. Cambridge: Cambridge University Press.

Morris, M. (1981). *Saying and meaning in Puerto Rico: Some problems in the ethnography of discourse*. Oxford: Pergamon.

Ochs, E. (1986). Introduction. In B. Schieffelin & E. Ochs (Eds.), *Language socialization across cultures*. Cambridge: Cambridge University Press.

Okabe, R. (1983). Cultural assumptions of East and West: Japan and the United States. In W. Gudykunst (Ed.), *Intercultural communication theory*. Beverly Hills, CA: Sage.

Park, M. (1979). *Communication styles in two different cultures: Korean and American*. Seoul: Han Shin.

Prothro, E. (1970). Arab-American differences in the judgement of written messages. In A. Lutfiyya & C. Churchill (Eds.), *Readings in Arab Middle-Eastern societies and cultures*. The Hague: Mouton.

Ramsey, S. (1984). Double vision: Nonverbal behavior in East and West. In A. Wolfgang (Ed.), *Nonverbal behavior: Perspectives, application, and intercultural insights*. Lewiston, NY: Hogrefe.

Rosaldo, M. (1973). I have nothing to hide: The language of Ilongot oratory. *Language in Society, 11*, 193–223.

Rosaldo, M. (1980). *Knowledge and passion: Ilongot notions of self and social systems*. Cambridge: Cambridge University Press.

Shouby, E. (1970). The influence of the Arab language on the psychology of the Arabs. In A. Lutifiyya & C. Churchill (Eds.), *Readings in Arab Middle-Eastern societies and cultures.* The Hague: Mouton.

Ting-Toomey, S. (1980). Talk as a resource in the Chinese-American speech community. *Communication, 9,* 193–203.

Wiemann, J., Chen, V., & Giles, H. (1986). *Beliefs about talk and silence in a cultural context.* Paper presented at the Speech Communication Association, Chicago.

Wolfson, N. (1981). Compliments in cross-cultural perspective. *TESOL Quarterly, 15,* 117–124.

Young, L. (1982). Inscruitability revisited. In J. Gumperz (Ed.), *Language and social identity.* Cambridge: Cambridge University Press.

Yum, J. (1987b). The practice of uye-ri in interpersonal relationships in Korea. In D. L. Kincaid (Ed.), *Communication theory from eastern and western perspectives.* New York: Academic Press.

Speech and the Communal Function in Four Cultures

Gerry Philipsen

. . . The long history of communication study is marked by an enduring concern with how symbolic action can serve the needs of individuals and societies. Typically, this concern has been directed to the informative, persuasive, aesthetic, and heuristic functions of communication. Recently, increased attention has been paid to the communal function—that is, to communication as a means for linking individuals into communities of shared identity. Eastman (1985) refers to communal identity as the achievement of "subjective social identity and community membership" (p. 5). She is concerned with how (a) shared attitudes, (b) knowledge and use of culturally specific vocabulary, and (c) competence to speak about context-sensitive topics are efficacious for individuals in such achievements. Philipsen (1987) has defined this as the cultural function of communication, the use of communication in the creation, affirmation, and negotiation of shared identity (p. 249). His emphasis is on the individual's knowledge and use of community-specific discursive forms such as episodic sequences, stories, and aligning actions as sources of insight into and models for situated communal practice. Such approaches have in common a concern with how the individual's understanding and use of linguistic behavior function in the process of identifying the individual with a social group.

Ong (1982) has pointed to the special role of speech, the use of language in social situations, in performing the communal function:

> Because in its physical constitution as sound, the spoken words proceeds from the human interior and manifests human beings to one another as conscious interiors, as persons, the spoken word forms human beings into close-knit groups. (p. 74)

Source: Abridged from Chapter 4 in S. Ting-Toomey & F. Korzenny (Eds.), *Language, Communication, and Culture* (pp. 79–92). Newbury Park, CA: Sage, 1989.

Ong's statement is a stimulus for this essay, as a source of inspiration and as a point of contention. It inspires the strategy of inquiring into the cultural function of communication—the examination of how speech, one important medium of communication, joins individuals into communities of shared identity. But so much of what has been learned in the empirical study of speech behavior suggests that *how* speech functions, in lives and societies, *varies* across speech communities (Hymes, 1962, 1972). Thus Ong's statement prompts me to ask: What can be learned about the communal function of speech by studying it in diverse societies?

For the past several years a group of investigators has been studying different cultures and how speaking functions within them. For each of these four cultures the available data include a completed doctoral dissertation plus a book or published papers. Each study involved one or more years of intensive fieldwork in a speech community, with the aim of discovering and describing cultural symbols and meanings, premises, and rules pertaining to speaking. Although the studies were not explicitly or exclusively directed to the communal function, each member of the group has been concerned with the themes developed in Philipsen (1987) and, thus, each study includes some data that are pertinent to the question raised in this essay.

An important feature of each of the projects reviewed here is its use of an ethnography of speaking model (Hymes, 1962). This is a model of description that directs the investigator to study communities of discourse in terms of their distinctive systems of resources and rules pertaining to communicative conduct. Of particular importance is the discovery and description of culturally shaped "ways of speaking" (Hymes, 1974), a term that joins the Whorfian idea of "fashions of speaking" with the commonsense notion of ways of life. It is assumed that the spoken life of various people is so richly varied that knowledge of how spoken life is conceptualized, enacted, and interpreted in a given community is a matter of empirical investigation.

Although the ethnographer of speaking treats a culture as *sui generis* (i.e., as its own thing), assumptions and procedures are used heuristically in the study of a given culture. An assumption guiding the projects summarized here is that cultural premises and rules about speaking are intricately tied up with cultural conceptions of persons, agency, and social relations—that is, rules and beliefs about speech articulate with a larger cultural code defining the nature of persons, whether and how it is that humans can act efficaciously in the world of practice, and what are the possible and appropriate ways in which individuals are linked together in social units. In this sense a code of speaking is a code of personhood and society as well.

SPEAKING IN PLACE IN TEAMSTERVILLE

The following have been observed as patterns in Teamsterville culture (Philipsen, 1972, 1975, 1976, 1986):

(1) the expression of a belief that neighborhood speech practices—and therefore the speaker's speech—are substandard in relation to the mainstream speech of

American society, accompanied by an aggressive persistence in the use of the neighborhood practices and the aggressive negative sanctioning of neighborhood residents who deviate from neighborhood practices;

(2) a reluctance on the part of community members to engage in conversation with persons who live outside the four-block space of the speech community and, within the community, a restriction of the spoken part of one's life to meetings of groups of people with whom the interlocutor shares the identity features of age, gender, ethnicity, and location of residence (usually defined in terms of an area of approximately one city block);

(3) the practice of infusing a concern with "place" in every speech episode, such that descriptions of others, attributions of intent to self and others, and decisions about whether and how to interact with others are consistently and systematically expressed in terms of ethnicity, residence, and gender; and

(4) the belief that speech is an efficacious resource for affirming and enacting ties of solidarity and that it is, for ordinary community members, inefficacious in economic and political assertions, such as in making a living and in disciplining children.

These beliefs and practices can be summarized in terms of the idea of "place" as a fundamental theme and motive in Teamsterville spoken life. Teamstervillers perceive the world as being shaped by a finely developed sense of place. They see boundaries, social and physical, where some others do not, and this vision serves a major unifying perception in their worldview. The centrality of place in the cultural outlook is reflected in a strong concern for locating people in social-physical space, in a view of places as locales whose boundaries rightly enclose and shelter some people and deny entry to others, and in a pervasive concern that oneself and others know and stay in their proper place both hierarchically and socially.

How, in such a social world, is the cultural function performed? Taken from the perspective of the individual speaker, the following can be specified. The use of the neighborhood style of speaking is one obvious practical act that can be performed by individuals to instantiate "subjective social identity and community membership" (Eastman, 1985, p. 5). Each time a speaker speaks in the neighborhood style, that speaker performs an act of identification; she or he identifies with the social group by using a way of speaking that historically has defined that group. It is historical in that the practice is handed down from generation to generation and in that there are written reports, widely publicized, about the neighborhood speech style. These widely publicized reports make at least a superficial knowledge of Teamsterville speech ways a part of the larger common culture of Chicago.

The use of neighborhood speech style is an act of identification in two mutually reinforcing ways. First, it is an act by which the speaker "gives off" to others the impression that the speaker is a member, is "from around here" and "belongs around here." That is, as directed to one's interlocutors the use of neighborhood speech makes an identity claim. Second, it is an act by which speakers themselves hear their own speech as similar to the speech of a particular group of others. Thus, the use of neighborhood speech is an act in which one experiences oneself as a member. Taking both ways together, such acts of speech are powerful acts of what I call "membering"—a word that captures something that the verbs *enact, announce, affirm, establish,* and the like do not quite express alone.

A second principle governing membering through language use in Teamsterville is that the person must spend a great deal of time in sociable interaction among a group of people with whom the person has a matched social identity—matched in terms of age, gender, ethnicity, and residence. The purpose of such groups is "to hang together in times of fun and trouble" for the sake of pure association. It is in the company of such a group that the member feels most alive, most "a person," as some outsiders might say.

In Teamsterville culture the model person is a *persona,* that is, a person with a specified set of social attributes, who is acting out his or her prescribed role among a specified *dramatis personae.* The model person has a place and is in place. Speech activity through which the speaker signals that he or she is in the proper place is efficacious in expressing to others and in affirming to the speaker the identification of the speaker with the group. The key principles of action by which such membering is accomplished are (a) the use of the local, nonstandard dialect and (b) being copresent with others of one's own cohorts.

EXPRESSING ONESELF IN NACIREMA CULTURE

Shortly after completing the Teamsterville fieldwork, I initiated a long-term study of mainstream American culture. *American culture* here refers to the system of symbols and premises that has been reported in such well-known studies as those of Varenne (1977) and Yankelovich (1982). Using Horace Miner's well-known term, I refer to this as Nacirema culture (*Nacirema* is *American* spelled backward).

One of the core themes that stimulated our group's studies of Nacirema culture is the idea of the deep structure of a Nacirema communal event. It was my intent to formulate the underlying principles of speaking operative in a speech event in which Nacirema interlocutors would experience a sense of "subjective social identity and community membership" (Eastman, 1985, p. 5). These principles can be expressed as follows: (a) Every individual in the event should be given a period of time to say to the group whatever it is that is of concern to the individual, and (b) it is the responsibility of all individuals to be attentive to what each other individual expressed during his or her turn to talk.

In an unpublished study conducted in 1975, Mary Jo Rudd and I investigated rules for speaking in middle-class families in a community in Southern California. We observed and listened intently to tape recordings of Nacirema conversation at family "dinner time," a speech event in which the participants relentlessly insisted that all family members be allowed a turn to talk—because each person "has something to contribute." We found that the people we observed believed strongly that one's place in the family, defined by a role, such as "father," should not be a basis for interrupting or curtailing the speech of others because each person's utterance is believed to be uniquely valuable. For these Nacirema individuals, speech is a way to express one's psychological uniqueness, to acknowledge the uniqueness of others, and to bridge the gap between one's own and another's uniqueness; it is a means by which family members, for example, can manifest their equality and demonstrate that they pay little heed to differences in status—practices and beliefs that would puzzle and offend a proper Teamsterviller.

In Seattle, Washington, five years later, Tamar Katriel and I listened to many Nacirema tell their life stories—stories in which great moral weight was placed upon interpersonal "relationships." Each party was not only free, but also felt a sense of pressure, to express and celebrate her or his uniqueness and to explore and understand the other's distinctive individuality. This was manifested most sharply in what we came to call the "communication ritual," a structured sequence of communicative acts in which intimate partners take turns disclosing difficulties experienced with self and relationship. In the ideal version of the ritual, both interlocutors disclose and listen intently to the disclosures of the other. If both parties are close (disclosive), supportive (of the other's "real self"), and flexible (willing to change their view of self or other in the face of interpersonal "feedback"), then the ideal is further realized.

"Dinner time" and the "communication ritual" are speech events whose rule structure and associated beliefs illustrate what I had proposed as the deep structure of a Nacirema speech event in which individuals experienced a sense of social identification through the use of language. Of course, each of these is an intimate, not a communal, event, but this intimate ideal is being pressed as the ideal for other, more communal, relationships; that is, it is being transferred to, or imposed upon, the public domain (see Sennett, 1978). The transference of this deep structure from the intimate to the public domain is revealed in an application of the structure to a prominent Nacirema public scene, the television talk show *Donahue*, hosted by Phil Donahue.

Katriel and Philipsen (1981) introduced the idea that *Donahue* is a public ritual that expresses and affirms core North American concepts and values pertaining to personhood, society, and communication. It is a widely-viewed, and widely-understood, enactment of an episodic sequence that is meaningful to bearers of Nacirema culture. It displays an episodic sequence by which interlocutors can experience a sense of subjective identity and community membership, a sense that can be vicariously experienced by those viewers who are code bearers.

Carbaugh (1984, 1987) has presented a detailed analysis and interpretation of the culture displayed on *Donahue*. One part of that culture is a system of communication rules, invoked on the show, which he articulates as follows:

- *Rule 1*: In the conversations of *Donahue*, (a) the presentation of "self" is the preferred communication activity, and (b) statements of personal opinions count as proper "self" presentations.
- *Rule 2*: Interlocutors must grant speakers the moral "right" to present "self" through opinions.
- Rule 3: The presentation of "self" through opinions should be "respected," that is, tolerated as a rightful expression.
- *Rule 4*: Asserting standards that are explicitly transindividual, or societal, is dis-

preferred since such assertions are heard (a) to constrain the preferred presentations of "self" unduly, (b) to infringe upon the "rights" of others, and (c) to violate the code of proper respect.

These rules for self-presentation on *Donahue* reflect important features of the culture displayed on that show. One is an emphasis on the existential and moral standing of the "self" as a distinctive, autonomous, and powerful but delicate entity. A second is the importance placed on attentiveness to the distinctiveness of others. A third is the insistence that "society" not be allowed to constrain "self," as reflected in Rule 4, which proscribes the use of transindividual standards for inhibiting or evaluating individual expression. To speculate on how Carbaugh's findings apply to the present concern, I propose that when a Nacirema participates in a speech event in which she or he hears self and others following these rules, that is a point at which membering is experienced.

The *Donahue* rule structure, like the rule structure of family dinner time and of the communication ritual, is a particular expression of the more general, underlying deep structure, posited above, for Nacirema speech events in which the communal function is performed. One contribution of Carbaugh's study is to show this culture at work in a public speech event that is widely experienced as intelligible and consequential in American society.

In Nacirema culture, the model person is a unique *self* whose uniqueness is expressed and affirmed in and through "communication" (close, supportive, flexible speech) with others. "Communication," as a culturally defined way of speaking, constitutes a dialogic relationship in which the self not only is expressed but is actively engaged in the other's experience of the speaker and of a distinctive other. The ideal social relationship is one constituted by dialogic commitments rather than one defined by a set of transpersonal, historically determined expectations. To experience a sense of shared identity, from the standpoint of this code, requires speech events in which these central values and beliefs about persons, social relationships, and communication are articulated and affirmed. Such events are those in which the individuals experience themselves and others expressing their distinctive selves, and in which, they experience themselves and others aggressively attending to the distinctiveness of others' selves.

ISRAELI DUGRI SPEECH

In her ethnographic study of Israeli ways of speaking, Katriel (1983, 1986) has systematically described and interpreted the cultural meanings of *dugri* speech, translated from the Hebrew as straight or direct talk. She specifies its cultural meanings in terms of five dimensions—as sincere, assertive, natural, solidary, and matter-of-fact speech. It involves speech acts in which one person confronts another in such a way as to display images of honesty, in the sense of being true to one's feelings; of assertiveness, in the sense of strength or determination to express a view that is unpalatable to the hearer; of naturalness, in the sense of spontaneous, simple, unadorned speech;

of solidarity, in the sense of suspending roles and rules in the creation of egalitarian, undifferentiated, individuating relations; and matter-of-factness or antistyle, in the sense of a preference for deeds over words.

Dugri is a way of speaking intimately bound up with the subculture of the Sabras, native-born Israelis of Jewish heritage, mainly of European descent. "To speak dugri," as one of Katriel's informants put it, "is to act like a Sabra." The Sabra represents the construction, in Israel, of a new Jew who had "come to the Land of Israel to build and be both personally and communally rebuilt in it" (Katriel, 1986, p. 17). Sabras, the children of pioneers settling in a new Jewish state, developed a unique culture that features a rejection of the genteel European culture from which they were descended and, in particular, of the European Jews' way of relating to the larger European society, a way characterized by defensiveness, restrictiveness, and passivity as an adaptive mechanism.

It is in the spirit of the Sabra cultural agenda that the dugri way of speaking can be understood as communal speech. That agenda consists of the building, in Israel, of a new Jewish identity as well as a new Jewish society that can stand strong in opposition to external forces of various kinds, including externally imposed standards of evaluation and conduct. The new Jew would be productive in labor and would strive to create a just and egalitarian society. Dugri speech, which consists of one person speaking to another in such a way as to suspend the usual requirements of politeness and decorum associated with their role relationship, enacts this cultural agenda symbolically. Its sincerity, in speaking from the heart, reveals the speaker in his or her fundamental humanness; its assertiveness enacts a commitment to shake off the stance of passivity; its naturalness flaunts convention and artifice; its solidariness thematizes the ideal of building a society; and its matter-of-factness underlines the desire to take people, things, and conditions as they are.

Where it is enacted, talking dugri is a powerful way for Sabras to experience a subjective sense of shared identity and community membership. It is in such moments that speaker and listener can project and reaffirm their identity as Sabras.

Images of personhood, society, and communication are expressed in the cultural meanings of dugri speech. Society is elevated in dugri to a position of paramount importance, a position that necessarily, even happily, is superior to the individual person. The individual is stripped of any pretension to preciousness and fragility, as in the Nacirema code, but is, like the Nacirema person, characterized in terms of equality with and differentiation from others. But the Sabra person is not, like the Nacirema person, defended or protected from the restraining forces of society—rather, the Sabra's rationale for living is, to a great degree, his or her potential for serving and, in and through his or her social life, constituting the new Israeli society. Dugri speech symbolizes how individuals can, ideally, be linked together in social ties: The speaker, in flaunting the conventions associated with the old society, in suspending the conventional procedures for treating individuals with the respect for which the old code qualified them by virtue of their achieved or ascribed status, "disassociates himself [or herself] from a given structural relationship or social paradigm, while at the same time asserting a deeper affiliation with a more basic and encompassing one" (Katriel, 1986, p. 66).

COMMUNAL SPEECH IN AN
APPALACHIAN COMMUNITY

The affirmation and construction of communal ties is an important function of speech in the Appalachian community of Bond, Kentucky, studied by George B. Ray (1983, 1987). On the basis of ethnographic participant observation for a period of two years, Ray described in detail the structure of the community's prominent speech situations and speech events, with an eye to interpreting the means and meanings of speech to residents of Bond. The practice of "huddling," the speech situations of "porch talk" and "supper," and the community ideals of egalitarianism and respect all contribute to a cultural pattern of speaking that has specific implications for the communal function of speech.

One of the most striking features of the community's social life is the expressed desire "to experience life with others" (Ray, 1983, p. 167). To experience life with others, for a member of the Bond speech community, requires people (a) to be together in the same scene and (b) to signal to others that one is "all right." The signaling of one's own and the experiencing of others' being "all right" is effected through many tactics and realized in many different speech events.

"Huddling" in Bond suggests a key to understanding communal speech there. Huddling means that people get together to talk in small public or private gatherings. Huddling groups consist of interlocutors who are well known to each other, such as close friends or family, but are not necessarily segregated as to age or gender. The basic rules of huddling are that no one should speak too much, no one should do anything to upset others, one should appear reserved and modest, and one should not exaggerate. Perhaps the fundamental rule of huddling is that each participant give her- or himself up to the experience of simply "passing the time" with others, with no instrumental agenda or purpose. The ideal of huddling is realized to the extent that each participant makes of the event no more and no less than phatic communion.

The enactment of huddling and of "passing the time" is illustrated in several different speech situations, including "porch talk" and family "supper." In the former, there is an implicit episodic sequence of four steps: (a) Participants inquire about each other's overall condition ("You all right today?"), (b) there is an extended period of general conversation about topics of local interest (neighbors, weather, crops), (c) leave-taking is negotiated, and (d) leaving is consummated. The sequence provides for unlimited time to be together and is begun with an inquiry into the well-being of each participant, thus satisfying the key criteria for a huddling event in Chestnut Flat.

Family supper is an event in which the family is together. It is not necessary that serious discussion takes place. Although there is not, in Bond, evidence for the Nacirema concern that every person takes a turn at talk, there is a concern, particularly on the part of parents, that everyone be together so that the parents can reassure themselves that everyone is "all right." This is manifested in (a) presence at the meal time, (b) the general physical appearance of the child, and (c) whether or not the child eats the usual portion of food. As one of Ray's (1983) adult informants said about going to the parents' home to have supper with them:

I think when we go there [home] you don't have to say a lot. If you see each other, you know if they are well, if they are sick or have a cold. Mom always said, "You look so thin. Have you been sick?" It doesn't take long. Just to look at you and make sure you are all right. It doesn't matter if you stay long or not. It's just the effect to be there and see them. (p. 171)

The Bond code of persons emphasizes the essential equality of persons as well as the importance of "respect" for the feelings and well-being of others. Particular, known individuals are vitally important to social life because they are the personnel for one of the community's fundamentally important social processes, huddling, and thus important communication processes are devoted primarily to discovering and verifying that one's present, and potentially future, interlocutors are "all right." In moments of sociation in which one experiences life with others, for its own sake, without the intrusion of other mental, emotional, or linguistic tasks, the residents of Bond enact a fundamentally communal sequence of actions. Thus it is in such moments that one experiences a subjective sense of social identity and community membership. For the individual in Bond, then, the strategy for performing the communal function consists of the following injunctions: (a) Spend time in the presence of other known interlocutors; (b) during such time spent together, devote oneself primarily to the "task" of being together without imposing any purpose that would compete with the phatic one; (c) engage in those acts that would signal attentiveness to the well-being of others and that would signal one's own well-being; and (d) modulate one's own linguistic action (safe topics, no exaggeration, appear reserved) so as to avoid engaging in any activity that would disturb the equanimity of the interlocutors, and thus of the occasion.

CONCLUSION

. . . These studies suggest that each of the four cultures reviewed here includes culture-specific episodic sequences for experiencing a subjective sense of social identity and community membership. This finding is consistent with the thesis advanced by Philipsen (1987) that each culture provides a distinctive way to perform the communal function. The implication of this is that although Ong's (1982) thesis that speech unites humans into groups is supported by the data reviewed here, Ong's thesis is seriously qualified in the light of cross-cultural data that suggest that *how* speech performs the communal function is subject to considerable cultural variation.

REFERENCES

Carbaugh, D. (1984). *On persons, speech, and culture: Codes of "self," "society," and "communication" on Donahue.* Unpublished doctoral dissertation, University of Washington.
Carbaugh, D. (1987). Communication rules in Donahue discourse. *Research on Language and Social Interaction, 21,* 31–61.

Eastman, C. (1985). Establishing social identity through language use. *Journal of Language and Social Psychology, 4*, 1–20.

Hymes, D. (1962). The ethnography of speaking. In T. Gladwin & W. Sturtevant (Eds.), *Anthropology and human behavior* (pp. 13–53). Washington, DC: Anthropological Society of Washington.

Hymes, D. (1972). Models of the interaction of language and social life. In J. Gumperz & D. Hymes (Eds.), *Directions in sociolinguistics: The ethnography of communication* (pp. 35–71). New York: Holt, Rinehart & Winston.

Hymes, D. (1974). Ways of speaking. In R. Bauman & J. Sherzer (Eds.), *Explorations in the ethnography of speaking* (pp. 433–451). Cambridge: Cambridge University Press.

Katriel, T. (1983). *Towards a conceptualization of ways of speaking: The case of Israeli "Dugri" speech.* Unpublished doctoral dissertation, University of Washington.

Katriel, T. (1986). *Talking straight: Dugri speech in Israeli Sabra culture.* Cambridge: Cambridge University Press.

Katriel, T., & Philipsen G. (1981).What we need is communication: "Communication" as a cultural category in some American speech. *Communication Monographs, 48*, 301–317.

Ong, W. (1982). *Orality and literacy: The technologizing of the word.* London: Methuen.

Philipsen, G. (1972). *Communication in Teamsterville, a sociolinguistic study of speech behavior in an urban neighborhood.* Unpublished doctoral dissertation, Northwestern University.

Philipsen, G. (1975). Speaking "like a man" in Teamsterville: Culture patterns of role enactment in an urban neighborhood. *Quarterly Journal of Speech, 61*, 13–22.

Philipsen, G. (1976). Places for speaking in Teamsterville. *Quarterly Journal of Speech, 62*, 15–25.

Philipsen, G. (1986). Mayor Daley's council speech: A cultural analysis. *Quarterly Journal of Speech, 72*, 247–260.

Philipsen, G. (1987). The prospect for cultural communication. In D. Kincaid (Ed.), *Communication theory: Eastern and Western perspectives* (pp. 245–254). New York: Academic Press.

Ray, G. (1983). *An ethnography of speaking in an Appalachian community.* Unpublished doctoral dissertation, University of Washington.

Ray, G. (1987). An ethnography of nonverbal communication in an Appalachian community. *Research on Language and Social Interaction, 21*, 171–188.

Sennett, R. (1978). *The fall of public man.* New York: Random House.

Varenne H. (1977). *Americans together: Structured diversity in a midwestern town.* New York: Teachers College Press.

Yankelovich, D. (1982). *New rules: Searching for self-fulfillment in a world turned upside down.* New York: Random House.

Language Attitudes, Behaviour and Research
John Edwards

INTRODUCTION

. . . Central to much of what follows here is the concept of *attitude* which, though widespread in social psychology, is not one about which there has been universal agreement. At a general level, however, one might agree with Sarnoff (1970) who views attitude as 'a disposition to react favourably or unfavourably to a class of objects' (p. 279). This disposition is often taken to comprise three components: thoughts (the cognitive element), feelings (affective) and predispositions to act (behavioural), i.e. one knows or believes something, has some emotional reaction to it and, therefore, may be assumed to act on this basis (see e.g. Secord & Backman, 1964). Two points should be made here. First, there is often inconsistency between assessed attitudes and actions presumably related to them (one reason, incidentally, for seeking confirmatory data). Second, there is often confusion between belief and attitude; strictly speaking, *attitude* includes *belief* as one of its elements. . . .

SOME VIEWS OF LANGUAGE AND IDENTITY

. . .

Ethnic-Group Members

Although the lives and views of ordinary group members are clearly of the greatest importance in understanding *their* language, identity and social relationships, we do not have much formal information here. Fishman (1977a) has noted, for example, that 'the only aspect of bilingual education that has been even less researched than student attitudes and interests is that of parental attitude and interests' (p. 45). Nevertheless, the informal record is useful. In the United States, we have noted the gradual lessening of the influence of specifically ethnic institutions and societies as group need for them decreased (Edwards, 1977a). As regards ethnic language itself, there has not been much legal or official pressure on ethnic-group speakers to abandon the mother-tongue; the important factor here has typically been the perceived advantage of life in the mainstream. The few moves to suppress immigrant languages in the last century were unpopular and soon revoked. . . . This is not to say that minorities would not have preferred a Utopian society with mainstream accessibility *and* complete cultural and linguistic retention. Choices had to be made. These were not always easy or welcomed in themselves but it is clear that communicative language, at any rate, was a dispensable commodity for most groups. However regrettable this may be,

Source: Abridged from Chapter 6 in J. Edwards, *Language, society and identity* (pp. 139–153). London: Basil Blackwell, 1985.

we must remember that, in areas generally untouched by legal compulsion, immigrants Americanised of their own volition, to the extent desired or made necessary by attractive options (see Ravitch, 1976). Providing we acknowledge the public-private and communicative-symbolic distinctions (see chapter 4), we can see that American groups have been largely assimilationist in their attitudes.

The picture for immigrants in other settings is not unlike that obtaining in the United States. Changing attitudes in Great Britain have inexorably affected linguistic transmission, even where the first generation remains committed. Just as the culturally active Chinese immigrant in San Francisco laments the lack of interest in Chinese among children (Morrison & Zabusky, 1980), so Mascarenhas (1983) reports that the editor of a Punjabi weekly newspaper in Great Britain does not have Punjabi-speaking children. The Asian vernacular press in Great Britain is shrinking, despite a good deal of concern and interest, and the young Asian boy who delivers Urdu newspapers in Birmingham does not read the language himself.

So far as indigenous minorities are concerned, perceptions of ordinary group members confirm what is mentioned above. It is true that group languages have suffered persecution (but see Petyt, 1975) or, at least, ignorance. But even here we should not neglect the elements of choice and volition. Languages may, through force of circumstance, come to play a very reduced communicative role or only a symbolic one, and only group members themselves can save them (Fennell, 1981; Price, 1979); but, we observe that ordinary group members are not, typically, language activists. They are not generally swayed by abstract or romantic appeals which cannot compete with more immediate exigencies; the attitudinal stance is clear.

Most minority groups are, above all, pragmatic and this usually implies a considerable assimilationist sentiment (see Gaarder, 1981). A recent book provides some first-hand accounts which support this. Morrison and Zabusky (1980) interviewed 140 first-generation immigrants to the United States and one is struck by the overwhelming desire to learn English. Many of the interviewees had regrets connected with emigration and not all of them preferred to describe themselves as American— although many, even in this first generation, did so—but the pragmatic desire to make the act of emigration worthwhile is clear.

A lengthier description of adaptation to life in the larger society is given in an autobiography by Rodriguez (1983 . . .). He discusses the public-private distinction I have discussed here: home was Spanish and outside was English. Rodriguez considers that having to learn English at school, although painful, established his right to speak the language of *los gringos*. This, as he makes quite clear, created a loosening of ties with parents and relatives who remained Spanish-speaking, for as his English improved his Spanish declined. For Rodriguez, 'public individuality' (via English) caused a diminished 'private individuality' (via Spanish). Whether this need be so for all ethnic group members is doubtful, and Rodriguez's case might be taken as an example of the need for bilingual education. If so, however, it would be of the transitional variety, for he is critical of those who reject assimilation; they are 'filled with decadent self-pity . . . they romanticize public separateness' (p. 27). Besides, Rodriguez was to find that family life and intimacy could indeed be expressed through English— 'intimacy is not created by a particular language; it is created by intimates' (p. 32). His linguistic cost-benefit analysis will not be to everyone's taste but it is an honest account and, I think, generalisable.

Less temperate reactions by other 'ethnics' towards policies intended to affect their language and identity can also be found, often in the popular press. Thus, Zolf (1980) proclaimed himself against the Canadian multicultural policy: 'I don't need a multiculturalism grant to be Jewish' (p. 6). Multiculturalism, he feels, is a political sop to ethnic voters, encourages fragmented loyalties, and attempts to maintain what can only be sustained by groups themselves. Hayakawa (1980), commenting on bi-lingualism in the United States, states that it is a good thing in itself, but should not be *officially* supported. He is particularly exercised by politicians stressing their own ethnic roots.

In general, the adjustments made by minority groups—as revealed in the historical record and discussed in this book—give a rather clear assessment of attitudes towards language and identity. At the risk of belabouring the point, I note again that their views are the products of altered environments. In this sense, and especially during periods of transition, they may not always reflect ideal preferences. They *do* reflect practical and necessary choices.

Ethnic-Group Spokesmen [and Women]

I have already discussed the gradually increasing gap between the lives of ethnic-group members and the societies, churches and schools which were once so important to them. The fact that these institutions remain means that there exist persons who feel themselves to be group spokesmen [or women] and leaders, but who may also be some way removed from grassroots sentiment. These individuals, furthermore, are often ones who have prospered in the larger society; indeed, their role as spokesmen [or women] often reflects an admired ability to straddle two cultures. Relatively secure, these activists endorse cultural pluralism because they feel that 'permanent minority status might be advantageous' (Higham, 1975, p. 211; . . .). The reader will also recall here the results of the Irish survey (Committee on Irish Language Attitudes Research, 1975) which found markedly different viewpoints held by ordinary people and those involved in pro-Irish activities. All of this is not to deny that spokesmen [or women] may reflect the wishes of less articulate or visible group members and that they may galvanise latent desires—leaders are always a minority, after all. But it is surely worth noting that, in an area as sensitive as language and identity, care should be taken to see how far and in what form enthusiasm extends.

Mann (1979) has outlined in some detail the distance between group spokesmen [or women] and the masses. Noting that rank-and-file ethnics in the United States were not swept into the cultural renaissance, he cites the view of Myrdal that, far from being a people's movement, the new ethnicity is supported by well-established intel-lectuals and writers. While they may be sincere, they are hardly typical. Mann suggests that they are too ready to see mass support for their ideas in public ethnic activities and festivals—celebrations which have in most cases become thoroughly Americanised. The fact that intellectuals and leaders present an articulate, powerful and visible source of influence should not confuse us into thinking that they represent large-scale opinion. . . .

The Mainstream Population

What do majority-group members think of cultural pluralism and of the retention of minority language and identity? Historically, the evidence shows little tolerance or concern for such matters at all and, as we should expect, such a stance is still prevalent in many quarters. Reactions in the popular press to issues relating to ethnic diversity show a continuing fear of social fragmentation (see Edwards, 1980b); the title of one of Greeley's books, *Why can't they be like us?* (1971), surely summarises the view of many.

There is, however, a more recent tolerance for diversity. The surveys of O'Bryan *et al.* (1976) and Berry *et al.* (1977) on unofficial languages and multiculturalism in Canada demonstrate a growing awareness that diversity can be a strength. A similar interpretation could be placed upon the findings of the report of the Committee on Irish Language Attitudes Research (1975). In fact, we might say that in many parts of the world a liberalism which is, at least in part, the product of relative affluence and security is now ready to accept ethnic diversity. This is not always based upon a great deal of knowledge, however—many people surveyed in the Canadian work knew very little about multiculturalism *per se* (see also Edwards & Chisholm, in preparation). When we reflect further on the meaning and implications of tolerance for diversity, we should consider at least three important questions: (a) is current tolerance necessarily a stable quantity; (b) does tolerance extend equally across all majority-minority and minority-minority relationships; and (c) can we equate tolerance with active support for diversity, especially in language matters?

Tolerance for diversity has not been something which minority groups could always count upon. The findings of scapegoats when times are bad has been a regrettably common occurrence and it surely needs no documentation here. As well, the sort of tolerance which Skutnabb-Kangas (1984) discusses in the case of European guest-workers—where, when industrial productivity slows, workers are retained to serve as a cushion for economic shocks at the lowest end of the social hierarchy—operates from a base of self-interest and not from one of altruism. We should be careful, therefore, if we attempt to erect an enduring social policy upon public attitudes which may shift quite rapidly. At the very least we should be concerned not to build false hopes, and not to dash minority-group expectations which have been encouraged to rise on unstable foundations.

We should also understand that, while there may be a greater degree of tolerance by majorities of minorities in general, this does not imply equal tolerance for all groups. Nor does it imply uniformity of goodwill within and across minority groups themselves. Kopan (1974) notes that antipathy to new immigrants in the United States came from those who had been new immigrants themselves only a little earlier. Kolack (1980), in a study of ethnic communities in Massachusetts, refers to the often violent feelings between minority groups (see also Dinnerstein *et al.*, 1979). Again, inter-minority hatred does not require extensive documentation here.

Finally, we should not equate tolerance for diversity with a desire to see *active* promotion of ethnic-group interests (especially where support comes from government sources). Where there is general support for bilingual education, for example, it is for a compensatory or transitional variety. Drake (1979) feels that there has *not* been a shift towards active support for pluralism in the United States (see also Mann, 1979; Sowell, 1978). The implications of accepting the equation are obvious (see Edwards, 1982b). . . .

LANGUAGE ATTITUDES

In sociolinguistics and the social psychology of language, attitudes have traditionally been of great importance. This is because people's reactions to language varieties can reveal their perceptions of the *speakers*; in this way, language attitudes are linked to views of identity. . . .

Language-Attitudes Research

In 1960, Lambert *et al.* introduced the 'matched-guise' technique as a means of assessing language attitudes. Judges evaluate—on a number of dimensions—a tape-recorded speaker's personality after hearing him or her read the same passage in each of two or more language varieties. That the speaker is, for all 'guises', the same person is not revealed to the judges and, typically, they do not guess this. Their judgements are then considered to represent stereotyped reactions to the given language varieties, since potentially confounding elements are constant across guises. While the technique has been criticised, mainly for its alleged artificiality, it does seem to provide useful information which can be confirmed by other means (e.g. by questionnaires, or by ratings of actual speakers *not* adopting guises). In general then, the technique presents to the listener samples of speech which are thought to act as identifiers allowing the expression of social stereotypes.

The study by Lambert *et al.* considered reactions towards French and English guises in Montreal. The English-speaking judges generally reacted more favourably to English than to French guises; more interestingly, the French-speaking evaluators *also* rated English guises more favourably. Lambert and his colleagues concluded that the findings demonstrated not only favourable reactions from members of the high-status group towards their own speech but also that these reactions had been adopted by members of the lower-status group. This 'minority group reaction' is a revealing comment on the power and breadth of social stereotypes in general, and on the way in which these may be assumed by those who are themselves the objects of negative stereotypes.

A study by Giles (1970) investigated reactions of British secondary-school children to a variety of accents, including the non-regional RP (Received Pronunciation), Irish, German and West Indian. In terms of status, aesthetic quality and communicative content (a measure of the perceived ease of interaction with the speakers), RP was rated most favourably, regional accents (e.g. South Welsh and

Somerset) were in the middle ranks, and urban accents (e.g. Cockney, Birmingham) were at or near the bottom of the scale. These results agree largely with an earlier suggestion by Wilkinson (1965) that there exists in Great Britain a tripartite accent prestige hierarchy: at the top is RP, then come various regional accents and, finally, accents associated with heavily urbanised areas (see also Trudgill, 1975a).

Earlier, Lambert (1967) had introduced a refinement which seems to clarify this work. He categorised the many personality dimensions on which judges typically rate speech and speakers into three groups. Thus, some are seen to reflect a speaker's *competence* (e.g. dimensions like intelligence and industriousness), some *personal integrity* (helpfulness, trustworthiness) and some *social attractiveness* (friendliness, sense of humour). An investigation by Giles (1971) considered reactions to RP, South Welsh and Somerset accents along these lines. Although RP received the highest ratings in terms of *competence*, the other two were perceived more favourably on *integrity* and *attractiveness*; the assessments were made by judges who were themselves from either South Wales or Somerset. In a later study, Giles (1973) presented the same three accents, plus a Birmingham variety, to groups of South Welsh and Somerset school-children whose views on capital punishment had earlier been ascertained; the guises in this study all presented arguments against capital punishment. Giles was interested to measure both the children's views of the quality of the arguments presented, and any changes in their stance on the topic. It was found that the higher the status of an accent, the more favourable were the ratings of the quality of the argument. However, in terms of attitude change among the children, only the regional accents proved effective. The study thus suggests that messages can be seen as high in quality without necessarily being persuasive; or, to use Lambert's terminology, accents judged as reflecting high speaker *competence* need not always have greater influence upon listeners than regional varieties associated with *integrity* and *attractiveness* (see also Giles & Powesland, 1975).

Carranza and Ryan (1975) studied the reactions of Mexican-American and Anglo-American students to speakers of Spanish and English. Although the topic discussed by speakers had some influence upon the ratings, English was generally rated more favourably than Spanish on both status-related and *solidarity* (i.e. integrity and attractiveness) dimensions. However, Spanish *was* seen more favourably on the solidarity than on the status traits. Similar results were found in a study by Ryan and Carranza (1975) in which evaluations of standard English and Spanish-accented English were made by Mexican-Americans, Blacks and Anglos (i.e. White, English speakers). Arthur *et al.* (1974) found that White, Californian college students downgraded the so-called 'Chicano' English on several personality dimensions. Ryan *et al.* (1977) have also shown that the *degree* of accent may affect ratings; as Spanish-American 'accentedness' increased, reactions of English-speaking students became less favourable (see also Brennan & Brennan, 1981a, b; Ryan & Carranza, 1977).

Studies involving Black speakers in the United States have also shown that language-attitude ratings reveal social perceptions. Tucker and Lambert (1969) presented a number of American English dialect varieties to northern White, southern White and southern Black college students. All groups rated 'Network' speakers most favourably—'Network English' being roughly equivalent here to British RP—and Black speakers were downgraded (see also Fraser, 1973). Irwin (1977) found that White judges perceived Black college students less favourably than their White counterparts on dimensions of voice quality, fluency and confidence. We could also note here the work of V. Edwards (1979), since her studies of evaluations of Black speakers in Great Britain show a similar pattern—both teachers and West Indian adolescents perceived West Indian speakers less favourably then they did working-class and middle-class English speakers.

Overall, these studies of language evaluation show that speech can evoke stereotyped reactions reflecting differential views of social groups. Standard accents and dialects usually connote high status and competence; regional, ethnic and lower-class varieties are associated with greater speaker integrity and attractiveness. The trust and liking apparently reflected in such varieties may be related to conceptions of ingroup solidarity. It is important to remember in all this that the social context in which evaluations occur is not a static entity; as it changes, one should expect to see alterations in attitudes too. Recent movements like the new ethnicity, French-Canadian nationalism and 'Black pride' can, for example, be expected to reveal revitalised group perceptions through linguistic evaluation.

However, the process by which speakers of nonstandard varieties adopt the stereotyped views of the majority continues (Edwards, 1979b). We do not observe, though, the large-scale defection from these varieties to which this might be expected to lead. In this connection, we should recall that *all* varieties—standard or non-standard—can serve that bonding or solidarity function which is a part of group identity; we now see that this is reflected in evaluations along *integrity* and *social attractiveness* dimensions. There may also, of course, be practical difficulties and psychological penalties involved in attempts to leave one dialect group and join another . . . . Finally here, we can note that an association between lower-class speech patterns and masculinity accounts for a 'covert prestige' (in the United States and Great Britain at least) attaching to non-standard speech. . . . This phenomenon seems to cross class lines; middle-class speakers often report using *more* non-standard forms than they actually do. In any event, it appears that the overt downgrading of non-standard varieties may co-exist with more latent positive connotations.

Recently, Ryan *et al.* (1982; see also Ryan *et al.*, 1984) have attempted to summarise language attitude studies by providing an 'organisational framework'. They suggest that there are two determinants of language perceptions: *standardisation* and *vitality*. A standard is one whose norms have been codified and is associated with dominant social groups. Vitality (see also next section) refers to the number and importance of functions served, and is clearly bolstered by the status which standards possess; it can also be a feature, however, of non-standard varieties, given sufficient numbers of speakers and community support. There are also two main evaluative dimensions: *social status* and *solidarity*. We have already noted that standard varieties usually connote high status, while non-standard ones may reflect group solidarity. Finally, the authors suggest three major measurement techniques: *content analysis* and *direct* and *indirect* assessment. The first of these is seen to include historical and sociological observation, as well as ethnographic studies. Direct assessment usually involves questionnaire or interview methods, while the 'matched-guise' approach is the best example of indirect measurement of language attitudes. . . .

LANGUAGE BEHAVIOUR AND IDENTITY

The study of language attitudes reveals, with some regularity, that different varieties evoke different perceptions, i.e. speakers' identities are evaluated largely in terms of status and solidarity. The discussion so far has indicated that, in minority-majority contexts, language shift occurs. With regard to dialect and accent, however, where language assimilation need not happen, it is apparent that retention of negatively stereotyped varieties is at least partly due to the continuing value they possess for group solidarity and identity (see Ryan, 1979). Still, there are many examples of people 'losing' such varieties once they move away from the contexts where these are vernaculars. It is also the case that many speakers of non-standard forms become, to a greater or lesser degree, bidialectal, retaining the original variety while adding another for instrumental purposes. Individuals may thus alter their dialects depending upon the situations they are in. . . .

Linguistic Accommodation

Giles and Powesland (1975) suggest that the essence of the theory of speech accommodation derives from social psychological studies of similarity-attraction and social exchange. Byrne (1971), for example, describes a series of studies demonstrating that personal similarity increases the likelihood of attraction and liking—we like others who are like ourselves. This insight was supplemented by findings that reduction of existing dissimilarities will lead to more favourable evaluation. Since the desire for social approval is 'assumed to be at the heart of accommodation' (Giles & Powesland, 1975, p. 159), we see that the model involves reducing linguistic differences in order to be better perceived by others. However, accommodation means change, and change costs something; consequently, Giles and Powesland draw upon the social-exchange literature (e.g. Homans, 1961) and note that accommodation will only likely be initiated if a favourable cost-benefit ratio can be achieved. Thus, 'accommodation through speech can be regarded as an attempt on the part of the speaker to modify or disguise his [or her] persona in order to make it more acceptable to the person addressed' (Giles & Powesland, 1975, p. 158).

Three more relevant points are brought out by Giles and Powesland. First, the speaker is not necessarily 'consciously aware' of his [or her] accommodative plan. Some strategies may be quite overt, but covert accommodation is also possible and here the *listener* may not always detect its operation either. Second, accommodation can imply divergence as well as convergence; just as a speaker may become linguistically more like the listener whose approval is desired, so divergent accommodation can occur where dissociation is wanted. Third, convergent accommodation does not *always* lead to social approval. Giles and Powesland cite an example in which an English-speaking European addresses an East African official in Swahili. In this case, accommodation is seen as condescension and implies that the official is incapable of dealing in English.

In terms of the mechanics of accommodation, Giles and Smith (1979) observe that obvious 'intralingual convergences' are those of pronunciation (i.e. accent), speech rate and message content. They also acknowledge the importance of Tajfel's theory of intergroup relations and social change, particularly with regard to divergence (see e.g. Tajfel . . . 1981). . . . Tajfel proposed that groups in contact compare themselves, and want to see themselves, as distinct and positively valued entities. Members of a subordinate group, in trying to achieve a more positive identity, have a number of strategies available to them (assuming, of course, that any changes are seen as actually possible). They may move into the other group (assimilation), may redefine negative qualities as positive (e.g. negatively marked group features like colour or dialect may become positive, in a process of revitalised group pride), or may create altogether new evaluative dimensions which will favour their group. Outright group competition is also seen as a possibility.

Speech accommodation, as discussed by Giles and his colleagues, can thus be seen—in either its divergent or convergent mode—as an identity adjustment made to increase group status and favourability. . . . *Convergence* reflects a desire for approval, occurs when perceived benefits outweigh costs, and varies in magnitude according to the extent of the available linguistic repertoire and the degree of need for approval. It is favourably received by listeners (i.e. where they are conscious of its operation; Giles and Powesland, 1975) to the extent to which positive intent is attributed. *Divergence* (or at least speech maintenance) reflects a desire for personal dissociation or an emphasis upon positive ingroup identity (if the encounter is defined in intergroup terms). Magnitude constraints are as above and unfavourable reactions can be expected when listeners perceive negative intent.

Ethnolinguistic Vitality

For present purposes, the accommodation model is most interesting as it relates to a further development, that of *ethnolinguistic vitality*. Giles et al. (1977) outline three variables pertinent to group vitality: status (particularly socioeconomic), demography (number, concentration and proportion of group members) and institutional support (e.g. the use of group language in education, government, religion, etc.). When the notion of vitality is connected with Tajfel's theory of group relations and with the accommodation perspective, the authors propose that a unified model for understanding language and ethnic group relations emerges. Thus, Tajfel provides the primary conceptual framework of group strategies, these are examined in their linguistic contexts through accommodation theory, and the vitality factors provide the social background.

The next important treatment is that of Giles and Johnson (1981). Here a theoretical approach to language and ethnic identity is given, having four components. The first is Tajfel's theory of social identity and group relations (see above) which involves strategies of social creativity (i.e. in the redefinition of negatively valued dimensions or the creation of new ones) and social competition. The second is *perceived* ethnolinguistic vitality . . . , i.e. in addition to the actual variables affecting vitality (above), Giles and Johnson now append group members' perceptions of vitality; they suggest that while objective and subjective conceptions of vitality often overlap, they need not always do so, and subjective assessments may prove a revealing refinement. Third, Giles and Johnson refer to the distinctiveness, strength and value of group boundaries; taken together, these are seen to contribute to the perceived 'hardness' or 'softness' of boundaries. Boundary permeability, in turn, affects the strength and potential changeability of group membership . Fourth, Giles and Johnson acknowledge that ethnic-group membership is not the only salient category in people's lives and may not, therefore, be of explanatory value in all social interactions. Thus, they discuss the importance of *multiple*-group membership.

Giles and Johnson then propose that individuals are more likely to define encounters with outgroup members in ethnic terms, and will try to maintain positive linguistic distinctiveness (i.e. maintain identity) when they: (a) identify strongly with an ethnic group which has language as an important group dimension; (b) are aware of alternatives to their own group status; (c) consider their group to have high vitality; (d) see their group's boundaries as hard and closed; and (e) identify strongly with few other social categories. . . . It follows that, when the alternative to each of these propositions is considered, linguistic attenuation is to be expected, and possibly assimilation by the outgroup. . . .

REFERENCES

Agheyisi, R. & Fishman, J. Language attitude studies. *Anthropological Linguistics*, 1970, *12*, 131–57.

Arthur, B., Farrar, D. & Bradford, G. Evaluation reactions of college students to dialect differences in the English of Mexican-Americans. *Language and Speech*, 1974, *17*, 255–70.

Berry, J., Kalin, R. & Taylor, D. *Multiculturalism and ethnic attitudes in Canada*. Ottawa: Supply & Services, 1977.

Brennan, E. & Brennan, J. Accent scaling and language attitudes: Reactions to Mexican American English Speech. *Language and Speech*, 1981, *24*, 207–21. (a)

Brennan, E. & Brennan, J. Measurements of accent and attitude toward Mexican-American speech. *Journal of Psycholinguistic Research*, 1981, *10*, 487–501. (b)

Byrne, D. *The attraction paradigm*. New York, Academic Press, 1971.

Carranza, M. & Ryan, E. Evaluation reactions of bilingual Anglo and Mexican American adolescents toward speakers of English and Spanish. *International Journal of the Sociology of Language*, 1975, *6*, 83–104.

Carroll, J. International comparisons of foreign language learning in the IEA project. In J. Alatis (ed.), *Georgetown University Round Table on language and linguistics*. Washington, DC: Georgetown University Press, 1978.

Committee on Irish Language Attitudes Research. *Report*. Dublin: Government Stationery Office, 1975.

Cooper, R. & Fishman, J. The study of language attitudes. *International Journal of the Sociology of Language*, 1974, 3, 5-19.

Dinnerstein, L., Nichols, R. & Reimers, D. *Natives and strangers*. New York: Oxford University Press, 1979.

Drake, G. Ethnicity, values and language policy in the United States. In H. Giles & B. Saint-Jacques (eds), *Language and ethnic relations*. New York: Pergamon, 1979.

Edwards, J. Ethnic identity and bilingual education. In H. Giles (ed.), *Language, ethnicity and intergroup relations*. London: Academic Press, 1977. (a)

Edwards, J. *Language and disadvantage*. London: Edward Arnold, 1979. (b)

Edwards, J. Critics and criticism of bilingual education. *Modern Language Journal*, 1980, 64, 409-15. (b)

Edwards, J. Language attitudes and their implications among English speakers. In E. Ryan & H. Giles (eds), *Attitudes toward language variations*. London: Edward Arnold, 1982. (a)

Edwards, J. Bilingual education revisited: A reply to Donahue. *Journal of Multilingual and Multicultural Development*, 1982, 3, 89-101. (b)

Edwards, V. *The West Indian language issue in British schools*. London: Routledge & Kegan Paul, 1979.

Fennell, D. Can a shrinking linguistic minority be saved? In E. Haugen, J. McClure & D. Thomson (eds), *Minority languages today*. Edinburgh: Edinburgh University Press, 1981.

Fishman, J. The social science perspective. In Center for Applied Linguistics (ed.), *Bilingual education: Current perspectives (Vol. 1)*. Arlington, Virginia: CAL, 1977. (a)

Fraser, B. Some "unexpected" reactions to various American- English dialects. In R. Shuy & R. Fasold (eds), *Language attitudes*. Washington, DC: Georgetown University Press, 1973.

Gaardner, A. A review of *Bilingual education: Theories and issues* (C. Paulston). *Modern Language Journal*, 1981, 65, 205-206.

Gardner, R. Language attitudes and language learning. In E. Ryan & H. Giles (eds), *Attitudes toward language variations*. London: Edward Arnold, 1982.

Gardner, R. & Lambert, W. *Attitudes and motivation in second-language learning*. Rowley, Massachusetts: Newbury House, 1972.

Giles, H. Evaluative reactions to accents. *Educational Review*, 1970, 22, 211-27.

Giles, H. Patterns of evaluation in reactions to RP, South Welsh and Somerset accented speech. *British Journal of Social and Clinical Psychology*, 1971, 10, 280-1.

Giles, H. Communicative effectiveness as a function of accented speech. *Speech Monographs*, 1973, 40, 330-1.

Giles, H., Bourhis, R. & Taylor, D. Towards a theory of language in ethnic group relations. In H. Giles (ed.), *Language, ethnicity and intergroup relations*. London: Academic Press, 1977.

Giles, H. & Byrne, J. An intergroup approach to second language acquisition. *Journal of Multilingual and Multicultural Development*, 1982, 3, 17-40.

Giles, H. & Johnson, P. The role of language in ethnic-group relations. In J. Turner & H. Giles (eds), *Intergroup behavior*. Oxford: Basil Blackwell, 1981.

Giles, H. & Powesland, P. *Speech style and social evaluation*. London: Academic Press, 1975.

Giles, H. & Smith, P. Accommodation theory: Optimal levels of convergence. In H. Giles & R. St. Clair (eds), *Language and social psychology*. Oxford: Basil Blackwell, 1979.

Hayakawa, S. Pay for your own tongue. *Maclean's*, 1980, 93(29), 12.

Homans, G. *Social behavior*. New York: Harcourt, Brace & World, 1961.

Irwin, R. Judgements of vocal quality, speech fluency, and confidence of southern Black and White students. *Language and Speech*, 1977, *20*, 261–6.

Kolack, S. Lowell, an immigrant city. In R. Bryce-Laporte (ed.), *Sourcebook on the new immigrants*. New Brunswick, New Jersey: Transaction, 1980.

Kopan, A. Melting pot: Myth or reality? In E. Epps (ed.), *Cultural pluralism*. Berkeley: McCutchan, 1974.

Labov, W. *Language in the inner city*. Philadelphia: University of Pennsylvania Press, 1976.

Lambert, W. A social psychology of bilingualism. *Journal of Social Issues*, 1967, *23(2)*, 91–109.

Lambert, W., Hodgson, R., Gardner, R. & Fillenbaum, S. Evaluational reactions to spoken languages. *Journal of Abnormal and Social Psychology*, 1960, *60*, 44–51.

Macnamara, J. Attitudes and learning a second language. In R. Shuy & R. Fasold (eds), *Language attitudes*. Washington, DC: Georgetown University Press, 1973.

Mann, A. *The one and the many: reflections on the American identity*. Chicago: University of Chicago Press, 1979.

Mascarenhas, A. The news in many tongues by satellite and bicycle. *The Sunday Times*, 3 April 1983.

Morrison, J. & Zabusky, C. *American mosaic*. New York: Meridian, 1980.

O'Bryan, K., Reitz, J. & Kuplowska, O. *Non-official languages: A study in Canadian multi-culturalism*. Ottawa: Supply & Services Canada, 1976.

Peyt, K. Romania, a multilingual nation. *International Journal of the Sociology of Language*, 1975, *4*, 75–101.

Price, G. The present position and viability of minority languages. In A. Alcock, B. Taylor, & J. Welton (eds), *The future of cultural minorities*. London: Macmillan, 1979.

Ravitch, D. On the history of minority group education in the United States. *Teachers College Record*, 1976, *78*, 213–28.

Rodriuquez, R. *Hunger of memory*. New York: Bantam, 1983.

Ryan, E. & Carranza, M. Evaluative reactions of adolescents toward speakers of Standard English and Mexican American accented English. *Journal of Personality and Social Psychology*, 1975, *31*, 855–63.

Ryan, E. & Carranza, M. Ingroup and outgroup reactions to Mexican American language varieties. In H. Giles (ed.), *Language, ethnicity and intergroup relations*. London: Academic Press, 1977.

Ryan E., & Carranza, M. & Moffie, R. Reactions towards varying degrees of accentedness in the speech of Spanish-English bilinguals. *Language and Speech*, 1977, *20*, 267–73.

Sarnoff, I. Social attitudes and the resolution of motivational conflict. In M. Jahoda & N. Warren (eds), *Attitudes*. Harmondsworth, Middlesex: Penguin, 1970.

Secord, P. & Backman, C. *Social psychology*. New York: McGraw-Hill, 1964.

Skutnabb-Kangas, T. Children of guest workers and immigrants: Linguistic and educational issues. In J. Edwards (ed.), *Linguistic minorities, policies and pluralism*. London: Academic Press, 1984.

Sowell, T. Ethnicity in changing America. *Daedalus*, 1978, *107(1)*, 213–37.

Street, R. & Giles, H. Speech accommodation theory: A social cognitive approach to language and speech behavior. In M. Roloff & C. Berger (eds), *Social cognition and communication*. Beverly Hills: Sage, 1982.

Tajfel, H. *Human groups and social categories*. Cambridge: Cambridge University Press, 1981.

Trudgill, P. *Accent, dialect and the school*. London: Edward Arnold, 1975. (a)

Tucker, G. & Lambert, W. White and Negro listeners' reactions to various American-English dialects. *Social Forces*, 1969, *47*, 463–8.

Van den Berghe, P. *Race and racism*. New York: Wiley, 1967.
Wilkinson, A. Spoken English. *Educational Review*, 1965, *17 (supplement)*.
Zolf, L. Mulling over multiculturalism. *Maclean's*, 1980, *93(15)*, 6.

Speech Accommodation

Howard Giles, Anthony Mulac, James J. Bradac, and Patricia Johnson

The first publications concerning "speech accommodation theory" (SAT) emerged in 1973. Giles (1973) . . . demonstrated the phenomenon of interpersonal accent convergence in an interview situation. . . . [I]n that same year, Giles, Taylor, and Bourhis (1973) published a paper that confirmed empirically some fundamental ideas inherent in what subsequently was to be labeled *SAT*. In a bilingual context, they found that the more effort in convergence a speaker was perceived to have made, the more favorably that person was evaluated and the more listeners would converge back in turn. Moreover, a plethora of convergent strategies was discovered even in what for some would be described as a socially sterile laboratory setting. . . .

Convergence has been defined as a linguistic strategy whereby individuals adapt to each other's speech by means of a wide range of linguistic features, including speech rates, pauses and utterance length, pronunciations and so on. Divergence refers to the way in which speakers accentuate vocal differences between themselves and others. Both of these linguistic shifts may be either *upward* or *downward*, where the former refers to a shift in a societally valued direction and the latter refers to modifications toward more stigmatized forms.

Beyond these basic distinctions several more specific accommodative forms can be indicated. The complexity level increases. Thus in any interaction, convergence can be mutual (A-> <-B) and if mutual can result in style matching (A-> <-B) or, probably less commonly, style switching (A—>B; A<—B). Convergence can be nonmutual (A->B). Both interactants can maintain their dissimilar styles, neither converging nor diverging (A B). Divergence can be mutual (<-A B->) or nonmutual (<-A B). And one person can attempt to converge as the other diverges (<-A <-B). Further, convergence can refer to a speaker's attempt to move toward the other's manifest speech style (Seltig, 1983) or to a speaker's attempt to move toward a style suggested by a belief, expectation, or stereotype regarding the other's style. The *response to a manifest* style versus *response to a belief* about other's style, and so on, distinction can be offered for divergence as well. Additionally, the distinction between partial and total convergence or divergence can be offered (Street, 1982). Thus, for example, a speaker initially exhibiting a rate of 50 words per minute can move to match exactly another speaker's rate of 100 words per minute (total con-

Source: Abridged from Chapter 1 in M. McLaughlin (Ed.), *Communication Yearbook 10* (pp. 13-48). Newbury Park, CA: Sage, 1987.

vergence) or can move to a rate of 75 words per minute (partial convergence). Finally, we can distinguish between unimodal and multimodal divergence or convergence. The former distinction indicates that a speaker can converge to or diverge from one aspect of the other's speech, for example, rate, whereas the latter distinction indicates convergence or divergence at two or more levels, for example, rate and accent.

The central notion of the framework . . . is that during interaction individuals are motivated to adjust (or to accommodate) their speech styles as a strategy for gaining one or more of the following goals: evoking listeners' social approval, attaining communicational efficiency between interactants, and maintaining positive social identities. In addition, it is the individual's *perception* of the other's speech that will determine his or her evaluative and communicative responses. . . .

CONVERGENCE

Convergence and Desire for Social Approval

SAT proposes that speech convergence be considered a reflection (often non-conscious) of a speaker's or group's need for social integration or identification with another. The theory has its basis in research on similarity attraction which, in its simplest form, suggests that as one person becomes more similar to another, this increases the likelihood that the second will like the first. Thus interpersonal convergence through speech is one of many strategies that may be adopted in order to become more similar to another. It involves the reduction of linguistic dissimilarities between two people in terms of most language features from dialects (Coupland, 1980) to nonverbal behaviors (von Raffler-Engel, 1979). Thus, for example, Welkowitz and Feldstein (1969, 1970) reported that dyadic participants who perceived themselves to be similar in terms of attitudes and personality converged durations of internal pauses (those within a conversational turn) and of switching pauses more than did those participants perceiving dissimilarity. Dyadic interactants who perceived themselves to be similar were more able and willing to coordinate and influence one another's speech patterns and timing than other dyads, presumably because these perceived similar dyads were initially more positively oriented and more certain of one another (Byrne, 1971). In addition to pause duration, Welkowitz, Feldstein, Finkelstein, and Aylesworth (1972) found that dyadic participants perceiving themselves as similar converged vocal intensity more than subjects randomly paired. . . .

A compelling set of illustrations in like manner comes from a large-scale naturalistic study of code-switching in Taiwan by Berg (1985), who examined 8,392 interactions across many markets, department stores, shops, and banks. In general, the most common pattern of communication in these situations was *mutual* accommodation to the other's dialect, the nature of which depended on the particular setting involved. For instance, customers would downwardly converge to salespeople in the market place and would receive upward convergence in return, but in banks (given the sociolinguistic and socioeconomic attributes of the salespeople there) customers would now upwardly converge to the clerks who would downwardly converge to them. Of particular interest to SAT is the continual finding that in many of these settings where customers, of course, hold the relative monetary reins, salespeople converged much *more* to customers than vice versa. Of course in times of commodity scarcity and economic hardship, one might expect the reverse pattern to be operative in view of the social approval (and even survival) motive.

An exception to the convergent style/social approval connection is the case in which a speaker "makes fun of" another by mocking his or her communicative behavior (see Basso, 1979). In this case, the speaker typically will signal the intention to mock the other's style through the use of various meta-communicative devices. Kathryn Shields (personal communication) has observed Jamaican schoolteachers (who usually adopt a standardized form in the classroom) converging/mimicking their pupils' creolized forms when the latter are deemed disruptive, inattentive, or lacking in academic effort. This suggests that one's perception of a speaker's intention is crucial to specifying the consequences of both convergence and divergence.

For affective reasons again, people converge to where they *believe* their partners are linguistically. For example, Bell (1982) reported that New Zealand broadcasters would read the same news phonologically quite differently depending on which socioeconomic bracket they thought their listening audience derived from (see also Seltig, 1985). Often of course we are quite accurate in pinpointing the linguistic attributes of our recipients, yet on other occasions we are quite wrong. Beebe (1981), for instance, found that Chinese Thai bilingual children would use Chinese phonological variants when being interviewed by an objectively sounding Standard Thai speaker who looked ethnically Chinese. Similarly, some Singaporeans' and Australian immigrants' attempts lexically, grammatically, and prosodically to match "upwardly" the speech of native English speakers may miscarry, and in other cases, native English speakers mismanage their *downward* convergent attempts toward what they believe Singaporeans and Aborigines sound like (Platt & Weber, 1984). . . .

From these examples it can be argued that speech convergence is often cognitively mediated by our stereotypes of how socially categorized others will speak (see Hewstone & Giles, 1986), and "foreigner talk" and speech to certain ethnic minorities and young children can be examplars of this. . . .

A vivid demonstration of stereotypical convergence at a different lifespan stage is reported by Caporael, Lukaszewski, and Culbertson (1983), who found that some nurses would use baby talk to the institutionalized elderly, irrespective of the latter's actual capabilities, if these nurses had generally unfavorable views of their charges' functional autonomy (see also, Ryan, Giles, Bartolucci, & Henwood, 1986). Blind persons also often report being the recipients of such stereotyped convergence, as urged by Klemz (1977, p. 8):

> The blind are discriminated against in less formal situations. All too often strangers
> address them as though they were deaf, or mentally deficient; or refuse to address
> them at all, and talk to their companions instead. Most people are prepared to help

the blind, but they are not prepared to accept them as normal colleagues and companions. They *expect* the blind to be helpless and offer them help, whether they need it or not. (emphasis added)

By contrast, in some cases convergence may reflect one speaker's attempt to reciprocate another's *actual* communicative behavior, which may be either consistent or inconsistent with an appropriate stereotype. For example, a student may converge to a particular professor's extremely rapid rate of speech even though the professorial stereotype may dictate cautious and thoughtful utterance. More will be said later about convergence to actual behavior versus stereotypical convergence. . . .

However, there are differential evaluations of convergence depending on its magnitude and the dimensions on which it occurs. Giles and Smith (1979) presented eight versions of a taped message to an English audience. The taped voice was a Canadian exhibiting varying degrees and combinations of convergence on three linguistic dimensions (pronunciation, speech rate, and message content). Listeners appreciated convergence on each linguistic level, but upgraded the speaker most when he converged on speech rate and *either* content *or* pronunciation. Convergence on all three dimensions, however, was perceived negatively as patronizing. Thus convergence does not seem to be necessarily linearly related to positive evaluations and there appear to be optimal levels, and possibly optimal *rates* in some situations as well (see also Bradac, Hosman, & Tardy, 1978). It seems that listeners have ranges of acceptable or preferred behavior (Cappella & Greene, 1982). For example, Street (1982) found that observers tolerated differences between interviewer and interviewee speech rates of up to 50 words a minute, but beyond those limits the speaker was downgraded.

. . . . [A]ccepting the notion that people find approval from others satisfying and that speech convergence goes some way toward achieving this, it is likely that there is a tendency for people to converge toward one another in many situations, albeit some people are more "person-centered/receiver-focused" (O'Keefe & Delia, 1985) and "rhetorically sensitive" (Ward, Bluman, & Dauria, 1982) communicators than others. Indeed, Higgins's (1980) "communication games" approach to interpersonal communication, in essence, posits such a conversational rule, and certainly the phenomenon appears ubiquitous in the sense of its early ontogenetic (e.g., Street, Street, & Van Kleeck, 1983), cross-sex (Brouwer, Gerritsen, & De Haan, 1979), and cross-cultural (Scollon & Scollon, 1979) appearances. It follows from this that the greater the speaker's need to gain another's approval or attraction, the greater the degree of convergence there will be, up to a certain optimal level. Interestingly, it could be argued that not only do speakers converge to where they believe others to be, but in some (as yet, unspecified) conditions to where they believe others *expect them* to be linguistically. In any event, factors that may influence the intensity of the social approval need include the probability of future interactions with the other, the extent of their social power over the speaker, capacities for empathy, previous experience of converging toward that person, as well as interindividual variability in the need for social approval. . . .

Developing the notion of social approval further, the *power* dimension is among the most crucial determinants of the degree to which convergence will be manifest (see Berg, 1985). Thus, for example, Wolfram (1973) reports that in New York City, where both Puerto Ricans and Blacks agree that the latter hold more power and prestige than the former, Puerto Ricans assimilate the dialect of Blacks far more than vice versa. Josiane Hamers (personal communication), using role-taking procedures in a Quebec industrial setting, has demonstrated greater bilingual convergence to a recipient who was an occupational superior than one who was a subordinate; foremen converged more to managers than workers and managers converged more to higher managers than foremen. Similarly, research on the linguistic assimilation of immigrants in alien-dominant cultures suggests that language shifts are typically unilateral (see Giles, 1978), with subordinate groups converging to the dominant group in their use of language far more than vice versa (for example, Taylor, Simard, & Papineau, 1978). From a different perspective, Kincaid, Yum, Woelfel, and Barnett (1983) demonstrated that at the level of culturally held beliefs and values, Korean immigrants in Hawaii "converge" over time toward the equilibrium point of the host society. In terms of Tajfel and Turner's (1979) social identity theory, convergent language shifts have been considered as a tactic for achieving a positive self-image (Giles & Johnson, 1981). Seeking social approval is the main element of the individual mobility strategy that may be adopted by certain members of subordinate groups who perceive their ingroup's social position as legitimate and immutable (see also Albo, 1979; Giles & Bourhis, 1976). . . .

Situational Constraints on Speech Convergence

Convergent behavior will not always be the most appropriate or positvely evaluated strategy, however, even in situations in which the speaker is seeking approval. Ball, Giles, Byrne, and Berechree (1984) point out that much of the previous research on SAT has centered around the dynamics of situations where norms are ambiguous or nonexistent, even at the social evaluational level (for example, Bourhis, Giles, & Lambert, 1975; Street, 1982). And perhaps this is not surprising given that SAT arose in part as a reaction against the theoretical bias in sociolinguistic theory favoring normative explanations (Giles & Hewstone, 1982). Indeed, as Scotton (1976) argues, it is a moot point as to when many situations are so normatively constrained that there still does not exist a wide latitude of acceptable communicative behaviors. Moreover, language behaviors are often used negotiatively so as to determine creatively what social norms are operating. Hence, in contexts of social ambiguity, people are likely to converge on others present (usually those with more status or dominance) by social comparison (Suls & Miller, 1977) so as to sound as though they "fit in" and say the "right thing." Admittedly, although this could be just another manifestation of the need for social approval, it does come about by a quite different mechanism and is worthy of elevation into the propositional format of SAT.

Some research has explored the situational boundaries of SAT. For example, Genesee and Bourhis (1982) showed in a Quebec study that situational norms were a strong factor in the evaluative reactions of listeners to a French Canadian salesman who either converged toward an English Canadian customer or maintained his own ingroup language over a sequence of interactive exchanges. For instance, the salesman was *not* upgraded on many dimensions for converging toward the customer. This was so apparently because of the established situational norm "the customer is always right." Space precludes an adequate critique of this factorially complex, two-study paper by Genesee and Bourhis. However, suffice it to say that careful examination of their findings (which are couched heavily in situational preeminence terms) shows that many accommodative tendencies were apparent in their data that were not highlighted by the authors. This was especially the case among those listening groups who could best identify with the target speakers on audiotape. For instance, even given the above mentioned situational norm, the immediately converging salesman was upgraded by monolingual English Canadian observers in terms of how positively they felt the customer would experience that situation. Nevertheless, the Genesee and Bourhis study is a pioneering landmark in its consideration not only of interpersonal accommodation with respect to (actually different, competing) social norms, but also in its attention to ingroup biases, the sociostructural statuses of the languages involved, and the sequential nature of accommodative exchanges. There is a need to explore the ways in which normative and accommodative processes combine and interact *sequentially* (see Bourhis, 1985) during the different trajectories of interpersonal development and their demise.

With some of those initial ends in mind, Ball, Giles, Byrne, and Berechree (1984) conducted a study in which listeners rated an interviewee who was heard outside and inside an interview speaking with either a "refined" or "broad" Australian accent. He either maintained his accent, or converged downward or upward, or diverged downward or upward toward the interviewer who spoke (in a factorial experimental design) with either a "broad" or "refined" accent. The results showed that the perception of the interviewee's speech was markedly affected by the subjects' supposed normative expectations that the interviewee would adhere to social pressures of sounding more refined inside the interview. This was evidenced to the extent that when the interviewee actually maintained his refined accent he was *perceived* to have become more refined in accent. The interviewee was rated as more competent, eager, and determined when using a refined accent, largely irrespective of whether he upwardly diverged or converged to the refined accent. That is, adherence to the sociolinguistic norms for an interview was the valued event, and little judgmental significance was attributed (at least in terms of the traits used therein) for accent shifts in terms of interpersonal accommodation. . . .

Speech Convergence, Attributions, and Intentions

Convergence and divergence can be produced, as discussed above, for a number of reasons. It is therefore pertinent for SAT to draw upon research on causal attribution which, in general terms, suggests that we understand people's behaviors, and hence evaluate them, in terms of the motives and intentions we attribute as being the cause of their actions (Heider, 1958). It has been proposed that a perceiver takes into account three factors when attributing motives to an act: the other's ability, effort, and external pressures impelling the person to act in a particular way (Kelley, 1973).

Simard, Taylor, and Giles (1976) examined the implications of attribution principles for the evaluation of convergence. They found that listeners who attributed another's convergence toward them as a desire to break down cultural barriers perceived this act very favorably. When this same shift was attributed externally to situational pressures forcing the speaker to converge, then the convergent act was perceived less favorably. Similarly, when a non-convergent act (that is, maintaining one's speech) was externally attributed to situational pressures, the negative responses were not so pronounced as when the behavior was attributed internally to the speaker's lack of effort. It should be noted, although being cognizant of actor- [or actress]-observer differences in making attributions about the same behavioral events (Farr & Anderson, 1983), that we require far more information as regards what social cues different recipients of accommodative acts utilize *for what attributional purposes.* When, for example, do listeners attribute nonconvergence to a personally-insulting maneuver; a failure to perceive the appropriate situational norm; an inflexible or even decayed speech repertoire; or a successful social rejection of speech characteristic of a particular contrastive group? As the last alternative implies, motives and intentions are attributed often for more *social* than *situational* or *individualistic* reasons as being due to interactants' memberships in various social groups and the historically determined meanings they have for them (see also Hewstone & Jaspars, 1984). . . .

Speech Maintenance and Divergence

It may appear from the foregoing, superficially at least, that the absence of convergence, speech maintenance (Bourhis, 1979), is a passive response of a nonattending, or disagreeable, social being. . . . Although this could sometimes be the case, it is far from representative of those other occasions in which people (for example, ethnic minorities) deliberately use their language or speech style as a symbolic tactic for maintaining their identity, cultural pride, and distinctiveness (Ryan, 1979). Moreover, repertoire constraints or certain personality factors might dictate nonconvergence. . . .

It has been suggested further that in certain situations individuals may wish to go beyond this communicative stage and actually *accentuate* the linguistic and social differences between themselves and outgroup members (see also Doise, 1978). Scotton (1985) recently introduced the term *dis-accommodation* to refer to those occasions where people rephrase or repronounce something uttered by their partners so as to maintain their own integrity, distance, or identity. For example, a speaker might say, "OK, man, let's get it together at my pad around 2:30 tomorrow afternoon," and receive the reply, "Fine, sir, we'll relocate, 14:30, at your cottage, tomorrow." Now whether this apparent refusal to converge is a different phenomenon from, or a special, more consciously conceived case of, the general notion of *speech divergence* (Giles, 1973), a term coined for the modification of speech *away from* interlocutors, is a moot point. In any case, an example of divergence is found in Putman and Street's (1984) study in which interviewees who role-played sounding dislikable were found predictably to diverge in noncontent speech features away from their interviewers. Seltig (1985), in an analysis of a German radio program, has indicated how interviewers diverge from supposed experts as a signal of their own identification with the opposing (lay) views of members of the interactive audience.

In many instances, albeit of course not all, divergent strategies are adopted in dyads—or indeed larger groups (see Ros & Giles, 1979)—where the participants are members of different social or ethnic groups (Fitch & Hopper, 1983). Thus Tajfel and Turner's (1979) social identity theory of intergroup relations and social change provides an appropriate framework from which to consider the processes of speech maintenance and divergence (see Giles & Johnson, 1981).

Tajfel and Turner (1979) suggest that people do not always react to others as individuals so much as reacting to them as representatives of different social groups. They proposed that encounters could be seen as lying along an interindividual/ intergroup continuum where those at the former extreme would be encounters between two or more people that were fully determined by their interpersonal relationships and individual characteristics, and those at the latter extreme (the intergroup pole) would be encounters determined by certain social categories. The more participants perceive an encounter toward the intergroup end of the continuum, "the more they tend to treat members of the outgroup as undifferentiated items in a unified social catergory rather than in terms of their individual characteristics" (Tajfel & Turner, 1979, p. 36). Thus Hogg (1985) found that males were judged to sound more "masculine" (by an independent group of observers) when talking to females when gender was made salient than when it was not; in other words, they appeared to be diverging vocally from their opposite sex interlocutors.

Turner (1982) suggests that under these same depersonalizing conditions, ingroup members also take on the characteristics in a *self-stereotyping* manner of their own social group. As a mediating factor, then, the examination of *linguistic* self-stereotyping would seem to be a topic worthy of further empirical inquiry as it holds out the promise of explaining some of the variance in individuals' divergent strategies. It is most likely that people's views of what is prototypical ingroup speech vary considerably, and may often be quite incorrect from an objective standpoint.

Social identity theory is concerned with behavior found at *this* level of extreme prototypicality and enables predictions that the more individuals define situations in intergroup terms and desire to maintain or achieve a positive ingroup identity, the more likely it will be that speech divergence will occur. The precise psychological climate necessary for, and the extent of, such divergence, Giles and Johnson (in press b) claim in their ethnolinguistic identity theory, is a function of a number of intergroup variables, most prominently individuals' perceptions of (1) the social structural forces operating in their own group's favor (see Bourhis & Sachdev, 1984) and (2) the legitimacy, as well as the stability, of their ingroup's position in the intergroup status hierarchy (see Giles & Johnson, in press b).

The sequence of processes central to social identity theory (social categorization-identification-social comparison-psychological distinctiveness) suggest that when one of an individual's social group memberships is construed as situationally salient, he or she will attempt to differentiate from relevant outgroup individuals on dimensions that are valued as core aspects of their group identity. Should language be a salient dimension of that group membership, as it so often is for ethnic groups (see Taylor, 1976), then differentiation by means of speech or nonverbal divergence (see also LaFrance, 1985) will ensue (on one or more of the following dimensions: language, dialect, slang, phonology, discourse structures, isolated words and phrases, posture, and so on) in order to achieve a positive psycholinguistic distinctiveness (Giles, Bourhis, & Taylor, 1977).

A demonstration of speech divergence was provided by Bourhis and Giles (1977) with Welsh people in an interethnic context. Welsh people who placed a strong value on their Welsh group membership and who were learning the Welsh language took part in a survey on the techniques of second-language learning. In a language laboratory setting they heard questions presented verbally to them individually in their language booths by a Standard English speaker who at one point challenged their reasons for learning what he called "a dying language with a dismal future." These Welsh subjects, in contrast to a control group who did not value the Welsh language in any integrative sense (Gardner & Lambert, 1972), broadened their Welsh accents in their replies compared with earlier emotively neutral questions. In addition, some used Welsh words and phrases, and one simply conjugated particular Welsh verbs in response! Previously, in response to a neutral question, many of the subjects had emphasized their Welsh group membership to the English-sounding speaker in terms of the *contents* of their responses. The study demonstrates that psycholinguistic distinctiveness can occur (see however Cacioppo & Petty, 1982), like convergence, in many different linguistic forms. Other studies have shown that many social groups positively evaluate representative ingroup speakers on audiotape who diverge in speech style when interacting with members of relevant outgroups (Bourhis, Giles, & Lambert, 1975; Doise, Sinclair, & Bourhis, 1976). Conversely, and not surprisingly, divergence from an outgroup member is often viewed as insulting, impolite, or downright hostile (Deprez & Persoons, 1984; Sandilands & Fleury, 1979).

An interesting example of divergence is provided by Escure's (1982) study of interactional patterns of Belize Creole, in which choice of dialect by Creoles fulfills identity maintenance functions. She showed that a speaker's speech act is often defined as a power relationship with the interlocutor (see above), and that the interlocutor's ethnic membership narrows the Creole speaker's choices. In interaction with Caribs, the selection of the mesolect is determined by a combination of linguistic insecurity (the stigma attached by outgroups and some ingroup members as "raw" Creole) and of social dominance relative to the neighboring Carib group. The Caribs often respond by sneers and asides delivered in neutral tones in their own language, incomprehensible to the Creoles, but understood and responded to by other Carib bystanders.

It is likely that there is a hierarchy of strategies for psycholinguistic distinctiveness varying in the degree of social dissociation that they indicate (Hewstone & Giles, 1986). These may range from a few pronunciation and content differentiations, through forms of accent and dialect divergences to verbal abuse and naming, abrasive humor, and the maintenance or switch to another language in response to an outgroup speaker. Clearly, the degree of linguistic divergence that can be manifested will depend also on the verbal repertoires of the speakers. . . .

Divergence and Cognitive Organization

As with speech convergence, divergence has been examined empirically, as well as theoretically, more from the perspective of the (affective) identity maintenance function than in terms of cognitive organization (Giles, Scherer, & Taylor, 1979). However, divergence may function not only as an expression of attitudes but also to put order and meaning into the interaction and to provide a mutually understood basis for communication. For example, the accentuation of accent, as well as content differentiation in certain contexts, or other forms of divergence, may serve to indicate that speakers are not members of the host community or familiar with the current situation in which they find themselves. This kind of self-handicapping tactic (Weary & Arkin, 1981) thereby increases the probability that any norms inadvertently broken can be attributed externally and that a greater latitude of acceptance will be made available for the speaker; divergence here has some social utility (Ryan, personal communication). This divergence, moreover, acts as a form of self-disclosure to indicate that certain norms and spheres of knowledge and behavior may not be shared and intersubjectivity is at a premium (see also Rommetveit, 1979).

In other situations speech divergence may be a strategy employed to bring another's behavior to an acceptable level or to facilitate the coordination of speech patterns. Two studies have indicated that sometimes interactants (for example, therapists and adults) may diverge in the amount they talk in order to encourage their partners (that is, clients and children) to talk more (Matarazzo, Weins, Matarazzo, & Saslow, 1968; Street, Street, & Van Kleeck, 1983). Anecdotally, it is common for people to slow down their speech rate with extremely fast-talking others in order to "cool them down" to a more comfortable communicative and cognitive level. . . .

In other situations, dissimilarities between interactants' speech may not only be acceptable, but even expected (Grush, Clore, & Costin, 1985). Ball et al. (1984) showed in their study that an interviewee maintaining his standard accent with an interviewer who spoke with a broad accent was more positively evaluated than when he converged "down" to the interviewer. In this case, it seems that situational norms override other evaluative considerations such as convergence as a strategy for increased similarity and attraction. Other contexts also typically involve differential speech behavior (Miller & Steinberg, 1975; Watzlawick, Beavin, & Jackson, 1967) yet do maintain a similar or complementary pattern of speech. For example, in interviews, the speech behaviors of interviewer and interviewee differ but the speakers may adjust their speech to maintain complementary speech patterns (Matarazzo & Weins, 1972; Putman & Street, 1984). That is, speakers may diverge or maintain dissimilar speech patterns in dyads when a role or power discrepancy exists. These speech differences may indicate optimal sociolinguistic distances and be psychologically acceptable and comfortable for both participants. This analysis may explain the finding (Mulac et al., in press) that women failed to converge toward men's lower level of gaze while silent in mixed-sex dyads, although women, unlike men, otherwise displayed convergence in same- and mixed-sex settings. Further instances where so-called speech complementarity is likely to occur are interactions between doctor-patient, employer-employee, teacher-pupil, parent-child, as well as in young, male-female romantic encounters. Indeed, those physicians who subscribe to possessing a patient-oriented (rather than to a doctor-oriented) communicative style (Tate, 1983) may well be competent in their capacities to converge and complement either sequentially or simultaneously with their clientele. As Giles (1980) argued, it is not entirely impossible to concoct instances in which people may wish to converge, diverge, and complement each other with regard to various verbal, vocal, and nonverbal forms *simultaneously*. . . .

REFERENCES

Albo, X. (1979). The future of the oppressed languages in the Andes. In W. C. Cormack. & S. Wurm (Eds.), *Language and society: Anthropological issues* (pp. 309–330). The Hague: Mouton.

Ball, P., Giles, H., Byrne, J. L., & Berechree, P. (1984). Situational constraints on the evaluative significance of speech accommodation: Some Australian data. *International Journal of the Sociology of Language, 46*, 115–130.

Basso, K. H. (1979). *Portraits of "The Whiteman."* Cambridge: Cambridge University Press.

Beebe, L. (1981). Social and situational factors affecting communicative strategy of dialect code-switching. *International Journal of Sociology of Language, 32*, 139–149.

Bell, A. (1982). Radio: The style of news language. *Journal of Communication, 32*, 150–164.

Berg, M. E. van de (1985). *Language planning and language use in Taiwan.* Dordrecht: ICG Printing.

Bourhis, R. Y. (1979). Language in ethic interaction: A social psychological approach. In H. Giles & B. Saint-Jacques (Eds), *Language and ethnic relations* (pp. 117–141). Oxford: Pergamon.

Bourhis, R. Y., & Giles, H. (1977). The language of intergroup distinctiveness. In H. Giles (Ed.), *Language, ethnicity and intergroup relations* (pp. 119–135). London: Academic Press.

Bourhis, R. Y., Giles, H., & Lambert, W. E. (1975). Social consequences of accommodating one's style of speech: A cross-national investigation. *International Journal of the Sociology of Language, 6*, 55–72.

Bourhis, R. Y., & Sachdev, I. (1984). Vitality perceptions and language attitudes. *Journal of Language and Social Psychology, 3*, 97–126.

Bradac, J. J., Hosman, L. A., & Tardy, C. H. (1978). Reciprocal disclosures and language intensity: Attributional consequences. *Communication Monographs, 45*, 1–17.

Brouwer, D., Gerritesen, M., & De Hann, D. (1979). Speech differences between men and women: On the wrong track? *Language in Society, 8*, 33–50.

Byrne, D. (1971). *The attraction paradigm.* New York: Academic Press.

Cacioppo, J., & Petty, R. (1982). Language variables, attitudes, and persuasion. In E.G. Ryan & H. Giles (Eds.), *Attitudes towards language variation: Social and applied contexts* (pp. 189–207). London: Edward Arnold.

Caporael, L. R., Lukaszewski, M. P., & Culbertson, G. H. (1983). Secondary baby talk: Judgments by institutionalized elderly and their caregivers. *Journal of Personality and Social Psychology, 44,* 746–754.

Cappella, J. N., & Greene, J. (1982). A discrepancy-arousal explanation of mutual influence in expressive behavior for adult-adult and infant-adult interaction. *Communication Monographs, 49,* 89–114.

Coupland, N. (1980). Style-shifting in a Cardiff work-setting. *Language in Society, 9,* 1–12.

Deprez, K., & Persoons, K. (1984). On the identity of Flemish high school students in Brussels. *Journal of Language and Social Psychology, 3,* 273–296.

Doise, W. (1978). *Groups and individuals.* Cambridge: Cambridge University Press.

Doise, W., Sinclair, A., & Bourhis, R. Y. (1976). Evaluation of accent convergence and divergence in cooperative and competitive intergroup situations. *British Journal of Social and Clinical Psychology, 15,* 247–252.

Escure, G. (1982). Interactional patterns in Belize Creole. *Language in Society, 11,* 239–264.

Farr, R., & Anderson, T. (1983). Beyond actor-observer differences in perspective: Extensions and applications. In M. Hewstone (Ed.), *Attribution theory: Social and functional extensions* (pp. 45–64). Oxford: Blackwell.

Fitch, K., & Hopper, R. (1983). If you speak Spanish they'll think you are a German: Attitudes towards language choice in multilingual environments. *Journal of Multilingual and Multicultural development, 4,* 115–128.

Gardner, R. C., & Lambert, W. E. (1972). *Attitudes and motivation in second language learning.* Rowley, MA: Newbury House.

Genesee, F., & Bourhis, R. Y. (1982). The social psychological significance of code-switching in cross-cultural communication. *Journal of Language and Social Psychology, 1,* 1–28.

Giles, H. (1973). Accent mobility: A model and some data. *Anthropological Linguistics, 15,* 87–105.

Giles, H. (1978). Linguistic differentiation between ethnic groups. In H. Tajfel (Ed.), *Differentiation between social groups* (pp. 361–393). London: Academic Press.

Giles, H. (1980). Accommodation theory: Some new directions. *York Papers in Linguistics, 9,* 105–136.

Giles, H., & Bourhis, R. Y. (1976). Black speakers with white speech—a real problem? In G. Nickel (Ed.), *Proceedings of the 4th International Congress on Applied Linguistics* (Vol. 1, pp. 575–584). Stuttgart: Hochschul Verlag.

Giles, H., & Hewstone, M. (1982). Cognitive structures, speech and social situations: Two integrative models. *Language Sciences, 4,* 187–219.

Giles, H., & Johnson, P. (1981). The role of language in ethnic group relations. In J. C. Turner, & H. Giles (Eds.), *Intergroup behavior* (pp. 199–243). Oxford: Blackwell.

Giles, H., & Johnson, P. (in press b). New directions in language maintenance: A social psychological approach. *International Journal of the Sociology of Language.*

Giles, H., & Powesland, P. F. (1975). *Speech style and social evaluation.* London: Academic Press.

Giles, H., Scherer, K. R., & Taylor, D. M. (1979). Speech markers in social interaction. In K. R. Scherer & H. Giles (Eds.), *Social markers in speech* (pp. 343–381). Cambridge: Cambridge University Press.

Giles, H., Smith, P. M. (1979). Accommodation theory: Optimal levels of convergence. In H. Giles & R. St. Clair (Eds.), *Language and social psychology* (pp. 45–65). Oxford: Blackwell.

Giles, H., Taylor, D. M., & Bourhis, R. Y. (1973). Towards a theory of interpersonal accommodation through language: Some Canadian data. *Language in Society, 2,* 177–192.

Grush, J. E., Clore, G. L., & Costin, F. (1975). Dissimilarity and attraction: When difference makes a difference. *Journal of Personality and Social Psychology, 32,* 783–789.

Heider, F. (1958). *The psychology of interpersonal relations.* New York: John Wiley.

Hewstone, M., & Giles, H. (1986). Social groups and social stereotypes in intergroup communication: Review and model of intergroup communication breakdown. In W. B. Gudykunst (Ed.), *Intergroup communication* (pp. 10–26). London: Edward Arnold.

Hewstone, M., & Jaspars, J. (1984). Social dimensions of attribution. In H. Tajfel (Ed.), *The social dimension* (Vol. 2, pp. 379–404). Cambridge: Cambridge University Press.

Higgins, E. T. (1980). The "communication game": Implications for social cognition and persuasion. In E. T. Higgins, C. P. Herman, & M. P. Zanna (Eds.), *Social cognition: The Ontario symposium* (pp. 343–392). Hillsdale, NJ: Lawrence Erlbaum.

Hogg, M. (1985). Masculine and feminine speech in dyads and groups: A study of speech style and gender salience. *Journal of Language and Social Psychology, 4,* 99–112.

Kelley, H. H. (1973). The process of causal attribution. *American Psychologist, 28,* 107–128.

Kincaid, D. L., Yum, J. O., Woelfel, J., & Barnett, G. A. (1983). The cultural convergence of Korean immigrants in Hawaii: An empirical test of a mathematical model. *Quality and Quantity, 18,* 59–78.

Klemz, A. (1977). *Blindness and partial sight.* Cambridge: Woodhead-Faulkner.

LaFrance, M. (1985). Postural mirroring and intergroup relations. *Personality and Social Psychology Bulletin, 11,* 207–217.

Matarazzo, J. D., Weins, A. N., Matarazzo, R. G., & Saslow, G. (1968). Speech and silence behavior in clinical psychotherapy and its laboratory correlates. In J. Schlier, J. D. Matarazzo, & C. Savage (Eds.), *Research in psychotherapy* (Vol. 3). Washington, DC: American Psychological Association.

Matarazzo, J. D., & Weins, A. W. (1972). *The interview: Research on its anatomy and structure.* Chicago: Aldine-Atherton.

Miller, G. R., & Steinberg, M. (1975). *Between people: A new analysis of interpersonal communication.* Chicago: Science Research Associate.

O'Keefe, B. J., & Delia, J. G. (1985). Psychological and interactional dimensions of communicative development. In H. Giles & R. St. Clair (Eds.), *Recent advances in language, communication and social psychology* (pp. 41–85). London: Lawrence Erlbaum.

Platt, J., & Weber, H. (1984). Speech convergence miscarried: An investigation into inappropriate accommodation strategies. *International Journal of the Sociology of Language, 46,* 131–146.

Putman, W., & Street, R. (1984). The conception and perception of noncontent speech performance: Implications for speech accommodation theory. *International Journal of the Sociology of Language, 46,* 97–114.

Rommetveit, R. (1979). On the architecture of intersubjectivity. In R. Rommetveit & R. M. Blakar (Eds.), *Studies of language, thought, and communication* (pp. 93–107). London: Academic.

Ros, M., & Giles, H. (1979). The language situation in Valencia: An accommodation framework. *ITL: Review of Applied Linguistics, 44,* 3–24.

Ryan, E. B. (1979). Why do low-prestige language varieties persist? In H. Giles, & R. St. Clair (Eds.), *Language and social psychology* (pp. 145–175). Oxford: Blackwell.

Ryan E. B., Giles, H., Bartolucci, G., & Henwood, K. (1986). Psycholinguistic and social psychological components of communication by and with the elderly. *Language and Communication, 6*, 1–22.

Sandilands, M. L., & Fleury, N. C. (1979). Unilinguals in des milieux bilingues: Une analyse des attributions. *Canadian Journal of Behavioral Science, 11*, 164–168.

Scollon, R., & Scollon, S. B. (1979). *Linguistic convergence: An ethnography of speaking at Fort Chipewyan, Alberta.* New York: Academic.

Scotton, C. M. (1976). Strategies of neutrality: Language choice in uncertain situations. *Language, 52*, 919–941.

Scotton, C. M. (1980). Explaining linguistic choices as identity negotiations. In H. Giles, W. P. Robinson, & P. M. Smith (Eds.), *Language: Social psychological perspectives.* Oxford: Pergamon.

Seltig, M. (1983). Institutionelle Kommunikation: Stilwechsel als Mittel strategischer Interaktion. *Linguistische Berichte, 86*, 29–48.

Seltig, M. (1985). Levels of style-shifting exemplified in the interaction strategies of a moderator in a listener participation programme. *Journal of Pragmatics, 9*, 179–197.

Simard, L., Taylor, D. M., & Giles, H. (1976). Attribution processes and interpersonal accommodation in a bilingual setting. *Language and Speech, 19*, 374–387.

Street, R. L., Jr. (1982). Evaluation of noncontent speech accommodation. *Language and Communication, 2*, 13–21.

Street, R. L., Jr., Street, N. J., & Van Kleeck, A. (1983). Speech convergence among talkative and reticent three-year-olds. *Language Sciences, 5*, 79–86.

Suls, J. M., & Miller, R. L. (1977). *Social comparison processes.* New York: John Wiley.

Tate, P. (1983). Doctors' style. In D. Pendleton & J. Hasler (Eds.), *Doctor-patient communication* (pp. 75–85). London: Academic.

Tajfel, H., & Turner, J. C. (1979). An integrative theory of intergroup conflict. In W. G. Austin & S. Worchel (Eds.), *The social psychology of intergroup relations* (pp. 33–47). Monterey, CA: Brooks/Cole.

Taylor, D. M. (1976). Ethnic identity: Some cross-cultural comparisons. In J. W. Berry & W. J. Lonnev (Eds.), *Applied cross-cultural psychology.* Amsterdam: Swets and Zeitlinger.

Taylor, D. M., Simard, L., & Papineau, D. (1978). Perceptions of cultural differences and language use: A field study in a bilingual environment. *Canadian Journal of Behavioral Science, 10*, 181–191.

Turner, J. C. (1982). Towards a cognitive redefinition of the social group. In H. Tajfel (Ed.), *Social identity and intergroup behavior.* Cambridge: Cambridge University Press.

von Raffler-Engel, W. (1979). The unconscious element in inter-cultural communication. In R. St. Clair & H. Giles (Eds.), *The social and psychological contexts of language* (pp. 101–130). Hillsdale, NJ: Lawrence Erlbaum.

Ward, S. A., Bluman, D. L., & Dauria, A. F. (1982). Rhetorical sensitivity recast: Theoretical assumptions of an informal interpersonal rhetoric. *Communication Quarterly, 30*, 189–195.

Watzlawick, P., Beavin, J. H., & Jackson, D. (1967). *Pragmatics of human communication.* New York: Norton.

Weary, G., & Arkin, R. M. (1981). Attributional self-presentation. In J. H. Harvey, M. J. Ickes, & R. Kidd (Eds.), *New directions in attribution theory and research* (Vol. 3). Hillsdale, NJ: Lawrence Erlbaum.

Welkowitz, J., & Feldstein, S. (1969). Dyadic interaction and induced differences in perceived similarity. *Proceedings of the 77th Annual Convention of the American Psychological Association, 4,* 343–344.

Welkowitz, J., & Feldstein, S. (1970). Relation of experimentally manipulated interpersonal perception and psychological differentiation to the temporal patterning of conversation. *Proceedings of the 78th Annual Convention of the American Psychological Association, 5,* 387–388.

Welkowitz, J., Feldstein, S., Finkelstein, M., & Aylesworth, L. (1972). Changes in vocal intensity as a function of interspeaker influence. *Perceptual and Motor Skills, 35,* 715–718.

Wolfram. W. (1973). Sociolinguistic aspects of assimilation: Puerto Rican English in East Harlem. In R. W. Shuy & R. W. Fasold (Eds.), *Language attitudes: Current trends and prospects.* Washington, DC: Georgetown University Press.

CHAPTER 9

Nonverbal Behavior

Just as our verbal behaviors are conditioned by our culture, our nonverbal behaviors reflect the cultural patterns we acquire throughout the socialization process. The way in which we move about in space and time when communicating with others is based primarily on our physical and emotional responses to environmental stimuli. Whereas our verbal behaviors are mostly explicit and are processed cognitively, our nonverbal behaviors are spontaneous, ambiguous, often fleeting, and often beyond our conscious awareness and control.

When we communicate with strangers, our understanding of the interaction is limited by the strangers' unfamiliar nonverbal behaviors. From greeting and gesturing to expressions of feelings and body postures, we may find ourselves at odds with strangers. Because nonverbal behaviors are rarely conscious phenomena, it may be difficult for us to know exactly why we are feeling uncomfortable.

Hall (1966) refers to the largely unconscious phenomenon of nonverbal communication as the "hidden dimension" of culture. It is considered hidden because, unlike verbal messages, nonverbal messages are embedded in the context of our communication. In addition to the situational and relational cues of a particular communication transaction, nonverbal messages provide us with important contextual cues. Together with verbal and other contextual cues, nonverbal messages help us interpret the total meaning of a communication experience.

The purpose of the readings in this chapter is to increase our awareness of, and sensitivity to, the influence of this implicit, nonverbal dimension of our communication with strangers. In the first reading, Gudykunst and Ting-Toomey discuss general aspects of how nonverbal phenomena vary across cultures. They examine how we regulate privacy, how we use space and time, and how we synchronize our behavior with others.

In the second reading, Matsumoto, Wallbott, and Scherer examine how emotions vary across cultures. They examine what conditions lead to specific emotions, how we deal with various emotions, and the consequences our emotions have on our behavior. Matsumoto, Wallbott, and Scherer also look at cultural universals in facial expressions.

REFERENCES

Hall, E. T. (1966). *The hidden dimension.* New York: Doubleday.

Nonverbal Dimensions and Context-Regulation
William B. Gudykunst and Stella Ting-Toomey

Nonberbal context provides the background in which verbal messages can be meaningfully encoded and decoded. A verbal message such as "don't touch me" can occur in the context of an angry tone of voice, an informative tone, and a teasing tone. The verbal message, in conjunction with the paralinguistic signals, can unfold in the context of dramatic or restrained kinesic movements, animated or controlling facial expressions, and close or distant proxemic interaction. Finally, both verbal and nonverbal messages occur in the context of environment, space, and time dimensions.

Context-regulation, in this chapter, refers to the regulation of the nonverbal aspects of environment, space, and time. Nonverbal communication is defined as the simultaneous multimodal, multilevel message transmission and message interpretation process. . . .

ENVIRONMENT: A DIALECTICAL PERSPECTIVE

Kurt Lewin (1936) focused attention on the importance of environment in influencing human behavior, arguing that $B = f(P,E)$, where B = behavior, P = person, and E = environment. In other words, Lewin believes that human behavior is defined by the persons interacting, as well as the environment in which the interaction takes place.

The Dialectical Perspective

Altman and Gauvain (1981) studied the relationship among culture, human behavior, and home environment, proposing a dialectical perspective to the study of the three constructs. The three theoretical assumptions that guided the development of the dialectical theory of the nonverbal environment are (1) the world, universe, and human affairs involve various oppositional tensions; (2) these oppositional processes function as a unified system—oppositional poles help define one another, and without such contrasts neither would have meaning; and (3) the relationships between opposites are dynamic—changes occur over time and with circumstances (Altman & Gauvain, 1981). While verbal communication is a digital communication process,

Source: Abridged from Chapter 6 in W. B. Gudykunst and S. Ting-Toomey, *Culture and interpersonal communication* (pp. 117–133). Newbury Park, CA. Sage, 1988.

nonverbal communication is a multilayered, multimodal, multidimensional, analogic process. The oppositional poles such as identity-communality and accessibility-inaccessibility govern the use of mixed nonverbal signals. The use of interaction space, for example, may signal the need for individual privacy or identity, while at the same time hand gestures and facial expressions may signal accessibility or openness for the purpose of minimizing relational distance or status difference.

Altman and Gauvain (1981) suggest that the environment of a culture typically reflects the degree to which the culture and its members attempt to cope with two sets of dialectical opposites: the identity-communality dimension and the accessibility-inaccessibility dimension. The identity-communality dialectic reflects the "uniqueness and individuality of its occupants; that is, their personal identity as individuals and as a family, along with their ties, bonds, and affections with the communality and larger cultures of which they are part" (p. 288). The accessibility-inaccessibility dialectic involves the degree to which the home environment emphasizes the openness or closedness of occupants to outsiders. . . .

The identity-communality dimension echoes the individualism-collectivism dimension, and the accessibility-inaccessibility dimension reflects the power distance and uncertainty avoidance dimensions. Individualistic cultures foster identity-type nonverbal behaviors and collectivistic cultures encourage communal-type nonverbal behaviors. In addition, people in low power distance, low uncertainty avoidance cultures tend to engage in an explicit nonverbal style that may create an impression of accessibility, while people in high power distance, high uncertainty avoidance cultures tend to engage in implicit nonverbal style that may create an impression of inaccessibility. The . . . model includes four nonverbal style possibilities: unique-explicit nonverbal style, unique-implicit nonverbal style, group-explicit nonverbal style, and group-implicit nonverbal style. The degree of identity-communality continuum refers to the use of contexts (environment, space, time) to assert individual identity or communal identity, while the degree of accessibility-inaccessibility continuum refers to the use of specific nonverbal behaviors (such as parlinguistics or kinesics) explicitly or implicitly to regulate the nonverbal meanings of immediacy, potency, and responsiveness (Mehrabian, 1972). According to Mehrabian, immediacy refers to the like-dislike dimension, potency refers to the high-low-status dimension, and responsiveness refers to the active-passive energy dimension.

Unique-explicit nonverbal style refers to the use of nonverbal behavior to regulate individual privacy, as well as the use of expressive nonverbal gestures to signal immediacy, potency, and responsiveness. Unique-implicit nonverbal style refers to the use of nonverbal behaviors to protect individual privacy while simultaneously using subdued nonverbal gestures and movements to display relational liking and power distance. Group-explicit nonverbal style refers to the use of nonverbal behaviors to ensure group norms and regulate public face and the use of expressive nonverbal gestures to signal immediacy, potency, and responsiveness. Finally, group-implicit style refers to the use of nonverbal behaviors to uphold group norms and public face while at the same time using subdued nonverbal behaviors to display relational liking and power distance.

Overall, we may conclude that members of individualistic, low power distance, and low uncertainty avoidance cultures (such as Australia and the United States) are likely to engage in the unique-explicit nonverbal style of interaction, and members of individualistic, high power distance, and high uncertainty avoidance cultures (such as Belgium and France) are likely to engage in unique-implicit nonverbal style of interaction. Conversely, members of collectivistic, low (to moderate) power distance, and low uncertainty avoidance cultures (such as Hong Kong and Singapore) are likely to use a group-explicit style of nonverbal communication, while members from collectivistic, high power distance, and high uncertainty avoidance cultures (such as Japan and Korea) are likely to use group-implicit style of nonverbal communication.

In fact, reviews of past cross-cultural nonverbal research (LaFrance & Mayo, 1978a, 1978b; Ramsey, 1979, 1984) point out clearly that members of individualistic cultures tend to engage in more privacy-regulation nonverbal behaviors, while members of collectivistic cultures tend to engage in more public face-regulation nonverbal behaviors. Further, while people in low power distance, low uncertainty avoidance cultures tend to use explicit nonverbal gestures to signal accessibility, people in high power distance, high uncertainty avoidance cultures tend to use implicit nonverbal gestures to regulate status positions and relational power. . . .

Home Environments

In applying the dialectical theory to the study of home environments across cultures, Altman and Gauvain (1981) found that the middle-class home environment in individualistic cultures is very different from the middle-class home environment in collectivistic cultures. In individualistic cultures, the middle-class home environment typically is separated from the community at large through the use of front yards, backyards, gates, and lawns. In collectivistic cultures, the middle-class home environment is developed in such a way that the architectural design of the home is integrated with a central plaza, a community center, or a neighborhood dwelling. Altman and his associates (Altman & Gauvain, 1981; Werner, Altman, & Oxley, 1985) further observe that the decor and furnishings of North American middle-class suburban homes symbolize the desire of the owners to differentiate themselves from one another, while the decor and furnishing of Indian, Japanese, and Mexican middle-class homes tend to express the communal desire of getting together, of interconnecting, and of group identity. Ramsey (1979) points out that while Northern European middle-class homes tend to emphasize edges, boundaries, and the segmentation of individual spaces and norms for each household member, Southeast Asian middle-class homes tend to emphasize communal spaces between objects in interior design. Finally, Altman and Gauvain (1981) found that while suburban North American homes can be identified by their individualized landscapes, by their locations in the middle or rear part of a lot, and by their separate entranceways, the Pueblo Indian homes are clusters of dwellings that surround a central courtyard or plaza where work, community activities, and religious events take place. . . .

PRIVACY-REGULATION, PROXEMICS, AND HAPTICS

Privacy-Regulation

Privacy-regulation is concerned with the identity expressiveness dimension and the information accessibility dimension. Altman (1975) defines privacy-regulation as the "selective control of access to the self or to one's group" (p. 18). Privacy-regulation can be achieved through both concrete and behavioral means. On the concrete level, the use of closed doors in the United States, the use of soundproof, double doors in the German culture (Hall, 1966), the use of large, carved doors in Norway, and the use of high shrubbery, trees, and fences to shield the home from public in Canada and England (Altman & Gauvin, 1981), all display the high need for personal privacy and individual identity in these cultures. Conversely, in Javanese (Geertz, 1973), Japanese, and many Southeast Asian cultures, population density and crowded environmental conditions make it virtually impossible for members of these cultures to manipulate the concrete environment to maintain and create personal privacy. Furthermore, personal privacy might not be as major a concern for people in collectivistic cultures as it is for people in individualistic cultures. A compensatory norm also appears to exist among privacy-regulation, environmental manipulation, and self-disclosure in collectivistic cultures. Many studies (Barnlund, 1975a; Gudykunst, Yang, & Nishida, 1985; Won-Doornink, 1985), for example, have found that members of individualistic cultures are more accessible in disclosing private information during initial interactions than members of collectivistic cultures. Conjointly, members of individualistic cultures also tend to engage in environmental control to assert their unique identity and to claim private space than do members of collectivistic cultures. Whereas in collectivistic cultures, individuals do not necessarily manipulate the environment to ensure individual privacy, they compensate by monitoring their self-disclosure process more judiciously and cautiously. As Derlega and Chaikan (1977) suggested, the reconceptualization of self-disclosure in the direction of nonverbal privacy-regulation may yield more fruitful avenues for future research into self-disclosure and interpersonal development process. In identity-based cultures, where people tend to use barriers and proxemic space to ensure individual privacy, the verbal self-disclosure process becomes more free-flowing, spontaneous, and accessible. In communal-based cultures, where people are less likely to use environmental space to assert individual privacy, the verbal self-disclosure process then becomes more regulated and inaccessible.

Proxemics

Claiming a space for oneself means injecting a sense of identity or selfhood into a place with clear boundaries surrounding it. According to Hall's (1966) proxemic theory, the use of interpersonal space or distance helps individuals regulate intimacy by controlling sensory exposure. Altman (1975) views the study of proxemics as the claiming of personal territory that includes the "personalization of or marking of a place or object and communication that it is 'owmed' by a person or group" (p. 107). While members of all cultures engage in the claiming of space for self or collective effort, the experience of spaciousness and crowdedness and the perception of space-violation and space-respect vary from one culture to the next. The key mediating variable appears to rest with the need for sensory exposure and contact in different cultures.

Intimacy by sensory exposure (and therefore the need for close personal space) "is reported to be high among South Americans, Southern and Eastern Europeans, and Arabs, and low among Asians, Northern Europeans, and North Americans" (Sussman & Rosenfeld, 1982, p. 66). Andersen (1987) provides a further explanation by arguing that high-contact cultures, wherein members prefer to stand close and touch, tend to be located in warmer climates or regions; while low-contact cultures, wherein members prefer to stand further apart and touch little, tend to be located in cooler climates or regions. He concludes that cultures in cooler climates tend to be more task-oriented and interpersonally "cool," whereas cultures in warmer climates tend to be more interpersonally oriented and interpersonally "warm" (p. 10). In short, people in low-contact cultures have a low need for sensory exposure and people in high-contact cultures have a high need for sensory exposure.

Sussman and Rosenfeld (1982) tested the proxemic theory of sensory exposure by examining the use of interpersonal distance in Japanese, Venezuelan, and North American students. They found that (a) when speaking their native languages, Japanese sit further apart than Venezuelans, with North Americans at an intermediate distance; (b) females sit closer than males; and (c) when speaking English, respondents from other cultures use personal distances more closely approximating North American conversational distance norms than when speaking their native languages. While Venezuela is a high-contact culture, Japan is a low-contact culture. It seems that when individuals converse in their native language, the use of their native language also triggers a broader package of culturally appropriate behaviors.

Engebretson and Fullmer (1970) found that Japanese prefer greater interaction distances with their friend, father, and professor than do Japanese-Americans in Hawaii and Caucasian Americans. Little (1968) also found that members of Mediterranean cultures (such as Greeks and Southern Italians) prefer closer distances than do Northern Europeans. LaFrance and Mayo (1978a) commented that Argentineans make greater differentiations between the use of personal distance and relationship type, while Iraqis make little distinction between the use of personal space and relationship type. In terms of spatial violation behavior, a series of studies by Bond and Shiraishi (1974), Bond and Komai (1976), and Bond and Iwata (1976) suggest that members of individualistic cultures tend to take an active, aggressive stance when their space is violated, while members of collectivistic cultures tend to assume a passive, withdrawal stance when their personal space is intruded.

Burgoon (1978, 1983) developed a theory of spatial violation behavior based on the violations of expectations model. She argues that the manner in which one reacts to violations is dependent upon the characteristics of the perpetrator of the violations, whether the violation is closer or farther than expected, and its extremity. The process of arousal labeling, the message value of proximity shift, and competing privacy and affiliation needs also affect individuals' expectations (Burgoon, 1983). The model, however, has not been tested in cultures where status relationships may assert a stronger influence on the expectation violation model than in the North American setting (e.g., cultures high in power distance). The assumption that "given a rewarding initiator, optimal communication outcomes are achieved by violating the expected distance rather than conforming to it" (p. 105) may be applicable in individualistic, low power distance cultures (such as the United States), but not in other cultures. Different behavioral outcomes may occur in collectivistic, high power distance cultures (such as Japan), for example, when the rewarding initiator (defined as a high-status person) attempts to violate the personal space of a low-status person. A high-status person, in violating the personal space of a low-status person in collectivistic, high power distance cultures is acting totally out of his or her ascribed role performance, and in turn, will bring stress and anxiety to the asymmetrical relationship. . . .

Haptics

Different cultures encode and interpret touch behavior in different ways. Low-contact cultures engage in less touch behavior than high-contact cultures. People in collectivistic cultures with high-intimacy sensory exposure need tend to engage in more tactile interaction than people in individualistic cultures with low-intimacy sensory exposure need. Hall (1983), for example, found that Arabs typically feel a strong sense of "sensory deprivation" and alienation at the lack of close, intimate contact with North Americans, while North Americans find Arabs' need for close personal space anxiety-provoking and disturbing. Almaney and Alwan's (1982) and Cohen's (1987) work supports Hall's observation concerning the nonverbal personalism and impersonalism dimension of Arab and North American cultures. As Almaney and Alwan (1982) conclude:

> To the Arab, to be able to smell a friend is reassuring. Smelling is a way of being involved with another, and to deny a friend his [or her] breath would be to act ashamed. In some rural Middle Eastern areas, when Arab intermediaries call to inspect a prospective bride for a relative, they sometimes ask to smell her. Their purpose is not to make sure that she is freshly scrubbed; apparently what they look for is any lingering odor of anger or discontent. The Burmese show their affection during greeting by pressing mouths and noses upon the cheek and inhaling the breath strongly. The Samoans show affection by juxtaposing noses and smelling heartily. In contrast, the [North] Americans seem to maintain their distance and suppress their sense of smell. (p. 17)

The tendency for North Americans to remain outside the appropriate olfactory zone of Arabs often leads to Arabs suspecting the speakers' genuine intentions, whereas the close contact need of the Arabs often constitutes a violation of the personal space and privacy of the North Americans. Similar to the Arab cultures' need for sensory intimacy, studies (Engebretson & Fullmer, 1970; Mayo & LaFrance, 1977;

Shuter, 1976; Watson, 1970) on touch behaviors in Latin American cultures and the U.S. culture reveal that people in Latin American cultures tend to engage in more frequent tactile behavior than people in the United States. In comparing touch behavior in Japan and the United States, Barnlund (1975a) found that Japanese tend to engage in same-sex touch behavior more often than North Americans, while North Americans tend to engage in opposite-sex touch behavior more often than Japanese. Further, Japanese females tend to touch more than do Japanese males. Conversely, in the Mediterranean cultures, LaFrance and Mayo (1978a) concluded that male-male touch behavior is used more frequently than female-female touch behavior.

Jones and Remland (1982) used the Touch Avoidance Measure (Andersen & Leibowitz, 1978) to analyze touch avoidance behaviors in Mediterranean, Near Eastern, Far Eastern, and U.S. cultures. They found that people in the Mediterranean are more touch-avoidant to opposite-sex touching than people in the United States. People in the Near East are less touch-avoidant to opposite-sex touching than both Mediterranean and Far Eastern groups. Finally, the Far Eastern group is the most touch-avoidant cultural group in opposite-sex touch behavior among the four groups. These findings support Watson's (1970) contention that the Far Eastern cultures are low-contact cultures, the North American culture is a moderate-contact culture, and the Arab and the Mediterranean cultures are high nonverbal contact cultures. Of course, variables such as gender, age, and relational distance will have an effect on the initiation and the receptivity levels of touch behavior, as well as on the variations of nonverbal touch forms.

The norms and rules employed regarding nonverbal touch behavior in high power distance, high-masculine cultures are more stringent than the norms and rules used in low power distance, low-masculine cultures. While tight relational norms and rules regulate tactile behavior in high uncertainty avoidance cultures, loose relational norms and rules govern tactile behavior in low uncertainty avoidance cultures. . . .

CHRONEMICS

Beyond the use of space and touch, time is reflective of the psychological environment in which communication occurs (see Jones, 1988, and LeVine, 1988, for recent cross-cultural comparisons). Time flies when two friends are enjoying themselves and having a good time. Time crawls when two ex-friends stare at each other and have nothing to say to one another. Hall (1983) distinguished two patterns of time that govern different cultures: Monochronic Time Schedule (M-time) and Polychronic Time Schedule (P-time).

According to Hall (1983), the M-time and P-time are empirically quite distinct, "like oil and water, they don't mix" (pp. 45–46). He elaborates, arguing that

> each has its strengths as well as its weaknesses. I have termed doing many things at once, Polychronic, P-time. The North European system—doing one thing at a time—is Monochronic, M-time. P-time stresses involvement of people and

completion of transactions rather than adherence to preset schedules. Appointments are not taken as seriously and, as a consequence, are frequently broken. P-time is treated as less tangible than M-time. For polychronic people, time is seldom experienced as "wasted," and is apt to be considered a point rather than a ribbon or a road, but that point is often sacred. (p. 46)

For Hall (1983), Latin American, Middle Eastern, Japanese, and French cultures are representatives of P-time patterns, while Northern European, North American, and German cultures are representatives of M-time patterns. People that follow M-time patterns usually engage in one activity at a time, they compartmentalize time schedules to serve self-needs, and they tend to separate task-oriented time from socio-emotional time. People that follow P-time tend to do multiple tasks at the same time, they tend to hold more fluid attitudes toward time schedules, and they tend to integrate task need with socio-emotional need. Members of individualistic cultures such as Denmark, Finland, Germany, and Norway tend to follow the M-time pattern, while members of collectivistic cultures such as Greece, Iran, Turkey, the Philippines, and Thailand tend to follow the P-time pattern. While members of individualistic cultures tend to view time as something that can be possessed, killed, and wasted, members of collectivistic cultures tend to view time as more contextually based and relationally oriented. People who follow M-time schedules tend to emphasize individual privacy, schedules, and appointments. People who follow P-time schedules, in contrast, tend to emphasize human connectedness, fluidity, and flextime.

Beyond M-time and P-time, Hall (1959) also differentiates five time intervals for arriving late for appointments: (1) mumble something time, (2) slight apology time, (3) mildly insulting time, (4) rude time, and (5) downright insulting time. For people who follow M-time schedules, if they are five minutes late for an appointment, they mumble something. If they are 10 to 15 minutes late, they would probably make a slight apology. For people who follow P-time schedules, it is not unusual for a person to be 45 or 60 minutes late and not even "mumble something," or to express a slight apology. While individualistic cultures are time-oriented, collectivistic cultures are relationally oriented. Members of individualistic cultures view time from a linear past-present-future perspective and members of collectivistic cultures tend to view time from a spiral, cyclical perspective. From the perspective of people in individualistic cultures, time can be controlled and wasted by individuals. From the perspective of people in collectivistic cultures, time regenerates itself without the necessary control and imposition by individuals. . . .

INTERPERSONAL SYNCHRONIZATION PROCESSES

According to Argyle (1979), the five basic nonverbal communication functions are (1) conveying interpersonal attitudes, (2) expressing emotional states, (3) managing conversations, (4) exchanging rituals, and (5) regulating self-presentation. One of the key concepts that may tie all these five nonverbal functions together is "interpersonal synchrony." According to Hall (1983), interpersonal synchrony refers to convergent rhythmic movements between two people on both the verbal and the nonverbal levels. Every facet of human behavior is involved in the rhythmic process. As Hall commented:

> It can now be said with assurance that individuals are dominated in their behavior by complex hierarchies of interlocking rhythms. Furthermore, these same interlocking rhythms are comparable to fundamental themes in a symphonic score, a keystone in the interpersonal processes between mates, co-workers, and organizations of all types on the interpersonal level within as well as across cultural boundaries. (p. 153)

Based on kinesic and proxemic film research, Hall (1983) found that conversational distances between individuals always are mentioned with incredible accuracy, that the process is rhythmic, and that the individuals are locked together in a "dance" that functions almost totally out of awareness. He also observed that people in Latin American, African, and Asian cultures seem to be more conscious of these rhythmic movements than are people in Northern European and North American cultures. The fact that synchronized rhythmic movements are based on the "hidden dimensions" of nonverbal behavior might explain why people in African and Latin American cultures (as high-context nonverbal cultures) are more in tune and display more sensitivity toward the synchronization process than people in low-context verbal cultures, such as those in Northern Europe and the United States.

Members of high-context, collectivistic cultures that are relational and group-oriented tend to have a higher need to contextualize the rhythmic pattern of an event from beginning, middle, and ending. It takes people in collectivistic cultures a longer time to engage in greeting and goodbye rituals, a longer time to move the relationship level from a low degree of intimacy to a higher degree of intimacy, and a longer time to terminate the action chain of an event than it takes people in individualistic cultures. Conversely, members of individualistic cultures have a relatively low need to complete an action chain; approach greeting, maintenance, and goodbye rituals with a fast pace; and approach the initiation, maintenance, and termination of a relationship with a faster pace than do members of collectivistic cultures. Whatever members of individualistic cultures do not accomplish on the nonverbal level, they can rely on words to convey.

Interpersonal synchrony or convergence is achieved when the nonverbal behavior between two individuals moves toward broadness, uniqueness, efficiency, flexibility, smoothness, personalness, and spontaneity, and when overt judgment is suspended (Knapp, 1983). Interpersonal misalignment or divergence occurs when the nonverbal behavior between two individuals moves toward narrowness, stylized behavior, difficulty, rigidity, awkwardness, publicness, and hesitancy, and when overt judgment is given (Knapp, 1983). Interpersonal synchrony signifies increased liking, rapport, and attention, while interpersonal misalignment signifies increased disliking, rejection, and indifference. While members of individualistic, low-context cultures emphasize speech convergence, members of collectivistic, high-context cultures emphasize the importance of nonverbal convergence. People in individualistic, low-context cultures emphasize the assertion of individual identities in the manipulation of environment, space, touch, and time dimensions. People in collectivistic, high-context cultures, in contrast, emphasize the importance of communal identities in the use of environment, space, touch, and time dimensions. Finally, while members of low-context, individualistic cultures tend to be more accessible through explicit verbal self-disclosure, members of high-context, collectivistic cultures tend to be more accessible through either explicit or implicit means of nonverbal interaction.

The concept of communication competence (Hymes, 1972; Spitzberg & Cupach, 1984) indeed takes on a cultural-specific meaning when the norms and values of verbal and nonverbal patterns in different cultural systems are examined. Researchers examining communication competence in individualistic, low-context cultures would place a higher value on verbal communication competence. Researchers analyzing communication competence in collectivistic, high-context cultures would place a higher emphasis on the study of nonverbal communication competence. . . .

REFERENCES

Almaney, A., & Alwan, A. (1982). *Communicating with the Arabs.* Prospect Heights, IL: Waveland Press.

Altman, I. (1975). *The environment and social behavior.* Monterey, CA: Brooks/Cole.

Altman, I, & Gawain, M. (1981). A cross-cultural dialectical analysis of homes. In L. Liben, A. Patterson, & N. Newcombe (Eds.), *Spatial representation and behavior across the life span.* New York: Academic Press.

Andersen, P. (1987, November). *Explaining intercultural differences in nonverbal behavior.* Paper presented at the Speech Communication Association Convention, Boston.

Andersen, P., & Leibowitz, K. (1978). The development and nature of the construct touch avoidance. *Environmental Psychology and Nonverbal Behavior, 3,* 89–106.

Argyle, M. (1979). New developments in the analysis of social skills. In A. Wolfgang (Ed.), *Nonverbal behavior: Applications and cultural implications.* New York: Academic Press.

Barnlund, D. (1975a). *Public and private self in Japan and the United States.* Tokyo: Simul.

Bond, M., & Iwata, Y. (1976). Proxemics and observation anxiety in Japan: Nonverbal and cognitive responses. *Psychologia, 19,* 119–126.

Bond, M., & Komai, H. (1976). Targets of gazing and eye contact during interviews. *Journal of Personality and Social Psychology, 34,* 1276–1284.

Bond, M., & Shiraishi, D. (1974). The effect of body lean and status of interviewer on the nonverbal behavior of Japanese interviewees. *International Journal of Psychology, 9,* 117–128.

Burgoon, J. (1978). A communication model of personal space violations: Explication and an initial test. *Human Communication Research, 4,* 129–142.

Burgoon, J. (1983). Nonverbal violations of expectations. In J. Wiemann & R. Harrison (Eds.), *Nonverbal interaction.* Beverly Hills, CA: Sage.

Burgoon, J. (1985). Nonverbal signals. In M. Knapp & G. Miller (Eds.), *Handbook of interpersonal communication.* Beverly Hills, CA: Sage.

Cohen, R. (1987). Problems of intercultural communication in Egyptian-American diplomatic relations. *International Journal of Intercultural Relations, 11,* 29–47.

Dergla, V., & Chaikin, A. (1977). Privacy and self-disclosure in social relationships. *Journal of Social Issues, 3*, 102–115.

Engebretson, D., & Fullmer, D. (1970). Cross-cultural differences in territorality. *Journal of Cross-Cultural Psychology, 1*, 261–269.

Geertz, C. (1973). *The interpretation of cultures.* New York: Basic Books.

Gudykunst, W. B., Yang, S. M., & Nishida, T. (1985). A cross-cultural test of uncertainty reduction theory. *Human Communication Research, 14*, 7–36.

Hall, E. T. (1959). *The silent language.* Garden City, NY: Anchor Books.

Hall, E. T. (1966). *The hidden dimension.* Garden City, NY: Anchor Books.

Hall, E. T. (1983). *The dance of life.* Garden City, NY: Anchor Books.

Henly, N., & LaFrance, M. (1984). Gender as culture. In A. Wolfgang (Ed.), *Nonverbal behavior: Perspectives, applications, and intercultural insights.* Lewiston, NY: Hogrefe.

Hymes, D. (1972). Models of the interaction of language and social life. In J. Gumperz & D. Hymes (Eds.), *Directions of sociolinguistics.* New York: Holt, Rinehart, and Winston.

Jones, J. (1988). Cultural differences in temporal patterns. In J. McGrath (Ed.), *The social psychology of time.* Newbury Park, CA: Sage.

Jones, T., & Remland, M. (1982, May). *Cross-cultural differences in self-reported touch avoidance.* Paper presented at the Eastern Communication Association Convention, Hartford, CT.

Knapp, M. (1983). Dyadic relationship development. In J. Wiemann & R. Harrison (Eds.), *Nonverbal interaction.* Beverly Hills, CA: Sage.

LaFrance, M., & Mayo, C. (1978a). Cultural aspects of nonverbal communication. *International Journal of Intercultural Relations, 2*, 71–89.

LaFrance, M., & Mayo, C. (1978b). Gaze direction in interracial dyadic communication. *Ethnicity, 5*, 167–173.

LaFrance, M., & Mayo, C. (1979). A review of nonverbal behaviors of men and women. *Western Journal of Speech Communication, 43*, 96–107.

LeVine, D. (1988). The pace of life across cultures. In J. McGrath (Ed.), *The social psychology of time.* Newbury Park, CA: Sage.

Lewin, K. (1936). *Principles of topological psychology.* New York: Harper and Row.

Little, K. (1968). Cultural variations in social schemata. *Journal of Personality and Social Psychology, 10*, 1–7.

Mayo, C., & LaFrance, M. (1977). *Evaluating research in social psychology.* Monterey, CA: Brooks/Cole.

Mehrabian, A. (1972). *Nonverbal communication.* Chicago: Aldine.

Poyatos, F. (1983). *New perspectives in nonverbal communication.* Oxford: Pergamon.

Ramsey, S. (1979). Nonverbal behavior: An intercultural perspective. In M. Asante, E. Newmark, & C. Blake (Eds.), *Handbook of intercultural communication.* Beverly Hills, CA: Sage.

Ramsey, S. (1984). Double vision: Nonverbal behavior east and west. In A. Wolfgang (Ed.), *Nonverbal behavior: Perspectives, applications, and intercultural insights.* Lewiston, NY: Hogrefe.

Shuter, R. (1976). Too close for comfort: Proxemics and tactility in Latin America. *Journal of Communication, 26*, 46–52.

Spitzberg, B., & Cupach, W. (1984). *Interpersonal communication competence.* Beverly Hills, CA: Sage.

Sussman, N., & Rosenfeld, H. (1982). The influence of culture, language, and sex on conversational distance. *Journal of Personality and Social Psychology, 42*, 66–74.

Tuan, Y. (1982). *Segmented worlds and self.* Minneapolis: University of Minnesota.

Watson, O. (1970). *Proxemic behavior: A cross-cultural study.* The Hague: Mouton.

Werner, C., Altman, I., & Oxley, D. (1985). Temporal aspects of homes. In I. Altman & C. Werner (Eds.), *Home environments.* New York: Plenum.

Wiemann, J., & Harrison, R. (Eds.). (1983). *Nonverbal interaction.* Beverly Hills, CA: Sage.

Wolfgang, A. (Ed.). (1984). *Nonverbal behavior: Perspectives, applications, and intercultural insights.* Lewiston, NY: Hogrefe.

Won-Doornink, M. (1985). Self-disclosure and reciprocity in conversation: A cross-cultural study. *Social Psychology Quarterly, 48,* 97–107.

Emotions in Intercultural Communication

David Matsumoto, Harald G. Wallbott, and Klaus R. Scherer

Emotions are not only markers of special episodes in subjective individual experience, they are also motivators and regulators of social interaction. Research on the emotions, especially in the cross-cultural realm, is becoming increasingly abundant. They are a particularly fascinating topic for intercultural study, because their antecedents, reactions, display, perception, and roles, in terms of both individual experience and social/motivational phenomena, can differ substantially across cultures.

Most studies to date have investigated the communication of emotion through facial expressions. But research on other aspects of emotion is also becoming popular. All of the research aims to elucidate cultural similarities and differences in the experience, expression, perception, and consequences of emotion, in the hopes of clarifying the nature and function of emotion in different cultures. . . .

CROSS-CULTURAL STUDIES OF FACIAL EXPRESSIONS

Background

For more than 100 years scientists argued about whether facial expressions are universal or specific to each culture. Until recently, the prevalent view in psychology was that facial expressions were culture-specific, learned differently across cultures, like language. Research from the past twenty years, however, has provided evidence for both universal *and* culture-specific aspects of facial expressions of emotion.

Three different types of cross-cultural studies have documented the universality of (at least) six different emotions (anger, disgust, fear, happiness, sadness, and surprise). In one type, members of one culture were asked to show how their face would look if they were the person in each of a number of different situations designed to elicit certain emotions (e.g. "you feel sad because your child died"—see Ekman &

Source: Abridged from Chapter 10 in M. Asante & W. Gudykunst (Eds.), *Handbook of International and Intercultural Communication* (pp. 225–246). Newbury Park, CA: Sage, 1989.

Friesen, 1971). Universality was demonstrated when observers in another culture did far better than chance in identifying which emotional contexts the expressions were intended to portray. This study had unusual import because the persons displaying the expressions were members of a visually isolated culture in New Guinea, and the observers were Americans who had had no previous exposure to New Guineans.

In a second type of experiment, the spontaneous facial expressions shown by Japanese and Americans while they watched stress-inducing (bodily mutilation) and neutral films (nature scenes) were measured (Ekman, 1972). Universality was demonstrated when virtually the same facial responses were emitted by members of both cultures, as the subjects in each culture watched the films alone, unaware of a hidden camera.

In a third type of experiment, photographs of facial expressions were shown to observers in a number of different cultures (Ekman, 1972, 1973; Ekman & Friesen, 1971; Ekman, Sorenson, & Friesen, 1969; Izard, 1971). This set of studies was different from others in that a large number of cultures and a full range of emotional expressions were tested. Universality in expression was documented because very high agreement was found across twelve literate cultures in the specific emotions attributed to facial expressions. Unlike the first two types of studies, this line of research has been repeated in different cultures, with different researchers, using different photographs of facial expression.

Cultural differences in the *display* of emotion have also been documented in the study described above concerning the spontaneous expressions of Japanese and American subjects as they viewed stress-inducing films. When a scientist was present while the subjects watched the films a second time, the Japanese more than the Americans masked negative expressions with smiles (Friesen, 1972). This study was the first to show how cultural differences in the management of facial expressions can mask universal emotions. Ekman and Friesen called these "display rules" (Ekman, 1972, 1973; Ekman & Friesen, 1969).

Recent Findings

Cross-cultural research on facial expressions continues to generate new information about cultural similarities and differences, particularly in regard to the perception of emotion. Here we present the most recent findings from a new series of cross-cultural studies.

A Possible Seventh Universal Facial Expression: Contempt Two studies from a total of 11 cultures (Ekman & Friesen, 1986; Ekman & Heider, in press) have reported evidence from a study involving 10 cultures and two judgment tasks suggesting the universality of a contempt expression: a unilateral smile. This finding was totally unexpected, as several different expressions thought to portray contempt were tested. These were originally included in the study to document the existence of culture-specific emotions.

Cultures Agree on the Most Salient Emotion Portrayed When Judgments Are Made with Intensity Ratings Findings from two recent studies (Ekman et al., 1987; Matsumoto & Ekman, in press) have indicated that cultures agree on the mòst salient emotion portrayed in the universal expressions, even when judgments are made using intensity ratings. In these studies, observers were allowed to register multiple emotion judgments for seven different emotion categories, using multiscalar intensity ratings. The findings provided were the first evidence of cross-cultural agreement about the most intense emotion when observers were able to choose more than one emotion.

Cultures Agree on the Second Most Salient Emotion Portrayed Analysis of the multiscalar intensity ratings described above from Ekman et al.'s (1987) study indicated that a majority of subjects in each of the 10 cultures tested agreed about the second most salient emotion. For example, contempt was the second strongest emotion judged by every culture for every disgust expression. Surprise was the second strongest in fear expressions. By contrast, happy and sad expressions did not have discernible second emotions. This finding provides stronger evidence in favor of the notion of universal aspects of emotion recognition.

Cultures Agree on the Relative Intensity of Emotion Portrayed Ekman et al. (1987) also reported that there was high agreement across cultures concerning which expression of two of the same emotion was the more intense. This provides an even stronger test of the notion of universality in recognition of these emotions, as not only did the cultures have to agree on which emotion was the most intense in each of the expressions separately, but they also had to agree on which expression was more intense.

Cultures Agree on the Universal Expressions of Emotion When Portrayed by Members of Another Culture High cultural agreement concerning the judgment of the most salient emotion has been reported in a recent study comparing American and Japanese observers viewing Caucasian and [Asian] posers portraying the universal expressions (Matsumoto, 1986; Matsumoto & Ekman, in press). While this study was not the first to document this finding (see "American Judgments of New Guinean Faces"—Ekman, 1972), it was the first to use expressions of posers of two different cultures in obtaining judgments of members of both cultures.

Cultures Disagree on How Intensely They Perceive the Emotions Findings from several studies have shown that cultures differ in their intensity ratings of the universal expressions (Ekman et al., 1987; Matsumoto, 1986; Matsumoto & Ekman, in press). These studies indicate that the cultural differences exist regardless of whether judgments are made of someone of the same or of a visibly different culture, and regardless of possible differences in the affect lexicons of the cultures. Matsumoto and Ekman (in press) expanded on the concept of display rules (Ekman, 1972; Ekman & Friesen, 1969; Friesen, 1972) for emotional expressions in explaining these differences in the perception of emotion. . . .

CROSS-CULTURAL STUDIES ON THE ANTECEDENTS OF AND REACTIONS TO EMOTIONS

Background

Emotional expression is one facet of a whole gamut of complex emotional processes that play important roles in everyday functioning and interpersonal communication. Other aspects of emotional processes include the antecedents of emotions; the evaluation of antecedent events; verbal and nonfacial nonverbal reactions, and perceived physiological symptoms and sensations; the subjective experience of the emotions; and the conscious regulation or control of emotions. In recent years, our laboratories have engaged in several large cross-cultural research programs focused on these processes, for both theoretical and practical reasons. Theoretically, these studies investigate whether aspects of emotion other than facial expressions are universal, and give us ideas concerning the possible impact of innate biological or culture-specific learning processes in emotion. Pragmatically, this line of research offers us insight into the cultural similarities and differences in emotion elicitation and experience. These, in turn, have direct relevance to our actual interactions with people of different cultures. . . .

Findings Implicating Universal Aspects of Emotional Experience

The Antecedents of Emotional Experience Just as there was debate concerning the origin of facial expressions of emotion, similar controversies existed concerning the nature of emotion antecedents. On one hand, previous work by Osgood and his colleagues concerning universals of affective meaning suggested universals across cultures in the ways antecedent events are interpreted (see Osgood, May, & Miron, 1975). On the other hand, the documentation of possible cultural differences in emotional expression through display rules and the neurocultural model of expression suggests that antecedent events to specific emotions may be specific to culture (see Ekman, 1972).

Research concerning the antecedents of emotional experience within cultures was sparse, and cross-cultural research on this topic was even rarer. Those few who attempted to examine antecedents of emotion across cultures were limited in their sampling of either cultures or emotions. Boucher, for example, did obtain cross-cultural agreement concerning the judgment of antecedent events to six emotions (Boucher & Brandt, 1981). But only two cultures were surveyed in this study (Malay and the United States).

The antecedent situations reported in the ESI [Emotion in Social Interaction] study (but not ISEAR [International Study of Emotion Antecedents and Reactions] as of yet) have been analyzed, and provide us with interesting information concerning the possible universality in antecedents. Because of the large number of responses obtained in the ESI studies, a coding scheme was developed for these antecedent situations. Broad categories of descriptions were used, as an attempt was made to code themes applicable to all four emotions (e.g., "relations with friends" or "achievement-related situations"). Of course, some categories specific only to one or two emotions had to be included. Detailed information concerning the codes and their development can be found in Ellgring and Baenninger-Huber (1986).

In the European sample, we found that there was surprisingly strong agreement across cultures concerning the types of antecedent situations that were major elicitors of each of the four emotions tested. For example, cultural pleasures, birth of new family members, body-centered "basic pleasures," and achievement-related situations were frequent antecedents of joy. Sadness was elicited by death of family members or friends, relationship problems, and world news. Fear was elicited most frequently by traffic, strangers, novel situations, achievement-situations, and risky situations. Finally, anger was elicited most frequently by relationship problems, injustice, and strangers.

Characteristics of Emotional Experience Participants were asked to report for each of the emotions how long ago the event occurred, how long and intensely they felt the emotion, and the degree to which they made a conscious effort to control or regulate their reactions to the situation. Their responses to how long ago the event occurred were considered to be indicative of the frequency of the occurrence of that emotion, because emotions that are reported to have happened further in the past may be experienced less frequently.

Emotion effects are consistently strong concerning the characteristics of emotion. . . . Situations eliciting anger and disgust occur most frequently, while situations eliciting fear occur least frequently. Situations eliciting sadness are experienced most intensely, while situations eliciting shame and guilt are experienced least intensely. Also, situations eliciting sadness and joy are experienced for the longest duration, while disgust and fear are experienced for the shortest duration. Finally, shame and guilt experiences require the greatest degree of control and regulation of reactions, while experiences eliciting joy require the least.

Cognitive Evaluation of the Emotions In the ISEAR project, respondents were asked a series of closed-ended questions concerning their cognitive evaluations of the antecedent situations they described. The selection of the questions was guided by Scherer's (1984, 1986) theory of emotion elicitation, which postulates different stimulus appraisals or evaluation checks for the antecedents of emotion. For each of the emotions, subjects were asked to rate how *expected* and *pleasant* the situations were, the degree to which *plans* were hindered as a result of these situations, how *fair* they thought the situations were, who or what was *responsible* for the situations, how they *coped* with the situations, how *moral* or *immoral* the situations were, how one's *self-image* was affected by the situations, and how one's *relations* with others were affected.

Each of the emotions were differentiated according to the respondents' evaluations of the antecedent situations of that emotion. For example, joy-producing situations were the most expected and pleasant. Joy also produced the most positive self-image changes, while guilt and shame produced the least positive changes in self-image. Joy also had positive influence on relationships with others, while anger and disgust produced the least positive influence on relations. Anger and sadness produced the most hindrances to plans, and anger was also judged as most unfair. Disgust experiences were most immoral (see Gehm & Scherer, 1988).

There were also strong and consistent emotion effects concerning attributions of responsibility for the situations, and the evaluation of one's coping potentials. For responsibility, respondents were most likely to attribute responsibility for anger, disgust, and fear-producing situations to others, and to oneself second. Guilt, joy, and shame-producing experiences, however, were attributed mostly to the self. Sadness-producing experiences were attributed mostly to fate. Again, though these differences between emotions were very significant, Wallbott and Scherer (in press) reported some interesting cross-cultural differences, which we will discuss below.

For coping, respondents indicated that no action was necessary for disgust and joy experiences, and that they felt powerless for fear and sad experiences. It is interesting that the modal response for guilt, shame, and anger was that respondents felt they could have a positive influence on the situation through their actions.

Verbal and Nonverbal Reactions, and Physiological Symptoms Emotions were also differentiated by verbal and nonverbal reactions to them and physiological symptoms. . . .

Responses to fear resulted in the most predominant pattern of *physiological symptoms*, which clearly differentiates it from the other emotions. Participants reported a higher incidence of breathing symptoms, stomach symptoms, feelings of cold, heartbeat changes, perspiration, and tensing of the muscles. Joy was also characterized by a distinctive pattern of physiological symptoms, which included, on one hand, feelings of warmth and muscle relaxation, and on the other hand, an absence of such symptoms as a "lump in the throat," stomach problems, feelings of coldness, and tensed muscles.

Temperature symptoms, or symptoms having to do with feelings of being hot, warm, or cold, also distinguished the emotions. Joy was the only emotion experienced as warm. Fear and, to a lesser degree, sadness were experienced as cold emotions, while anger and especially shame were experienced as hot emotions. Differences in blood flow changes for each of these emotions may account for these sensation differences. This finding corroborates experimental data for differences in skin temperature between emotions (Ekman, Levenson, & Friesen, 1983).

Participants' *nonverbal* reactions, such as changes in facial expressions (e.g., laughing, crying), also differentiated the emotions. Joy and shame, for example, were characterized by laughing or smiling, while sadness, as one might expect, was characterized by crying. Other changes in facial expressions were found for all negative emotions, especially anger and disgust. *Voice changes* of all different types accompanied all emotions, and were especially predominant in sadness, anger, and fear. Anger and fear were also characterized by screaming. Different types of *movements* also differentiated the emotions: "moving toward" other people was typical of joy, "moving against" others was typical of anger, and withdrawing was typical of all other negative emotions.

The overall number of nonverbal reactions also differentiated the emotions. Participants reported the most nonverbal reactions for anger and joy, and the least for fear, disgust, shame, and guilt. These findings suggest that anger and joy are more "active" in terms of the nonverbal behaviors and reactions produced in these situations.

While *verbal reactions* did not differentiate among the emotions, they do add to the distinctions already made by nonverbal reactions and physiological symptoms. For example, lengthy utterances characterized joy and anger, and are congruent with the findings above concerning the high number of nonverbal reactions reported for these emotions. These findings suggest that not only are anger and joy the most active emotions, they are the most socially based emotions. Speech melody and tempo changes were also especially predominant for anger and joy.

A final set of analyses suggest how emotions may be differentiated by the degree to which subjective experience is internalized or externalized. In order to examine this possibility, a ratio of the number of motor expressive reactions reported to the number of physiological symptoms reported was computed. If this ratio is > 1, then the experience is predominantly external, because the number of reactions is greater than the number of symptoms. If the ratio is < 1, then the experience is predominantly internal, as the number of symptoms reported is greater than the number of reactions (Wallbott & Scherer, 1986). Using this index of internalization/externalization, we found that joy and anger are more externalized than the other emotions, while shame, guilt, and fear were internalized.

Findings Suggesting Cultural Differences in Emotional Experience

In the research reported above, significant cultural effects were often found, although they were generally smaller than the emotion effects. The culture effects indicate that cultures differ to some degree in the experience or evaluation of emotion. Three studies have formally examined culture effects to this date, one comparing a U.S., Japanese, and European sample using the ESI data (Scherer, Matsumoto, Wallbott & Kudoh, 1988), a second comparing the U.S. and Japan using the ISEAR data (Matsumoto, Kudoh, Scherer, & Wallbott, 1988), and a third comparing the "IS-EAR" country samples on an a posteriori basis (Wallbott & Scherer, in press). Below we report the findings, aggregated across studies, concerning cultural differences in the antecedents of emotional experience, the characteristics of emotion, the verbal and nonverbal reactions, and the physiological symptoms.

Antecedents of Emotional Experience   Cultural differences in the antecedents of emotion were studied only in our first comparison study. We had no hypotheses concerning cultural differences in the antecedents because our previous work with European countries did not yield any major cross-cultural differences and we expected that the antecedents that were frequent elicitors of the emotions in Europe would also be frequent elicitors of the emotions in the United States and Japan. While this was generally true, there were antecedent categories that produced significant cultural differences, particularly contrasting the Japanese sample with the American and European samples.

For example, cultural pleasures, birth of a new family member, body-centered basic pleasures, and achievement-related situations were important antecedents of joy in the United States and Europe. In Japan, however, they are less frequently elicitors of joy. For sadness, world news, temporary and permanent separations, and death were more frequent elicitors of sadness in the United States and European samples than in Japan. Relationships, however, was a more frequent elicitor of sadness in Japan than in the other two cultures.

Fear of strangers and risky situations elicited fear more frequently in the United States and Europe than in Japan. But relationships elicited fear more frequently in Japan than in the other two cultures.

The pattern of results for anger was interesting. On one hand, the Japanese were angered less frequently by relationships and situations of injustice than the Europeans or Americans. On the other hand, situations involving strangers elicited anger more frequently in the Japanese than in the Europeans and Americans.

Characteristics of Emotion Above we reported that anger and disgust experiences were reported as having occurred most recently, with fear experiences reported as occurring least frequently. The data from our first comparison study suggested that across joy, sadness, fear, and anger, the Japanese reported that their experiences occurred more recently than the Americans or the Europeans. When the cultures were compared on the intensity and duration of emotion in the first study, we found that the American respondents in general reported feeling their emotions more intensely and for longer periods of time than their European or Japanese counterparts. Finally, contrary to our expectations, no cultural differences were found concerning control or regulation of emotion.

Cognitive Evaluation of the Emotion-Eliciting Situations In order to examine possible cultural differences in the cognitive evaluation of the antecedents to emotion, the American and Japanese responses on each of the evaluation dimensions from the ISEAR study were compared. The two cultures did not differ on the expectation or pleasantness of the event, the degree to which the experiences facilitated goals, the unfairness of the event, on their judgments of the immorality of the event, or in their judgments of the events' effects on their relationships.

There were, however, provocative cultural differences in the effects of the events on self-esteem, attributions of responsibility, and evaluation of one's coping potential. The cultural effects on self-esteem indicated that American participants in general reported greater positive self-esteem and self-confidence for the emotion-eliciting events than did the Japanese participants. For attributions of responsibility, the only cultural difference was found for sadness: American respondents attributed their sadness-producing experiences to others or to fate, whereas the Japanese respondents attributed the cause of the event mostly to themselves. Analysis of the respondents' unwillingness to attribute responsibility also produced an interesting cultural difference: A significantly larger percentage of Japanese respondents compared to their American counterparts did not make any attribution of responsibility.

Finally, culture effects on respondents' evaluations of their coping potential indicated a consistent finding across most emotions: More Japanese respondents believed that no action was necessary than American respondents, even for strong negative emotions. This finding is consistent with the findings above concerning the attribution of responsibility of the event: If one is reluctant to make an attribution of responsibility, or attributes the responsibility of the event to others, then coping is indeed limited, and is reflected in the belief that no action would be necessary.

Verbal and Nonverbal Reactions, and Physiological Symptoms In our first set of studies, we made a gross differentiation according to the channel of the reaction (voice, face, whole body, and so on), without further specifying the nature of these changes. This was necessary because the open-ended format allowed for a varied range of responses that would have rendered specific categories meaningless. In the second study based on the ISEAR data, analyses were conducted on specific categories given to the respondents. These categories were based on the most frequently occurring open-ended responses given in the first set of studies. The findings indicate a consistent cultural difference between the Japanese and the Americans: Americans reported significantly more verbal and non-verbal reactions to each of the seven emotions than did their Japanese counterparts.

Grossly defined categories, such as pleasant arousal, feelings of warmth or cold, and perspiration, were also used to categorize the types of physiological sensations participants reported in the first set of studies. As we found with verbal and nonverbal reactions, Japanese reported fewer physiological symptoms and sensations on a number of different categories. More specifically, the Japanese reported less stomach troubles and muscle symptoms for all four emotions; less blood pressure changes for joy, fear, and anger; less pleasant arousal and pleasant rest for joy; less unpleasant arousal for sadness and fear; less feelings of cold for fear; and less feelings of warmth for anger. This pattern was repeated when we collapsed across specific precoded categories in the second study as well: American subjects reported significantly more symptoms and sensations than did the Japanese respondents. This may be related to the finding reported above that Japanese subjects in general judge emotional expressions as being of lower intensity than other cultures do. Because these differences were not predicted, only post hoc explanations based on stereotypical notions concerning the respective cultures could be offered at this point. A first attempt at the development of hypotheses based on these findings can be found in Matsumoto et al. (in press). . . .

A MODEL OF CULTURE

. . . Hofstede (1980, 1983) has provided an interesting model of cultural variation that may be applicable to studies of emotion. On the basis of a large-scale (40-country) value survey, Hofstede suggests that there are four dimensions along which cultures may vary: *power distance, uncertainty avoidance, individualism,* and *masculinity.*

Power distance reflects the way in which interpersonal relationships form and develop when differences in power are perceived. Uncertainty avoidance reflects the degree to which people in a culture feel threatened by ambiguous situations and have created beliefs and institutions that help to avoid them. Individualism is a major dimension of cultural variability postulated by other theorists as well (Kluckhohn & Strodtbeck, 1961; Marsella, DeVos, & Hsu, 1985; Parsons & Shils, 1951; Triandis, 1986). Individualistic cultures emphasize individual goals and independence, while collectivistic cultures stress collective goals and dependence on groups. Masculinity reflects the degree to which cultures delineate sex roles, with masculine cultures making clearer differentiations between genders.

Two attempts have been made at using these dimensions of cultural variability in accounting for cultural differences with respect to emotion. The first was conducted by Gudykunst and Ting-Toomey (1988). These researchers reanalyzed the data concerning antecedents and nonverbal reactions reported from eight cultures in the ESI study (Scherer, Wallbott, & Summerfield, 1986), coding each of the eight cultures in terms of Hofstede's dimensions. These were then correlated with the percentage of respondents from each culture giving the three most frequent antecedents for the four emotions surveyed. Several significant correlations were found, each of which provided a dimension with which to understand and interpret cultural differences in the percentage of antecedents reported by each culture for the emotions. For example, power distance was negatively correlated with injustice as an antecedent to anger. In high-power-distance cultures, inequality and injustice are expected and taken for granted, while they are not expected or acceptable in low-power-distance cultures. Thus a negative correlation would be predicted between power distance and injustice as an antecedent to anger.

Gudykunst and Ting-Toomey (1988) also computed correlations between the four dimensions and the percentage of respondents in each culture reporting a specific type of verbal reaction. Significant correlations were again found, each of which was interpretable according to the Hofstede (1980, 1983) dimensions. For example, nonvocal reactions and verbalization were positively correlated with individualism. Individualistic cultures place greater emphasis on the verbal dimension of communication, including directness of expression, whereas the verbal dimension is often not trusted in collectivistic cultures, and communication is indirect.

A recent study by Matsumoto (in press) represents a second attempt at using Hofstede's dimensions to account for cultural variability and emotion. This researcher examined each of the cultures sampled in previous cross-cultural studies of the perception of facial expression of emotion. Two correlational analyses were computed. One examined the relationship between the cultural dimensions and the percentage of respondents making correct judgments concerning the universal emotions. The second analysis examined the relationship between the cultural dimensions and cultural variation in intensity ratings of the universal expressions.

Results from the first set of analyses produced no more significant correlations than would be expected by chance. This finding indicated that the cultural differences in the percentage of respondents making correct judgments concerning the universal emotions was not related to the four cultural dimensions. This result suggests that the

basic perception and judgment of *which* emotion is portrayed in the universal expressions may be related to more innate processing perceptual abilities not influenced
by culture. The results from the second set of analyses, however, did indicate some
degree of relationship between the cultural dimensions and perceptions of intensity.
For example, more intense ratings of contempt were given by cultures that scored high
on power distance and low on individualism. More intense ratings of fear and sadness,
however, were associated with cultures that scored less on power distance and higher
on individualism. . . .

REFERENCES

Ax, A. F. (1953). The physiological differentiation between fear and anger in humans.
    Psychosomatic Medicine, 15, 433–442.
Boucher, J. D., & Brandt, M. E. (1981). Judgment of emotion: American and Malay antece-
    dents. *Journal of Cross-Cultural Psychology, 12* 272–283.
Brown, B. L. (1980). The detection of emotion in vocal qualities. In H. Giles, P. W.
    Robinson, & P. Smith (Eds.), *Language: Social psychological perspectives.* Oxford:
    Pergamon.
Darwin, C. (1965). *The expression of the emotions in man and animals.* Chicago: University of
    Chicago Press. (Reprinted from London: Murray, 1872).
Duffy, E. (1941). An explanation of "emotional" phenomena without the use of the concept
    "emotion." *Journal of General Psychology. 25*, 283–293.
Ekman, P. (1972). Universal and cultural differences in facial expression of emotion. In J. R.
    Cole (Ed.), *Nebraska Symposium on Motivation* (pp. 207–283). Lincoln: University of
    Nebraska Press.
Ekman, P. (1973). Darwin and cross-cultural studies of facial expression. In P. Ekman (Ed.),
    Darwin and facial expression (pp. 1–83). New York: Academic Press.
Ekman, P., & Friesen, W. V. (1969). Nonverbal leakage and clues to deception. *Psychiatry, 32*,
    88–106.
Ekman, P., & Friesen, W. V. (1971). Constants across cultures in the face and emotion.
    Journal of Personality and Social Psychology, 17, 124–129.
Ekman, P., & Friesen, W. V. (1986). A new pancultural expression of emotion. *Motivation and
    Emotion, 10*, 159–168.
Ekman, P., & Friesen, W. V. (1988). Who knows what about contempt? A reply to Izard and
    Maynes, *Motivation and Emotion, 12*, 17–22.
Ekman, P., Friesen, W. V., O'Sullivan, M. O., Chan, A., Diacoyanni-Tarlatzis, I., Heider,
    K., Krause, R., LeCompte, W. A., Pitcairn, T., Ricci-Bitti, P. E., Scherer, K., Tomita
    M., & Tzavaras, A. (1987). Universals and cultural differences in the judgments of facial
    expressions of emotion. *Journal of Personality and Social Psychology, 53*, 712–717.
Ekman, P., & Heider, K. (in press). The universality of a contempt expression: A replication.
    Motivation and Emotion.
Ekman, P., Levenson, R. W., & Friesen, W. V. (1983). Autonomic nervous system activity
    distinguishes between emotions. *Science, 221*, 1208–1210.
Ekman, P., Sorenson, E. R., & Friesen, W. V. (1969). Pancultural elements in facial displays
    of emotion. *Science, 164*, 86–88.
Ellgring, H., & Baenninger-Huber, E. (1986). The coding of reported emotional experiences:
    Antecedents and reactions. In K. R. Scherer, H. G. Wallbott, & A. B. Summerfield

(Eds.), *Experiencing emotion: A cross-cultural study* (pp. 39-49). Cambridge: Cambridge University Press.

Friesen, W. V. (1972). *Cultural differences in facial expressions in a social situation: An experimental test of the concept of display rules.* Unpublished doctoral dissertation, University of California, San Francisco.

Gehm, T., & Scherer, K. R. (1988). Relating situation evaluation to emotion differentiation: Nonmetric analyses of cross-cultural questionnaire data. In K. R. Scherer (Ed.)., *Facets of emotion,* Hillsdale, NJ: Lawrence Erlbaum.

Giovannini, D., & Ricci-Bitti, P. E. (1981). Culture and sex effect in recognizing emotions by facial and gestural cues. *Italian Journal of Psychology 8,* 95-102.

Gudykunst, W. B., & Ting-Toomey, S. (1988). Culture and affective communication. *American Behavioral Scientist, 31,* 384-400.

Hofstede, G. (1980). *Cultures consequences.* Beverly Hills, CA: Sage.

Hofstede, G. (1983). Dimensions of natural cultures in fifty countries and three regions. In J. Deregowski, S. Dziurawiec, & R. Annis (Eds.), *Expiscations in cross-cultural psychology.* Lisse: Swets & Zeitlinger.

Izard, C. E. (1971). *The face of emotion.* New York: Appleton-Century-Crofts.

Izard, C. E., & Maynes, O. M. (1988). On the form and universality of the contempt expression: A correction for Ekman and Friesen's claim for discovery. *Motivation and Emotion, 12,* 1-16.

Kluckhohn, F., & Strodtbeck, F. (1961). *Variations in value orientations.* New York: Row & Peterson.

Kudoh, T., & Matsumoto, D. (1985). A cross cultural examination of the semantic dimensions of body postures. *Journal of Personality and Social Psychology, 48,* 1440-1446.

Marsella, A. J., DeVos, G., & Hsu, F. L. K. (Eds.). (1985). *Culture and self: Asian and Western perspectives.* New York: Tavistock.

Matsumoto, D. (1986). *Cross-cultural communication of emotion.* Unpublished doctoral dissertation, University of California, Berkeley.

Matsumoto, D. (in press). Cultural influences on the perception of emotion. *Journal of Cross-Cultural Psychology.*

Matsumoto, D., & Ekman, P. (in press). American-Japanese cultural differences in intensity ratings of facial expressions of emotion. *Motivation and Emotion.*

Matsumoto, D., & Kudoh, T. (1987). Cultural similarities and differences in the semantic dimensions of body postures. *Journal of Nonverbal Behavior, 11,* 166-179.

Matsumoto, D., Kudoh, T., Scherer, K. R., & Wallbott, H. G. (1988). Antecedents of and reactions to emotions in the US and Japan. *Journal of Cross-Cultural Psychology, 19,* 267-286.

McCluskey, K. W., Albas, D. C., Niemi, R. R., & Cuevas, D. (1975). Cross-cultural differences in the perception of the emotional content of speech: A study of the development of sensitivity in Canadian and Mexican children. *Developmental Psychology, 11,* 551-555.

Mood, D. W., Johnson, J. E., & Shantz, C. U. (1978). Social comprehension and affect-matching in young children. *Merril-Palmer Quarterly, 24,* 63-66.

Osgood, C. E., May, W. H., & Miron, M. S. (1975). *Cross-cultural universals of affective meaning.* Urbana: University of Illinois Press.

Parsons, T., & Shills, E. A. (1951). *Toward a general theory of action.* Cambridge, MA: Harvard University Press.

Plutchik, R. (1980). *Emotion: A psychoevolutionary synthesis.* New York: Harper.

Ricci-Bitti, P. E., Boggi-Cavallo, P., & Brighetti, G. (1984). *Universals and facial expressions of emotion: The case of contempt.* Paper presented at the 8th International Congress of Psychology, Acapulco.

Riskind, J. H. (1984). They stoop to conquer: Guiding and self-regulatory functions of physical posture after success and failure. *Journal of Personality and Social Psychology, 47,* 479–493.

Russell, J. A. (1980). A circumplex model of affect. *Journal of Personality and Social Psychology, 39,* 1161–1178.

Saarni, C. (1979). Children's understanding of display rules for expressive behavior. *Developmental Psychology, 15,* 424–429.

Schachter, S. (1964). The interaction of cognitive and physiological determinants of emotional state. In L. Berkowitz (Ed.), *Advances in experimental social psychology* (Vol. 1, pp. 49–81). New York: Academic Press.

Scherer, K. R. (1981). Speech and emotional states. In J. Darby (Ed.), *Speech evaluation in psychiatry* (pp. 189–220). New York: Grune & Stratton.

Scherer K. R. (1984). On the nature and function of emotion: A component process approach. In K. R. Scherer & P. Ekman (Eds.), *Approaches to emotion* (pp. 293–318). Hillsdale, NJ: Lawrence Erlbaum.

Scherer, K. R. (1986). Vocal affect expression: A review and a model for future research. *Psychological Bulletin, 99,* 143–165.

Scherer, K. R., & Ekman, P. (Eds.). (1984). *Approaches to emotion.* Hillsdale, NJ: Lawrence Erlbaum.

Scherer, K. R., Matsumoto, D., Wallbott, H. G., & Kudoh, T. (1988). Emotional experience in cultural context: A comparison between Europe, Japan, and the USA. In K. R. Scherer (Ed.), *Facets of emotion.* Hillsdale, NJ: Lawrence Erlbaum.

Scherer, K. R., Summerfield, A. B., & Wallbott, H. G. (1983). Cross-national research on antecedents and components of emotion: A progess report. *Social Science Information, 3,* 355–385.

Scherer, K. R., Wallbott, H. G., & Summerfield, A. B. (Eds.). (1986). *Experiencing emotion: A cross-cultural study.* Cambridge: Cambridge University Press.

Schlosberg, H. A. (1954). Three dimensions of emotion. *Psychological Review, 61,* 81–88.

Triandis, H. C. (1986). Collectivism vs. individualism: A reconceptualization of a basic concept in cross-cultural psychology. In C. Bagley & G. Verma (Eds.), *Personality, cognition, and values: Cross-cultural perspectives of childhood and adolescence.* London: Macmillan.

van Bezooijen, R. (1984). *The characteristics and recognizability of vocal expressions of emotion.* Dortrecht: Foris.

Wallbott, H. G. (1988). Faces in context: The relative importance of facial expression and context information in determining emotion attributions. In K. R. Scherer (Ed.), *Facets of emotion.* Hillsdale, NJ: Lawrence Erlbaum.

Wallbott, H. G., & Scherer, K. R. (1985). Differentielle situations: und Reaktionscharakteristika in Emotionserinnerungen: Ein neuer Forschungsansatz. *Psychologische Rundschau, 36,* 83–101.

Wallbott, H. G., & Scherer, K. R. (1986a). How universal and specific is emotional experience? Evidence from 27 countries on five continents. *Social Science Information, 25,* 763–796.

Wallbott, H. G., & Scherer, K. R. (1986b). Cues and channels in emotion recognition. *Journal of Personality and Social Psychology, 51,* 690–699.

Wallbott, H. G., & Scherer, K. R. (in press). Emotion and economic development: Data and speculations concerning the relationship between emotional experience and socioeconomic factors. *European Journal of Social Psychology.*

Weisfeld, G. E., & Beresford, J. M. (1982). Erectness of posture as an indicator of dominance or success in humans. *Motivation and Emotion, 6,* 113–131.

Wundt, W. (1905). *Grundzuege der physiologischen Psychologie* (Vol. 3). Leipzig; Wilhelm Engelmann.

PART 4

INTERACTION WITH STRANGERS

CHAPTER 10

Interpersonal Relationships with Strangers

Interpersonal relationships are sources of social contact and intimacy, two integral elements of human survival in any culture. We form many different types of relationships with others. To illustrate, we develop some relationships we call acquaintances and some we call friendships. Friendships, however, should not be confused with friendly relations. As Kurth (1970) points out, friendly relations are an outgrowth of role relationships and are possibly a prelude to friendship, whereas friendships are intimate relationships involving two people as individuals. These two types of relationships, therefore, differ with regard to the level of intimacy present—friendships being more intimate than friendly relations.

Another way in which friendly relations and friendships differ is with respect to the temporal dimension. Friendly relations, according to Kurth (1970), involve a present orientation, which focuses on the encounter that is taking place. In a friendship participants engage in interaction regarding the past and future, as well as the present. Further, the two types of relationships differ with respect to the cultural norms guiding them. There are cultural norms specifying what constitutes friendly relations. In the United States, for example, if we want to appear friendly in our relations with others we are expected to indicate that we are paying attention when others are talking. "The development of friendship," in contrast, "is based upon private negotiations and is not imposed through cultural values or norms" (Bell, 1981, p. 10). Suttles (1970) takes a similar position; he claims friendships are the least "programmed" relationships we form. We do not mean to suggest that culture plays no role in the development of friendships; rather, culture plays a much less important role in friendships than it does in friendly relations.

In defining the term *friendship*, Wright (1978) focuses on two aspects of the relationship: (1) the voluntary nature of the interaction, and (2) the personalistic focus of the interaction. The voluntary nature of the interaction means friendships are entered into voluntarily and friends informally agree to get together often in the absence of external constraints or pressures. Friendships, according to Wright, also involve a focus on the person; friends react to each other as "whole persons," not as occupants of roles.

The readings in this chapter are designed to examine different aspects of developing intimate relationships with strangers. In the first reading, Gudykunst overviews the process of developing intimate relationships with strangers. He examines the factors that contribute to our satisfaction with our communication with strangers and summarizes the factors that contribute to developing intimate relationships.

Rose, in the second reading, examines the factors that affect the quality of interethnic relationships in the United States. He looks at the factors that contribute to developing intimate relationships and acceptance of people from different ethnic backgrounds.

In the final reading in this section, Pogrebin discusses relationship development between the disabled and nondisabled, the young and old, as well as between heterosexuals and homosexuals. She points to one thing that happens when we develop relationships with people who are different than us: that we have to explain ourselves to those who are like us because members of our ingroups do not expect us to form relationships with members of outgroups.

REFERENCES

Bell, R. (1981). *Worlds of friendship*. Beverly Hills, CA: Sage.

Kurth, S. (1970). Friendships and friendly relations. In G. McNall (Ed.), *Social relationships*. Chicago: Aldine.

Wright, P. (1978). Toward a theory of friendship based upon a conception of the self. *Human Communication Research, 4,* 196–207.

Developing Relationships with Strangers
William B. Gudykunst

Most of our close interpersonal relationships are with people who are relatively similar to us. Part of the reason for this is that we do not have a lot of contact with strangers. Another reason why we do not have many close relationships with strangers is that our initial interactions and superficial contacts with strangers often result in ineffective communication. Since our communication with strangers is not as effective and satisfying as we would like, we do not try to develop intimate relationships with strangers. If we understand the process of relationship development, however, we can make an informed conscious decision as to whether or not we want to have intimate

Source: Abridged from Chapter 7 in W. B. Gudykunst, *Bridging Differences: Effective Intergroup Communication* (pp. 135–141). Newbury Park, CA: Sage, 1991.

relationships with strangers. In making such a decision, it is important to keep in mind that the more we know about strangers, the more accurately we can predict their behavior (Honeycutt, Knapp, & Powers, 1983).

COMMUNICATION SATISFACTION

One aspect of developing relationships with strangers is the degree to which we are satisfied with strangers' communication with us and strangers are satisfied with our communication with them. Satisfaction is an affective (i.e., emotional) reaction to communication that meets or fails to meet our expectations (Hecht, 1978). Tsukasa Nishida, Elizabeth Chua, and I (Gudykunst, Nishida & Chua, 1986, 1987) examined factors that contribute to communication satisfaction in interpersonal relationships between Japanese and North Americans.

Our research indicates that the more communication in a relationship is personalized and synchronized, and the less difficulty people experience in communicating with their partner, the more satisfied they are with the communication in their relationship. We also found that the more partners self-disclose to each other, the more they are attracted to each other, the more similarities they perceive, and the more uncertainty they reduce about each other, the more satisfied they are. Finally, the more "competent" the partners judge each others' communication to be, the more satisfied they are.

Michael Hecht and Sydney Ribeau and their associates examined satisfaction with interethnic conversations in the United States. Hecht, Ribeau, and Alberts (1989), for example, isolated seven factors that contribute to Afro-Americans' satisfaction with their conversations with whites. The first factor necessary for satisfaction is "acceptance." To be satisfied, Afro-Americans need to feel that they are respected, confirmed, and accepted by the whites with whom they communicate. Satisfying conversations with whites also included "emotional expression" and the whites being "authentic" (i.e., whites in satisfying conversations were perceived as "genuine" and whites in dissatisfying conversations were perceived as "evasive"). Afro-Americans also perceived that there was "understanding" (i.e., shared meanings) and "goal attainment" in satisfying conversations. They perceived "negative stereotyping" and felt "powerless" (e.g., manipulated or controlled) in dissatisfying conversations.

Hecht, Ribeau, and Sedano (1990) conducted a similar study with Mexican-Americans. They also found seven factors associated with satisfying and dissatisfying conversations. Similar to Afro-Americans, Mexican-Americans see "acceptance" as an important aspect of satisfying conversations. Satisfying conversations with whites also included the "expression of feelings" and "behaving rationally." The presence of "self-expression" and "relational solidarity" also contributed to satisfaction in conversations. "Negative stereotyping" and failure to discover a shared "worldview" (i.e., absence of perceived similarities) emerged as important factors in dissatisfying conversations.

Three themes are common to these studies. It, therefore, appears clear that

TABLE 1 Assessing Your Communication Satisfaction with Strangers

The purpose of this questionnaire is to help you assess the satisfaction you have when you communicate with strangers.* Respond to each statement by indicating the degree to which it is true of your communication with strangers: "Always False" (answer 1), "Usually False" (answer 2), "Sometimes True and Sometimes False" (answer 3), "Usually True" (answer 4), or "Always True" (answer 5).

_____ 1. I am satisfied with my communication with strangers.
_____ 2. I am able to present myself as I want to when I communicate with strangers.
_____ 3. I enjoy communicating with strangers.
_____ 4. Conversations flow smoothly when I communicate with strangers.
_____ 5. I get to say what I want to say when I communicate with strangers.

To find your score, add the numbers you wrote next to each statement. Scores range from 5 to 25. The higher your score, the greater your satisfaction in communicating with strangers.

* Adapted from Hecht (1978).

whites need to communicate acceptance, express emotions, and avoid negative stereotyping in order for Afro-Americans and Mexican-Americans to be satisfied with their conversations with them. While it was not specifically examined, we can infer that these three factors must be present for Afro-Americans and Mexican-Americans to perceive their white conversational partners as "competent."

The questionnaire in Table 1 is designed to help you assess your satisfaction with your communication with strangers. Take a couple of minutes to complete the questionnaire now.

Scores on the questionnaire range from 5 to 25. The higher your score, the greater your satisfaction with communicating with strangers. Even though your perceptions of how your communications with strangers are different than the strangers' perceptions, you also can "reverse" the statements in Table 1 and assess your perceptions of your communication with strangers. Remember, however, that how you think you are coming across to strangers may not be the same as how they perceive your communication with them.

DEVELOPING INTIMATE RELATIONSHIPS

There are differences and similarities in how people communicate in interpersonal relationships across cultures. Tsukasa Nishida and I (Gudykunst & Nishida, 1986b), for example, found that people in Japan (a collectivistic culture which emphasizes group membership) perceive ingroup relationships (i.e., co-worker and university classmate) to be more intimate than people in the United States (an individualistic culture which emphasizes the individual). The differences in perceived intimacy of relationships affect the way people communicate.[1] To illustrate, there is a difference in how people in Japan communicate with members of their ingroups and with members of an outgroup, with communication being the most "personal" with ingroup members. In the United States, in contrast, there is not a large difference in how we communicate with members of our ingroups and outgroups, except when outgroup membership is determined by cultural background or ethnicity (Gudykunst & Hammer, 1988b; Gudykunst et al., in press).

In addition to the cultural differences in perceived intimacy, there are many similarities across cultures. People in Japan and the United States, for example, rate relationships with people they have never met as less intimate than relationships with acquaintances, relationships with acquaintances as less intimate than relationships with friends, and relationships with friends as less intimate than relationships with close friends (Gudykunst & Nishida, 1986b). The similarities in the perceived intimacy of relationships are manifested in our communication. Communication in both cultures becomes more "personal" as the perceived intimacy of the relationship increases (Gudykunst & Nishida, 1986a,b). To illustrate, we talk about more intimate things about ourselves with friends than acquaintances.

Given these similarities and differences across cultures, what happens when people from different cultures communicate? Research suggests that as relationships between people from different cultures become more intimate (i.e., move from initial interactions to close friend), communication becomes more personal; for example, there are increases in self-disclosure, interpersonal attraction, perceived similarities, and uncertainty reduction (Gudykunst, Nishida, & Chua, 1986, 1987). Cultural dissimilarities appear to have a major influence on our communication in the early stages of relationship development (i.e., initial interactions and acquaintance relationships), but not in the final stages (e.g., close friend; Gudykunst, Chua, & Gray, 1987).[2]

I do not want to imply here that cultural and ethnic differences are not "problems" in close relationships. Cultural and ethnic differences can be sources of misunderstandings in intimate relationships, particularly in marital relationships. How to raise children, for example, is a central issue in intercultural or interethnic marriages. Cultural and ethnic differences can be major problems if the partners are not mindful of their communication around core issues like this. While there may be problems in close relationships due to cultural or ethnic differences, cultural and ethnic differences have less of an effect on communication in close friendships than in acquaintance relationships.[3] The nature of the relationship development process itself appears to offer a reasonable explanation as to why cultural and ethnic dissimilarities do not influence communication in close friendships as much as earlier stages of relationships.[4]

In early stages of relationship development, we must rely on cultural and sociological data to predict another person's behavior because we do not have sufficient information to use psychological data in making predictions. As the relationship develops and we gather information about the other person, we begin to use psychological data. When we use psychological data, we are differentiating how the other person is similar to and different from other members of his or her groups. In other words, we no longer rely on our stereotypes to predict the other person's behavior.

What is it about our initial interactions and our communication with acquaintances who are from other groups that allows the relationship to develop into a "friendship"? Research suggests that we must communicate in a way that signals we accept the other person, we must express our feelings, and we must avoid negative

TABLE 2 Assessing Your Communication with Strangers

The purpose of this questionnaire is to help you assess how you communicate with strangers. Respond to each statement by indicating the degree to which it is true of your communication with strangers: "Always False" (answer 1), "Usually False" (answer 2), "Sometimes True and Sometimes False" (answer 3), "Usually True" (answer 4), or "Always True" (answer 5).

_____ 1. I accept strangers as they are.
_____ 2. I express my feelings when I communicate with strangers.
_____ 3. I avoid negative stereotyping when I communicate with strangers.
_____ 4. I find similarities between myself and strangers when we communicate.
_____ 5. I accommodate my behavior to strangers when we communicate.

To find your score, add the numbers you wrote next to each statement. Scores range from 5 to 25. The higher your score, the greater your potential for developing intimate relationships with strangers.

---

stereotyping. All of these factors combined suggested that our communication with the other person helps him or her have positive personal and social identities. Stated differently, we support the other person's self-concept.[5]

Research several colleagues and I conducted (Sudweeks, Gudykunst, Ting-Toomey, & Nishida, 1990; Gudykunst, Gao, Sudweeks, Ting-Toomey, & Nishida, 1991) further suggests that we must perceive some degree of similarity between ourselves and the other person if an intimate relationship is to develop.[6] The display of empathy and mutual accommodation regarding differences in communication styles (i.e., adapting each other's style to the other person) also appear to be critical.[7] It is also important that at least one person have some competency in the other's language or dialect and that both parties demonstrate some interest in the other's culture or ethnic group.

Other factors that appear to be important are similar to those in developing relationships with people from our own groups. We must, for example, make time available to interact with the other person and consciously or unconsciously attempt to increase the intimacy of our communication (i.e., talk about things that are important to us).[8]

When we communicate on automatic pilot, we filter out strangers as potential friends simply because they are different and our communication with them is not as effective as our communication with people from our own group. Whether or not we want to act differently depends on our motivation. Do we want to approach people who are different, or continue to avoid them? I believe that relationships with strangers provide a chance for us to grow as individuals. The choice about developing these relationships, however, is yours.

I encourage you to make a conscious choice about whether or not you want to communicate effectively and develop relationships with strangers rather than relying on your unconscious, mindless decisions. If you choose to approach strangers and are mindful of your communication, you will eventually discover similarities between yourselves and the strangers with whom you communicate. The similarities you discover provide the foundation for developing intimate relationships.

Table 2 contains a questionnaire designed to help you assess your communication with strangers. Take a few minutes to complete it now.

Scores on the questionnaire range from 5 to 25. The higher your score, the greater your potential to develop intimate relationships with strangers.

NOTES

1 This research was an extension of Knapp, Ellis, and Williams' (1980) research in the United States.
2 There are differences in the relationship labels used in the various studies. I have used the labels isolated above for illustrative purposes.
3 There obviously will be exceptions here. A man may want an "Oriental" wife, for example, because he thinks she will be passive and serve him.
4 Much of the argument I make in this section is drawn from Gudykunst (1989).
5 Self-concept support has been found to be critical in relationship development. See Cushman and Cahn (1985) for a summary of this research. These factors also are related to Bell and Daly's (1984) "concern and caring" affinity-seeking strategy.
6 See Gudykunst (1989) for a summary of this research. Similarity is part of Bell and Daly's (1984) "commonalities" affinity-seeking strategy.
7 This is related to Bell and Daly's (1984) "politeness" affinity-seeking strategy.
8 These issues are related to Bell and Daly's "other involvement" affinity-seeking strategy.

REFERENCES

Bell, R., & Daly, J. (1984). The affinity-seeking function of communication. *Communication Monographs, 51,* 91–115.

Cushman, D. P., & Cahn, D. (1985). *Interpersonal communication.* Albany: State University of New York Press.

Gudykunst, W. B. (1989). Culture and communication in interpersonal relationships. In J. Anderson (Ed.), *Communication yearbook 12.* Newbury Park, CA: Sage.

Gudykunst, W. B., Chua, E., & Gray, A. (1987). Cultural dissimilarities and uncertainty reduction processes. In M. McLaughlin (Ed.), *Communication yearbook 10.* Beverly Hills, CA: Sage.

Gudykunst, W. B., Gao, G., Schmidt, K., Nishida, T., Bond, M., Leung, K., Wang, G., & Barraclough, R. (in press). The influence of individualism-collectivism on communication in ingroup and outgroup relationships. *Journal of Cross-Cultural Psychology.*

Gudykunst, W. B., Gao, G., Sudweeks, S., Ting-Toomey, S., & Nishida, T. (1991). Themes in opposite-sex Japanese–North American relationships. In S. Ting-Toomey & F. Korzenny (Eds.), *Cross-cultural interpersonal communication.* Newbury Park, CA: Sage.

Gudykunst, W. B., & Hammer, M. R. (1988b). The influence of social identity and intimacy of interethnic relationships on uncertainty reduction processes. *Human Communication Research, 14,* 569–601.

Gudykunst, W. B., & Nishida, T. (1986a). Attributional confidence in low- and high-context cultures. *Human Communication Research, 12,* 525–549.

Gudykunst, W. B., & Nishida, T. (1986b). The influence of cultural variability on perceptions of communication behavior associated with relationship terms. *Human Communication Research, 13,* 147–166.

Gudykunst, W. B., Nishida, T., & Chua, E. (1986). Uncertainty reduction processes in Japanese–North American relationships. *Communication Research Reports, 3,* 39–46.

Gudykunst, W. B., Nishida, T., & Chua, E. (1987). Perceptions of social penetration in Japanese–North American relationships. *International Journal of Intercultural Relations, 11,* 171–190.

Hecht, M. (1978). The conceptualization and measurement of communication satisfaction. *Human Communication Research, 4,* 253–264.

Hecht, M., Ribeau, S., & Alberts, J. (1989). An Afro-American perspective on interethnic communication. *Communication Monographs, 56,* 385–410.

Hecht, M., Ribeau, S., & Sedano, M. (1990). A Mexican-American perspective on interethnic communication. *International Journal of Intercultural Relations, 14,* 31–55.

Honeycutt, J. M., Knapp, M. L., & Powers, W. G. (1983). On knowing others and predicting what they say. *Western Journal of Speech Communication, 47,* 157–174.

Knapp, M., Ellis, D., & Williams, B. (1980). Perceptions of communication behavior associated with relationship terms. *Communication Monographs, 47,* 262–278.

Sudweeks, S., Gudykunst, W. B., Nishida, T., & Ting-Toomey, S. (1990). Relational themes in Japanese–North American relationships. *International Journal of Intercultural Relations, 14,* 207–233.

The Quality of Interracial Interactions

Terrence L. Rose

In his review of the contact literature, Ashmore (1970) noted the tendency to misperceive the behavior of others and, as a result, fail to revise, adequately, prejudicial attitudes following intergroup contact. He suggests that it is not enough to have contact with members of a group whose behavior is inconsistent with existing stereotypes; the contact must be frequent and intimate enough to preclude perceptual distortion.

   Ashmore (1970) suggests that such distortions may be overcome most effectively when the interactants are cooperatively interdependent and when they are placed into an intimate relationship with each other. When two people share common goals they should be less likely to misperceive the other's behavior, because such distortions could undermine their chances of reaching their shared goal. They must accurately assess the other's behavior, abilities, and personality to ensure effective integration of their individual efforts. They must also remain open to information from each other and, consequently, they are more likely to be susceptible to social influence attempts of the other. In general, cooperative interdependence is expected to promote each

Source: Abridged from "Cognitive and Dyadic Processes in Intergroup Contact" in D. L. Hamilton (Ed.), *Cognitive Processes in Stereotyping and Intergroup Behavior,* (pp. 280–302). Hillsdale, NJ: Lawrence Erlbaum, 1981.

person's receptiveness to information from the other and facilitate the development of homogeneity of behavior and attitudes. The end result is a minimization of perceptual distortion and actual differences between the interactants.

These elements are present whenever two people enter into a close interpersonal relationship in which each person is dependent on the other for his or her outcomes (Thibaut & Kelley, 1959). However, other effects also may occur when two people come to be close friends. Attraction to a member of a minority group not only may make one more open to information from the other, but this attraction may generalize to other members of the group. Moreover, a developing friendship may lead to interaction in settings other than those necessary for the accomplishment of group goals. Broadening the range of contact may then provide a greater range of information about the other and lessen the possibility of situation-specific attitude change (Ashmore, 1970).

These considerations suggest that cooperative interdependence and intimate relationships that promote such interdependence could promote favorable relationships between the members of different social groups and lessen the biases discussed in the previous section. However, there are other reasons to expect the formation of intimate intergroup relationships to foster a reduction in prejudicial beliefs and behavior.

One of these reasons is integrally related to a distinction typically made in the contact literature between intimate and superficial contact (Amir, 1969). Earlier conceptualizations often viewed the contact setting as being either intimate or superficial and stressed the importance of intimate contact in promoting positive intergroup relations. However, intimacy might better be conceptualized as the attainment of a particular state in an ongoing relationship (Levinger & Snoek, 1972; Thibaut & Kelley, 1959) rather than a property of the setting itself. Certain environments may promote the development of intimate relationships better than others but they are not inherently intimate or superficial. For example, within the most superficial settings two friends may break out of the roles they each play in these settings and behave as they might in other contexts. The question addressed in the present chapter is not so much how different settings promote or inhibit the development of intimate relationships, but how the formation of intimate relationships between the members of different social groups may reduce intergroup prejudice.

Given this distinction between settings and relationships there is another basis for espousing the virtues of intimacy. When an intimate relationship is fostered between two people, each becomes familiar with various aspects of the other's personality. In more superficial relationships the range of knowledge acquired about the other is restricted largely because that interaction is confined to a limited number of social contexts. That this difference may have significant implications from the study of intergroup contact is suggested by results reported by Gurwitz and Dodge (1977). They found that stereotyped attributions to a target person were less frequent when evidence disconfirming the stereotype for her [or his] social group was concentrated in the description of a single group member rather than dispersed across different members of the group. However, the opposite relationship was found when the evidence confirmed stereotypic beliefs about the target person's social group: Information dispersed across different members of the group enhanced stereotypic attributions to the target person to a greater extent than when the same information was conveyed in the description of a single group member.

Because an intimate intergroup relationship offers the possibility of multiple disconfirmations of the stereotype from the behavior of only one member of the group, Gurwitz & Dodge's findings suggest that such relationships may be more effective in changing that stereotype. Superficial relationships, in contrast, would have greater potential to confirm the stereotype, because with a larger number of superficial relationships, it is likely that there could be multiple confirmations of the stereotype across different members of the group.

There is yet another reason for favoring the development of intimate rather than more superficial relationships between the members of different groups. With superficial contact the members of each group are likely to have little information about each other except for that conveyed by surface characteristics, such as the other's skin color, physical attractiveness, dress, or language. Given only these types of information, however, it is reasonable to expect that a perceiver will tend to categorize others using these distinctive characteristics and differentiate people along traditional group lines, such as race, ethnicity, social class, and sex. In essence, then, surface contact would serve to prime or activate (see Higgins et al. 1977) categories of group membership and evoke stereotypic schemata for processing the behavior of others. In other words, by limiting intergroup interaction to more superficial forms and inhibiting the development of intimate relationships, it is more likely that people will continue to think about others in terms of their group membership. With more intimate relationships a more differentiated view develops of others in which a variety of categories can be used to process their behavior. The reason this is important is that the biases in information processing discussed earlier result from the application of schemata in long-term memory. To the extent stereotypes and categories of group membership are accessible during intergroup interaction, these stereotypes may be bolstered and the other's behavior misperceived in line with these stereotypes. The reasoning offered here suggests that this process would [be] more likely with less intimate contact between the members of different social groups.

These considerations suggest a number of possible bases for the efficacy of intimate relationships between members of different social groups to reduce existing intergroup prejudice. The question that arises at this point is to what extent we can expect such relationships to develop when the members of different social groups are placed in desegregated contexts.

THE DEVELOPMENT AND MAINTENANCE OF INTERPERSONAL RELATIONSHIPS

One particularly useful approach to the study of interpersonal relationships is Thibaut and Kelley's (1959) theory of social exchange. Thibaut and Kelley propose that dyadic interaction and the development of interpersonal relationships are a function of the rewards and costs expected from the relationship. If relatively unfavorable outcomes are expected the individual will avoid intimate encounters with others and discourage the development of potential relationships with them. One the other hand, if relatively favorable outcomes are expected, then greater intimacy will be desired and attempts will be made to initiate or expand the relationship beyond its current state. Changes in an ongoing relationship and the development of new relationships depend on the individuals' current level of satisfaction and the availability of more favorable alternatives.

In order for each member of a dyad to know what outcomes are available from a relationship they must possess some information about the other that will enable them to forecast and predict what these outcomes might be. In the case where no real relationship yet exists, one tends to rely heavily on social stereotypes invoked by the physical characteristics of the person (Levinger & Snock, 1972). When a relationship already exists, information acquired in past interactions can be used to guide future interactions.

According to Thibaut and Kelley (1959) initial interactions tend to be highly uniform and stereotyped in that most people behave similarly in such settings. Such interactions are characterized by formality, constraint, and politeness and consequently are conventional and highly predictable. As a result, they offer a limited amount of information that can be used to forecast the outcomes potentially available from a relationship. Although normative, socially desirable behavior is relatively uninformative about the other person (Jones & Davis, 1965), Thibaut and Kelley suggest that these forms of interactions are functional for the actor [or actress]. They allow him [or her] to enter into a potentially unstable relationship and gain additional information without incurring heavy costs. With increasing confidence in the viability of a new relationship, the members of the dyad shift from the self-presentation strategies characterizing initial interactions to more revealing patterns of behavior. This shift is necessary because new information must be acquired that will allow the interactants to predict the other's behavior and respond in such a way as to maximize the available outcomes. It is also necessary in order to reduce any remaining uncertainty about the stability of present outcomes and those that are likely to become available in the future. What this implies is that with increasing interaction and increased commitment to a relationship there should be a corresponding increase in the amount of self-disclosure between the interactants (Chaikin & Derlaga, 1976). Eventually, the members of the dyad may each obtain an extensive knowledge base for predicting the other's behavior and forecasting the outcomes associated with various types of interaction.

Within interracial settings perhaps one of the most salient features of the other person would be his or her race. Given that this is so, it is likely that inferences made about the other would be influenced by the stereotype of his or her racial group. If the stereotype is favorable, then positive outcomes would probably be expected from a relationship with members of the group. However, if the stereotype is unfavorable, as it is for most racial stereotypes, then negative outcomes would be forecast. One prediction, then, from Thibaut and Kelley's (1959) framework is that interracial interaction typically might be avoided. Evidence for this proposal comes from studies of desegregated neighborhoods that show that interracial contact tends to be less frequent than contact between the members of the same racial group (Bradburn et al., 1971; Hamilton & Bishop, 1976).

One would also expect on this basis that, in cases where contact is unavoidable, the members of interracial dyads would be less likely to develop an intimate relationship and might actively avoid an expansion of the relationship beyond its current state. One manifestation of this avoidance would be the display of few signs of intimacy or acceptance in interracial interactions. This strategy of interaction would help the reluctant individual to discourage the development of the relationship. One way of measuring the degree of acceptance or intimacy afforded another person is through nonverbal indices of immediacy (Mehrabian, 1969). Word, Zanna, and Cooper (1974) utilized a number of these nonverbal measures in an experiment where white subjects played the role of interviewers and interviewed either black or white job applicants. These investigators found that less nonverbal immediacy was displayed and less time was spent in the interviews with the black job applicants. Thus, less intimacy was displayed toward the black than white job applicants and the interracial setting was avoided relative to the intraracial one.

Another way of measuring the amount of intimacy during interaction is by measuring the amount of self-disclosure between the interactants (Chaikin & Derlega, 1976). Chaikin, Derlega, Harris, Gregorio, and Boone (1973; cited in Chaikin & Derlega, 1976) obtained evidence of both avoidance and restricted communication in interracial dyads. They had white subjects converse with a black or white confederate, who either disclosed highly personal information about himself [or herself] or who was relatively impersonal. Consistent with other research (Derlega, Harris, & Chaikin, 1973), the subjects reciprocated a white confederate's personal disclosures and revealed more personal information about themselves when he [or she] was more intimate with them. However, when the confederate was black, the subjects failed to match his [or her] disclosure level and were actually somewhat less intimate when he [or she] was more intimate with them. Thus, there is less self-disclosure within interracial settings than typically is found between members of the same racial group, at least in the initial stages of a relationship. As a consequence of this restricted flow of communication, there is little information available in the interactants that they might use to predict effectively the other's future behavior. Uncertainty would therefore remain high and the relationship would be unlikely to develop beyond its current state.

In failing to reciprocate the other's personal disclosures of information, or in failing to initiate a process of mutual self-disclosure, a white actor may be viewed by the black as cold and unfriendly (Chaikin & Derlega, 1974). This appraisal would receive additional confirmation if the white also displayed signs of nonverbal rejection, as was seen in the study by Word et al. (1974). The ultimate outcome of this process would be the confirmation of the black's negative beliefs about whites. Moreover, having formed a negative impression of the actor [or actress] and feeling rejected by him or her, it is likely that signs of rejection would be reciprocated by the black. This reaction could then serve as confirmation of the white actor's [or actress's] initial beliefs, leading to a self-fulfilling prophecy (Merton, 1948) and further undermining the future development of the relationship.

Support for this line of reasoning was obtained in a second experiment by Word et al. (1974). White confederates, acting as interviewers, were trained to behave in either a more or less immediate fashion toward white subjects, who role-played job applicants. In a high immediacy condition the confederates modeled their nonverbal behavior after those subjects who had interviewed white job applicants in the previous study and thus acted in a relatively accepting manner. In the low immediacy condition the confederates modeled the behavior displayed toward black job applicants in the previous study and were relatively unaccepting on a nonverbal level. Word et al. found that the nonverbal behavior of the less immediate interviewer resulted in a reciprocal pattern of nonverbal rejection by the subjects. These subjects also liked the interview less, performed less effectively in the setting, and showed greater signs of discomfort or uneasiness compared to subjects in the high immediacy group.

This study provides but one demonstration of how self-fulfilling prophecies may originate during interpersonal interaction. Studies have demonstrated the operation of self-fulfilling prophecies in a variety of contexts (Jones, 1977) and have shown that these patterns of interaction may originate from the stereotypes of the interactants. . . . These studies clearly show that an actor [or actress] may, without realizing his or her own part in this process, elicit confirmation of his or her existing beliefs by constraining the partner's behavior and precluding alternative responses.

The emergence of a self-fulfilling prophecy during interaction represents a case in which an individual receives a biased sample of information about another person and is misled into thinking his or her erroneous expectancies about the other are correct. Thibaut and Kelley (1959) have presented an informational analysis of dyadic interaction in which they discuss how information becomes biased by strategies of self-presentation. They suggest that when favorable outcomes are expected from a relationship the members of a dyad will each try to portray themselves in a favorable light so as to encourage the other's interest; this will not be the case when negative outcomes are forecast. In other words, when people expect relatively favorable outcomes, they will try to act in such a way as to convince a partner that the relationship will be a rewarding one for him or her in return. This strategy of self-presentation obviously results in a biased sample of information being provided. However, Thibaut and Kelley suggest that this enables the development of the relationship beyond its current state by stimulating a greater exchange of information between the members of the dyad.

One way of encouraging another's interest is to demonstrate that one possesses those characteristics that are valued by the other. An illustration of this process has been supplied by Zanna and Pack (1975). They found that when women perceived a male partner as being highly desirable, they portrayed themselves as being consistent with his view of the "ideal woman." However, when he was not seen as being a desirable partner, the women acted in ways consistent with their true beliefs. Thus it appears as though the women's predictions regarding the outcomes available from any potential relationship with the male target person resulted in a pattern of self-presentation that was biased. This probably would have served to attract the more desirable target person to the relationship, but it also resulted in a distorted representation of these women's typical attitudes and behavior.

A number of other strategies for encouraging the interest of a potential partner are available to a person. For example, one might adopt similar attitudes, conform to a partner's requests, or otherwise display a liking for the partner and what he or she stands for. In each case one may be viewed as acting in such a way as to convince a prospective partner that, by establishing or developing a mutual relationship, he or she will be able to obtain favorable outcomes.

When the individual holds negative racial stereotypes about the members of a social group and these are salient during intergroup interaction, one would expect few instances of such behavior. Unfavorable or unacceptable outcomes would be inferred and, rather than encouraging friendships with the group's members, any potential relationships would be discouraged. Interaction might occur in such cases, but unless the person received new information more favorable in nature, or individuating information that might discourage reliance on group stereotypes. . ., the interaction would probably remain formal, constrained, and uninformative for the interactants, or possibly degenerate into unpleasant interaction through the processes already discussed. Only when favorable outcomes are expected from the relationship will the person actively seek the other's interest and an expansion of the relationship. Thus Thibaut and Kelley's framework provides a basis for predicting discriminatory behavior.

VERBAL ACCEPTANCE AND REVERSE DISCRIMINATION IN INTERRACIAL SETTINGS

The studies of interracial interaction reviewed in the previous section were presented as though their findings reflected manifestations of racial prejudice and deliberate attempts by the subjects to avoid more intimate relations with members of a different racial group. Although such reactions might be expected from highly prejudiced persons, the subjects in this research have been college students who represent perhaps one of the most liberal populations in the United States. Rather than freely espousing extremely negative stereotypes of blacks, these individuals are reluctant to express such beliefs (Sigall & Page, 1971) and typically score low on measures of racial prejudice.

A series of studies by Dutton and his colleagues (Dutton, 1976) has shown that people who considers themselves unprejudiced tend to guard this self-image and actually may "bend over backwards" to demonstrate to themselves that they adhere to egalitarian values. In two studies it was shown that when these individuals were threatened by the suggestion that they might be prejudiced, they responded by showing preferential treatment to the member of a discriminated minority group (Dutton & Lake, 1973; Dutton & Lennox, 1974). This pattern of behavior appears to be especially likely when the person is in a position to be publicly evaluated (Dutton & Yee, 1974). According to these authors, the reverse discrimination exhibited by these subjects represents an attempt to discredit this threatening inference about themselves. That is, by responding very favorably toward a member of the minority group in question, the subjects may provide themselves with new data that disconfirms the implication that they hold discriminatory attitudes.

Other research suggests that, rather than discouraging the interest of black partners, the liberal white may try very hard to gain their acceptance. For example, Poskocil (1975) has shown that white subjects express more liberal racial attitudes in interracial than all-white "discussion groups." This attempt to gain the other's acceptance and approval may represent still another method [of] gaining assurance that one is lacking in racial prejudice.

A similar phenomon is apparent in laboratory studies of aggression (Donnerstein & Donnerstein, 1972; Donnerstein, Donnerstein, Simons, & Ditrichs, 1972). For example Donnerstein et al. found that direct aggression by white subjects was stronger when displayed toward black than white victims but only when the subjects' identities remained anonymous. If the black victim knew the aggressor's identity or could later retaliate, the subjects inhibited direct expressions of aggression and actually aggressed against him or her less than they did toward a white victim. These findings provide additional evidence that under certain conditions people will inhibit displays of preference for their own group's members and actually respond more favorably toward members of a different racial group.

These findings would seem to indicate that, at least under some conditions, the white person may actually go out of the way to gain a black partner's liking and approval. But will such attempts be successful? Poskocil (1975, 1977) suggests that such attempts will often fail to elicit a black person's approval: Rather than being a sign of friendship and acceptance these overtures are likely to be perceived as signs of white hypocrisy and guilt. As we have seen, this perception appears to have some basis. That is, although the white person may show overt agreement, compliance, and preferential treatment toward the black partner, he or she may also fail to reciprocate the latter's attempts at more intimate exchanges (Chaikin et al., 1973), display nonverbal signs of rejection (Word et al., 1974), and seek escape from the interaction (Word et al., 1974). Furthermore, once the person has reasserted his or her egalitarian values, less compliance actually may be seen in response to another request from a member of the same minority group (Dutton & Lennox, 1974). The person may act prejudiced when not under evaluative pressures (Donnerstein & Donnerstein, 1972; Donnerstein, et al., 1972; Dutton & Yee, 1974) and, when under such pressures, may simply substitute less direct signs of prejudice for more direct forms (Donnerstein & Donnerstein, 1972; Donnerstein, et al., 1972).

This conflictual quality present in the white's behavior is also evident in findings reported by Weitz (1972). She examined nonverbal (voice quality, behavioral measures) and verbal measures of acceptance toward black and white "interaction partners," and found that all of these measures were positively correlated when the subject's partner was white; however, when the partner was black, there was an inverse relationship between the nonverbal and verbal measures. In other words, those subjects displaying the most direct form of acceptance also showed the least acceptance on behavioral and nonverbal measures. In discussing this finding, Weitz (1972) emphasized the negative outcomes of verbal acceptance accompanied by nonverbal restraint:

> For the black in real interracial interaction, the above pattern leads to a situation of conflicting cues: positive verbal approach coupled with negative voice tone and behavior. For the white, this conflicted situation doubtlessly leads to anxiety and discomfort, and perhaps even to a tendency to avoid interracial contact [p. 17].

Weitz interpreted this finding using the concept of *ambivalence* (Katz, 1970). Ambivalence refers to a state of conflict that results when a person holds both positive and negative attitudes toward the same person, group, or object. Weitz proposes that her subjects were ambivalent toward their black partners and that they tended to repress their hostile feelings toward them. Weitz maintains that this repressed affect then was expressed through less easily monitored or consciously controlled channels. Thus positive affect was expressed verbally while repressed hostility toward the partner "leaked out" through less controllable nonverbal and behavioral channels.

Accompanying the ambivalence notion is the concept of *amplification* (Katz, 1970). Katz proposes that when the person has ambivalent attitudes toward another person his or her responses toward this person will be exaggerated in magnitude. Thus the person who is ambivalent toward blacks should display more favorable reactions toward a black partner than someone who holds uniformly positive attitudes toward that person's racial group. Similarly, when unfavorable reactions are performed, these should be more extreme than those performed by persons holding uniformly unfavorable attitudes toward the other's racial group.

This framework provides one basis for interpreting the findings reviewed thus far. It can account for Weitz's findings and those cases of reverse discrimination discussed earlier. Poskocil (1977) has suggested that some black people in interracial settings adopt a similar interpretation of white people's behavior. They construe the white person's exaggerated verbal acceptance as signs of guilt, his or her nonverbal behavior as evidence of concealed racism, and generally view expressions of liking and acceptance as insincere. . . .

These findings suggest that, despite the potential of intimate relationships to provide disconfirmation of negative stereotypes, interracial interactions may often be characterized by negative or conflicting communications. Rather than providing the type of information that could invalidate stereotypes, they may provide evidence that further bolsters prejudicial beliefs, discourages future interaction, and further restricts communication across group boundaries. Studying the nature of both verbal and nonverbal communications in interracial settings, and how information is processed by the participants, provides a valuable means of understanding the dynamics of interracial interactions.

REFERENCES

Amir, Y. Contact hypothesis in ethnic relations. *Psychological Bulletin*, 1969, *71*, 319–342.

Ashmore, R. D. Solving the problem of prejudice. In B. E. Collins, *Social Psychology*. Reading, Mass.: Addison-Wesley, 1970.

Bradburn, N. M., Sudman, S., Gockel, G. L., & Noel, J. R. *Side by Side.* Chicago: Quadrangle Books. 1971.

Chaikin, A. L., & Derlega, V. J. Self-disclosure. In J. W. Thibaut, J. T. Spence, & R. C. Carson (Eds.), *Contemporary Topics in Social Psychology.* Morristown, N.J.: General Learning Press, 1976.

Chaikin, A. L., Derlega, V. J., Harris, M. S., Gregorio, D., & Boone, P. *Self-disclosure in biracial dyads.* Unpublished manuscript, Old Dominion University, 1973.

Derlega, V. J., Harris, M. S., & Chaikin, A. L. Self-disclosure reciprocity, liking, and the deviant. *Journal of Experimental Social Psychology,* 1973, *9,* 277–284.

Donnerstein, E., & Donnerstein, M. White rewarding behavior as a function of the potential for black retaliation. *Journal of Personality and Social Psychology,* 1972, *24,* 327–334.

Donnerstein, E., Donnerstein, M., Simon, S., & Ditrichs, R. Variables in interracial agression: Anonymity, expected retaliation, and a riot. *Journal of Personality and Social Psychology,* 1972, *22,* 236–245.

Dutton, D. G. Tokenism, reverse discrimination, and egalitarianism in interracial behavior. *Journal of Social Issues,* 1976, *32,* 93–107.

Dutton, D. G., & Lake, R. A. threat of own prejudice and reverse discrimination in interracial situations. *Journal of Personality and Social Psychology,* 1973, *28,* 94–100.

Dutton, D. G., & Lennox, V. L. Effect of prior "token" compliance on subsequent interracial behavior. *Journal of Personality and Social Psychology,* 1974, *29,* 65–71.

Dutton, D. G., & Yee, P. The effect of subject liberalism, anonymity, and race of experimenter on subject's rating of oriental and white photos. *Canadian Journal of Behavioral Science,* 1974, *6,* 332–341.

Gurwitz, S. B., & Dodge, K. A. Effects of confirmations and disconfirmations on stereotype-based attributions. *Journal of Personality and Social Psychology,* 1977 *35,* 495–500.

Hamilton, D. L., & Bishop, G. D. Attitudinal and behavioral effects of initial integration of white suburban neighborhoods. *Journal of Social Issues,* 1976, *32,* 47–67.

Higgins, E. T., Rholes, W. S., & Jones, C. R. Category accessibility and impression formation. *Journal of Experimental Social Psychology,* 1977, *13,* 141–154.

Jones, R. A. *Self-Fulfilling Prophecies.* Hillsdale, N.J.: Lawrence Erlbaum Associates, 1977.

Katz, I. Experimental studies of Negro-white relationships. In L. Berkowitz (Ed.), *Advances in Experimental Social Psychology* (Vol. 5). New York: Academic Press, 1970.

Levinger, G., & Snoek, J. D. *Attraction in Relationship: A New Look at Interpersonal Attraction,* Morristown, N.J.: General Learning Press, 1972.

Mehrabian, A. Some referents and measures of nonverbal behavior. *Behavior Research Methods and Instrumentation,* 1969, *1,* 203–207.

Poskocil, A. *White racial attitudes in a liberal milieu as a function of group racial composition.* Paper presented at the annual meeting of the American Psychological Association, Chicago, 1975.

Poskocil, A. Encounters between black and white liberals: The collision of stereotypes. *Social Forces,* 1977, *55,* 715–727.

Thibaut, J. W., & Kelley, H. H. *The Social Psychology of Groups.* New York: Wiley, 1959.

Weitz, S. Attitude, voice and behavior: A repressed affect model of interracial interaction. *Journal of Personality and Social Psychology,* 1972, *24,* 14–21.

Word, C. O., Zanna, M. P., & Cooper, J. The nonverbal mediation of self-fulfilling prophecies in interracial interaction. *Journal of Experimental Social Psychology,* 1974, *10,* 109–120.

Zanna, M. P., & Pack, S. J. On the self-fulfilling nature of apparent sex differences in behavior. *Journal of Experimental Social Psychology,* 1975, *11,* 583–591.

The Same and Different:
Crossing Boundaries of Color, Culture, Sexual Preference, Disability, and Age
Letty Cottin Pogrebin

On August 21, 1985, as they had several times before, twenty-one men from a work unit at a factory in Mount Vernon, New York, each chipped in a dollar, signed a handwritten contract agreeing to "share the money equaly [sic] & fairly to each other," and bought a ticket in the New York State Lottery. The next day, their ticket was picked as one of three winners of the largest jackpot in history: $41 million.

The story of the Mount Vernon 21 captivated millions not just because of the size of the pot of gold but because of the rainbow of people who won it. Black, white, yellow, and brown had scribbled their names on that contract—Mariano Martinez, Chi Wah Tse, Jaroslaw Siwy, and Peter Lee—all immigrants from countries ranging from Paraguay to Poland, from Trinidad to Thailand.

"We're like a big family here," said Peter Lee. "We thought by pooling our efforts we would increase our luck—and we were right."[1]

The men's good fortune is a metaphor for the possibility that friendships across ethnic and racial boundaries may be the winning ticket for everyone. This is not to say that crossing boundaries is a snap. It isn't. There are checkpoints along the way where psychic border guards put up a fuss and credentials must be reviewed. We look at a prospective friend and ask, "Do they want something from me?" Is this someone who sees personal advantage in having a friend of another race at his school, in her company, at this moment in history? Is it Brotherhood Week? Does this person understand that "crossing friendships" require more care and feeding than in-group friendship, that it takes extra work?

EXPLAINING

Most of the extra work can be summed up in one word: *explaining.* Whatever the boundary being crossed—both partners in a crossing friendship usually find they have to do a lot of explaining—to themselves, to each other, and to their respective communities.

Explaining to Yourself

One way or another, you ask yourself, "What is the meaning of my being friends with someone not like me?"

Source: Abridged from *Among Friends* (pp. 189–226). New York: McGraw-Hill, 1987.

In his clasic study, *The Nature of Prejudice*, Gordon Allport distinguishes between the in-group, which is the group to which you factually belong, and the reference group, which is the group to which you relate or aspire.[2] Allport gives the example of Blacks who so wish to partake of white skin privilege that they seek only white friends, disdain their own group, and become self-hating. One could as easily cite Jews who assume WASP identity or "Anglicized Chicanos" who gain education and facility in English and then sever their ties of kinship and friendship with other Mexican-Americans.[3]

When you have a friend from another racial or ethnic group, you ask yourself whether you are sincerely fond of this person or might be using him or her as an entrée into a group that is your unconscious reference group. The explaining you do to yourself helps you understand your own motivations. It helps you ascertain whether the friend complements or denies your identity, and whether your crossing friendships are in reasonable balance with your in-group relationships.

Explaining to Each Other

Ongoing mutual clarification is one of the healthiest characteristics of crossing friendships. The Black friend explains why your saying "going ape" offends him, and the Jewish friend reminds you she can't eat your famous barbecued pork. Both of you try to be honest about your cultural sore points and to forgive the other person's initial ignorance or insensitivities. You give one another the benefit of the doubt. Step by step, you discover which aspects of the other person's "in-groupness" you can share and where you must accept exclusion with grace.

David Osborne, a white, describes his close and treasured friendship with an American Indian from Montana: "Steve was tall and athletic—the classic image of the noble full-blooded Indian chief. We were in the same dorm in my freshman year at Stanford at a time when there were only one or two other Native Americans in the whole university. He had no choice but to live in a white world. Our friendship began when our English professor gave an assignment to write about race. Steve and I got together to talk about it. We explored stuff people don't usually discuss openly. After that, we started spending a lot of time together. We played intramural sports. We were amazingly honest with each other, but we were also comfortable being silent.

"When I drove him home for spring vacation, we stopped off at a battlefield that had seen a major war between Chief Joseph's tribe and the U.S. Cavalry. Suddenly it hit me that, had we lived then, Steve and I would have been fighting on opposite sides, and we talked about the past. Another time, an owl flew onto our windowsill and Steve was very frightened. He told me the owl was a symbol of bad luck to Indians. I took it very seriously. We were so in touch, so in sync, that I felt the plausibility of his superstitions. I was open to his mysticism."

Mutual respect, acceptance, tolerance for the faux pas and the occasional closed door, open discussion and patient mutual education, all this gives crossing friendships—when they work at all—a special kind of depth.

Explaining to Your Community of Origin

Accountability to one's own group can present the most difficult challenge to the maintenance of crossing friendships. In 1950 the authors of *The Lonely Crowd* said that interracial contact runs risks not only from whites but from Blacks who may "interpret friendliness as Uncle Tomism."[4] The intervening years have not eliminated such group censure.

In her article "Friendship in Black and White," Bebe Moore Campbell wrote: "For whites, the phrase 'nigger lover' and for Blacks, the accusation of 'trying to be white' are the pressure the group applies to discourage social interaction."[5] Even without overt attacks, people's worry about group reaction inspires self-censorship. Henry, a Black man with a fair complexion, told me he dropped a white friendship that became a touchy subject during the Black Power years. "We'd just come out of a period when many light-skinned Negroes tried to pass for white and I wasn't about to be mistaken for one of them," he explains. "My racial identity mattered more to me than any white friend."

Black-white friendships are "conducted underground" says Campbell, quoting a Black social worker, who chooses to limit her intimacy with whites rather than fight the system. "I'd feel comfortable at my white friend's parties because everybody there would be a liberal, but I'd never invite her to mine because I have some friends who just don't like white people and I didn't want anybody to be embarrassed."

If a white friend of mine said she hated Blacks, I would not just keep my Black friends away from her, I would find it impossible to maintain the friendship. However, the converse is not comparable. Most Blacks have at some point been wounded by racism, while whites have not been victimized from the other direction. Understanding the experiences *behind* the reaction allows decent Black people to remain friends with anti-white Blacks. That these Blacks may have reason to hate certain whites does not excuse their hating all whites, but it does explain it. . . .

Historically, of course, the biggest enemies of boundary-crossing friendships have not been Blacks or ethnic minorities but majority whites. Because whites gain the most from social inequality, they have the most to lose from crossing friendships, which, by their existence, deny the relevance of ethnic and racial hierarchies. More important, the empowered whites can put muscle behind their disapproval by restricting access to clubs, schools, and businesses.

If you sense that your community of origin condemns one of your crossing friendships, the amount of explaining or justifying you do will depend on how conformist you are and whether you feel entitled to a happiness of your own making. . . .

THE SAME BUT NEVER QUITE THE SAME

"I go coon hunting with Tobe Spencer," said former police officer, L. C. Albritton about his Black friend in Camden, Alabama. "We're good friends. We stay in town during the day for all the hullabaloo and at night we go home and load up the truck with three dogs and go way down into the swamps. We let the dogs go and sit on a log, take out our knives and a big chew of tobacco . . . and just let the rest of the world go by."

Looking at a picture of himself and Spencer taken in 1966, Albritton mused: "It's funny that a police officer like me is standing up there smiling and talking to a nigger because we were having marches and trouble at that time. . . . Old Tobe Spencer—ain't nothing wrong with that nigger. He's always neat and clean as a pin. He'll help you too. Call him at midnight and he'll come running just like that."[6]

Two friends with the same leisure-time pleasures, two men at ease together in the lonely night of the swamps. Yet race makes a difference. Not only does the white man use the derogatory "nigger," but he differentiates his friend Tobe from the rest of "them" who, presumably, are not neat and clean and helpful. *The same but never quite the same.*

Leonard Fein, the editor of *Moment,* a magazine of progressive Jewish opinion, gave me "the controlling vignette" of his cross-ethnic friendships: "An Irish-Catholic couple was among our dearest friends, but on that morning in 1967 when we first heard that Israel was being bombed, my wife said, 'Who can we huddle with tonight to get through this ordeal,' and we picked three Jewish couples. Our Irish friends were deeply offended. 'Don't you think we would have felt for you?' they asked 'Yes,' we said, 'but it wasn't sympathy we wanted, it was people with whom, if necessary, we could have mourned the death of Israel—and that could only be other Jews.'

"The following week, when the war was over, my wife and I went to Israel. The people who came to live in our house and take care of our children were our Irish friends. They had understood they were our closest friends yet they could never be exactly like us.". . .

For Raoul, a phenomenally successful advertising man, crossing friendships have been just about the only game in town. He reminisced with me about growing up in a Puerto Rican family in a Manhattan neighborhood populated mostly by Irish, Italians, and Jews:

"In the fifties I hung out with all kinds of guys. I sang on street corners—do-wopping in the night—played kick the can, and belonged to six different basketball clubs, from the Police Athletic League to the YMCA. My high school had 6000 kids in it—street kids who hung out in gangs like The Beacons, The Fanwoods, The Guinea Dukes, The Irish Lords, and The Diablos from Spanish Harlem and Jewish kids who never hung out because they were home studying. The gang members were bullies and punks who protected their own two-block area. They wore leather jackets and some of them carried zip guns and knives. I managed to be acceptable to all of them just because I was good at sports. I was the best athlete in the school and president of the class. So I was protected by the gangs and admired by the Jewish kids and I had a lot of friends."

Raoul's athletic prowess won him a scholarship to a large midwestern university where he was the first Puerto Rican to be encountered by some people. "They wanted me to sing the whole sound track of *West Side Story.* They asked to see my switchblade. And I was as amazed by the midwesterners as they were by me. My first hayride was a real shock. Same with hearing people saying 'Good morning' to each other. Every one of my friends—my roommate, teammates, and fraternity brothers, Blacks from Chicago and Detroit and whites from the farms—they were all gentle and nice. And gigantic and strong. Boy, if one of them had moved into my neighborhood back home, he'd have owned the block.

"After graduation, a college friend went to work in a New York City ad agency that played in a Central Park league and needed a softball pitcher. He had me brought in for an interview. Even though I knew nothing about advertising, I was a helluva pitcher, and the owner of the agency took sports seriously. So he hired me. I always say I had the only athletic scholarship in the history of advertising. I pitched for the agency, I played basketball with the owner, and I learned the business. So I found my friends and my career through sports. Even though I may have been a Spic to most everyone, sports opened all the doors."

The same but never quite the same. . . .

"At the beginning, because of difficulties of adaptation, we immigrants protect ourselves by getting together with people from the same culture who speak the same language," says Luis Marcos, a psychiatrist, who came to the United States from Seville, Spain. "Next, when we feel more comfortable, we reach out to people who do the same work we do, mostly those who help us or those we help in some way. Then we have a basis for friendship. My mentor, the director of psychiatry at Bellevue, is a native-born American and a Jew. He helped me in my area of research and now he's one of my best friends. I also began to teach and to make friends with my medical students as they grew and advanced."

That Marcos and his friends have the health profession in common has not prevented misunderstandings. "When we first went out for meals together, my impulse was to pay for both of us," he says of another doctor, a Black woman who taught him not to leave his own behavior unexamined. "It wasn't that I thought she couldn't afford to pay; we were equally able to pick up the check. It was just that the cultural habit of paying for a woman was ingrained in my personality. But she misconstrued it. She felt I was trying to take care of her and put her down as a Black, a professional, and a woman. In order for our friendship to survive, she had to explain how she experiences things that I don't even think about."

MOVING IN ONE ANOTHER'S WORLD

Ethnotherapist Judith Klein revels in her crossing friendships. "My interest in people who are different from me may be explained by the fact that I'm a twin. Many people look to be mirrored in friendship; I've had mirroring through my sister, so I can use friendship for other things. One thing I use it for is to extend my own life. People who aren't exactly like me enhance my knowledge and experience. They let me be a vicarious voyager in their world."

As much as friends try to explain one another's world, certain differences remain particular barriers to intimacy.

Luis Marcos mentions the language barrier. "No matter how well I speak, I can never overcome my accent," he says. "And some people mistake the way I talk for lack of comprehension. They are afraid I won't understand an American joke, or if I choose to use aggressive words, they don't think I mean it, they blame my 'language problem.'"

While many Americans assume people with an accent are ignorant, many ethnics assume, just as incorrectly, that someone *without* an accent is smart. Some Americans have a habit of blaming the other person for doing or saying whatever is not understandable to Americans. Ethnics also have been known to blame their own culture—to use their "foreignness" as an excuse for behavior for which an American would have to take personal responsibility. "I can't help it if we Latins are hot-tempered" is a way of generalizing one's culpability.

Of course, the strongest barrier to friendship is outright resistance. After two years of off-and-on living in Tokyo, Angie Smith came to terms with the fact that "the Japanese do not socialize the way we do." She found, as many have, that in Japan friendship is considered an obligation more than a pleasure and is almost always associated with business.[7]

"Three times I invited two couples for dinner—the men were my husband's business associates—and three times the men came and the women didn't," Smith recalls. "They sent charming little notes with flowers, but they would not have been comfortable in our house for an evening of social conversation. Yet these same Japanese women would go out to lunch with me and tell me more intimate things than they tell each other. While we were in Japan, I just had to get used to sex-divided socializing and not having any couple friendships."

When people's differences are grounded in racism rather than alien styles of socializing, it can be especially painful to move in the other person's world.

"I felt myself a slave and the idea of speaking to white people weighed me down," wrote Frederick Douglass a century ago.[8] Today, most Blacks refuse to be weighed down by whites. They do not "need" white friends. Some doubt that true friendship is possible between the races until institutional racism is destroyed. Feminists of every shade have debated the question "Is Sisterhood Possible?" Despite the issues that affect *all* women, such as sexual violence, many Black women resist working together for social change or organizing with white women because they believe most whites don't care enough about welfare reform, housing, teen pregnancies, or school dropouts—issues that are of primary concern to Blacks.

Bell Hooks, a writer and a professor of Afro-American studies, wrote: "All too frequently in the women's movement it was assumed one could be free of sexist thinking by simply adopting the appropriate feminist rhetoric; it was further assumed that identifying oneself as oppressed freed one from being an oppressor. To a very great extent, such thinking prevented white feminists from undertsanding and overcoming their own sexist-racist attitudes toward black women. They could pay lip service to the idea of sisterhood and solidarity between women but at the same time dismiss black women."[9]

Phyllis Marynick Palmer, a historian, says white women are confounded by Black women's strong family role and work experience, which challenge the white stereotype of female incapacity. White women also criticize Black women for making solidarity with their brothers a priority rather than confronting Black men's sexism. In turn, Black women get angry at white women who ignore "their own history of racism and the benefits that white women have gained at the expense of black women."[10] With all this, how could sisterhood be possible? How can friendship be possible?

"I would argue for the abandonment of the concept of sisterhood as a global construct based on unexamined assumptions about our similarities," answers Dill, "and I would substitute a more pluralistic approach that recognizes and accepts the objective differences between women."

Again the word "pluralistic" is associated with friendship. An emphasis on double consciousness, not a denial of differences. The importance of feeling both the same and different, of acknowledging "the essence of me," of understanding that friends need not *transcend* race or ethnicity but can embrace differences and be enriched by them. The people who have managed to incorporate these precepts say that they are pretty reliable guidelines for good crossing friendships. But sometimes it's harder than it looks. Sometimes, the "vicarious voyage" into another world can be a bad trip.

The Hazards of Crossing

"Anglo wannabes" are a particular peeve of David Hayes Bautista. "These are Anglos who wanna be so at home with us that they try too hard to go native. For instance, Mexicans have a certain way that we yell along with the music of a mariachi band. When someone brought along an Anglo friend and he yelled "Yahoo, Yahoo' all night, every Chicano in the place squirmed."

Maxine Baca Zinn gives the reverse perspective: of a Chicano in an Anglo environment. "Once, when I was to speak at the University of California, a Chicana friend who was there told me that the minute I walked into that white academic world my spine straightened up. I carried myself differently. I talked differently around them and I didn't even know it." Was Zinn just nervous about giving her speech or did she tighten up in anticipation of the tensions Chicanos feel in non-Hispanic settings? She's not certain.

When Charlie Chin, a bartender, started work in a new place, a white coworker quipped, "One thing you have to watch out for, Charlie, are all the Chinks around here." I winced when Chin said this, but he told me, "I just smiled at the guy. I'm used to those jokes. That's the way whites break the ice with Asians. That's the American idea of being friendly.". . .

For another pair of friends, having different sensitivities did not destroy the relationship but did create a temporary misunderstanding. Yvonne, a Black woman, was offended when her white friend, Fran, came to visit, took off her shoes, and put her feet up on the couch. "I felt it showed her disregard for me and I blamed it on race," says Yvonne. "Black people believe the way you behave in someone's home indicates the respect you have for that person. Also, furniture means a lot to us because we buy it with such hard-won wages." Weeks later, Yvonne saw one of Fran's white friends do the same thing while sitting on Fran's couch. Yvonne realized that the behavior had nothing to do with lack of respect for Blacks. "For all I know millions of whites all over America put their feet up when they relax—I'd just never seen that part of their world before."

What Bill Tatum discovered about a couple of his white friends was not so easy to explain away. When the couple asked Tatum to take some food to Helen, their Black housekeeper who was sick, he asked her name and address. They knew her only as "Helen" but were able to get her address from their 6-year-old who had spent a week at her apartment when they had been on vacation.

"I arrived to find a filthy, urine-smelling building, with addicts hanging out on the front stoop. Rags were stuffed in the broken windows in Helen's apartment. She was wearing a bag of asafetida around her neck, a concoction made by southern Blacks to ward off back luck and colds. She was old, sick, and feverish. She said she'd never been sick before and her employers—my friends—had provided her with no health insurance. Obviously, they'd never imagined where or how this poor woman might live—or else they wouldn't have left their little girl with her. They treated their Black housekeeper with none of the respect and concern they showed me, their Black *friend* and a member of their economic class."

Until that experience, if anyone had ever accused the couple of racism, Tatum says he'd have gone to the mat defending them. Now he has to square what he's seen with his old love for them and he is finding it very, very difficult.

He makes another point about moving in the world of white friends. "Some whites make me feel completely comfortable because they say exactly what they think even if it contradicts whatever I've said. But other whites never disagree with me on anything. They act as if Blacks can't defend their positions, or they're afraid it would look like a put-down to challenge what I say even though they would challenge a white person's opinion in a minute."

While Tatum resents whites' misguided protectiveness, he also finds fault with "many Blacks who are climbing socially and are too damned careful of what *they* say. They won't advance an opinion until they have a sense of what the white friend is thinking." Not only is that not good conversation, he says, "that's not good friendship."

THE PROBLEM WITH "THEM" IS "US"

If you're a young, heterosexual, nondisabled person and you do not have one friend who is either gay, old, or disabled, there might be something wrong with *you*. If you're gay, old, or disabled and all your friends are just like you, it may not be because you prefer it that way.

Gay people, the elderly, and disabled people get the same pleasure from companionship and intimacy and have the same problems with friendship as does anyone else. They merit a separate discussion in this book for the same reason that class, race, and ethnicity required special discussion: because on top of the usual friendship concerns, they experience additional barriers.

In essence, the barriers exist because we don't *know* each other. Many people—some of whom are homophobic (have a fear of homosexuality)—reach adulthood without ever to their knowledge meeting a homosexual or a lesbian. Many have neither known someone who is blind or deaf or who uses a wheelchair nor spent time with an old person other than their grandparents. That there are such things as Gay Pride marches, disability rights organizations, and the Gray Panthers does not mean that these groups have achieved equal treatment under the law or full humanity in the eyes of the world. To a large degree, our society still wants to keep them out of sight—the gays for "flaunting their alternative life-styles," the disabled for not "getting better," and the old for reminding us of our eventual fate.

As a result of our hang-ups, these populations may be even more segregated than racial or ethnic minorities. When these groups are segregated, "we" don't have to think about "them." Out of sight, out of mind, out of friendship. People told me they had no gay, elderly, or disabled friends because "we live in two different worlds" or because "they" are so different—meaning threatening, unsettling, or strange. Closer analysis reveals, however, that we *keep* them different by making this world so hard for them to live in and by defining human norms so narrowly. It is our world—the homophobic, youth-worshipping, disability-fearing world—that is threatening, unsettling, and strange to them. In other words, their biggest problem is us.

To make friends, we have to cross our self-made boundaries and grant to other people the right to be both distinctive and equal.

Gay-Straight Friendship

Forming relationships across gay-straight boundaries can be as challenging as crossing racial and ethnic lines because it too requires the extra work of "explaining":

* Explaining to yourself why, if you're gay, you need this straight friend ("Am I unconsciously trying to keep my heterosexual credentials in order?"), or why, if you're straight, you need this gay friend ("Am I a latent homosexual?")
* Explaining to each other what your lives are like—telling the straight friend what's behind the words "heavy leather" or explaining to the gay friend just why he *cannot* bring his transvestite lover to a Bar Mitzvah
* Explaining to your respective communities why you have such a close relationship with one of "them"

Gay-straight friendship is a challenge not only because the heterosexual world stigmatizes gays but because homosexual society is a culture unto itself. Straights who relate comfortably with their gay friends say they get along so well because they respect the distinctive qualities of gay culture—almost as if it were an ethnic group. Interestingly enough, a Toronto sociologist has determined that gay men have the same institutions, "sense of peoplehood," and friendship networks as an ethnic community; all that gays lack is the emphasis on family.[11] And in places where lesbians congregate, such as San Francisco, there are women's bars, music, bookstores, publications, folklore, and dress styles—an elaborate self-contained culture.[12]

Since gay men and lesbians have to function in a straight world during most of their lives, it's not too much to ask a straight friend to occasionally accommodate to an environment defined by homosexuals. But even when both friends accommodate, gay-straight relations can be strained by disagreements over provocative issues.

Gay-Straight Debate

The Gay's View	The Straight's View
On Homophobia	
You're not relaxed with me. You think gayness rubs off or friendship might lead to sex. You act like every gay person wants to seduce you. You fear others will think you're gay. You are repulsed by gay sex though you try to hide it. You bear some responsibility for the discrimination against gays and if you're my friend, you'll fight it with me.	I am the product of a traditional upbringing. I cannot help being afraid or ignorant of homosexuality. My religion taught me that homosexuality is a sin. I'm trying to overcome these biases and still be honest with you about my feelings. I support gay rights, but I cannot be responsible for everyone else's homophobia.
On AIDS	
Ever since the AIDS epidemic, you have not touched me or drunk from a glass in my house. I resent your paranoia. I shouldn't have to watch my gay friends die and at the same time feel that my straight friends are treating me like a leper. If I did get AIDS, I'm afraid you would blame the victim and abandon me. Can I trust a friend like that?	I *am* afraid. I don't know how contagious the AIDS virus is or how it's transmitted. From what I read, no one does. All I know is that AIDS is fatal, homosexuals are the primary victims, and you are a homosexual. I'm caught between my affection for you and my terror of the disease. I don't know what's right and you're in no position to tell me.
On Lesbian Politics	
Lesbianism is not just sexual, it's political. Every woman should call herself a lesbian, become woman-identified, and reject everything masculinist. Women who love men and live in the nuclear family contribute to the entrenchment of patriarchal power and the oppression of women. Authentic female friendship can only exist in lesbian communities. If you don't accept "lesbian" as a positive identity, it will be used to condemn all woman who are not dependent on men.	I support lesbian rights and even lesbian separatism if lesbians choose it. I believe lesbian mothers must be permitted to keep their children. I oppose all discrimination and defamation of lesbians. I believe that lesbian feminists and straight women can work together and be friends, *but* I resent lesbian coercion and political strong-arming. I also resent your more-radical-than-thou attitude toward heterosexuals. Like you, what I do with my body is my business.
On Acceptance	
You want me to act straight whenever having a gay friend might embarrass you. I'm not going to tone down my speech or dress to please your friends or family. I do not enjoy being treated as a second-class couple when my lover and I go out with you and your spouse. If you can kiss and hold hands, we should be able to show affection in public. If straights ask each other how they met or how long they have been married, they should ask us how we met and how long we've been together.	You refuse to understand how difficult it is to explain gay life-styles to a child or an 80-year-old. You make me feel like a square in comparison with your flashy gay friends. You treat married people like Mr. and Mrs. Tepid, as if the only true passion is gay passion. Your friends make me feel unwanted on gay turf and at political events when I'm there to support gay rights. You put down all straights before you know them. It's hard to be your friend if I can't introduce you to other people without your feeling hostile or judging their every word. . . .

Disabled and Nondisabled Friendship

About 36 million Americans have a disabling limitation in their hearing, seeing, speaking, walking, moving, or thinking. Few nondisabled people are as sensitive to the experiences of this population as are those with close friends who are disabled.

"Last week," recalls Barbara Spring, "I went to have a drink at a midtown hotel with a friend who uses a wheelchair. Obviously it's not important to this hotel to have disabled patrons because we had to wait for the so-called accessible elevator for thirty minutes. Anyone who waits with the disabled is amazed at how long the disabled have to wait for everything."

"In graduate school, one of my friends was a young man with cerebral palsy," says Rena Gropper. "Because he articulated slowly and with great difficulty, everyone thought he was dumb and always interrupted him, but if you let him finish, you heard how bright and original his thinking was."

Terry Keegan, an interpreter for the deaf, has become friends with many deaf people and roomed for two years with a coworker who is deaf. "If they don't understand what we're saying it's not because they're stupid but because we aren't speaking front face or we can't sign." Keegan believes all hearing people should learn 100 basic words in Ameslan, American Sign Language. "Historically, this wonderful language has been suppressed. Deaf people were forced to use speech, lipreading, and hearing aids so they would not look handicapped and would 'fit in' with the rest of us. Their hands were slapped when they tried to sign. This deprived them of a superior communication method. Deafness is not a pathology, it's a difference. When we deny deaf people their deafness, we deny them their identity."

Many nondisabled people have become sensitized to idioms that sound like racial epithets to the disabled, such as "the blind leading the blind" or "that's a lame excuse." Some find "handicapped" demeaning because it derives from "cap in hand." A man who wears leg braces says the issue is accuracy. "*I'm* not handicapped, people's attitudes about me handicap me." Merle Froschl, a nondisabled member of the Women and Disability Awareness Project, points out that the opposite of "disabled" is "*not* disabled"; thus, "nondisabled" is the most neutral term. Disabled people are infuriated by being contrasted with "normal" people—it implies that the disabled are "abnormal" and everyone else is perfect. And the term "able-bodied" inspires the question, Able to do what: Run a marathon? See without glasses? Isn't it all relative?

"Differently abled" and "physically challenged" had a brief vogue, but says Harilyn Rousso, those terms "made me feel I really had something to hide." Rousso, a psychotherapist who has cerebral palsy, emphasizes, "Friends who care the most sometimes think they're doing you a favor by using euphemisms or saying 'I never think of you as disabled.' The reason they don't want to acknowledge my disability is that they think it's so negative. Meanwhile, I'm trying to recognize it as a valid part of me. I'm more complex than my disability and I don't want my friends to be obsessed by it. But it's clearly there, like my eye color, and I want my friends to appreciate and accept me with it."

The point is not that there is a "right way" to talk to people who are disabled but that friendship carries with it the obligation to *know thy friends*, their sore points and their preferences. That includes knowing what words hurt their feelings as well as when and how to help them do what they cannot do for themselves.

"Each disabled person sends out messages about what they need," says Froschl. "One friend who is blind makes me feel comfortable about taking her arm crossing the street, another dislikes physical contact and wants to negotiate by cane. I've learned not to automatically do things for disabled people since they often experience help as patronizing."

"I need someone to pour cream in my coffee, but in this culture, it's not acceptable to ask for help," says Rousso, adding that women's ordinary problems with dependency are intensified by disability. "I have to feel very comfortable with my friends before I can explain my needs openly and trust that their reaction will not humiliate both of us. For some people it raises too many anxieties."

Anxieties that surround the unknown are dissipated by familiarity. Maybe that explains why so many disabled-nondisabled friendships are composed of classmates or coworkers who spend a lot of time together.

"There are those who can deal with disability and those who can't," says Phil Draper, a quadriplegic whose spinal cord was injured in a car accident. "If they can't— if they get quiet or talk nervously or avoid our eyes—the work of the relationship falls entirely on us. We need friends who won't treat us as weirdo asexual second-class children or expect us to be 'Supercrips'—miracle cripples who work like crazy to make themselves whole again. Ninety-nine percent of us aren't going to be whole no matter what we do. We want to be accepted the way we are."

To accept friends like Phil Draper, the nondisabled have to confront their unconscious fears of vulnerability and death. In one study, 80 percent of nondisabled people said they would be comfortable having someone in a wheelchair as their friend. But "being in a wheelchair" came immediately after "blind" and "deaf-mute" as the affliction they themselves would least want to have.[13] If we fear being what our friend is, that feeling is somewhere in the friendship.

Nondisabled people also have to disavow the cult of perfectability. Disabled people are not going to "get better" because they are not "sick"; they are generally healthy people who are not allowed to function fully in this society—as friends or as anything else.

"Friendship is based on people's ability to communicate," says Judy Heumann, the first postpolio person to get a teacher's license in New York City and now a leader of the disability rights movement. "But barriers such as inaccessible homes make it hard for disabled people to just drop in. Spontaneity is something disabled people enjoy infrequently and the nondisabled take for granted.

"While more public places have ramps and bathrooms that accommodate wheelchairs, many parties still occur in inaccessible spaces. If I have to be carried upstairs or if I can't have a drink because I know I won't be able to use the bathroom later, I'll probably decide not to go at all. One way I measure my friends is by whether they have put in the effort and money to make their houses wheelchair-accessible. It shows their sensitivity to me as a person.

"Good friends are conscious of the fact that a movie theater or concert hall has to be accessible before I can join them; they share my anger and frustration if it's not. They understand why I'm not crazy about big parties where all the nondisabled are standing up and I'm at ass-level. It makes me able to function more as an equal within the group if people sit down to talk to me. I can't pretend I'm part of things if I can't hear anyone. I don't want to *not* be invited to large parties—I just want people to be sensitive to my needs.

"I always need help cooking, cleaning, driving, going to the bathroom, getting dressed. I pay an attendant to do most of those things for me but sometimes I have to ask a friend for help, which presents a lot of opportunities for rejection. Often, the friends who come through best are other disabled people whose disabilities complement mine. I can help a blind woman with her reading, child care, and traveling around town; she can do the physical things I need. And we don't have to appreciate each other's help, we can just accept it.". . .

Cross-Age Friendship

I am now 46, my husband is 51. Among our good friends are two couples who are old enough to be our parents. One woman, a poet, can be counted on for the latest word on political protests and promising writers. She and I once spent a month together at a writers' colony. The other woman—as energetic and as well-read as anyone I know— is also involved in progressive causes. Although the men of both couples have each had a life-threatening illness, the one with a heart condition is a brilliant civil liberties lawyer and the one who had a stroke is a prize-winning novelist with stunning imaginative powers. The lawyer taught our son to play chess when he was 5. The novelist has encouraged our daughters to write stories ever since they could read. The men have been fine surrogate grandfathers.

When I described these couples to someone my own age, he said, "Ah, it's easy to be friends with *interesting* old people, but what about the dull ones?" The answer is, I am not friends with dull young or middle-aged people so why should I want to be friends with dull old people? And why does he immediately think in terms of old people *not* being interesting? Perhaps the crux of the problem with cross-generational friendship is this *double* double standard. First, to think we "ought" to be friends with the elderly—as a class—denies old people the dignity of individuality and devalues their friendship through condescension. But second, to assume that those who are young or in mid-life will necessarily be more interesting and attractive than those over 65 maintains a double standard of expectation that cheats younger people of friends like ours.

Ageism hurts all ages. And it begins early: Studies show that 3-year-olds already see old people as sick, tired, and ugly and don't want to associate with them.[14] Older people also have their biases about youthful behavior. Some 70-year-olds think children are undependable, unappreciative, ask too many questions, and must be told what to do. They believe teenagers are callow, impatient, and unseasoned.[15]

The authors of *Grandparents/Grandchildren* write, "We shouldn't blame adolescents for not being adults. To become adults, the young need to be around adults."[16]

But age segregation keeps us apart. Without benefit of mutual acquaintance, stereotypes mount, brick by brick, until there is a wall high enough to conceal the real human beings on either side.

Another big problem is miscommunication. Conversations between young and old often founder because "sensory, physical, or cognitive differences" cause "distortion, message failure, and social discomfort."[17] That's a fancy way of saying they can't understand each other. And anyone who has ever talked with a young person whose span of concentration is the length of a TV commercial or with an old person whose mind wanders to the blizzard of '48 when asked how to dress for today's weather will understand how each generation's communication style can be a problem for the other.

But stereotypes and miscommunication do not entirely account for the gulf between young and old. Homophily—the attraction to the similar self—is the missing link. Those who are going through the same thing at the same time find it comforting to have friends who mirror their problems and meet their needs, and, usually, people of similar chronological age are going through parallel experiences with wage-earning, setting up house, child-rearing, and other life-cycle events.

Age-mates also tend to have in common the same angle of vision on history and culture. Two 65-year-olds watching a film about the Depression or World War II can exchange memories and emotional responses that are unavailable to a 30-year-old who did not live through those cataclysms. And while a person of 18 and one of 75 might both love Vivaldi, their simultaneous appreciation for Bruce Springsteen is unlikely.

Claude Fischer's studies reveal that more than half of all friend-partners are fewer than five years apart. But the span is reduced to two years if their relationship dates back to their youth when age gradations matter the most and the places where youngsters meet—school, camp, military service, and entry-level jobs—are more age-segregated. Contrary to popular wisdom, elderly people, like the rest of us, prefer friends of their own age. The more old people there are in a given community, the more likely it is that each one will have a preponderance of same-age friends. And, believe it or not, a majority of old people say they think it's more important for them to have age-mates than family as their intimates.

Given this overwhelming preference for homophily at every age, why am I on the bandwagon for cross-generational friendship? Because when it's good, it's very, very good—both for friends of different ages who are undergoing similar experiences at the same time and for friends of different ages who are enjoying their differences.

- A 38-year-old woman meets 22-year-olds in her contracts class at law school.
- A couple in their early forties enrolled in a natural childbirth course make friends with parents-to-be who are twenty years younger.
- Three fathers commiserate about the high cost of college; two are in their forties, the third is a 60-year-old educating his second family.

Age-crossing friendships become less unusual as Americans follow more idiosyncratic schedules for marrying, having children, and making career decisions.

But there are other reasons for feeling that age is immaterial to friendship. Marie Wilson, a 45-year-old foundation executive who has five children of high school age or older, told me, "My friends are in their early thirties, and they have kids under 8. But these women are where I am in my head. We became close working together on organizing self-help for the poor. Most women my age are more involved in suburban life or planning their own career moves."

Sharing important interests can be as strong a basis for friendship as is experiencing the same life-cycle events. However, without either of those links, the age difference can sit between the young and the old like a stranger. I'm not asking that we deny that difference but that we free ourselves from what Victoria Secunda calls "the tyranny of age assumptions"[18] and that we entertain the possibility of enriching ourselves through our differences. . . .

As we cross all these lines and meet at many points along the life cycle, people of diverse ages, like people of every class and condition, are discovering that we who are in so many ways "the same and different" can also be friends.

NOTES

1 L. Rohter, "Immigrant Factory Workers Share Dream, Luck and a Lotto Jackpot," *New York Times*, August 23, 1985.
2 G. Allport, *The Nature of Prejudice*, Doubleday, Anchor Press, 1958.
3 J. Provinzano, "Settling Out and Settling In." Papers presented at annual meeting of the American Anthropological Association, November 1974.
4 D. Riesman, R. Denney, and N. Glazer, *The Lonely Crowd: A Study of the Changing American Character*, Yale University Press, 1950.
5 B. M. Campbell, "Friendship in Black and White," *Ms.*, August 1983.
6 B. Adelman, *Down Home: Camden, Alabama*, Times Books, Quadrangle, 1972.
7 R. Atsumi, "Tsukiai—Obligatory Personal Relationships of Japanese White Collar Employees," *Human Organization*, vol. 38, no. 1 (1979).
8 F. Douglass, *Narrative of the Life of Frederick Douglass, an American Slave*, New American Library, Signet, 1968.
9 B. Hooks, *Ain't I a Woman: Black Women and Feminism*, South End Press, 1981.
10 P. M. Palmer, "White Women/Black Women: The Dualism of Female Identity and Experience in the United States," *Feminist Studies*, Spring 1983.
11 S. O. Murray, "The Institutional Elaboration of a Quasi-Ethnic Community," *International Review of Modern Sociology*, vol. 9, no. 2 (1979).
12 J. C. Albro and C. Tully, "A Study of Lesbian Lifestyles in the Homosexual Micro-Culture and the Heterosexual Macro-Culture," *Journal of Homosexuality*, vol. 4, no. 4 (1979).
13 L. M. Shears and C. J. Jensema, "Social Acceptability of Anomalous Persons," *Exceptional Children*, October 1969.
14 R. K. Jantz et al., *Children's Attitudes Toward the Elderly*, University of Maryland Press, 1976.
15 A. G. Cryns and A. Monk, "Attitudes of the Aged Toward the Young," *Journal of Gerontology*, vol. 1 (1972); see also, C. Seefeld et al., "Elderly Persons' Attitude Toward Children," *Educational Gerontology*, vol. 8, no. 4 (1982).
16 K. L. Woodward and A. Kornhaber, *Grandparents, Grandchildren: The Vital Connection*

(Doubleday, Anchor Press, 1981), quoted in "Youth Is Maturing Later," *New York Times*, May 10, 1985.

17 L. J. Hess and R. Hess, "Inclusion, Affection, Control: The Pragmatics of Intergenerational Communication." Paper presented at the Conference on Communication and Gerontology of the Speech Communication Association, July 1981.

18 V. Secunda, *By Youth Possessed: The Denial of Age in America,* Bobbs-Merrill, 1984.

CHAPTER 11

Strangers Adaptation

Life requires a series of adaptations. No two events are quite alike, and we must continually adapt ourselves to the changing environment. When we come into contact with strangers and develop an interpersonal relationship, we are, consciously or unconsciously, adapting ourselves to the strangers and the relationship.

The readings in the preceding chapter focused on various aspects of how we develop interpersonal relationships with strangers. We are now going to shift the focus of our attention to the strangers' perspective and examine how they cope with a new cultural environment and how their communication influences the overall adaptation process.

The communication process discussed in this chapter is a special case of human adaptation—namely, that which is required for a stranger to cope with a new and unfamiliar culture. Usually this adaptation is associated with a change from one society, or subsection of a society, to another, as well as with changes in the social environment. It is concerned with major cultural gaps that occur either as a result of a stranger's move from one culture to another or because of substantial changes in his or her environment.

An extensive list of examples of situations that involve cultural adaptation is presented by Taft (1977) under five headings: sojourning, settling, subcultural mobility, segregation, and change in society. Whereas the first two imply geographical mobility, the latter three do not. Examples of changes requiring adaptation even when the person does not change locations include such situations as change of profession, retirement, marriage, divorce, aging, transition from school to work, and starting at a university. Also included are the processes of accepting major social and technological innovations, such as computerized information-processing systems. There are also situations in which strangers are incorporated into a new social system, such as the armed services, religious orders, residential universities, prisons, concentration camps, rehabilitation centers, and mental hospitals.

Situations that result from physically moving to new locations include those of foreign exchange students, Peace Corps volunteers, foreign business personnel, missionaries, diplomats, technical advisors, and administrators. Further, there are immigrants and refugees who have voluntarily or involuntarily moved from one society to another with the intention of becoming full members of the new society on a permanent basis. Also, individuals moving from a small rural town to a large metro-politan area, or vice versa, are in a situation that involves some degree of cultural adaptation, although their adaptive processes as strangers in the new environment are generally considered less difficult and encompassing than those of international migrants.

International migration, whether for a long or short term, represents a classic situation where the newly arrived strangers are required to cope with substantial cultural change. Of course, situations of international migration vary in the abrupt-ness of the transition. For example, an abrupt cultural transition was experienced by many refugees from Southeast Asia after the Vietnam War. Owing to the involuntary and sudden nature of their departure from their home country, most refugees had little change to prepare themselves psychologically for life in the host society. At least during the initial resettlement phase, many of them suffered from a deep psychological dislocation and sense of loss (Kim, 1980).

Even when the transition is a voluntary one, international migrants differ in their motivation to adapt to the new environment and to make the host society their "second home." This motivation to adapt depends largely on the degree of perma-nence of the new residence. In the case of immigrants, their move from their original culture to the host society is a permanent one. Because they must make their living and attain social membership in the host society, they need to be concerned with their relationship to the new environment in the same way as the members of the native population are. On the other hand, a peripheral contact with the new culture is typical of the situation of many sojourners. Reasons for a sojourn in a new culture are often specific—to pursue a vocation, to obtain a degree, or merely to enhance one's prestige in the eyes of the folks back home. This may require less adaptation to the host cultural system. Foreign students, for example, can reduce their cultural adapta-tion to the bare minimum in order to fulfill their role as student and may confine their social contact to fellow students from their home country. A similar observation can be made about military personnel and their families in foreign countries. They may perceive less need to adapt to the host culture because their stay is only temporary.

Regardless of the circumstantial variations in the degree of necessary adaptation, every individual in a new culture must respond and adapt to environmental changes at least minimally. Primary attention here is given to what is perhaps the most profound situation of cultural adaptation—the adaptation of sojourners and immigrants (includ-ing refugees) who were born and raised in one culture and who have moved to another culture for an indefinite stay. By understanding the adaptive processes of international migrants, we can make inferences about the nature of other similar adaptive life situations.

In the first reading, Furnham overviews research on the short-term adaptation of sojourners. He summarizes what we know about "culture shock," one of the major concepts studied as part of the adaptation process. Furnham also presents the major "theories" used to explain the short-term adaptation process.

Kim, in the second reading, examines factors that facilitate long-term immi-grant adaptation to new cultural environments. She overviews the role of the strangers' use of mass and interpersonal communication systems in the host culture. She also discusses characteristics of strangers that facilitate adaptation.

In the final reading in this chapter, Gudykunst and Sudweeks apply Gudykunst and Hammer's (1988) theory of intercultural adaptation. They provide practical suggestions based upon the theory that we can use to adapt in another culture.

REFERENCES

Gudykunst, W. B., & Hammer, M. R. (1988). Strangers and hosts. In Y. Y. Kim & W. B. Gudykunst (Eds.), *Cross-cultural adaptation*. Newbury Park, CA: Sage.

Kim, Y. Y. (1980). *Psychological, social, and cultural adjustment of Indochinese refugees* (Vol. 4 of Indochinese refugees in the State of Illinois). Chicago: Travelers Aid Society.

Taft, R. (1977). Coping with unfamiliar cultures. In N. Warren (Ed.), *Studies in cross-cultural psychology* (Vol. 1). New York: Academic Press.

The Adjustment of Sojourners

Adrian Furnham

. . . A review of the extensive, diffuse literature on sojourner adjustment begs the question as to the definition of a sojourner. As usual the dictionary is of limited help. It defines *sojourn* as a temporary stay at a place and offers various synonyms: a delay or digression; to tarry, lodge, rest, or quarter. The word *sojourner* usually has been used to denote a traveler and a sojourn is often thought to be an unspecified period of time in a new (different, unfamiliar) environment. What is missing from the dictionary and necessary to begin any analysis of sojourner adjustment are (1) a clear distinction between sojourners and other types of travelers such as tourists, migrants, and refugees; (2) some idea of the motives of sojourners for traveling; (3) a taxonomy of the different types of sojourners and how they are related to each other; and (4) some idea (albeit imprecise and subjective) of the temporal extremes distinguishing, for instance, tourists and migrants from sojourners. Of course these questions are mutually dependent and are all part of the need for a clear conceptual definition of the term *sojourner.*

In order to get a useful working definition of *sojourner*, it is important to identify those dimensions that are useful (discriminatory) and to specify the independent variables that define *sojourn*. Various dimensions have been proposed, including the nature of stranger-host relationships (Gudykunst, 1983), frequency of contact (Bochner, 1982), and geographic distance (Furnham & Bochner, 1986). These dimensions neither discriminate sojourners from other groups nor suggest what differ-

Source: Abridged from Chapter 2 in Y. Y. Kim & W. B. Gudykunst (Eds.), *Cross-Cultural Adaptation* (pp. 42–61). Newbury Park, CA: Sage, 1988.

ent sojourner groups have in common. The first and most salient dimension is temporal—a sojourner spends a medium length of time (six months to five years) at a place, usually intending to return "home." Thus tourists spend too brief a period overseas to be thought of as sojourners, and migrants (and refugees) too long a period. The second dimension, more difficult to define, is specifically of purpose or motive. By and large, tourists travel for a variety of nonspecific motives (for example, relaxation, self-enlightenment) as do migrants, whose motives are equally vague and complex. Comparatively, sojourners' motives are more specific and goal-oriented.

Thus the independent variables in the sojourner experience are length of time and purpose. The dependent variables include the amount of difficulty or stress experienced, the quality of contact with the native or host population, and changes in self-concept and way of life. This chapter will be concerned with these dependent and independent variables.

MOTIVES OF SOJOURNERS

A number of different groups of people may be classified as sojourners: businesspeople, diplomats, foreign workers, students, and voluntary workers. Psychological research, however, has concentrated on some more than others. For instance, there is very little literature on diplomats, a limited (but increasing) amount on foreign workers and businesspeople, but a large amount on students and voluntary workers.

People usually have various motives and expectations when living in a foreign place. These motives and expectations help shape their reactions to their environment (Furnham & Bochner, 1986; Torbiorn, 1982).

As part of a major study, 69 Asian students who had returned from pursuing higher academic degrees overseas were interviewed in their homeland by Bochner (1973). They were asked why they had accepted their scholarships, and what they had hoped to get out of the experience of study abroad. Several measures of motivation (some direct and others indirect) were used. Of the 69 responses, 64 suggested that it was to get a degree or gain academic experience. Only two said their main reason was culture learning, and three (all from the Philippines) listed personal development (for example, to gain insight, to become better people, to find themselves). Similarly, in a large study of 2,536 foreign students in 10 different countries by Klineberg and Hull (1979), 71% of the respondents said that obtaining a degree or diploma was important. Again the acquisition of qualifications and experience ranked as the single most important reason for going to a foreign university.

Thus the overwhelming majority of foreign students are primarily interested in getting a degree or professional training rather than learning a second culture or achieving personal growth. What is utmost in their minds are concerns about the tangible payoffs a sojourn might provide in the shape of career advancement, prestige, and upward mobility. They withstood various hardships in their educational sojourn to achieve their purposes (Bochner, 1979; Bochner, Lin, & McLeod, 1979).

An examination of the motives of Peace Corp volunteers also revealed specific motivations for their sojourn. In a study, of approximately 300 trainees, Guthrie (1966) reports that about 80% evinced interests closely resembling those of the typical social worker. When interviewed they freely acknowledged that they had joined the Peace Corps because they wanted to do something significant and because they had not found a satisfying career at home. At the same time, many brought with them highly unrealistic notions as to what they could achieve, how quickly they could solve the problems of the region in which they served, or what tangible results could be expected from their work.

CULTURE SHOCK

Nearly all sojourners suffer from culture shock. The culture shock "hypothesis" or "concept" suggests that the experience of a new culture is a sudden, unpleasant feeling that may violate expectations of the new culture and cause one to evaluate one's own culture negatively. Nearly all users of the term have suggested that the experience is negative—though this may not necessarily be the case.

The anthropologist Oberg (1960) was first accredited with using the term. In a brief and largely anecdotal article he mentions at least six aspects of culture shock.

(1) *strain*, as a result of the effort required to make necessary psychological adaptation
(2) *a sense of loss* and *feelings of deprivation* in regard to friends, status, profession, and possessions
(3) *rejection* by and/or rejection of members of the new culture
(4) *confusion* in role, role expectations, values, feelings, and self-identity
(5) *surprise, anxiety*, even *disgust* and *indignation* after becoming aware of culture differences
(6) *feelings of impotence*, as a result of not being able to cope with the new environment

Some years later, Cleveland, Mangone, and Adams (1963) offered a similar analysis relying heavily on personal experiences, especially those at the two extremes—that is, those (American) migrants who act as if they "never left home" and those who immediately "go native."

Others have attempted to improve upon Oberg's (1960) multifaceted definition of culture shock. Guthrie (1975) has used the term "culture fatigue"; Smalley (1963), "language shock"; Byrnes (1966), "role shock"; and Ball-Rokeach (1973), "pervasive ambiguity." In doing so, different researchers have simply placed the emphasis on slightly different problems—language, physical irritability, role ambiguity—rather than actually helping to specify *how* or *why* or *when* different people do or do not experience different aspects of culture shock. No one has attempted to specify the *relationships* among the various facets of culture shock; to order the *importance;* to suggest in which *order* they are most likely to occur; whether certain *groups* are more vulnerable to one type of shock or another.

Bock (1970) has described culture shock as primarily an emotional reaction that is consequent upon not being able to understand, control, and predict behavior, which appears to be a basic need. When people cannot do this, their usual accustomed, unthinking behavior changes to becoming unusual and unfamiliar as does that of others. This lack of familiarity extends to both the physical (design of buildings, parks) and the social environment (etiquette, clothing, and so on). Furthermore, the experience and use of time (mealtimes, time keeping) may all change (Hall, 1959), which may be profoundly disturbing. This theme is picked up by all of the writers in the field (Lundstedt, 1963; Hays, 1972)—many view culture shock as a stress reaction where salient psychological and physical rewards are generally uncertain and difficult to control or predict. Sojourners remain anxious, confused, and sometimes apathetic or angry until they have had time to develop a new set of assumptions that help them to understand and predict the behavior of others.

Others have attempted to describe culture shock in terms of individuals lacking points of reference, social norms, and rules to guide their actions and understand others' behavior. Hence the concept of *alienation* or *anomie* and idea of powerlessness, meaninglessness, normlessness, self- and social estrangement, and social isolation (Seeman, 1959) are seen to apply. But even more salient are constructs, ideas associated with *anxiety* that pervade the culture-shock literature. A "free-floating" anxiety, lack of self-confidence, distrust of others, and mild psychosomatic complaints are common (May, 1970). Furthermore, people appear to lose their inventiveness and spontaneity and become obsessively concerned with orderliness (Nash, 1967). In-depth case studies, just as much as large surveys, on sojourners have again and again come up with findings such as this.

Central to the very concept of culture shock is change and adaptation. The fairly extensive literature on the U curve, the W curve, and the inverted U curve (Church, 1982; Torbiorn, 1982) have been proposed to describe adaptation over time. By and large, the empirical literature is highly equivocal, providing only very modest support for any one pattern. Part of the problem lies in the failure to differentiate between distinct subgroups of sojourners as well as adaptation to quite different phenomena such as food, language, climate, and so on.

Most attempts to investigate culture shock then have been descriptive. Little or no attempt has been made to explain *for whom* the shock will be more or less intense; what determines *which reaction* a person is likely to experience; *how long* they remain in a period of shock; what factors *inoculate against* shock, and the like. It is often suggested that *all* people will suffer culture shock, yet some do not experience any negative aspects of sojourning, indeed they *seek out* these experience[s] for *enjoyment*. Sensation-seekers for instance might be expected not to suffer any adverse affects but to enjoy the highly arousing stimuli of the unfamiliar (Zuckerman, 1978).

Adler (1975) and David (1972) have offered an alternative view of culture shock, arguing that although it is most often associated with negative consequences it is often important for self-development and personal growth. Culture shock is seen as a transitional experience that can result in the adoption of new values, attitudes, and behavior patterns. The implication is that although it may be strange and possibly difficult, sojourning makes a person more adaptable, flexible, and insightful.

Although different writers have put emphasis on different aspects of culture shock (for example, alienation versus anxiety). Very few writers have stressed the positive or beneficial side of culture shock either for those individuals who revel in exciting and different environments or for those whose initial discomfort leads to personal growth. . . .

THEORIES OF SOJOURNER ADJUSTMENT

Despite the lack of any fully developed, formal theory that adequately explains sojourner adjustment, there are a number of theoretical approaches that have been fruitfully applied to this topic. Furnham and Bochner (1986) have identified eight such theoretical orientations.

Movement as Loss (Bereavement)

The geographic movement of the sojourner means the loss of specific relationships and significant objects (family, friends, occupational status, familiar foods, etc.). This loss is followed by individual grief or by more conventional types of mourning. Many particularly psychoanalytically oriented researchers have pointed to the similarities among typical grief reactions—intense anxiety, reduced resistance to stress, apathy and withdrawal, and anger. However, there are a number of problems with the analogy between grief and sojourner adjustment.

First, it is presumed that all sojourners experience negative, grieflike reactions. This is clearly not the case, as many sojourners thrive on the experience. Second, although the literature pertaining to the grief of the sojourner does not take into account individual and cultural differences, it makes no specific predictions as to what types of people suffer more or less grief, over what period, or what form the grief will take. Third, counseling for the grieving would seem highly inappropriate for sojourners who need information and support as much as therapy.

Fatalism (Locus of Control Beliefs)

This approach argues that many sojourners (particularly those from the Third World) have fatalistic, external locus of control beliefs before traveling, and that the initial experience of being a sojourner leads one to adopt fatalistic beliefs, along with passive and impaired coping strategies, and psychological distress. Sojourners tend to experience a loss of control and, therefore, lack the opportunity to manipulate the outcomes of their behavior.

The fatalism or locus of control explanation for the relationship between sojourning and adjustment is interesting but presents potential problems. The explanation does not account for the distress rates of different sojourning groups. Sojourners from a country in which the religious outlook is fatalistic or whose experiences render them more helpless should have more difficulty in adjusting than should migrants from a country where personal responsibility is valued. Also, most people who migrate have, by definition, an internal locus of control and are therefore relatively homogeneous without respect to their culture or origin. In order to migrate voluntarily (as a sojourner) one has to assume considerable personal responsibility and control over one's own affairs—financial, social, and familial. There must be other factors that account for the relationship between geographical movement and psychological well-being.

Selective Migration (Natural Selection)

This view is appealing in its simplicity and potential power. It suggests that those people who cope best with the exigencies of new environments become the prevailing type—the survival of the fittest. Hence the most carefully selected, or those who had the most hurdles to overcome in becoming a sojourner, will cope and adapt the best. This theory has a number of limitations, however. The theory stresses the relationship between selection processes and coping strategies. The evidence presented, however, is usually retrospective and the thesis itself more tautological than explanatory. Considering the selection obstacles of the sojourners, it is not clear which barriers or obstacles select for adaptation and which do not. The sheer number of obstacles alone does not imply that those people who necessarily overcome them will adapt well. For instance, education, physical fitness, language ability, and financial security may be important positive factors with regard to selection, while others, such as religion, may not. Rarely, if ever, do the optimally adaptive selectors exist in isolation from those factors that do not discriminate.

Positive selector obstacles may differ from country to country, from time to time, or from one sojourner group to another. Most receiving nations have specific general criteria of their own for the admission of sojourners. There are social, political, and economic reasons for these criteria that change over time. Hence it is extremely difficult to test the usefulness of this approach unless the precise nature of the adaptive selectors in both departure and arrival countries are specified and examined.

Appropriate Expectations

This approach suggests that the relationship between a sojourner's expectations (social, academic, economic) for sojourn and the fulfillment (or lack of fulfillment) is a crucial factor in determining adjustment. It has been shown that high (even unrealistic) expectations that cannot or do not get fulfilled are related to poor adjustment and that low expectations that are exceeded are related to good adjustment.

Again this approach is not without its problems. First, all sojourners have a wealth of expectations, some relating to social, economic, geographic, and political aspects of life in their new country. They are bound to be wrong about some, expecting too much or too little. What is unclear is *which* expectations about *what* aspect of life in the new country are most important to adjustment than others.

Second, the process by which unfulfilled expectations lead to poor adjustment is far from clear. Third, having low expectations may be better for short-term adjustment but worse for overall social mobility (which would mean poor long-term adjustment).

Negative Life Events

This approach emphasizes that any *change* (major or minor, positive or negative) in one's daily routine is associated with adaptation stress and strain and associated psychological and physical illness. Sojourning involves drastic changes and the absolute amount of adjustment is directly related to the speed and type of adaptation. Problems of this approach lie in measurement of life events (quality versus quantity, various dimensions), identifying possible intervening variables, and the relatively small percentages of variance accounted for, among others. There is a problem in establishing cause and effect: Do psychologically distressed people cause the occurrence of many negative events, or do randomly occurring life events lead to depression? The cause relationship is likely to be bidirectional though the major causal direction may be from events to illness. Surprisingly, literature in the area of life events has not paid attention to the sojourner adjustment phenomena.

Social Support (Breakdown in Support Networks)

This explanation argues that social support is directly related to increased psychological well-being and to a lower probability of physical and mental illness. This approach draws on various traditions, including attachment theory, social network theory, and various ideas in psychotherapy. Because sojourning usually involves leaving one's family, friends, and acquaintances (work colleagues and neighbors), sources of social support are considerably reduced, hence a dramatic increase in physical and mental illness. Although few researchers claim that social support is the only, or the most important, determinant of sojourner adjustment, there is sufficient evidence to suggest that it is an important feature. This "theory," however, has to specify the quality as well as the quantity of social support in relations to aspects of adjustment. Also, the mechanism or process whereby social support prevents psychological problems needs to be spelled out.

A Clash of Values

The differences in values (social, moral, work, and so on) that exist among many cultures have been used to account for the misunderstandings, distress, and difficulties experienced by cross-cultural sojourners. Differences in values between the person's country of departure and country of arrival are assumed to be directly proportional to the amount of difficulty experienced by that person. Sociologists and psychologists have for many years seen links among deviance, delinquency, mental disorder, and a conflict in cultural values. There is a rich interdisciplinary literature on the definition and consequences of values. The idea is simply that differences in value systems cause related stress.

This approach also suggests that certain values (for example, stoicism, self-help) are more adaptive than others. It may, however, be that such values relate more to the reporting or not reporting of illness and unhappiness than they do to actual capacity to cope with stress. Value systems may be useful and necessary but not sufficient in predicting how much strain travelers feel.

Social Skills Deficit

It has been shown that socially inadequate or unskilled individuals have not mastered the social conventions of their society. They are unaware of or unable to abide by the rules of social behavior that regulate interpersonal conduct in their culture. From this prospective, socially unskilled persons are often like strangers in their own land and new arrivals in an alien culture or subculture are in a position similar to indigenous socially inadequate individuals. There is now considerable empirical evidence to indicate that the elements of social interaction listed earlier vary among cultures, and that many travelers do not easily learn the conventions of another culture. Ironically, individuals in this predicament (such as foreign students, businesspeople, diplomats, and missionaries) often tend to be highly skilled in the customs of their own society and find their sudden inadequacy in the new culture to be quite frustrating. The culture-learning, social skills model has clear implications for the comprehension and management of cross-cultural difficulties. Cross-cultural problems arise because sojourners have trouble negotiating everyday social encounters.

The social skills approach is favored by Furnham and Bochner (1986) not only for its explanatory power but also for its implications for culture learning. First, coping difficulties are attributed to a lack in appropriate skills rather than to some deficiency in the personality or cultural socialization of the sojourner. Second, the notion of "adjustment," with its ethnocentric overtones, is eliminated because sojourners are not expected to adjust themselves to a new culture. Rather, they learn selected aspects for instrumental reasons, which need not become part of their permanent repertoire. Culture learning makes a distinction between skills and values, between performance and compliance. Third, established courses exist for teaching second-culture skills, an extension of the developed and empirically assessed field of intracultural social skills training. Fourth, cultural social skills training is easier, more economic, and more effective than many other remedial approaches based on counseling and psychotherapy. Finally, the training can be used specifically to help people acquire bicultural competence.

CONCLUSION

This chapter has argued for the necessity of distinguishing among various groups of travelers such as tourists, sojourners, and migrants. In doing so, two dimensions, *motives* for travel and the *length* of time spent in the foreign country, have been presented. Although the latter is moderately straightforward and simple to measure, the former is highly complex. Indeed the many agencies who sponsor sojourners are quite unaware of the real aims and motives of those whom they support. Implicit in a great deal of literature on sojourners is that they will suffer from culture shock—a multifaceted negative reaction to changes in language, role, environment, and the like. Two major problems have been highlighted with regard to the concept of culture shock: (1) It is highly vague and imprecise, not specifying *how, why, who,* or *when* different people experience it, and (2) most researchers stress only the negative rather than the positive aspects of adaptation in a new culture. Also, the mental health in the adaptation of foreign students has been discussed, considering demographic, cultural, personality, social, and situational factors. Finally, eight plausible approaches to sojourners have been presented and evaluated. By and large this area of research has been atheoretical, with few major theories guiding research. Nevertheless, the eight perspectives have been borrowed from other areas of study by researchers in studying sojourner adjustment.

Research findings in this relatively new area are often ambiguous and inconsistent. In future studies, individual differences need to be taken more into account. First, researchers need to consider psychological differences in personality (for example, self-concept and beliefs) of sojourners before and after any sojourning experiences. Second, there are demographic differences (for example, age, sex, national group, religion, and schooling) that condition a sojourner's worldview and expectations. Third, actual experiential differences in the new country need to be examined, including the native population's reactions. All of these variables have been examined in the past. The problem has been that, in concentrating on one set of variables, others have been ignored (or worse still, confounded). For a more systematic and comprehensive understanding of the sojourn experience, these and other relevant variables must be investigated simultaneously in a given research.

REFERENCES

Adler, P. (1975). The transitional experience: An alternative view of culture shock. *Journal of Humanistic Psychology, 15,* 13-23.

Ball-Rokeach, S. (1973). From pervasive ambiguity to a definition of the situation. *Sociometry, 36,* 43-51.

Bochner, S. (1973). *The mediating man: Cultural interchange and transnational education.* Honolulu: Culture Learning Institute.

Bochner, S. (1979). Cultural diversity: Implications for modernization and international education. In K. Kumar (Ed.), *Bonds without bondage.* Honolulu: University of Hawaii Press.

Bochner, S. (Ed.). (1982). *Cultures in contact: Studies in cross-cultural interaction.* Oxford: Pergamon.

Bochner, S., Lin, A., & McLeod, B. (1979). Cross-cultural contact and the development of an international perspective. *Journal of Social Psychology, 107,* 29-41.

Bock, P. (Ed.). (1970). *Culture shock: A reader in modern anthropology.* New York: Knopf.

Byrnes, F. (1966). Role shock: An occupational hazard of American technical assistants abroad. *Annals of the American Academy of Political and Social Science, 368,* 95-108.

Church, A. (1982). Sojourner adjustment. *Psychological Bulletin, 91,* 540-572.

Cleveland, H., Mangone, G., & Adams, J. (1963). *The overseas Americans*. New York: McGraw-Hill.

David, K. (1972). Intercultural adjustment and applications of reinforcement theory to problems of "culture shock." *Trends, 4*, 1-64.

Furnham, A., & Bochner, S. (1986). *Culture shock: Psychological reactions to unfamiliar environments*. London: Methuen.

Gudykunst, W. (1983). Toward a typology of stranger-host relationship. *International Journal of Intercultural Relations, 7*, 401-413.

Guthrie, G. (1966). Cultural preparation for the Philippines. In R. Textor (Ed.), *Cultural frontiers of the Peace Corps*. Cambridge: MIT Press.

Guthrie, G. (1975). A behavioral analysis of culture learning. In R. Brislin, S. Bochner, & W. Lonner (Eds.), *Cross-culture perspectives on learning*. New York: Wiley.

Hall, E. (1959). *The silent language*. Garden City, NY: Doubleday.

Hays, R. (1972). Behavioral issues in multinational operations. In R. Hayes (Ed.), *International business*. Englewood Cliffs, NJ: Prentice-Hall.

Klineberg, O., & Hull, W. (1979). *At a foreign university: An international study of adaptation and coping*. New York: Praeger.

Lundstedt, S. (1963). An introduction to some evolving problems in cross-cultural research. *Journal of Social Issues, 19*, 1-9.

May, R. (1970). The nature of anxiety and its relation to fear. In A. Elbing (Ed.), *Behavioral decisions in organizations*. New York: Scott, Foresman.

Nash, D. (1967). The fate of Americans in a Spanish setting: A study of adaptation. *Human Organization, 26*, 3-14.

Oberg, K. (1960). Culture shock: Adjustment to new culture environments. *Practical Anthropology, 7*, 197-182.

Seeman, M. (1959). On the meaning of alienation. *American Sociological Review, 24*, 783-791.

Torbiorn, I. (1982). *Living abroad: Personal adjustment and personnel policy in the overseas setting*. New York: Wiley.

Zuckerman, M. (1978). Sensation seeking and psychopathy. In R. Hare & D. Schalling (Eds.), *Psychopathic behavior*. New York: Wiley.

Facilitating Immigrant Adaptation:
The Role of Communication
Young Yun Kim

. . .

THE PROCESS OF IMMIGRANT ADAPTATION

Through the process of socialization, individuals acquire the collective entity called "culture," enabling them to respond to various environmental messages. Internalized cultural attributes provide individuals in a given society with a common set of beliefs,

Source: Abridged from Chapter 9 in T. L. Albrecht & M. B. Adelman (Eds.), *Communicating Social Support* (pp. 192-211). Newbury Park, CA: Sage, 1987.

values, norms, language, and verbal and nonverbal modes of communication. Although no two individuals in a given culture are identical, the basic commonality of their internalized culture enables them to communicate with one another with fidelity and to develop and maintain a multitude of interpersonal relationships.

Of the many relational ties that individuals maintain at a given time, ties with "significant others" play a particularly crucial role in providing social support. The term *personal network* refers to *an individual's social network that consists of close, supportive, relational ties with significant others.* This network generally includes family, relatives, and close friends who provide the individual with social support in some major ways. As Albrecht and Adelman (1984, p. 10) state, the personal network helps the individual "to reduce uncertainty through the process of social comparison, the exchange of information for problem solving, and to meet needs for affiliation and affection." Social support channeled through the personal network lessens stress by improving the "fit" between the person and the environment (Caplan, 1979; French, Rodgers, & Cobb, 1974).

The majority of new immigrants find themselves without an adequate support network, particularly during the initial stage of adaptation when they are confronted with the highly uncertain and stressful conditions of the host environment (Schuetz, 1944/1963; Zwingmann & Pfister-Ammende, 1973). Uprooted from their supportive ties in the home country, and accustomed to seeing and doing things in a manner different from that of the natives, many immigrants meet the challenges of the new environment almost single-handedly. Even if some members of the original personal network from the home country (such as family members) are still with them, the immigrants are faced with having to develop a new set of significant relationships with native members of the host environment.

Host Communication Competence and Interpersonal Relationships

One of the most critical factors that promote or deter the immigrants' development of interpersonal relationships with the natives is host communication competence. Most immigrants "know" very well their inadequacies in communicating with the natives and their lack of ability to express, to be understood, and to develop meaningful interpersonal relationships with the natives. *Host communication competence, then, refers to an immigrant's overall capability to decode and encode messages effectively in interacting with the host environment.* It is the primary vehicle through which the immigrant is able to understand and respond adequately to various challenges of the host environment. This capability enables the immigrant to transform mental and behavioral resources into functional ways of dealing with inputs from the environment (Ruesch, 1951/1968).[1] As the immigrant becomes increasingly proficient in the host communication system, the effectiveness in managing his or her various life activities correspondingly increases.

This theoretical relationship also operates in the reverse direction, that is, the process of developing host communication competence is enhanced by participating in interpersonal relationships with the natives. One learns to communicate by communicating, so to speak, as one learns to swim by swimming. There is simply no

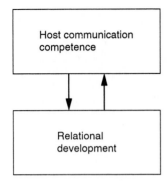

FIGURE 9.1 Mutal facilitation of host communication competence and relational development.

better, more efficient way to acquire host communication competence than by engaging in communication activities with the natives. *Indeed, the development of host communication competence, and the cultivation of interpersonal relationships with the natives, occur side by side in the ongoing process of immigrant adaptation.* This mutual causation between host communication competence and relational development of immigrants should not necessarily be viewed pessimistically as a catch-22. Rather, the two interrelated activities should be viewed as both inseparable and mutually enhancing dimensions of the same process, that is, immigrants' second-cultural adaptation. In doing one, the other follows as well (see Figure 9.1).

This close association between the development of interpersonal ties with the natives and the development of host communication competence has been amply demonstrated in previous studies. For instance, studies of Korean immigrants (Kim, 1977a, 1977b, 1978b, 1979b) and of Indochinese refugees (Kim, 1980b) have suggested that the indicators of psychological adaptation (e.g., alienation, social distance, and attitudes toward the host society) are clearly related to the extent that they have developed interpersonal ties with the natives. The better-adjusted immigrants are more involved with the natives in interpersonal relationships.

Dimensions of Host Communication Competence

The immigrant's host communication competence can be viewed as consisting of three interrelated dimensions: *cognitive, affective,* and *behavioral* (Gudykunst & Kim, 1984; Kim, 1979a, 1982). First, the immigrant must acquire cognitive information about codes and their meanings in the host communication system, particularly its language, verbal and nonverbal modes of expression, and rules of interaction. This knowledge will increase the immigrant's "perspective-taking" abilities (Fogel, 1979) and "coorientation" (Oshagan, 1981; Pearce & Stamm, 1973) with the natives. Second, the immigrant must acquire the motivational and attitudinal orientation that is compatible with that of the host culture. The emotional tendencies, aesthetic sensibilities, humor, and values of the host culture must be shared by the immigrant if he or she is to participate in meaningful relationships with the natives. Third, the immigrant must learn to perform in the various communication situations of the host

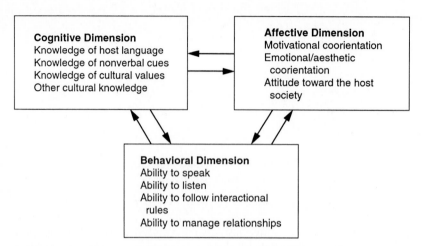

FIGURE 9.2 Interrelated dimensions of host communication competence.

society. This behavioral competence includes the ability (or skill) to speak, listen, read, and write the host language, to express and understand various nonverbal expressions in the manner acceptable to the natives, and to carry out social transactions in accordance with the appropriate interaction norms and rules of the host culture.

These three dimensions are organically interdependent. The way an immigrant communicates with native members of the host culture reflects the simultaneous interplay of his or her cognitive, affective, and behavioral capabilities. Together, the three dimensions of host communication competence contribute to the immigrant's overall effectiveness in dealing with the natives (see Figure 9.2).

Realistically, the average immigrant will not become fully competent in the host communication system to the extent that his or her communication modes are identical with those of the natives. The first-generation children of immigrants, however, are more fully adapted than their parents because they have been exposed to, and have acquired, host communication competence from early childhood.[2] Immigrants, on the other hand, make a workable adaptation as a result of their many trials and errors. They gradually become more capable of approaching the natives to elicit their responses, of responding to their approaches adequately, and of taking on various social roles they must perform. All of these adaptive changes help the immigrants to enhance their chances of achieving personal goals and aspirations.

Host Communication Competence, Relational Development, and Adaptation

Adaptation, then, can be viewed as occurring through a process of individual transformation toward an increasing level of host communication competence and of relational development with natives.[3] Generally, the process of change is sufficiently subtle so that the person may hardly recognize it. Adaptive changes in immigrants occur even when they

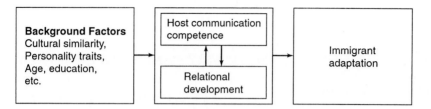

FIGURE 9.3 Background factors facilitating adaptation.

actively resist. Adherence to an ideology, such as cultural separatism or pluralism, that emphasizes deliberate resistance against losing the original cultural identity, may minimize adaptive changes. Nevertheless, existing evidence clearly demonstrates that immigrants do transform themselves in the direction of increased similarity to host cultural characteristics and of greater integration into the host social structure (Alba, 1976; Crispino, 1977).

Thus adaptation occurs *naturally* regardless of the intentions of immigrants as long as they are functionally dependent on, and interacting with, the host sociocultural system for survival and self-fulfillment. It is similar to the case of family members who, as a result of an extensive exposure to each other and of sharing common life experiences, manifest many similar attributes with or without their conscious awareness.

Not all immigrants, of course, begin the process of adaptation with the same degree of preparedness and receptivity. Previous studies have identified a number of background characteristics that tend to prepare the immigrants with greater adaptive potential (Kim, 1977a, 1980b; Snyder, 1976). These background factors include the similarity between the original culture and the host culture, a higher educational level, and younger age at the time of immigration. Also, such personal qualities as tolerance for ambiguity and risk taking (Fiske & Maddi, 1961), internal locus of control (Johnson & Sarason, 1978), gregariousness (Bradburn, 1969), and hardy or resilient personality (Quisumbing, 1982) have been found to facilitate an immigrant's cross-cultural adaptation (see Figure 9.3).

As such, individual immigrants begin the process of adapting at different starting points and with varying personal dispositions. All immigrants, however, face a common challenge—a challenge to maximize their life chances in the new environment by increasing their communication effectiveness and developing supportive ties with natives.

ETHNIC SUPPORT SYSTEMS

How, then, does the ethnic social support system influence the immigrant's overall adaptation process? Commonly, an immigrant today has access not only to native members of the host society but also to individuals of their national or ethnic origin. In the United States and other countries that have received a large number of immigrants, many immigrant communities provide some form of "mutual aid" or "self-help" activities. These community organizations render valuable services to those immigrants in need of material, informational, emotional, and other forms of social support (see DeCocq, 1976; University of Toronto, 1980; Weber & Cohen, 1982). The Vietnamese Association of Illinois, for example, assists with many of its members' needs by providing translation services, housing information, transportation, and counseling. Such community services are of particular importance to new arrivals who are lacking in host communication competence and other resources required for self-reliance. They also organize religious services and holiday festivities to promote a sense of ethnic identity and pride among its members. Frequently informal friendship networks also develop as immigrants continue participating in various organized ethnic community activities.

Ethnic Community and Initial Adaptation

In fact, many immigrants do have some ethnic ties (other than ties with members of their household) at arrival in the host society. In their initial migration into the host society, most immigrants find a place in which they have at least some access to an ethnic support system through family, relatives, friends, or visible community organizations. Snyder (1976) reported that a sizable personal network at arrival existed for most immigrants in five ethnic neighborhoods (blacks, Chicanos, whites, Arabs, and American Indians) in Los Angeles. (See also Smith, 1976, for a similar observation.)

It appears, then, that *new immigrants are naturally inclined to seek support among fellow immigrants within their ethnic community.* While interacting with natives involves a great deal of unfamiliarity and stress, ethnic relations are based on preacquired repertoires and, thus, are least stressful. The extensive reliance on other immigrants within the ethnic community for support has been frequently observed in previous studies. Valdez (1979), in a study of the relational patterns of Puerto Ricans in an industrialized city, reported the immigrants' high integration into ethnically homogeneous networks of family, friends, and coworkers. Le (1979, in Deusen, 1982, p. 238) also reported that the personal networks of Vietnamese refugees in Los Angeles consisted predominantly of other Vietnamese, and that they serve as a primary source of help for mental health problems. (See also Y. Kim, 1977b, 1978a, 1978b; King, 1984; Krause, 1978; Silverman, 1979; Yum, 1983, for similar findings.)

The natural inclination for immigrants to affiliate with fellow immigrants in their ethnic community is consistent with the view of Albrecht and Adelman (1984) on support-seeking behavior. Based on the uncertainty reduction theory, they hypothesized that individuals are likely to seek support from those with whom they perceive less relational uncertainty, and that those who share a stressful context will be perceived as more helpful than those who do not share the context (p. 20). Rather than taking the risk of performing inadequately in the unfamiliar modes of the host communication system, immigrants tend to prefer to seek social support from fellow immigrants.

The reliance of immigrants on fellow immigrants for social support has also been observed to be influenced by at least two additional factors: the immigrant's marital status and the "institutional completeness" of the ethnic community. Alba and Chamlin (1983) argued that those who are "in-married," that is, married to members of the same ethnic group, are likely to be more involved with other ethnic individuals for social support. A similar finding was reported by J. Kim (1980) in his study of Korean immigrants in the Chicago area. Institutional completeness of an ethnic community refers to the degree that the community is established in religious, media, welfare, business, political, and other organizations (Breton, 1964). Inglis and Gudykunst (1982) replicated Y. Kim's (1976) study of Korean immigrants in the Chicago area and among Korean immigrants in Hartford, Connecticut, and reported a significant difference between the two groups in the overall size of ethnic relational ties. The degree of ethnic involvement of the immigrants in Hartford, an area with less institutional completeness, was found significantly lower than that of the immigrants in Chicago, an area with greater institutional completeness.

Ethnic Community and Long-Term Adaptation

Although an ethnic support network clearly plays a vital role in providing social support to immigrants, it is generally regarded as either insignificant or dysfunctional to adaptation in the long run. Broom and Kitsuse (1955, p. 45) argue, "A large part of the acculturation experience of the members of an ethnic group may be circumscribed by the ethnic community." Similarly, Shibutani and Kwan (1965, p. 982) state: "To the extent that . . . a minority group participates in different sets of communication channels, they develop different perspectives and have difficulty in understanding each other."

Supporting this view, Y. Kim's (1980) study found a negative influence of ethnic communication on both early and later stages of the cultural adaptation of Korean immigrants. The variance in the immigrants' acculturation level explained by their participation in relationships with natives was two times the variance explained by the ethnic communication. Also, no statistically significant association was observed in Y. Kim's (1976) study of Korean immigrants between the degree of ethnic involvement and indices of adaptation to the American cultural environment. This and other empirical evidence suggests that, *in the long run, an immigrant's participation in ethnic communication activities does not substantially facilitate, and in some cases may even hinder, the adaptation process.* This tentative generalization, of course, recognizes that ethnic ties with highly adapted individuals can be greatly beneficial to the immigrant's learning not only during the initial phase, but throughout the adaptation process.

ADAPTIVE CHANGES IN PERSONAL NETWORKS

In spite of the supportive role played by ethnic ties at the beginning, it is ultimately from the native members that much of immigrants' adaptive capacities are acquired. The natives, knowingly or unknowingly, present feedback to immigrants as to whether they are in tune with the host communication modes. Often such feedback is given in the form of subtle nonverbal expressions of understanding or puzzlement, comfort or discomfort, and approval or disapproval. Based on such feedback, immigrants examine their own cognitive, affective, and behavioral tendencies and modify what they can.

As immigrants become increasingly proficient in communicating with the natives, they are better able to cultivate and maintain interpersonal relationships with them. In time, they incorporate natives into their personal network of supportive relationships in more meaningful ways. This means that, by examining their personal network patterns, we can understand the degree of their host communication competence. Indeed, the relational ties that an immigrant has developed at a given time is one of the most frequently used indicators of his or her overall adaptation (see Y. Kim, 1976, 1979a; Nagata, 1969; Yum, 1983).

Of many possible aspects of the nature of the immigrant's personal network, three are suggested here as reflecting, as well as facilitating, their host communication competence and adapatation most characteristically. The three aspects are network heterogeneity, strength of ties with natives, and the centrality of natives in the immigrant's network. (A fuller discussion of these network characteristics is presented in Y. Kim, 1986b.)

Heterogeneity The network *heterogeneity* generally refers to *the degree that nonethnic members of the host society are included in an immigrant's personal network.* It has been observed by identifying the size and the ratio of relational ties with outgroup members to the total number of ties in the immigrant's personal network. For example, Yum (1982), in her study of Korean immigrants in Hawaii, measured network heterogeneity by the degree of nonethnic members included in the personal network. In this study, "communication diversity," or the level of integration of Americans in the immigrants' information sources, was significantly influential in their acquiring the information necessary for their functioning in the United States. Y. Kim (1977b, 1978a, 1978b, 1980b) also reported an increasing number of natives in the interpersonal networks of Korean and Indochinese immigrants during the initial years.

Findings such as these are reinforced by the positive association between a greater network heterogeneity and the "cosmopolitan" (as opposed to local or provincial) psychological orientation proposed in nonimmigrant settings (Craven & Wellman, 1973; Fischer, 1982; Rogers & Kincaid, 1982). A higher-level inclusion of nonethnic individuals in an immigrant's personal network indicates a higher-level host communication competence. Conversely, someone whose personal network consists primarily of fellow ethnic individuals is likely to be less competent in communicating with the natives and less adapted to the host environment. Further, composition of a primarily ethnic personal network is indicative of the lack of facilitative influence on the immigrant's future interaction and relationship development with natives.

Tie Strength Once the heterogeneity of the personal network is determined, we may proceed to examine the content of each relational tie. One relational content relevant to the immigrant's host communication competence is "tie strength" (Granovetter, 1973; Marsden & Campbell, 1983). The term refers to *the level of "bondedness" or intimacy between individuals in a relationship.* It implies an overall level of interdependency between the involved persons, that is, the relative degree of difficulty to break the relationship. Altman and Taylor (1973) described such an attribute as indicating a high degree of "social penetration" in the relationship development. For the present analysis, individuals in a stronger relational tie are considered to exchange a greater amount of social support than those in a weaker relational tie.

Strength of ties with nonethnic persons can be assessed in a number of ways. One may focus on the amount (or rate) of interaction between the immigrant and each member of the personal network for a given period of time (e.g., daily, weekly, monthly). This is based on the assumption that, on the whole, intimacy is reflected in the amount of communication. Tie strength can also be assessed by the intensity of positive or favorable feelings that the individual attributes to a given relationship. Often this is done by asking the respondent to assess the strength of relational ties in a rank order, or in terms of a number of "intimacy zones" such as "acquaintances," "casual friends," and "intimate friends" (Alba, 1978; Y. Kim, 1976, 1978a, 1980b). If we were to focus only on the personal network of intimate friends, we could further differentiate the degree of tie strengths by assessing both the overall volume of communication and the ratings of perceived intimacy.

Research findings have shown the close association between the strength of ties with natives and the degree of an immigrant's host communication competence. Y. Kim (1977a, 1978a, 1980), for example, has consistently found that, as the immigrant becomes better adapted to the host environment, his or her interpersonal ties with natives tend to become more intimate. An increase in the immigrant's intimate American friends was significantly associated with indicators of English proficiency as well as the level of "cognitive complexity" (i.e., understanding of the American cultural system).

Centrality Another content attribute of relevance to immigrant adaptation is the degree of the "centrality" of natives in the immigrant's personal network. In network terms, *centrality refers to the degree that a person has a short distance to others in a personal network.* It represents the person's accessibility to other persons in the network, and thus the degree of information and influence within the network (Mariolis, 1979; Yum, 1984). This means that the higher a native's centrality in an immigrant's personal network, the higher the person's significance to the immigrant.

Even though few immigrant studies have used this centrality concept, *it is considered a potentially useful indicator of the extent that natives are integrated into the immigrant's personal support system.* As the centrality of ties with natives approaches or exceeds that of fellow ethnic ties in an immigrant's personal network, the immigrant's host communication competence and adaptation is considered to have increased as well. Together with the two other network characteristics (network heterogeneity and the strength of native ties), the centrality of native ties appears to serve as a useful framework in which an immigrant's host communication competence and adaptation can be understood. . . .

NOTES

1   Communication competence has been a topic of much research and academic debate in recent years. Earlier presentation of the concept was made by Ruesch in conceptualizing mental health/illness. More recently, Geyer (1980) integrated various social psychological theories of alienation using a general systems approach, and presented a comprehensive conceptualization of alienation. Geyer viewed alienation as essentially a result of the lack of competence in an individual's information-processing capacities. In the field of communication, Spitzberg and Cupach (1984) present a comprehensive review of diverse approaches to communication competence, along with their own model of interpersonal competence. See also Parks (1985) and Bostrom (1984) for articles that conceptualize and describe communication competence in a number of social seetings.

2 Many studies have examined the adaptation patterns across generations of immigrants. See, for example, Allen and Lambert (1972), Alba (1976), Chan (1978), and Conner (1977).

3 The term *adaptation* has been used (see Berry, 1980; Brody, 1970) along with other similar terms such as *acculturation* (see Broom & Kitsuse, 1955; Kim, 1982; Nagata, 1969; Padilla, 1980), *adjustment* (see Coelho, 1958; Deutsch & Wong, 1963), and *assimilation* (see Crispino, 1977; Decroos, 1979; Gordon, 1964). While these terms vary somewhat in their respective emphasis and focus of analysis, they all refer to the common process of change in immigrants in relation to the host environment. In this chapter, the term *adaptation* is used in the broadest sense of its meaning, encompassing the meanings of other terms.

REFERENCES

Alba, R. D. (1976). Social assimilation among American Catholic national religion groups. *American Sociological Review, 41,* 1030–1046.

Alba, R. D. (1978). Ethnic networks and tolerant attitudes. *Public Opinion Quarterly, 42,* 1–16.

Alba, R. D., & Chamlin, M. B. (1983). A preliminary examination of ethnic identification among whites. *American Sociological Review, 48,* 240–247.

Albrecht, T. L., & Adelman, M. B. (1984). Social support and life stress: New directions for communication research. *Human Communication Research, 11,* 3–32.

Allen, C., & Lambert, W. E. (1972). Ethnic identification and personality adjustment of Canadian adolescents of mixed English-French parentage. In J. W. Berry & G. J. S. Wilde (Eds.), *Social psychology: The Canadian context* (pp. 173–192). Toronto: McClelland & Stewart.

Altman, I., & Taylor, D. A. (1973). *Social penetration: The development of interpersonal relationships.* New York: Holt, Rinehart & Winston.

Atwater, E. (1983). *Psychology of adjustment: Personal growth in a changing world.* Englewood Cliffs, NJ: Prentice-Hall.

Bennet, J. W. (1976). *The ecological transition: Cultural anthropology and human adaptation.* New York: Pergamon.

Berry, J. W. (1980). Acculturation as varieties of adaptation. In A. M. Padilla (Ed.), *Acculturation: Theory, models and some new findings* (pp. 9–25). Washington, DC: Westview.

Berry, J. W., & Kalin, R. (1979). Reciprocity of inter-ethnic attitudes in a multi-cultural society. *International Journal of Intercultural Relations, 3,* 99–112.

Bostrom, R. N. (Ed.). (1984). *Competence in communication: A multidisciplinary approach.* Newbury Park, CA: Sage.

Bradburn, N. (1969). *The structure of psychological wellbeing.* Chicago: Aldine.

Breton, R. (1964). Institutional completeness of ethnic communities and the personal relations of immigrants. *American Journal of Sociology, 70,* 193–205.

Brody, E. B. (Ed.). (1970). *Behavior in new environments: Adaptation of migrant populations.* Newbury Park, CA: Sage.

Broom, L., & Kitsuse, J. (1955). The validation of acculturation. *American Anthropologist, 57,* 44–48.

Caplan, G. (1964). *Principles of preventive psychiatry.* New York: Basic Books.

Chan, Y. N. L. (1978). *Educational needs in intergenerational conflict: A study of immigrant families in N.Y. Chinatown.* Unpublished doctoral dissertation, Cornell University.

Coelho, G. V. (1958). *Changing images of America: A study of Indian students' perceptions.* New York: Free Press.

Conner, J. W. (1977). *Tradition and change in three generations of Japanese-Americans.* Chicago: Nelson-Hall.

Coombs, G. (1978–1979). Opportunities, information networks and the migration-distance relationships. *Social Networks, 1,* 257–276.

Craven, P., & Wellman, B. (1973). The network city. *Sociological Inquiry, 43,* 57–88.

Crispino, J. A. (1977). *The assimilation of ethnic groups: The Italian case.* Unpublished doctoral dissertation, Columbia University.

DeCocq, G. A. (1976). European and North American self-help movements: Some contrasts. In A. H. Katz & E. I. Bender (Eds.), *The strength in us: Self-help groups in the modern world* (pp. 202–208). New York: New Viewpoint.

Decroos, J. F. (1979). *The long journey: Assimilation and ethnicity maintenance among urban Basques in northern California.* Unpublished doctoral dissertation, University of Oregon.

Deusen, J. M. V. (1982). Health/mental health studies of Indochinese refugees. *Medical Antropology, 6,* 231–252.

Deutsch, S. E., & Wong, G. Y. M. (1963). Some factors in the adjustment of foreign nationals in the United States. *Journal of Social Issues, 19,* 115–122.

Donahue, T. S. (1982). Toward a broadened context for modern bilingual education. *Journal of Multicultural Development, 3,* 77–87.

Fischer, C. S. (1982). *To dwell among friends: Personal networks in town and city.* Chicago: University of Chicago Press.

Fiske, D., & Maddi, S. (Eds.). (1961). *Functions of varied experience.* Homewood, IL: Dorsey.

Fogel, D. (1979, November). *Human development and communication competencies.* Paper presented at the annual meeting of the Speech Communication Association, San Antonio, TX.

French, J. R. P., Jr., Rodgers, W., & Cobb, S. (1974). Adjustment as person-environment fit. In G. V. Coelho, D. A. Hamburg, & J. E. Adams (Eds.), *Coping and adaptation* (pp. 316–333). New York: Basic Books.

Geyer, R. F. (1980). *Alienation theories: A general systems approach.* New York: Pergamon.

Gordon, M. (1964). *Assimilation in American life.* New York: Oxford University Press.

Granovetter, M. S. (1973). The strength of weak ties. *American Journal of Sociology, 78,* 1360–1380.

Herberg, D. C. (1980). Multicultural workers' network: Taking ethno-culture seriously. In *Symposium on helping networks and the welfare state: Vol. 11. Community and state.* Toronto, Canada: University of Toronto.

Inglis, M., & Gudykunst, W. B. (1982). Institutional completeness and communication acculturation: A comparison of Korean immigrants in Chicago and Hartford. *International Journal of Intercultural Relations*, 6, 251–272.

Johnson, J. H., & Sarason, I. G. (1978). Life stress, depression and anxiety: Internal-external control as moderator variable. *Journal of Psychosomatic Research*, 22, 205–208.

Keefe, S. E., Padilla, A. M., & Carlos, M. L. (1978). *Emotional support systems in two cultures: A comparison of Mexican Americans and Anglo Americans*. Santa Barbara: University of California, Spanish Speaking Mental Health Research Center.

Kim, J. (1980). Explaining acculturation in a communication framework: An empirical test. *Communication Monographs*, 47, 155–179.

Kim, Y. Y. (1976). *Communication patterns of immigrants in the process of acculturation: A survey among the Korean population in Chicago*. Unpublished doctoral dissertation, Northwestern University, Evanston, IL.

Kim, Y. Y. (1977a). Communication patterns of foreign immigrants in the process of acculturation. *Human Communication Research*, 4, 66–77.

Kim, Y. Y. (1977b). Inter-ethnic and intra-ethnic communication. In N. Jain (Ed.), *International and intercultural communication annual* (Vol. 4). Falls Church, VA: Speech Communication Association.

Kim, Y. Y. (1978a). *Communication patterns of Mexican-Americans in the Chicago area*. Paper presented at the meeting of the Third World Conference, Chicago.

Kim, Y. Y. (1978b, Summer). A communication approach to the acculturation process: A study of Korean immigrants in Chicago. *International Journal of Intercultural Relations*, pp. 197–224.

Kim, Y. Y. (1979a). Toward an interactive theory of communication-acculturation. In D. Nimmo (Ed.), *Communication yearbook 3* (pp. 435–453). New Brunswick, NY: Transaction Books.

Kim, Y. Y. (1979b, November). *Dynamics of intrapersonal and interpersonal communication: A study of Indochinese refugees in the initial phase of acculturation*. Paper presented at the meeting of the Speech Communication Association, San Antonio, TX.

Kim, Y. Y. (1980). *Research project report on Indochinese refugees in the state of Illinois: Vol. IV. Psychological, social, and cultural adjustment of Indochinese refugees*. Chicago: Travelers Aid Society of Metropolitan Chicago.

Kim, Y. Y. (1982). Communication and acculturation. In L. A. Samovar & R. E. Porter (Eds.), *Intercultural communication: A reader* (pp. 359–372). Belmont, CA: Wadsworth.

Kim, Y. Y. (1986a). Communication, information, and adaptation. In B. D. Ruben (Ed.), *Information and behavior*, 1. New Brunswick, NJ: Transaction Books.

Kim, Y. Y. (1986b). Understanding the social context of intergroup communication: A personal network approach. In W. B. Gudykunst (Ed.), *Intergroup communication*. London: Edward Arnold.

King, S. S. (1984). *Natural helping networks among ethnic groups in Hawaii*. Washington, DC: National Institute of Mental Health.

Krause, C. A. (1978). Urbanization without breakdown: Italian, Jewish, and Slavic immigrant women in Pittsburgh, 1900–1945. *Journal of Urban History*, 4, 291–306.

Lum, J. (1982). Marginality and multiculturalism. In L. Samovar & R. Poll (Eds.), *Intercultural communication: A reader*. Belmont, CA: Wadsworth.

Marsden, P. V., & Campbell, K. E. (1983, September). *Measuring tie strength*. Paper presented at the annual meeting of the American Sociological Association, Detroit, MI.

Moos, R. H. (Ed.). (1976). *Human adaptation: Coping with life crises*. Lexington, MA: D.C. Heath.

Nagata, G. (1979). *A statistical approach to the study of acculturation of an ethnic group based on communication oriented variables: The case of Japanese Americans in Chicago.* Unpublished doctoral dissertation, University of Illinois, Urbana.

Oshagan, E. P. (1981). *Coorientation as a function of communication: An intercultural test.* Unpublished doctoral dissertation, University of Wisconsin-Madison.

Padilla, A. M. (Ed.). (1980). *Acculturation: Theory, models and some new findings.* Washington, DC: Westview.

Parks, M. R. (1985). Interpersonal communication and the quest for personal competence. In M. L. Knapp & G. R. Miller (Eds.), *Handbook of interpersonal communication* (pp. 171-204). Newbury Park, CA: Sage.

Pearce, W. B., & Stamm, K. (1973). Coorientational states and interpersonal communication. In P. Clark (Ed.), *New models for communication research* (pp. 177-203). Newbury Park, CA: Sage.

Quisumbing, M. (1982). *Life events, social support and personality: Their impact upon Filipino psychological adjustment.* Unpublished doctoral dissertation, University of Chicago, Chicago, IL.

Rogers, E. M., & Kincaid, D. L. (1981). *Communication networks: Toward a new paradigm for research.* New York: Free Press.

Ruesch, J. (1968). Values, communication, and culture: An introduction. In J. Ruesch & G. Bateson (Eds.), *Communication: The social matrix of psychiatry* (pp. 3-20). New York: W. W. Norton.

Schuetz, A. (1944/1963). The stranger. *American Journal of Sociology, 49.* 499-507. Reprinted in M. Stein & A. Vidich (Eds.), *Identity and anxiety.* Glencoe, IL: Free Press.

Shibutani, T., & Kwan, M. (1965). *Ethnic stratification.* New York: Macmillan.

Silverman, M. L. (1979, October). *Vietnamese in Denver: Cultural conflicts in health care.* Paper presented at the Conference on Indochinese Refugees, George Mason University, Fairfax, VA.

Smith, M. E. (1976). Networks and migration resettlement: Cherchez la femme. *Anthropology Quarterly, 49,* 20-27.

Snyder, P. A. (1976). Neighborhood gatekeepers in the process of urban adaptation: Cross-ethnic commonalities. *Urban Anthropology, 5,* 35-52.

Spitzberg, B. H., & Cupach, W. R. (1984). *Interpersonal communication competence.* Newbury Park, CA: Sage.

University of Toronto. (1980, May). *Symposium of helping networks and the welfare state.* Toronto, Canada: University of Toronto.

Valdez, A. (1979). *The social and occupational integration among Mexican and Puerto Rican ethnics in an urban industrial society.* Unpublished doctoral dissertation, University of California, Los Angeles.

Weber, G. H., & Cohen, L. M. (Eds.). (1982). *Beliefs and self-help: Cross-cultural perspectives and approaches.* New York: Human Sciences Press.

Yum, J. O. (1982). Communication patterns and information acquisition among Korean immigrants in Hawaii. *Human Communication Research, 8,* 154-169.

Yum, J. O. (1983). Social network patterns of five ethnic groups in Hawaii. In R. Bostrom (Ed.), *Communication yearbook 7* (pp. 574-591). Newbury Park, CA: Sage.

Yum, J. O. (1984). Network analysis. In W. B. Gudykunst & Y. Y. Kim (Eds.), *Methods for intercultural communication* (pp. 95-116). Newbury Park, CA: Sage.

Zwingmann, C., & Pfister-Ammende, M. (1973). *Uprooting and after.* New York: Springer-Verlag.

Applying a Theory of Intercultural Adaptation

William B. Gudykunst and Sandra Sudweeks

Gudykunst and Hammer's (1988) theory of intercultural adaptation has several important implications regarding how people adapt to living in another culture and
communicate effectively with people from other cultures. Our purpose in this paper is
to summarize some of the implications and, at the same time, illustrate how theories
can be applied to our everyday interactions.

Gudykunst and Hammer's major contention is that if we want to adapt successfully to living in another culture, we must be able to reduce uncertainty about host
nationals' behavior and reduce our anxiety about interacting with host nationals (this
has been empirically tested and supported; Gao & Gudykunst, 1990). Stated differently, we must be able to understand the people of the other culture (uncertainty
reduction) and be able to manage our emotional reaction to the cultural differences
that we encounter (anxiety reduction) if we are going to adapt to living in another
culture.

Many factors contribute to the reduction of uncertainty and anxiety when we
live in other cultures. We have control over several of the variables in the theory. By
"control" we mean that we have the ability to consciously choose how we want to
behave regarding these variables. The variables we can control include: (1) having the
ability to speak the language used in the host culture; (2) having knowledge of the
host culture (e.g., its communication rules, norms, etc.); (3) having open, flexible,
and accurate stereotypes; (4) having positive attitudes toward the other culture and its
people; (5) having intimate and rewarding contact with members of the other culture;
(6) perceiving similarities between our culture and the host culture; (7) sharing
communication networks with members of the host culture; and (8) having a positive
cultural identity of our own. Since we have control over these factors (i.e., we can
modify or change them), the theory can be used as a guide to help us adapt to living in
a new culture and communicate more effectively with members of other cultures. In
the remainder of this chapter, we "translate" the theory into six specific practical
suggestions for adapting to new cultural environments. The suggestions are divided
into two categories: understanding people in the host culture (reducing our uncertainty) and managing our emotional reactions (reducing our anxiety).

UNDERSTANDING PEOPLE IN THE HOST CULTURE

Our ability to understand the people in the other culture is influenced by our
knowledge of the culture and its language, our expectations about living in the other
culture (including our stereotypes of and attitudes toward people in the other culture),
and our understanding of ourselves as cultural beings (e.g., our own cultural identity).
Three practical suggestions can be generated from the theory regarding how we can
increase our understanding of people in the host culture.

Source: This paper was written for this volume. We want to thank Stella Ting-Toomey, Joyce Baker, Paula
Trubisky, Mark Cole, and David Doyle for helpful comments on an earlier version of the paper.

Describing Others' Behavior Leads to Understanding; Evaluating Others' Behavior Always Leads to Misunderstanding

If we want to adapt and communicate effectively, it is important that we try not to evaluate behavior before we understand it. It is important to remember that the natural human tendency is to evaluate others' behavior. Such evaluation, however, is inevitably based upon our own cultural standards. Using our own cultural standards to evaluate others' behavior usually inhibits our ability to understand them. To understand others, we must first describe what we observe.

Describing behavior refers to an actual report of what was observed with a minimum of distortion and without attributing significance to the behavior. Description includes what we see, hear, feel, touch, and taste. In other words, it is information that comes from our sense organs. "He breathed in my face when we talked" and "She did not look me in the eyes when we talked" are both descriptive statements. Neither attaches meaning to the behavior, both only describe the behavior observed.

An interpretation is the meaning or social significance attached to the behavior. It involves what we think about what we observed. There are multiple interpretations for any one description. To illustrate, consider the second description: "She did not look me in the eyes when we talked." What are the possible interpretations of this behavior? To develop a list of possible interpretations we must be "mindful," or deliberate, about our thinking processes. If we respond in a mindless, or automatic, fashion we will think only about the interpretations used in our own subculture. Not looking someone in the eye in the white, middle-class subculture of the United States, for example, usually is interpreted as the person is not telling the truth. Other possible interpretations in this subculture include, but are not limited to, she is shy, she is hiding something, and she is being disrespectful. If, however, the person who did not look us in the eye is from another culture/subculture, we should also consider the interpretation that she is being respectful.

After we have developed a list of possible interpretations, we must determine the most probable interpretation of the other person's behavior. If we know the other person, we can rely on individual information about him or her to make an "educated guess." If we do not know the other person, we must rely on the cultural and/or group-based information we have to make the interpretation.

Once we have determined the most probable interpretation, we can then evaluate the behavior. Obviously, in the preceeding example we would evaluate the interpretations "she is lying" or "she is showing respect" much differently.

To summarize, there are some general "steps" we can follow to try to better understand how people who are different from us conduct themselves and to improve our interpretation of our interactions with them. If we apply these steps, our knowledge of people who are different should increase. After we have an experience with a person who is different:

1. We must stop and observe what we have experienced. We must *describe* what we saw happening. Description is a report of what we observed with the minimum of distortion and without attributing social significance, or meaning.

2. We must then look for *alternative interpretations* (i.e., the social significance or

meaning) of the behavior we described. This requires that we try to figure out how the other person perceived what occurred, what it meant to him or her, and what he or she might have determined was appropriate behavior in that situation. If we have some knowledge of the other person and his or her group, we usually can make a reasonable guess as to how she or he interpreted what was going on and what would be appropriate behavior.

3. If we are unable to guess how the other person is interpreting what happened with a high degree of confidence, we must seek additional information (e.g., go to the library and find information on the other group; ask the other person directly; ask someone from his or her cultural group; ask someone from our own group who has had extensive experience with people from the other group, and so on). These strategies will be discussed in detail later in this chapter.

4. After we have obtained additional information, we must draw a conclusion as to how we think the other person interpreted what happened. Given our understanding of what happened, we can then *evaluate* the interaction. Do we like it or dislike it, given our understanding of how the other person interpreted it and behaved in response to that interpretation?

5. Lastly, we must incorporate our conclusions into our understanding of the other person or cultural group. It is important to remember, however, that our conclusions and understanding may be inaccurate, or may not always generalize to all people in the other group, owing to personality and situational differences.

Before proceeding, it is necessary to point out that describing behavior requires that we become mindful of our communication. We communicate normally at relatively low levels of awareness. That is, we do not think about how we are interpreting incoming messages; rather, we just interpret them and base our reaction on this interpretation. To figure out how people in the host culture may be interpreting what is going on, we must consciously think about what is happening (i.e., be mindful). Mindfulness requires paying attention: being deliberate about our thinking processes and making the unconscious aspects of the communication process conscious (Langer, 1989).

Ellen Langer (1989) believes that focusing on the process (how we do something) forces us to be mindful of our behavior and pay attention to the situations in which we find ourselves (see her article in Chapter 2 of this reader). It is only when we are mindful of our process of communication that we can determine how our interpretations of messages differ from others' interpretations of those messages.

Knowledge of the Culture and Its Language Are Necessary to Understand the Behavior of People in Another Culture

There are several ways we can gain knowledge about the other culture. One of the best ways to learn about people in other cultures is to study their language. Without understanding some of the host language, it is not possible to understand their behavior. We do not mean to say that it is necessary to speak the language fluently, but that the more language we understand, the more culture we can understand. Also, making an effort to speak the language usually is taken as a positive sign by the host nationals, and our attempts to use the language will increase their desire to get to know us as individuals.

Charles Berger (1979) isolated three general types of strategies we can use to gather information about people in other cultures and reduce our uncertainty about them and the way they will interact with us: passive, active, and interactive strategies. Passive strategies involve our taking the role of "unobtrusive observers" (i.e., we do not intervene in the situation we are observing). To illustrate this process, assume that we want to find out about Yoko, a Japanese we have just met.

Obviously, the type of situation in which we observe Yoko influences the amount of information we gain about her. If we observe Yoko in a situation where she is not interacting with others, we will not gain much information about her. Situations in which she is interacting with several people at once, in contrast, allow us to make comparisons of how Yoko interacts with different people.

If we know any of the people with whom Yoko is interacting, we can compare how Yoko interacts with them and how she might interact with us. It also should be noted that if other Japanese are present in the situation, we can compare Yoko's behavior with the Japanese to try to determine how she is similar to and different from other Japanese.

There is one more aspect of the situation that will influence the amount of information we can obtain by observing Yoko's behavior. In Japan, if the situation is a formal one, her behavior is likely to be a function of the role she is filling in the situation, so we will not learn much about Yoko as an individual. Situations where behavior is not guided by roles or social protocol, on the other hand, will provide useful information about Yoko's behavior.

The preceding examples all involve our taking the role of an observer. These are passive strategies of information seeking. The active strategies for reducing uncertainty require us to do something to acquire information about Yoko. One thing we could do to get information about Yoko is to ask questions of someone who knows her. When we ask others about someone we need to keep in mind that the information we receive may not be accurate. The other person may not really know Yoko well or may intentionally give us incomplete or inaccurate information.

We can also gather information about people from other groups by asking individuals from our own cultural group who have had contact with those groups or by gathering information from the library. In this example, we could gather information on Japan and Japanese people by questioning someone we know who has lived in Japan, by reading a book on Japanese culture, or by completing a Japanese cultural assimilator (e.g. a programmed learning process that teaches about Japanese culture). This would give us information about Yoko's cultural background that would allow us to make cultural level predictions about her behavior. Again, we must keep in mind that our informant may or may not have reliable information about Japanese people, and that Yoko may not be a "typical" Japanese.

Neither the passive nor the active strategies require that we actually interact with the person about whom we are trying to gather information. When we speak directly with that person, in contrast, we can use the interactive strategies of verbal interrogation (question asking) and self-disclosure to seek information.

One obvious way we can gather information about others is to ask them questions. There are limitations to this strategy that must be kept in mind. First, we can ask only so many questions. We are not sure of what the number is, but we always know when we have asked too many. Second, our questions must be appropriate to the nature of the interaction we are having and the relationship we have with the other person. When we are interacting with someone who is similar to us, we both have some sense of what is appropriate according to our common cultural understanding.

When we are communicating with people from other cultures the same limitations are present, but there may be other limitations of which we are unaware. The number and type of questions that people from other cultures consider acceptable may not be the same. People from other cultures also may not be able to answer our questions, especially if our questions deal with why they behave the way they do (the ultimate answer to "why" questions is "because—that's the way we do it here!"). When interacting with people from other cultures there is the additional problem of our not wanting to appear "stupid" or rude. We, therefore, often avoid asking questions of people from other cultures.

If we can overcome our fear of looking stupid, asking questions is an excellent way to gather information about people from other cultures. Generally speaking, people from other cultures will probably respond in a positive way as long as they perceive that our intent is to learn about them personally or about their group and *not* to judge them.

The other way we can gather information about another person when interacting with her or him is through self-disclosure—telling the other person unknown information about ourselves. Self-disclosure works as an information gathering strategy because of the reciprocity norm (Gouldner, 1960). Essentially, the reciprocity norm states that if I do something for you, you will reciprocate and do something for me. The reciprocity norm appears to be a cultural universal; it exists in all cultures.

In conversations between people who are not close (i.e., people we meet for the first time or acquaintances), we tend to reciprocate and tell each other the same information about ourselves that the other person tells us. If I disclose my opinion on a topic when we are talking, you will probably tell me your opinion on the same topic. There will, however, be some differences in how we communicate with people from other cultures and in how we communicate with people from our own culture. The topics that are appropriate to be discussed, for example, vary from culture to culture. If we self-disclose on a topic with a person from another culture and she or he does not reciprocate, there is a good chance we have found an inappropriate topic of conversation between individuals who are not close in that person's group.

When we are observing host nationals we need to engage in "active seeing." "Active seeing requires effort and reflection. It means absorbing your surroundings rather than casually encountering them" (Lauer & Lauer, 1988, p. 197). Lauer and

Lauer believe that active seeing can turn a potentially negative experience into a "watershed" (i.e., a crucial change point in life).

Our Expectations Influence Our Ability to Understand People of Other Cultures

The attitudes we have about other cultures in general and the culture in which we are going to live in particular create expectations about our experiences in the other culture. The stereotypes we have about the people also affect our expectations. If we are open to other cultures, have a positive attitude toward the specific culture, and have positive stereotypes about the people of the culture, we will probably have positive expectations about our experiences. If we have a negative attitude toward the other culture and hold negative stereotypes about the people, we will probably have negative expectations about our experiences.

We do not mean to suggest that there is anything wrong with having negative attitudes or stereotypes. The point is that negative attitudes and stereotypes create negative expectations. Negative expectations, in turn, tend to create self-fulfilling prophecies; that is, we will interpret the behavior of members of the other cultures negatively and, therefore, we will have negative experiences. If we find we have negative attitudes or stereotypes, we can try to hold them in check and allow ourselves to increase our understanding of the other culture (i.e., avoid evaluating the behavior we are observing) when we are interpreting the behavior of people in the culture.

Holding our negative expectations in check or replacing them with positive stereotypes is necessary to communicate effectively with people in other cultures. It also is necessary for us to grow as individuals. Virtually all psychologists writing on self-development suggest something like "replace the negative tape with a positive and logical thought" (Kavenaugh, 1985, p. 136).

MANAGING OUR EMOTIONAL REACTIONS

The ability to manage our emotional reactions in another culture is vital to successful adjustment. The anxiety or stress we experience when entering another culture is natural and necessary. Everyone experiences it to some degree. The degree to which we adjust to living in another culture depends on how we cope with the stress and anxiety, not whether we experience them. Three practical suggestions can be generated from the theory regarding managing our anxiety and stress.

Anxiety and Stress Are Natural Reactions to Living in Another Culture and Interacting with Members of Other Cultures

Experiencing anxiety and stress when we live in another culture is to be expected; everyone has these reactions to some degree. Anxiety and stress, therefore, are not "bad" in and of themselves. In fact, stress and anxiety can have positive consequences. To illustrate, a North American who is outgoing and greets everyone he or she passes on the street with "Hi, how are you?" would experience stress if this greeting is not reciprocated in another culture. The stress that is experienced should serve as a cue that something is not right. The stress, consequently, will motivate the North American to observe members of the culture to see what made him or her feel uncomfortable. Experiencing stress and anxiety, therefore, can provide the motivation one needs to gain the information necessary to understand people from the other culture.

Communication with people from other cultures frequently is based on negative expectations. Research indicates, for example, that actual or anticipated interaction with a member of a different culture leads to anxiety (Stephan & Stephan, 1985). Stephan and Stephan argue that we fear four types of negative consequences when interacting with people from other cultures.

First, we fear negative consequences for our self-concepts. In interacting with people from other cultures, we worry "about feeling incompetent, confused, and not in control . . . . anticipate discomfort, frustration, and irritation due to the awkwardness of intergroup interactions" (Stephan & Stephan, 1985, p. 159). We also may fear the loss of self-esteem, that our social identities will be threatened, and that we will feel guilty if we behave in ways that offend people from other cultures.

Second, we may fear that negative behavioral consequences will result from our communication with people from other cultures. We may feel that people from other cultures will exploit us, take advantage of us, or try to dominate us. We also may worry about performing poorly in the presence of people from other cultures or worry that physical harm or verbal conflict will occur.

Third, we fear negative evaluations of people from other cultures. We fear rejection, ridicule, disapproval, and being stereotyped negatively. These negative evaluations, in turn, can be seen as threats to our social identities. Recent research suggests that we perceive interpersonal communication as more agreeable and less abrasive than intergroup communication (Hoyle, Pinkley, & Insko, 1989).

Finally, we may fear negative evaluations by members of our own culture. If we interact with people from other cultures, members of our own culture may disapprove. We may fear that members of our culture will "reject" us, "apply other sanctions," or identify us "with the outgroup" (Stephan & Stephan, 1985, p. 160).

Stephan and Stephan (1985) point out that "intergroup anxiety often has a basis in reality. People sometimes do make embarrassing mistakes, are taken advantage of, and are rejected by ingroup and outgroup members" (p. 160) when communicating with people from other cultures. One of the emotional reactions we have to our expectations of being disconfirmed is that we become frustrated. "Frustration involves feelings of intense discomfort stemming from the blockage of paths toward goals. . . . Frustration, in turn, often leads to aggressive behavior as people try to vent their negative feelings" (Brislin, et al., 1986, p. 250).

The anxiety we experience when communicating with people from other cultures is largely unconscious. To be controlled, it must be brought to a conscious level (i.e., we must become mindful about our own feelings). To understand people from other cultures, we must cognitively manage our anxiety.

There are many ways to cope with the anxiety and stress we experience when living in another culture. One way is to "fight" the other culture and criticize the members of the other culture. This way of coping may make us feel better, but it will not help us to adjust to living in the other culture and get the most out of our stay. Another way to cope is to "take flight" from the culture and interact only with other members of our culture. Although this coping mechanism does work for some, it does not lead to an enjoyable learning experience in the other culture. The most successful way to cope with living in another culture is to try to be flexible.

The More Flexible We Are, the Better We Will Be Able to Deal with the Anxiety and Stress We Experience in Interacting with People from Another Culture

Being flexible does not mean "going native" (trying to act like a member of the other culture to an unnatural or excessive degree). Rather, being flexible means adjusting our behavior to the situation in an appropriate manner (keeping in mind that we are not members of the host culture). In order to know how to adjust our behavior, we must first observe the way things are done in the culture. What works in the host culture? How do the "natives" do things? What would be an appropriate way to adjust our behavior? In making our observations, we must keep in mind that all members of the host culture do not behave in the same way. Just as in the United States, there can be tremendous variation in acceptable behavior within a culture. These variations may occur because of age, social status, or gender differences. In adapting to these differences, we need to develop a tolerance for ambiguity.

Tolerance for ambiguity implies the ability to deal successfully with situations, even when a lot of information needed to interact effectively is unknown. Ruben and Kealey (1979) point out that

> the ability to react to new and ambiguous situations with minimal discomfort has long been thought to be an important asset when adjusting to a new culture . . . .
> Excessive discomfort resulting from being placed in a new or different environment—or from finding the familiar environment altered in some critical ways—can lead to confusion, frustration and interpersonal hostility. Some people seem better able to adapt well in new environments and adjust quickly to the demands of the changing milieu. (p. 19)

Ruben and Kealey's research indicates that the greater our tolerance for ambiguity, the more effective we are in completing task assignments in other cultures.

Our tolerance for ambiguity affects the type of information we try to find out about others. People with a low tolerance for ambiguity try to gather information that supports their own beliefs. People with a high tolerance for ambiguity, in contrast, seek "objective" information from others (McPherson, 1983). Objective information is necessary to understand and accurately predict others' behavior.

Being flexible also means that we must be able to adapt and accommodate our behavior to people in the host culture. One important aspect of adapting our behavior is the ability to speak another language (or at least use phrases in another language). If we always expect to speak our own language, we cannot be effective in communicating with others. Ernest Boyer (1990), Chair of the Carnegie Endowment for Teaching, points out that we "should become familiar with other languages and cultures so that [we] will be better able to live, with confidence, in an increasingly interdependent world" (p. B4).

The need to adapt our behavior is not limited to speaking another language. If we are from the white middle-class subculture of the United States and are communicating with someone from another culture who expects to stand much closer to us than we are comfortable (e.g., someone from a Latin or Arab culture), for example, we have two options.

First, we can choose to try to use our own interpersonal distance (e.g., we should stand at least at arm's length). If the other person keeps trying to use her or his social distance, however, we will "dance" around the room (i.e., the other person moves forward, we move back; to compensate and be at a distance that is comfortable for him or her, the other person then moves closer). If we are not mindful of our communication and willing to be flexible in our behavior, this is likely to occur.

Alternatively, we can choose to use a different pattern of behavior. We can decide to stand closer to the other person than we would if we were communicating with someone from our own culture. This option will, in all likelihood, lead to more effective communication. When people are following different norms, at least one of the parties must adapt for effective communication to occur.

Once we know how things are done in the host culture, we can try out these behaviors ourselves. After trying the new behaviors, we need to reflect on the degree to which they were successful and enjoyable. Based upon our reflections, we can then decide whether or not we want to continue the new behavior or try something different.

We Can Use the Same Coping Mechanisms to Deal with Anxiety and Stress in Another Culture That We Use in Our Own Culture

Many people assume that the coping mechanisms needed for adjusting to another culture are different from those they use to cope with stress and anxiety in their own culture. This is not so. The vast majority of coping mechanisms we use to adjust to new situations in the United States also will work in another culture. If we find ourselves at a loss as to how to cope with stress in another culture, we need to stop and think about how we cope with new situations in the United States. What, for example, did we do to adjust to college life or a move to a new city?

In addition to thinking about how we coped with new situations in the United States, we also can seek out activities we enjoy doing in the United States. Almost any activity we enjoy in the United States can be done in another culture. Although the form may differ a little, the activity is probably available. Some creativity may be necessary. It might be difficult, for example, to go horseback riding in Japan, but it is possible. Being creative in approaching problems of adjustment can help make our stay in another culture an enjoyable learning experience.

There is one other important factor that will help us cope with the anxiety we experience in another culture; namely, developing a social support network among the host nationals. Developing friendships with host nationals appears to be an important element of reducing anxiety. The main reason is that the friend gives us someone with whom we can discuss our anxiety and uncertainty. Host nationals are preferable because people from our own culture living in the host culture may be having the same problems we are. A person from our own culture who has adapted to the host culture can be a source of information and support, but he or she is not a substitute for a host national friend. In the absence of a host national friend, we can use nonintimate, "fringe" relationships with shopkeepers, bartenders, and hairdressers or barbers to fulfill many of our social support needs (Adelman, 1988).

CONCLUSION

Kurt Lewin often is quoted as saying "there is nothing so practical as a good theory." We have tried to illustrate practical implications of one theory of intercultural adaptation in this paper. To summarize, Gudykunst and Hammer's (1988) theory suggests that being able to describe what happens before interpreting and evaluating the behavior of those we encounter in other cultures, increasing our knowledge of other cultures and languages, holding positive expectations of our interactions in other cultures, and knowing how to manage our uncertainty and anxiety all help us to adapt and effectively communicate with people in other cultures. We can choose how to behave with respect to these processes if we are mindful of our communication when we are living and working in other cultures.

REFERENCES

Adelman, M. (1985). Cross-cultural adjustment: A theoretical perspective on social support. *International Journal of Intercultural Relations, 12*, 183–204.

Berger, C. R. (1979). Beyond initial interactions. In H. Giles & R. St. Clair (Eds.), *Language and social psychology*. Oxford: Blackwell.

Boyer, E. (1990, June 20). Letter to editor. *Chronicle of Higher Education*, p. B4.

Brislin, R. W., Cushner, K., Cherrie, C., & Yong, M. (1986). *Intercultural interactions: A practical guide*. Newbury Park, CA: Sage.

Gao, G., & Gudykunst, W. B. (1990). Uncertainty, anxiety, and adaptation. *International Journal of Intercultural Relations, 14*, 301–317.

Gouldner, A. (1960). The norm of reciprocity. *American Sociological Review, 25*, 161–179.

Gudykunst, W. B., & Hammer, M. R. (1988). Strangers and hosts: An uncertainty reduction based theory of intercultural adaptation. In Y. Y. Kim & W. B. Gudykunst (Eds.), *Cross-cultural adaptation: Current approaches*. Newbury Park, CA: Sage.

Hoyle, R., Pinkley, R., & Insko, C. (1989). Perceptions of social behavior: Evidence of differing expectations for interpersonal and intergroup behavior. *Personality and Social Psychology Bulletin, 15*, 365–376.

Kavenaugh, R. (1985). *Search*. New York: Harper and Row.

Langer, E. (1989). *Mindfulness*. Reading, MA: Addison-Wesley.

Lauer, R., & Lauer, J. (1988). *Watersheds: Mastering life's unpredictable crises*. New York: Ivey Books.

McPherson, K. (1983). Opinion-related information seeking. *Personality and Social Psychology Bulletin, 9*, 116–124.

Ruben, B., & Kealey, D. (1979). Behavioral assessment of communication competency and the perception of cross-cultural adaptation. *International Journal of Intercultural Relations, 3*, 15–48.

Stephan, W. G., & Stephan, C. W. (1985). Intergroup anxiety. *Journal of Social Issues, 41*, 157–166.

CHAPTER 12

Communicating
Effectively with
Strangers

To say we have communicated does not imply an outcome. Communication is a process involving the exchange of messages and the creation of meaning. When we communicate, we attach meaning to (or interpret) messages we construct and transmit to others. We also attach meaning to (or interpret) messages we receive from others. We are not always aware of this process, but we do it nevertheless. For two people to communicate effectively, the two must attach relatively similar meanings to the messages sent and received (e.g., they interpret the messages similarly). Powers and Lowrey (1984) refer to this as "basic communication fidelity"—"the degree of congruence between the cognitions [or thoughts] of two or more individuals following a communication event" (p. 58). It is important to point out, however, that the meaning one person attaches to a message is never totally the same as the meaning another person attaches to the same message. "To say that meaning in communication is never totally the same for all communicators is not to say that communication is impossible or even difficult—only that it is imperfect" (Fisher, 1978, p. 257).

In order to interpret strangers' messages accurately, we must be able to differentiate among a description of what we observed, how we interpreted it, and our evaluations. When we communicate with others we do not describe their behavior. Rather, when we decode incoming messages, we immediately interpret those messages. Because we tend to use our own symbolic system to interpret incoming messages, we often misinterpret messages transmitted by people who are different. In order to understand people who are different, we must become mindful and try to figure out the meaning they attached to the message transmitted to us.

Describing behavior refers to an actual report of what was observed with a minimum of distortion and without attributing meaning to the behavior. Description includes what we see, hear, feel, touch, and taste. In other words, it is information that comes from our sense organs. "He breathed in my face when we talked" and "She did not look me in the eyes when we talked" are both descriptive statements. Neither attaches meaning to the behavior; both only describe the behavior observed.

An interpretation is the meaning or social significance attached to the behavior. It involves what we think about what we observed. There are multiple interpretations for any one description. To illustrate, consider the second description: "She did not look me in the eyes when we talked." What are the possible interpretations of this behavior? To develop a list of possible interpretations we must be mindful. If we respond in a mindless fashion, we will only think about the interpretations used in our subculture. Not looking someone in the eye in the white, middle-class subculture of the United States, for example, usually is interpreted as the person is not telling the truth. Other possible interpretations in this subculture include, but are not limited to, she is shy, she is hiding something, and she is being disrespectful. If, however, as in the example presented earlier, the person who did not look us in the eye is black, we should also consider the interpretation that she is being respectful.

After we have developed a list of possible interpretations, we must determine what is the most probable interpretation that the other person is placing on the message. If we know the other person, we can rely on psychological data about him or her to make an "educated guess." If we do not know the other person, we must rely on the cultural and sociological data we have to make an educated guess.

Once we have determined the most probable interpretation, we can then evaluate the behavior. Obviously, we would evaluate the interpretations "she is lying" and "she is showing respect" in the preceding example much differently.

Only by separating descriptions, interpretations, and evaluations of behavior can we understand strangers. If we interpret their behavior without describing it first, we inevitably use our own symbol system to interpret their behavior. This will lead to misinterpretations a large percent of the time.

We are emphasizing how to differentiate description, interpretation, and evaluation because we think it is critical to communicating effectively with strangers, and it is not discussed in the readings that follow.

The first two readings in this chapter present two alternative perspectives on the nature of communication effectiveness. In the first reading, Kim suggests that communication competence is a characteristic of the person communicating. She sees competence as an individual's ability to manage cultural differences and the stress associated with communicating with strangers.

Gudykunst, in the second reading, takes another approach to intercultural competence. He argues that competence is not within the communicator. Rather, competence is an impression we form of ourselves and others. Gudykunst discusses the motivation, knowledge, and skills we need to be perceived as competent when we communicate with strangers. (The last half of the discussion of effectiveness in Chapter 12 in the second edition of *Communicating with Strangers* was adapted from this reading. This reading, therefore, should be omitted if that chapter in the text has been read.)

Whereas the first two readings are broad, the final reading focuses on a specific issue in communicating effectively with strangers. Fisher and Brown lay out a prescriptive approach for building better relationships when we negotiate. They suggest that we must be unconditionally accepting. Based on this principle, they provide specific suggestions for improving our effectiveness when we negotiate with strangers (e.g., balance emotions with reason).

REFERENCES

Fisher, B. A. (1978). *Perspectives on human communication*. New York: Macmillan.
Powers, W., & Lowrey, D. (1984). Basic communication fidelity. In R. Bostrom (Ed.), *Competence in communication*. Beverly Hills, CA: Sage.

Intercultural Communication Competence: A Systems-Theoretic View
Young Yun Kim

CONCEPTUAL GROUNDING

The systems perspective emphasizes the dynamic, interactive nature of the communication process between two or more individuals. The relationship between the individual communication system and the multiperson (including two-person) communication system is multidirectional and multilateral in causality. Like the relationship of the mind and the reality it experiences, the relationship between the person and the environment is viewed as mutually affecting and being affected by each other. All parties involved in a given encounter, including the conditions of the social context in which the encounter takes place, codetermine the communication outcomes. This means that no one element in a multiperson communication system can be singled out for being solely responsible for the outcomes. Each person has a reality of his/her own and its own tokens of significance, with which the individual comes to organize new experiences.

Competence vs. Successful Outcome

From this systems principle of multilateral causality, the commonly accepted views that regard ICC [intercultural communication competence] as identical or exchangeable in meaning with successful interaction outcome (such as effectiveness and

Source: Abridged from S. Ting-Toomey & F. Korzenny (Eds.), *Cross-Cultural Interpersonal Communication* (pp. 259–275). Newbury Park, CA: Sage, 1991.

appropriateness) presents a possible problem of conceptual validity (e.g., Abe & Wiseman, 1986; Hammer & Martin, 1989; Imahori & Lanigan, 1989). Addressing this issue is crucial to any attempt to solidify the concept of ICC, particularly in light of the fact that implicit assumptions in equating competence with successful interaction outcome have not been closely examined in the past.

One of the most elaborate presentations of the correspondence between competence and successful interaction outcome has been made by Spitzberg and Cupach (1984) and Spitzberg (1988, 1989). In this view, communication competence means "evaluative impression of communication quality," or judgments of the decoder's communication competence on the bases of perceived effectiveness and appropriateness. This outcome-oriented conceptualization of communication competence, however, does not take into account the fact that different decoders may assess the same person's competence differently, and that the same person may be evaluated differently by a same decoder in different situations. . . . [A] given individual's performance is affected not only by his/her own communicative abilities, but also by many external factors operating in a given communication context—such as the biases in the decoder's perception that is likely to be influenced by the level of his/her own level of competence. The decoder's perception should be further affected by the nature of the relationship and the interaction goal, and the degree of incompatibility of the normative cultural expectations about what is effective and appropriate communication behavior.

Accordingly, conceptualizing ICC as identical to or exchangeable with performance outcomes—subjective or objective—tends to blur the principle of multilateral causality in the interpersonal communication system. Although a given individual's competence should clearly facilitate successful outcomes, it cannot necessarily produce them. Equating ICC with successful interaction outcome—whichever indicators may be employed as its indicators—allows the domain of ICC to "float" and be confounded by contextual and relational conditions, and, thus, cannot contribute to developing a definition of ICC that is consistent across varied types and situations of intercultural encounter.

Comparatively, the present systems-theoretic view suggests that ICC must be conceptually separated from communication outcomes. It emphasizes that ICC should be located *within* a person as his/her overall *capacity* or *capability* to facilitate the communication process between people from differing cultural backgrounds and to contribute to successful interaction outcomes. Here, ICC is considered a necessary, but not sufficient, condition for achieving success in intercultural encounters—just as a highly competent driver may not always be able to prevent accidents due to factors external to the driver (such as hazardous road conditions or serious mistakes made by other incompetent drivers).

Cultural vs. Intercultural Communication Competence

Another source of divergence observed in current approaches to ICC is the "mixing" of cultural (or culture-specific) communication competence (CCC) in conceptualizing ICC. Many ICC models have been derived from the empirical data obtained from a specific cultural context for the purpose of predicting "overseas success" of temporary sojourners such as Peace Corps volunteers, Navy personnel, and technical advisors (cf. Furnham & Bochner, 1986; Kealey & Ruben, 1983). Such studies and the resultant conceptualizations of ICC parallel those in the culture-specific approaches common in cultural anthropology, cross-cultural psychology, and sociolinguistics. Field studies in these areas have provided extensive knowledge of cultural patterns characteristic of different societies. Notably, cultural anthropological studies have provided ample ethnographic insights into implicit communication patterns in varied cultures. Hall (1976), for example, derived an analytic concept, "contexting," on which he compared various cultural communication systems along a continuum of high-context and low-context. Similarly, sociolinguistic ethnographers have described how people use the linguistic means specific to their speech community to communicate (cf. Knapp & Potthoff, 1987). Among cross-cultural psychologists, Triandis (1972) has provided extensive data on various "subjective cultures," and has presented an analytic framework that identifies the "essentials" of cultural elements including: patterns of dress, child rearing, decision making, language, philosophy, and aesthetics (Triandis, 1983).

The knowledge generated from the cultural studies provides useful insights into improving communication competence in dealing with specific cultural groups. To enhance the chances of successful communication and functioning in the United States, for example, college students from China must equip themselves with abilities to communicate with Americans. To be successful in the Japanese market, American business men and women must equip themselves with abilities to communicate with their Japanese counterparts. Based on such culture-specific goals of individuals, training programs have been developed to enhance the individual's cultural communication competence, utilizing such culture-specific methods as "intercultural sensitizer" or "culture assimilator" (cf. Albert, 1983; Triandis, 1973).

What is important for the present exploration of ICC, however, is that intercultural competence and cultural competence must be clearly distinguished as separate conceptual domains, even though both operate together in any given intercultural encounter. While the content of CCC clearly varies from culture to culture, the content of ICC should remain constant across all intercultural situations regardless of specific cultures involved.

From this viewpoint, some of the variables included in the existing lists of ICC indicators (or factors) are questionable in their conceptual validity. We may, for instance, question the validity of "self-disclosure" as a crucial element of ICC that is universally applicable in all intercultural encounters. Research has shown that high-context and low-context cultures do differ in self-disclosure behavior (and related information-seeking behavior) in initial interactions, and that, even within a cultural group, individuals vary their self-disclosure behavior depending on whether their interaction partners are from within or outside their own culture (e.g., Gudykunst, 1986; Hall, 1976). Other ICC-related concepts such as "expressiveness" (e.g., Hammer, 1989) may also be subject to a similar evaluation, based on the fact that many of the "high-context" cultures emphasize formalized and stylized interaction rituals and discourage unnecessary verbal expressiveness particularly during initial encounters between strangers.

Similar questions can be raised about the very notion that communication competence is exchangeable with interactants' evaluation of each other's performance (e.g., Spitzberg & Cupach, 1984; Spitzberg, 1989). This assumption may reflect the humanistic-democratic-individualistic value prevalent in the North American and Western European academic subcultures, in which a competent communicator is expected to behave in a way that is satisfactory to all parties involved. This normative interpersonal value may not be a significant factor in intercultural encounters that involve people from cultures where uneven distribution of power and "undemocratic" communication practices may be more readily accepted by individual communicators. Even within the humanistic cultural group, competent interpersonal communication does not always lead to mutual satisfaction, as in the case of parents having to "punish" and discipline their children.

From the present systems perspective, then, ICC must be conceptually distinguished from successful interaction outcomes, and from culture-specific communication competence (CCC). Instead, ICC must be anchored *within* a person as his/her capacity to manage the varied contexts of intercultural encounter regardless of the specific cultures being interfaced.

TOWARD A GENERAL THEORY

As we begin to solidify the meaning of ICC by distinguishing it from the commonly accepted definitions, we are able to "ground" the concept in its most basic, generic, and value-neutral level. Having proposed distinctions between what is and what is not within the domain of ICC, an attempt is made next to explore the key dimensions of ICC itself. Specifically, the nature of ICC is viewed in terms of the key challenges that individuals must manage in all intercultural encounters in varying degrees: namely, cultural difference/unfamiliarity, intergroup posture, and the accompanying stress.

Key Challenges of Intercultural Encounters

By definition, intercultural communication presents a significant amount of differences between interactants' cultural backgrounds. Relatedly, cultural differences that enter into a given encounter introduce a high degree of *unfamiliarity* with each other's messages and meanings. Such cultural difference and unfamiliarity between culturally dissimilar interactants brings the experiences of anxiety or lack of "attributional confidence" to the interactants (cf. Gudykunst, 1988c; Lalljee, 1987 . . .). The gap between respective experiential backgrounds limits the interactant's ability to encode and decode messages with fidelity. In cybernetic terms, "The limitations of man's [woman's] communication are determined by the capacity of his [her] intrapersonal network, the selectivity of his [her] receivers, and the skill of his [her] effector organs."

(Ruesch, 1968/1951, p. 17). As such, the number of incoming and outgoing message signals, as well as the signals that can be transmitted within each person's intrapersonal system, is limited in many intercultural encounters.

An assumption here, of course, is that individuals who have been socialized within the same culture are more similar and familiar with each other's system of meaning and behavior. Although no two individuals within a culture are alike, they are likely to share many common denominators that will help them encode and decode the messages. They may differ or even argue about individual preferences, but by and large they do understand each other satisfactorily. Comparatively, individuals from different cultures frequently are faced with a potentially greater problem of understanding each other. Recognition of verbal and nonverbal codes, behaviors, and interpretation of the hidden assumptions underlying those behaviors are likely to be more difficult.

In addition, intercultural communication is viewed distinct from (intra)cultural communication in that the psychological posture the interactants take is based on each other's cultural identity (cf. Collier & Thomas, 1988; Collier, 1989). As articulated extensively in studies of social identity theory, intercultural interactants tend to see themselves, as well as their interaction partners, in light of the respective cultural group membership (cf. Brewer & Miller, 1984; Gudykunst, 1988a, 1988b; Kim, 1986, 1989b; Ross, 1988; Tajfel, 1974; Turner & Giles, 1981). The differing cultural identities of the interactants psychologically position them into "intergroup" (as compared to "interpersonal") relational orientations, which in turn encourage them to perceive each other as a group representative rather than as a unique person.

The interfacing of group identities and intergroup postures creates a "psychological distance" that places each interactant apart from the other. Such intergroup postures often are accompanied by "ingroup loyalties" and "outgroup discrimination" (cf. Brewer & Miller, 1984; Brown & Turner, 1981). The "we-they" intergroup orientation influences the intercultural context to be less personalized (or individualized) and more impersonal. Empirical studies have reported the tendencies of intercultural interactants to shy away from requesting intimate information about each other and to accentuate mutual differences in perceiving each other's attributes. . . . Ross (1977) and Pettigrew (1979), for example, have labelled such psychological tendencies of intergroup posture as "attribution errors," which is closely related to "ethnocentrism" and other similar concepts such as "prejudice" (cf. Brewer & Miller, 1984; Milner, 1981).

Intergroup posturing tendencies have been observed to be particularly acute when the interactants come from groups that have a history of dominance/subjugation or a significant discrepancy in the present power status or prestige of the respective groups (cf. Kim, 1989b), as in the case of encounters between a person from the West Indies and one from Great Britain, or between an Anglo American and an American Indian. The actual and perceived power discrepancy between the interactants' group memberships tends to be further accentuated when the physically observable cultural differences, or cultural (or ethnic) "markers" (such as dress, physical features, and behavioral idiosyncracy) are strongly present in intercultural encounters.

The above intercultural challenges—cultural difference and intergroup posture—lead to stress. Stress experiences, no matter how minimal, are inherent in the
very nature of the intercultural communication context, since stress is a generic
process of a human system that is experienced whenever the capabilities of the system
are not adequately equipped to manage the demands of an environment (including an
interaction partner). Stress, indeed, is considered part-and-parcel of intercultural
encounters, disturbing the internal equilibrium of the individual system. Accordingly,
to be interculturally competent means to be able to manage such stress, regain the
internal balance, and carry out the communication process in such a way that
contributes to successful interaction outcomes. In fact, managing stressful experiences
is a precondition for managing the challenges of cultural difference and unfamiliarity
as well as intergroup posture. The importance of the ability to manage stress in
intercultural encounters is clearly demonstrated in the numerous studies that have
examined such stress-related phenomena as: "intergroup anxiety" (Barna, 1983;
Gudykunst, 1988c; Stephan & Stephan, 1985) and "culture shock" (cf. Furham &
Bochner, 1986; Kim, 1988, 1989a).

Intercultural stress, along with cultural difference and intergroup posture, vary
in different encounters. Yet these challenges do serve as key challenges of intercultural
communication, suggesting that the domain of ICC must refer to that capacity of an
individual to manage the challenges. In other words, individuals who hope to carry
out effective intercultural interactions must be equipped with a set of abilities to be
able to understand and deal with the dynamics of cultural difference, intergroup
posture, and the inevitable stress experiences.

Adaptability and Intercultural Communication Competence

In the present systems perspective, the capacity of an individual to manage intercultural challenges is referred to as "adaptability"—the capability of an individual's
internal psychic system to alter its existing attributes and structures to accommodate
the demands of the environment. In this view, each person is an "open system" with
fundamental goals to adapt to its environment through its inherent homeostatic drive
to maintain an equilibrium, both internally and in relation to the environment
(including the other person). When the system is challenged by the environment, its
internal equilibrium is temporarily disturbed as the person-environment symmetry is
broken. Under such conditions, a person experiences stress and begins the process of
regaining internal equilibrium by adapting (acting upon), or adapting to (accommodating), the environmental challenges.

As such, stress and adaptation of a person's internal system are inseparably
linked, jointly and interactively facilitating the process of new learning and of
developing new capabilities to deal with new challenges (cf. Burns & Farina, 1984;
Kim, 1988). This adaptive, "self-organizing" (Jantsch, 1980) characteristic enables
human thought to generate more adaptive alternatives than lower animals are capable
of generating. More meanings can be attributed to objects and ideas, and a greater

number of connections between meanings arise achieving a greater complexity, and thus a greater number of alternative, creative outcomes in managing itself vis-à-vis the environment.

In intercultural encounters, therefore, adaptability means the individual's capacity to suspend or modify some of the old cultural ways, and learn and accommodate some of the new cultural ways, and creatively find ways to manage the dynamics of cultural difference/unfamiliarity, intergroup posture, and the accompanying stress. Indeed, this adaptability—the self-altering and creative capacity—can be placed at the heart of ICC as a meta-competence. A person equipped with greater adaptability is likely to be more open to learning different cultural patterns with less intergroup posturing—less ethnocentric and discriminatory of the other person based on his/her cultural identity. Such an interculturally competent person is likely to be less defensive and rigid in the face of differences, unfamiliarity with the differences, and the intergroup posturing of cultural identities.

Further, the individual's adaptability is synonymous with his/her capacity to stretch beyond the internalized cultural parameters and to absorb the psychological "pain" in the process. As Jourard (1974) stated, "temporary disorganization, or even shattering, of one way to experience the world, is brought on by new disclosure . . ." (p. 426). In this regard, facing intercultural challenges is a significant way to achieve psychic growth beyond the conditions that are already known, familiar, and comfortable into those that are unknown, strange, and unsettling.

A variety of specific concepts exist in the psychological and communication literature that are directly or indirectly related to the systems-theoretic concept of adaptability. Such specific concepts, particularly the ones identified below, offer promising usefulness as indicators of ICC as defined in terms of adaptability. Essentially, these concepts range from cognitive, affective, to operational (or behavioral) realms of the individual's internal information processing (cf. Goss, 1989; Kim, 1988).

The *cognitive dimension* refers to the "sense-making" activities for ascertaining the meaning of various verbal and nonverbal codes one receives. In this dimension, psychological concepts—such as "cognitive simplicity/complexity" (Applegate & Sypher, 1988; Burleson, 19897; Schroder, Driver & Streufert, 1975), "narrow/broad category width" (Detweiler, 1986), "cognitive rigidity/flexibility" (Kim, 1988), and "perspective taking" (Pearce & Stamm, 1973)—correspond in meaning to the adaptability of an individual's internal system in intercultural encounters.

The *affective dimension* focuses on the emotional and aesthetic tendencies of an individual's internal system. In psychological terms, it refers to the motivational and attitudinal predisposition in responding to external stimuli. In intercultural encounters, in particular, the affective dimension of competence would mean "readiness" to accommodate the intercultural challenges. Existing concepts that are related to this dimension include: "adaptive motivation" (Kim, 1988), "affirmative self/other attitude" (Kim, 1988), "ambiguity tolerance" (Ruben & Kealey, 1979), "empathy" (Ruben & Kealey, 1979), "empathic motivation" (Burleson, 1983), "psychological

distance" (Amir, 1969), and "intergroup anxiety" (Gudykunst, 1986; Stephan &
Stephan, 1985), "ethnocentrism" (Brewer & Campbell, 1976), and "prejudice"
(Tajfel, 1974; Weigel & Howes, 1985).

In the *operational* (or behavioral) dimension, an individual's adaptive capacity is
defined as his/her abilities to be flexible and resourceful in actually carrying out what
he/she is capable of in the cognitive and affective dimensions. Here, concepts such as
"behavioral complexity" (Applegate & Sypher, 1988), "behavioral flexibility"
(Samter, Burleson & Basden-Murphy, 1989), "communication accommodation"
(Gallois, Franklyn-Stokes, Giles & Coupland, 1988), "message complexity" (Applegate & Sypher, 1988), "person-centered communication" (Applegate & Delia, 1980),
"interpersonal management" (Applegate & Leichy, 1984), and "interaction involvement" (Cegala, Savage & Brunner & Conrad, 1982) are potentially relevant to the
present conceptualization of the behavioral dimension of ICC. Additional concepts of
possible relevance to the behavioral dimension of ICC include: "non-judgmental
interaction posture," "self-oriented role behavior," and "interaction management"
(Ruben & Kealey, 1979; Olebe & Koester, 1989).

Collectively, the cognitive, affective, and behavioral dimensions of adaptive
capacity are viewed to constitute the present conceptual domain of ICC. Each of these
dimensions refers to a process that is generic to each person's internal communication
system, promoting the individual capacity to manage environmental challenges. . . .

REFERENCES

Albert, R. (1983). The intercultural sensitizer or culture assimilator: A cognitive approach. In
    D. Landis & R. Brislin (Eds.), *Handbook of intercultural training, Vol. II: Issues in training
    methodology* (pp. 186–217). New York: Pergamon.
Amir, Y. (1969). Contact hypothesis in ethnic relations. *Psychological Bulletin, 7*(5), 319–342.
Applegate, J., & Delia, J. (1980). Person-centered speech, psychological development, and the
    contexts of language usage. In R. St. Clair & H. Giles (Eds.), *The social and psychological
    contexts of language* (pp. 245–282). Hillsdale, NJ: Lawrence Erlbaum.
Applegate, J., & Leichty, G. (1984). Managing interpersonal relationships: Social cognitive
    and strategic determinants of competence. In R. Bostrom (Ed.), *Competence in commu-
    nication: A multidisciplinary approach* (pp. 33–55). Beverly Hills, CA: Sage.
Applegate, J., & Sypher, H. (1988). A constructivist theory of communication and culture. In
    Y. Kim & W. Gudykunst (Eds.), *Theories in intercultural communication* (pp. 41–65).
    Newbury Park, CA: Sage.
Barna, L. (1983). The stress factor in intercultural relations. In D. Landis & R. Brislin (Eds.),
    Handbook of intercultural training, Vol. II: Issues in training methodology (pp. 19–49). New
    York: Pergamon.
Bertalanffy, L. (1975), General system theory. In B. Ruben & J. Kim (Ed.), *General systems
    theory and human communication* (pp. 6–20). Rochelle Park, NJ: Hayden Book.
Brewer, M., & Campbell, D. (1976). *Ethnocentrism and intergroup attitudes.* New York: John
    Wiley & Sons.

Brewer, M., & Miller, N. (1984). Beyond the contact hypothesis: Theoretical perspectives on desegregation. In N. Miller & M. Brewer (Eds.), *Groups in contact: The psychology of desegregation* (pp. 281–302). New York: Academic Press.

Brown, R., & Turner, J. (1981). Interpersonal and intergroup behavior. In J. Turner & H. Giles (Eds.), *Intergroup behavior* (pp. 33–65). Chicago: The University of Chicago Press.

Burlson, B. (1983). Social cognition, empathic motivation, and adults' comforting strategies. *Human Communication Research, 10,* 295–304.

Burlson, B. (1987). Cognitive complexity. In J. McCroskey & J. Delia (Eds.), *Personal and interpersonal communication* (pp. 305–349). Beverly Hills, CA: Sage.

Burns, G., & Farina, A. (1984). Social competence and adjustment. *Journal of Social and Personal Relationships, 1,* 99–113.

Cegala, D., Savage, G., Brunner, C., & Conrad, A. (1982, December). An elaboration of the meaning of interaction involvement: Toward the development of a theoretical concept. *Communication Monographs, 49,* 229–248.

Collier, M. (1989). Cultural and intercultural communication competence: Current approaches and directions for future research. *International Journal of Intercultural Relations, 13*(3), 287–302.

Collier, M., & Thomas, M. (1988). Cultural identity: An interpretive perspective. In Y. Kim & W. Gudykunst (Eds.), *Theories in intercultural communication* (pp. 99–120). Newbury Park, CA: Sage.

Detweiler, R. (1986). Categorization, attribution and intergroup communication. In W. Gudykunst (Ed.), *Intergroup communication* (pp. 62–73). London: Edward Arnold.

Dinges, N. (1983). Intercultural competence. In D. Landis & R. Brislin (Eds.), *Handbook of intercultural training, Vol. I: Issues in theory and design* (pp. 176–202). New York: Pergamon.

Dinges, N., & Lieberman, D. (1989). Intercultural communication competence: Coping with stressful work situations. *International Journal of Intercultural Relations, 13*(3), 371–386.

Furnham, A., & Bochner, S. (1986). *Culture shock: Psychological reactions to unfamiliar environments.* London: Methuen.

Gallois, C., Franklyn-Stokes, A., Giles, H., & Coupland, N. (1988). Communication accommodation in intercultural communication. In Y. Kim & W. Gudykunst (Eds.), *Theories in intercultural communication* (pp. 157–185). Newbury Park, CA: Sage.

Goss, B. (1989). *The psychology of human communication.* Prospect Heights, IL: Waveland.

Gudykunst, W. (1986). Ethnicity, types of relationship, and intraethnic and interethnic uncertainty reduction. In Y. Kim (Ed.), *Interethnic communication* (pp. 201–224). Newbury Park, CA: Sage.

Gudykunst, W. (Ed.) (1988a). *Language and ethnic identity.* Clevedon, England: Multilingual Matters.

Gudykunst, W. (Ed.) (1988b). *Intergroup communication* London: Edward Arnold.

Gudykunst, W. (1988c). Uncertainty and anxiety. In Y. Kim & W. Gudykunst (Eds.), *Theories in intercultural communication* (pp. 123–156). Newbury Park, CA: Sage.

Gudykunst, W., & Ting-Toomey, S. (1989). *Culture and interpersonal communication.* Newbury Park, CA: Sage.

Hall, E. (1976). *Beyond culture.* Garden City, NY: Anchor/Doubleday.

Hammer, M. (1989). Intercultural communication competence. In M. Asante & W. Gudykunst, *Handbook of international and intercultural communication* (pp. 247–260). Newbury Park, CA: Sage.

Hammer, M., Gudykunst, W., & Wiseman, R. (1978). Dimensions of intercultural effectiveness: An exploratory study. *International Journal of Intercultural Relations, 2,* 382–392.

Imahori, T., & Lanigan, M. (1989). Relational model of intercultural communication competence. *International Journal of Intercultural Relations, 13*(3), 269–286.

Jantsch, E. (1980). *The self-organizing universe: Scientific and human implications of the emerging paradigm of evolution.* New York: Pergamon.

Jourard, S. (1974). Growing awareness and the awareness of growth. In B. Patton & K. Griffin (Eds.), *Interpersonal communication* (pp. 456–465). New York: Harper & Row.

Kealey, D., & Ruben, B. (1983). Cross-cultural personnel selection criteria, issues, and methods. In D. Landis & R. Brislin (Eds.), *Handbook of intercultural training, Vol. I: Issues in theory and design* (pp. 155–175). New York: Pergamon.

Kim, Y. (1986) (Ed.). *Interethnic communication.* Newbury Park, CA: Sage.

Kim, Y. (1988). *Communication and cross-cultural adaptation: An integrative theory.* Clevedon, England (Philadelphia): Multilingual Matters.

Kim, Y. (1989a). Intercultural adaptation. In M. Asante & W. Gudykunst (Eds.), *Handbook of international and intercultural communication* (pp. 225–294). Newbury Park, CA: Sage.

Kim, Y. (1989b). Explaining interethnic conflict. In J. Gittler (Ed.), *The annual review of conflict knowledge and conflict resolution,* Vol. 1 (pp. 101–125). New York: Garland.

Knapp, K., & Knapp-Potthoff, A. (1987). Instead of an introduction: Conceptual issues in analyzing intercultural communication. In K. Knapp, W. Enninger, & A. Knapp-Potthoff (Eds.), *Analyzing intercultural communication* (pp. 1–13). New York: Mouton de Gruyter.

Lalljee, M. (1987). Attribution theory and intercultural communication. In K. Knapp, W. Enninger & A. Knapp-Potthoff (Eds.), *Analyzing intercultural communication* (pp. 37–49). New York: Mouton de Gruyter.

Martin, J. (Ed.). (1989). *Intercultural communication competence.* A special issue of *International Journal of Intercultural Relations, 13*(3).

Martin, J., & Hammer, M. (1989). Behavioral categories of intercultural communication competence: Everyday communicators' perceptions. *International Journal of Intercultural Relations, 13*(3), 303–332.

Miller, N., & Brewer, M. (1984). The social psychology of desegregation: An introduction. In N. Miller & M. Brewer (Eds.), *Groups in contact: The psychology of desegregation* (pp. 1–27). New York: Academic Press.

Milner, D. (1981). Racial prejudice. In J. Turner & H. Giles (Eds.), *Intergroup behavior* (pp. 102–143). Chicago: The University of Chicago Press.

Munroe, R., & Munroe, R. (1980). Perspectives suggested by anthropological data. In H. Triandia & W. Lambert (Eds.), *Handbook of cross-cultural psychology* (pp. 253–317). Boston: Allyn & Bacon.

Olebe, M., & Koester, J. (1989). Exploring the cross-cultural equivalence of the behavioral assessment scale for intercultural communication. *International Journal of Intercultural Relations, 12,* 233–246.

Pearce, B., & Stamm, K. (1973). Communication behavior and coorientation relation. In P. Clarke (Ed.), *New models for mass communication research* (pp. 177–203). Beverly Hills, CA: Sage.

Pettigrew, T. (1979). The ultimate attribution error: Extending Allport's cognitive analysis of prejudice. *Personality and Social Psychology Bulletin, 5,* 461–476.

Ross, E. (1977). The intuitive psychologist and his shortcomings: Distortions in the attribution process. In L. Berkowitz (Ed.), *Advances in experimental social psychology.* Vol. 10. New York: Academic Press.

Ross, E. [(Ed.).] (1988). *Interethnic communication.* Athens: University of Georgia Press.

Ruben, B. (1975). Intrapersonal, interpersonal, and mass communication processes in individual and multi-person systems. In B. Ruben & J. Kim (Eds.), *General systems theory and human communication* (pp. 164-90). Rochelle Park, NJ: Hayden.

Ruben, B. (1989). The study of cross-cultural competence: Traditions and contemporary issues. *International Journal of Intercultural Relations, 13*(3), 229-240.

Ruben, B., & Kealey, D. (1979). Behavioral assessment of communication competency and the prediction of cross-cultural adaptation. *International Journal of Intercultural Relations, 3,* 15-48.

Ruesch, J. (1951/1968). Values, communication, and culture: An introduction. In J. Ruesch & G. Bateson, *Communication: The social matrix of psychiatry* (pp. 1-20). New York: W. W. Norton.

Samter, W., Burleson, B., & Basden-Murphy, L. (1989). Behavioral complexity is in the eye of the beholder: Effects of cognitive complexity and message complexity on impressions of the source of comforting message. *Human Communication Research, 15*(4), 612-629.

Schroder, H., Driver, M., & Streufert, S. (1975). Intrapersonal organization. In B. Ruben & J. Kim (Eds.), *General systems theory and human communication* (pp. 96-113). Rochelle Park, NJ: Hayden.

Segall, M., Dasen, P., Berry, J., & Poortinga, Y. (1990). *Human behavior in global perspective.* New York: Pergamon.

Spitzberg, B. (1988). Communication competence: Measures of perceived effectiveness. In C. Tardy (Ed.), *A handbook for the study of human communication* (pp. 67-105). Norwood, NJ: Ablex.

Spitzberg, B. (1989). Issues in the development of a theory of interpersonal competence in the intercultural context. *International Journal of Intercultural Relations, 13*(3), 241-269.

Spitzberg, B., & Cupach, W. (1984). *Interpersonal communication competence.* Beverly Hills, CA: Sage.

Stephan, W., & Stephan, C. (1985). Intergroup anxiety. *Journal of Social Issues, 41*(3), 157-175.

Tajfel, H. (1974). Social identity and intergroup behavior. *Social Science Information, 13,*

Triandis, H. (1972). *The analysis of subjective culture.* New York: Wiley.

Triandis, H. (1973). Culture training, cognitive complexity, and interpersonal attitudes. In D. Hoopes (Ed.), *Readings in intercultural communication* (Vol. 2, pp. 55-67). Pittsburgh: Regional Council for International Education.

Triandis, H. (1983). Essentials of studying cultures. In D. Landis & R. Brislin (Eds.), *Handbook of intercultural training, Vol. I: Issues in theory and design* (pp. 203-223). New York: Pergamon.

Turner, J., & Giles, H. [(Eds.).] (1981). *Intergroup behavior.* Chicago: The University of Chicago Press.

Weigel, R., & Howes, P. (1985). Conceptions of racial prejudice: Symbolic racism reconsidered. *Journal of Social Issues, 4*(3), 117-138.

Being Perceived as a Competent Communicator

William B. Gudykunst

. . . John Wiemann and James Bradac (1989) point out that in everyday usage competence implies "adequate," "sufficient," and/or "suitable." Given this usage, competent communicators are people who "get by" and manage to avoid the "pitfalls" and "traps" of communication.

. . . [M]isinterpreting others' messages is one of the major pitfalls or traps of the communication process. I, therefore, see effectiveness (i.e., minimizing misunderstandings) as one of the major factors involved in our perceptions of competence. Effectiveness, as I use the term, is related closely to the notions of adequacy and sufficiency in the everyday usage of competence.[1] Suitability implies that our communication is appropriate; we communicate in ways that meet the minimum contextual requirement of the situation in which we find ourselves. . . .

Our view of our communication competence may not be the same as that of the person with whom we are communicating. I, for example, might see myself as a very competent communicator and when we interact you may perceive me as not being very competent. An "outside" observer might have still a different perception of my competence. Understanding communication competence, therefore, minimally requires that we take into consideration our own and the other person's perspective.

If we have different views of our competence than the people with whom we are communicating, then competence is an impression we have of ourselves and others. Stated differently, "competence is not something intrinsic to a person's nature or behavior" (Spitzberg & Cupach, 1984, p. 115). . . . This view of competence clearly suggests that the specific skills we have do not ensure that we are perceived as competent in any particular interaction. Our skills, however, do increase the likelihood that we are able to adapt our behavior so that others see us as competent (Wiemann & Bradac, 1989). . . .

Brian Spitzberg and William Cupach (1984) isolate three components of communication competence: motivation, knowledge, and skills. Motivation refers to our desire to communicate appropriately and effectively with others. Of particular importance to the present analysis is our motivation to communicate with people who are different. Knowledge refers to our awareness or understanding of what needs to be done in order to communicate appropriately and effectively. Skills are our abilities to engage in the behaviors necessary to communicate appropriately and effectively.

We may be highly motivated and lack the knowledge and/or the skills necessary to communicate appropriately and effectively. We also may be motivated and have the knowledge necessary, but not the skills. If we are motivated and have the knowledge and skills, this does not ensure that we will communicate appropriately or effectively. There are several factors that may intervene to affect our behavior. We may, for example, have a strong emotional reaction to something that happens. Our

Source: Abridged from Chapter 6 in W. B. Gudykunst, *Bridging Differences: Effective Intergroup Communication*, (pp. 101–127). Newbury Park, CA: Sage, 1991.

emotional reaction, in turn, may cause us to "act out" a script we learned earlier in life that is dysfunctional in the situation in which we find ourselves. . . .

The person with whom we are communicating may also be a factor in our ability to be perceived as competent. If the other person communicates with us in a way that suggests we are not competent, we will, in all likelihood, act in an incompetent fashion.[2] It is also possible that we may act appropriately and effectively without actually having the knowledge necessary to engage in the behaviors by imitating the behavior of another person. While this can work when communicating with people who are different when we do not have sufficient knowledge of the other person's group, it is not the best strategy. I agree with Wiemann and Kelly (1981), "knowledge without skill is socially useless, and skill cannot be obtained without the cognitive ability to diagnose situational demands and constraints" (p. 290). . . .

MOTIVATION

Jonathan H. Turner (1987) suggests that certain basic "needs" motivate us to interact with others. Needs are "fundamental states of being in humans which, if unsatisfied, generate feelings of deprivation" (p. 23). The needs that serve as motivating factors are: (1) our need for a sense of security as a human being; (2) our need for a sense of trust (this need involves issue of predictability; I trust you will behave as I think you will); (3) our need for a sense of group inclusion; (4) our need to avoid diffuse anxiety; (5) our need for a sense of a common shared world; (6) our need for symbolic/material gratification; and (7) our need to sustain our self-conception. These needs vary in the degree to which we are conscious of them. We are the least conscious of the first three, moderately conscious of the fourth, and the most conscious of the last three.

Each of the needs, separately and in combination, influences how we want to present ourselves to others, the intentions we form, and the habits or scripts we follow.[3] The needs also can influence each other. Anxiety, for example, can result from not meeting our needs for group inclusion, trust, security, and/or sustaining our self-concept. Turner argues that our "overall level of motivational energy" is a function of our level of anxiety produced by these four needs.

Managing Our Anxiety

While avoiding anxiety is an important motivating factor in our communication with people who are similar, it is critical in our communication with strangers. . . . [I]ntergroup anxiety is largely a function of our fear of negative consequences when we interact with people who are different. As our anxiety becomes high, our need for a sense of a common shared world and our need to sustain our self-conception become central (J. H. Turner, 1987). Having a sense of a common shared world and sustaining our self-concept are much more difficult when we communicate with strangers than when we communicate with people who are similar. High anxiety, therefore, leads us to avoid communicating with strangers.

The combination of our need to avoid anxiety and our need to sustain our self-conception leads to an approach-avoidance orientation toward intergroup encounters.[4] Most of us want to see ourselves as "nonprejudiced" and "caring" people. We may, therefore, want to interact with strangers to sustain our self-concept. At the same time, however, our need to avoid anxiety leads us to want to avoid interactions which are not predictable. Holding both attitudes at the same time is not unusual.

Most of us spend the vast majority of our time interacting with people who are relatively similar to us. Our actual contact with people who are different is limited; it is a novel form of interaction (Rose, 1981). If our attempts to communicate with strangers are not successful and we cannot get out of the situations in which we find ourselves easily, then our unconscious need for group inclusion becomes unsatisfied. This leads to anxiety about ourselves and our standing in a group context (J. H. Turner, 1987). The net result is that we retreat into known territory and limit our interactions to people who are similar.

The critical thing that we need to keep in mind is that we can cognitively control our initial anxiety by increasing our tolerance for ambiguity and/or becoming mindful of our communication. . . . [B]ecoming mindful involves the creation of new categories, openness to new information, and awareness of more than one perspective. One way we can create new categories is to look at similarities we share with strangers rather than focusing on the differences. Does the person from the other group, for example, have children who go to the same school as ours? Does he or she belong to the same social clubs we do? Does she or he experience similar frustrations in her or his professional and personal life as we do? Does he or she have similar worries about his or her family as we do? The first two questions search for shared group memberships, while the second two focus on shared values, attitudes, or beliefs.

Robert Bellah, Richard Madsen, William Sullivan, Ann Swidler, and Steven Tipton (1985) point out that we need to seek out commonalities because "with a more explicit understanding of what we have in common and the goals we seek to attain together, the differences between us that remain would be less threatening" (p. 287). Finding commonalities requires that we be mindful of our prejudices. "Racism and sexism and homophobia and religious and cultural intolerance . . . are all ways of denying that other people are the same kind as ourselves" (Brodie, 1989, p. 16).

The position that Bellah and his associates advocate vis-à-vis cultural and/or ethnic differences is consistent with Langer's (1989) contention that

> because most of us grow up and spend our time with people like ourselves, we tend to assume uniformities and commonalities. When confronted with someone who is clearly different in one specific way, we drop that assumption and look for differences. . . . The mindful curiosity generated by an encounter with someone who is different, which can lead to exaggerated perceptions of strangeness, can also bring us closer to that person if channeled differently. (p. 156)

Langer's research suggests that once individuals satisfy their curiosity about differences, understanding can occur. She, therefore, argues that what is needed is a way to make mindful curiosity about differences not taboo. One way that each of us can contribute to the acceptance of mindful curiosity is by accepting others' questions about us and our groups as "requests for information" until we are certain there is another motivation.

We also can become open to new information by modifying our expectations. If, for example, we have an inflexible negative stereotype of another group, we can either modify the content of the stereotype or hold it more flexibly. We can consciously recognize that our stereotype may be inaccurate and does not apply to *all*, or even most, members of the other group. . . .

KNOWLEDGE

The knowledge component of communication competence refers to our awareness of what we need to do to communicate in an appropriate and effective way. This includes a specific awareness of the "skills" discussed in the next section and how they can be used when communicating with strangers. When communicating with strangers, we also need to have knowledge about the other person's group. My focus is this section, therefore, is on how we can gather information about strangers and their groups so that we can interpret their messages accurately. . . .

Information Seeking Strategies

Charles Berger (1979) isolated three general types of strategies we can use to gather information about others and reduce our uncertainty about them and the way they will interact with us: passive, active, and interactive strategies. When we use passive strategies we take the role of "unobtrusive observers" (i.e., we do not intervene in the situation we are observing). To illustrate this process, assume that we want to find out about Yoko, a Japanese to whom we have just been introduced.

Obviously, the type of situation in which we observe Yoko influences the amount of information we gain about her. If we observe Yoko in a situation where she does not have to interact with others, we will not gain much information about her. Situations in which she is interacting with several people at once, in contrast, allow us to make comparisons of how Yoko interacts with the different people.

If we know any of the people with whom Yoko is interacting, we can compare how Yoko interacts with the people we know and how she might interact with us. It should also be noted that if other Japanese are present in the situation, we can compare Yoko's behavior with theirs to try to determine how she is similar to and different from other Japanese.

There is one other aspect of the situation that will influence the amount of information we obtain about Yoko's behavior. If the situation is a formal one, her behavior is likely to be a function of the role she is filling in the situation and we will not learn much about Yoko as an individual. Situations where behavior is not guided by roles or social protocol, on the other hand, will provide useful information on Yoko's behavior.

The preceding examples all involve our taking the role of an observer. The active strategies for reducing uncertainty require us to do something to acquire information about Yoko. One thing we could do to get information about Yoko is to ask questions of someone who knows her. When we ask others about someone we need to keep in mind that the information we receive may not be accurate. The other person may intentionally give us wrong information or the other person may not really know Yoko well.

We can also gather information about other groups by asking people who have had contact with those groups or gathering information from the library. In this example, we could gather information on Japan by questioning someone we know who has lived in Japan, reading a book on Japanese culture, or completing a Japanese cultural assimilator. . . . This would give us information about Yoko's cultural background that would allow us to make cultural level predictions about her behavior. Again, we need to keep in mind that our informant may or may not have good information about Japan and that Yoko may not be a typical Japanese. . . .

When we use active strategies to gather information we do not actually interact with the people about whom we are trying to gather information. The interactive strategies of verbal interrogation (question asking) and self-disclosure, in contrast, are used when we interact with the other person.

One obvious way we can gather information about others is to ask them questions. When we are interacting with someone who is similar, there are limitations to this strategy that have to be kept in mind. First, we can ask only so many questions. I am not sure of what the number is, but I always know when I have asked too many. Second, our questions must be appropriate to the nature of the interaction we are having and the relationship we have with the other person.

When we are communicating with strangers, the same limitations are present, and there are others. The number and type of questions that strangers consider acceptable may not be the same as what we consider acceptable. . . . Strangers also may not be able to answer our questions, especially if our questions deal with why they behave the way they do [the ultimate answer to why questions is "because!" (that is the way we do it here)]. When interacting with strangers there is also the added problem of our not wanting to appear "stupid" or be "rude." We, therefore, often avoid asking questions of strangers.

If we can overcome our fear of looking "stupid," asking questions is an excellent way to gather information about strangers. Generally speaking, strangers will probably respond in a positive way as long as they perceive that our intent is to learn about them personally or their group and *not* to judge them.[5]

The other way we can gather information about another person when interacting with her or him is through self-disclosure—telling the other person unknown information about ourselves.[6] Self-disclosure works as an information gathering strategy because of the reciprocity norm.[7] Essentially, the reciprocity norm states that if I do something for you, you will reciprocate and do something for me. The reciprocity norm appears to be a cultural universal; it exists in all cultures.[8]

In conversations between people who are not close (i.e., people we meet for the first time, acquaintances), we tend to reciprocate and tell each other the same information about ourselves that the other person tells us. If I disclose my opinion on a topic when we are talking, you will probably tell me your opinion on the same topic. There will, however, be some differences when we communicate with strangers than when we communicate with people from our own group. The topics that are appropriate to be discussed, for example, vary from culture to culture and ethnic group to ethnic group. If we self-disclose on a topic with a stranger and she or he does not reciprocate, there is a good chance we have found an inappropriate topic of conversation in that person's group. Since the timing and pacing of self-disclosure varies across cultures and ethnic groups, it is also possible that our timing is off or we have tried to self-disclose at an inappropriate pace. . . .

Uncertainty Orientation

There is one cognitive/affective process, uncertainty orientation, that appears to influence whether or not we try to gather information about others that needs to be discussed before addressing skills. Richard Sorrentino and Judith-Ann Short (1986) point out

> that there are many people who simply are not interested in finding out information about themselves or the world, who do not conduct causal searches, who could not care less about comparing themselves with others, and who "don't give a hoot" for resolving discrepancies or inconsistencies about the self. Indeed, such people (we call them certainty oriented) will go out of their way not to perform activities such as these (we call people who *do* go out of their way to do such things uncertainty oriented). (pp. 379–380).

Uncertainty oriented people integrate new and old ideas and change their belief systems accordingly.[9] They evaluate ideas and thoughts on their own merit and do not necessarily compare them with others. Uncertainty oriented people want to understand themselves and their environment. Certainty oriented people, in contrast, like to hold on to traditional beliefs and have a tendency to reject ideas that are different. Certainty oriented people maintain a sense of self by not examining themselves or their behavior.

The more uncertainty oriented we are, the more likely we are willing to question our own behavior and its appropriateness when communicating with strangers. Also, the more uncertainty oriented we are, the more we would try to gather information about strangers so we can communicate effectively with them . . . .

SKILLS

The skills necessary to communicate effectively and appropriately with strangers are those that are directly related to reducing our uncertainty and anxiety.[10] Reducing and/or controlling our anxiety requires at least two skills: becoming mindful and developing a tolerance for ambiguity. Reducing uncertainty minimally requires three skills: empathy, behavioral flexibility, and the ability to reduce uncertainty itself (the first two skills, however, are necessary to develop the third).

Becoming Mindful

By now, it should be clear that I believe becoming mindful is an important aspect of communicating effectively with strangers. We must be cognitively aware of our communication if we are to overcome our tendency to interpret strangers' behavior based on our own system. . . . [W]e are seldom highly mindful of our communication.

When we interact with strangers, we do become somewhat mindful of our communication. Our focus, however, is usually on the outcome ("Will I make a fool of myself?"), rather than the process of communication. Even when we communicate with people close to us, we are not mindful of the process. Mihaly Csikszentmihalyi (1990) contends that

> there are few things as enjoyable as freely sharing one's most secret feelings and thoughts with another person. Even though this sounds commonplace, it in fact requires concentrated attention [mindfulness], openness, and sensitivity. In practice, the degree of investment of psychic energy in a friendship is unfortunately rare. (p. 188).

He goes on to argue that we must "control" our own lives if we want to improve our relationships with others. Such control requires that we be mindful. . . .

Tolerance for Ambiguity

Tolerance for ambiguity implies the ability to deal successfully with situations, even when a lot of information needed to interact effectively is unknown. Brent Ruben and Daniel Kealey (1979) point out that

> the ability to react to new and ambiguous situations with minimal discomfort has long been thought to be an important asset when adjusting to a new culture. . . .
> Excessive discomfort resulting from being placed in a new or different environment— or from finding the familiar environment altered in some critical ways—can lead to confusion, frustration and interpersonal hostility. Some people seem better able to adapt well in new environments and adjust quickly to the demands of the changing milieu. (p. 19)

Ruben and Kealey's research indicates that the greater our tolerance for ambiguity, the more effective we are in completing task assignments in other cultures.

Our tolerance for ambiguity affects the type of information we try to find out about others. People with a low tolerance for ambiguity try to gather information that supports their own beliefs. People with a high tolerance for ambiguity, in contrast, seek "objective" information from others (McPherson, 1983). Objective information is necessary to understand strangers and accurately predict their behavior. . . .

Empathy

The one skill that consistently emerges in discussions of competence in communicating with strangers is empathy. To understand empathy, we need to contrast it with sympathy. Sympathy refers to "the imaginative placing of ourselves in another person's position" (Bennett, 1979, p. 411). When we sympathize we use our own frame of reference to try to figure out how the other person is feeling. Milton Bennett (1979) argues that if we apply the Golden Rule ("Do unto others as you would have done unto you") when communicating with strangers, we are being sympathetic because the referent is our own standard of appropriate behavior.

In contrast to sympathy, empathy is "the imaginative intellectual and emotional participation in another person's experience" (Bennett, 1979, p. 418). The referent for interpreting the experience is not our own, but rather the other person's. Bennett proposes that we substitute the "Platinum Rule" ("Do unto others as they themselves would have done unto them"; p. 422) for the Golden Rule. This is a reasonable approach as long as what others want done unto them does not violate our basic moral principles or universally accepted principles of human rights.[11] . . .

Behavioral Flexibility

To gather information about and adapt our behavior to strangers requires that we are flexible in our behavior.[12] As suggested in the discussion of knowledge, we must be able [to] select strategies that are appropriate to gather the information we need about strangers in order to communicate effectively with them. This requires that we have different behavioral options open to us. Do I sit back and watch the other person or go interact with him or her? Which strategy will provide the information I need to know to communicate effectively?

We also must be able to adapt and accommodate our behavior to people from other groups if we are going to be successful in our interactions with them. One important aspect of adapting our behavior is the ability to speak another language (or at least use phrases in another language). If we always expect strangers to speak our language, we cannot be effective in communicating with them. Ernest Boyer (1990), Chair of the Carnegie Endowment for Teaching, points out that we "should become familiar with other languages and cultures so that [we] will be better able to live, with confidence, in an increasingly interdependent world" (p. B4).

Harry Triandis (1983) points out that the importance of speaking another language depends, at least in part, on where you are:

> In some cultures foreigners are expected to know the local language. A Frenchman [or woman] who arrives in the United States without knowing a word of English, or an American who visits France with only a bit of French, is bound to find the locals rather unsympathetic. For example, I have found a discrepancy between my friends' and my own experience in Paris. Their accounts stress discourtesy of the French while I have found the French to be quite courteous. I suspect the difference is that I speak better French than the majority of visitors and am therefore treated more courteously.

In contrast, in other cultures the visitor is not expected to know the local language. In Greece, for example, one is not expected to know the language although a few words of Greek create delight, and increase by order of magnitude (a factor of ten) the normal hospitable tendencies of that population. (p. 84)

Some attempt at using the local language is necessary to indicate an interest in the people and/or culture.

The need to adapt our behavior is not limited to speaking another language. If I (a white male from the United States) am communicating with someone from another culture who wants to stand much closer to me than I want him or her to stand (e.g., someone from a Latin or Arab culture), I have two options if I am mindful of my communication.

First, I can choose to try to use my own interpersonal distance (e.g., the other person should stand at least at arms length from me). If the other person keeps trying to use her or his distance, however, he or she will "dance" me around the room (i.e., the other person moves forward, I move back; to compensate and be at a distance that is comfortable for him or her, the other person moves closer). If I am not mindful of my communication, this is what is likely to occur.

Alternatively, I can choose to use a different pattern of behavior. I can decide to stand closer to the other person than I would if I was communicating with someone from my own culture. This option will, in all likelihood, lead to more effective communication. When people are following different norms, at least one of the parties has to adapt for effective communication to occur. . . .

Ability to Reduce Uncertainty

The final skill to be discussed is the ability to reduce uncertainty itself. If you can empathize and have behavioral flexibility you can gather the information necessary to reduce uncertainty. As indicated earlier, reducing uncertainty requires that we be able to describe others' behavior, select accurate interpretations of their messages, accurately predict their behavior, and be able to explain their behavior. When we also are controlling our anxiety, these abilities should lead to appropriate and effective communication. . . .

NOTES

1 Spitzberg and Cupach (1984) use the term effectiveness to refer to task outcomes (e.g., goal achievement).
2 Watzlawick, Beavin, and Jackson (1967), for example, point out that the way members of a family communicate with each other can create mental illness.
3 J. H. Turner (1987) uses different labels for some of the terms (including the needs). He uses the [term] ethnomethods, for example, to refer to what I call habits or scripts. I believe my terms capture the essence of his idea, but are not as full of academic jargon.
4 Spitzberg and Cupach (1984) also talk about approach avoidance as a factor in motivation. They, however, assume that it is a basic orientation to any encounter rather than deriving it from more basic needs as I am here.

5 Langer notes that there appear to be "taboo" questions. I believe, however, that most of the taboos are in our minds.
6 Berger (1979) actually isolates a third interactive strategy, deception detection, that I am not discussing.
7 See Gouldner (1960) for an extensive discussion.
8 There are some differences in how it is manifested in different cultures. See Gudykunst and Ting-Toomey (1988) for a detailed discussion.
9 This summary is drawn from Sorrentino and Short (1986).
10 The theory (Gudykunst, 1988) suggests that effectiveness and adaptation are a function of reducing uncertainty and anxiety. Other variables (e.g., expectations) affect our level of uncertainty and anxiety and are not linked directly to effectiveness. Gao and Gudykunst (1990) tested this assumption in an adaptation context and it was supported. There are numerous other skills that could be discussed if I did not select the skills based on the theory. There is some overlap between those selected on the basis of the theory and atheoretically derived lists of skills. Ruben (1976), for example, listed seven skills: (1) empathy, (2) tolerance for ambiguity, (3) display of respect, (4) interaction posture, (5) orientation to knowledge, (6) role behavior, and (7) interaction management.
11 Space does not permit an elaborate discussion of ethical issues here. A complete discussion of ethical relativity theory can be found in *Communicating with Strangers* (first edition: Gudykunst & Kim, 1984; second edition: Gudykunst & Kim, 1992).
12 The way I am talking about behavioral flexibility is very similar to Lennox and Wolfe's (1984) notion of ability to modify self-presentations (which is a subscale in their revised self-monitoring scale). Spitzberg and Cupach (19984) included Snyder's (1974) notion of self-monitoring as a skill in communication competence. I have not called this self-monitoring or ability to modify self-presentations because I think the idea of behavioral flexibility is more general. The concepts, however, are interrelated.

REFERENCES

Beck, A. (1988). *Love is never enough.* New York: Harper and Row.

Bellah, R. N., Madsen, R., Sullivan, W. M., Swidler, A., & Tipton, S. M. (1985). *Habits of the heart: Individualism and commitment in American life.* Berkeley: University of California Press.

Bennett, M. (1979). Overcoming the Golden Rule: Sympathy and empathy. In D. Nimmo (Ed.), *Communication yearbook 3.* New Brunswick, NJ: Transaction.

Berger, C. R. (1979). Beyond initial interactions. In H. Giles & R. St. Clair (Eds.), *Language and social psychology.* Oxford: Blackwell.

Boyer, E. (1990, June 20). Letter to the editor. *Chronicle of Higher Education,* p. B4.

Brodie, H. K. (1989, September 9). No we're not taught to hate, but we can overcome instinct to fear "the other." *Los Angeles Times,* Part II, p. 16.

Carroll, R. (1988). *Cultural misunderstandings: The French-American experience.* Chicago: University of Chicago Press.

Csikszentmihalyi, M. (1990). *Flow: The psychology of optimal experience.* New York: Harper and Row.

Gao, G., & Gudykunst, W. B. (1990). Uncertainty, anxiety, and adaptation. *International Journal of Intercultural Relations, 14,* 301–317.

Gouldner, A. (1960). The norm of reciprocity. *American Sociological Review, 25,* 161–179.

Gudykunst, W. B. (1988). Uncertainty and anxiety. In Y. Kim & W. Gudykunst (Eds.), *Theories in intercultural communication*. Newbury Park, CA: Sage.

Gudykunst, W. B., & Kim, Y. Y. (1984). *Communicating with strangers: An approach to intercultural communication*. New York: McGraw-Hill.

Gudykunst, W. B. & Kim, Y. Y. (1992). *Communicating with strangers* (2nd ed.). New York: McGraw-Hill.

Gudykunst, W. B., & Ting-Toomey, S., with Chua, E. (1988). *Culture and interpersonal communication*. Newbury Park, CA: Sage.

Hofman, T. (1985). Arabs and Jews, blacks and whites: Identity and group relations. *Journal of Multilingual and Multicultural Development, 6*, 217–237.

Langer, E. (1989). *Mindfulness*. Reading, MA: Addison-Wesley.

Lennox, R., & Wolfe, R. (1984). Revision of the self-monitoring scale. *Journal of Personality and Social Psychology, 46*, 1349–1364.

McFall, R. (1982). A review and reformulation of the concept of social skills. *Behavioral Assessment, 4*, 1–33.

McPherson, K. (1983). Opinion-related information seeking. *Personality and Social Psychology Bulletin, 9*, 116–124.

Rose, T. (1981). Cognitive and dyadic processes in intergroup contact. In D. Hamilton (Ed.), *Cognitive processes in stereotyping and intergroup behavior*. Hillsdale, NJ: Erlbaum.

Ruben, B. (1976). Assessing communication competency for intercultural adaptation. *Group and Organizational Studies, 1*, 334–354.

Ruben, B., & Kealey, D. (1979). Behavioral assessment of communication competency and the prediction of cross-cultural adaptation. *International Journal of Intercultural Relations, 3*, 15–48.

Sorrentino, R. M., & Short, J. A. (1986). Uncertainty orientation, motivation, and cognition. In R. M. Sorrentino & E. T. Higgins (Eds.), *Handbook of motivation and cognition*. New York: Guilford.

Spitzberg, B., & Cupach, W. (1984). *Interpersonal communication competence*. Beverly Hills, CA: Sage.

Triandis, H. C. (1983). Essential of studying culture. In D. Landis & R. Brislin (Eds.), *Handbook of intercultural training* (Vol. 1). Elmsford, NY: Pergamon.

Turner, J. H. (1987). Toward a sociological theory of motivation. *American Sociological Review, 52*, 15–27.

Watzlawick, P., Beavin, J., & Jackson, D. (1967). *The pragmatics of human communication*. New York: Norton.

Wiemann, J. M., & Backlund, P. (1980). Current theory and research in communication competence. *Review of Educational Research, 50*, 185–199.

Wiemann, J. M., & Bradec, J. (1989). Metatheoretical issues in the study of communicative competence. In B. Dervin (Ed.), *Progress in communication sciences* (Vol. 9). Norwood, NJ: Ablex.

Wiemann, J. M., & Kelly, C. (1981). Pragmatics of interpersonal competence. In C. Wilder-Mott & J. Weaklund (Eds.), *Rigor and imagination*. New York: Praeger.

A Strategy for Building Better Relationships As We Negotiate

Roger Fisher and Scott Brown

. . . Most of the time we carry on our various relationships without following any conscious strategy—specific rules of conduct or guidelines that we think will improve the relationship. We may simply react to what others do. Or emotions may dominate logic and keep us from pursuing any strategy we might have in mind. Sometimes, however, we will be following a deliberate strategy—a theory of how to have better relations—without realizing it is a poor one.

To achieve the kind of relationship we want, we are likely to need a few explicit guidelines. At a minimum, we will want to avoid two common mistakes.

1. Ignoring partisan perceptions. We forget how differently people can see things.
2. Relying on reciprocity. We try to build a relationship by expecting others to follow our lead or by following theirs.

BEWARE OF PARTISAN PERCEPTIONS; DON'T FORGET HOW DIFFERENTLY PEOPLE SEE THINGS

Each of us needs the kind of relationship with someone else that will enable us to cope successfully with whatever problems come along. As I seek such a working relationship with you, there is a great risk that I will fail to appreciate how differently you view the world. If our disagreements are significant, we will almost certainly have strikingly dissimilar perceptions of ourselves, of each other, of what is important, of what our relationship is today, and of what it might become. Unless I understand these differences, they will interfere with our ability to solve problems.

Each of us tends to see things in ways that take our own interests disproportionately into account. And the facts we know best are those closest to us. The more we know about something, the more important it is likely to appear. An auto accident just outside our house is more important to us than an earthquake ten thousand miles away. A drizzle on our picnic looms larger in our lives than a typhoon in the Far East.

The process of perceiving things and building up our beliefs is highly personal. Each of us:

- observe different events;
- focuses attention on different aspects of these events;
- tends to concentrate on evidence that supports our prior views;
- filters and labels information so that it is easy to store;
- remembers information so that it fits a coherent "story"; and
- reshapes information previously stored to fit new needs.

Source: Abridged from Chapter 3 in R. Fisher and S. Brown, *Getting Together: Building Better Relationships As We Negotiate* (pp. 24–39). Boston: Houghton Mifflin, 1988.

Psychologists have found that all people, in varying degrees, need consistency in the way they relate their perceptions and their beliefs. There is a great deal of truth to the adage, "Where you stand depends on where you sit." Union leaders, looking at the facts of a labor-management dispute, may see underpaid workers, price inflation, and management hostility. Management may see highly paid workers, rising costs, and a history of union threats. Even two individuals whose lives are extremely close observe, note, and remember quite different things. For example, if we were to stop and read the minds of a middle manager and a higher executive on a Friday afternoon after a bad week, we might find them to have [different] perceptions. . . .

Once their differences are brought to their attention, the middle manager and higher executive ought to be able to understand each other's perceptions without difficulty. When people in a relationship are further apart—in terms of distance, culture, background, and role—the contrast between their perceptions will be greater, and each will find it more difficult to appreciate how the other sees things.

A successful strategy for building a working relationship has to recognize that partisans will perceive their differences differently. In this respect, the U.S.-Soviet relationship is particularly difficult. Officials of the two countries, living in different cultures, observing some facts at close range and others at a distance, and approaching those facts with different ideologies, values, and interests, cannot possibly have the same perceptions.

Consider the element of reliability. Everyone recognizes that it is difficult to work with someone who cannot be trusted, someone who makes misleading statements or makes promises that are not fulfilled. The U.S.-Soviet problem, however, involves not just questionable reliability, but also highly different perceptions of reliability. To improve the working relationship between the two governments, we need a strategy that will work despite those conflicting perceptions. The objective truth about which is more reliable (as scientific investigators, historians, and legal scholars might later decide) is only one bit of data. In a given situation, it may not even be important. What is important is that we can predict with confidence that each government will see itself as being more reliable than the other, and certainly as being more reliable than the other perceives it to be.

The chart on page 395 illustrates American and Soviet perceptions in 1987.

The fact that perceptions are going to differ, and with a strong partisan bias in favor of the side holding them, is a serious obstacle in building a relationship that can deal well with differences. Partisan perceptions about substantive matters create some differences and make others more difficult to solve.

Partisan perceptions about the way we interact can be even more damaging. If I value cooperation, understanding, and honesty, I am almost certain to see my conduct as more cooperative, more understanding, and more honest than you see it. Likewise, if I have serious differences with you, I am likely to see your behavior as lacking those qualities. As a result, I am likely to blame you for problems in the relationship and to justify my own faults as better than yours: "You never listen to me, so it's not worth talking to you." When partisan perceptions create negative reactions in the relationship, it deteriorates.

Partisan perceptions

U.S. Reliability

A U.S. view	A Soviet view
The Salt II treaty is not binding because it was never ratified.	The U.S. signed the Salt II treaty but then did not even ask for Senate approval.
The U.S. is free to reinterpret the language of the ABM Treaty since the Soviets would be free to do so.	The U.S. signed the ABM Treaty and then, 14 years later, "reinterpreted" it in a way contrary to what all the negotiators and the U.S. Senate understood.
Since no comprehensive test ban treaty has been concluded, the U.S. is free to continue testing.	The U.S. signed the Non-Proliferation Treaty, committing it to seek an end to all nuclear testing for all time. It now ignores that obligation, saying that it wants to continue testing as long as nuclear weapons exist.
In view of Soviet threats and subversion, the U.S. must be free to act in self-defense against terrorism and aggression.	The U.S. treats itself as free to violate international law by mining Nicaraguan harbors, bombing Libya, and using force to try to overthrow even legal governments that it recognizes.

Soviet Reliability

A U.S. view	A Soviet view
The radar facility at Krasnoyarsk constitutes a violation of the Anti-Ballistic Missile Treaty.	The radar facility is a space-tracking device permitted by the ABM Treaty.
A number of Soviet nuclear tests constitute likely violations of the 150-kiloton limit set by the 1974 Threshold Test Ban Treaty.	U.S. studies consistently overestimate the magnitude of Soviet nuclear tests. Unofficial American experts agree that none has exceeded the 150-kiloton limit.
The Soviet Union consistently violates its promises.	The Soviet Union carefully honors its legal obligations.
They care nothing for the spirit of an agreement.	We adhere to the letter of every treaty.

As the next section points out, the consequences of partisan perceptions are particularly acute if either side uses reciprocity as a guide for behavior.

DON'T RELY ON RECIPROCITY TO BUILD A RELATIONSHIP BY EXPECTING OTHERS TO FOLLOW OUR LEAD OR BY FOLLOWING THEIRS

The good relationship that we seek is reciprocal. Two people will deal more skillfully with their differences if both behave rationally, both fully understand each other's perceptions, both communicate effectively, both are reliable, neither tries to coerce the other, and each accepts the other as someone whose interests and views deserve to be taken into account.

The principle of reciprocity is familiar in substantive negotiations, where a favor or concession by one side is exchanged for a similar favor or concession by the other. If I shovel the snow off my neighbor's walk when he [or she] is away in the winter, I can fairly ask him [or her] to mow my lawn when I am away in the summer. Fairness suggests that if the Soviet Union asks the United States to cut its nuclear missiles by 50 percent, it should offer to cut its own missiles by the same percentage. We may disagree about exactly what is reciprocal. (If you did me a favor by driving my children home from school last week, do I owe you the favor of looking after your son, Buster, all day Saturday?) But the principle of reciprocity is a generally accepted external standard of fairness in substantive negotiations.

Since a reciprocal relationship is our goal, and since reciprocity is a sound basis for substantive agreements, there is a natural tendency to rely on some form of reciprocity as the key to building an effective working relationship. This tendency, however, is dangerous. In one form, a reciprocal strategy looks like an application of the Golden Rule: "Do unto others as you would have them do unto you." In another form, it constitutes a hostile policy of "an eye for an eye": I will treat you as badly as you have been treating me. Either policy is risky.

. . . The Golden Rule is a useful rule of thumb in helping me understand how my behavior is likely to affect you and how you might want me to behave. If you, as a middle manager, appreciate being consulted by your superiors before they make major decisions that affect you, then you can safely predict that I, a subordinate, would like similar treatment. But the Golden Rule is *not* based on the premise that if I behave as you would like, I can safely predict that you will behave the same way. If I avoid criticizing you in public, I cannot safely assume that you will avoid criticizing me. If I try to build a working relationship based on such an optimistic view—that you will reciprocate my actions—I will make dangerous mistakes. . . .

No one seriously recommends this strategy—although some who work for better relations are accused of doing so, and others may favor bits of it, such as not talking about differences. To pursue a comprehensive approach resting on the premise that others will follow our example is highly risky and unwise. I might think I want your actions to be based wholly on affection for me, but we will not solve serious differences if I act wholly on the basis of affection for you. I may *think* that I would like you to accept without question my understanding of a situation, but it will not help us deal with reality for me to accept yours. As unpleasant as discussing differences may sometimes be, it is the only way to deal with them successfully. And if we were to trust everybody simply because we would like everybody to trust us, we would certainly be disappointed—and broke. Reliance on reciprocal good will is not a sound foundation on which to build a working relationship.

This is particularly true when partisan perceptions are taken into account. If I pursue a strategy that depends on your equivalent behavior, I will probably find that you fail the test. Even if you believe your behavior is as good as mine, I am likely to see it as worse. I may then become discouraged and turn to a different, more hostile strategy. . . .

REQUIREMENTS OF A SUCCESSFUL STRATEGY

If the analysis . . . is sound, a strategy for building a better working relationship must pass some difficult tests:

Independent of disagreement. In no way should our guidelines require substantive agreement. While agreement makes relationships more comfortable, the more serious our disagreements, the more we need a good working relationship to cope with them. We need an "all weather" strategy.

Independent of concessions. Our strategy should neither require us to give in nor demand that others do so.

Independent of partisan perceptions. We should take into account the extent to which we and they will see things differently. The value of our guidelines should not rest on the premise that we see the truth and they are wrong. Although on each occasion we may firmly believe that we are right, it is impossible to build a relationship on the premise that the other side is always wrong.

Independent of reciprocity. We should not wait for the other side to engage in exemplary behavior, nor should we assume that our example will be followed.

Independent of permanent "sides." If our goal involves full understanding and being open to persuasion, a good strategy should also leave us open to revising our views about who is on our side and who is not. Just as a neighbor may become a member of the family, so business adversaries may become joint venturers and former enemies may become military allies. Relationship-building should be open-ended.

A PRESCRIPTIVE APPROACH: BE UNCONDITIONALLY CONSTRUCTIVE

The balance of this chapter outlines a strategy that meets the tests set out above. This is no miracle strategy that will turn criminals into trustworthy friends, business adversaries into reliable colleagues, and enemies into allies. No such strategy exists. What we offer is a framework for thinking about the problem, a general approach that seems to make sense, and some rules of thumb that may prove helpful in many situations.

In any relationship, I want to be able to take steps that will both improve our ability to work together and advance my substantive interests, whether or not you respond as I would like. In short, I am looking for guidelines I can follow that will be both good for the relationship and good for me, *whether or not you follow the same guidelines.* In that sense, this strategy is "unconditionally constructive."

Finally, because we will be better able to settle our differences wisely and easily if both of us approach the relationship constructively, I would like the guidelines to be good for you, too. In fact, I would like them to be the best that you could follow. They should be as good for you as they are for me.

To meet these rigorous tests, the strategy cannot be as bold, trusting, and venturesome as some would like. It must be risk averse. (We, the authors, do not know with whom you, the readers, may be dealing.) In some circumstances, it will not be as quick or successful in improving a relationship as a bolder—and riskier—approach might be. In baldest outline, it is as follows:

An Unconditionally Constructive Strategy

Do only those things that are both good for the relationship
and good for us,
whether or not they reciprocate.

1. *Rationality.* Even if they are acting emotionally,
   balance emotions with reason.
2. *Understanding.* Even if they misunderstand us,
   try to understand them.
3. *Communication.* Even if they are not listening,
   consult them before deciding on matters that affect them.
4. *Reliability.* Even if they are trying to deceive us, neither trust them nor deceive them; *be reliable.*
5. *Noncoercive modes of influence.* Even if they are trying to coerce us, neither yield to that coercion nor try to coerce them;
   be open to persuasion and try to persuade them.
6. *Acceptance.* Even if they reject us and our concerns as unworthy of their consideration, *accept them as worthy of our consideration,*
   care about them, and
   be open to learning from them.

These guidelines are not advice on how to be "good," but rather on how to be effective. They derive from a selfish, hard-headed concern with what each of us can do, in practical terms, to make a relationship work better. The high moral content of the guidelines is a bonus. I can feel good about improving the way we deal with differences.

In every relationship, we are bound to encounter significant conflicts of interest. But we will almost always share an interest in dealing skillfully with those conflicts. Neither partner in a relationship wants the other to bungle. It is not inconsistent for me to want to advance selfish interests that conflict with yours and at the same time want to improve our joint ability to deal with those conflicting interests. . . .

CHAPTER 13

Becoming Intercultural

We live in a world where we constantly are exposed to international events through the mass media and other advanced information systems. What happens in a small nation in South America can be, directly and indirectly, a significant part of the political reality of many nations around the world. Diplomats and international business personnel work closely with strangers of other cultures and need to be keenly aware of the changing realities of the world. In urban centers, many of us find ourselves working side by side with strangers from various national, racial, ethnic, and religious backgrounds.

In addition to adjusting to the technological connectedness of our international and domestic environments, all of us have to adapt to changes in many aspects of our lives—in social structure, values, politics, and, most of all, in our human relations. Even in less technological societies, change has encroached on nearly every pattern of life—on many traditional values, on the structure and functions of the family, and on the relations between generations. Every index suggests that the rate of change will increase up to the as-yet untested limits of human adaptability. Our relationship to our personal and collective past is increasingly becoming one of dislocation, of that peculiar mixture of freedom and loss that inevitably accompanies massive change.

Increasingly we are placed in positions in which the culture of our youth cannot be depended on to produce reliable predictions about what other people are going to do next. There is little convincing evidence that decreasing physical distance and increasing informational proximity brings improvement in the quality of human life. We continue to see international and domestic conflicts, in spite of the fact that people across cultural and subcultural boundaries perhaps know more about one another now than at any other time in history.

What we see, instead, are many different ways in which people try to cope with, and adapt to, the complexities of life. There are those who feel lost in the midst of all this change and who shy away from such concepts as "social consciousness" or "world consciousness." Others busily organize people to join together to fight for traditional values and to reverse the changing trends. There are also those who try desperately to keep up with the changes that occur around them, often finding only experiences of failure and despair.

What appears to be lacking in our efforts to cope with the changes and complexities of our contemporary world is a clear understanding of its fundamental dynamics and a definite sense of direction for change. We fail to recognize the pervasive "interculturalness" of our domestic and international realities, and instead we try to deal with many intercultural problems in a manner shaped by our own culture. Even though the problems we face demand an intercultural orientation and new ways of dealing with one another, we try to "force" our own cultural ways on others. Such seems to be the case with many international problems and domestic clashes of diverse interest groups, as well as with our attempts to resolve conflicts between individuals.

What we need to do in order to be more effective in our changing world is to make a conscious decision concerning our basic attitudes toward ourselves and toward our relationships to others and the world at large. This means we need to search for a new image of ourselves that will help us develop specific strategies for daily activities and problems. Reorienting ourselves and becoming less ethnocentric is, of course, a difficult challenge. For most of us, who have grown up in one cultural milieu during our formative years, it is difficult to change our cultural inertia and habits even if we would like to.

Yet is is crucial that we do our utmost to work toward becoming less ethno-centric if we are to become more functional and effective in our intercultural environ-ment. To be an effective business manager in a multinational company, for example, one cannot be highly ethnocentric. To be an effective teacher in a multiethnic urban school, one must be able to deal with children and their parents whose cultural attributes are different from one's own. To be an effective ambassador to another country, one must be an effective communicator with a great deal of sensitivity, understanding, and the social skills of the local culture.

Experiences of immigrants and sojourners who successfully adapt to new cultural environments are invaluable in providing us with insights into the fundamental changes we must undergo if we are to develop an intercultural perspective. The readings in this chapter are designed to examine selected issues in developing an intercultural perspective. In the first reading, Kim and Ruben outline the intercultural transformations individuals go through. They contend that gradual changes take place within us when we communicate extensively with strangers. The "stress-adaptation-growth" process we go through leads to increases in our interculturalness.

In the second reading, Boulding discusses the possibility of developing a species identity. She argues that if we recognize our common species identity we can over-come the obstacles (e.g., our identities as members of nation-states) to peace in the world. Boulding looks at the idea of species identity from several different cultural perspectives.

Intercultural Transformation
Young Yun Kim and Brent D. Ruben

. . . An increasing number of attempts have been made to explore ideologies and worldviews that are larger than national and cultural interests and that embrace all humanity. As early as 1946, Northrop (1946/1966), in *The Meaning of the East and the West,* proposed an "international cultural ideal" to provide intellectual and emotional foundations for what he envisioned as "partial world sovereignty." Among contemporary critics of culture, Thompson (1973) explored the concept "planetary culture" in which Eastern mysticism was integrated with Western science and rationalism. Similarly, Capra (1975), in *The Tao of Physics,* showed an essential harmony between these two complementary manifestations of the human mind.

Additional philosophical ideas have been proposed by Gebser (see Feuerstein, 1987), who projected "integral consciousness" as an emerging mode of experiencing reality. In this mode, the "rational," "mythical," "magical," and "primal" modes are simultaneously present and integrated. Elgin's (1981) idea of "voluntary simplicity" echoes Gebser, portraying an emerging "global common sense" and a practical life-style to reconcile the willful, rational approach to life of the West and the holistic, spiritual orientation of the East. Other concepts such as "international" (Lutzker, 1960), "universal" (Walsh, 1973), "multicultural" (Adler, 1982), and "marginal" (Lum, 1982) have been presented to project similar images of personhood, with varying degrees of descriptive and explanatory value.

Paralleling these philosophical and ideological visions of intercultural personhood, many behavioral scientists have investigated experiences of individuals extensively exposed to foreign cultures. Stimulated by the post-Second World War boom in student exchange and international migration, the Peace Corps movement in the 1960s, the expansion of multinational trade, and the increase in civil and military government personnel, extensive literature has approached the investigation. Studies of the intercultural communication experiences of sojourners and immigrants can be broadly categorized into two approaches—the "intercultural communication-as-problem" approach; and the "intercultural communication-as-learning/growth" approach, as briefly reviewed next.[1]

INTERCULTURAL COMMUNICATION-AS-PROBLEM APPROACH

Because encounters with alien cultural environments present surprises and uncertainties (in varying degrees depending on the severity of cultural dislocation experiences), there have been ample discussions, essays, and empirical studies dealing with this

Source: Abridged from Chapter 13 in Y. Y. Kim & W. B. Gudykunst (Eds.), *Theories in Intercultural Communication* (pp. 299–321). Newbury Park, CA: Sage, 1988.

phenomenon. The concept *culture shock*, has been used by anthropologists, communication researchers, sociologists, and psychologists, among others, to explain many of
the frustrations encountered in the early part of the sojourner's stay abroad. Many
writers have described the various psychological, social, and physical reactions associated with culture shock. Other similar terms also have been employed to refer to
variations of such "shock" experiences, including *role shock* (Byrnes, 1966; Higbee,
1969), *language shock* (Smalley, 1963), *culture fatigue* (Guthrie, 1966, 1975), and
transition shock (Bennett, 1977).

Essentially, culture shock has been used to refer to "a form of personality
maladjustment which is a reaction to a temporary unsuccessful attempt to adjust to
new surroundings and people" (Lundstedt, 1963, p. 8) and a natural consequence of
the state of a human organism's inability to interact with the new and changed
environment in an effective manner (Bennett, 1977). Taft (1977) identified a number
of common reactions to cultural dislocation: (1) "cultural fatigue," as manifested by
irritability, insomnia, and other psychosomatic disorders; (2) a sense of loss arising
from being uprooted from one's familiar surroundings; (3) rejection by the individual
members of the new environment; and (4) a feeling of impotence from being unable to
competently deal with the environmental unfamiliarity. Similarly, many immigrant
studies have looked into the phenomena related to "mental illnesses" of immigrants.
Descriptions of encounters with the Southeast Asian refugees in mental health
settings have appeared in the literature (see Kinzie, Tran, Breckenridge, & Bloom,
1980; Williams & Westermeyer, 1986). In each of these cases, the features associated
with environmental change are the "shock" effects involving heightened emotions
and intense suffering.

Closely related to the studies of culture shock are studies examining the process
of individual adjustment in unfamiliar cultural environments. Many attempts have
been made to identify the "stages" of adjustment that individuals go through in a
foreign environment. Oberg (1960), for instance, described four stages: (1) a "honey-
moon" stage characterized by fascination, elation, and optimism; (2) a stage of
hostility and emotionally stereotyped attitudes toward the host society and increased
association with fellow sojourners; (3) a recovery stage characterized by increased
language knowledge and ability to get around in the new culture; and (4) a final stage
in which adjustment is about as complete as possible, anxiety is largely gone, and new
customs are accepted and enjoyed.

Others have depicted the stages of adaptive change individuals go through in
"curves." These curves indicate the patterns of change over time in the degree of
satisfaction in living in the alien environment. Some empirical support has been
found, for instance, for what has been described as a U curve of adjustment (Lysgaard,
1955), depicting the initial optimism and elation in the host culture, the subsequent
dip or "trough" in the level of adjustment, followed by a gradual recovery to higher
adjustment levels. Gullahorn and Gullahorn (1963) extended this curve further and
proposed a W curve, indicating that sojourners often undergo a reacculturation
process (a second U curve in their home environment similar to that experienced
abroad). (See Church, 1982, for a detailed review.)

A common viewpoint in these studies of culture shock and adaptation has been that life is difficult in foreign lands. These studies also shared a common concern for minimizing the psychological difficulties and maximizing effective performance in an unfamiliar environment. Few agreements exist, however, as to patterns and processes of adaptive changes that can be determined from the existing studies. Adjustment stage models also present inherent conceptual difficulties in classifying individuals. As Church (1982) pointed out, the existing models do not adequately address crucial questions, such as "Is the order of stages invariant?" and "Must all stages be passed through or can some be skipped by some individuals?" . . .

INTERNATIONAL COMMUNICATION-AS-LEARNING/ GROWTH APPROACH

Countering the preceding "problem-oriented" studies, an alternative approach was proposed by Adler (1987) who viewed culture shock in a broader context of intercultural learning and growth. In Adler's view,

> Culture shock is thought of as a profound learning experience that leads to a high degree of self-awareness and personal growth. Rather than being only a disease for which adaptation is the cure, culture shock is likewise at the very heart of the cross-cultural learing experience. It is an experience in self-understanding and change. (p. 29)

Similarly, Ruben (1983) questioned the problem-oriented perspective as he discussed the results of a study of Canadian technical advisers and their spouses on two-year assignments in Kenya (Ruben & Kealey, 1979). In this study, the intensity and directionality of culture shock was found to be unrelated to patterns of psychological adjustment at the end of the first year in an alien culture. Of still greater interest was the finding that, in some instances, the magnitude of culture shock was positively related to social and professional effectiveness within the new culture. These findings suggested implications that directly contradict the problem-oriented perspective on the nature of culture shock.

In the intercultural communication-as-learning/growth approach, then, culture shock experiences are viewed as the core or essence, though not necessarily the totality, of the cross-cultural learning experience. The culture-shock process is regarded as fundamental in that the individual must somehow confront the social, psychological, and philosophical discrepancies one finds between his or her own internalized cultural disposition and that of the new environment. The cross-cultural learning experience, accordingly, is viewed in large part as a transitional experience reflecting a "movement from a state of low self- and cultural awareness to a state of high self- and cultural awareness" (Adler, 1972/1987, p. 15).

Based on this perspective, Adler (1975) described five phases of encompassing and progressive changes in identity and experiential learning. Briefly, the five phases are: (1) a *contact phase* characterized by excitement and euphoria during which the individual views the new environment ethnocentrically; (2) a *disintegration phase* marked by confusion, alienation, and depression, during which cultural differences become increasingly noticeable; (3) a *reintegration phase* characterized by strong rejection of the second culture, defensive projection of personal difficulties, and an existential choice to either regress to earlier phases or to move closer to resolution and personal growth; (4) an *autonomy stage* marked by increasing understanding the host culture along with a feeling of competence; and (5) a final *independence stage* marked by a cherishing of cultural differences and relativism, creative behavior, and increased self- and cultural awareness. . . .

INTERCULTURAL TRANSFORMATION

. . . *Intercultural communication* is defined as the communication process that takes place in a circumstance in which communicators' patterns of verbal and nonverbal encoding and decoding are significantly different because of cultural differences. Although many intercultural experiences occur indirectly through being exposed to messages that we read, see, and hear in mass media (including books, journals, magazines, movies, television programs, and newspapers), we are primarily concerned here with communication situations of direct, face-to-face encounters between individuals of differing cultural backgrounds. The term *culture* is used broadly and inclusively to refer to the collective life patterns shared by people in social groups such as national, racial, ethnic, socioeconomic, regional, and gender groups. Communication situations are considered intercultural to the extent that the participants carry different cultural and subcultural attributes. The more the participants differ in their cultural and subcultural attributes, the more intercultural the communication is (see Gudykunst & Kim, 1984; Ruben, 1983; Sarbaugh, 1979).

   Intercultural transformation refers to the process of change in individuals beyond the cognitive, affective, and behavioral limits of their original culture. As a process, the concept implies differential levels of *interculturalness*. The term *intercultural* is preferred here to other similar terms such as *multicultural, universal,* and *marginal.* Simply projecting a personhood that transcends any given cultural group, the term is not bounded by any specific cultural attributes.[2] . . .

   For the present purpose, individuals are viewed as systems and are understood to function through ongoing interactions with the environment and its inhabitants. In this perspective, *communication* refers to the process of information decoding (receiving, processing, and transforming) and encoding (expressing verbally and nonverbally) necessary to function in a given environment. Through communication, an individual is linked with the environment informationally. This continual give-and-take process of communication is necessary to the emergence and survival of all humans as social beings. As such, each person is viewed as an *open system.*[3]

   Like all other living systems, humans are characteristically *homeostatic,* attempting to hold constant a variety of variables in our internal meaning structure to achieve an ordered whole. When individuals receive messages that disrupt their existing internal order, they experience *disequilibrium*. In this state of disequilibrium, *stress* confronts the individual, and he or she struggles to regain internal equilibrium. Stress, then, is a manifestation of a generic process that occurs whenever the capabilities of an open system are not totally adequate to the demands of the environment. In stressful situations, the so-called defensive mechanism is activated in individuals as an attempt to hold the internal structure constant by some kind of psychological maneuvering. People attempt to avoid or minimize the anticipated or actual "pain" of disequilibrium and stress by self-deception, denial, avoidance, and withdrawal (Lazarus, 1966, p. 262).

When the environmental challenges continue to threaten internal equilibrium, individuals by necessity continue to strive to "meet" and manage the challenge through their *adaptive activities* of acting on the environment as well as of responding to it. Unlike animals that commonly respond to environmental challenges with passivity, human adaptive activities include both alteration of internal conditions and alteration of environmental conditions (Chomsky, 1972). With the reflexive" and "self-reflexive" capacities of the human mind that reviews, anticipates, generalizes, analyzes, and plans, individuals are capable of creatively transforming their internal as well as external conditions. This uniquely human adaptive capacity is called by Jantsch (1980) "self-organizing," and is viewed as the key to internal growth. "We live, so to speak, in co-evolution with ourselves, with our own mental products" (p. 177).

Through iterative communication processes between the inner and outer world, individuals' internal structures evolve and grow. They learn to see a situation "with new eyes." This self-organizing (or reflexive and self-reflexive) characteristic of human systems enables human thought to generate more adaptive alternatives than lower animals are capable of generating. More meanings can be attributed to objects, and a greater number of connections between meanings arise, and, thus, a greater number of outcomes. Whereas the moth has no alternative when faced with a light and immediately flies toward it, a person engaging in complex thought processes can perceive a stimuli in many ways and can consider many ways of interrelating these perceptions for adaptive purposes.

The *stress-adaptation-growth* process is cyclic and continual. Once an environmental threat propels the system into disequilibrium, the person acts to restore harmony by restructuring his or her internal communication system in order to accommodate the challenge. Internal equilibrium is thus regained until the system is confronted by new environmental challenges. Implicit in this view is the notion that there is simply no way to derive the benefits of growth without the concomitant experiences of stress. This principle presents the unity in which stress and growth are integrated in the adaptation process because neither occurs without the other, and each occurs because of the other.

The dynamic tension between stress and adaptation and the resultant internal growth essentially characterizes the life processes of humans (as well as all living systems). It is this tension that is necessary for the continued existence of individuals facing environmental challenges. It is the resolution of stressful difficulties that promises the qualitative transformation of a person toward a greater internal capacity to cope with varied environmental conditions. The increased internal capacity, in turn, facilitates the subsequent handling of stress and adaptation. . . .

FROM CULTURAL TO INTERCULTURAL . . .

As human infants grow, they adapt to a cultural environment composed largely of the symbols and objects whose meaning and significance are the product of the communication activities of other humans. Over time, individuals develop and internalize the cognitive, affective, and behavioral attributes that are commonly shared by people in the cultural milieu. Such attributes, in turn, serve as necessary means of communication in managing themselves and their environment.

In this process, the individuals become cultural beings. Cultural attributes become a large part of their unconscious patterns of communication, particularly the cognitive patterns of categorizing and sorting information from the environment. As cultural persons, they are further conditioned by the collective ways of feeling and behaving. Humans, thus, have limited freedom in experiencing what is beyond the borders of their cultural consciousness.

The internalized cultural imprinting that governs individuals' internal conditions remain largely unrecognized, unquestioned, and unchallenged until they encounter people with different cultural attributes. As Boulding (1956/1977) stated, the human nervous system is structured in such a way that the patterns that govern behavior and perception come into consciousness only when there is a deviation from the familiar (p. 13). Intercultural encounters provide such situations of deviation from the familiar as individuals are faced with things that do not follow their hidden program.

The Intercultural Stress-Adaptation-Growth Process

In communicating interculturally, people inevitably experience a multitude of difficulties as they experience communication patterns that challenge their taken-for-granted assumptions. Individuals who are seriously engaged in intercultural encounters (such as immigrants and sojourners who must by necessity operate effectively in an alien environment) are challenged to change at least some of their culturally conditioned ways of thinking, feeling, and behaving. The extent of such challenges of intercultural communication are at least partly dependent on the degree of heterogeneity of the participants' cultural attributes in a particular encounter. The more incongruent and heterogeneous the cultural attributes of the communicators, the more intercultural their communication experiences will be.[4]

As such, intercultural communication experiences are inherently stressful. Understanding and being understood interculturally often involves a substantial challenge, which introduces internal disequilibrium and stress in participants. Confronted with situations in which assumptions and premises acquired in childhood are called into question, the communicators experience uncertainty and conflict. In the case of immigrants who have moved to an alien culture, there will be a dramatic increase in symbolic as well as physical challenges. Conservative estimates suggest that, within the first year in a new culture, an individual may experience nearly one third of what Holmes and Rahe (1967) considered the 43 most significant life changes.

This phenomenon is what is commonly referred to as culture shock, typically viewed, as we pointed out earlier, as a negative, problematic, and undesirable phenomenon to be avoided. Viewed in the present system's terms, however, culture shock is a manifestation of a generic process that occurs whenever the capabilities of a living system are not sufficiently adequate to the demands of an unfamiliar cultural environment. It is a necessary precondition to change and growth, as individuals strive to regain their inner balance by adapting to the demands and opportunities of the intercultural situation.

In facing culture shock situations, then, individuals must, at least temporarily, alter some of their existing cultural patterns of communication in order to make communication work as they intend. To put it differently, such situations require us to suspend or change some of the old cultural ways and accommodate some of the new cultural ways. This necessity is commonly met with conscious or unconscious resistance of the individuals engaged in intercultural communication, which adds to the stress they already experience. Yet insisting on the old cultural ways and trying to avoid stress is like "wanting to have one's cake and eat it, too."

Culture shock—or the generic intercultural stress—is, indeed, part and parcel of the intercultural adaptation cycle. New and unfamiliar environmental conditions of culture differences naturally produce strain in individuals' internal systems as they strive to adapt. The psychological movements of individuals into new dimensions of perception and experience often produce forms of temporary personality disintegration, or even "breakdown" in some extreme cases. Intercultural stress is therefore viewed as the internal resistance of the human organism against its own cultural evolution.

To the extent that stress is said to be responsible for suffering, frustration, and anxiety, it also must be credited as an impetus for learning, growth, and creativity for the individual. Temporary disintegration is thus viewed as the very basis for subsequent growth in the awareness of life conditions and ways to deal with them. Jourard (1974) described this dynamic process as integration—disintegration-reintegration:

> Growth is the dis-integration of one way of experiencing the world, followed by a reorganization of this experience, a reorganization that includes the new disclosure of the world. The disorganization, or even shattering, of one way to experience the world, is brought on by new disclosure from the changing being of the world, disclosures that were always being transmitted, but were usually ignored. (p. 456)

Similarly, Hall (1976), in proposing a psychic growth of individuals beyond their own cultural parameters, calls this process "identity-separation-growth dynamism." (See, also, Dabrowski, 1964, for a similar view.)

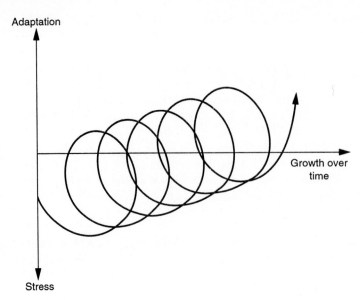

FIGURE 13.1 Stress-adaptation-growth dynamics of the process of intercultural transformation.

The stress-adaptation-growth process lies at the heart of intercultural communication experience in a forward-upward movement of a cycle of "draw-back-to-leap." Each stressful experience is responded to with a "draw back," which then activates one's adaptive energy to "leap forward." . . . The shifting between the breakup of the old internalized cultural system and the creation of a new system enables the individual to be better adapted to subsequent intercultural encounters. Ultimately, the intercultural communication experiences of individuals contribute to the evolution of the social systems of which they are a part.

This process of growth is strongly evidenced in numerous immigrants, refugees, and missionaries, who, of necessity, have had to incorporate within themselves the communication patterns of the new environment and thus have restructured their internal conditions. When possible, they have also managed the conditions of the host environment in accordance with their prior cultural attributes. Through continuous intercultural stress-adaptation experiences stimulated by the environmental challenges, they have expanded their internal capacities to function in the changed environment.

Empirical research has provided some supportive indication, although indirect and rudimentary, that the stresses in adapting to a different culture indeed lay the groundwork for subsequent adaptive growth. For example, Eaton and Lasry (1978) reported that the stress level of more upwardly mobile immigrants was greater than those who were less upwardly mobile. Among Japanese-Americans (Marmot & Syme, 1976) and Mexican-American women (Miranda & Castro, 1977), the better adapted immigrants had a somewhat greater frequency of stress-related symptoms (such as anxiety and need for psychotherapy) than the less adapted group. Additionally, some of the findings from the study of Ruben and Kealey (1979) suggested that the Canadians in Kenya who would ultimately be the most effective in adapting to a new culture underwent the most intense culture shock during the transition period. Other acculturation studies of immigrants and foreign students in the United States have shown that, once the initial phase has been successfully managed, individuals demonstrate an increased cognitive complexity, positive orientation toward the host environment and themselves, and behavior capacities to communicate with the natives (see, for example, Coelho, 1958; Kim, 1976, 1978, 1980).

Readers must be reminded, at this point, that not all individuals are successful in making transitions toward becoming intercultural. Certain individuals, although in the minority, may strongly resist such internal change, thereby increasing the stress level further and making the stress-adaptation-growth cycle intensely difficult. Some may not be able to cope with intense stress experiences because of a lack of psychological resilience. Others may find themselves in intercultural situations that present too severe a challenge to manage. Most individuals in most circumstances, however, are viewed to undergo the stress-adaptation-growth cycle as just postulated.

Consequences of Intercultural Transformation

As has just been explained, the process of becoming intercultural—of personal transformation from cultural to intercultural—is a process of growth beyond one's original cultural conditioning. One consequence of extensive communication experiences and the subsequent internal transformation is the development of a cultural identity that is far from being "frozen." An intercultural person's cultural identity is characteristically open to further transformation and growth. This does not mean that a highly intercultural person's identity is culture-free or cultureless. Rather, it is not rigidly bound by membership to any one particular culture. Adler (1982), in his explication of "multicultural" person, characterizes this unique identity:

> The identity of multicultural man [woman] is based, not on "belongingness" which implies either owning or being owned by culture, but on a style of self-consciousness that is capable of negotiating ever new formations of reality. In this sense multicultural man [woman] is a radical departure from the kinds of identities found in both traditional and mass societies. He [She] is neither totally *a part of* nor totally *apart from* his [her] culture; he [she] lives, instead, on the boundary. (p. 391)

A second consequence of extensive intercultural communication experiences and adaptive change is a cognitive structure that enables a broadened and deepened understanding of human conditions and cultural differences and a view of things that are larger than any one cultural perspective. Yoshikawa (in press) described such cognitive growth in intercultural communication as a creative process that shares an analogous structural relationship with the scientific discovery process and the religious enlightenment process. In this view, Yoshikawa postulated the developmental stages as a movement from an ethnocentric (or dualistic) perception to a nondualistic, "metacontextual" perception. At this stage of cognitive development, a person is able to experience the dynamic and dialogical interaction between the original culture and the new culture.

The increased cognitive depth and breadth is, in turn, likely to facilitate corresponding emotional and behavioral capacities as well. The inherent drive toward internal balance (or harmony) in individuals as open systems will lead to a congruence between cognitive, affective, and behavioral domains of an individual's internal system. In the moment of calm and relaxation, the process of what we may call the *inner alchemy* takes place: As the "old" person breaks up, the intercultural knowledge, attitudes, and behavioral capacities construct a "new" person at a higher level of integration.

Thus the intercultural person who has benefited from extensive intercultural communication and adaptive transformation often possesses an affirmative (or accepting) attitude toward cultural differences, as well as the emotional and behavioral openness and capacity to participate in the other person's experiences. Even when the person is not aware of the cultural customs of the other person, a highly intercultural person is likely to have the affective and behavioral flexibility to adapt to the situation and creatively manage or avoid conflicts that could result from inappropriate switching between cultures. Houston (1981), a Japanese-American writer, spoke of her personal interculturalness as follows:

> Now I entertain according to how I feel that day. If my Japanese sensibility is stronger, I act accordingly and feel OK. If I feel like going all American, I can do that too and feel OK. I've come to accept the cultural hybrid of my personality and recognize it as a strength, not as a weakness. Because I am culturally neither pure Japanese nor pure American . . . does not mean that I am less of a person. It seems that I have been enriched by the heritages of both.

As has been pointed out, it is our view that this internal growth beyond the parameters of any one culture characterizes an "intercultural person." As such, an intercultural person achieves what Harris (1979) referred to as an "optimal level of communication competence." At this stage, one achieves the maximum capacity to communicate with individuals who are significantly different in cultural backgrounds, and are able to make deliberate choices of actions in specific situations rather than simply being dictated by the normative courses of actions in a given culture. Becoming intercultural, therefore, can be viewed as a process of reaching out beyond culture for a full blossoming of the uniquely human adaptive capacity. . . .

NOTES

1 See, for example, Adler (1975), Brislin (1981), Church (1982), Furnham (1984), Furnham & Bochner (1986), and Kim (1988) for more thorough literature reviews in this area.

2 The present term *intercultural personhood* is preferred because it is more general and inclusive than other similar terms without implying any specific cultural attributes. It portrays personal

characteristics that transcend any given cultural group. Unlike the term *multicultural person*, it does not imply that the individual necessarily "possesses" characteristics of more than one culture. Unlike the term *universal person*, it does not suggest an awareness and appreciation of all groups of the world. The term *international person* focuses on the expanded psychological orientation beyond a national boundary, but it does not emphasize numerous ethnic, racial, and other subcultural groups within a nation. The term *marginal person* suggests a sense of inferiority or alienation, which is not considered an attribute of intercultural personhood.

3 For discussions of human communication based on the General Systems perspective, see Boulding (1977) and Ruben & J. Kim (1975).

4 In theorizing the adaptation process of immigrants and sojourners in the host culture, Kim (1979; 1988) has taken the individual background factors, relationship factors, and host environmental factors into account.

REFERENCES

Adler, P. S. (1975). The transition experience: An alternative view of culture shock. *Journal of Humanistic Psychology, 15*(4), 13–23.

Adler, P. S. (1982). Beyond cultural identity: Reflections on cultural and multicultural man. In L. A. Samovar & R. E. Porter (Eds.), *Intercultural communication: A reader* (pp. 389–408). Belmont, CA: Wadsworth.

Adler, P. S. (1987). Culture shock and the cross-cultural learning experience. In L. F. Luce & E. C. Smith (Eds.), *Toward internationalism* (pp. 24–35). Cambridge, MA: Newbury. (Original work published in 1972)

Barnlund, D. (1982). Communication in a global village. In L. Samovar & R. Porter (Eds.), *Intercultural communication: A reader*. Belmont, CA: Wadsworth.

Bateson, G. (1972). *Steps to an ecology of mind.* New York: Ballantine.

Becker, T. (1968). Patterns of attitudinal changes among foreign students. *American Journal of Sociology, 73,* 431–442.

Bennett, J. (1977). Transition shock: Putting culture shock in perspective. In N. Jain (Ed.), *International and Intercultural Communication Annual, 4,* 45–52.

Boulding, K. E. (1977). *The image: Knowledge in life and society.* Ann Arbor: The University of Michigan Press. (Original work published in 1956)

Breitenbach, D. (1970). The evaluation of study abroad. In I. Eide (Ed.), *Students as links between cultures.* Paris: UNESCO.

Brislin, R. W. (1981). *Cross-cultural encounters.* Elmsford, NY: Pergamon.

Byrnes, F. C. (1966). Role shock: An occupational hazard of American technical assistants abroad. *Annals, 368,* 95–108.

Capra, F. (1975). *The Tao of physics.* Boulder, CO: Shambhala.

Chomsky, N. (1972). *Language and mind.* New York: Harcourt, Brace, Jovanovich.

Church, A. T. (1982). Sojourner adjustment. *Psychology Bulletin, 91*(3), 540–572.

Coelho, G. V. (1958). *Changing images of America: A study of Indian students' perceptions.* New York: Free Press.

Dabrowski, K. (1964). *Positive disintegration.* Boston: Little, Brown.

Dubin, R. (1969). *Theory building.* New York: Free Press.

Eaton, W. W., & Lasry, J. C. (1978). Mental health and occupational mobility in a group of immigrants. *Science and Medicine, 12,* 53–58.

Elgin, D. (1981). *Voluntary simplicity.* New York: Bantam.

Feuerstein, G. (1987). *Structures of consciousness: The genius of Jean Gebser: An introduction and critique.* Lower Lake, CA: Integral.

Furnham, A. (1984). Tourism and culture shock: *Annals of Tourism Research, 11*(1), 41-57.

Furnham, A., & Bochner, S. (1982). Social difficulty in a foreign culture. In S. Bochner (Ed.), *Cultures in contact.* Elmsford, NY: Pergamon.

Furnham, A., & Bochner, S. (1986). *Culture shock: Psychological reactions to unfamiliar environments.* London: Methuen.

Gudykunst, W. B., & Kim, Y. Y. (1984). *Communicating with strangers: An approach to intercultural communication.* New York: Random House.

Gullahorn, J. T., & Gullahorn, J. E. (1963). An extension of the U-curve hypothesis. *Journal of Social Issues, 19*(3), 33-47.

Guthrie, G. M. (1966). Cultural preparation for the Philippines. In R. B. Textor (Ed.), *Cultural frontiers of the Peace Corps.* Cambridge: MIT Press.

Guthrie, G. M. (1975). A behavioral analysis of culture learning. In R. W. Brislin, S. Bochner, & W. J. Lonner (Eds.), *Cross-cultural perspectives on learning.* New York: John Wiley.

Hall, E. T. (1976). *Beyond culture.* New York: Doubleday.

Harris, L. M. (1979, May). *Communication competence: An argument for a systemic view.* Paper presented at the annual conference of the International Communication Association, Philadelphia.

Higbee, H. (1969). Role shock—a new concept. *International Educational and Cultural Exchange, 4*(4), 71-81.

Holmes, T. H., & Rahe, R. H. (1967). The social readjustment rating scale. *Journal of Psychometric Research, 11,* 213-218.

Houston, J. W. (1981, May). *Beyond Mansamar: A personal view on the Asian-American womanhood.* Lecture presented at Governors State University, University Park, IL. (audio recording available)

Jantsch, E. (1980). *The self-organizing universe: Scientific and human implications of the emerging paradigm of evolution.* New York: Pergamon.

Jourard, S. (1974). Growing awareness and the awareness of growth. In B. Patton & K. Giffin (Eds.), *Interpersonal communication.* New York: Harper & Row.

Kim, Y. Y. (1976). Communication patterns of foreign immigrants in the process of acculturation. *Human Communication Research, 4*(1), 66-77.

Kim, Y. Y. (1978). Toward a communication approach to the acculturation process. *International Journal of Intercultural Relations,* 192-224.

Kim, Y. Y. (1979). Toward an interactive theory of communication-acculturation. In B. D. Ruben (Ed.), *Communication yearbook 3* (pp. 435-453). New Brunswick, NJ: Transaction Books.

Kim, Y. Y. (1980). *Psychological, social, and cultural adjustment of Indochinese refugees.* In *Indochinese refugees in the State of Illinois* (Vol. IV of 5 volumes). Chicago: Travelers Aid Society of Metropolitan Chicago.

Kim, Y. Y. (1985a). Communication, information, and adaptation. In B. D. Ruben (Ed.), *Information and behavior* (Vol. 1. pp. 324-340). New Brunswick, NJ: Transaction Books.

Kim, Y. Y. (1985b). Intercultural personhood: An integration of Eastern and Western perspectives. In L. A. Samovar & R. E. Porter (Eds.), *Intercultural communication: A reader* (4th ed., pp. 400-410). Belmont, CA: Wadsworth.

Kim, Y. Y. (1988). *Communication and cross-cultural adaptation.* Clevedon, England: Multilingual Matters.

Kinzie, J. D., Tran, K. A., Breckenridge, A., & Bloom, J. L. (1980). An Indochinese refugee psychiatric clinic: Culturally accepted treatment approaches. *American Journal of Psychiatry, 137,* 1429–1432.

Klineberg, O., & Hull, W. F. (1979). *At a foreign university: An international study of adaptation and coping.* New York: Praeger.

Lazarus, R. S. (1966). *Psychological stress and the coping process.* New York: McGraw-Hill.

Lum, J. (1982). Marginality and multiculturalism. In L. Samovar & R. Porter (Eds.), *Intercultural communication: A reader* (3rd ed.). Belmont, CA: Wadsworth.

Lundstedt, S. (1963). An introduction to some evolving problems in cross-cultural research. *Journal of Social Issues, 19*(3), 1–9.

Lutzker, D. (1960). Internationalism as a predictor of cooperative behavior. *Journal of Conflict Resolution, 4*(4), 426–430.

Lysgaard, S. (1955). Adjustment in a foreign society: Norwegian Fulbright grantees visiting the United States. *International Social Science Bulletin, 7*(1), 45–51.

Marmot, M. G., & Syme, S. L. (1976). Acculturation and coronary heart disease in Japanese-Americans. *American Journal of Epidemiology, 104*(3), 225–247.

Miranda, M. R., & Castro, F. G. (1977). Culture distance and success in psychotherapy with Spanish speaking clients. In J. L. Martinez Jr. (Ed.), *Chicano Psychology* (pp. 249–262). New York: Academic Press.

Northrop, F. (1966). *The meeting of the East and the West.* New York: Collier. (Original work published in 1946).

Oberg, K. (1960). Cultural shock: Adjustment to new cultural environments. *Practical Anthropology, 7,* 170–179.

Piaget, J. (1977). Problems of equilibriation. In M. Appel & L. Goldberg (Eds.), *Topics of cognitive development.* New York: Plenum.

Ruben, B. D. (1975). Intrapersonal, interpersonal and mass communication process in individual and multi-person systems. In B. D. Ruben & J. Y. Kim (Eds.), *General systems theory and human communication* (pp. 164–190). Rochelle Park, NJ: Hayden.

Ruben, B. D. (1978). Communication and conflict: A system-theoretic perspective. *The Quarterly Journal of Speech, 64*(2), 202–210.

Ruben, B. D. (1980, March). *Culture shock: The skull and the lady—reflections on cultural adjustment and stress.* Paper presented at the annual conference of the Society for Intercultural Education, Training, and Research, Mount Pocono, PA.

Ruben, B. D. (1983). A system-theoretic view. In W. B. Gudykunst (Ed.), *Intercultural communication theory* (pp. 131–145). Beverly Hills, CA: Sage.

Ruben, B. D. (1988). *Communication and human behavior* (2nd ed.). New York: Macmillan.

Ruben, B. D., & Kealey, D. J. (1979). Behavioral assessment of communication competency and the prediction of cross-cultural adaptation. *International Journal of Intercultural Relations, 3*(1), 15–47.

Ruben, B. D., & Kim, J. Y. [(Eds.).] (1975). *General systems theory and human communication.* Rochelle Park, NJ: Hayden.

Sarbaugh, L. (1979). *Intercultural communication.* Rochelle Park, NJ: Hayden.

Smalley, W. A. (1963). Culture shock, language shock, and the shock of self-discovery. *Practical Anthropology, 10,* 49–56.

Spaulding, S., Flack, M. J., & Associates (1976). *The world's students in the United States: A review and evaluation of research on foreign students.* New York: Praeger.

Taft, R. (1977). Coping with unfamiliar cultures. In N. Warren (Ed.), *Studies in cross-cultural psychology* (Vol. I, pp. 121–153). London: Academic Press.

Thompson, W. (1973). *Passages about earth: An exploration of the new planetary culture.* New York: Harper & Row.

Walsh, J. E. (1973). *Intercultural education in the community of man.* Honolulu: University of Hawaii Press.

Williams, C. L., & Westmeyer, J. (1986). Psychiatric problems among adolescent Southeast Asian refugees: A descriptive study. *Pacific/Asian American Mental Health Research Center Newsletter,* 4(3/4), 22–24.

Beyond Diversity:
The Development of Species Identity
Elise Boulding

Is it possible to conceptualize a common identity while acknowledging differences? Of course. We do it all the time. I have a common identity with anyone from the town I live in, which is Boulder, Colorado. Regardless of how different the life ways and values of its roughly 80,000 residents may be, we are all Boulderites. I certainly have a common identity with all my fellow citizens in the United States, which includes people of different races and ethnic groups, who speak different languages, and who are of very diverse religious beliefs and employments. I myself was born in Norway and am a naturalized citizen, but that does not affect my commitment to acknowledging certain common obligations to anyone who is a fellow citizen of the United States, including the obligation to pay taxes to support the services from which we all benefit.

One of the extraordinary realities of living in the modern world is that we all have multiple identities. Some of these identities take up only a small part of our lives, such as the associations we belong to. Others are part of our core identity, such as our family identity. The INGOs [international nongovernmental organizations] we belong to give us transnational identities. Sometimes our different identities come in conflict with one another, and then we have role conflicts. How much time should we give to our family identity, our career identity, our organizational identities? And what might a species identity mean?

In looking for answers to some of these questions, we can search for sources of species identity in some traditional conceptions of the international order. We will turn to this shortly, but first we must have an understanding of the concept of *species*, which denotes a category of biological classification. Its simplest meaning is "a class of individuals having common attributes and designated by a common name" (Webster, 1979). The species designation for humans is *homo* (add *mulier*, for women) *sapiens*. Because of our special mental capacities, humans have a more highly evolved concept of *kind* than any other species. Yet our common humanness is rarely thought of as a key part of our individual identities. Once we have moved past our own core identity

Source: Abridged from Chapter 4 in Elise Boulding, *Building a Global Civic Culture,* (pp. 64–71). New York: Teachers College Press, Columbia University, 1988.

in family and community, most of us let our national identity absorb the residuals of our sense of self. Therein lies the problem of the human species itself. Nations become empires and evolve identities that come to be seen as univeral/species identities, which the nations then feel called to impose on others who have not experienced that particular historical evolution. Competing empires offer competing "species identities," legitimated by cultural/religious traditions that also are experienced by their adherents as universal. Since every religious and cultural tradition has some component of authentic (civilization-transcending) universalism, this sets the stage for the struggle in every society between those who have an intuitive experience of authentic universalism, and those who equate species identity with their own historical sense of mission. Out of those struggles the world civic culture is emerging. Let us see how the claims of the nation-state conflict with the claims of species identity.

As the core political unit in the modern world, the nation-state is able to make demands that are normally considered to override all other demands. This is particularly the case in wartime; our identities as United States citizens then become overriding. However, if a person's religious beliefs include the teaching that all human life is sacred, thus forbidding the taking of lives in war, then the state may acknowledge the religious identity as an overriding one and allow conscientious objectors to fulfill their obligations to their country by giving alternative service of a nonmilitary kind. This does not involve a denial of obligations to the state; rather, it is their fulfillment in the broader context of obedience to what is sometimes called a "higher law." This higher law is thought of by religious conscientious objectors as the law of God. However, there are also secular conscientious objectors who base their beliefs in the inviolability of human life on ethical teachings in a humanist tradition.

Whether based on religious or secular-humanist beliefs, there are people in all countries who feel allegiance to a community that in one sense does not exist—the community of humankind. It is this allegiance that we are calling species identity. The community of humankind is a country without borders, with no capital city and with only one law—to avoid doing harm to any fellow human being. However, one cannot feel allegiance to an abstraction. That is where the concept of civic culture comes in. This allegiance can only become operational through a set of common understandings developed on the basis of interaction in all the ways we have been describing in these chapters: between governments, in the United Nations, and between people across national borders. We have to enter into more social interaction and become more consciously linked across national borders, to give substance to that civic culture.

Each cultural tradition has ways of thinking about this hoped-for community of humankind. The shared civic culture has to be built up out of each of those traditions, with no one predominating. The World Order Models Project of the World Policy Institute is one very important effort in building up that shared civic culture. Mendlovitz (1975) gives an overview of the efforts of a transnational group of scholars to visualize preferred future worlds that allow for diversity.

Let us examine the concepts of the international order that have emerged in the West, in India, in China, and in Islam, to see what materials we have to work with in the forming of a species identity.

A VIEW FROM THE WEST

The concept of the social order in Roman law was of an ideal universal state that would administer a rule of law for the world. This concept of a universal state survived in the ideology of the Holy Roman Empire and was conceived of as a universal Christian state in the Middle Ages. Divisions in Christendom after the Reformation brought that idea to an end, so the ideal shifted to a "concert of states."

Since the Treaty of Westphalia in 1648, the development of a plurality of democratic nation-states has been seen as the endpoint of a process of freeing human beings from the tyranny of despotism. In the United States, sometimes called the "first new nation,'" the ideal was that each individal was free to seek "life, liberty, and the pursuit of happiness," so long as that pursuit did not injure others. The nation-state was thus seen as the ideal vehicle for creating and safeguarding the liberties of each citizen. The French Declaration of the Rights of Man (1780) defined these liberties as basic human rights.

Since separate nation-states might discover conflicting interests in the course of protecting their citizenry, it therefore became necessary to accept a common constraint of international law which all states would acknowledge. Originally, that law was conceived as based on Roman law; however, by the late nineteenth century it came to be seen that international law, to be acceptable, could not be based on the laws of any one national or civilizational tradition. It must therefore be a synthesis of the legal traditions of all civilizations. This would provide "the broader intellectual foundations necessary to give it worldwide authority in an age which is no longer prepared to accept the leadership of any one nation, culture, ideology or legal system" (Larson & Jenks, 1965, p. 3). The process by which this synthesis was to take place began at the Hague Peace Conferences, which included China, Japan, Ethiopia, Turkey, and Mexico, as well as the nations of Europe and North America. It continued with the formation of the League of Nations and its successor, the United Nations. From the perspective of the West, the Roman law tradition is seen as dominant, but other traditions are to be taken account of. The system of sovereign nation-states guaranteeing the liberty of their citizens, living at peace with one another, and abiding by international law is seen as both generating and maintaining that minimal degree of world civic culture required to assure a stable future order. World government—the ceding of sovereignty to a central power—is not seen as desirable but rather as a regression to tyranny and despotism.

A VIEW FROM INDIA

India has never had a tradition of a universal state. Experiencing successive invasions over the centuries from the North and the West, India has historically conceived of itself rather as a society of many races in continual adjustment. Tagore (1924), who wrote about the dangers of the incursion of Western ideas concerning the nation-state long before India's independence from England, maintained that kings and emperors were never important in India until the West arrived. Tagore saw India's genius as precisely in *not* being a nation, and in being a society focused on the social regulation of differences and the spiritual recognition of unity. In the Hindu tradition, rulers are subject to the law, the Dharma; the law is not subject to the will of rulers. There is divine authority first, and state authority is strictly secondary. Tagore saw the Western nation-state as being a political and economic mechanism for competition, conquest, and acquisition—in short, essentially anti-people.

As a leading internationalist in the 1920s, Tagore valued the spirit of the West but not its mechanisms. The ideal he held forth, also upheld by Gandhi and by the leaders of India today, is of the world as an assembly of societies, not nations. India's own 1,652 racial groups, and its border problems with other ethnic groups, assure a focus on finding ways of living together across deep and often bitter differences. As Tagore (1924) said, what India has been, the world is now. The world must find a basis of unity that is not political. The world civic culture must be rooted in an acceptance of a great diversity of life ways. The multicultural society, rather than the nation-state, is the ideal. This is also an attractive ideal for many African and some Asian countries that face similar problems.

A VIEW FROM CHINA

China, like the West, held an ideal of a universal state with one ruler. The Chinese, however, arrived at the concept of the universal state in a very different way from the West. Western political development, from the Greek city-state to the modern military-industrial security state, is seen from the Chinese perspective as one that has weakened interpersonal bonds and made people individualistically competitive rather than mutually cooperative.

Facing the dilemma of a fractionated world community, some Chinese thinkers feel that their own historial traditions offer an alternative and more peaceful developmental path toward a modernized international system (Xiaotaong, 1987). While the endpoint is not unlike that visualized by many Westerners, the path is different, and therefore some characteristics of the resulting order would also be different. The Chinese path builds on ever-widening circles of familial relationships, from clan to society. In the clan-based patterns of the East, it is suggested, we may find some clues for overcoming the blocks to creating a mature civic culture which have emerged in the West.

In Confucian thought the universal state is called the "land under heaven." A core saying is, "Everybody in the land under heaven serves the public interest." There are three important concepts in this saying. One is the concept of the land under heaven, which implies that land is a whole, an indivisible entity, without boundaries, belonging to everyone. The second is that dwellers in this boundaryless land all share a common public interest. The third, which provides the integrative dynamic for the other two, is the kinship principle. The folk who live in the land under heaven belong to extended families organized as clans interlinked in one macrofamily. The kinship principle provides the basis for the precept that the love, respect, and obligations one exercises toward one's own family are also to be exercised toward all other families within the total social order. One respects not only one's own parents, but all parents. One cares not only for one's own children, but all children.

In one sense traditional Chinese society was very hierarchical, operating on an explicit center-to-periphery model. The ruler, who was responsible for the good order of society, lived at the center. Clans built up relationships in ever-widening circles from the enlightened moral center where the *huaxia* or the *han* people lived, outward to the peoples of the border, the *manyi*. What is different from the center-to-periphery models of the West, however, is that exactly the same obligations and rules of behavior applied to the relationships between center and periphery peoples as applied among center people. One did not have different sets of obligations to different classes of people.

It might be said that there is no public/private interface in such a social order because carrying out family duties according to the highest standards of morality provides the model for carrying out civic duties; the obligations are the same. One puts the state in order by beginning with the family and expanding outward.

This approach turns on its head the Western concept of "development" as a movement away from kinship-based and toward contract-shaped relationships. The Chinese political tradition would leave family and clan intact as building blocks of the larger society. While the clan formula may appear regressive to Westerners, it facilitates the coexistence of many nationalities within the larger society without breaking the moral bonds of interclan responsibility. Chinese tradition uses the family in an instrumental way as a means to a world bond, a world civic culture. Today the universal-state idea has been abandoned, as in the West, but the coexistence of natioins is cemented by an interclan bond and a sense of world public interest ("the land under heaven") that is unlike the concept of a loose association of autonomous states in the West. While West and East both use the concept of family, China uses it instrumentally and the West metaphorically.

A VIEW FROM ISLAM

The original Muslim concept of gradual movement toward a universal Islamic state, *dar al-Islam,* has been replaced by the concept of the coexistence of *dar al-Islam* and *dar al-harb*—the peoples that remain outside Islam. The treaty between Francis I of France and Sulayman the Magnificent in 1535, providing for the coexistence of Christianity and Islam, marked the end of the earlier universalist idea. In this respect Islam, China, and the West have all followed the same path. At the same time, the state does not have the central importance in Islamic tradition that it has in China and the West because the rule of Allah takes preeminence and the state is subservient to divine law. This is more like Hindu doctrine. Islamic society tends to be very localist, organized around local mosques and their resident teachers. Scholar-teachers have a central importance in Islamic society. The authority of the *ulama,* a central core of scholars, is as significant as that of the ruling *caliph* (Rahman, 1966).

Islam is in many ways an unusually egalitarian society, a legacy of its nomadic origins. This egalitarianism is translated into a strong feeling of responsibility on the part of every Muslim for the welfare of the *umma,* the total community of the faithful, and a keen sense of social justice. Muslims are said to do better at tithing than any other religion. One interesting application of this egalitarianism is the unusual extent of the provisions for the freedom of non-Muslims living in a Muslim land. Devices such as the *aman* and the *millet* system gave legal protection in premodern times for non-Muslim residents and made provision for them to live under their own laws. There was no comparable system at the time for non-Christians living in Christian lands. However, the egalitarianism is very unevenly applied to women. In some countries, strict *purdah* (seclusion) of women is practiced, while in others there is no seclusion at all. Generally, upper-middle-class Muslim women have good opportunities for professional training (as doctors and teachers, for example), sometimes because of, sometimes in spite of *purdah* traditions.

The Muslim religious obligation to extend principles of social justice to non-Muslims provides a strong basis for the development of a peaceful society of nations. The lack of emphasis on the state itself, and the great importance given to the quality of life as lived in the local mosque-centered community, provide a basis for an international community of peoples, somewhat along the lines of the Hindu concept of a multicultural international order. The system of dialogue at the local level, linked to a national dialogue process, would have to be more fully extended beyond the *umma,* to make its full contribution to a world civic culture. While this is already happening in the Non-Aligned Movement, the present high levels of conflict within Islam make further developments along these lines seem highly unlikely at the moment. In the longer term, the social inventiveness of Islam will be very important to the emerging civic culture of the future. For examples of this promise, see Khan (1985).

HOW THESE FOUR VIEWS CONTRIBUTE TO SPECIES IDENTITY

We have looked at the facts of diversity in the social order in terms of ethnicity, religion, and gender differences. These diversities have caused deep conflicts, but in each case we have also found approaches to managing that diversity that reduce conflict and enhance the common interests of adversary groups.

Moving on to the more difficult question of species identity, we first looked at ideas about world order in four major civilizational traditions. The assumption behind that examination was that community in the sense of common fate and shared expectations on a world scale is an important basis for the development of both civic culture and species identity.

Earlier concepts of a universal state have been rejected by the West and also by China and Islam, as the impossibility of imposing one cultural pattern on the world as a whole has become clear. India, more aware of diversity from its inception, never even developed such a concept. Each tradition has subsequently sought to define a common bond based on common survival needs, through structuring the recognition of diversity and accepting common rules about protecting that diversity. In the West the tradition of international law has developed out of common self-interest, with an underpinning of Judeo-Christian ethics. For China, India, and Islam, the recognition of humans as spiritual beings "under heaven," under the Dharma, or under Allah, has been primary. This recognition has been accompanied by practical recognition of the need for local community. China uses the family/clan nexus as the model for community at every level, from local to planetary. Hinduism and Islam focus on the protection of diverse local ethnic groups and communities and the fostering of mutual recognition and respect. The interesting thing is that none of these traditions depend primarily on spiritual transformation to achieve a peaceful world order and a common species identity. Each is operating in terms of the everyday realities of diversity and conflict, to achieve awareness of a common interest, a common bond in the diversity itself, that will make gradually increasing levels of cooperation possible across the diversity. . . .

REFERENCES

Khan, I. (Ed.). (1985). *World Muslim Gazetteer.* Karachi: World Muslim Congress.

Larson, A., & Jenks, W. (1965). *Sovereignty within the law.* New York: Oceana.

Mendlovitz, S. (1975). *On the creation of a just world order.* New York: Free Press.

Rahman, F. (1966). *Islam.* Chicago: University of Chicago Press.

Tagore, R. (1924). *Nationalism.* London: Macmillan.

Webster. (1979). *New collegiate dictionary.* Springfield, MA: G & C Merriam.

Xiaotaong, P. (1987). *Human identity.* Unpublished report prepared for the Committee for a Just World Peace, World Policy Institute, New York.

CHAPTER 14

Building Community

Conflict between people of different ethnic and cultural groups is occurring throughout the world today. Examples of intergroup conflict include, but are not limited to, recent racial harassment on university campuses in the United States, nationality conflicts in the Soviet Union (e.g., between the Azerbaijanis and the Armenians), conflicts between Protestants and Catholics in Northern Ireland, and clashes between Arabs and Jews in Israel, to name only a few.

Whereas the specific "causes" of intergroup conflict differ depending upon the situation, all incidents share one thing in common: namely, they involve *polarized communication.* Arnett (1986) argues that

> the major problem of the human community for the remainder of this century and into the next . . . [is] communication from polarized positions. Polarized communication can be summarized as the inability to believe or seriously consider one's view as wrong and the other's opinion as truth. Communication within human community becomes typified by the rhetoric of "we" are right and "they" are misguided or wrong. (pp. 15–16)

Polarized communication, therefore, exists when groups or individuals look out for their own interests and have little concern for that of others.

Lack of concern for others' interests leads to moral exclusion. "Moral exclusion occurs when individuals or groups are perceived as *outside the boundary in which moral values, rules, and considerations of fairness apply.* Those who are morally excluded are perceived as nonentities, expendable, or undeserving; consequently, harming them appears acceptable, appropriate or just" (Optow, 1990, p. 1). Lack of concern for others and moral exclusion are a function, at least in part, of "spiritual deprivation" (i.e., the feeling of emptiness associated with separation from our fellow humans) that Mother Teresa sees as the major problem facing the world today (Jampolsky, 1989).

There is a tendency for many of us to think that cultural and ethnic diversity inevitably lead to polarized communication and hinder the development of community. This, however, is not the case. Cultural and ethnic diversity are necessary for community to exist. For community to develop, cultural and ethnic differences must be dealt with in a constructive fashion. The term *community* is derived from the Latin *communitas,* which has two related, but distinct, interpretations: (1) the quality of "common interest and hence the quality of fellowship," and (2) "a body of people having in common an external bond" (Rosenthal, 1984, p. 219). Yankelovich (1984) argues that community evokes the "feeling that 'Here is where I belong, these are my people, I care for them, they care for me, I am part of them' . . . its absence is experienced as an achy loss, a void . . . feelings of isolation, falseness, instability, and impoverishment of spirit" (p. 227).

The readings in this chapter were selected to illustrate different aspects of building community. In the first reading, Opotow looks at the issue of moral exclusion and injustice. Moral exclusion involves not applying our moral principles to selected groups (e.g., selected outgroups). Opotow examines the antecedents and consequences of moral exclusion. It is important to recognize that being morally inclusive is necessary for developing an intercultural perspective and for building community in our lives.

In the second reading, Peck outlines the characteristics of community. He points out, for example, that building community requires that we be inclusive, that we are committed to others, that we examine our behavior, and that we learn to fight gracefully.

In the final reading, Bellah, Madsen, Sullivan, Swidler, and Tipton examine the culture of separation that exists in the United States. They outline transformations that are necessary for a sense of community to increase.

REFERENCES

Arnett, R. (1986). *Communication and community*. Carbondale: Southern Illinois University Press.
Jampolsky, G. (1989). *Out of darkness into the light*. New York: Bantam.
Opotow, S. (1990). Moral exclusion and injustice. *Journal of Social Issues, 46*(1), 1–20.
Rosenthal, P. (1984). *Words and values*. Cambridge: Cambridge University Press.
Yankelovich, D. (1981). *New rules: Searching for self-fulfillment in a world turned upside down*. New York: Random House.

Moral Exclusion and Injustice
Susan Opotow

. . . Moral exclusion occurs when individuals or groups are perceived as *outside the boundary in which moral values, rules, and considerations of fairness apply*. Those who are morally excluded are perceived as nonentities, expendable, or undeserving; consequently, harming them appears acceptable, appropriate, or just. Moral exclusion (a term proposed by Ervin Staub, 1987) links a wide range of social issues, such as

Source: Abridged from *Journal of Social Issues*, 1990, *46(1)*, 1–20.

abortion, species conservation, nuclear weapons, and immigration policies, because our position on these issues depends on whom we include in or exclude from our moral boundaries. . . .

Moral exclusion can be mild or severe. Severe instances include violations of human rights, political repression, religious inquisitions, slavery, and genocide. The person or group excluded ("the other') is perceived as a plague or threat, and harm doing can take such extreme forms as torture and death. Milder instances of moral exclusion occur when we fail to recognize and deal with undeserved suffering and deprivation. The other is perceived as nonexistent or as a nonentity. In this case, harm doing results from unconcern or unawareness of others' needs or entitlements to basic resources, such as housing, health services, respect, and fair treatment. Although harms that result from unconcern or from efforts to achieve one's own goals may not involve malevolent intent, they can nevertheless result in exploitation, disruption of crucial services, suffering, the destruction of communities, and death. Outwardly, severe and mild forms of moral exclusion are different, but they share vital underlying characteristics. In both, the perpetrators perceive others as psychologically distant, lack constructive moral obligations toward others, view others as expendable and undeserving, and deny others' rights, dignity, and autonomy. . . .

ANTECEDENTS OF MORAL EXCLUSION

Conceptual Origins of Moral Exclusion: The Scope of Justice

Although we rarely think about them, we each have beliefs about the sorts of beings that should be treated justly. Moral values, rules, and considerations of fairness apply only to those within this boundary for fairness, called our "scope of justice" or "moral community." Membership within this boundary, therefore, has profound implications. People who are slaves, children, women, aged, Black, Jewish, mentally retarded, physically handicapped, and insane constitute a partial list of beings whose rights have been abrogated or eliminated because of their exclusion from the scope of justice.

Deutsch (1974, 1985) defines the scope of justice as the psychological boundary of one's moral community; a narrow conception of community results in a constricted scope of situations in which considerations of justice govern one's conduct. Walzer (1983) asserts that distributive justice begins with allocation of membership in the community; denial of membership results in the tyranny of insiders over outsiders, and begins "the first of a long train of abuses" (p. 62). Therefore, the extent of our moral community is fundamental to the psychology of justice.

People who morally exclude others are often viewed as evil or demented, but we each have boundaries for justice and can morally exclude others in some spheres of our lives. Typically, we feel strong moral obligations to family and friends, but not to strangers, enemies, or members of disadvantaged groups, so we are more likely to exclude them from our moral universe. . . . [A]dverse social circumstances create the conditions necessary for ordinary people to dehumanize, harm, and act with incredible cruelty toward others.

What then, in concrete terms, is moral inclusion? An empirical study of the scope of justice approached this question by using principal components analysis of attitudes and behaviors (Opotow, 1987). The findings indicated a coherent cluster of attitudes that comprised moral inclusion: (1) believing that considerations of fairness apply to another, (2) willingness to allocate a share of community resources to another, and (3) willingness to make sacrifices to foster another's well-being. This definition is consistent with Regan's (1983) proposition that members of the moral community are those whose well-being concerns us, and with Fineberg's (1986) assertion that those with rights (i.e., members of the moral community) exercise them not only through asserting claims, but also through surrendering these rights to others. . . .

Although the scope of justice is largely ignored in psychology, it is debated among moral philosophers. Nozick (1974) and Rawls (1971) assert that membership in the human species is the appropriate boundary. This psychologically salient boundary is widely accepted by philosophers, psychologists, and the lay public, but recently it has become less distinct and more controversial. Advances in fetal medicine have raised questions about when one becomes a member of the category "human," with its attendant rights (Callahan & Callahan, 1984). Regan (1983) and Singer (1975) argue that cognitive awareness, rather than species membership, is a more just boundary; therefore, nonhuman sentient animals such as higher mammals are entitled to their lives and to fair treatment. This view is gaining increasing acceptance as research reveals that nonhuman animals have more sophisticated intellectual capacities than previously suspected (see Hoage & Goldman, 1986). More extensive boundaries are proposed by Schweitzer and the Jainists, who argue that all forms of life should be treated with reverence. Stone (1974) and Leopold (1949) argue for still wider boundaries that include inanimate natural objects. This v.. v "enlarge[s] the boundaries of the community to include soils, water, plants, and animals, or collectively, the land" (Leopold, 1949, p. 204). Until recently, this view was considered radical; it is gaining increased public acceptance (e.g., Bryant, 1989) as our moral boundaries expand.

In addition to differences between philosophical positions, the boundaries of the moral community also vary between cultures and historical periods. To some extent, we each construct our own moral code, but prevailing cultural norms also shape our beliefs about which categories of beings are entitled to considerations of fairness (Bandura, 1986; Edward, 1987; Shweder, Mahapatra, & Miller, 1987). As an example on a current moral frontier, many North Americans are outraged when Japanese fishermen slaughter whales and porpoises, which are now included in our moral community but not in theirs. Yet, relatively recently, whaling was a major industry in the U.S.A. Similarly, although the slaughtering of farm animals is not widely viewed as an injustice in Western countries, it is ethically repugnant in other traditions such as Buddhism. As Austin and Hatfield state,

It is easy for us to feel appalled at the way nobles exploited their serfs, plantation owners exploited their slaves, and male chauvinists exploited women. But were these landowners, slaveowners, and male chauvinists fundamentally different from us, or were they simply responding to different pressures and a different *status quo?* The prevailing power balances, then, seem to affect even the most aloof reformers' conceptions of social justice. (1980, p. 43)

. . .

Psychological Origins of Moral Exclusion

Apart from the moral fashions of the moment, are there enduring psychological factors that predict moral exclusion? Although we lack a cohesive literature on moral exclusion, research in a number of related areas suggests that two factors modify our moral boundaries. The first, severity of conflict, results from our perceptions of situations. The second, feelings of unconnectedness, results from our perceptions of relationships.

Conflict Justice during conflict is different than during times of calm. Danger, conflict, and stress reinforce group boundaries and change information processing strategies and the choice of justice rules (Coser, 1956; Leventhal, 1979; Staub, 1985). As conflict escalates, cohesion within groups increases, but concern for fairness between groups shrinks. Because moral constraints on behavior are weak for those outside the scope of justice, outsiders are increasingly endangered. Dominance can take extreme forms, such as exploitation, slavery, and extermination (Lerner & Whitehead, 1980).

Consistent with work on conflict and ethnocentrism (Bar-Tal, this issue; Brewer, 1979; LeVine & Campbell, 1972), and work on "enemy images" (Holt & Silverstein, 1989; White, 1984), those within the community perceive their own group as more moral, honest, peaceful, virtuous, and obedient than outgroup members. The outgroup's perceived moral failings justify utilitarian, self-maximizing decisions that dispense with concerns about their well-being. Consequently, conflict with those within the moral community takes a different form than conflict with those outside it. With those inside, conflict is the regulated competition of equals, conducted according to rules of fair play, such as a duel or a bidding war; with those outside, conflict is an unregulated, no-holds-barred power struggle among unequals, such as guerrilla warfare (Deutsch, 1985).

The body of work on conflict predicts a simple negative relationship between severity of conflict and the scope of justice. Opotow (1987) found that increasing conflict constricted subjects' scope of justice. Less is known about decreasing the severity of conflict. Hallie (1971) suggested that diminished conflict offers an opportunity to enlarge moral boundaries:

The justifications the victimizers believe in usually crumble only after the victimizer has been put into some kind of danger, has been coerced. When one's self-interest is at issue, guilt, if it comes at all, frequently follows danger . . . . After Abolition many planters piously asserted their long-standing conviction that the slaves should be freed, and many Nazis stated stoutly, after the unconditional surrender, that they always thought destroying Jews was unnecessary or even wrong. Unfortunately for our species, victimizers need to experience contradiction in the form of coercion and moral guilt. (p. 260)

Empirical investigation of the effects of decreased conflict on moral boundaries could advance theory and have practical relevance to deterrence of moral exclusion.

Unconnectedness Moral exclusion emerges from our innate tendency to differentiate objects (Tajfel & Wilkes, 1963). Differentiation and categorization can often be innocuous, merely facilitating acquisition of information and memory. Social categorization becomes invidious when it serves as a moral rationalization for injustice. Race, for example, could be a neutral characteristic; as a criterion for social catgorization, however, it becomes a value-loaded label that generates unequal treatment and consequences for members of different groups (Archer, 1985; Tajfel, 1978).

Perceiving another as unconnected to oneself can trigger negative attitudes, destructive competition (Deutsch, 1973), discriminatory responses (Tajfel, 1978), and aggressive, destructive behavior (Bandura, Underwood, & Fromson, 1975)— attitudes and behaviors consistent with moral exclusion. Conversely, perceiving another as connected to oneself in any way can hinder moral exclusion. Belonging to the same community, perceiving another as a worthwhile being, or discerning any thread of connectedness creates bonds, even with strangers. Research on cooperation and competition (Deutsch, 1973), prosocial behavior (Staub, 1978), interpersonal attraction (Byrne, 1971), ethnocentrism (Brewer, 1979; LeVine & Campbell, 1972), and value similarity (Schwartz & Struch, 1989) supports the idea that connection leads to attraction, empathy, and helpful behavior—attitudes and behavior consistent with moral inclusion.

From the above research, it would seem that perceiving another as beneficial or as similar should exert roughly comparable effects on measures of moral inclusion. However, an empirical examination of the scope of justice did not support this hypothesis (Opotow, 1987). In an experiment that examined how moral boundaries were modified by severity of conflict, perceiving another as similar or dissimilar ("similarity"), and perceiving another as beneficial or harmful ("utility"), the findings indicated that conflict and utility were significant and consistent predictors of moral inclusion, but similarity was not. An isolated finding, an interaction between conflict and similarity, suggested that moral inclusion based on similarity is highly reactive to severity of conflict. This finding contradicted common wisdom and research that predicts similarity should foster moral inclusion. Here, similarity increased moral *exclusion* as conflict escalated. These data question the assumption that all variables that engender connectedness will lead to moral inclusion in a similar fashion; instead, they suggest that each type of connectedness has a distinctive phenomenological path to moral inclusion. . . .

THE OCCURRENCE OF MORAL EXCLUSION

In *The Devil's Dictionary*, Ambrose Bierce (1906/1978) defines *moral* as "Conforming to a local and mutable standard of right. Having the quality of general expediency" (p. 169). This ironic definition has the ring of truth. We prefer to think of our ethical ideals as stable and unwavering, but in reality they are more reactive to situations than we notice. Social success depends upon knowing which moral rules are appropriate for different kinds of relationships. Therefore, we unconsciously choose from our repertory of moral responses, depending on salient characteristics of each situation (Staub, this issue). Stage theorists of moral development (e.g., Kohlberg, 1976) assume that moral reasoning is stable at each stage, but Bandura (1986) questions this assumption, stating "the standards for moral reasoning are much more amenable to social influence than stage theories would lead one to expect" (p. 493).

Moral flexibility has both assets and liabilities. Those who can conceive of alternative definitions of a situation and its requirements can break away from the unquestioning conformity to orders and norms that permits people to carry out crimes of obedience (Kelman & Hamilton, 1989). Moral flexibility may also have some of the assets of cognitive flexibility. In negotiation (Pruitt, 1981) and conflict resolution (Deutsch, 1973), recognizing alternatives can fortify one's negotiating stance and generate integrative solutions. In social relations, recognizing moral alternatives may strengthen social influence; however, it can have the dangerous by-product of a "double standard." For example, in instances of sexism and racism, what constitutes "fair" behavior differs, based on group membership. An extreme and odious example of moral flexibility was "doubling," in which Nazi doctors created an "ordinary self" (healer) and an "Auschwitz self" to avoid the conscious awareness that they were killers (Lifton, 1986). For Auschwitz doctors, some people remained patients who should be healed; others, simultaneously excluded from the categories of "medical patient" and "human," were removed from the doctors' moral community and from medicine's ethical obligations. In moral flexibility, doubling, and the double standard, splitting one's moral obligations results in decent behavior for those in one's moral community but harm for those outside.

Moral exclusion not only relies on moral flexibililty, but also on the appearance of moral legitimacy. Moral reasoning in the service of moral exclusion is typically self-serving, utilizes trivial criteria to justify harm, and implicitly asserts that particular moral boundaries are correct. For example, the professed goal of "protecting the purity of one's community" designates moral boundaries with unflattering contrasts and implicit devaluation. If is difficult to find moral values that do not imply moral boundaries. Even higher values, such as enhancing human dignity, imply that there is a moral boundary that excludes other species of animals.

Excusing harm doing with arguments that justify implicit moral boundaries is common. For example, minorities are often excluded when they seek to rent or buy a residence. Community members rationalize their exclusionary practices with negative characterological attributions about outgroup members that provide a false moral

TABLE 1 Processes of Moral Exclusion

Process	Manifestation in moral exclusion
Exclusion-specific processes	
Biased evaluation of groups	Making unflattering comparison between one's own group and another group; believing in the superiority of one's own group
Derogation	Disparaging and denigrating others by regarding them as lower life forms or inferior beings—e.g., barbarians, vermin
Dehumanization	Repudiating others' humanity, dignity, ability to feel, and entitlement to compassion
Fear of contamination	Perceiving contact with others as posing a threat to one's own well-being
Expanding the target	Redefining "legitimate victims" as a larger category
Accelerating the pace of harm doing	Engaging in increasingly destructive and abhorrent acts to reduce remorse and inhibitions against inflicting harm
Open approval of destructive behavior	Accepting a moral code that condones harm doing
Reducing moral standards	Perceiving one's harmful behavior as proper; replacing moral standards that restrain harm with less stringent standards that condone or praise harm doing
Blaming the victim	Displacing the blame for reprehensible actions on those who are harmed
Self-righteous comparisons	Lauding or justifying harmful acts by contrasting them with morally condemnable atrocities committed by the adversary
Desecration	Harming others to demonstrate contempt for them, particularly symbolic or gratuitous harm
Ordinary processes	
Groupthink	Striving for group unanimity by maintaining isolation from dissenting opinion that would challenge the assumptions, distortions, or decisions of the group
Transcendent ideologies	Experiencing oneself or one's group as exalted, extraordinary, and possessed of a higher wisdom, which permits even harmful behavior as necessary to bring a better world into being

justification for discrimination. Harmful outcomes accrue to minority group members, who experience prejudice and reduced mobility (Danielson, 1976). These moral justifications for harm also injure the perpetrators and those they ostensibly protect by shielding them from an opportunity to conquer their fear of those who differ from them on some characteristic, and by losing an opportunity to enlarge and enrich their restricted subculture (see Fine, this issue).

Symptoms of Moral Exclusion

The rationalizations and justifications that support moral exclusion render it difficult to detect. Therefore, it is important to be able to recognize its characteristic symptoms, and this ability may also offer opportunities to arrest its advance. There is a literature on sanctioned harm doing that, although neither large nor cohesive, can provide insight into the symptoms of moral exclusion. In analyses of mass murders and

TABLE 1 *(Continued)*

Process	Manifestation in moral exclusion
Deindividuation	Feeling anonymous in a group setting, thus weakening one's capacity to behave in accordance with personal standards
Moral engulfment	Replacing one's own ethical standards with those of the group
Psychological distance	Ceasing to feel the presence of others; perceiving others as objects or as nonexistent
Condescension	Regarding others as inferior; patronizing others, and perceiving them with disdain—e.g., they are childlike, irrational, simple
Technical orientation	Focusing on efficient means while ignoring outcomes; routinizing harm doing by transforming it into mechanical steps
Double standards	Having different sets of moral rules and obligations for different categories of people
Unflattering comparisons	Using unflattering contrasts to bolster one's superiority over others
Euphemisms	Masking, sanitizing, and conferring respectability on reprehensible behavior by using palliative terms that misrepresent cruelty and harm
Displacing responsibility	Behaving in ways one would normally repudiate because a higher authority explicitly or implicitly assumes responsibility for the consequences
Diffusing responsibility	Fragmenting the implementation of harmful tasks through collective action
Concealing the effects of harmful behavior	Disregarding, ignoring, disbelieving, distorting, or minimizing injurious outcomes to others
Glorifying violence	Viewing violence as a sublime activity and a legitimate form of human expression
Normalizing violence	Accepting violent behavior as ordinary because of repeated exposure to it and societal acceptance of it
Temporal containment of harm doing	Perceiving one's injurious behavior as an isolated event—"just this time"

genocides, particularly the Holocaust and the My Lai massacre (e.g., Arendt, 1963; Bandura, 1990; Bar-Tal, 1989; Duster, 1971; Kelman, 1973; Kelman & Hamilton, 1989; Lifton, 1973, 1986; Sanford & Comstock, 1971; Smelzer, 1971; Staub, 1987, 1989; Thompson & Quets, 1987), the authors highlight different symptoms, but there is much overlap (for detailed descriptions, see Bandura, this issue; Lifton, 1986; Staub, this issue).

To create a codebook of symptoms that would define moral exclusion operationally for empirical research, I distilled a list of more than two dozen symptoms from this literature on sanctioned harm doing (see Table 1). Not all the symptoms have equal importance, the list is not exhaustive, and it is merely a list, not a description of how the symptoms cluster. For example, scapegoating, an ordinary form of moral exclusion for children, can include blaming the victim, fear of contamination, derogation, deindividuation, moral engulfment, condescension, and other processes. Yet the list is useful to recognize and study moral exclusion.

Considered as a group, these symptoms can be categorized in several ways. They are *exclusion-specific* and unlikely to be employed in common interpersonal relations, or they are *ordinary* and frequently occur in everyday life. I describe this distinction in more detail in the next paragraphs. In addition, at least four other dimensions on which the symptoms can be categorized are interesting to consider: (1) They are predominantly *cognitive*, i.e., categorizations of people and social situations based on beliefs and expectations, or they are predominantly *moral*, i.e., based on rules of conduct concerning the mutual obligations, rights, and entitlements of those in relationships. (2) They are largely *individual* symptoms, or they are *group* symptoms. (3) They are mere *symptoms* or moral exclusion, or they actively *advance* it. This distinction, an important one for understanding the progression of moral exclusion, is not readily apparent and could be clarified by systematic study. (4) They *eliminate self-deterrents,* they *promote self-approval,* or like moral justifications, they are especially powerful because they *do both* (Bandura, this issue). Discovering stable clusters of these symptoms would contribute coherence to the literature on sanctioned harm, and provide useful categories for theorists and researchers. Bandura's model (this issue) includes many of these symptoms and identifies four categories that group them.

Nearly half the symptoms are exclusion-specific. Examples are dehumanization, fearing contamination from social contact, and reducing one's moral standards. Although these symptoms can occur in everyday relations, they signal that interpersonal or intergroup conflict is taking a destructive course. In his Crude Law of Social Relations, Deutsch (1973) states that the "characteristic processes and effects elicited by a given type of social relationship tend also to elicit that type of relationship" (p. 365). This law applies particularly well to these potent symptoms, in which there is likely to be a reciprocal relation between symptoms and effects. In other words, symptoms that provoke moral exclusion are also triggered by moral exclusion, instigating a vicious cycle. Concrete actions that obstruct the exclusion-specific symptoms may also arrest moral exclusion. It is possible that there may be certain critical symptoms to halt, particularly if they occur in a relatively invariant pattern. However, lacking systematic empirical studies, we still have much to learn about the course that moral exclusion takes.

Ordinary symptoms associated with moral exclusion can occur in everyday life. Examples are psychological distancing, displacing responsibility, group loyalty, and normalizing and glorifying violence. These symptoms can be part of the work routine in certain societal institutions, for example, normalizing violence in the military, transcendent ideologies in religious establishments, technical thinking in business organizations, displacement of responsibility by nurses in hospitals, and psychological distancing by doctors. These and numerous other institutions routinely employ euphemisms to discuss unpleasant topics. Although these ordinary exclusion symptoms can occur without people necessarily perceiving others as outside the moral community, their ordinariness poses a special risk; those who habitually employ them can perceive some people as objects and imperceptibly cross a threshold that excludes these others from their moral universe.

Interaction of Psychological and Social Factors

As the symptoms indicate, both social and individual elements contribute to moral exclusion. Moral exclusion emerges and gains momentum in a recursive cycle in which individuals and society modify each other. In one direction, individuals internalize the prevailing social order, reshape their perceptions of others, reconfigure their moral community, and engage in symptoms of moral exclusion such as dehumanization, victim blaming, psychological distancing, and condescension. In the other direction, moral exclusion emerges from individuals; their attitudes and behaviors reshape the social order, redefining group entitlements, narrowing the scope of justice, and reinforcing the perceptual distortions that gave rise to them. The interaction between individuals and society is evident even when isolated, psychopathic subgroups or individuals attack people (as in the 1989 murder of "feminists" in Montreal). They are, to some extent, acting on societal norms that condone some forms of mistreatment, such as devaluation of women. In these tragic attacks, perpetrators employ elaborate and obviously flawed moral justifications to support their distorted contention that they are rooting out an evil.

Such individual rationalizations, although outrageous, are not very different from the reasons given to defend state-supported harm that occurs in violations of human rights. Both covert and overt institutionalization of moral exclusion, such as racism and apartheid, are far more virulent and dangerous than the individual manifestation because institutionalized harm occurs on a much larger scale. Yet moral exclusion can engender widespread harm within a society only when people *individually* engage in moral restructuring. The bidirectional influence between individuals and society in perpetuating moral exclusion suggests possible ways to interrupt the cycle of harm.

Outcomes of Moral Exclusion

Those who are morally excluded are perceived as undeserving, expendable, and therefore eligible for harm. Although both those inside and outside the moral community can experience wrongful harm, harm inflicted on insiders is more readily perceived as an injustice and activates guilt, remorse, outrage, demands for reparative response, self-blame, or contrition. When harm is inflicted on outsiders, it may not be perceived as a violation of their rights, and it can fail to engage bystanders' moral concern.

As severity of conflict and threat escalates, harm and sanctioned aggression become more likely. As harm doing escalates, societal structures change, the scope of justice shrinks, and the boundaries of harm doing expand. Because conflict with unequals is an unregulated, no-holds-barred power struggle (Deutsch, 1985) and because moral constraints on behavior are weak for those outside the scope of justice, outsiders are increasingly endangered (Lerner & Whitehead, 1980).

In sum, moral exclusion can occur in degree, from overt evil to passive unconcern. In this broad conceptualization, moral exclusion is neither an isolated nor inexplicable event, but occurs with great frequency, depends on ordinary social and psychological processes to license previously unacceptable attitudes and behavior, and can cause great harm, from personal suffering to widespread atrocities.

REFERENCES

Archer, D. (1985). Social deviance. In G. Lindzey & E. Aronson (Eds.), *The handbook of social psychology* (3rd ed., Vol. 2, pp. 743–804). New York: Random House.

Arendt, H. (1963). *Eichmann in Jerusalem: A report on the banality of evil.* New York: Viking.

Austin, W., & Hatfield, E. (1980). Equity theory, power, and social justice. In G. Mikula (Ed.), *Justice and social interaction.* New York: Springer-Verlag.

Bandura, A. (1986). *Social foundations of thought and action: A social cognitive theory.* Englewood Cliffs, NJ: Prentice-Hall.

Bandura, A. (1990). Mechanisms of moral disengagement in terrorism. In W. Reich (Ed.), *The psychology of terrorism: Behaviors, world-views, and states of mind.* New York: Cambridge University Press.

Bandura, A., Underwood, B., & Fromson, M. E. (1975). Disinhibition of aggression through diffusion of responsibility and dehumanization of victims. *Journal of Research on Personality, 9,* 253–269.

Bar-Tal, D. (1989). Delegitimization: The extreme case of stereotyping and prejudice. In D. Bar-Tal, C. Graumann, A. W. Kruglanski, & W. Stroebe (Eds.), *Stereotyping and prejudice: Changing conceptions.* New York: Springer-Verlag.

Bierce, A. (1978). *The devil's dictionary.* Owings Mills, MD: Stemmer House. (Original work published 1906 under the title, *The cynic's word book.*)

Brewer, M. B. (1979). The role of ethnocentrism in intergroup conflict. In W. G. Austin & S. Worchel (Eds.), *The social psychology of intergroup relations.* Monterey, CA: Brooks/Cole.

Bryant, N. (1989, December 25). Outdoors: One of the richest evenings of the year. *New York Times,* p. 47.

Byrne, D. (1971). *The attraction paradigm.* New York: Academic Press.

Callahan, S., & Callahan, D. (1984). *Abortion: Understanding differences.* New York: Plenum.

Coser, L. (1956). *The functions of social conflict.* New York: Free Press.

Danielson, M. N. (1976). *The politics of exclusion.* New York: Columbia University Press.

Deutsch, M. (1973). *The resolution of conflict.* New Haven, CT: Yale University Press.

Deutsch, M. (1974). Awakening the sense of injustice. In M. Lerner & M. Ross (Eds.), *The quest for justice: Myth, reality, ideal.* Canada: Holt, Rinehart & Winston.

Deutsch, M. (1975). Equity, equality, and need: What determines which value will be used as the basis for distributive justice? *Journal of Social Issues, 31*(3), 137–150.

Deutsch, M. (1985). *Distributive justice: A social psychological perspective.* New Haven, CT: Yale University Press.

Duster, T. (1971). Conditions for a guilt-free massacre. In N. Sanford & C. Comstock (Eds.), *Sanctions for evil: Sources of social destructiveness.* San Francisco: Jossey-Bass.

Edwards, C. A. (1987). Culture and the construction of moral values: A comparative ethnography of moral encounters in two cultural settings. In J. Kagan & S. Lamb (Eds.), *The emergence of morality in young children.* Chicago: University of Chicago Press.

Fineberg, J. (1986). The nature and value of rights. In E. Bandman & B. Bandman (Eds.), *Bioethics and human rights: A reader for health professionals.* Lanham, MD: University Press of America.

Foa, U. G., & Foa, E. B. (1974). *Societal structures of the mind.* Springfield, IL: Thomas.

Hallie, P. P. (1971). Justification and rebellion. In N. Sanford & C. Comstock (Eds.), *Sanctions for evil: Sources of social destructiveness.* San Francisco: Jossey-Bass.

Hoage, R. L., & Goldman, L. (Eds.). (1986). *Animal intelligence: Insights into the animal mind.* Washington, DC: Smithsonian Institution Press.

Holt, R. R., & Silverstein, B. (1989). On the psychology of enemy images: Introduction and overview. *Journal of Social Issues, 45*(2), 1-11.

Homans, G. C. (1961). *Social behavior: Its elementary forms.* New York: Harcourt, Brace & World.

Kelman, H. (1973). Violence without moral restraint: Reflections on the dehumanization of victims and victimizers. *Journal of Social Issues, 29*(4), 25-61.

Kelman, H. C., & Hamilton, V. L. (1989). *Crimes of obedience.* New Haven, CT: Yale University Press.

Kohlberg, L. (1976). Moral stages and moralization. In T. Lickona (Ed.), *Morality, moral behavior and moral development: Basic issues in theory and research* (pp. 52-73). New York: Holt, Rinehart & Winston.

Leopold, A. (1949). *A Sand County almanac.* New York: Oxford University Press.

Lerner, M. J. (1970). The desire for justice and reactions to victims. In J. Macauley & L. Berkowitz (Eds.), *Altruism and helping behavior: Social psychological studies of some antecedents and consequences.* New York: Academic Press.

Lerner, M. J. (1980). *The belief in a just world.* New York: Plenum.

Lerner, M. J., & Whitehead, L. A. (1980). Procedural justice viewed in the context of justice motive theory. In G. Mikula (Ed.), *Justice and social interaction.* New York: Springer-Verlag.

Leventhal, G. S. (1979). Effects of external conflict on resource allocation and fairness within groups and organizations. In W. G. Austin & S. Worchel (Eds.), *The social psychology of intergroup relations.* Monterey, CA: Brooks/Cole.

LeVine, R. A., & Campbell, D. T. (1972). *Ethnocentrism: Theories of conflict, ethnic attitude, and group behavior.* New York: Wiley.

Lifton, R. J. (1973). *Home from the war—Vietnam veterans: Neither victims nor executioners.* New York: Simon & Schuster.

Lifton, R. J. (1986). *The Nazi doctors.* New York: Basic Books.

Lind, E. A., & Tyler, T. R. (1988). *The psychology of procedural justice.* New York: Plenum.

Mikula, G. (1980). Introduction: Main issues in the psychological research on justice. In G. Mikula (Ed.), *Justice and social interaction.* New York: Springer-Verlag.

Nozick, R. (1974). *Anarchy, state, and utopia.* New York: Basic Books.

Oliner, S. B., & Oliner, P. (1988). *The altruistic personality: Rescuers of Jews in Nazi Germany.* New York: Free Press.

Opotow, S. V. (1987). Limits of fairness: An experimental examination of antecedents of the scope of justice. *Dissertation Abstracts International, 48*(08B), 2500. (University Microfilms No. 87-24072.)

Opotow, S. (1989). [Exclusion from justice and destructive interpersonal conflict]. Unpublished raw data.

Pruitt, D. G. (1981). *Negotiation behavior.* New York: Academic Press.

Rawls, J. (1971). *A theory of justice.* Cambridge, MA: Belknap.

Regan, T. (1983). *The case for animal rights.* Berkeley: University of California Press.

Sanford, N., & Comstock, C. (1971). *Sanctions for evil: Sources of social destructiveness.* San Francisco: Jossey-Bass.

Schwartz, S., & Struch, N. (1989). Values, stereotypes and intergroup antagonism. In D. Bar-Tal, C. Graumann, A. W. Kruglanski, & W. Stroebe (Eds.), *Stereotyping and prejudice: Changing conceptions.* New York: Springer-Verlag.

Shweder, R., Mahapatra, M., & Miller, J. G. (1987). Culture and moral development. In J. Kagan & S. Lamb (Eds.), *The emergence of morality in young children.* Chicago: University of Chicago Press.

Singer, P. (1975). *Animal liberation: A new ethics for our treatment of animals.* New York: Avon.

Smelzer, N. J. (1971). Some determinants of destructive behavior. In N. Sanford & C. Comstock (Eds.), *Sanctions for evil: Sources of social destructiveness.* San Francisco: Jossey-Bass.

Staub, E. (1978). *Positive social behavior and morality: Vol. I. Social and personal influences.* New York: Academic Press.

Staub, E. (1985). The psychology of perpetrators and bystanders. *Political Psychology, 6,* 61–85.

Staub, E. (1987, August). *Moral exclusion and extreme destructiveness: Personal goal theory, differential evaluation, moral equilibration and steps along the continuum of destruction.* Paper presented at American Psychological Association meeting, New York.

Staub, E. (1989). *The roots of evil: Origins of genocide and other group violence.* New York: Cambridge University Press.

Stone, C. D. (1974). *Should trees have standing? Toward legal rights for natural objects.* Los Altos, CA: William Kaufmann.

Tajfel, H. [(Ed.).] (1978). *Differentiation between social groups: Studies in the social psychology of intergroup relations.* London: Academic Press.

Tajfel, H., & Wilkes, A. C. (1963). Classification and qualitative judgment. *British Journal of Psychology, 54,* 101–114.

Thibaut, J. W., & Walker, L. (1975). *Procedural justice: A psychological analysis.* Hillsdale, NJ: Erlbaum.

Thompson, J. L. P., & Quets, G. A. (1987, August). *Redefining the moral order: Towards a normative theory of genocide.* Paper presented at American Sociological Association meeting, Chicago.

Walster, E., & Walster, G. W. (1975). Equity and social justice. *Journal of Social Issues, 31*(3), 21–43.

Walster, E., & Walster, G. W., & Berscheid, E. (1978). *Equity: Theory and research.* Boston: Allyn & Bacon.

Walzer, M. (1983). *Spheres of justice: A defense of pluralism and equality.* New York: Basic Books.

White, R. K. (1984). *Fearful warriors: A psychological profile of U.S.-Soviet relations.* New York: Free Press.

The True Meaning of Community
M. Scott Peck

In our culture of rugged individualism—in which we generally feel that we dare not be honest about ourselves, even with the person in the pew next to us—we bandy around the word "community." We apply it to almost any collection of individuals—a town, a church, a synagogue, a fraternal organization, an apartment complex, a professional association—regardless of how poorly those individuals communicate with each other. It is a false use of the word.

If we are going to use the word meaningfully we must restrict it to a group of individuals who have learned how to communicate honestly with each other, whose relationships go deeper than their masks of composure, and who have developed some significant commitment to "rejoice together, mourn together," and to "delight in each other, make others' conditions our own." But what, then, does such a rare group look like? How does it function? What is a true definition of community?

We can define or adequately explain only those things that are smaller than we are. I have in my office, for instance, a very handy little electrical space heater. If I were an electrical engineer, I could take it apart and explain to you—define—exactly how it works. Except for one thing. That is the matter of the cord and plug that connect it with something called electricity. And there are certain questions about electricity, despite its known physical laws, that even the most advanced electrical engineer cannot answer. That is because electricity is something larger than we are.

There are many such "things": God, goodness, love, evil, death, consciousness, for instance. Being so large, they are many-faceted, and the best we can do is describe or define one facet at a time. Even so, we never seem quite able to plumb their depths fully. Sooner or later we inevitably run into a core of mystery.

Community is another such phenomenon. Like electricity, it is profoundly lawful. Yet there remains something about it that is inherently mysterious, miraculous, unfathomable. Thus there is no adequate one-sentence definition of genuine community. Community is something more than the sum of its parts, its individual members. What is this "something more?" Even to begin to answer that, we enter a realm that is not so much abstract as almost mystical. It is a realm where words are never fully suitable and language itself falls short.

The analogy of a gem comes to mind. The seeds of community reside in humanity—a social species—just as a gem originally resides in the earth. But it is not yet a gem, only a potential one. So it is that geologists refer to a gem in the rough simply as a stone. A group becomes a community in somewhat the same way that a stone becomes a gem—through a process of cutting and polishing. Once cut and polished, it is something beautiful. But to describe its beauty, the best we can do is to describe its facets. Community, like a gem, is multifaceted, each facet a mere aspect of a whole that defies description.

Source: Abridged from Chapter 3 in *The Different Drum: Community Making and Peace* (pp. 59–76). New York: Simon and Schuster, 1987.

One other caveat. The gem of community is so exquisitely beautiful it may seem unreal to you, like a dream you once had when you were a child, so beautiful it may seem unattainable. As Bellah and his coauthors put it, the notion of community "may also be resisted as absurdly Utopian, as a project to create a perfect society. But the transformation of which we speak is both necessary and modest. Without it, indeed, there may be very little future to think about at all."[1] The problem is that the lack of community is so much the norm in our society, one without experience would be tempted to think, How could we possibly get there from here? It *is* possible; we *can* get there from here. Remember that to the uninitiated eye it would seem impossible for a stone ever to become a gem.

The facets of community are interconnected, profoundly interrelated. No one could exist without the other. They create each other, make each other possible. What follows, then, is but one scheme for isolating and naming the most salient characteristics of a true community.

INCLUSIVITY, COMMITMENT, AND CONSENSUS

Community is and must be inclusive.

The great enemy of community is exclusivity. Groups that exclude others because they are poor or doubters or divorced or sinners or of some different race or nationality are not communities; they are cliques—atcually defensive bastions against community.

Inclusiveness is not an absolute. Long-term communities must invariably struggle over the degree to which they are going to be inclusive. Even short-term communities must sometimes make that difficult decision. But for most groups it is easier to exclude than include. Clubs and corporations give little thought to being inclusive unless the law compels them to do so. True communities, on the other hand, if they want to remain such, are always reaching to extend themselves. The burden of proof falls upon exclusivity. Communities do not ask " How can we justify taking this person in?" Instead the question is "Is it at all justifiable to keep this person out?" In relation to other groupings of similar size or purpose, communities are always relatively inclusive.

In my first experience of community at Friends Seminary, the boundaries between grades, between students and teachers, between young and old, were all "soft." There were no outgroups, no outcasts. Everyone was welcome at the parties. There was no pressure to conform. So the inclusiveness of any community extends along all its parameters. There is an "allness" to community. It is not merely a matter of including different sexes, races, and creeds. It it also inclusive of the full range of human emotions. Tears are as welcome as laughter, fear as well as faith. And different styles: hawks and doves, straights and gays, Grailers and Sears, Roebuckers, the talkative and the silent. All human differences are included. All "soft" individuality is nurtured.

How is this possible? How can such differences be absorbed, such different people coexist? Commitment—the willingness to coexist—is crucial. Sooner or later, somewhere along the line (and preferably sooner), the members of a group in some way must commit themselves to one another if they are to become or stay a community. Exclusivity, the great enemy to community, appears in two forms: excluding the other and excluding yourself. If you conclude under your breath, "Well, this group just isn't for me—they're too much this or too much that—and I'm just going to quietly pick up my marbles and go home," it would be as destructive to community as it would be to a marriage were you to conclude, "Well, the grass looks a little greener on the other side of the fence, and I'm just going to move on." Community, like marriage, requires that we hang in there when the going gets a little rough. It requires a certain degree of commitment. It is no accident that Bellah et al. subtitled their work *Individualism and Commitment in American Life.* Our individualism must be counterbalanced by commitment.

If we do hang in there, we usually find after a while that "the rough places are made plain." A friend correctly defined community as a "group that has learned to transcend its individual differences." But this learning takes time, the time that can be bought only through commitment. "Transcend" does not mean "obliterate" or "demolish." It literally means "to climb over." The achievement of community can be compared to the reaching of a mountaintop.

Perhaps the most necessary key to this transcendence is the appreciation of differences. In community, instead of being ignored, denied, hidden, or changed, human differences are celebrated as gifts. Remember how I came to appreciate Lily's "gift of flowing," and she my "gift of organization." Marriage is, of course, a small, long-term community of two. Yet in short-term communities of even fifty or sixty, while the timing and depth are almost opposite, I have found that the dynamics are the same. The transformation of attitudes toward each other that allowed Lily and me to transcend our differences took twenty years. But this same transcendence can routinely occur within a community-building group over the course of eight hours. In each case alienation is transformed into appreciation and reconciliation. And in each case the transcendence has a good deal to do with love.

We are so unfamiliar with genuine community that we have never developed an adequate vocabulary for the politics of this transcendence. When we ponder on how individual differences can be accommodated, perhaps the first mechanism we turn to (probably because it is the most childlike) is that of the strong individual leader. Differences, like those of squabbling siblings, we instinctively think can be resolved by a mommy or daddy—a benevolent dictator, or so we hope. But community, encouraging individuality as it does, can never be totalitarian. So we jump to a somewhat less primitive way of resolving individual differences which we call democracy. We take a vote, and the majority determines which differences prevail. Majority rules. Yet that process excludes the aspirations of the minority. How do we transcend differences in such a way as to include a minority? It seems like a conundrum. How and where do you go beyond democracy?

In the genuine communities of which I have been a member, a thousand or more group decisions have been made and I have never yet witnessed a vote. I do not mean to imply that we can or should discard democratic machinery, any more than we should abolish organization. But I do mean to imply that a community, in transcending individual differences, routinely goes beyond even democracy. In the vocabulary of this transcendence we thus far have only one word: "consensus." Decisions in genuine community are arrived at through consensus, in a process that is not unlike a community of jurors, for whom consensual decision making is mandated.

Still, how on earth can a group in which individuality is encouraged, in which individual differences flourish, routinely arrive at consensus? Even when we develop a richer language for community operations, I doubt we will ever have a formula for the consensual process. The process itself is an adventure. And again there is something inherently almost mystical, magical about it. But it works. And the other facets of community will provide hints as to how it does.

REALISM

A second characteristic of community is that it is realistic. In the community of marriage, for example, when Lily and I discuss an issue, such as how to deal with one of our children, we are likely to develop a response more realistic than if either of us were operating alone. If only for this reason, I believe that it is extremely difficult for a single parent to make adequate decisions about his or her children. Even if the best Lily and I can do is to come up with two different points of view, they modulate each other. In larger communities the process is still more effective. A community of sixty can usually come up with a dozen different points of view. The resulting consensual stew, composed of multiple ingredients, is usually far more creative than a two-ingredient dish could ever be.

We are accustomed to think of group behavior as often primitive. Indeed, I myself have written about the ease with which groups can become evil.[2] "Mob psychology" is properly a vernacular expression. But groups of whatever kinds are seldom real communities. There is, in fact, more than a quantum leap between an ordinary group and a community; they are entirely different phenomena. And a real community is, by definition, immune to mob psychology because of its encouragement of individuality, its inclusion of a variety of points of view. Time and again I have seen a community begin to make a certain decision or establish a certain norm when one of the members will suddenly say, "Wait a minute, I don't think I can go along with this." Mob psychology cannot occur in an environment in which individuals are free to speak their minds and buck the trend. Community is such an environment.

Because a community includes members with many different points of view and the freedom to express them, it comes to appreciate the whole of a situation far better than an individual, couple, or ordinary group can. Incorporating the dark and the light, the sacred and the profane, the sorrow and the joy, the glory and the mud, its conclusions are well rounded. Nothing is likely to be left out. With so many frames of reference, it approaches reality more and more closely. Realistic decisions, consequently, are more often guaranteed in community than in any other human environment.

An important aspect of the realism of community deserves mention: humility. While rugged individualism predisposes one to arrogance, the "soft" individualism of community leads to humility. Begin to appreciate each others' gifts, and you begin to appreciate your own limitations. Witness others share their brokenness, and you will become able to accept your own inadequacy and imperfection. Be fully aware of human variety, and you will recognize the interdependence of humanity. As a group of people do these things—as they become a community—they become more and more humble, not only as individuals but also as a group—and hence more realistic. From which kind of group would you expect a wise, realistic decision: an arrogant one, or a humble one?

CONTEMPLATION

Among the reasons that a community is humble and hence realistic is that it is contemplative. It examines itself. It is self-aware. It knows itself. "Know thyself" is a sure rule for humility. As that fourteenth-century classic on contemplation, *The Cloud of Unknowing*, put it: "Meekness in itself is nothing else than a true knowing and feeling of a man's [or woman's] self as he [or she] is. Any man [or woman] who truly sees and feels himself [or herself] as he [or she] is must surely be meek indeed."[3]

The word "comtemplative" has a variety of connotations. Most of them center upon awareness. The essential goal of contemplation is increased awareness of the world outside oneself, the world inside oneself, and the relationship between the two. A man [or woman] who settles for a relatively limited awareness of himself [or herself] could hardly be called contemplative. It is also questionable whether he [or she] could be called psychologically mature or emotionally healthy. Self-examination is the key to insight, which is the key to wisdom. Plato put it most bluntly: "The life which is unexamined is not worth living."[4]

The community-building process requires a self-examination from the beginning. And as the members become thoughtful about themselves they also learn to become increasingly thoughtful about the group. "How are *we* doing?" they begin to ask with greater and greater frequency. "Are *we* still on target? Are *we* a healthy group? Have *we* lost the spirit?"

The spirit of community once achieved is not then something forever obtained. It is not something that can be bottled or preserved in aspic. It is repeatedly lost. Remember how, toward the end of Mac Badgeley's Tavistock group in 1967, after enjoying hours of nurturing fellowship, we began to squabble again. But remember also that we were quick to recognize it because we had become aware of ourselves as a group. And because we were rapidly able to identify the cause of the problem—our division into Grailers and Sears, Roebuckers—we were rapidly able to transcend that division and recapture the spirit of community.

No community can expect to be in perpetual good health. What a genuine community does, however, because it is a contemplative body, is recognize its ill health when it occurs and quickly take appropriate action to heal itself. Indeed, the longer they exist, the more efficient healthy communities become in this recovery process. Conversely, groups that never learn to be contemplative either do not become community in the first place or else rapidly and permanently disintegrate.

A SAFE PLACE

It is no accident that I relearned "the lost art of crying" at the age of thirty-six while I was in a true community setting. Despite this relearning, my early training in rugged individualism was sufficiently effective that even today I can cry in public only when I am in a safe place. One of my joys, whenever I return to community, is that the "gift of tears" is returned to me. I am not alone. Once a group has achieved community, the single most common thing members express is: "I feel safe here."

It is a rare feeling. Almost all of us have spent nearly all our lives feeling only partially safe, if at all. Seldom, if ever, have we felt completely free to be ourselves. Seldom, if ever, in any kind of a group, have we felt wholly accepted and acceptable. Consequently, virtually everyone enters a new group situation with his or her guard up. That guard goes very deep. Even if a conscious attempt is made to be open and vulnerable, there will still be ways in which unconscious defenses remain strong. Moreover, an initial admission of vulnerability is so likely to be met with fear, hostility, or simplistic attempts to heal or convert that all but the most courageous will retreat behind their walls.

There is no such thing as instant community under ordinary circumstances. It takes a great deal of work for a group of strangers to achieve the safety of true community. Once they succeed, however, it is as if the floodgates were opened. As soon as it is safe to speak one's heart, as soon as most people in the group know they will be listened to and accepted for themselves, years and years of pent-up frustration and hurt and guilt and grief come pouring out. And pouring out ever faster. Vulnerability in community snowballs. Once its members become vulnerable and find themselves being valued and appreciated, they become more and more vulnerable. The walls come tumbling down. And as they tumble, as the love and acceptance escalates, as the mutual intimacy multiplies, true healing and converting begins. Old wounds are healed, old resentments forgiven, old resistance overcome. Fear is replaced by hope.

So another of the characteristics of community is that it is healing and convert-ing. Yet I have deliberately not listed that characteristic by itself, lest the subtlety of it be misunderstood. For the fact is that most of our human attempts to heal and convert prevent community. Human beings have within them a natural yearning and thrust toward health and wholeness and holiness. (All three words are derived from the same root.) Most of the time, however, this thrust, this energy, is enchained by fear, neutralized by defenses and resistances. But put a human being in a truly safe place, where these defenses and resistances are no longer necessary, and the thrust toward health is liberated. When we are safe, there is a natural tendency for us to heal and convert ourselves.

Experienced psychotherapists usually come to recognize this truth. As neophytes they see it as their task to heal the patient and often believe they succeed in doing so. With experience, however, they realize that they do not have the power to heal. But they also learn that it is within their power to listen to the patient, to accept him or her, to establish a "therapeutic relationship." So they focus not so much on healing as on making their relationship a safe place where the patient is likely to heal himself.

Paradoxically, then, a group of humans becomes healing and converting only after its members have learned to stop trying to heal and convert. Community is a safe place precisely because no one is attempting to heal or convert you, to fix you, to change you. Instead, the members accept you as you are. You are free to be you. And being so free, you are free to discard defenses, masks, disguises; free to seek your own psychological and spiritual health; free to become your whole and holy self.

A LABORATORY FOR PERSONAL DISARMAMENT

Toward the end of a two-day community experience in 1984 a late-middle-aged lady announced to the group: "I know Scotty said we weren't supposed to drop out, but when my husband and I got home yesterday evening we were seriously considering doing just that. I didn't sleep very well last night, and I almost didn't come here this morning. But something very strange has happened. Yesterday I was looking at all of you through hard eyes. Yet today for some reason—I don't really understand it—I have become soft-eyed, and it feels just wonderful."

This transformation—routine in community—is the same as that described in the story of the rabbi's gift. The decrepit monastery, a dying group, came alive (and into community) once its members began looking at each other and themselves through "soft eyes," seeing through lenses of respect. It may seem strange in our culture of rugged individualism that this transformation begins to occur precisely when we begin to "break down." As long as we look out at each other only through the masks of our composure, we are looking through hard eyes. But as the masks drop and we see the suffering and courage and brokenness and deeper dignity underneath, we truly start to respect each other as fellow human beings.

Once when I was speaking about community to the governing body of a church, one of the members wisely commented: "What I hear you saying is that community requires the confession of brokenness." He was correct of course. But how remarkable it is that in our culture brokenness must be "confessed." We think of confession as an act that should be carried out in secret, in the darkness of the confessional, with the guarantee of professional priestly or psychiatric confidentiality. Yet the reality is that every human being is broken and vulnerable. How strange that we should ordinarily feel compelled to hide our wounds when we are all wounded!

Vulnerability is a two-way street. Community requires the ability to expose our wounds and weaknesses to our fellow creatures. It also requires the capacity to be affected by the wounds of others, to be wounded by their wounds. This is what the woman meant by "soft eyes." Her eyes were no longer barriers, and she did, indeed, feel wonderful. There is pain in our wounds. But even more important is the love that arises among us when we share, both ways, our woundedness. Still, we cannot deny the reality that this sharing requires a risk in our culture—the risk of violating the norm of pretended invulnerability. For most of us it is a new—and, seemingly, potentially dangerous—form of behavior.

It may seem odd to refer to community as a *laboratory*. The word implies a sterile place filled not with softness but with hardware. A laboratory can better be defined, however, as a place designed to be safe for experiments. We need such a place, because when we experiment we are trying out—testing—new ways of doing things. So it is in community: it is a safe place to experiment with new types of behavior. When offered the opportunity of such a safe place, most people will naturally begin to experiment more deeply than ever before with love and trust. They drop their customary defenses and threatened postures, the barriers of distrust, fear, resentment, and prejudice. They experiment with disarming themselves. They experiment with peace—peace within themselves and within the group. And they discover that the experiment works.

An experiment is designed to give us new *experience* from which we can extract new wisdom. So it is that in experimenting with personally disarming themselves, the members of a true community *experientially* discover the rules of peacemaking and learn its virtues. It is a personal experience so powerful that it can become the driving force behind the quest for peace on a global scale.

A GROUP THAT CAN FIGHT GRACEFULLY

It may at first glance seem paradoxical that a community that is a safe place and a laboratory for disarmament should also be a place of conflict. Perhaps a story will help. A Sufi master was strolling through the streets one day with his students. When they came to the city square, a vicious battle was being fought between government troops and rebel forces. Horrified by the bloodshed, the students implored, "Quick, Master, which side should we help?"

"Both," the Master replied.

The students were confused. "Both?" they demanded. "Why should we help both?"

"We need to help the authorities learn to listen to the aspirations of the people," the Master answered, "and we need to help the rebels learn how not to compulsively reject authority."

In genuine community there are no sides. It is not always easy, but by the time they reach community the members have learned how to give up cliques and factions. They have learned how to listen to each other and how not to reject each other. Sometimes consensus in community is reached with miraculous rapidity. But at other times it is arrived at only after lengthy struggle. Just because it is a safe place does not mean community is a place without conflict. It is, however, a place where conflict can be resolved without physical or emotional bloodshed and with wisdom as well as grace. A community is a group that can fight gracefully.

That this is so is hardly accidental. For community is an amphitheater where the gladiators have laid down their weapons and their armor, where they have become skilled at listening and understanding, where they respect each others' gifts and accept each others' limitations, where they celebrate their differences and bind each others' wounds, where they are committed to a struggling together rather than against each other. It is a most unusual battleground indeed. But that is also why it is an unusually effective ground for conflict resolution.

The significance of this is hardly slight. There are very real conflicts in the world, and the worst of them do not seem to go away. But there is a fantasy abroad. Simply stated, it goes like this: "If we can resolve our conflicts, then someday we shall be able to live together in community." Could it be that we have it totally backward? And that the real dream should be: "If we can live together in community, then someday we shall be able to resolve our conflicts"?

A GROUP OF ALL LEADERS

When I am the designated leader I have found that once a group becomes a community, my nominal job is over. I can sit back and relax and be one among many, for another of the essential characteristics of community is a total decentralization of authority. Remember that it is antitotalitarian. Its decisions are reached by consensus. Communities have sometimes been referred to as leaderless groups. It is more accurate, however, to say that a community is a group of all leaders.

Because it is a safe place, compulsive leaders feel free in community—often for the first time in their lives—to *not* lead. And the customarily shy and reserved feel free to step forth with their latent gifts of leadership. The result is that community is an ideal decision-making body. The expression "A camel is a horse created by a committee" does not mean that group decisions are inevitably clumsy and imperfect; it does mean that committees are virtually never communities. . . .

The flow of leadership in community is routine. It is a phenomenon that has profound implications for anyone who would seek to improve organizational decision making—in business, government, or elsewhere. But it is not a quick trick or fix. Community must be built first. Traditional hierarchical patterns have to be at least temporarily set aside. Some kind of control must be relinquished. For it is a situation in which it is the spirit of community itself that leads and not any single individual.

A SPIRIT

Community *is* a spirit—but not in the way that the familiar phrase "community spirit" is usually understood. To most of us it implies a competitive spirit, a jingoistic boosterism, such as that displayed by fans of winning football teams or the citizens of a town in which they take great pride. "Our town is better than your town" might be taken as a typical expression of community spirit.

But this understanding of the spirit of community is profoundly misleading as well as dreadfully shallow. In only one respect is it accurate. The members of a group who have achieved genuine community do take pleasure—even delight—in themselves as a collective. They know they have won something together, collectively discovered something of great value, that they are "onto something." Beyond that the similarity ends. There is nothing competitive, for instance, about the spirit of true community. To the contrary, a group possessed by a spirit of competitiveness is by definition not a community. Competitiveness is always exclusive; genuine community is inclusive. If community has enemies, it has begun to lose the spirit of community— if it ever had it in the first place.

The spirit of true community is the spirit of peace. People in the early stages of a community-building workshop will frequently ask, "How will we know when we are a community?" It is a needless question. When a group enters community there is a dramatic change in spirit. And the new spirit is almost palpable. There is no mistaking it. No one who has experienced it need ever ask again "How will we know when we are a community?"

Nor will one ever question that it is a spirit of peace that prevails when a group enters community. An utterly new quietness descends on the group. People seem to speak more quietly; yet, strangely, their voices seem to carry better through the room. There are periods of silence, but it is never an uneasy silence. Indeed, the silence is welcomed. It feels tranquil. Nothing is frantic anymore. The chaos is over. It is as if noise had been replaced by music. The people listen and can hear. It is peaceful.

But spirit is slippery. It does not submit itself to definition, to capture, the way material things do. So it is that a group in community does not always feel peaceful in the usual sense of the word. Its members will from time to time struggle with each other, and struggle hard. The struggle may become excited and exuberant with little, if any, room for silence. But it is a productive, not a destructive, struggle. It always moves toward consensus, because it is always a loving struggle. It takes place on a ground of love. The spirit of community is inevitably the spirit of peace and love. . . .

NOTES

1 Robert Bellah et al., *Habits of the Heart* (Berkeley, Calif.: Univ. of California Press, 1985), p. 286.
2 M. Scott Peck, *People of the Lie: The Hope for Healing Human Evil* (New York: Simon and Schuster, 1983).
3 Trans. Ira Progoff (New York: Julian Press, 1969), p. 92.
4 J. W. Mackail, ed., *The Greek Anthology* (1906), Vol. III, *Apology,* p. 38.

Transforming American Culture

Robert N. Bellah, Richard Madsen, William M. Sullivan, Ann Swidler, and Steven M. Tipton

. . . [M]uch of the thinking about our society and where it should be going is rather narrowly focussed on our political economy. This focus makes sense in that government and the corporations are the most powerful structures in our society and affect everything else, including our culture and our character. But as an exclusive concern, such a focus is severely limited. Structures are not unchanging. They are frequently altered by social movements, which grow out of, and also influence, changes in consciousness, climates of opinion, and culture. We have followed Tocqueville and other classical social theorists in focussing on the mores—the "habits of the heart"— that include consciousness, culture, and the daily practices of life. It makes sense to study the mores not because they are powerful—in the short run, at least, power belongs to the political and economic structures—but for two other reasons. A study of the mores gives us insight into the state of society, its coherence, and its long-term viability. Secondly, it is in the sphere of the mores, and the climates of opinion they express, that we are apt to discern incipient changes of vision—those new flights of the social imagination that may indicate where society is heading.

A CHANGE OF ERAS?

In the course of this book, we have documented the latest phase of that process of separation and individuation that modernity seems to entail. John Donne, in 1611, at the very beginning of the modern era, with the prescience that is sometimes given to great poets, vividly described that process:

'Tis all in peeces, all cohaerence gone;
All just supply, and all Relation:
Prince, Subject, Father, Sonne, are things forgot,
For every man alone thinkes he hath got
To be a Phoenix, and that then can bee
None of that kinde, of which he is, but hee.[1]

Donne lived in a world where the ties of kinship and village and feudal obligation were already loosening, though only a few perceived how radical the consequences would be.

America was colonized by those who had come loose from the older European structures, and so from the beginning we had a head start in the process of moderniza-

Source: Abridged from Chapter 11 in *Habits of the Heart: Individualism and Commitment in American Life* (pp. 275–296). Berkeley: University of California Press, 1985.

tion. Yet the colonists brought with them ideas of social obligation and group formation that disposed them to recreate in America structures of family, church, and polity that would continue, if in modified form, the texture of older European society. Only gradually did it become clear that every social obligation was vulnerable, every tie between individuals fragile. Only gradually did what we have called ontological individualism, the idea that the individual is the only firm reality, become widespread. Even in our day, when separation and individuation have reached a kind of culmination, their triumph is far from complete. The battles of modernity are still being fought.

But today the battles have become half-hearted. There was a time when, under the battle cry of "freedom," separation and individuation were embraced as the key to a marvelous future of unlimited possibility. It is true that there were always those, like Donne, who viewed the past with nostalgia and the present with apprehension and who warned that we were entering unknown and dangerous waters. It is also true that there are still those who maintain their enthusiasm for modernity, who speak of the third wave or the Aquarian Age or the new paradigm in which a dissociated individuation will reach a final fulfillment. Perhaps most common today, however, is a note of uncertainty, not a desire to turn back to the past but an anxiety about where we seem to be headed. In this view, modernity seems to be a period of enormously rapid change, a transition from something relatively fixed toward something not yet clear. Many might find still applicable Matthew Arnold's assertion that we are

Wandering between two worlds, one dead,
The other powerless to be born.[2]

There is a widespread feeling that the promise of the modern era is slipping away from us. A movement of enlightenment and liberation that was to have freed us from superstition and tyranny has led in the twentieth century to a world in which ideological fanaticism and political oppression have reached extremes unknown in previous history. Science, which was to have unlocked the bounties of nature, has given us the power to destroy all life on the earth. Progress, modernity's master idea, seems less compelling when it appears that it may be progress into the abyss. And the globe today is divided between a liberal world so incoherent that it seems to be losing the significance of its own ideals, an oppressive and archaic communist statism, and a poor, and often tyrannical, Third World reaching for the very first rungs of modernity. In the liberal world, the state, which was supposed to be a neutral night-watchman that would maintain order while individuals pursued their various interests, has become so overgrown and militarized that it threatens to become a universal policeman [or woman].

Yet in spite of those daunting considerations, many of those we talked to are still hopeful. They realize that though the processes of separation and individuation were necessary to free us from the tyrannical structures of the past, they must be balanced by a renewal of commitment and community if they are not to end in self-destruction or turn into their opposites. Such a renewal is indeed a world waiting to be born if we only had the courage to see it.

THE CULTURE OF SEPARATION

One of the reasons it is hard to envision a way out of the impasse of modernity is the degree to which modernity conditions our consciousness. If modernity is "the culture of separation," Donne characterized it well when he said " 'Tis all in peeces, all cohaerence gone." When the world comes to us in pieces, in fragments, lacking any overall pattern, it is hard to see how it might be transformed.

A sense of fragmentariness is as characteristic of high intellectual culture as of popular culture. Starting with science, the most respected and influential part of our high culture, we can see at once that it is not a whole, offering a general interpretation of reality, as theology and philosophy once did, but a collection of disciplines each having little to do with the others. As Stephen Toulmin recently put it:

> From the early seventeenth century on, and increasingly so as the centuries passed, the tasks of scientific inquiry were progressively divided up between separate and distinct "disciplines." . . . Every independent scientific discipline is marked by its own specialized modes of abstraction: and the issues to be considered in each discipline are so defined that they can be investigated and discussed independently— in abstraction from—the issues belonging to other disciplines . . . As a result of this first kind of abstraction, the broad and general questions about "cosmic interrelatedness" which were the focus of the earlier debates about nature have been superseded by other, more specialized, disciplinary questions. . . . In its actual content (that is to say) the science of the nineteenth and early twentieth centuries became an aggregate, rather than an integration, of results from its component disciplines.[3]

What Toulmin has pointed out for the natural sciences is equally true of the social sciences and, indeed, of all the "disciplines" and "fields" into which contemporary intellectual culture is divided. As the French anthropologist Louis Dumont has observed:

> [I]n the modern world each of our particular viewpoints or specialized pursuits does not know very well—or does not know at all—what it is about and the reason for its existence or distinctness, which is more often a matter of fact than of consensus or rationality. Just as our rationality is mostly a matter of the relation of means and ends, while the hierarchy of ends is left out, so also our rationality manifests itself within each of our neatly distinct compartments but not in their distribution, definition and arrangement.[4]

The poet and critic Wendell Berry has described the consequences for the place of poetry in a culture of separation and specialization. Since science specializes in the external reality of the world, the poet is consigned to speak about his [or her] own feelings. He [or she] is himself [or herself] his [or her] chief subject matter and "the old union of beauty, goodness and truth is broken." Such poets can no longer be public persons, so that even when, as of late, some of them have turned to protest, it is a private protest. As Berry puts it, "In his [or her] protest, the contemporary poet is speaking publicly, but not as a spokesman [or woman]; he [or she] is only one outraged citizen speaking *at* other citizens who do not know him [or her], whom he [or she] does not know, and with whom he [or she] does not sympathize."[5] One recent poet who tried to integrate the world—politics, economics, culture—into one vast poem, taking Dante as his model, only showed how impossible such an integration is under modern conditions. According to Helen Vendler, Ezra Pound's huge *Cantos* are a "jumble of detail," a "mound of potsherds," of which Pound himself finally said, "I cannot make it cohere."[6]

These developments in the realm of high culture have had devastating consequences for education. Here, particularly in higher education, students were traditionally supposed to acquire some general sense of the world and their place in it. In the contemporary multiversity, it is easier to think of education as a cafeteria in which one acquires discrete bodies of information or useful skills. Feeble efforts to reverse these trends periodically convulse the universities, but the latest such convulsion, the effort to establish a "core curriculum," often turns into a battle between disciplines in which the idea of a substantive core is lost. The effort is thus more symptomatic of our cultural fracture than of its cure.

When we turn from intellectual culture to popular culture, particularly the mass media, the situation is, if anything, even more discouraging. Within the disciplinary and subdisciplinary "compartments" of intellectual culture, though there is little integration between them, there is still meaning and intensity in the search for truth. In popular culture, it is hard to say even that much. To take an extreme example, television, it would be difficult to argue that there is any coherent ideology or overall message that it communicates. There is a sense in which the broadcasters' defense of their role—that they are merely mirroring the culture—has a certain plausibility. They do not support any clear set of beliefs or policies, yet they cast doubt on everything. Certainly, they do not glorify "the power structure." Big business is not admirable: its leaders are frequently power-hungry bullies without any moral restraints (J. R. Ewing, for example). Government is under a cloud of suspicion: politicians are crooks. Labor is badly tarnished: labor leaders are mobsters. The debunking that is characteristic of our intellectual culture is also characteristic of the mass media. While television does not preach, it nevertheless presents a picture of reality that influences us more than an overt message could. As Todd Gitlin has described it,

> [T]elevision's world is relentlessly upbeat, clean and materialistic. Even more sweepingly, with few exceptions prime time gives us people preoccupied with personal ambition. If not utterly consumed by ambition and the fear of ending up as losers, these characters take both the ambition and the fear for granted. If not surrounded by middle-class arrays of consumer goods, they themselves are glamorous incarnations of desire. The happiness they long for is private, not public; they make few demands on society as a whole, and even when troubled they seem content with the existing institutional order. Personal ambition and consumerism are the driving forces of their lives. The sumptuous and brightly lit setting of most series amount to advertisements for a consumption-centered version of the good life, and this doesn't even take into consideration the incessant commercials, which convey the idea that human

aspirations for liberty, pleasure, accomplishment and status can be fulfilled in the realm of consumption. The relentless background hum of prime time is the packaged good life.[7]

Gitlin's description applies best to daytime and prime-time soaps. It does not apply nearly so well to situation comedies, where human relations are generally more benign. Indeed, the situation comedy often portrays people tempted to dishonesty or personal disloyalty by the prospect of some private gain, who finally decide to put family or friends ahead of material aggrandizement. Yet, finally, both soaps and situation comedies are based on the same contrast: human decency versus brutal competitiveness for economic success. Although the soaps show us that the ruthlessly powerful rich are often unhappy and the situation comedies show us that decent "little people" are often happy, they both portray a world dominated by economic competition, where the only haven is a very small circle of warm personal relationships. Thus the "reality" that looms over a narrowed-down version of "traditional morality" is the overwhelming dominance of material ambition.

Of course, in television none of these things is ever really argued. Since images and feelings are better communicated in this medium than ideas, television seeks to hold us, to hook us, by the sheer succession of sensations. One sensation being as good as another, there is the implication that nothing makes any difference. We switch from a quiz show to a situation comedy, to a bloody police drama, to a miniseries about celebrities, and with each click of the dial, nothing remains.

But television operates not only with a complete disconnectedness between successive programs. Even within a single hour or half-hour program, there is extraordinary discontinuity. Commercials regularly break whatever mood has built up with their own, often very different, emotional message. Even aside from commercials, television style is singularly abrupt and jumpy, with many quick cuts to other scenes and other characters. Dialogue is reduced to clipped sentences. No one talks long enough to express anything complex. Depth of feeling, if it exists at all, has to be expressed in a word or a glance.

The form of television is intimately related to the content. Except for the formula situation comedies (and even there, divorce is increasingly common), relationships are as brittle and shifting as the action of the camera. Most people turn out to be unreliable and double-dealing. Where strong commitments are portrayed, as in police dramas, they are only between buddies, and the environing atmosphere, even within the police force, is one of mistrust and suspicion.

If popular culture, particularly television and the other mass media, makes a virtue of lacking all qualitative distinctions, and if the intellectual culture, divided as it is, hesitates to say anything about the larger issues of existence, how does our culture hold together at all? The culture of separation offers two forms of integration—or should we say pseudo-integration?—that turn out, not surprisingly, to be derived from utilitarian and expressive individualism. One is the dream of personal success. As Gitlin has observed, television shows us people who are, above all, consumed by ambition and the fear of ending up losers. That is drama we can all identify with, at least all of us who have been (and who has not?) exposed to middle-class values. Isolated in our efforts though we are, we can at least recognize our fellows as followers of the same private dream. The second is the portrayal of vivid personal feeling. Television is much more interested in how people feel than in what they think. What they think might separate us, but how they feel draws us together. Successful television personalities and celebrities are thus people able freely to communicate their emotional states. We feel that we "really know them." And the very consumption goods that television so insistently puts before us integrate us by providing symbols of our version of the good life. But a strange sort of integration it is, for the world into which we are integrated is defined only by the spasmodic transition between striving and relaxing and is without qualitative distinctions of time and space, good and evil, meaning and meaninglessness. And however much we may for a moment see something of ourselves in another, we are really, as Matthew Arnold said in 1852, "in the sea of life enisled . . . / We mortal millions live *alone.*"[8]

THE CULTURE OF COHERENCE

But that is not the whole story. It could not be the whole story, for the culture of separation, if it ever became completely dominant, would collapse of its own incoherence. Or, even more likely, well before that happened, an authoritarian state would emerge to provide the coherence the culture no longer could. If we are not entirely a mass of interchangeable fragments within an aggregate, if we are in part qualitatively distinct members of a whole, it is because there are still operating among us, with whatever difficulties, traditions that tell us about the nature of the world, about the nature of society, and about who we are as people. Primarily biblical and republican, these traditions are, as we have seen, important for many Americans and significant to some degree for almost all. Somehow families, churches, a variety of cultural associations, and, even if only in the interstices, schools and universities, do manage to communicate a form of life, a *paideia,* in the sense of growing up in a morally and intellectually intelligible world.

The communities of memory of which we have spoken are concerned in a variety of ways to give a qualitative meaning to the living of life, to time and space, to persons and groups. Religious communities, for example, do not experience time in the way the mass media present it—as a continuous flow of qualitatively meaningless sensations. The day, the week, the season, the year are punctuated by an alternation of the sacred and the profane. Prayer breaks into our daily life at the beginning of a meal, at the end of the day, at common worship, reminding us that our utilitarian pursuits are not the whole of life, that a fulfilled life is one in which God and neighbor are remembered first. Many of our religious traditions recognize the significance of silence as a way of breaking the incessant flow of sensations and opening our hearts to the wholeness of being. And our republican tradition, too, has ways of giving form to time, reminding us on particular dates of the great events of our past or of the heroes who helped to teach us what we are as a free people. Even our private family life takes on a shared rhythm with a Thanksgiving dinner or a Fourth of July picnic.

In short, we have never been, and still are not, a collection of private individuals who, except for a conscious contract to create a minimal government, have nothing in common. Our lives make sense in a thousand ways, most of which we are unaware of, because of traditions that are centuries, if not millennia, old. It is these traditions that help us know that it does make a difference who we are and how we treat one another. Even the mass media, with their tendency to homogenize feelings and sensations, cannot entirely avoid transmitting such qualitative distinctions, in however muted a form.

But if we owe the meaning of our lives to biblical and republican traditions of which we seldom consciously think, is there not the danger that the erosion of these traditions may eventually deprive us of that meaning altogether? Are we not caught between the upper millstone of a fragmented intellectual culture and the nether millstone of a fragmented popular culture? The erosion of meaning and coherence in our lives is not something Americans desire. Indeed, the profound yearning for the idealized small town that we found among most of the people we talked to is a yearning for just such meaning and coherence. But although the yearning for the small town is nostalgia for the irretrievably lost, it is worth considering whether the biblical and republican traditions that small town once embodied can be reappropriated in ways that respond to our present need. Indeed, we would argue that if we are ever to enter that new world that so far has been powerless to be born, it will be through reversing modernity's tendency to obliterate all previous culture. We need to learn again from the cultural riches of the human species and to reappropriate and revitalize those riches so that they can speak to our condition today.

We may derive modest hope from the fact that there is a restlessness and a stirring in the intellectual culture itself. Stephen Toulmin tells us that "our own natural science today is no longer 'modern' science." It is a "postmodern" science in which disciplinary boundaries are beginning to appear as the historical accidents they are and the problems that are necessarily "transdisciplinary" are beginning to be addressed. This recognition is based on the realization that we cannot, after all, finally separate who we are from what we are studying. As Toulmin puts it, "We can no longer view the world as Descartes and Laplace would have us do, as 'rational onlookers,' from outside. Our place is within the same world that we are studying, and whatever scientific understanding we achieve must be a kind of understanding that is available to participants within the processes of nature, i.e., from inside."[9] Perhaps nature as perceived by the poet, the theologian, and the scientist may be the same thing after all. At least there is now room to talk about that possibility. And there are parallel developments in the social sciences. There, too, it appears that studying history and acting in it are not as different as we had thought. If our high culture could begin to talk about nature and history, space and time, in ways that did not disaggregate them into fragments, it might be possible for us to find connections and analogies with the older ways in which human life was made meaningful. This would not result in a neotraditionalism that would return us to the past. Rather, it might lead to a recovery of a genuine tradition, one that is always self-revising and in a state of development. It might help us find again the coherence we have almost lost. . . .

RECONSTITUTING THE SOCIAL WORLD

The transformation of our culture and our society would have to happen at a number of levels. If it occurred only in the minds of individuals (as to some degree it already has), it would be powerless. If it came only from the initiative of the state, it would be tyrannical. Personal transformation among large numbers is essential, and it must not only be a transformation of consciousness but must also involve individual action. But individuals need the nurture of groups that carry a moral tradition reinforcing their own aspirations. Implicitly or explicitly, a number of the communities of memory we have discussed in this book hold ethical commitments that require a new social ecology in our present situation. But out of existing groups and organizations, there would also have to develop a social movement dedicated to the idea of such a transformation. We have several times spoken of the Civil Rights movement as an example. It permanently changed consciousness, in the sense of individual attitudes toward race, and it altered our social life so as to eliminate overt expressions of discrimination. If the Civil Rights movement failed fundamentally to transform the position of black people in our society, it was because to do that would have required just the change in our social ecology that we are now discussing. So a movement to transform our social ecology would, among other things, be the successor and fulfill-ment of the Civil Rights movement. Finally, such a social movement would lead to changes in the relationship between our government and our economy. This would not necessarily mean more direct control of the economy, certainly not nationaliza-tion. It would mean changing the climate in which business operates so as to encourage new initiatives in economic democracy and social responsibility, whether from "private" enterprise or autonomous small- and middle-scale public enterprises. In the context of a moral concern to revive our social ecology, the proposals of the proponents of the Administered Society and Economic Democracy that we discussed in the preceding chapter could be considered and appropriate ones adopted. [10]

To be truly transformative, such a social movement would not simply subside after achieving some of its goals, leaving the political process much as it found it. One of its most important contributions would be to restore the dignity and legitimacy of democratic politics. We have seen in earlier chapters how suspicious Americans are of politics as an area in which arbitrary differences of opinion and interest can be resolved only by power and manipulation. The recovery of our social ecology would allow us to link interests with a conception of the common good. With a more explicit understanding of what we have in common and the goals we seek to attain together, the differences between us that remain would be less threatening. We could move to ameliorate the differences that are patently unfair while respecting differences based on morally intelligible commitments. . . .

SIGNS OF THE TIMES

Few of those with whom we talked would have described the problems facing our society in exactly the terms we have just used. But few have found a life devoted to "personal ambition and consumerism" satisfactory, and most are seeking in one way or another to transcend the limitations of a self-centered life. If there are vast numbers of a selfish, narcissistic "me generation" in America, we did not find them, but we certainly did find that the language of individualism, the primary American language of self-understanding, limits the ways in which people think.

Many Americans are devoted to serious, even ascetic, cultivation of the self in the form of a number of disciplines, practices, and "trainings," often of great rigor. There is a question as to whether these practices lead to the self-realization or self-fulfullment at which they aim or only to an obsessive self-manipulation that defeats the proclaimed purpose. But it is not uncommon for those who are attempting to find themselves to find in that very process something that transcends them. For example, a Zen student reported: "I started Zen to get something for myself, to stop suffering, to get enlightened. Whatever it was, I was doing it for myself. I had hold of myself and I was reaching for something. Then to do it, I found out I had to give up that hold on myself. Now it has hold of me, whatever 'it' is."[11] What this student found is that the meaning of life is not to be discovered in manipulative control in the service of the self. Rather, through the disciplined practices of a religious way of life, the student found his self more grasped than grasping. It is not surprising that "self-realization" in this case has occurred in the context of a second language, the allusive language of Zen Buddhism, and a community that attempts to put that language into practice.

Many Americans are concerned to find meaning in life not primarily through self-cultivation but through intense relations with others. Romantic love is still idealized in our society. It can, for course, be remarkably self-indulgent, even an excuse to use another for one's own gratification. But it can also be a revelation of the poverty of the self and lead to a genuine humility in the presence of the beloved. We have noted in the early chapters of this book that the therapeutically inclined, jealous though they are of their personal autonomy, nonetheless seek enduring attachments and a community within which those attachments can be nurtured. As in the case of self-cultivation, there is in the desire for intense relationships with others an attempt to move beyond the isolated self, even though the language of individualism makes that sometimes hard to articulate.

Much of what is called "consumerism," and often condemned as such, must be understood in this same ambiguous, ambivalent context. Attempts to create a beautiful place in which to live, to eat well and in a convivial atmosphere, to visit beautiful places where one may enjoy works of art, or simply lie in the sun and swim in the sea, often involve an element of giving to another and find their meaning in a committed relationship.[12] Where the creation of a consumption-oriented lifestyle, which may resemble that of "the beautiful people" or may simply involve a comfortable home and a camper, becomes a form of defense against a dangerous and meaningless world, it probably takes on a greater burden than it can bear. In that case, the effort to move beyond the self has ended too quickly in the "little circle of family and friends" of which Tocqueville spoke, but even so the initial impulse was not simply selfish.

With the weakening of the traditional forms of life that gave aesthetic and moral meanings to everyday living, Americans have been improvising alternatives more or less successfully. They engage, sometimes with intense involvement, in a wide variety of arts, sports, and nature appreciation, sometimes as spectators but often as active participants. Some of these activities involve conscious traditions and demanding practices, such as ballet. Others, such as walking in the country or jogging, may be purely improvisational, though not devoid of some structure of shared meaning. Not infrequently, moments of intense awareness, what are sometimes called "peak experiences," occur in the midst of such activities. At such moments, a profound sense of well-being eclipses the usual utilitarian preoccupations of everyday life. But the capacity of such experiences to provide more than a momentary counterweight to pressures of everyday life is minimal. Where these activities find social expression at all, it is apt to be in the form of what we have called the lifestyle enclave. The groups that form around them are too evanescent, too inherently restricted in membership, and too slight in their hold on their members' loyalty to carry much public weight. Only at rare moments do such largely expressive solidarities create anything like a civic consciousness, as when a local professional sports team wins a national championship and briefly gives rise to a euphoric sense of metropolitan belongingness. . . .

And while our universities are under greater pressure than ever to emphasize pragmatic results—technological achievements and career-oriented skills—there are voices calling for a reaffirmation of the classic role of education as a way to articulare private aspirations with common cultural meanings so that individuals simultaneously become more fully developed people and citizens of a free society. Eva Brann has recently given an eloquent defense of this understanding of education in her *Paradoxes of Education in a Republic.* She argues that in education at present, the choice is either tradition or technique, and that technique has become far too dominant.[13] The result is that in the multiversities of today, it is hard to find a single book, even a single play of Shakespeare's, that all the students in a large class know. When education becomes an instrument for individual careerism, it cannot provide either personal meaning or civic culture. And yet, somehow, the tradition does get transmitted, at least to students who seek it out.

Tradition gets transmitted because there are still teachers who love it and who cannot help transmitting it. Helen Vendler, in her 1980 presidential address to the Modern Language Association, took as her text a passage at the end of Wordsworth's *The Prelude:*

> What we have loved,
> Others will love, and we will teach them how.

She sums up her argument by saying:

It is not within our power to reform the primary and secondary schools, even if we have a sense of how that reform might begin. We do have it within our power, I believe, to reform ourselves, to make it our own first task to give, especially to our beginning students, that rich web of associations, lodged in the tales of majority and minority cultures alike, by which they could begin to understand themselves as individuals and as social beings. . . . All freshman English courses, to my mind, should devote at least half their time to the reading of myth, legend and parable; and beginning language courses should do the same. . . . We owe it to ourselves to show our students, when they first meet us, what we are: we owe their dormant appetites, thwarted for so long in their previous schooling, that deep sustenance that will make them realize that they too, having been taught, love what we love.[14]

If college education, and probably more than a few secondary schools as well, are still providing us with some of the help we need to make tradition a vital resource in our lives, it is hard to see how that other great cultural institution, television, which competes with the schools for the education of our youth and for the continuing education of adults, succeeds in doing so. Except for some notable contributions from public television, most programming is devoid of any notion of coherent tradition.

On the basis of our interviews, and from what we can observe more generally in our society today, it is not clear that many Americans are prepared to consider a significant change in the way we have been living. The allure of the packaged good life is still strong, though dissatisfaction is widespread. Americans are fairly ingenious in finding temporary ways to counteract the harsher consequences of our damaged social ecology. Livy's words about ancient Rome also apply to us: "We have reached the point where we cannot bear either our vices or their cure." But, as some of the more perceptive of the people to whom we talked believe, the time may be approaching when we will either reform our republic or fall into the hands of despotism, as many republics have done before us. . . .

NOTES

1 John Donne, "An Anatomie of the World: The First Anniversary."
2 Matthew Arnold, "Stanzas from the Grand Chartreuse" (1855).
3 Stephen Toulmin, *The Return to Cosmology: Postmodern Science and the Theology of Nature* (Berkeley and Los Angeles: University of California Press, 1982), pp. 228-29, 234.
4 Louis Dumont, *From Mandeville to Marx: The Genesis and Triumph of Economic Ideology* (Chicago: University of Chicago Press, 1977), p. 20.
5 Wendell Berry, *Standing by Words* (San Francisco: North Point Press, 1983), pp. 5, 20.
6 Helen Vendler, "From Fragments a World Perfect at Last," *New Yorker*, March 19, 1984, p. 143.
7 Todd Gitlin, *Inside Prime Time* (New York: Pantheon, 1983), pp. 268-69. Conversations with Todd Gitlin and Lisa Heilbronn were helpful in clarifying our views of television.
8 Matthew Arnold, "To Marguerite." Emphasis in original.
9 Toulmin, *Return to Cosmology*, pp. 254, 209-10.

10 On many of these issues, an approach refreshingly free of ideological narrowness is provided
    by recent Catholic social teaching. See the collection of documents from Vatican II and
    after: *Renewing the Earth: Catholic Documents on Peace, Justice, and Liberation*, ed. David J.
    O'Brien and Thomas A. Shannon (Garden City, N.Y.: Image Books, 1977). See also Pope
    John Paul II's 1981 encyclical letter *Laborem Exercens*, contained in Gregory Baum, *The
    Priority of Labor* (New York: Paulist Press, 1982), which provides a useful commentary.
    Charles K. Wilber and Kenneth P. Jameson use these teachings to reflect about the
    American economy in their *An Inquiry into the Poverty of Economics* (Notre Dame, Ind.:
    University of Notre Dame Press, 1983).

11 Steven M. Tipton, *Getting Saved From the Sixties* (Berkeley and Los Angeles: University of
    California Press, 1982), p. 115.

12 The differences between private vacations and public holidays, or holy days, illustrate the
    moral limits of expressive alternatives to traditional civic and religious forms of enacting our
    social solidarity. The vacation began its short, century-long history as a stylish middle-class
    imitation of the aristocrat's seasonal retreat from court and city to country estate. Its charac-
    ter is essentially individualistic and familial: "Everyone plans his [or her] own vacation, goes
    where he [or she] wants to go, does what he [or she] want to do," writes Michael Walzer.
    Vacations are individually chosen, designed, and paid for, regardless of how class-patterned
    vacation behavior may be or how many vacation spots depend on public funds for their
    existence. The experience vacations celebrate is freedom—the freedom to break away from
    the ordinary places and routines of the workaday world and "escape to another world" where
    every day is "vacant" and all time is "free time." There we have "our own sweet time" to do
    with as we will and empty days to fill at our own pace with activities of our own choosing.
    Public holidays, by contrast, were traditionally provided for everyone in the same form and
    place, at the same time, to celebrate together by taking part in the fixed communal rites,
    meals, and celebrations that already filled them. In ancient Rome, the *dies vacantes*, in a
    telling reversal of meaning, were those ordinary working days devoid of religious festivals or
    public games. Public holy days such as the Sabbath are the common property of all.
    "Sabbath rest is more egalitarian than the vacation because it can't be purchased: it is one
    more thing that money can't buy. It is enjoined for everyone, enjoyed by everyone," Walzer
    observes. The Sabbath requires a shared sense of obligation and solemnity, backed not only
    by a shared impulse to celebrate but by a common mechanism of enforcement. God created
    the Sabbath for everyone and *commanded* all of the faithful to rest, although in our society
    today individuals are free to choose to respect it or not. Nonetheless, the Sabbath signifies a
    freedom interwoven with civic equality and unity under an ultimate authority that is not
    merely a [hu]man-made social idea. (Walzer, *Spheres of Justice*, pp. 190–96.)

13 Eva T. H. Brann, *Paradoxes of Education in a Republic* (Chicago: University of Chicago Press,
    1979), p. 111.

14 Helen Vendler, "Presidential Address 1980," *PMLA* 96 (1981): 350. Vendler's aim is not to
    create more literature majors but to save us from going through life "unaccompanied by a
    sense that others have also gone through it, and have left a record of their experience." We
    need to be able to think about Job, Jesus, Antigone, and Lear "in order to refer private
    experience to some identifying frame or solacing reflection," to the classic stories of our
    culture's traditions that show us what it means to be a good person in practical relationships
    to others in particular situations (p. 349). More than laws or philosophical arguments, such
    stories shape the habits of our hearts by guiding us through example.